D1496515

BUYING AMERICA FROM THE INDIANS

BUYING AMERICA FROM THE INDIANS

Johnson v. McIntosh and the
History of Native Land Rights

Blake A. Watson

University of Oklahoma Press : Norman

Library of Congress Cataloging-in-Publication Data

Watson, Blake A., 1956–
    Buying America from the Indians : Johnson v. McIntosh and the history of Native
land rights / Blake A. Watson.
        p. cm.
    Includes bibliographical references and index.
    ISBN 978-0-8061-4244-9 (hardcover : alk. paper) 1. Johnson, Joshua, fl. 1819—
Trials, litigation, etc. 2. M'Intosh, William—Trials, litigation, etc. 3. Indian
title—United States—History—19th century. 4. Indian land transfers—Illinois—
History—19th century. 5. Vendors and purchasers—United States.—History—
19th century. I. Title.
    KF228.J644W38 2012
    346.7304'32—dc23
                                                                                    2011046419

1 2 3 4 5 6 7 8 9 10

For my parents, John and Barbara Watson

"And we declare to you that, we consider ourselves free
to make any bargain or cession of lands,
whenever and to whomsoever we please."

—Message from the Western Indians to the United States,
Foot of the Miami Rapids, August 13, 1793
(*American State Papers:* Indian Affairs, at 1:356)

"The Indian inhabitants are to be considered merely
as occupants, to be protected, indeed, while in peace,
in the possession of their lands, but to be deemed incapable
of transferring the absolute title to others."

—Chief Justice John Marshall, in *Johnson and Graham's
Lessee v. McIntosh,* February 28, 1823
(*Johnson,* 21 U.S. at 591)

CONTENTS

ILLUSTRATIONS

FIGURES

MAPS

PREFACE

My scholarly interest in Native land rights is reinforced by my teaching. I teach Property to first-year law students, and our textbook begins with *Johnson and Graham's Lessee v. McIntosh*, an 1823 decision of the United States Supreme Court. On October 18, 1775, eleven Piankeshaw chiefs deeded two large tracts to the royal governor of Virginia and nineteen other persons from Maryland, Pennsylvania, Great Britain, and the Illinois country. Thirty years later, on December 30, 1805, the Piankeshaws ceded much of the same land to the United States in a treaty negotiated by William Henry Harrison, governor of the Indiana Territory. A local land speculator, William McIntosh, subsequently purchased a portion of the land in question.

The plaintiffs in *Johnson* were the heirs of one of the original purchasers, and appeared to have the upper hand. After all, if the Piankeshaws sold the property in 1775, the tribe had nothing left to cede in 1805, and the United States had nothing to sell. *Nemo dat qui non habet* (he who hath not cannot give). Faced with these facts, the attorneys representing McIntosh argued that the 1775 purchase was invalid because Indians lacked the capacity to sell land to private individuals. In the words of Chief Justice John Marshall, the dispute concerned "the power of Indians to give, and of private individuals to receive, a title, which can be sustained in the courts of this country."

On behalf of a unanimous Supreme Court, Marshall announced that following the discovery of America, Indians no longer enjoyed the "power to dispose of the soil at their own will, to whomsoever they pleased."[1] The decision was a crushing defeat for the Illinois and Wabash Land Company, which in 1779 had united the investors in the Piankeshaw (or Wabash) purchase with an overlapping group of individuals who had acquired two large tracts of land in 1773 from the Illinois Indians. The quixotic pursuit of fortune by the Illinois-Wabash speculators, sustained for half a century, ended in complete failure.

Johnson v. McIntosh has been described as "the root of title for most real property in the United States." The decision has also been denounced as "conquest by judicial fiat" and an extraconstitutional fiction developed "to rationalize the subjugation of the Indian nations."[2] To better understand the impact of *Johnson* on Native land rights, I believe one must examine the historical context of the Illinois and Wabash purchases. I first conceived the idea of writing about *Johnson v. McIntosh* when I was an attorney with the United States Department of Justice in the 1990s and was involved in adversarial disputes concerning Indian property rights. I began my research after becoming a law professor in 1992. Since that time a considerable number of articles have been published regarding *Johnson* and its impact on indigenous land rights. I describe this body of scholarship in chapter 18 of this book. Of particular significance is Lindsay G. Robertson's *Conquest by Law: How the Discovery of America Dispossessed Indigenous Peoples of Their Lands* (2005), which broke new ground as the first booklength treatment of the history of *Johnson v. McIntosh*. Although I chose to finish my manuscript prior to reading *Conquest by Law*, I did read and benefit from Robertson's 1997 Ph.D. dissertation, upon which *Conquest by Law* is based. All persons interested in *Johnson v. McIntosh* are indebted to Professor Robertson's discovery of primary documents detailing the affairs of the Illinois and Wabash Companies, documents now part of the digital collections at the University of Oklahoma College of Law.

This book endeavors to complement Robertson's scholarship and other prior accounts of *Johnson v. McIntosh* by providing additional historical context. Consequently, the book examines the divergent views of Native land rights; the geopolitical dispute between the French, British, Indians, and the colonies over the future of the Ohio Valley; the existence and impact of other pre-Revolutionary speculative ventures; the rivalry between Virginia and Pennsylvania over western lands; the role of the Illinois-Wabash speculators in the ratification of the Articles of Confederation; the cession of Virginia's charter claims in the Ohio Valley; and the federal government's evolving policy regarding Indian lands. In addition, the book emphasizes that the Illinois-Wabash speculation was not only a purchase but also a sale. The role played by the Illinois and Piankeshaw tribes has heretofore not been adequately addressed. Why did the tribes agree to sell their homelands? How did the sales affect relationships with neighboring tribes? What did the tribal chiefs say about the sales during their visit in 1793 to Philadelphia? And finally, what became of the Illinois and Piankeshaw Indians?

The two concluding chapters examine the impact of *Johnson v. McIntosh* on Native land rights and the future of the doctrine of discovery. The *Johnson* decision figured prominently in the debate over the 1830 Indian Removal Act, which led to the tragic relocation of the southeastern tribes. The case is also connected to basic principles of federal Indian law, such as the doctrines of diminished tribal sovereignty, federal trust authority, and "plenary" power over Indian affairs. The Supreme Court in 1955 relied on *Johnson* to hold that Indian title is "not a property right" and may be terminated "without any legally enforceable obligation to compensate the Indians."[3]

Johnson v. McIntosh has also influenced indigenous land rights in Australia, New Zealand, and Canada. In recent years, however, the discovery doctrine has been viewed as an unfortunate relic of the age of European colonization. On September 13, 2007, the United Nations approved the Declaration on the Rights of Indigenous Peoples, which affirms indigenous peoples' rights to land. Although the declaration is not legally binding, it represents a movement away from *Johnson*, and a movement toward a reconceptualization of indigenous rights.

The permanence of land creates a personal connection for me with the Indians involved in *Johnson v. McIntosh*. From my office in Dayton, Ohio, I can see traffic on Interstate 75, which parallels the Miami River. In August 1749, Pierre-Joseph Céleron ascended the Miami to Pickawillany (near present-day Piqua) to persuade Memeskia to renounce his alliance with Great Britain. The defiance and subsequent death of the Piankeshaw tribal leader were pivotal events leading up to the French and Indian War. My high school years were spent in Robinson, Illinois, across the Wabash River from Vincennes, Indiana. I camped on the bank of the Embarrass River, where in 1788 some sixty Kentuckians killed nine Piankeshaw and Miami Indians who were friendly to the Americans. In junior high I resided in Olathe, Kansas, just a few miles north of where the Piankeshaws and Illinois lived from the 1830s until their relocation, after the Civil War, to present-day Miami, Oklahoma.

When I lived in these places, I was unaware of their history of Indian ownership. In writing this book, I have learned that the Piankeshaws moved down the Wabash River in the 1730s and established Chippekoke village at present-day Vincennes. Although there is a difference of opinion regarding the derivation of the Piankeshaw village name, some say it means "place of roots." The appellation is fitting, since federal ownership is "the root of most land titles in America today" and since government title in turn "flows from '[t]he great case of *Johnson v. M[']Intosh*.'"[4] Understanding the roots of the Illinois-Wabash purchase facilitates a critical assessment of the *Johnson* discovery rule and its impact on federal Indian law and Native land rights.

BUYING AMERICA FROM THE INDIANS

1

FEBRUARY 28, 1823

Daniel Webster was undoubtedly at ease when he walked through the short hallway leading to the United States Supreme Court chamber, then in the basement of the Capitol. There were, after all, several reasons for serenity as the forty-one-year-old lawyer-politician arrived to hear the Court's decision regarding Indian land rights in *Johnson and Graham's Lessee v. McIntosh*.

First of all, he was in familiar surroundings. Prior to *Johnson*, Webster had appeared in thirty-one cases before the Court. His first three Supreme Court cases had been argued in this room, located beneath the Senate chamber. When the British burned the Capitol in 1814, the Court had been compelled to meet elsewhere, including a cramped committee room described as "little better than a dungeon." Webster argued eight times there, including the case that gave him a national reputation: *Dartmouth College v. Woodward*.

Since February 1819, however, Webster had exhibited his oratorical skills in the courtroom he was now entering. The prominent architect Benjamin Latrobe had rebuilt the low-arched vaulted ceiling, which was supported by massive pillars. The slightly elevated mahogany desks of the seven justices were situated below three windows on the east wall, which provided insufficient light. In the back of the semicircular room was the plaster relief *Justice*, portraying a woman holding scales and a sword. To some observers, the room was splendid; to others, it had a "cellar-like aspect." One visitor remarked that *Justice* lacked the traditional blindfold because "it was too dark for her to see anyway."[1]

Old Supreme Court Chamber in the basement of the United States Capitol. Franz Jantzen, Collection of the Supreme Court of the United States.

Webster's preeminent status was the second reason for his calm demeanor as he watched the justices don their black gowns. To be sure, there was a great deal at stake in this case. Johnson, Graham, and the other shareholders of the Illinois and Wabash Land Company were asking the Supreme Court to uphold private purchases, made in 1773 and 1775, of immense tracts of Indian land. On the eve of oral arguments, a lawyer for McIntosh exclaimed at a White House dinner that "sevent[y] millions of acres of land are in controversy."[2] Yet no constitutional provision was at issue, not the Contract Clause, as in *Dartmouth College,* or the Necessary and Proper Clause, as in *McCulloch v. Maryland.* An unfavorable decision in *Johnson v. McIntosh* would not affect Webster's position as the unquestioned head of the Supreme Court bar.

Nevertheless, the Massachusetts congressman had done his best in a difficult case. On Saturday, February 15, Webster had endeavored to convince the five justices present—John Marshall, William Johnson,

Brockholst Livingston, Gabriel Duvall, and Joseph Story—that the Indians had lawfully deeded the lands at issue. According to one observer, George Rodney of Delaware, Webster "went into a discussion upon the origin of property and managed it skilfully for a bad cause." Rodney surmised that the Court "will doubtless [be] against the grant." Edward Ingersoll, a shareholder in the Illinois and Wabash Land Company, expressed his desire "to sell for present profits, [as] I calculate on an unfavorable decision."[3]

Webster settled himself as Marshall prepared to deliver the opinion. Two Supreme Court justices—Bushrod Washington and Thomas Todd—had not participated in the case. Justice Story had been absent on the third day of arguments, either "from indisposition or ill will."[4] Webster opened for the plaintiffs, and his co-counsel, Robert Goodloe Harper of Baltimore, concluded the case. Henry Murray and William Winder represented McIntosh. Both counsel and the audience awaited the Court's decision. There were no Indians in attendance.

John Marshall, age forty-seven, a Federalist from Virginia and a proponent of a strong national government, began as follows: "The plaintiffs in this cause claim the land . . . under two grants . . . by the chiefs of certain Indian tribes, constituting the Illinois and the Piankeshaw nations; and the question is, whether this title can be recognised in the Courts of the United States?" The chief justice then proceeded to address the source of law that would govern the Court's decision: "It will be necessary . . . to examine, not singly those principles of abstract justice . . . ; but those principles also which *our own government has adopted* in the particular case, and given us as the rule for our decision."

This did not sound promising. The rights of Indians to own property and to transfer title were natural rights in the view of the plaintiffs, based on the principles of "abstract justice" that Marshall was subordinating to the principles "our own government has adopted." But which principles did Marshall have in mind? The chief justice chose to emphasize the right of discovery: "This principle was, that *discovery gave title* to the government by whose subjects, or by whose authority, it was made, against all other European governments, which title might be consummated by possession. . . . Those relations which were to exist between the discoverer and the natives, were to be regulated by themselves."

Webster was familiar with Marshall's circuitous reasoning. After declaring as determinative the principles adopted by the government, Marshall turned to the doctrine of discovery—a doctrine of *international* law that gave the discovering nation rights "against all other European governments." International law, however, should not have determined the validity of the deeds held by the Illinois and Wabash Land Company, as Marshall seemingly acknowledged when he stated that the relations between the discoverer and the Natives "were to be regulated by themselves." Marshall had come full circle, but he had not yet provided the answer. Would the Supreme Court uphold the Illinois-Wabash purchase? In the following passage, Marshall denied the right of Indians to convey legal title to the lands they occupy:

> They were admitted to be the rightful occupants of the soil, with a legal as well as just claim to retain possession of it, . . . but their rights to complete sovereignty, as independent nations, were necessarily diminished, and *their power to dispose of the soil at their own will, to whomsoever they pleased, was denied by the original fundamental principle, that discovery gave exclusive title to those who made it.*[5]

Although eighty-two paragraphs were to follow, the fundamental question was answered: the 1773 and 1775 sales were invalid. The United States, in subsequent treaties, obtained a complete title to the lands at issue, which was thereafter transferred to William McIntosh. The shares in the Illinois and Wabash Land Company were worthless.

The outcome in *Johnson v. McIntosh* most likely did not upset Daniel Webster, who made no mention of the decision in his correspondence. After fulfilling his role, Webster lost interest in the proceedings. During the next day's argument he sent John Quincy Adams an extract of a letter stating that Adams "is gaining fast upon the affections of the people."[6] Thus, while the fate of the Illinois and Wabash Land Company was before the Court, the outcome of the 1824 election was on the mind of Daniel Webster.

Robert Goodloe Harper was also on familiar ground as he listened glumly to Marshall's depiction of land law in America "from its discovery to the present day." The fifty-eight-year-old elder statesman of the Federalist Party had appeared in more Supreme Court cases than any other person between 1800 and 1815 and was considered one of the great lawyers of the era. Most notably, Harper had successfully contended, in *Fletcher v. Peck*, that a Georgia statute had impaired vested property rights in violation of the Contract

Clause. Typically dressed in a dark blue outercoat, buff waistcoat, and pol-
ished boots, Harper was viewed by many as a "dandy in dress" and "in some
degree artificial."[7] At the same time, contemporaries praised him as a gifted
debater who possessed a first-rate command of the law.

Harper, like Webster, would end the day with his reputation intact. As
the chief justice exclaimed that the 1763 Royal Proclamation constituted
"an additional objection to the title of the plaintiffs," Harper may have
reacted by reflecting on his military, political, and legal careers. At age
sixteen, he had served during the Revolution under General Nathaniel
Greene. When the British attacked Baltimore in 1814, Harper was "in the
hottest of the fight" and commanded troops in the battle at North Point.
At this time he attained the rank of major-general and was customarily addressed as "General Harper" for the rest of his life.

His political career had two phases, beginning as a Republican from
South Carolina and ending as a Federalist from Maryland. From 1794
until 1801 Harper served as chairman of the House Committee of Ways
and Means, supported the alien and sedition laws, and voted for Aaron
Burr in the election of 1800. After moving to Baltimore, Harper was
elected to the Senate in 1816, but he served less than a year due to the
press of private concerns, not least his role in the Illinois and Wabash Land
Company. In both 1816 and 1820 he received consideration as the Federalist candidate for vice president.[8]

Harper's legal career blossomed in Baltimore, where he opened a law office in 1799. Aside from *Fletcher v. Peck*, Harper's most celebrated achieve-
ment was his speech of seven hours made during the 1805 impeachment
trial of Justice Samuel Chase. His abilities were unquestioned, and Edward
Ingersoll informed a fellow shareholder that Harper's argument in *Johnson*
"has been everything that could be desired; full, powerful and elegant."[9]
No one would dispute that Harper, like his co-counsel Daniel Webster,
had done his best under discouraging circumstances.

There was one critical difference, however, between the two men:
Robert Goodloe Harper was a shareholder in the Illinois-Wabash Land
Company. As a young man Harper had developed an interest in western
lands and invested in several unsuccessful ventures. For the remainder of
his life the desire for wealth and the harsh reality of debt were constant
companions. By retiring from Congress and moving to Baltimore, he
had hoped not only to establish a lucrative law practice but also to wed
Catherine Carroll, the daughter of one of the richest men in America.[10]

Charles Carroll of Carrollton initially opposed the match but eventually consented. During the course of their marriage "Kitty" received eighty-seven thousand dollars from her father, yet her husband had outstanding single debts as large as ten thousand dollars.[11]

The Illinois-Wabash purchase beckoned as the means to a lavish, debt-free lifestyle. The primary investors were from Pennsylvania and Maryland, the two states where Harper had spent much of his adult life. In the 1790s he met Robert Morris and John Nicholson of Philadelphia, who both purchased shares in the Illinois and Wabash venture. He may also have had dealings with Supreme Court Justice James Wilson, who served as the company's president. Harper's subsequent involvement with the Illinois-Wabash purchase was likely sparked by the presence in Maryland of his father-in-law and other prominent shareholders, such as Governor Thomas Johnson and Supreme Court Justice Samuel Chase. By the time he argued *Fletcher v. Peck* in 1809, Robert Goodloe Harper was spearheading efforts to obtain confirmation of the 1773 and 1775 sales.

Perhaps his ambitious nature caused Harper to overlook the fact that the company's claims had been repeatedly rejected for over forty years. Harper himself crafted memorials in 1810 and 1816 that failed to persuade Congress. Only one alternative remained: litigation in the federal courts. When Illinois statehood in 1818 was followed by the death of Thomas Johnson in 1819, the final option was at hand. Largely stage-managed by Harper, litigation was commenced by Johnson's heirs in order to confirm their right to lands purchased in 1775 from the Piankeshaws.

Because the stakes were so high, and possible fortunes so immense, Harper and his fellow shareholders convinced themselves that they had a chance. Harper maintained in 1810 that the claim "can be sustained in a court of Law," and a shareholder noted in 1811 that "Mr. Harper is as sanguine as a reasonable person can probably be." Three days after oral arguments concluded, Harper ignored prevailing sentiment and discussed the measures to be taken "should we obtain a favourable decision."[12] On Friday, February 28, 1823, in the basement chamber of the Supreme Court, Robert Goodloe Harper finally realized there would not be "a favourable decision" in the matter of the Illinois-Wabash purchase.

Johnson v. McIntosh offers divergent rationales for its conclusion that Indians are mere occupants of their lands and thus "incapable of transferring the absolute title to others." Marshall vacillates between discovery ("discovery gave exclusive title") and conquest (conquest "gives a title which the courts of the conqueror cannot deny"), yet acknowledges the *"pretension* of converting the discovery of an inhabited country into conquest."[13] The Court also concludes that the Virginia "sea to sea" royal charter and the 1763 Royal Proclamation divested the Illinois and Piankeshaws of their rights of proprietorship.[14] On one hand, Marshall defends the result as supported by the "character and habits" of the Natives, the "superior genius" of the Europeans, and the "soundest principles of wisdom and national policy."[15] On the other hand, he views the matter as a fait accompli, declaring that "however this restriction may be opposed to natural right, and to the usages of civilized nations, yet, if it be indispensable to that system under which the country has been settled, and be adapted to the actual condition of the two people, *it may, perhaps, be supported by reason,* and certainly cannot be rejected by Courts of justice."[16]

Given such conflicting signals, it is not surprising that *Johnson* has been characterized as "one of the most misunderstood cases in the Anglo-American law." Although the decision has been defended as "a brilliant compromise" that "poses little or no restriction on the tribes," most commentators have criticized *Johnson v. McIntosh* and its endorsement of the doctrine of discovery. Robert Williams, Jr., characterizes Marshall's opinion as an "abusive, anachronistic and racist vision of Indian status and rights." Steven Newcomb posits that *Johnson* was premised on "a distinction between paramount rights of 'Christian people' and subordinate rights of 'heathens' or non-Christians." The Supreme Court's adoption of the doctrine of discovery, Lindsay Robertson points out, "led to political catastrophe for Native Americans."[17]

Maurice Baxter, a biographer of Daniel Webster, characterizes *Johnson v. McIntosh* as "a hopeless case from the beginning," and describes the legal dispute as follows: "Did the Indians have such a title to their lands that they could sell to private individuals? And if so, was the sale legal in the face of the British Proclamation of 1763 and of subsequent Virginia legislation prohibiting these transactions? Webster elaborately maintained the affirmative to both questions. *But the whole history of Indian relations was against him, and a decision in his favor would have caused a more chaotic situation than one could imagine."*[18] Baxter overstates Webster's role. For Daniel Webster, *Johnson* was just another case, a chance to earn a fee. It was not one of the cases that defined him as the "Defender of the Constitution." The legal positions Webster "elaborately maintained" before the Court were based on arguments and theories that were crafted by others.

For Robert Goodloe Harper, however, *Johnson v. McIntosh* was *not* just another case: it represented the culmination of years of effort to confirm—and profit from—the Illinois-Wabash purchase. Harper devoted a considerable portion of his legal career to the issue of Indian land rights. His efforts, of course, were not expended on behalf of Indian tribes but rather for the benefit of private speculators who purchased Indian lands.

For John Marshall, the litigation provided an opportunity to legitimize the process of land acquisition in the United States. Marshall's opinion defies succinct appraisal, but the central message of *Johnson v. McIntosh* is that "discovery" divested Indians of "their power to dispose of the soil at their own will, to whomsoever they pleased." Baxter asserts that "the whole history of Indian relations" led inexorably to this result, and Marshall justified his holding on the basis of "the actual condition of the two people."[19] These statements are misleading: actual practices varied regarding the sale of Indian lands to private individuals, and the result in *Johnson*—while predictable—was not foreordained.

For the Illinois and Piankeshaw Indians, the result in *Johnson* had no direct impact. The tribes had twice sold their rights to the lands at issue; first by private sale, second by treaty. On February 28, 1823, the Illinois and Piankeshaws no longer inhabited their historic homelands. They had been removed to Missouri and would be removed again, to Kansas, and ultimately to the Indian Territory. In the process their separate identities were lost; but their descendants—now members of the Peoria Tribe of Oklahoma—remain.

For all Indians, the legacy of *Johnson v. McIntosh* continues to have a significant impact. The litigation is inextricably connected to the prevailing legal view of Native land rights in America. The right of Indians to their lands—to possess, use, exclude, own, and sell—was "one of the most intensely contested issues in the life of the early Republic."[20] The historical process of buying America from the Indians has been largely concluded, but the legitimacy of America's conception of Indian land rights persists as one of the most important issues in Indian country and federal Indian law.

2

"THE *SINNE* OF THE *PATTENTS*"

John Marshall was a historian as well as a jurist. In 1804, in the introductory volume of *The Life of George Washington*, Marshall set forth a lengthy narrative "of the principal events preceding our revolutionary war."[1] Almost twenty years later, when crafting the decision in *Johnson v. McIntosh*, Marshall relied heavily on his history of America to proclaim "the universal recognition" of two legal principles: (1) that European discovery of lands in America "gave exclusive title to those who made it"; and (2) that such discovery "necessarily diminished" the power of Indian nations "to dispose of the soil at their own will, to whomsoever they pleased." The chief justice's claim of "*universal recognition*" of these principles, however, is belied by the historical record. The acquisition of Illinois and Piankeshaw lands by private individuals and without government approval was by no means unprecedented.

The founder of Rhode Island, Roger Williams, is a case in point. Within six years after arriving in America, Williams found himself banished from the Massachusetts Bay Colony and a grantee—by virtue of a private transaction with the Narragansett Indians—of lands in present-day Providence. In this brief period of time Williams formulated the simple, yet profoundly radical, view that Europeans could "justly occupy lands in the Americas only by purchasing those lands from their rightful owners, the Indians."[2]

"THE NATIVES ARE TRUE OWNERS OF ALL THEY POSSESS OR IMPROVE"

Roger Williams arrived in Massachusetts in 1631. At that time there were three primary English settlements: Plymouth, Salem, and Boston. The

Plymouth Colony was founded in 1620 by the *Mayflower* Pilgrims, members of a separatist Puritan sect who had secured a land patent from the London Virginia Company. The Pilgrims settled beyond the domain of the Virginia Company but came to an agreement with the Plymouth Council for New England, which had been granted a royal charter. Without mention of Indians, King James I granted the Plymouth Council an exclusive title "from Sea to Sea" to lands located between 40 and 48 degrees north latitude.[3]

James was succeeded in 1625 by his son Charles, who bestowed upon the Massachusetts Bay Company certain lands "from the Atlantick . . . on the Easte Parte, to the South Sea on the West Parte."[4] Although the 1629 charter failed to acknowledge the Indian occupants, John Winthrop and his fellow Puritans were aware of their presence. In a 1621 tract Robert Cushman declared Indian lands to be "spacious and void," and thus available for settlement. Winthrop advanced similar arguments eight years later, prior to his departure to the New World: "As for the Natives in New England, they inclose noe Land, neither have any setled habytation, . . . and . . . if we leave them sufficient for their use, *we may lawfully take the rest.*"[5] Most land in America was thought to be *vacuum domicilium*, or empty space. Referring to smallpox, Winthrop observed that "God hath consumed the natives with a miraculous plague, whereby the greater part of the country is left void of inhabitants." John Cotton, a contemporary of Winthrop, also embraced the doctrine of *vacuum domicilium*, writing that "in a vacant soyle, hee that taketh possession of it, and bestoweth culture and husbandry upon it, his Right it is."[6]

The legalities of colonization appeared settled: Massachusetts belonged to England by virtue of discovery, and the King's right to grant lands was justified by *vacuum domicilium*. Yet even prior to Williams's arrival in 1631, Englishmen were transacting with Indians. In 1625 colonists asked the Pemaquids to grant them twelve thousand acres, which the tribe did in "the first deed of Indian land to English colonists." John Whelewright and others, by private purchase, were deeded land by the Pisquataquas, and Winthrop transacted with Natives in 1642 for land along the Concord River. These purchases, however, were based on expediency rather than a change in legal principle. In 1629 the Salem Colony was instructed from London that "if any of the savages *pretend* right of inheritance to all or any part of the land granted in our patent, we pray you endeavor to purchase their title, that we may *avoid the least scruple of intrusion.*"[7] Indian title was never officially acknowledged as equivalent (or superior) to title to lands held under royal patent.

The question of Indian land rights was not foremost on the mind of Roger Williams when he arrived in America. After brief stays in Boston and Salem, Williams settled in Plymouth Colony, where he sought the "liberty of conscience" denied him in England. While at Plymouth he befriended Massasoit, sachem of the Wampanoags, and Canonicus, the aged leader of the Narragansetts. Already familiar with Latin, Greek, French, and Dutch (which he had taught John Milton in exchange for Hebrew lessons), Williams became conversant in local languages. In fact, his first published book—*A Key into the Language of America*—does not focus on the theological positions for which he is most famous but instead describes Native dialects and customs.[8] In chapter VII ("Of their Persons and parts of body"), Williams expresses his views in verse:

> *Bòast not proud* E[n]glish, *of thy birth & blood,*
> *Thy brother* Indian *is by birth as Good.*
> Of one blood God made Him, and Thee & All,
> As wise, as faire, as strong, as personall.

Williams also noted that the Natives "are very exact and punctuall in the bounds of their Lands . . . notwithstanding a sinfull opinion amongst ma[n]y that Christians have right to *Heathens* Lands: but of the delusion of that phrase, I have spoke in a discourse."[9]

The aforementioned "discourse" was written in 1632. The Plymouth governor, William Bradford, had asked Williams to express his views on the right of Puritans to be in America, and Williams responded with "a large Book in Quarto."[10] The treatise, which was destroyed, condemned the royal patents as illegal expropriations. The New World belonged to the Indians, "from whom alone a valid title could be derived," and therefore colonists should "repent of receiving title by patent from a king who had no right to grant it."[11] Neither possession of waste lands (*vacuum domicilium*) nor patent sufficed; purchase alone justified occupation.

Williams had laid down the gauntlet: if Europeans wished to own America, they must buy America from the Indians. His treatise, which challenged colonial legitimacy, prompted a rebuke from John Winthrop: "But if our title be not good, neither by Patent, nor possession of these parts as *vacuum Domicilium,* nor by good liking of the natives, I mervayle by what title Mr. Williams himselfe holdes. & if God were not pleased with our inheritinge these partes, why did he drive out the natives before us?"[12]

Winthrop resolved that Williams should be censured for expressing the view that Englishmen "could have no title . . . except as they compounded with the natives." However, when Williams appeared at General Court on March 4, 1634, he "gave satisfaction of his intention and loyalty." On the same day, the court enacted a law prohibiting the purchase of Indian lands "without License first had and obtained of the General Court."[13]

As it turned out, Williams's penitence was short-lived. Returning to Salem, he protested the "sinfulness" of using royal patents to "usurp land from the natives." On November 27, 1634, Winthrop noted in his journal that Williams "had broken his promise to us, in teaching publickly against the king's patent . . . [and by claiming that] the Natives are true owners of all they possess or improve." The General Court declared that Williams had divulged "new & dangerous opinions" and ordered him to leave the colony within six weeks.[14]

Rather than return to England, Williams found refuge among the Indians. Both Massasoit and Canonicus provided aid as he traveled south to present-day Rhode Island. As noted by Edwin Gaustad, "here he would occupy land only by agreement with the Indians (no patent from King Charles); here he would bring family and send for friends and neighbors; here he would name his village Providence."[15] The land grant was affirmed in 1638 when Canonicus and Miantonomo declared in a deed that, "having two years since sold unto Roger Williams the land and meadows, upon . . . Mooshassuc and Woonasquatucket, do now . . . confirm the bounds of these lands." Conflicting claims, however, caused Williams to go to England in 1643 and secure a charter for "Providence Plantations." Williams presumably considered the charter a *confirmation* of his purchase and not a *grant* of land. The 1643 charter makes no mention of any prior right of the Crown, and the subsequent 1663 charter states that the land was obtained "by purchase and consent of the said natives." In contrast to other colonial charters, the 1663 charter acknowledges the rights of the Indians to the soil.[16]

In chapter XXV of *A Key into the Language of America* ("Of buying and selling"), Roger Williams relates the grievous fears of his Native friends:

Oft have I heard these Indians say,
These English *will deceive us.*

Of all that's ours, our lands and lives.
In th' end, they will bereave us.[17]

In 1652 Williams again decried "the *sinne* of the *Patents*, wherein *Christian Kings* (so calld) are invested with Right by virtue of their Christianitie, to take and give away the Lands and Countries of other men."[18] The steadfast position of Roger Williams stands in rebuttal to John Marshall's claim of "universal recognition" of the view that discovery divested Indian nations of their full rights of property. Williams believed—as did the shareholders of the Illinois and Wabash Land Company—that Indians owned the lands they occupied and could sell their rights to any purchaser.

Marshall was wrong: there was no consensus regarding the rights of the Native inhabitants of the New World. The degree of emphasis placed on discovery, patent, possession, and purchase varied among the colonizing nations. A survey of European views of Indian land rights during "the age of discovery" reveals divergent opinions on two related issues: whether Native Americans owned the lands they occupied, and if so, whether such ownership rights could be sold or otherwise transferred to private individuals.

SPANISH VIEWS OF INDIAN LAND RIGHTS

Spanish views of Indian land rights were based largely on the "Catholic conceptualization of the rights of non-Christian peoples." Robert Williams, Jr., in *The American Indian in Western Legal Thought*, traces the "discourses of conquest" back to the thirteenth century, when Pope Innocent IV asked whether it was "licit to invade a land that infidels possess, or which belongs to them?" The polar positions considered were (1) that "infidels . . . possessed no rights to *dominium* that Christians were required to recognize"; and (2) that "infidels possessed the natural-law right to hold property and exercise lordship." Innocent IV adopted the position that wars could not be waged against infidels because of their nonbelief, but declared that the Church could deprive non-Christians of their property in certain situations, such as the failure to admit missionaries. Otherwise, all persons had the right under natural law to own property.[19]

The opposing point of view was championed by Hostiensis, cardinal of Ostia and the most important canonist of the thirteenth century. Hostiensis argued that infidels "were presumed to lack rights to property and lordship." As noted by Olive Dickason, it was the assertion of papal authority over nonbelievers that initially "fueled the ideological motor of Europe's expansion."[20] Christopher Columbus inaugurated the "Age of Discovery" on October 12, 1492, by landing on an island inhabited by Arawak Natives. He made no offer of purchase but instead announced that the island was the property of the Catholic sovereigns of Spain: "The officers and crews came on shore and immediately took over the territory, making it out as a free gift to the King and Queen of Spain. . . . The natives from whom they took it watched the proceedings without resentment, for they had not the least idea what was happening. Having not yet arrived at the conception of property they were unable to conceive the idea of theft."[21]

By the papal bull *Inter Caetera* of May 4, 1493, Pope Alexander VI drew a line of demarcation one hundred leagues west of the Cape Verde islands and granted to Spain all countries "hitherto discovered." Lands located to the east of the line—"so long as they had not already been seized by any other Christian Prince"—were awarded to Portugal.[22] The initial papal documents concerning the New World do not refer to the property rights of the Native inhabitants. Martín Fernández de Enciso, an author of a book on America published in 1519, reported that a group of Natives, "upon being informed of the papal donation, laughed and wondered that the pope would be so liberal with what was not his." The Spanish theologian Domingo de Soto similarly exclaimed that "the Pope did not grant, nor could he grant, our kings dominion over these peoples and their affairs, because he had no right to it (himself)."[23]

Francisco de Vitoria likewise advocated that title to Native lands could not be "traced through the Supreme Pontiff." In a series of lectures delivered in 1532 at the University of Salamanca, Vitoria considered whether the aborigines of the New World "were true owners of private property." Consistent with Innocent IV's natural law ideology, the Dominican Basque argued that "certain basic rights inhere in men . . . by reason of their humanity." In addition to denying that title to the New World could be claimed by papal grant, Vitoria declared that discovery "gives no support to a seizure of the aborigines any more than if it had been they who had discovered us."[24]

Vitoria's influence is debatable. Pope Paul III, in the papal bull *Sublimis Deus* (1537), proclaimed that Indians "may and should, freely and legitimately, enjoy . . . the possession of their property." On the other hand, most European nations recognized title to new terrain "simply by reason of its discovery." Vitoria's death prevented his participation in the debate over the nature of Indian rights that took place in 1550 in Valladolid under the aegis of Charles V, the grandson of Ferdinand and Isabella. The royal historiographer Juan Ginés de Sepúlveda contended that the *hombrecillos* ("little men") of the New World were barbaric and lacked private property. Bartolomé de Las Casas, a Dominican priest, rejected the argument that Native peoples are incapable of enjoying rights of ownership. Las Casas, who spent most of the first half of the sixteenth century in the New World, argued instead that natural law applies to Indians as it does to all human beings.[25]

In discussing Spain's views on Indian land rights, Marshall stated in *Johnson v. McIntosh* that "Spain did not rest her title solely on the grant of the Pope," but instead "placed it on the rights given by discovery." However, as Robert Williams, Jr., points out, "Marshall's assertion that discovery vested exclusive title in the discoverer deviated from the accepted principles of the Law of Nations." The discoverer did *not* obtain title but instead was accorded an exclusive entitlement to deal with the native inhabitants as against other European nations.[26]

FRENCH VIEWS OF INDIAN LAND RIGHTS

French exploration of the New World began in 1524 when King Francis I authorized a voyage along the east coast of North America. As a Catholic ruler, Francis was restricted by the *Inter Caetera*, but an opening was provided when Pope Clement VII was persuaded in 1533 to reinterpret the bull and limit its meaning. By 1540 Francis challenged not just the scope of the *Inter Caetera* but its legitimacy, asserting that popes had no power to distribute lands. The French ruler belittled the notion that the Catholic Church could grant ownership of the New World to Spain and Portugal, asking "to see Adam's will to learn how he had partitioned the world."[27]

John Marshall states in *Johnson v. McIntosh* that France "founded her title to the vast territories she claimed in America on discovery" and "asserted her right of dominion over a great extent of country not actually settled by Frenchmen, and her *exclusive right to acquire and dispose of the soil which remained in the occupation of Indians*."[28] The French monarchs thus claimed all of Canada, Arcadia, and Louisiana by virtue of discovery. By describing France's title as the "exclusive right to acquire and dispose of the soil which remained in the occupation of Indians," however, Marshall acknowledges that something remained to be acquired. Rather than obtaining an absolute and complete title by discovery, France at most claimed an exclusive—or preemptive—right to transact with the Natives. Rights of preemption certainly impacted Indian land rights, by limiting potential purchasers, but were nevertheless rights *to acquire* Indian soil, not rights *to* Indian soil. Moreover, such preemptive rights operated to exclude other European nations, leaving open the possibility that *private individuals* could purchase Indian lands.

Jacques Cartier's exploration of Canada in the 1530s was followed by Samuel de Champlain's settlement at Quebec and by subsequent journeys into the Great Lakes region and Mississippi Valley by Jacques Marquette, Louis Jolliet, and René-Robert Cavelier, Sieur de La Salle. According to historian Francis Parkman, La Salle stood at the mouth of the Mississippi River on April 9, 1682, and claimed possession of "this country of Louisiana."[29] The assertion of ownership was not accompanied by a deed or bill of sale. The French would eventually establish New Orleans at the mouth of the Mississippi, in addition to settlements and outposts along the St. Lawrence and in the Great Lakes region.

Because the French were focused on trade, they were able to find a "middle ground" with the Natives in the *pays d'en haut* (upper country). In contrast to the British focus on settlement, there were few grants of Indian lands to Frenchmen, in either a public or private capacity. A reputed transaction, however, involved the Piankeshaws—the tribe who sold the lands at issue in *Johnson v. McIntosh*. In 1742 the Piankeshaws supposedly granted the French a large tract along the Wabash River. In April of 1773, British general Thomas Gage expressed to Lord Dartmouth his firm conviction that private purchases of Indian lands "cannot be admitted by us, without establishing a very dangerous Precedent."[30] Just two months thereafter, the Illinois Indians assembled near the Mississippi River and sold most of their lands to William Murray and his twenty-one partners.

As discussed in the next chapter, the French in 1749 attempted to bolster their claim to the Ohio Valley by sending down the Ohio River an expedition led by Pierre-Joseph Céleron, Sieur de Blainville. At several points during the journey Céleron left behind lead plates on which French claims to the region were recorded. The engraved inscriptions asserted rights of possession to "the said river Ohio and of all those [rivers] that therein fall, and of all the lands on both sides as far as the sources of the said rivers."[31] Neither the Indians nor the English, however, were persuaded.

DUTCH AND SWEDISH VIEWS OF INDIAN LAND RIGHTS

The Netherlands based its claims to the New World on purchase of Native lands. Hugo Grotius wrote two treatises in the seventeenth century that furthered Dutch interests in settling the New World. In 1608 he published *Mare Liberum* (Freedom of the Seas) in order to demonstrate "that the Dutch . . . have the right to sail to the East Indies." Grotius agreed with Vitoria that the doctrine of discovery applied only to vacant lands and was thus inapplicable to land occupied by Indians. In *De Jure Belli ac Pacis* (The Law of War and Peace, 1625), Grotius again denounced efforts to claim, by right of discovery, "what is held by another, even though the occupant may be wicked, may hold wrong views about God, or may be dull of wit."[32]

The Protestant Dutch—who could not rely on papal grants—resolved to purchase land in America from the Indians. As William MacLeod points out, the Dutch took the position that "the Indian tribes or nations were owners of the land—*as of course they were.*" The most famous sale took place in 1626, when Peter Minuit of the Dutch West India Company purchased Manhattan Island for goods valued at twenty-four dollars. Three years later, the Colony of New Netherland provided that all patroons "shall be bound to purchase . . . the soil where they propose to plant their colonies." In light of such practices, the Dutch have been given credit for establishing the principle of purchasing the title to Indian lands in North America.[33]

The policy of the Swedes was similar to that of the Dutch. The governor of New Sweden acknowledged that the Natives owned the lands they inhabited. Accordingly, the Swedes acquired land by purchase and established Fort Christina (present-day Wilmington, Delaware) in 1638 after transacting with the Lenape Indians.[34] In 1655 the colony was lost to the Dutch, who surrendered it to the English in 1664.

EARLY ENGLISH AND COLONIAL VIEWS OF INDIAN LAND RIGHTS

Henry VII, who reigned from 1485 to 1509, was "a pious son of the Church, obedient to its decree in any matter of religion." The exploration of the New World, however, was a different issue. The Tudor king recognized the rights of Spain and Portugal in the southern seas but claimed the English could reach the Americas by crossing the North Atlantic. In 1496

John Cabot was authorized to find lands "unknown to all Christians" and acquire the "title and jurisdiction of the [lands] so discovered." In *Johnson v. McIntosh*, Marshall states that Cabot "discovered the continent of North America, along which he sailed as far south as Virginia," and observes that it is to this discovery that "the English trace their title."[35]

In the royal patent of December 9, 1502, explorers were barred from lands "first discovered by the King of Portugal or other friendly princes *and now in their possession.*" England thus maintained that the claims to the New World were defensible only when supported by settlement. In an exchange with the Spanish ambassador, Queen Elizabeth claimed that touching ground and naming rivers were "acts which cannot confer property." However, as John Juricek points out, the English came to believe that the king himself could take possession of overseas territories through the medium of royal charters.[36]

King James I relied on his personal authority to grant territory in the New World. The charter issued in 1606 to the Virginia Company was followed, three years later, by a larger grant "in absolute property." The 1609 charter is directly relevant to the *Johnson v. McIntosh* litigation, since its grant "from Sea to Sea, West, and Northwest" encompassed the lands purchased from the Illinois and Piankeshaws in 1773 and 1775. The grants of land from "Sea to Sea"—which created six of the thirteen colonies (Massachusetts, Connecticut, Virginia, North Carolina, South Carolina, and Georgia)—were vast preemptive claims designed to thwart the ambitions of other European powers.[37]

Tracing ownership to royal grants cohered with the fundamental principle of English land law that the king was the ultimate source of title. Feudalism was based on the theory that individuals held property "of the king" and were required to perform services to their lord. Land in British America was typically granted "in free and common socage," which required the payment of quitrents to the Crown. Although the rents often were not collected, the quitrent system served as a means of asserting royal authority. Indeed, both John Adams and Thomas Jefferson addressed this contentious issue in pre-Revolution publications and condemned the purported transfer of feudalism to America.[38]

The charters were silent as to Indian land rights. Nathan Dane, in his *General Abridgment and Digest of American Law* (1824), declared that all colonists "settled with the Indians as of convenience, of equity, or humanity, and not as a matter in law essential to his title." Dane's sweeping statement is incorrect, as evidenced by the actions of Roger Williams in New England. But neither the Tudors nor the Stuarts believed it was necessary to buy America from the Indians. The Pennsylvania charter of 1681 declared William Penn and his successors *"the true and absolute Proprietaries."* Penn did announce, on October 28, 1681, his intention to "buy Land of the true Owners wch I think is the Susquehanna People." Just ten days earlier, however, in his letter to the Indians, Penn stated that Charles II *"hath given unto me a great Province."* The Quaker proprietor acknowledged that his authority came from England and had no qualms about selling tracts in Pennsylvania *before* transacting with the Indians.[39]

Appearing contemporaneously with the royal charters were various theories propounded by Englishmen to justify the dispossession of the Indians. At first, the focus was on the Natives themselves: because of their heathenism they had no right to the lands they occupied. Sir Edward Coke announced in *Calvin's Case* (1608) that "when an infidel country is conquered, there being no established law among infidels which a Christian people can recognize, the rules laid down by the king apply."[40] Coke endorsed the view that heathen lands could be regarded in law as vacant. In 1640 the inhabitants of Milford, Connecticut, passed three resolves that also invoked religion to justify dispossession: "Voted, that the earth is the Lord's and the fulness thereof; voted, that the earth is given to the Saints; voted, we are the Saints."[41]

Other Englishmen focused on Native land use. Writing in the early part of the sixteenth century, Thomas More placed his *Utopia* in the New World, and stated that it was a just cause for war "when a people which does not use its soil . . . forbids the use and possession of it to others." John Winthrop and the Puritans likewise criticized the failure of the Indians to "improve" the land. John Locke, in his *Two Treatises of Government* (1690), developed the idea of a natural right to property and, in so doing, defended England's claim to Indian lands. According to Locke, "in the beginning all the world was America," and those who enclosed and cultivated the soil would be its owners. English claims to "waste" lands were based not on papal or royal authority but on natural right. As James Tully points out, Locke defined property "in such a way that Amerindian customary land use [was] not a legitimate type of property."[42]

When Reverend John Bulkley of Colchester, Connecticut, delivered his Christmas Eve sermon in 1724, he preached that the English had an absolute right to appropriate all lands in America "*as lay Wast or Unimproved by the Natives.*"[43] In the same fashion, the defendants in *Johnson v. McIntosh* relied on John Locke to argue that the Illinois and Piankeshaws had "acquired no proprietary interest in the vast tracts of territory which they wandered over." John Marshall characterized Indians as nomadic savages and declared that "to leave them in possession of their country, was to leave the country a wilderness." The iconic American actor John Wayne held a similar view in the twentieth century: "Our so-called stealing of this country from them was just a matter of survival. There were great numbers of people who needed new land, and the Indians were selfishly trying to keep it for themselves."[44]

The foregoing authorities supported the view that Indians lacked property rights. Yet, if the English could claim title to lands in America by virtue of discovery, royal patent, and natural right, why was so much property purchased from the Indians? More than seventy Indian deeds from Maine survive from the seventeenth century, dating as far back as 1639. Norwalk Indians sold land on March 5, 1640, to Roger Ludlow, a resident of Fairfield, Connecticut. In 1644, Native occupants sold the site of Harvard College. In 1678 four Indians deeded an island in the Delaware River to Elizabeth Kinsey. Edmund Cartlidge in 1725 purchased a "plantation" from Wiggoneeheehan, a Delaware Indian. Numerous transactions took place, and Governor Josiah Winslow of Plymouth Colony remarked, as early as 1676, that "the English did not possess one foot of land in this colony but what was fairly obtained by honest purchase of the Indian proprietors."[45]

While many persons did not consider "Indian title" to be a legally recognizable title, there were exceptions. In his role as colonial agent for Massachusetts and Connecticut, Jeremiah Dummer in 1721 published his *Defence of the New-England Charters*, arguing that only those who purchased land from "the native Lords of the Soil" held lawful title. According to Dummer, the Crown "neither did nor could grant the Soil," having no right to do so by virtue of inheritance, conquest, purchase, discovery, or Christianity. Rather, the "only fair and just" title was the "*Indian title*" that Dummer claimed had been purchased by "honest *New-England* Planters." Quaker minister Thomas Chalkley, in 1738, likewise acknowledged the primacy of Indian land rights, asserting that "no People . . . ought to take away, or settle, on other Mens Lands or Rights, without Consent, or purchasing the same."[46] In adherence to such principles, Jesuit Thomas Copley of Maryland acquired land in 1639 from the Patuxent Indians. This challenge to the absolute title of Lord Baltimore evoked a response comparable to the reaction of Puritan officials to Roger Williams. Such transactions were condemned as contemptuous of the proprietor's "dignity & rights" and productive of "dangerous consequence if not timely prevented."[47]

Even if Indians held property rights in their lands, the question remained whether English law would permit the Indians to sell their land to private parties. Eventually every colony regulated the purchase of Native lands. One reason for government oversight was to minimize fraudulent and unfair dealings, which produced resentment and undermined Indian relations. However, as John De Forest observed in his *History of the Indians of Connecticut*, such regulations were promulgated not only for the benefit of Indians but also "for the purpose of asserting and preserving the jurisdiction power of the General Court over the unbought and unoccupied lands of the colony." More recently, Eric Kades has argued that the enactment of such restrictions "makes perfect sense as a tool of efficient expropriation of Indian lands."[48]

Because Virginia asserted jurisdiction over the lands occupied by the Illinois and Piankeshaws, it is instructive to examine Virginia law concerning Indian purchases. Virginia passed a law in 1652 stating that "noe Indians [may] Sell their lands but at quarter Courts." Eastern Shore Indians were authorized two years later to sell land to individuals; however, a 1656 law provided that "no such alienations or bargaines and sales [shall] be valid without the assent of the Assembly."[49] Six years later, the General Assembly acknowledged that its prior laws had "proved fruitless and ineffectual," and declared that "no English *for any cause whatsoever* [shall] purchase or buy any land then claimed or possessed by any Indians." Virginia thereafter vacillated with respect to acquisition of Indian land. Between 1705 and 1778 regulation of Indian land purchases was controlled by an act that "declared it unlawful 'for an Indian king, or any other *of the said tributary Indians* whatever,' to sell or lease to non-Indians any lands 'now actually possessed, or justly claimed and pretended to by the said Indians.'"[50]

If the 1705 act applied only to "tributary" Indians, it had no effect on the sales by the Illinois and Piankeshaws. In June 1776 the revolutionary Virginia Convention resolved "that no purchases of lands within the chartered limits of Virginia shall be made, under any pretence whatever, from *any Indian tribe or nation*, without the approbation of the Virginia legislature" and, five days later, adopted a constitution providing that "no purchase of lands should be made of the Indian natives but in behalf of the public by authority of the General Assembly."[51] However, unless retroactive, these laws did not impact the Illinois-Wabash purchases. Thus there was real doubt as to whether the land sales at issue in *Johnson v. McIntosh* were prohibited by Virginia law. Whether the sales were prohibited by *British* law, however, was a more troublesome issue for the shareholders of the Illinois and Wabash Land Company.

"THE *SINNE* OF THE *PATTENTS*" REDUX

Protest against "the *sinne* of the *Pattents*" did not die with Roger Williams. The question resurfaced in the 1660s in New Jersey, where landowners defended the validity of Indian title. This lesser known dispute was reminiscent of the Williams controversy: the assertion that the Indians could convey a valid title was opposed by government officials, who viewed it as a challenge to Crown authority. The New Jersey conflict also foreshadowed the struggle of the Illinois and Wabash Land Company to overcome government resistance to its title claims. In both instances, ownership of land was contested on the basis of competing chains of title. In both instances, Native land rights were championed by recipients of Indian deeds. And in both instances, natural rights to property were opposed by the doctrine of discovery, feudal law, statutory prohibitions, and royal authority.

In 1666 Puritans from Connecticut settled along the Passaic River, naming their town Newark. On July 11, 1667, the transplanted colonists purchased twenty thousand acres from the Lenni Lenape Indians in exchange for goods in kind, including "four barrells of beere." The lands in question, however, had previously granted by Charles II to his brother James, who in turn had granted the proprietary rights to Sir George Carteret and Lord John Berkeley.[52] When the proprietors attempted to collect quitrents, the settlers resisted. In 1675 six prominent English lawyers were asked to render their legal opinion on "Wither the Grant from ye Indians be Sufficient to any planter without a Grant from ye King or his Assignes." The lawyers denied the validity of private purchases of Indian lands, arguing that "the Prince . . . who make the Discovery hath the Right of the Soyle & Govermt of that place." Legislation prohibiting the purchase of Indian lands without a license from the governor was passed in 1683 and again in 1703. Nevertheless, the settlers continued to insist that they could hold property solely by their Indian purchase.[53]

The controversy was revived in the 1740s when settlers petitioned for confirmation of their title to lands purchased from Indians. The proprietors countered by filing suit in the Chancery of New Jersey. A flash point finally occurred when Samuel Baldwin of Newark was jailed for cutting timber on a proprietary tract. Baldwin denied that he was trespassing, claiming title by virtue of an Indian deed. A midafternoon riot ensued on September 19, 1745, when a mob "flooded into town armed with clubs, axes and crowbars, . . . brushed aside the sheriff, broke open the jail door and freed Baldwin, without the nicety of bail."[54]

What followed was an escalating war of words. In February 1746 Griffin Jenkins published "*A Brief Vindication of the Purchasers against the Proprietors, in a Christian Manner*," appealing to the royal conscience to "do Justice amongst his Subjects, by giving every one his Right and Title . . . bought of the Natives." In response, the proprietors denounced the "setting up sham Deeds, procured from stroling Indians, in Place of the Title of the Crown of England." The proprietors argued that reliance on Indian title was an affront to the Crown: "To pretend to hold Lands by an Indian Deed only, is not that declaring the Indian Grantor to be the Superior Lord of that Land, and disavowing the Crown of England to be so? . . . And do not those Overt Acts . . . approach to High Treason?"[55]

Still the proponents of Indian title persevered. In 1746 an unsigned letter published in a New York newspaper argued that John Locke's labor theory legitimated the *Native title* to the lands in question, because the Indians worked the property prior to its sale. A year later the Newark settlers presented a defense of their title, beginning with the contention that their purchases were fairly obtained, "not of some Strolling Indians, or for some few Bottles of Rum, . . . but of their Chiefs, at a dear Rate." Then, in the true spirit of Roger Williams, the settlers questioned the authority of Charles II to grant the lands without first purchasing them from the native occupants: "We hope you'll give us leave to ask how he came by them, was it by Discovery, by Conquest, by Gift, or by Contract, was the Discovery made in his Day? . . . Can it be supposed [the Indians] had no Right unto . . . their Lands[?] . . . Yes, Doubtless they had, from the Great and Absolute Proprietor of the Whole Universe."[56]

The argument of the Newark purchasers is as radical as the view espoused by Roger Williams a century earlier, and as straightforward as the position taken by the Illinois and Wabash Land Company three-quarters of century thereafter. The legal dispute with the proprietors was never resolved, yet it serves as a postscript to Williams's banishment by the Massachusetts Bay Colony and as a prelude to the Supreme Court's decision in *Johnson v. McIntosh*. Most of the basic arguments for and against Indian title were now in place. Significant developments, however, still lay ahead, such as the rise (and fall) of the speculative land companies; the regulation of Indian land sales by the Crown itself; the American Revolution; and the ensuing struggle between the national government and several of the states for control of the newly acquired territory in the Ohio and Mississippi valleys.

The issue of Native land rights was central to the struggle for control of the trans-Appalachian west. The shareholders of the Illinois and Wabash Land Company were not alone in contending that private individuals could acquire Native lands directly. Puritan Roger Williams, Jesuit Thomas Copley, and Quaker Thomas Chalkley had insisted upon the primacy of Indian title. Jeremiah Dummer and the Newark settlers, for more worldly reasons, also relied upon Indian deeds. The England writer Arthur Young reached the same conclusion just prior to the American Revolution, pointing out the "absurdity" of the discovery doctrine, and arguing that "the *right* every where is in the natives [and] all other rights are fictitious."[57]

It is thus evident that John Marshall's unyielding pronouncement in *Johnson v. McIntosh*—that Indian tribes are "incapable of transferring the absolute title to others"—was by no means universally accepted prior to the Supreme Court's 1823 decision.[58] Marshall's legal views were certainly not shared by the Illinois Indians, who in 1773 sold most of their lands to twenty-two individuals who formed the Illinois Land Company. Nor were his views accepted by the Piankeshaw Indians, who in 1775 sold most of their lands to the twenty individuals who became the original shareholders in the Wabash Land Company.

3

THE ILLINOIS AND
PIANKESHAWS

Why did the tribes in *Johnson v. McIntosh* consent to sell vast portions of their homeland to private purchasers? The grantors received an assortment of goods, valued by the parties at twenty-four thousand dollars for the Illinois purchase and thirty-one thousand dollars for the Wabash (Piankeshaw) purchase.[1] Were the chiefs fraudulently induced to sign the deeds? Or did the tribes willingly transact with foresight of the impending wave of trans-Appalachian settlement?

The Illinois and Wabash conveyances, to be better understood from the Native perspective, must be placed in historical context. The Iroquois, French, and British presence in the Ohio and Mississippi Valleys fractured the political cohesion of the local tribes, and disease and warfare led to dramatic reductions in population. The Illinois and Miami confederacies were unable to protect their homelands and were incapable of preventing the influx of settlers. While perhaps inevitable, the sales in 1773 and 1775 nevertheless led to the demise of the Illinois and the Piankeshaws as separate tribal identities.

THE ILLINOIS INDIANS PRIOR TO 1763

The Illinois dominated the mid-Mississippi Valley prior to European contact. At the height of their power, the tribes of this loosely organized confederation ranged east to the Wabash River, south to the Ohio River, northward into Wisconsin, and west some 150 miles beyond what the Illinois called the Missi-sippiwe, the "Great River." The French identified as many as twelve tribes as members of the Illini nation, but only five tribes remained in the 1830s: the Kaskaskia, Peoria, Cahokia, Tamaroa, and Michigamea.[2]

John Marshall, in *Johnson v. McIntosh*, declared that the subsistence of Indians "was drawn chiefly from the forest." Allison Dussias, however, notes that the Illinois combined farming with hunting and fishing and suggests that Marshall's statement "was inaccurate with respect to the very tribes whose land conveyances were at issue."[3] The Illinois were drawn into the fur trade during the last half of the seventeenth century. At this time their primary enemies were the Osage, Pawnee, Winnebago, and Dakota peoples, and while warfare could be devastating, it was constrained by the lack of European weaponry. With the arrival of French the Illinois became embroiled in a series of wars with increasingly deadly results, and the list of their enemies grew to include, among other tribes, the Five Nations of the Iroquois League.

The five Iroquois peoples, from east to west in upstate New York, were the Mohawk, Oneida, Onondaga, Cayuga, and Seneca tribes. During the "Beaver Wars" of the seventeenth century the Iroquois drove the Mahicans from the Hudson Valley and fought with Algonquians, Hurons, and Eries for control of the St. Lawrence. After subduing the neighboring tribes, the Iroquois turned to the west. The Illinois could not match the firepower of the invaders and were forced to retreat temporarily across the Mississippi River.[4]

France was also interested in extending its presence into the Illinois country. At a Chippewa village near Sault Ste. Marie, Simon François Daumont, Sieur de St. Lusson, proclaimed in 1671 the annexation "of all countries discovered or to be discovered between the Northern, Western, and Southern Seas." Thereafter, Father Jacques Marquette and Louis Jolliet undertook the task of exploring the claimed territory. On June 17, 1673, their expedition reached the Mississippi by way of the Fox and Wisconsin rivers. As their small entourage descended to the mouth of the Arkansas River, the adventurers encountered the Peoria Indians. Returning by way of the Illinois River, they came to a Kaskaskia village and received an enthusiastic welcome. Marquette promised to return and establish a mission and did so in the spring of 1675.[5]

In order to present a united front against the Five Nations, other tribes joined the Kaskaskia, and by 1680 a "grand village" was situated on the west bank of the river, near present-day Utica, Illinois. Seven or eight thousand Indians lived there, but on September 10, 1680, less than five hundred warriors were in residence, and only one hundred were armed with muskets. Six Europeans were also present, including Henri de Tonti, the trusted lieutenant of French explorer René-Robert Cavelier, Sieur de La Salle, who had returned to Canada the previous March.[6]

A large war party approached, consisting of Iroquois and Miami Indians. Their objective was to subjugate the region and monopolize the fur trade. During the night the Illinois sent their women and children downstream to an island in the Illinois River. Negotiations ensued, and the Europeans departed. The warring nations then moved downstream, toward the mouth of the Illinois River, where the tribes of the Illinois confederacy separated with tragic results: "Some descended the Mississippi; some, more prudent, crossed to the western side. One of their principal tribes, the Tamaroas, . . . had the fatuity to remain near the mouth of the Illinois, where they were speedily assailed by all the force of the Iroquois. The men fled, and very few of them were killed; but the women and children were captured to the number, it is said, of several hundred."[7] As noted by James Scott, "the Illinois never again gained any numerical or political significance," and in 150 years the tribes would no longer inhabit their namesake state.[8]

When La Salle reached the "grand village" in December, he was greeted by silence. The explorer traveled farther south and came upon the remains of several hundred Indians. He returned to Canada, reunited with Tonti, and set forth in 1681 on his most famous expedition. After claiming "Louisiana" for France near the Gulf of Mexico in April 1682, La Salle returned north to defend the Illinois (and French fur trade) against renewed Iroquois warfare. In December construction began on a new fort atop a sheer outcrop of rock—known today as Starved Rock—located across the Illinois River from the Kaskaskia village. Fort St. Louis was completed in the spring of 1683 and soon attracted Algonquian tribes seeking protection from the Iroquois. Several tribes of the Miami confederacy settled nearby, including the Piankeshaws (Peanghichia). By 1684 there was a Native population of approximately twenty thousand, and Fort St. Louis was without question the focal point of French authority between Canada and Louisiana.[9]

The September 1680 attack marked the last important military success of the Iroquois in the Great Lakes region. The Illinois and other

Algonquian tribes retaliated in 1687, aided by the French. In order to protect their territory, the Five Nations agreed to peace terms in 1701 with Great Britain and France. Based on the treaty, Great Britain contended that the Iroquois were under the aegis of the British Crown. Cadwallader Colden, in *The History of the Five Indian Nations Depending on the Province of New York in America* (1727), depicted Iroquois history as a chronicle of conquest, thereby extending British influence to the Ohio country and Great Lakes region. The "Beaver Wars" actually ended in failure, yet were transformed into the myth of Iroquois conquest, which enabled England and her colonies to fortify claims to trans-Appalachia by securing land cessions from the "conquering" Iroquois rather than from the actual inhabitants.[10]

When the Iroquois were put on the defensive, the need lessened for the Illinois tribes to congregate for mutual protection. The Peorias remained, but by 1703 the Cahokias, Tamaroas, and Kaskaskias were settled near present-day St. Louis. The French at this time established forts and missions extending from the Great Lakes to the confluence of the Ohio and Mississippi. In 1699 the Seminarians of Quebec founded a mission at the village of Cahokia, twenty miles below the mouth of the Illinois River. The Jesuits thereafter accompanied the Kaskaskia Indians to the Kaskaskia River, and French officials responded by building Fort Chartres, located sixteen miles away on the Mississippi.[11]

The divided tribes were susceptible to attack, and by 1710 the total population of the confederacy was reduced to approximately 6,200 persons. Over the next forty years the population continued to decline, in large part due to the cumulative effects of warfare and disease. During most of the first half of the eighteenth century the Illinois participated in French campaigns against the Fox Indians and their allies, the Kickapoo and Mascouten tribes. The Illinois also fought the English and their colonies during the French and Indian War, raiding settlements in Pennsylvania and Georgia and attacking English forces in the Carolinas.[12]

The French presence remained strong in the southern part of the Illinois country, where settlers brought with them the twin killers of malaria and smallpox. Recurrent epidemics ravaged the Illinois, and the population dropped to about 2,000 in 1750. The Peoria were estimated at a total of just 250 persons in 1736, and the combined warrior strength of the Kaskaskia, Michigamea, and Cahokia tribes was put at two hundred men in 1759. Carol Spindel attributes the dramatic decline to "exacerbated intertribal warfare, a declining birthrate, epidemics of diseases to which they had no immunity, alcoholism, and the departure of splinter groups."[13] Helen Tanner contends that "the most important factor was the constant raiding and warfare upon the Illinois by their anti-French tribal enemies."[14] The Illini Nation was a shell of its former self when the Illinois country was added to the British Empire at the conclusion of the French and Indian War.

The Illinois and the British

The Illinois country was not directly affected when the French surrendered Canada in 1760. The British victory, however, helped end the great imperial conflict known as the Seven Years' War. In the 1763 Treaty of Paris, France ceded Canada, the Illinois country, and—with the exception of New Orleans—all other lands east of the Mississippi River. By a prior secret treaty France had transferred New Orleans and lands west of the Mississippi to Spain. Consequently, after ninety years of French "rule" and alliance, the Illinois Indians were faced with the unwelcome prospect of interacting with new European powers.

The arrival of the British was delayed, however, by Native efforts to push troops and settlers back across the Alleghenies. The Ottawa leader Pontiac led the uprising, and within weeks every western post except Detroit and Fort Pitt had fallen. The resistance was fueled in part by opposition to the presumptuous transfer of Indian territory. In 1765 an Illinois chief expressed his surprise "that the great emperor of the French has given away *our land*." When four hundred soldiers under Major Arthur Loftus ascended the Mississippi from New Orleans, the Illinois and neighboring tribes forced the British to retreat. Lieutenant John Ross became the first British officer to complete the trip, arriving in the Illinois country from Mobile. However, when the Illinois returned from their winter quarters, they informed Ross "that *these lands are ours* and no one claims them, not even other red men."[15] Fearing for his life, the lieutenant departed for New Orleans.

It was Sir William Johnson, superintendent for Indian affairs, who proposed to General Thomas Gage, the commander in chief of British forces in North America, that a remarkable Irishman by the name of George Croghan be sent to take charge of the French-built Fort Chartres on the Mississippi. Croghan, who participated in numerous schemes to acquire

Indian lands, was Johnson's deputy superintendent. Gage commissioned Alexander Fraser to accompany Croghan, with instructions to bring presents to the Indians, pacify the French inhabitants, and effect a formal transfer of governmental authority.

The expedition was ultimately successful, but only after a series of missteps. Fraser left Fort Pitt without Croghan in March of 1765, reaching Fort Chartres one month later. He was harshly received and fled to New Orleans. In his report Fraser described the Illinois in unflattering terms, characterizing them as "cruel, treacherous, and cowardly," and "in general great Drunkards."[16] George Croghan, who held a higher opinion of Indians, never made it to Fort Chartres. He was captured and tomahawked, but he survived and was allowed to travel to the Illinois country. Croghan met Pontiac in eastern Illinois on July 18, 1765. The assembled group, which included deputies "from the four Nations living in the Illinois Country," thereafter held conferences on the Wabash River and at Detroit, where a formal end to the rebellion was arranged. The "four Nations"—the Kaskaskia, Peoria, Michigamea, and Cahokia tribes—informed Croghan that "they had allowed the French to settle in areas, but that they had not sold any part of their country to the French."[17]

British occupation of the Illinois country finally occurred on October 10, 1765, when Louis Bellerive, Sieur de St. Ange, surrendered Fort Chartres to Captain Thomas Stirling of the Forty-Second Highlanders regiment. In a letter to General Gage, Stirling noted that the French were without "possessions in this Country, Except the Ground the Forts stands on, as no Lands were ever bought from the Indians, who Claim the whole as their property."[18] Even as their numbers were decreasing, the confederated tribes continued to claim ownership of the Illinois Country.

The Illinois attended the August 1766 conference at Fort Chartres, where Croghan urged the tribes to trade with English merchants, such as the Philadelphia firm of Baynton, Wharton, and Morgan (with whom Croghan was associated). In the summer of 1767 the Kaskaskias chose an additional chief, Jean Baptiste DuCoigne, who would lead his people well into the next century. By this time many Kaskaskias and Peorias had moved to the west bank of the Mississippi, which was nominally Spanish but occupied primarily by French farmers and traders. Other Illinois Indians remained east of the Mississippi, near Kaskaskia and Cahokia. It was in the latter village where, on April 20, 1769, a Peoria Indian killed the famed Pontiac.[19]

On July 5, 1773, after a month of public conferences, the Illinois Indians sold two large tracts of land—one lying between the Ohio and Mississippi rivers and the other on the Illinois River. The deed was signed by six Kaskaskia chiefs (including DuCoigne), three Peoria chiefs, and one Cahokia chief. Anna Edith Marks provides the following colorful—if perhaps imaginative—description of the event: "The bronzed Indians with their blankets wound about them—some standing in majestic dignity, others lounging about smoking their long pipes; the red coated soldiers; the buckskin clad Frenchman—all gazing upon the purchase price consisting of piles of bright red blankets, shirts, stockings, shining brass kettles, steel knives, sacks of flour; and even cattle and horses—must have formed a peculiarly striking and impressive setting for the signing of the agreement."[20] At this time the Kaskaskia tribe numbered about 210 persons with just 60 warriors. The Peorias and Michigameas were reduced to 170 warriors.[21] The diminished confederacy held only a small fraction of its formerly extensive domain and was struggling to survive.

THE PIANKESHAWS

The name Piankeshaw is said to have originated from the Miami word *payunggishah*, meaning "those who separated and formed a tribe."[22] Early French accounts divide the Miami confederation into six tribes: the Atchatchakangouen, Kilatika, Mengakonkia, Ouiatenon, Pepikokia, and Piankeshaw tribes. The four that survived to sign treaties with the United States were the Miami (Atchatchakangouen), Eel River (Kilatika), Wea (Ouiatenon), and Piankeshaw tribes. The English called the confederacy the Twightwee (cry of the crane) or, more generally, the Wabash Indians.

In spite of their participation in the 1680 attack on the Illinois, the Miamis were persuaded by La Salle and Tonti to settle near Fort St. Louis. By 1684 the fortification had attracted nearly 4,000 warriors, including 1,300 Miamis, 600 Kilatakas, 500 Ouiatenons, 160 Pepikokias, and 150 Piankeshaws. However, the Piankeshaws left prior to 1688 and settled on the Vermilion and Wabash rivers in present-day Indiana. One reason behind their eastward migration was the emergence of English competition for Indian trade. As Eric Hinderaker has noted, the tribes of the Miami confederacy "quickly learned that they could receive European manufactures on better terms from the English than they enjoyed with the French."[23] This attraction to English goods proved a fatal attraction, because the Anglo-Americans desired not only to trade with Indians but also to acquire their lands.

Marquis de Vaudreuil, the governor-general of New France, reported in 1712 that he had sent Jean-Baptiste Bissot, Sieur de Vincennes, to the Miami "to prevent them from approaching the English." Vincennes relocated to the headwaters of the Maumee River but died during the winter of 1718–19. By this time the Wea Indians were settled next to Fort Ouiatenon, near present-day West Lafayette, Indiana. Some of the Piankeshaws were also living in this area, while other tribal members resided farther south along the Vermilion River.[24]

In spite of French protests, the Miami solicited English traders, and Fort Oswego was established in 1724 on the southeast shore of Lake Ontario to facilitate the fur trade. Pennsylvania and Virginia were beginning to focus on the Ohio Valley, and the French were further alarmed by English overtures to the Chickasaw of Mississippi and western Tennessee. In response, François Marie Bissot de Vincennes, who had assumed the duties of his father, was ordered to establish a fort near the confluence of the Wabash (Ouabache) and the Ohio. The youthful Vincennes persuaded a number of Piankeshaws to accompany him, although the Indians were wary of the Chickasaws and refused to move as far south as the Ohio River. As a compromise, the new post was established in 1731 or 1732 at present-day Vincennes, Indiana. The fort was intended to impede Chickasaw intrusions, safeguard the Wabash-Ohio route, and stop the advance of English colonial traders.[25]

The governor of Louisiana, Jean-Baptiste Le Moyne de Bienville, declared the post at Vincennes to be "one of the more important ones of the Colony." The French could travel the Great Lakes, ascend the Maumee River in northeast Indiana, portage to the Wabash, descend to the Ohio, and then proceed either to the Illinois country or to New Orleans. A disapproving Englishman characterized the French in North America "'as rats in a good old cheese,' who, having gained entrance via the St. Lawrence and Mississippi, were busy gnawing their way to the center to 'claim the whole as their own.'" The French, of course, saw things differently, viewing British Americans as trespassers and troublemakers.[26]

Vincennes was not provided sufficient goods to hold the post, and he struggled to keep the Piankeshaws from returning to their former villages. To make matters worse, the Chickasaws threatened to cut off travel between Canada and Louisiana. Bienville consequently ordered Vincennes to descend the Mississippi with a force of Piankeshaw and Illinois Indians and rendezvous with him in March 1736 near present-day Memphis, Tennessee. The Louisiana governor was delayed, however, and the Chickasaws pressed their advantage, capturing and killing Vincennes. Most of the Piankeshaws elected to return to the Vermilion River, and just fifteen warriors remained.[27]

Louis Bellerive, Sieur de St. Ange, who in 1765 would surrender Fort Chartres to the British, was chosen as the new commander of Fort Vincennes. In addition to Native protectors, the fledgling post needed settlers, who were reluctant to come unless they could purchase land. In order to solve this problem, St. Ange apparently convinced the Piankeshaws in 1742 to grant a large tract of land along the Wabash. The deed, or treaty, was allegedly lost during the French and Indian War, and the lack of any record casts doubt on whether the transaction occurred. The putative 1742 grant is alluded to in the 1775 deed by which the Piankeshaws sold the lands at issue in *Johnson v. McIntosh*. In the 1775 deed—which was prepared by the speculators—the earlier grant is expressly excepted from the sale of land. The existence of the 1742 grant is also supported by the fact that St. Ange considered himself empowered to issue deeds for small plots. The post gradually attracted farmers, merchants, and tradesmen, and the surrounding area included a village, commons, and arable strips of land.[28]

PIANKESHAW REBELLION AND REPRISAL

The Piankeshaw leader Memeskia led an exodus from Vincennes after a disastrous 1736 expedition against the Chickasaws. By 1745 Memeskia and his followers resided near Kekionga (Fort Wayne). The leader of the local Indian village, Le Pied Froid, was regarded by the French as the chief of the Miami confederacy. Le Pied Froid remained loyal, in contrast to Memeskia, who would soon acquire another name—Old Briton—in recognition of his new allegiance. As Andrew Cayton observes, although Memeskia had no hereditary right to be a prominent chief, he was a "clever diplomat" who led by decisive action, and his rise "reflected a new pattern of leadership, one based on ability."[29]

Memeskia had three reasons for believing that living conditions could be improved by joining with the English. France required merchants to pay for the privilege of using trading posts, which increased the cost of their goods. Second, eastern Indians had recently founded the village of

Chiningue (Logstown) on the upper Ohio River, cutting short the travel time for Pennsylvania traders and Iroquois and Shawnee middlemen. Finally, the capture of Louisbourg, Nova Scotia, in 1745 enabled the British to cut off supplies bound for French forts.[30]

The chief of the Hurons, Orontony, was the first to break with the French. The Hurons were driven westward by the Iroquois and eventually came to be known as the Wyandot Indians. Orontony, who was also called Nicholas, moved his people to Sandusky Bay on the shore of Lake Erie, where they were visited by George Croghan and other British traders. In 1747 Orontony conspired with other Indians, including Memeskia, to revolt against the French. The Hurons killed five traders, but failed to capture a French post, and thereafter sought sanctuary in eastern Ohio and western Pennsylvania.[31]

Memeskia, on the other hand, had more success, burning part of Fort Miami and seizing eight soldiers from the garrison. This irrevocable break with France produced a schism within the Miami confederacy, and in 1747 Memeskia led his followers to the confluence of the Great Miami River and Loramie's Creek, near the modern town of Piqua, Ohio. The new settlement, Pickawillany, could be reached by British traders and soon became populated by Indians from various tribes. Memeskia, who was called the Piankeshaw King as well as Old Briton, was fast becoming a threat to French interests in the Ohio Valley.[32]

Once ensconced at Pickawillany, Memeskia expressed his desire to be admitted to the British alliance. Delegates from Pickawillany traveled east to Lancaster, Pennsylvania, the largest inland town in the colonies. The conference was a success, and both sides were elated with the 1748 Lancaster Treaty. Pennsylvania officials believed it would extend British influence westward and aid the province in its rivalry with Virginia over the Indian trade. Memeskia was undoubtedly pleased, because his settlement would soon become an important trading center, and because his diplomacy enabled him to maintain his independence from the French. Pickawillany welcomed defectors from the Eel River, Ouiatanon, and Piankeshaw tribes on the upper Wabash, and when news of the treaty reached Vincennes, the Piankeshaws residing nearby "moved in a body to the White River, reducing the distance between them and Pickawillany by half."[33]

The 1748 Treaty of Aix-la-Chapelle formally ended King George's War, but tensions soon increased when the British Board of Trade approved a large grant of Appalachian territory to the Ohio Company of

Virginia. The acting governor of Canada, Marquis de La Galissonière, responded by authorizing an expeditionary force to claim ownership of trans-Appalachia. The man chosen for the task, Captain Pierre-Joseph Céleron, Sieur de Blainville, arrived at the head of the Allegheny River on June 29, 1749, where he "tacked up a metal sign decorated with the king's arms and buried his first lead plate of claim." A month later the expedition reached the mouth of the Great Miami River, which led to Memeskia's village. Upon arrival Céleron discovered that his military strength could not compel Memeskia to return to Fort Miami from Pickawillany and its ready access to British trade. Relegated to persuasion, Céleron relayed the governor's edict that "the English . . . may no longer approach this land, *which belongs to me.*" But Memeskia declined to accompany Céleron, who reported that the Indians "are entirely devoted to the English."[34]

In November 1749 George Croghan led a contingent of traders to Pickawillany and constructed storehouses and a small stockade. According to Dorothy Libby, "all during 1750 rumors and reports of Piankashaw activities and collaboration with the English were circulating among the French and in the Illinois country." The governor-general of New France, Marquis de la Jonquière, reported in September 1750 that the Indians were "more angry than ever against the French." Whereas in 1749 the population of Memeskia's village was less than two hundred persons, a year later there were perhaps as many as four hundred families present. To add insult to injury, when French officials resorted to bribery, the Piankeshaw King accepted the trade goods but remained at Pickawillany.[35]

The governor of Pennsylvania, James Hamilton, instructed George Croghan in November 1750 to "renew the chain of friendship" and counter French efforts to curry favor with Old Briton. During his westward journey Croghan was joined by Christopher Gist, who had been employed by the Ohio Company of Virginia to explore the western territory. On February 17, 1751, the small party arrived at Pickawillany, which Gist described as "one of the strongest Indian Towns upon this Part of the Continent." According to Croghan, a delegation of Weas and Piankeshaws from the Wabash Valley "requested to be admitted into the chain of friendship." Although unauthorized, an agreement was drawn up on behalf of the Pennsylvania governor that declared the Weas and Piankeshaws to be "good Friends and Allies of the English Nation."[36]

Croghan's "treaty" was subsequently rejected by the Pennsylvania House of Assembly, and Croghan himself was reproved by Governor

Hamilton "for acting in publick matters without his orders." Nevertheless, the recent events bolstered Memeskia's confidence. The Piankeshaw King's aura of invincibility grew larger after the French attacked Pickawillany but failed to breach the stockade walls. Memeskia responded by killing three French soldiers and cutting off the ears of another as a warning. The French ministry named Marquis Duquesne as the governor-general of New France and instructed him to shift the focus from Memeskia to the English. Unaware of this change in strategy, Charles-Michel Mouet de Langlade of Michilimackinac, the twenty-two-year-old son of a prominent French trader and an Ottawa Indian, concocted a plan to head south with 250 warriors and catch the Piankeshaw King by surprise.[37]

The plan worked. Most of the men were away hunting when the attack commenced on the morning of June 21, 1752. Within minutes the outcome was determined, as described by David Edmunds: "Within the palisade, Old Briton found he commanded a force of only twenty fighting men, including a handful of British traders. . . . The attackers outnumbered them more than ten to one. Moreover, Langlade held another trump card: he had captured many of the defenders' families."[38] In the afternoon Langlade promised to depart if Memeskia would surrender the Englishmen in the fort. Lacking water and heavily outnumbered, five white men agreed to come out, while two others hid themselves. The Indians stabbed one unfortunate trader, scalped him, and then cut out his heart and ate it. After seizing and killing Memeskia, the victors dismembered and boiled the Piankeshaw King, and then proceeded to consume his body in front of his horrified followers. In the words of Thomas Burney, one of the traders who avoided detection, "for his attachment to the English, they boiled, and eat him all up."[39]

The sudden and violent death of the Piankeshaw King changed the balance of power in the Ohio Valley. His wife and son fled eastward, but most followers returned to the French. As noted by Jack Stagg, their concern for survival "superseded any advantage the British could offer." The Piankeshaws lost political power, and two decades later—when they transacted with the future members of the Wabash Land Company—the tribe was a subordinate member of the Miami confederacy. In terms of the larger geopolitical dispute, Langlade's attack has been characterized as "the first battle of the impending French and Indian War."[40] The final clash between the French and British for control of North America was about to begin.

"QUARRELING ABOUT LANDS WHICH BELONG TO US"

The Illinois and the Piankeshaws, like other tribes east of the Mississippi, were caught up in the ensuing warfare between France and Great Britain. Eric Hinderaker, in *Elusive Empires: Constructing Colonialism in the Ohio Valley, 1673–1800*, contrasts the French "empire of commerce," which focused on Indian trade, with the British "empire of land," which endeavored to transplant Europeans and exploit American resources. British Americans placed a higher value on land ownership than did their French counterparts, in part due to sheer numbers: the colonial population was approaching one million, whereas only about eighty thousand French were scattered along the St. Lawrence, the Great Lakes, and the rivers of interior America.[41] The contrast between their viewpoints, however, can be overstated: the French focus on commerce did not preclude ownership of Native lands (such as the 1742 Vincennes grant), and acquisition of tribal lands by the British usually followed or accompanied extensive trading.

The French message to the Indians was straightforward: the duplicitous English talked about a "chain of friendship" but schemed "to invade the territories *which do not belong to them*," But if the lands occupied by the western tribes did not belong to the English, who owned such lands? La Galissonière had declared that the land "*belongs to me*." On the other hand, Céleron was careful to assure the Indians that the French "will not invade your lands nor drive you away from them." The Indians, in response, spoke defiantly of "our lands."[42] Yet it is evident from Céleron's journal that the Natives were more concerned about the loss of trade goods. Memeskia broke from the French to trade with the English, and the Weas and Piankeshaws sought a commercial alliance from George Croghan and Pennsylvania. English traders, however, were inevitably followed by Englishmen seeking Indian lands. The latter made their appearance, in the case of the Illinois and the Piankeshaws, in 1773 and 1775.

Native Americans were never oblivious to the impact of land cessions. Chief Powhatan in 1607 declared to John Smith that "your comming is not for trade, but to invade my people and possess my Country." George Croghan wrote in 1749 that "the Indians Does nott Like to hear of there Lands being Setled over Allegany Mountain." Two Delaware chiefs confronted Christopher Gist in 1752 and asked "where the Indians' land lay, for that the French claimed all the Land on one Side the River Ohio and the English on the other Side." Twenty-two-year-old George Washington told a lie in June 1754 when he assured Indians that the English presence in the Ohio country was only "to maintain your Rights." Two weeks later, at the Albany Congress, the Mohawk chief Hendrick observed that the "Governor of Virginia, and the Governor of Canada are both quarrelling about lands which belong to us, and such a quarrel as this may end in our destruction."[43]

In light of the foregoing, it is evident that the transactions in *Johnson v. McIntosh* were neither unprecedented nor unusual. The 1773 and 1775 purchases were preceded by a quarter of a century of schemes involving Indian lands. As discussed in the chapters that follow, some speculators sought grants of land directly from the Crown, whereas others requested royal confirmation of title to lands previously acquired from Native grantors. In a few instances, however, the speculative ventures depended entirely upon private purchases from tribal owners.

4

"AN UNACCOUNTABLE THIRST
FOR LARGE TRACTS OF LAND"

Land in the Americas was initially viewed by Europeans as territory containing resources, not as a commodity in itself. In the eighteenth century, however, wealthy individuals began to regard the New World as an investment opportunity. In France a Scotsman named John Law persuaded King Louis XV to grant a trade monopoly to the Company of the Indies (Compagnie des Indes), known popularly as the Mississippi Company. Law and his cohorts circulated a glowing report of Louisiana, sold stock at swiftly rising prices, and created a "bubble" that inevitably burst and ruined French investors: "So numerous were the private fortunes gained that a new word was invented to describe them. The word 'millionaire' was coined at this time to describe the rich Mississippians, first appearing in print in the lawyer Marais' journal in 1720. . . . [However, when] shares plunged the public was incandescent with fury."[1]

Speculation in trade was followed by speculation in land. Merrill Jensen points out that "land speculation was the major get-rich-quick activity of the eighteenth century." Wealthy Anglo-Americans, who had few other investment options, purchased land in hopes that rising prices would yield substantial profits. In 1756 Peter Wraxall, a British official who attended the Albany Congress, declared the "unaccountable thirst for large Tracts of Land" to be "one of the most fatal Causes of the decrease of our Indian Interest & Influence."[2]

Virginia and Pennsylvania colonists were especially keen to obtain western lands. Prominent Virginians interpreted their 1609 "sea-to-sea" charter as encompassing the Ohio and the upper Mississippi valleys, and applied to the Crown for vast tracts in Indian country. Speculators from Pennsylvania, who were constrained by fixed boundaries, focused instead on making connections: with the Indians through trade, with British officials in America, and with London businessmen and members of the English ministry. In contrast to the homogeneous Anglican planters of Virginia, the Pennsylvanians were a more varied group: Irish and Scottish traders on the frontier as well as Jewish and Quaker merchants in Lancaster and Philadelphia. Individuals from both colonies assumed that royal approval was essential to their settlement schemes.

The Crown, in turn, was faced with the daunting task of governing the lands secured by the 1763 Treaty of Paris. Several intractable issues surfaced, which ultimately became intertwined with other causes of the American Revolution. Should settlement of Indian lands be permitted? Should quitrents be collected, and taxes imposed, to finance the maintenance of military outposts? Were additional colonies desirable, or would the establishment of transmontane governments encourage rebellion?

As described in the sections that follow, English policy regarding Indians and western settlement was by no means static. On October 7, 1763, King George III barred private purchases of Indian lands west of the Allegheny Mountains; however, within a decade, the king responded favorably to the petition of the Grand Ohio Company and issued an order establishing the colony of Vandalia in West Virginia and Kentucky. The colony never materialized, and the settlement schemes of other land companies likewise failed. During this period, some individuals chose to follow the path blazed by Roger Williams and the Newark settlers: they argued that a private purchase of Indian lands sufficed to vest "as full and ample a title as could be obtained."[3] Prominent colonists—including Benjamin Franklin and Patrick Henry—championed the "natural liberty" of Indians to own and sell property. The argument for buying America from the Indians was developed in letters, pamphlets, and legal opinions, and the stage was set for the Illinois and Wabash purchases of 1773 and 1775.

VIRGINIA SPECULATION PRIOR TO THE PROCLAMATION OF 1763

Thomas Lee was an aristocratic Virginia landowner who was not averse to profiting from his connections. By 1711, at the age of twenty-one, he was both a Crown collector of shipping duties and the local land agent for

Thomas Fairfax, the sixth Lord Fairfax of Cameron. In 1749 Lee became the acting governor of Virginia. Among those who survived him were his six sons, including Richard Henry Lee and Francis Lightfoot Lee, who both signed the Declaration of Independence; and Arthur Lee, a signatory to the 1778 Treaty of Alliance with France. Other prominent members of the Lee family include Charles Lee, third attorney general of the United States; Henry "Light-Horse Harry" Lee, revolutionary war hero; and Robert E. Lee, famed Confederate general.[4]

Thomas Lee was a man "spurred by a restless drive, a relentless ambition, and a proud nature." An opportunity to act on his ambitions arose in 1744 when Lee and William Beverley attended a conference with the Six Nations of the Iroquois League at Lancaster, Pennsylvania.[5] Virginia sought a cession of territory in the upper Ohio Valley from the Iroquois, who claimed the area by right of conquest. During the negotiations Lee pointed to a chest of goods and stated that "the key is in our pockets." Whether it was this statement that produced the desired effect is unknown; however, the Six Nations relinquished their claim to "all the lands . . . in the Colony of Virginia." In exchange for signing a deed to this effect on July 2, 1744, the Iroquois received £200 in goods and £200 in gold.[6]

The Iroquois thought they were relinquishing rights only to the Shenandoah Valley, but as Anthony Wallace observes, the Lancaster deed was viewed by Virginians as "a license to speculate and settle new lands west of the Alleghenies." In 1747 Thomas Lee and eleven others petitioned the Governor's Council for 200,000 acres, but soon thereafter added investors and formed the Ohio Company of Virginia, which in 1748 petitioned the Crown for a half million acres. On March 16, 1749, King George II granted 200,000 acres to the Ohio Company and promised an additional 300,000 acres if the company settled one hundred families within seven years and erected a fort.[7]

The king may have been influenced by the fact that the petitioners were among Virginia's elite in terms of landed wealth and political power. In addition to members of the Lee family, Lawrence and Augustine Washington were associates, and George Washington, George Mercer, and George Mason were later added. What ultimately swayed the Crown, however, was the fact that settlement of western lands would undermine French claims to the area. The British government desired to expand its North American empire, and officials hoped that the grant would encourage similar endeavors.[8]

La Galissonière countered in 1749 by authorizing Céleron's expedition, which traveled down the Ohio and ascended the Great Miami River to Pickawillany. Céleron's lead plates were buried in land claimed by Virginia, and the Ohio Company venture contributed to the escalating tensions between France and Great Britain. As interim governor, Thomas Lee reported to the Privy Council that Virginia's boundaries extended "to the West including California," and he predicted that settlers would transform the Ohio Valley into "the strongest frontier . . . of the King's Dominions in America." As the president of the Ohio Company, Lee instructed Christopher Gist in September 1750 to inspect the western lands in order to discover the areas most conducive to settlement.[9]

When Gist traveled to Logstown in November, he grew fearful because inhabitants of the tribal village sensed he had "come to settle the Indians' Land." He journeyed farther west to Pickawillany, where in 1751 he witnessed George Croghan's unauthorized treaty with the Weas and Piankeshaws. Gist returned in the spring but was sent on a second scouting expedition in November. It was during this trip that Gist was asked "where the Indians' land lay" in light of the French and English claims to the Ohio Valley.[10]

The prospects of the Ohio Company improved in June of 1752 when Virginia commissioners traveled to Logstown and secured a deed confirming the 1748 Lancaster Treaty. The Indians acknowledged the 1744 cession, and Virginia in return promised to build a fort on the Ohio for trade and protection. The beneficial effects of the Logstown Treaty, however, were short-lived. On June 21, 1752, the balance of power tilted toward France when Indian allies surprised Memeskia and consumed the Piankeshaw King. Heartened by this turn of events, the French began building several forts along Lake Erie and the upper Allegheny River. The lieutenant governor of Virginia, Robert Dinwiddie, reacted by sending twenty-one-year-old George Washington into the wilderness to tell the French to depart from Virginia territory. When Washington returned without success in January 1754, he was ordered to proceed to the forks of the Ohio and assist William Trent in building the promised fort. To promote enlistment in the colonial troops, Dinwiddie proclaimed that 200,000 acres on the east side of the Ohio River would be granted "to such persons who by their voluntary engagements and good behavior in the said service shall deserve the same." The chief beneficiary turned out to be George Washington, who received over 20,000 acres for his services and purchased another 25,000 acres from other soldiers.[11]

The hopes of the Ohio Company faded in April when Trent was forced to yield the partially constructed fort, and hopes were all but extinguished when Washington surrendered to the French on July 4, 1754. After permitting Washington to return home, the French destroyed the Ohio Company's storehouse and occupied western Pennsylvania.[12] The French and Indian War had begun, and the Ohio Company was unable to fulfill the conditions of its royal grant.

After a series of defeats, General John Forbes in 1758 constructed a road through Pennsylvania with the objective of subduing the French at Fort Duquesne. Prior to his arrival, two events occurred that ensured victory. First, on August 26, the British isolated western Canada by capturing Fort Frontenac on Lake Ontario. Second, in the Treaty of Easton, dated October 24, 1758, Pennsylvania pacified local Indians by returning lands that had been purchased four years earlier, and by pledging that it would make no further grants west of the Allegheny Mountains. One month later Forbes occupied the remains of Fort Duquesne, which was rechristened Fort Pitt. Although Montreal was not taken until 1760, the victories in 1758 proved decisive and enabled the British to take control of the upper Ohio Valley.[13]

With the removal of the French from the area, the Ohio Company attempted to revive its royal grant, but struggled due to the new policy of appeasing the Indians by restricting settlement. Colonel Henry Bouquet, the commander at Fort Pitt, was offered financial inducements if he would favor the company, but he refused, pointing out that the Crown had confirmed the Treaty of Easton. In July 1763 George Mercer sailed to England in an attempt to revive the fortunes of the Ohio Company. Although his efforts were unavailing, Mercer was able to secure the lucrative position of stamp collector for Maryland and Virginia. However, when he arrived in Williamsburg in October 1765, Mercer was confronted by colonists enraged by the Stamp Act. He immediately returned to England and continued to press the company's claims.[14]

Undaunted by such setbacks, several members of the Ohio Company decided in 1763 to embark on another venture involving lands in the Illinois country. George Washington, Richard Henry Lee, and thirty-six other gentlemen founded the Mississippi Land Company, and in September the self-styled "adventurers" submitted a petition for 2,500,000 acres. However, before the petition could be considered, King George III issued the Proclamation of October 7, 1763. British subjects were barred from purchasing western lands "*without our especial leave and licence for that purpose first obtained*."[15] The Virginia speculators, hopeful that "leave and licence" could be obtained, continued to lobby the Crown to approve their ventures.

PENNSYLVANIA SPECULATION PRIOR TO THE PROCLAMATION OF 1763

In 1744, the year Thomas Lee traveled in style to Lancaster to further his colony's territorial ambitions, George Croghan traveled on foot and horseback into the dense Ohio forests. Croghan was born in Ireland, came to America around 1741, settled on the Pennsylvania frontier, and established himself as the "King of the Traders." One of his biographers, Albert Volwiler, considers Croghan "the leading exponent of the expansion of the Anglo-Saxon race into the Ohio region during the generation before 1775." Eric Hinderaker has shed further light on this colorful and complex individual: "He was a flamboyant, hard-drinking man . . . [who] won allies among Indians and colonists . . . with an unusual combination of shrewd calculation and open-handed affability. . . . Croghan was an energetic self-promoter with little regard for order, careful recordkeeping, or, to hear some of his associates tell it, fair dealing."[16]

George Croghan's fortunes as an Indian trader and land speculator waxed and waned throughout his life, and on several occasions he faced imprisonment for debt. In the 1740s Anglo-American traders earned French enmity by trading with Indian tribes, such as the Miami confederacy, who were drawn to less expensive English goods. Croghan purchased his stock on credit from numerous merchants, including Joseph Simon, Levy Andrew Levy, David Franks, Barnard and Michael Gratz, and the firm of Baynton, Wharton, and Morgan of Philadelphia. Croghan often combined forces with others, including Robert Callender, Samuel Wharton, and William Trent. As discussed in later chapters, Wharton and Trent joined Croghan in many of his land speculations, and while Croghan was not involved in the Illinois or Wabash purchases, David Franks invested in both transactions, and Joseph Simon, Levy Andrew Levy, Robert Callender, and the Gratz brothers were shareholders in the Illinois Land Company.

Rather than wait for Indians to come to him with their furs, Croghan transported his goods to tribal villages. He established trading posts on Lake Erie, at the forks of the Ohio, and at Pickawillany. Pennsylvania officials twice rejected Croghan's counsel in 1751: first by repudiating his treaty with the Weas and Piankeshaws, signed at Memeskia's village in February, and then by declining to erect a fort on the Ohio River. A year later, in the Logstown Treaty, Virginia agreed to build the desired fort and supplanted Pennsylvania as the dominant influence in the area.[17]

The Iroquois in August of 1749 sold Croghan three tracts of land in western Pennsylvania: 40,000 acres east of Fort Pitt, 60,000 acres on both sides of the Youghiogheny at the mouth of Sewickly Creek, and 100,000 acres west of the lower Monongahela. At some point prior to July 1754 Croghan completed another transaction with the Six Nations, acquiring 4,000 acres west of Carlisle on Aughwick Creek. The Irishman did not obtain prior authorization for his purchases, but he did acknowledge Crown authority and sought royal confirmation until about 1770, when he began to contend that the private purchases from the Indians transferred full title. Proprietor Thomas Penn at first refused to recognize the title "of that vile man," stating that if Indians were allowed to sell their lands to whomsoever they chose, "we shall have Indians practiced upon for the private advantage of every worthless fellow that goes among them." However, Penn relented when third parties bought portions of the Aughwick purchase.[18]

Croghan's ventures were put on hold during the French and Indian War. The firm of Croghan and Trent furnished George Washington with powder and lead, but Washington commandeered their packhorses, causing merchandise to be left in the woods. The omnipresent Irishman joined Braddock's expedition and was present when General Edward Braddock was mortally wounded on July 9, 1755. Croghan was thereafter made a captain, and the Pennsylvania council forwarded a law to England, for royal approval, exempting him for ten years from arrest for debt. In 1756 Croghan's experience in Indian affairs led to his appointment as deputy superintendent under Sir William Johnson. In light of his financial troubles, Philadelphia merchants were "not a little surprized" by Croghan's procurement of the coveted Crown office.[19]

In October 1758 at the Easton conference, colonial officials acceded to Croghan's recommendation that Richard and Thomas Penn disclaim most of their 1754 purchase of southwestern Pennsylvania. The Penn brothers agreed to deed back to the Indians the portion for which they had not yet paid, a decision that "knocked the French in the head." Croghan's services, however, did not prevent King George II from disapproving the law exempting him from arrest, and by the end of the war Croghan was desperately seeking to raise funds. The irrepressible trader enticed the firm of Baynton, Wharton, and Morgan with prospects of immense profits by extending trade to the recently conquered Illinois country.[20] The Philadelphia firm was interested, but hostilities postponed the project until 1766.

As far back as the 1750s, Pennsylvania traders and merchants suffered losses due to Indian warfare, and further setbacks occurred as a result of Pontiac's rebellion. The "suffering traders of 1754 and 1763" joined forces with their creditors on December 7, 1763, at the Indian Queen Tavern in Philadelphia. Since Croghan had already decided to travel to London to seek confirmation of his Iroquois purchases, it was resolved that he would apply to the Crown for relief. William Trent and Samuel Wharton prepared a memorial arguing that British officials had encouraged Indian trade to thwart the French; and that the only thing of value that could compensate for trade losses was Indian land. Croghan and his colleagues requested George III to grant them a large tract of land, just as the king's grandfather had granted a large tract of land to the Ohio Company of Virginia.[21]

George Croghan set sail for England on December 29, 1763. It is not certain whether news of the Royal Proclamation of 1763 had reached Philadelphia. Croghan, in any event, would not be stopped by a royal edict. Fierce storms left him shipwrecked off the coast of France, yet the plucky Croghan managed to save his important papers and reached London in February 1764. The overextended Irishman was welcomed by English officials and by wealthy noblemen who desired to speculate in American lands.[22]

ROYAL REGULATION OF INDIAN LAND SALES AND THE DEMARCATION OF INDIAN COUNTRY

Prior to the French and Indian War the acquisition of Indian lands was chiefly regulated by the colonies. Royal commissions, however, were occasionally convened to deal with the issue of Native rights. Charles II had appointed a commission to investigate conditions in Massachusetts, and this body had declared that Indians lacked rights to undeveloped lands. The royal commissioners disagreed and stated in 1665 that "the country is theirs till they give it or sell it, though it be not improoued."[23] Forty years later, in a dispute between the Mohegan Tribe and Connecticut, Queen Anne's royal commission held for the tribe, rejecting the colony's contention that it held title to the tribe's lands through conquest. A reconstituted Court of

Commissioners announced in 1743 that Indian lands were not "impropriated" in British subjects "till they have made *fair and honest* purchases of the natives." However, in the same year the commission found for Connecticut on the merits, and George III rejected the tribe's final appeal in 1773.[24]

Whereas royal commissions were convened on an ad hoc basis, the Crown relied on government councils for routine management of the colonies. Charles II replaced the Joint Council for Trade and Plantations in 1675 with the Committee of the Privy Council on Trade and Plantations. King William III in 1696 created the Board of Trade, which made recommendations to the Privy Council through the secretary of state for the Southern Department. The board also drafted instructions for royal governors and reported on laws passed by colonial legislatures.[25]

Soon after its creation the Board of Trade informed colonial governors that private purchases of Indian lands would not be tolerated. The New York governor was told in 1697 to prohibit private purchases of Iroquois lands, and similar instructions were generally circulated in 1702. The board in 1753 wrote to Sir Danvers Osborn, the newly appointed governor of New York, and ordered him to examine allegations of fraudulent transactions. At the 1754 Albany Congress, delegates proposed that "all future purchases of lands from the Indians be void unless made by the Governt where such lands lye."[26]

Peter Wraxall, in his 1756 report to the Board of Trade, declared that the grant to the Ohio Company was "one of most material articles of discontent & Jealousy to the confederate Nations and their allies." Although Pennsylvania, in the Treaty of Easton, promised that it would not allow future settlements west of the Alleghenies, the capture of Fort Duquense led to renewed interest in the upper Ohio Valley. The commander at Fort Pitt, Colonel Bouquet, responded in 1761 with a military proclamation that prohibited British subjects from settling west of the Allegheny Mountains "unless such have obtained leave in writing from the general, or the governors of their respective provinces." Two months later the Board of Trade informed the royal colonies that future purchases of Indian lands must be authorized before Crown grants would be made and confirmed for new settlements.[27]

Thus, by the end of 1761, the basic principles underlying regulation of Indian lands were in place. The Crown had approved land grants prior to 1754 as an antidote to the French presence in the Ohio Valley, but once hostilities commenced, the focus shifted to appeasing the Indians by prohibiting settlement of their lands. The Easton treaty and Bouquet's proclamation established boundaries separating "Indian country" from lands open to colonists. The purchase of Indian lands, when permitted, was subjected to government approval. However, once victory over France in North America was assured, the question arose whether such restrictions would remain in place. The answer came on October 7, 1763, in the form of a royal proclamation issued by King George III.

The Proclamation of 1763 "formalized the elements of an Indian policy that had already taken shape during the years of conflict." News of Pontiac's rebellion reached England in July or August 1763, several months after William Petty, earl of Shelburne, assumed the presidency of the Board of Trade. Shelburne had proposed in June that a boundary be fixed between English settlements and the Indian nations of the Ohio Valley. Shelburne resigned in September and was replaced by Wills Hill, earl of Hillsborough. Hillsborough added the prohibition of private purchases of Indian lands, which was accompanied by qualifying phrases. After obtaining the assent of Attorney General Charles Yorke—who asked "whether so many words are necessary?"—the document was approved by the Privy Council and issued by the king.[28]

The 1763 Proclamation addresses the governance of new subjects, provision of land grants to soldiers, and legal status of acquired lands. With respect to the last issue, the proclamation declares that officials are—"*for the present, and until our further pleasure be known*"—barred from granting warrants or patents for lands "beyond the heads or sources of any of the rivers which fall into the Atlantic Ocean from the west or north-west." The proclamation also prohibited British subjects "from making any purchases . . . of any of the lands above reserved, without our especial leave and licence for that purpose first obtained." If and when the Indians should desire to sell their lands, "the same shall be purchased only for us, in our name, at some public meeting or assembly of the said Indians."[29]

Reaction to the Royal Proclamation of 1763 depended upon one's point of view. Hillsborough, who owned vast properties in Ireland, was hopeful that it would stem mass emigration to America. Thomas Gage predicted that the British would "avoid Many future Quarrells with the Savages by this Salutary Measure," and George Montague-Dunk, earl of Halifax and secretary of state for the Southern Department, believed the proclamation would protect the Indians by restraining "fraudulent Purchase of

Their Lands." Settlers, on the other hand, felt betrayed, and land speculators were "horrified at the effects the proclamation would have on their
claims to the west."[30] Opposition to the proclamation was tempered by
the belief that the restrictions were temporary. The boundary line would
undoubtedly be redrawn, since it reflected "neither the actual state of
settlement nor the respective claims of the tribes and the whites."[31] The
proclamation barred trans-Appalachian settlement "until our further pleasure be known" and stated only that subjects could not purchase Indian
lands without "our especial leave and licence." This language encouraged
speculators such as George Washington, who in 1767 stressed the imper-
manence of the decree in a letter to his land agent, William Crawford:
"I can never look upon that proclamation in any other light . . . than as
a temporary expedient to quiet the minds of the Indians. . . . Any person, therefore, who neglects the present opportunity of hunting out good
lands, and in some measure marking and distinguishing them for his own,
in order to keep others from settling them, will never regain it." Washington was not alone in this assessment. Some thirty thousand settlers
moved across the Proclamation Line from 1765 to 1768, and as Jack Sosin
has observed, "speculators soon were covertly marking out tracts on the
headwaters of the Ohio."[32]

John Marshall, in *Johnson v. McIntosh*, relied chiefly on the discovery doctrine to reject the claims of the Illinois and Wabash Land Company but
did state that the Royal Proclamation of 1763 constituted "an additional
objection to the title of the plaintiffs." The lands at issue were subject to the
prohibition on private purchases without "especial leave and licence." The
proclamation assumed the Crown held the underlying *title* to the land, subject to Native occupancy.[33] Speculators eventually rejected this premise and
contended that the Indians held the "underlying" title. One obstacle, however, remained: even if the Indians held title to their lands, the proclamation
barred English subjects from purchasing such lands without Crown approval.
As is described in chapter 13, Robert Goodloe Harper, in order to overcome
this problem, would draw deeply upon his legal skills and argue that the 1763
Royal Proclamation was an invalid action without force of law.[34]

THE CAMDEN-YORKE OPINION OF 1757

James Fenimore Cooper, in *The Last of the Mohicans*, chronicles the August
1757 surrender of Fort William Henry, a significant setback for England.[35]

The Seven Years' War was a global contest, however, and British interests fared better on the other side of the world. On June 23, 1757, Robert Clive led soldiers of the British East India Company to victory over the Nawab of Bengal, virtually destroying French claims in India. In the aftermath of this triumph, the company requested advice from the Crown with regard to its rights in the "Fortresses, Districts, and Territories" that were acquired from the natives.[36] In a sequence of events still shrouded in mystery, the legal opinion provided in 1757—regarding the right of the East India Company to acquire lands from "the *Mogul*, or any of the *Indian* Princes"—was edited and brandished in the 1770s by proponents of the right to purchase Indian lands in America. Because it plays a prominent role in the Illinois and Wabash purchases, the 1757 "Camden-Yorke" opinion warrants further examination.

The British East India Company operated under a royal charter that granted it a monopoly over trade in the East Indies. The company noted in its petition that it had acquired "Plunder and Booty" and "some Districts of Land." With respect to the latter, the company sought approval of its right to own "such Fortresses, Districts, and Territories . . . as they have acquired, or may hereafter acquire, from any Nation, State, or People, by Treaty, Grant, or Conquest." The petition was laid before England's top two legal officers: Solicitor General Charles Yorke, and Attorney General Charles Pratt (who later became Lord Camden).[37] On December 24, 1757, Pratt and Yorke declared that the king had no property right in the lands at issue:

> In respect to such Places as have been, or shall be acquired by Treaty, or Grant from the Mogul, or any of the Indian Princes, or Governments, Your Majesty's Letters Patents are not necessary, the Property of the Soil vesting in the Company by the *Indian* Grants, subject only to Your Majesty's Right of Sovereignty.[38]

The Camden-Yorke (or Pratt-Yorke) opinion thus held that a grant by an "Indian" transferred land rights to the grantee. There is no indication that anyone considered whether the opinion's reasoning should apply as well to Native Americans. By serendipity, however, British subjects in the last half of the eighteenth century were acquiring "Indian" lands on not one but two continents. As discussed later, speculators had no qualms about relying on the 1757 legal opinion to sanction grants by the "*Indian*

Princes" of the Ohio and Mississippi valleys. The Camden-Yorke opinion, after it surfaced in the 1770s as putative authority for private transactions with Indian tribes, remained "in play" for at least a half century. It was a catalyst for the Illinois and Wabash purchases and was not finally laid to rest until February 28, 1823, when John Marshall declared it to be "entirely inapplicable to purchases made in America."[39]

SPECULATION AFTER THE PROCLAMATION: 1764–1768

George Croghan, after surviving the shipwreck that concluded his Atlantic crossing, proceeded to conduct official business and pursue personal affairs—although not necessarily in that order—from February 1764 until the following September. As William Johnson's deputy, Croghan assisted the Board of Trade in shaping its "Plan for the Management of Indian Affairs." The plan, which was abandoned in 1768, called for imperial control of the Indian trade and a more exact demarcation of Indian country. In order to pay for the costs of administering the newly acquired territories, England enacted the Sugar Act of 1764 and the Stamp Act of 1765. The laws were the first in a series of revenue measures that provoked increasingly hostile responses in America. Viewing these in conjunction with the 1763 Proclamation, many colonists wondered why they should "pay taxes to garrison a frontier to keep themselves out."[40]

With regard to his personal affairs, Croghan sought to obtain restitution for the "suffering traders" in the form of a large tract of land, and secure a grant of 200,000 acres in Mohawk country in exchange for his 1749 purchase of 200,000 acres in the Ohio Valley. He failed on both accounts. The board held that it could not sanction Croghan's private purchase of Iroquois land and declined to grant land as compensation for the traders' losses. Undaunted, Croghan returned in the fall of 1764 to Philadelphia, where he persuaded Samuel Wharton that the traders and their creditors could instead obtain restitution *directly* from the Six Nations. Croghan also convinced Wharton and his partners, John Baynton and George Morgan, to pursue business opportunities in the Illinois country. As he did so often, Croghan planned to use his official position to further his own affairs and the interests of his colleagues. In anticipation of better times, he purchased a large manor outside Philadelphia and furnished it with Irish linens, carpets from Scotland, mahogany furniture, backgammon tables, a spinet, and other expensive items.[41]

Whether fortuitously or by design, William Johnson proposed to General Thomas Gage in 1764 that Croghan was the ideal person to reconcile the western Indians with the impending British control of the Mississippi Valley. Croghan left Fort Pitt on May 15, 1765, with members of the Seneca, Delaware, and Shawnee tribes, who promised to use their influence with the Wabash and Illinois Indians. Prior to departure Croghan learned that his furtive plan to profit from the trip—by smuggling a shipment of knives, firearms, and Indian goods provided by Baynton, Wharton, and Morgan—had been discovered by angry Pennsylvania frontiersmen, who threatened Croghan's life if he returned to Cumberland County.[42]

This financial disaster was soon supplanted by other concerns. On the morning of June 8, 1765, while camping below the mouth of the Wabash River, Croghan's party was attacked by eighty Kickapoo and Mascouten Indians, who killed three Shawnees and two white men. The veteran fur trader was tomahawked, but as he later observed, "I got the Stroke of a hatchett on the Head, but my Scull being pretty thick the hatchett wou'd not enter, so you may see a thick Scull is of Service on some Occasions."[43] When the attackers discovered the identity of the murdered Indians, they realized that the Shawnee, Delaware, and Iroquois were at peace with the English, and they became alarmed. Through his understanding of the situation Croghan was able to complete his mission and transform his capture into a diplomatic triumph.

As Albert Volwiler points out, Croghan kept separate journals during his trip: "one journal, emphasizing the Indian negotiations, was evidently prepared for English officials; the other, emphasizing topography, soil, trees, game, etc., was evidently prepared for land speculators and projectors of inland colonies." Croghan and his fellow captives were transported up the Wabash River and came into contact with some Piankeshaw Indians whom Croghan had befriended at Pickawillany. According to his official journal, the warriors were displeased and declared that "they would not be concerned in the affair." Shortly thereafter, Croghan and his colleagues were set free.

At this point Croghan conferred with the Weas, Piankeshaws, Kickapoos, Mascoutens, and Miamis. He then held a conference with Pontiac "in which I settled all matters with the Ilinois Indians." In August, at a council at Detroit, western tribesmen informed Croghan that the French "never conquered us neither did they purchase a foot of our Country."[44] The intrepid Irishman left in September to report to Johnson and Gage.

Shortly thereafter, on October 10, 1765, British troops under Captain Thomas Stirling occupied Fort Chartres. Because of Croghan's diplomatic success, Crown officials ignored the smuggling fiasco in Pennsylvania. The "King of the Traders" had managed to extricate himself once again from a difficult situation, and he focused anew on the two mainstays in his life: Indian trade and Indian lands.

Croghan was undoubtedly pleased to learn, when he returned to Philadelphia, that during his absence the policy of restricting Indian trade to public posts had ended, thus legalizing commercial transactions in the Illinois country. The firm of Baynton, Wharton, and Morgan put together a shipment of goods that arrived in Kaskaskia in April 1766. Croghan and George Morgan accompanied the next shipment and reached Illinois in August. At the height of its operations, the Quaker firm used six hundred packhorses to move goods from Philadelphia to Fort Pitt and employed hundreds of sawyers, shipwrights, and boatmen to transport merchandise to sell to French *habitants*, British soldiers, and the Indians. However, for several interrelated reasons, the Illinois venture eventually led to the ruin of the Baynton, Wharton, and Morgan partnership.[45]

Personality clashes, business competition, and unanticipated changes in British policy doomed the enterprise. George Morgan antagonized Croghan, fell out of favor with the commandant at Fort Chartres, and came to be "universally hated" by the French *habitants*. More significant, the Quaker firm was dealt a major blow when the contract for supplying provisions to the British garrison was awarded in 1768 to David Franks and Company of Philadelphia. Further setbacks occurred when William Murray of Pennsylvania began selling goods in Illinois for Franks and the Gratz brothers. Finally, the Crown acted contrary to expectations by returning the management of Indian trade to the colonies, reducing the British military presence, and discouraging the creation of an Illinois colony. In the summer of 1767 Baynton, Wharton, and Morgan acceded to the appointment of trustees to secure the interests of creditors, and Morgan proposed in 1770 to dispose of all goods in Illinois.[46]

Croghan had not only persuaded Baynton, Wharton, and Morgan to stake a fortune on the Indian trade but also promoted the idea of a new colony in the Illinois country. In his private journal Croghan noted that a colony in the Mississippi Valley would "curb the machinations of the French and Spaniards." His enthusiasm was contagious, and the Illinois Company was organized in 1766 for the purpose of petitioning the Crown for a grant of 1,200,000 acres at the confluence of the Mississippi and Ohio. In addition to Croghan, investors included Baynton, Wharton and Morgan, Joseph Galloway, John Hughes, Joseph Wharton, Joseph Wharton, Jr., and William Franklin, the royal governor of New Jersey (and illegitimate son of Benjamin Franklin). Indian Superintendent William Johnson and the elder Franklin became secret members. Based on his personal observations in 1764, Croghan assured Johnson that "one half of England is now Land Mad & Everybody there has thire eys fixt on this Cuntry."[47]

Benjamin Franklin complained in September of 1766 that the "Illinois affair goes forward but slowly" but was encouraged when Lord Shelburne proposed that there be formed two new colonies, one in the Illinois country and the other at Detroit. After obtaining the approval of the Board of Trade for the Illinois colony, Shelburne laid the proposal before the king, and the creation of a fourteenth American colony appeared imminent. However, Shelburne thereafter lost jurisdiction over colonial affairs when a new cabinet position, secretary of state for the American Department, was created. It was filled by Wills Hill, the earl of Hillsborough. In March 1768 Hillsborough reported adversely on the idea of inland colonies. The report was taken under advisement by the Privy Council, but it soon became evident that the Illinois colony would not be approved.[48]

When Samuel Wharton learned of Hillsborough's report, he immediately asked Benjamin Franklin to drop "the Illinois affair" and devote his lobbying efforts to the "Indian restitution." As far back as 1765 the "suffering traders" had sent memorials to General Gage and Sir William Johnson, requesting reparations in the form of an Indian land grant. Johnson eventually convinced the Six Nations and the Delaware Indians to cede a large tract of land on the Ohio River. Since the area in question was west of the Proclamation Line, Johnson urged the tribes to agree to a new boundary, assuring them that they would receive "a Considerable Present in return for your Friendship."[49]

The news from London galvanized the traders and their creditors, who organized a new speculative venture—the Indiana Company—which included David Franks, Levy Andrew Levy, Robert Callender, Joseph Simon, John Baynton, George Croghan, William Franklin, George Morgan, William Trent, and Samuel Wharton. Croghan, Trent, and Wharton spent the summer distributing presents among the chiefs of the Six Nations, and on September 19, 1768, twenty boatloads of Indian goods arrived at Fort Stanwix (present-day Rome, New York). More than two thousand Indians met with representatives from New Jersey, Pennsylvania, Virginia, and the Crown.[50]

Ray Billington describes the Fort Stanwix treaty of 1768 as "one of the worst treaties in the history of Anglo-Indian relations," but from the point of view of George Croghan and the Indiana Company, the conference was a tremendous success. Pursuant to a carefully orchestrated plan, the Iroquois first transacted with the speculators and then incorporated the terms of the private grants in the treaty of cession. The 1749 sale of 200,000 acres by the Iroquois to Croghan was ratified, and it was provided that if the Penn proprietors claimed the land at issue, the Crown should grant Croghan an equal amount of property elsewhere. With respect to the Indiana Company, the Indians granted an immense area in what is now West Virginia and eastern Kentucky. The grant was subject to royal approval, but the deed itself conditioned any subsequent land cession to the Crown on the prior rights of the named grantees, in the hope of forcing the English ministry to accept the private transaction in order to obtain the benefits of the treaty.[51]

Two days later, on November 5, 1768, the Six Nations executed a treaty of cession, agreeing to a new boundary line running from northern New York to Fort Pitt, down the southern bank of the Ohio River, and all the way to the mouth of Tennessee River in western Kentucky. British officials pointed out that William Johnson obtained more land than he had been authorized to purchase. The Cherokee and Shawnee objected to the treaty as well, because most of the ceded lands did not belong to the Six Nations. As Michael McConnell points out, "the Six Nations maintained their own territorial integrity by selling land occupied by people on the fringes of the Iroquois world."[52]

George Croghan was cautiously optimistic but still avoided his numerous creditors. William Trent, Samuel Wharton, and other members of the Indiana Company were in similar situations. The Indiana grant was their salvation; however, the grantees still believed that royal confirmation was needed before they could enter into possession. Consequently, on December 30, 1768—five years and one day after Croghan had sailed to England—articles of agreement were drawn up in Philadelphia guaranteeing the expenses of Trent and Wharton for a similar journey.[53] During their unexpectedly long stay in England, the political and legal landscapes underwent dramatic transformations: the thirteen colonies moved inexorably toward independence, and the widely held assumption that Indians could not convey a title without royal approval was questioned.

SPECULATION AFTER THE PROCLAMATION: 1769–1773

When Samuel Wharton and William Trent sailed for England in 1769, their objective was clear-cut: to obtain royal confirmation of their Indian grant in order to claim a marketable title to the lands in question. However, at the same time that the Pennsylvania speculators vied for the favor of British officials, the necessity of securing approval of private purchases of Indian land was challenged. In a letter to George Croghan, dated September 4, 1770, Wharton deemed it "indisputable" that the Iroquois had *"an inherent and undoubted power to grant the lands to us"* and declared that "our title is certainly good against the King." During this same period, the edited Camden-Yorke opinion was circulated among select individuals, including George Washington, who transcribed the opinion on a blank page at the beginning of his 1773 diary.[54] Thus, while speculators continued to seek imperial approbation for land grants, support was also building for the notion that an Indian deed sufficed to transfer full title. This competing legal view was the impetus for the private purchase, on July 5, 1773, of two tracts of land from the Illinois Indians.

Lord Hillsborough, who served both as president of the Board of Trade and as secretary of state for the American Department, was the chief obstacle for the Indiana Company. On April 25, 1769, the board censured William Johnson for exceeding his instructions at Fort Stanwix, and Hillsborough thereafter announced that the grants to Croghan and the Indiana Company were to be reserved for further consideration. Trent was certain that all was lost, but Wharton rejected the despairing sentiments of his colleague (whom he considered a social embarrassment) and enlisted the assistance of a highly connected Englishman, Thomas Walpole. Wharton and Walpole devised a scheme that promised to enrich prominent individuals in Great Britain and secure royal confirmation of the Iroquois grants. Pursuant to their plan, eighteen individuals—including Benjamin Franklin, Moses Franks, Jacob Franks, and Napthali Franks—petitioned the king for 2.4 million acres of the lands ceded at Fort Stanwix.[55]

The Walpole petition was referred to the Board of Trade. To everyone's surprise, Lord Hillsborough suggested that the petitioners *enlarge* their request and purchase lands in the Ohio Valley sufficient for the establishment of a fourteenth colony. The "Grand Ohio Company" was quickly organized, and in January 1770 the company responded to Hillsborough's proposition by asking for approximately 20 million acres. The colony—which would include and uphold the Indiana and Croghan grants—was named Vandalia in honor of Queen Charlotte, who claimed descent from the Vandals.[56]

On April 20, 1771, Benjamin Franklin informed his son that "the Ohio affair seems now near a conclusion" but warned that "many things happen between the Cup and the Lip." His words proved prophetic, as the Board of Trade sat on the petition for months and then urged that the grant be rejected. The interminable delay was disastrous for the financially strapped speculators. George Croghan responded to creditors' suits by mortgaging his New York lands and by drawing bills payable to Wharton, which came back from England marked for nonpayment. Wharton and Trent "feared arrest unless they could raise funds to pay their tailor, shoemaker, and other tradesmen."[57] Between April 1769, when the board objected to the Fort Stanwix treaty, and April 1772, when the board reported adversely on the Walpole petition, it appeared unlikely that the English ministry would approve any land grants. Not coincidentally, during this same period Samuel Wharton first declared that Indians in America could convey a valid title without royal approval.

Did desperation prompt Wharton to gravitate toward the view that Native Americans had unfettered authority to sell their lands? What role, if any, did the Camden-Yorke opinion of 1757 play? It is unclear who initially recognized that a legal opinion concerning the East India Company could be of service to persons interested in Indian lands in America, but the most probable candidate is none other than Benjamin Franklin.[58] What is beyond dispute is that private individuals continued to purchase land from Indians after the Royal Proclamation of 1763. In 1765 Pontiac sold land near Detroit to four individuals, and in 1767 a Captain Jonathan Carver was deeded a large tract of Sioux land in present-day Minnesota and Wisconsin. In both instances the claimants unsuccessfully sought royal ratification of title; with respect to the Carver grant, arguments were later presented to Congress that such ratification was not necessary to transfer title.[59]

Legal justifications for the right of Indians to sell their lands also appeared with more frequency after the issuance of the 1763 Proclamation.

William Johnson acknowledged in 1765 that the Indians put "their Lands under the protection of the Crown" but contended nonetheless that "the right of Soil always remained to the Indians."[60] John Adams, writing in 1775 under the pseudonym Novanglus, argued that New England settlers understood that the Crown held no title to North America and "therefore honestly purchased their lands of the natives."[61] Adams's position echoed the views of the English author Arthur Young, who stated in 1772 that title to lands in America could only be "founded on purchase."[62]

The two individuals who gave the most consideration to Indian property rights, however, were Benjamin Franklin and Samuel Wharton. Franklin's fame preceded him when he arrived in London in July 1757: he had already developed his renowned stove and was elected a Fellow of the Royal Society in recognition of his work with electricity. The Camden-Yorke opinion was written on December 24, 1757, but there is no evidence that Franklin was immediately aware of its issuance. But when the British Parliament in 1767 examined the rights of the East India Company, the Camden-Yorke opinion was invoked during the debates. Franklin attended the April debates at the House of Lords and was thus aware of the company's claim of right to "territory and dominion" acquired. On April 11, 1767, the *London Chronicle* published an article by "Benevolus" (Franklin) contending that the right to the territory in America "was in the tribes of Indians who inhabited it, and from whom the settlers were obliged to purchase." Franklin's position was unequivocal: after reading a pamphleteer's assertion that Americans received their lands "by the bounty of the crown," he wrote in the margin: "False! The Lands did not belong to the Crown but to the Indians, of whom the Colonists either purchased them at their own Expence, or conquer'd them without Assistance from Britain."[63]

The first indication that Franklin appreciated the potential value of the Camden-Yorke opinion comes in a letter written several years after the fact. On April 5, 1773, in a letter lost to posterity, William Franklin must have referred to the 1757 opinion, because his father's reply, dated July 14, 1773, declares that "the Opinion of Pratt and Yorke . . . is undoubtedly a good One, so far as it allows the Indian Power of Grant in their own Lands."[64] Most significant, the elder Franklin's letter reveals that he understood the significance of the opinion as early as the spring of 1769 and had discussed it with Samuel Wharton: "I gave the same Opinion to Mr. Wharton when he arrived here with respect to the Retribution Grant, and advised his not applying for a Confirmation. . . . My Advice farther was to proceed immediately to sell and settle the Lands, without supposing any Occasion for such Confirmation; and he has frequently acknowledged the Propriety of the Advice, and wished he had followed it."[65]

Franklin's view of the matter was echoed in letters written by Samuel Wharton in 1770 and 1771. Wharton assured George Croghan in 1770 that even if the Crown refused to ratify their Indian deeds, "the grantors [have] an inherent and undoubted power to grant the lands to us, as well as to the King. . . . And Dr. F says, that if the property was his, he would not seek for any other title, but sell or settle on it as was most agreeable to him."[66] In separate letters to Croghan, both dated July 21, 1771, Wharton reiterated his belief in the validity of Indian title, stating in one letter that men "laugh at the idea of coming to England to get a title to lands in the Indian country," and announcing in the other missive that prominent officials had assured him "of the indispensable goodness of our Indian title." Although Wharton made no reference to the Camden-Yorke opinion in his letters to Croghan, there is little doubt that the Quaker merchant was aware of it.[67]

Wharton, Trent, Croghan, and Franklin all realized there would be no need to rely on the controversial Camden-Yorke opinion if a favorable decision was rendered on behalf of the Grand Ohio Company. On June 5, 1772, the three Pennsylvania speculators, along with Thomas Walpole, defended the Vandalia proposal before a Privy Council committee. Samuel Wharton delivered a "brilliantly presented" argument, and the committee (which included several members of the Grand Ohio Company) recommended that the petition be granted. King George III accepted Hillsborough's resignation in August and issued an order for the establishment of the colony. George Croghan, in December, remarked to William Johnson that the new colony should produce "a handsome profit," and he had no reason to think otherwise in May 1773 when the Board of Trade forwarded its report on the plan of government for Vandalia to the Privy Council. However, by the end of 1774, it was all but certain that the Irishman's dream of wealth had been dashed yet again. The opposition of Virginia, the delaying tactics of Crown officials, and the dramatic events heralding the American Revolution all combined to ensure that the Vandalia project would never proceed, as Franklin put it–from "the Cup" to "the Lip."[68]

Virginia speculators undermined the Vandalia proposal by asserting conflicting claims and protesting the creation of the colony. George

Mason in particular worked to revive the Ohio Company and in 1773 penned "Extracts from the Virginia Charters with Some Remarks on Them," asserting that lands in question were part of Virginia and "no new Government or Proprietary can legally be established there." Meanwhile, the Vandalia proposal moved forward at a glacial pace. On September 23, 1774, Thomas Wharton, in a letter to Thomas Walpole, criticized the "determined obstinacy" of the Crown's lawyers. What Wharton did not know was that the quest of the Grand Ohio Company had already ended: on August 12, 1774, a final petition was referred by the Privy Council to a committee, which took no further action.[69]

The Vandalia colony had been cursed with bad timing. On the evening of December 16, 1773, individuals disguised as Mohawk Indians boarded the *Dartmouth* and dumped 342 chests of tea into Boston Harbor. Thomas Wharton wrote to Samuel on the first day of 1774 and expressed his wish that "thou may be in possession of the grant, before the arrival of the full accounts respecting the conduct of the Americans touching the tea."[70] Following the closure of the port of Boston, the Massachusetts House of Representatives proposed a colonial congress, and when Thomas Wharton wrote to Walpole in September, the First Continental Congress had already been in session for two weeks. Under such circumstances, there would be no more colonies and no more grants of land by the Crown.

It is not surprising, therefore, that the Pennsylvania speculators began to promote the idea that a grant by an "Indian" was all that was necessary to transfer land rights to the grantee. Samuel Wharton and William Trent wrote pamphlets that championed the right of Indians in America to sell land to private persons. George Croghan went even further, borrowing funds to purchase 1.5 million acres in 1773, and another 6 million acres in 1775, directly from the compliant Six Nations. Croghan was never able to reap substantial profits from his purchases, despite selling portions of his 1749 and 1754 acquisitions.[71] In 1777 the veteran fur trader and Indian agent was bedridden with gout and unable to escape from Philadelphia during its occupation by the British. In 1778 Croghan was accused of treason but was cleared in a Pennsylvania court. In 1779 and 1780 he resided in Lancaster, in a house without a chimney, and survived by the grace of the Gratz brothers. When he died on August 31, 1782, he was virtually penniless, and there was no mention of his death in the newspapers. Nicholas Wainwright summed up the life of George Croghan as follows:

"He had dreamed vast dreams. He had stimulated men of note with his visions of western development . . . through his relentless energy, his restless imagination, and his daring courage. The rub was, he had done it all on borrowed money."

George Croghan, in the last years of his life, testified before Congress on behalf of the Illinois and Wabash Land Company, which was seeking recognition of the purchases from the Illinois and Piankeshaw Indians. The "King of the Traders" was introduced with yet another distinctive moniker: the "foremost living expert on the western Indian country."[72] Although Croghan was not able to profit from his private purchases of Indian lands, he maintained to his death that in each transaction he had received a valid and marketable title. The shareholders of the Illinois and Wabash Land Company agreed with Croghan's position—which echoed the views of Roger Williams, the Newark rioters, Benjamin Franklin, Samuel Wharton, and others—that Indian tribes own the lands they occupy and possess the legal capacity to sell such lands to private individuals.

5

THE ILLINOIS PURCHASE OF 1773

The origins of the Illinois purchase are not clearly documented. What is certain is that several individuals, on April 7, 1773, agreed in writing that William Murray should "as soon as convenient" return to the Illinois country and "purchase from the Native Indian proprietors or Owners, a large quantity of Lands on the Mississippi River." Murray carried the edited version of the Camden-Yorke opinion with him from Philadelphia to Pittsburgh and presented it to the British officer at Kaskaskia on the eleventh of June. After three weeks of negotiations the Illinois Indians conveyed two immense tracts of land to Murray and twenty-one other named grantees.[1]

Who was William Murray, and how did he obtain a copy of the Camden-Yorke opinion? Historians have theorized that Captain William Murray of the 42nd Regiment of the Royal Highlanders, who commanded Fort Pitt between 1764 and 1767, thereafter left the British Army and became the merchant William Murray, who sold goods in the Illinois country prior to negotiating the aforementioned land purchase. Military records prove that Captain William Murray had nothing to do with the Illinois purchase, but information regarding the merchant William Murray prior to 1768 is unfortunately scant, although his connection with David Franks can be traced as far back as 1763. Furthermore, although it was Murray who carried the Camden-Yorke opinion to Kaskaskia and purchased the land from the Illinois, logic suggests that the plan to engage in large-scale land speculation was formulated by someone else—most likely Barnard Gratz, Michael Gratz, David Franks, or Moses Franks of London.

In any event, by the spring of 1773 twenty-two individuals residing in England, Pennsylvania, and the Illinois country were convinced of their right to acquire land directly from the Native inhabitants.

A British soldier by the name of William Murray was the commander of Fort Pitt from November 1764 to August 1767. A few months later, on May 25, 1768, a "William Murray of the City of Philadelphia" appointed Barnard Gratz as "my true and lawful Attorney" and then departed for the Illinois country. William Byars, in his 1916 biography of the Gratz brothers, states that "circumstantial evidence is strong enough to justify considering Captain William Murray . . . as the William Murray." Other historians have concurred. It is certain, however, that the British officer William Murray was *not* the land speculator of the same name who purchased lands from the Illinois Indians in 1773.[2]

According to British military records, a "William Murray . . . of Lintrose" was commissioned in 1758 as a captain in the 42nd Royal Highland (Black Watch) Regiment. Captain Murray received a temporary promotion to major, and thereafter took command of Fort Pitt in 1764.[3] The regiment was sent to Ireland in 1767. It appears possible that Murray left the army and became the merchant who worked with the Gratz brothers and David Franks, but in August 1776 several companies of the Black Watch regiment landed at Staten Island, New York, where they were "formed into two temporary battalions, the command of one being given to Major William Murray (Lintrose)."[4]

Who then was the merchant William Murray? The editor of Henry Bouquet's papers, Louis Waddell, states that William Murray became the Fort Pitt commissary in the spring of 1763. Murray also served as a clerk for William Plumsted and David Franks of Philadelphia, who delivered provisions to the troops and served as agents for the English firm of Colbrooke, Nesbitt, and Franks. It is not known when or under what circumstances Murray commenced his association with Plumsted and Franks, although in a letter sent in 1769 to Murray in Illinois, the sister of David Franks—Miss Richi (or Richea) Franks of New York City—is described as his "old and esteemed friend."[5]

After establishing himself at Fort Pitt in August of 1763, Bouquet informed Plumsted and Franks that "Mr Murray your Agent" had engaged in "unpardonable Neglect" in not reporting a deficiency of flour, "which might have Occasioned the loss of this Post." A court of inquiry was convened, and Murray remained at Fort Pitt at least through October. At some point thereafter he returned to Philadelphia, as evidenced by the marriage records of St. Paul's Church, which indicate that a William Murray married Martha McEntire on May 31, 1764.[6] This is undoubtedly the merchant, since the minutes of the Illinois and Wabash Land Company indicate that ten years later, on May 31, 1774, "William Murray and his wife Martha" sold one share in the company to Samuel Chase "for 300 pounds sterling money of Great Britain."[7]

It is not clear whether Murray returned to Fort Pitt. What is certain is that by November of 1768, William Murray had relocated to the Illinois country. During the next five years Murray had dealings with several future members of the Illinois and Wabash land companies, including Barnard and Michael Gratz, David Franks, Moses Franks of London, Joseph Simon, Levy Andrew Levy, James Milligan, David Sproat, Alexander Ross, Robert Callender, William Thompson, and James Rumsey.[8] As Michael Gratz informed his brother Barnard in 1769, their association with Murray and the Illinois trade was "turning out to great advantage."[9]

In December 1771, however, General Gage was told to evacuate Fort Pitt and Fort Chartres to reduce expenses, and by the following September just fifty British soldiers were stationed at Kaskaskia. The reduction of troops dealt a severe blow to the Illinois trade, and William Murray returned to Philadelphia, where he was appointed, on April 3, 1773, as an attorney for David Franks and Company in order to settle the company's business in Illinois.[10] Four days later a document titled "Subscription for a Land Purchase in the Illinois Country" was agreed to by the following twenty-two subscribers:

William Murray	Illinois Country
George Castles	Illinois County
James Rumsey	Illinois Country
Moses Franks	London
Jacob Franks	London
David Franks	Philadelphia
Moses Franks	Philadelphia
Barnard Gratz	Philadelphia
Michael Gratz	Philadelphia
Andrew Hamilton	Philadelphia
William Hamilton	Philadelphia

John Inglis	Philadelphia
Alexander Ross	Philadelphia
David Sproat	Philadelphia
James Milligan	Philadelphia
Edmund Milne	Philadelphia
Joseph Simon	Lancaster
Levy Andrew Levy	Lancaster
Thomas Minshall	York County
Robert Callender	Cumberland County
William Thompson	Cumberland County
John Campbell	Pittsburgh

The document states that William Murray "knows of lead and copper mines in the Illinois" and directs Murray to purchase "a large Quantity of Lands on the Mississippi River (taking in some of those mines)." By their signatures the subscribers agreed to pay for the purchase and Murray's expenses. Payment was due "as soon as the Indian Grant . . . is produced to us at Philadelphia."[11]

When William Murray returned to the Illinois country, he carried with him a version of the Camden-Yorke opinion, which stated that it was "a true Copy compared by Mr Wm Trent in London the 1st of April 1772."[12] There is no reason to believe that Trent sent the opinion directly to Murray. Some historians have argued that Murray obtained it from George Croghan, but the evidence suggests otherwise. It is more likely that the one of the subscribers heard about the opinion while in England. Someone—Franklin, Trent, or Wharton—may have shown a copy of the opinion to Moses and Jacob Franks of London, or perhaps to Barnard Gratz, who went to England in 1769. If so, the information would have been shared with David Franks or Michael Gratz. What seems most likely is that one or more of the subscribers came into possession of the Camden-Yorke opinion, and then formulated the idea of using it in connection with the purchase of mineral-rich Indian lands in the Illinois country.[13]

THE ILLINOIS PURCHASERS

The twenty-two subscribers to the Illinois purchase were a varied lot in terms of location, occupation, and background: three men from the Illinois country, six from western Pennsylvania, eleven from Philadelphia, and two living in London. Some were businessmen, others frontiersmen; several were related by family or marriage; and when independence was declared, a significant number remained loyal to Great Britain. A brief description of the Illinois purchasers follows.

William Murray signed the agreement on behalf of the other two subscribers from the Illinois country, George Castles and James Rumsey. Like Murray, both were familiar with the tribes of the Illinois confederacy. Castles sold an assortment of items used in the purchase, including five bottles of Taffia, a cheap rum distilled in the West Indies.[14] Rumsey served in the 42nd Royal Highland Regiment and was a member of the 1765 expedition to Fort Chartres. After retiring from the army, he returned to the Illinois country, where he first worked for Baynton, Wharton, and Morgan, and subsequently with Murray, David Franks, and the Gratz brothers.[15]

James Milligan, Alexander Ross, Thomas Minshall, Robert Callender, William Thompson, and John Campbell served in various capacities as intermediaries between Philadelphia and the backcountry. Milligan traded goods at Fort Pitt, where he associated with Joseph Simon, Levy Andrew Levy, John Campbell, and others. Ross is listed on the agreement as being from Philadelphia but was involved in the western fur trade and had served as commissary at Fort Pitt. As a loyalist, he had his lands confiscated in 1778.[16] Minshall and Callender were "suffering traders" and members of the Indiana Company. Thompson and Campbell combined military careers with fur trading and land speculation. Of the six men, only John Campbell had any substantial connection with the Illinois and Wabash Land Company.[17]

John Inglis, David Sproat, and Edmund Milne were successful Philadelphia businessmen. Inglis was a merchant and an associate of Alexander Ross and David Franks. Sproat was in the shipping business prior to the Revolution but left Philadelphia in 1777 to join other loyalists in New York, where he served as the commissary for American prisoners of war.[18] Milne was a silversmith who died in his ninety-eighth year, on February 4, 1822, just one year prior to the Supreme Court's decision in *Johnson v. McIntosh*. The minutes of the Illinois and Wabash Land Company between 1778 and 1793 list Milne as the most dutiful attendee of meetings in Philadelphia.

Four of the remaining subscribers—Simon and Levy of Lancaster and the Gratz brothers of Philadelphia—were Jewish merchants with business ties to David Franks. Joseph Simon also formed partnerships with

Michael Gratz. National Portrait Gallery, Smithsonian Institution; gift of Richard N. Tetlie.

George Croghan, William Trent, James Milligan, and John Campbell. Levy Andrew Levy, who emigrated from England, worked for Simon as a clerk and later became his son-in-law and business partner.[19] The Gratz brothers were born in Upper Silesia, near the German-Polish border. The older brother, Barnard, was employed as a clerk for David Franks shortly after his arrival in Philadelphia in 1754.[20] Michael Gratz, who emigrated in 1759, also worked briefly for Franks but soon joined forces with his brother, who had started a business. The youthful brothers became "merchant venturers," conducting business in the colonies, Europe, and the West Indies. Barnard, the "cautious man of business," tended to remain in Philadelphia, while Michael, the "audacious speculator," often traveled to Lancaster and elsewhere in North America.[21]

In 1760 Barnard married a member of Joseph Simon's extended family, and in 1769 Michael married one of Simon's daughters. By this time the brothers were leaders in the Jewish community in Philadelphia. In protest of the Stamp Act, Barnard and Michael signed the 1765 Non-Importation Agreement. In 1766 the Gratzes employed George Croghan to sell merchandise at Fort Pitt in exchange for furs, and in 1768 the brothers enlisted William Murray to engage in the Illinois trade.[22] During this period Croghan's debts to the Gratzes became a significant concern, and it was agreed that Barnard would travel to London to look after the Irishman's interest in the Indiana Company. The elder Gratz arrived in England in 1769, shortly after Benjamin Franklin had informed Wharton and Trent of the Camden-Yorke opinion. It is possible that Barnard Gratz also learned of the 1757 opinion during his stay.

The remaining investors were David and Moses Franks of Philadelphia, Jacob and Moses Franks of London, and Andrew and William Hamilton of Philadelphia. Clarence Alvord and Clarence Carter, who co-authored a history of Illinois, assert that the 1773 purchase "was the work of the firm of Franks and Company of Philadelphia." Jacob Rader Marcus, a leading historian of colonial American Jews, concurs with this assessment, noting that "David Franks was far more influential than the Gratzes, for with him came the London branch of his family and his politically powerful kinsmen, the Hamiltons of Pennsylvania."[23] David Franks was also a former employer of William Murray, who informed the subscribers about the lead and copper mines in the Illinois country.

The patriarch of the Franks family, Jacob, lived in New York and prospered by supplying the British Army during King George's War. His son Moses moved to England and became a partner in the firm of Nesbitt, Colebrook, and Franks, which earned substantial profits in the colonies. Moses Franks was not averse to speculation and lent assistance to like-minded individuals who endeavored to obtain land grants from the Crown—individuals such as Croghan, Franklin, Wharton, Trent, and Barnard Gratz. His younger brother David also speculated in lands but chose to remain in America. He moved from New York to Philadelphia, married a Christian woman from a prominent family, and became a member of the prestigious Philadelphia Dancing Assembly. Franks shipped timber, furs, and agricultural products to Great Britain in exchange for goods, which he sold at his store on High Street. He also profited by supplying British troops stationed at Fort Pitt and elsewhere, which sparked his interest in the west.[24]

When the firm of Nesbitt, Colebrook, and Franks was appointed as commissary to the British forces during the French and Indian War, David Franks became their agent, which led him to employ William Murray. As one of the "suffering traders" of 1763, Franks was named as a grantee in the deed executed by the Six Nations at Fort Stanwix and later served as president of the Indiana Company.[25] In addition to Murray, Franks had business dealings with several of the subscribers to the Illinois purchase, including Joseph Simon, Robert Callender, and the Gratz brothers. David Franks was both wealthy and well connected, and his stature rose even higher when his eldest daughter married Andrew Hamilton III, the nephew of James Hamilton, the former Philadelphia mayor and governor of Pennsylvania.

Andrew Hamilton and his brother William both subscribed to the Illinois purchase. Moses Franks of Philadelphia was a son of David Franks, who in 1779 joined his namesake uncle in England and in his later years became the chief justice of the Bahamas. The final subscriber, Jacob Franks of London, was most likely another son of David Franks, although he may have been Jacob Henry Franks, who was the son of David's brother Naphtali, a London merchant.[26]

In April 1773, when the aforementioned individuals signed the subscription agreement for the Illinois land purchase, it appeared certain that Vandalia would soon become the fourteenth colony. The British government had presumably changed its position regarding western settlements. It is not surprising, therefore, that the subscribers were willing to provide William Murray with the financial support necessary to travel to the Illinois country and convince the Indians to sell their land.

THE PURCHASE

William Murray's journey to the Illinois country required him to navigate the falls of the Ohio, near present-day Louisville; float past the mouth of the Wabash—where George Croghan suffered "the Stroke of a hatchett on the Head"; and then struggle up the Mississippi to the mouth of the Kaskaskia River. The trip was fraught with peril and was especially dangerous in the spring of 1773. Lord Dunmore, the royal governor of Virginia, had commissioned a survey party to explore lands in the Ohio Valley, a confrontational move that in May had led to altercations with the Shawnees. At about the same time, Murray was completing his journey from Philadelphia to Pittsburgh, stopping in Lancaster to pick up supplies at the store of Joseph Simon. Once in Pittsburgh, Murray awaited the ten boatmen hired to take his supplies downriver, but only three appeared. Retaining his optimism despite such setbacks, Murray sought to reassure the Gratz brothers by relaying Croghan's claim that the Vandalia colony "is fixed" as well as his declaration that Camden and Yorke had personally confirmed their opinion respecting "Indian titles" when Croghan was in England in 1764. "So courage, my boys," Murray wrote in his letter to the Gratzes in Philadelphia.[27]

On June 11, 1773, Murray arrived at Kaskaskia, where he was met by Captain Hugh Lord of the 18th Royal Irish Regiment. In September 1771, former commander Lieutenant Colonel John Wilkins had been discharged for misappropriating funds and had been succeeded by Major Isaac Hamilton, who oversaw the recall of all but fifty soldiers. Hamilton in turn was relieved in June of 1772 by Captain Lord, who shortly thereafter was ordered by General Gage to inquire into suspected fraudulent activity by Wilkins's friend and confidant, William Murray. Although there is no record of action taken against Murray, it is thus likely that the greeting exchanged between the two men was not warm.[28]

Upon arrival, William Murray presented the edited Camden-Yorke opinion to Captain Lord, in which the Crown's highest lawyers had declared that the king's "Letters Patents are not necessary" to acquire land by grant from "the *Indian* Princes." Murray soon held public conferences with the Illinois confederacy and invited the British officers and French residents to attend. The negotiations were not without expense, and one of his local suppliers billed Murray for liquors distributed at the conferences, for the use of his house, and for a French interpreter. In a letter written shortly after the purchase, Murray assured the other subscribers that the negotiation "was carried on with the greatest deliberation, solemnity and in the most public manner possible, all which hundreds can testify."[29]

As described by Eric Kades, Murray "dealt with the shells that remained of the once great Illinois tribes. Their population had fallen from around 10,500 in 1680 to 2,500 in 1736 and to 500 in 1800, as they fell victim to European diseases and Indian enemies on all sides." Their claim to the lands of the Illinois River valley, and to most of the remaining Illinois country, was based on the fact that neighboring tribes had not yet encroached and established permanent settlements. In 1765 the chiefs of the Illinois confederacy had defiantly informed the British that "these lands are ours and no one claims them."[30] However, tribal population and fortunes continued to decline in the ensuing years, and after three weeks of negotiations with Murray, the Illinois Indians were willing to sell their homelands.

The conveyance was effected on July 5, 1773, pursuant to a warranty deed containing the customary language of English property law. The Illinois were represented by six Kaskaskia chiefs, three Peoria chiefs, and one Cahokia chief.[31] The consideration received included a nominal sum of five shillings and the following goods:

> two hundred and sixty strouds, two hundred and fifty blankets, three hundred and fifty shirts, one hundred and fifty pairs of stroud and half thick stockings, one hundred and fifty stroud breech cloths, five hundred pounds of gunpowder, four thousand pounds lead, one gross of knives, thirty pounds of vermilion, two thousand gun flints, two hundred pounds of brass kettles, two hundred pounds of tobacco, three dozen gilt-looking glasses, one gross of gun-worms, two gross of awls, one gross of fire-steels, sixteen dozen of gartering, ten thousand pounds of flour, five hundred bushels of Indian corn, twelve horses, twelve horned cattle, twenty bushels of salt, and twenty guns.[32]

Other goods and services included blankets presented to the chiefs after the purchase, one hog, two saddles, approximately twenty gallons of rum, expenses for interpreters, and miscellaneous provisions given to the Indians "to keep them in good temper."[33]

The first tract is described with recognizable reference points, such as the Mississippi and Ohio rivers, as well as more obscure points of reference, including the "Crab Tree Plains" and the "Salt Lick creek" (Saline River). This tract begins at the mouth of the Mary's River, just below Chester, Illinois; connects to the Wabash River below Old Shawneetown; goes down the Ohio to the Mississippi; and then travels up the Mississippi to its beginning point. The second (or upper) parcel likewise mentions vague locations, such as the site of a battle "between the Pewaria and Renard Indians" (outside Arrowsmith, Illinois), and "a great mountain, to the northwest of the White Buffalo Plain" (Elkhart, Illinois). This tract begins at the mouth of the Missouri River, travels up the Mississippi and the Illinois rivers (to Channahon, Illinois); and then returns to its point of origin after passing near the modern towns of Arrowsmith and Elkhart.[34]

The value of the goods and merchandise exchanged for the two parcels is also unclear. Although the litigants in *Johnson v. McIntosh* valued the consideration at "24,000 dollars, current money of the United States, and upwards," the Illinois and Wabash Land Company had previously estimated the goods to be worth over $37,000. On the other hand, according to the statement of expenses submitted by William Murray, the total cost of the purchase was £3,113, Pennsylvania currency, or £141.10.3 per subscriber. Included in this amount was £500 in expenses claimed by Murray "for my Extraordinary Trouble, Fatigue, Risque & &. Having Done no other Business during an Absence of nine months from my family."[35]

The twenty-two subscribers are listed individually, and the Illinois Land Company is not mentioned because it did not yet exist. It is evident from the face of the deed, however, that the subscribers were not entirely convinced of their right to purchase land directly from the Indians. Significantly, the deed grants the lands to the named grantees, "their heirs and assigns, in severalty, *or unto His Most Sacred Majesty George III . . . for the use, benefit, and behoof of all the said above-named grantees, their heirs and assigns, in severalty, as aforesaid, (by whichever of these tenures the said grantees may most legally hold the same)*." The deed was subsequently recorded at Kaskaskia in the office of the notary public. In a letter penned shortly after the conveyance, Murray reported that he had been told about a vein of copper "about the size of a barrell" that was part of the lands purchased. "I flatter myself," Murray wrote, "that I shall have the approbation of all the Partys concerned for my Negotiation."[36]

THE EMPIRE STRIKES BACK

Captain Hugh Lord must have pondered his options as Murray conferred with the Indians. Lord was well aware of the restrictions on purchase of Indian lands set forth in the 1763 Proclamation. Yet Murray had presented him with an opinion authored by the Crown's highest legal authorities, indicating that "*Indian* princes" could grant land to private parties without royal sanction. Two days prior to the conveyance, Lord wrote to General Gage to request further instructions: "Mr. Murray on his arrival here showed me the opinion . . . that His Majesty's subjects were at liberty to purchase whatever quantity of lands they chose of Indians. . . . I told

Mr. Murray that . . . I should not suffer him to *settle* any of the lands as it was expressly contrary to His Majesty's orders. . . . I shall wait your Excellency's orders for my conduct towards this great purchaser."[37] On the third of September Lord sent Gage another letter, informing his superior that two Frenchmen followed the example of Murray and purchased lands belonging to one of the Illinois tribes.[38]

Lord's first letter did not reach New York until the fourteenth of September, after Gage had left for England. His replacement, Major General Frederick Haldimand, immediately wrote to William Johnson regarding "the very Extraordinary proceedings of Mr. Murray." Haldimand enclosed a copy of Lord's letter and urged the Indian superintendent to convince "the Chiefs of the different Nations . . . to disavow what has been done." In reply, Johnson warned that it is "so easy to get Deeds from a few [Indians] . . . that it is in Fact the rigorous Hand of Government alone that can effectually prevent it."[39]

News of the Illinois land purchase did not reach England until November 1773. Haldimand wrote to both Gage and William Legge, the earl of Dartmouth, and expressed concern about purchases "of such a dangerous tendency," particularly when "carried on under the sanction of the opinion of persons so conspicuous for their knowledge of the law as Lord Camden and late Lord Morden [Yorke]."[40] There appears to be no public response by Lord Camden to the use of the opinion in North America. Dartmouth, as secretary of state for the colonies, informed the king of the purchase and declared in a letter to William Johnson that the purchase was "in open violation and contempt of his Royal Authority."[41]

The approval of the Vandalia colony in 1772 led the Illinois subscribers to believe that the Crown had acknowledged the transitory nature of the 1763 Proclamation. The Camden-Yorke opinion reinforced the view that Indian lands were available for purchase, particularly if one was unfamiliar with the opinion's history and its unedited language. Consequently, William Murray and his colleagues may not have anticipated the forceful denunciation of their purchase by Crown officials. The subscribers certainly did not anticipate the "Boston tea party" of December 16, 1773, which not only sealed the fate of the Vandalia colony but also spurred the enactment of the Coercive Acts that contributed to the escalating tensions between Great Britain and her colonies. Matters went from bad to worse on February 3, 1774, when the Crown prohibited colonial officials from issuing licenses for the purchase by private persons of any lands from the Indians without special orders. The revised policy ordered all Crown lands to be surveyed and sold at public auctions in lots ranging from one hundred to one thousand acres. These restrictions were assailed by Thomas Jefferson in his 1774 pamphlet *A Summary View of the Rights of British America* as a deliberate ploy to check westward expansion, and were later included in the Declaration of Independence as one of the "long train of abuses and usurpations" imposed upon the colonists.[42]

General Haldimand also took measures aimed specifically at the "clandestine" purchases. On March 9, 1774, he instructed Captain Lord to order the notary public to erase all references to the purchases from the official records. The next day Haldimand proclaimed that all purchases of Indian lands without royal approval "will be considered as void and fraudulent."[43] As far as the Crown was concerned, William Murray and his fellow purchasers received no property rights in return for the goods and merchandise provided to the Illinois Indians.

The twenty-two subscribers—and the tribes of the Illinois confederacy—viewed the matter differently. According to Murray, when Captain Lord informed the Indians that they should consider their recent transactions as having no effect, the tribal leaders rejected the suggestion. The subscribers found no fault with Murray's actions and approved his expenses. The next logical step was to ward off opposition to the purchase. Consequently, on February 17, 1774, several of the grantees resolved that Murray should "wait upon the Earl of Dunmore at Williamsburg, Virginia, and offer him in the name of the whole, one, two, or three equal proprietary shares in the said purchase for his Lordship & his Friends in Great Britain."[44] The Vandalia land scheme had moved forward only after influential London bankers and politicians were brought into the fold. The Illinois purchasers likewise believed that including the royal governor of Virginia and other important Englishmen in their speculative venture would make the Crown less inclined to disapprove the conveyance. Although it turned out that Lord Dunmore never became a partner to the Illinois purchase, he was approached by William Murray, and he did become a participant in a subsequent transaction: the October 1775 purchase by twenty individuals of two large tracts of land near the Wabash River from the Piankeshaw Indians.

6

LORD DUNMORE,
THE WABASH PURCHASE
OF 1775, AND REVOLUTION

The decision made in February 1774 by the grantees of the Illinois purchase—to buttress their title by soliciting the favor of the royal governor of Virginia—was consistent with the tactics employed by the Grand Ohio Company, which had offered shares to influential Englishmen in order to secure the Crown's approval of the Vandalia grant. David Franks, William Murray, and their fellow speculators determined to proceed in a similar fashion, although rather than Lord Dunmore being provided with a financial stake in the Illinois purchase, the governor was instead brought into another venture: the acquisition in October 1775 of two large tracts of land in southern Illinois and Indiana from the Piankeshaw Indians. As will be seen, this association with Dunmore, while quite promising at first, ultimately proved to be a mistake.

Following the Boston Tea Party in December 1773, colonists continued to protest the exercise of parliamentary power in America and also took issue with the notion that the Crown owned the lands occupied by Indians. Leading political figures, such as Franklin, Adams, Jefferson, and Henry, espoused views that appeared favorably disposed toward the idea that Indians could sell their lands without royal sanction. A lesser-known individual, Richard Henderson of North Carolina, acted on such principles in March of 1775, joining with eight other individuals to purchase a large portion of present-day Kentucky directly from the Cherokees. Shortly thereafter David Franks, William Murray, and a new group of speculators put into motion their plan for the "Wabash purchase" from the Piankeshaws, which transpired at Vincennes in October.

John Murray: "Our Worthy Governor"

The title of earl of Dunmore was conferred on Charles Murray in 1686 by James II. His son John Murray served in the army of King George II, but another son, William, supported Charles Stuart in the uprising of 1745. As a result William was placed under house arrest. William became the third earl of Dunmore in 1752, and when he died four years later, he was succeeded by his son, John, the viscount of Fincastle.[1]

John Murray was a young man when his father rebelled against the Crown. He chose a different path, serving in his uncle's former regiment, becoming a Whig, and rejecting Stuart pretensions. In 1770 Dunmore was commissioned as the royal governor of New York. As noted by John Selby, the Scotsman came to America "to enhance the patrimony of his children." Soon after Dunmore arrived, Benjamin Franklin was informed that "only money talked" when dealing with the new governor. The Scottish earl allied with New York speculators and soon was in possession of some fifty thousand acres of land. According to William Smith of the New York Council, Dunmore was not only enriching his family but was also enjoying himself. In his diary entry following the Feast of St. Andrew, Smith noted that the governor was "clamorous in giving the Toasts" and had "sunk himself to the vilest baudy Healths."[2]

Shortly thereafter it was determined that Dunmore should govern Virginia. On February 11, 1771, Crown officials set forth detailed instructions for this new position, admonishing Dunmore that private purchases of Indian land "may endanger the peace and security of our said colonies." Given his good fortune in New York, Dunmore responded to the news with dismay. According to Smith, "my Lord took too Chearful a Glass" at his farewell dinner and cried out, "Damn Virginia—Did I ever seek it? Why is it forced upon me? I ask'd for New York—New York I took, & they robbed me of it without my Consent."[3]

Dunmore was in an unenviable position when he arrived in Williamsburg: his desultory remarks preceded him, and the man he was replacing, the late Lord Botetourt, had been highly respected by Virginians. However, as Clarence Alvord noted, "Virginia speculators had found their patron."[4] In particular, Dunmore pursued two courses of action that delighted colonists and exasperated royal authorities. First, he aggressively exercised his authority to grant western lands. When the colonial governors were instructed that no lands were to be granted except to officers and soldiers of the French and Indian War, Dunmore announced

Lord Dunmore (John Murray, fourth Earl of Dunmore). Portrait by Sir Joshua
Reynolds. Scottish National Portrait Gallery, purchased in 1992 with contributions
from the Art Fund and the National Heritage Fund.

that Virginian veterans as well as British regulars were entitled to locate lands. The primary beneficiary was George Washington, who laid claim to over two hundred thousand acres. His western properties accounted for more than half of his landed wealth, and for Christmas in 1773, the grateful Washington presented the governor with a barrel of whitethorn berries.[5]

Dunmore also vigorously asserted Virginia's territorial rights, claiming authority over lands on both sides of the Ohio River and also over the area surrounding Fort Pitt. The fort had been abandoned in 1772, which created a jurisdictional void. Virginia's claim prompted Pennsylvania to create Westmoreland County and set up a civil government, which did not go unnoticed. Just a few weeks after William Murray departed to negotiate the Illinois purchase, Lord Dunmore traveled to Fort Pitt, arriving in August 1773. He authorized William Thompson to survey lands in Kentucky, promised John Campbell some two thousand acres at the falls of the Ohio, and publicly pledged to uphold the land claims of veterans and squatters. Privately Dunmore conferred with George Croghan about opportunities for land speculation. Croghan apparently discussed his prior purchases of Indian lands, since word was circulating by January of 1774 that the Virginia governor was of the view that "Colo. Croghans Grant was good."[6] The Irish trader may have presented the Camden-Yorke opinion to Dunmore, who in turn may have shared it with George Washington.

Thus when William Murray presented the petition of the Illinois grantees to Dunmore, he must have anticipated a favorable response. The petition, dated April 19, 1774, requested Dunmore "to take the Petitioners, and their settlements into the protection of your Lordships Government of Virginia." To support their claim the petitioners relied on the Camden-Yorke opinion "relative to Titles, derived by his Majesty's Subjects from the Indians." It appears that Dunmore was also offered two shares—for himself and his oldest son—in the incipient scheme to acquire lands from the Piankeshaws. By May 16, 1774, Murray was back in Philadelphia, and he informed Barnard Gratz that "eight in Maryland have signed to the new affair."[7]

Dunmore dutifully transmitted to the earl of Dartmouth the petition "of a set of gentlemen who have purchased from the Indians a considerable tract of land." Hesitant to place too much reliance on the Camden-Yorke opinion, the governor warned that by rejecting the petition, British officials would encourage "the people to adopt a form of government of their own." According to Dunmore, there was no stopping western settlement in any event, and the Illinois grantees were willing to accede to—rather than resist—British authority.[8]

The Virginia governor was not to learn of the Crown reaction until December of 1774. In the intervening months the dispute between Virginia and Pennsylvania became further complicated by rising tensions between settlers and Indians. The Shawnee in particular viewed with hostility the surveying parties descending the Ohio. On March 3, 1774, Alexander McKee at Fort Pitt (renamed Fort Dunmore by Virginia supporters) warned William Johnson that the rapid settlement "may in the End draw on a Quarrell." In an open letter printed in a Williamsburg newspaper, "Virginius" described the situation as a "golden opportunity" and suggested that bold action would "render the name of *Dunmore* as memorable in *Virginia* as that of *Marlborough* is in *Great Britain.*"[9]

Dunmore needed little prompting. His western agent, John Connolly, had already organized frontiersmen into a militia. When the family of Logan, a Mingo chief, was brutally murdered, Dunmore asked the Virginia legislature to provide troops for an expedition against the anticipated retaliation. When this request was refused, Dunmore decided to conduct a campaign with militia drawn from the western counties. The governor desired war for several reasons: to frustrate the impending establishment of the Vandalia colony; to strengthen Virginia's territorial claims by conquest; to force the Ohio Indians to cede their lands as a condition of peace; and to secure a large grant for his family.[10]

On July 10, 1774, Lord Dunmore left Williamsburg, not to return for five months. He arrived in Pittsburgh in September, where he expressed to Alexander Ross his "great hopes of success" with regard to the Illinois petition. Ross relayed this information to Matthew Ridley of Baltimore, an investor in the "new affair," and further noted that Dunmore counseled against bribing English officials, at least for the time being: "Lord Dunmore has not thought proper to offer any share yet to Lords Gower & Dartmouth, that it may not appear we wanted to influence them by interested motives to promote the matter. But hereafter, when the business is either forwarded, or finished, to make a tender then will appear in the more favourable light of an acknowledgement for a favor received."[11]

Dunmore left Pittsburgh by the end of September but saw no action in his namesake war. The pivotal encounter was fought at Point Pleasant (West Virginia), where a historical marker commemorates the engagement

as "the most important battle ever waged between the forces of civilization and of barbarism in America." Hyperbole and racism aside, the failure
to defeat the Virginian forces caused the Shawnee to capitulate. Chief
Cornstalk met with Dunmore and agreed to a peace that was ponderously
memorialized in verse:

> The Indians with aching hearts, on bended knees did fall
> And for his Lordship's mercy, so loudly they did call
> His Lordship with compassion, forgave them from that day,
> If all the costs and charges amongst them they would pay.[12]

The "costs and charges" included the relinquishment of Shawnee claims
to Kentucky, thus establishing the Ohio River as the de facto boundary
between the Ohio Indians and the settlers.

Lord Dunmore's War was over, and the governor returned to Williamsburg in early December. Upon his arrival Dunmore garnered accolades,
including a letter from the College of William and Mary that conveyed
"such expressions of affection as can be derived only from applauding and
grateful hearts!" In January Dunmore presided over an elegant ball that
celebrated the christening of his daughter—named Virginia in honor of
the colony. The governor stood at the height of his fame, and was, according to a fellow countryman, "as popular as a Scotsman can be among weak
prejudiced people."[13]

Not everything was going Governor's way, however: the response from
London concerning the Illinois purchase was not favorable. When Dunmore endorsed the purchase in May 1774 he was unaware that news of
the transaction had reached England the previous November and that
Secretary of State Dartmouth had denounced the affair in letters sent to
William Johnson and Frederick Haldimand. Dartmouth's first letter to
Dunmore regarding the petition arrived in Pittsburgh during the Shawnee campaign. The secretary of state expressed his personal view that the
purchase was "a violation of the King's rights," but Dunmore took solace
in the fact that Dartmouth promised to "obey such commands as I shall
receive from the King thereupon."[14] On September 8, 1774, Dartmouth
wrote again, communicating "His Majesty's Disapprobation" and stating
that purchases beyond the Proclamation Line "can be considered in no
light than that of a gross indignity and dishonour to the Crown and of an
Act of equal inhumanity and injustice to the Indians."[15]

In response to this rebuke Dunmore wrote fifty pages of folio manu-script, completed on Christmas Eve, reporting on the war against the Shawnees, the territorial dispute with Pennsylvania, and his land poli-cies. The governor truthfully stated that "the purchases of Murray and others . . . [were completed] long before I became acquainted with any circumstance of either," but he spoke falsely by denying having "been concerned in any scheme for obtaining of land." Dunmore advised the Crown to reverse the policy set forth in the 1763 Proclamation, arguing that angry colonists would otherwise "form a set of democratical govern-ments of their own upon the backs of the old colonies." Dartmouth was not convinced. He commanded Dunmore to "signify the King's Dis-allowance of the Indian Purchase upon the Ohio."[16]

The earl of Dunmore had failed to persuade the Crown to accept the Illi-nois purchase, and events soon unfolded that transformed their patron from an apparent asset to an unequivocal liability. On March 21, 1775, Dun-more issued a proclamation forbidding Richard Henderson "and other dis-orderly persons" from occupying lands "under any purchase, or pretended purchase, made from *Indians.*" The governor also published the Order of the Privy Council, dated February 3, 1774, concerning the disposition of Crown lands. The long-suppressed instructions proved so unpopular that "raising the conditions of new Appropriations of Lands" became one of the twenty-seven grievances set forth in the Declaration of Independence.[17]

The governor's proclamation and the Crown's land policy were received with displeasure by the delegates to the second Virginia convention. On March 23 Patrick Henry delivered his famous oration, exclaiming, "Give me liberty or give me death!" in support of his motion that the mili-tia should be put into a state of defense. The motion passed by a single vote, reflecting the lingering doubts of his compatriots. Indeed, two days later the convention resolved to thank "our worthy Governor . . . for his truly noble, wise, and spirited conduct on the late expedition against our Indian enemy." These sentiments, however, proved to be the final plau-dits Virginia provided Lord Dunmore. Before the end of March the del-egates elected representatives to attend the Second Continental Congress in Philadelphia.[18] Before the first of May Dunmore removed gunpowder from the public magazine in Williamsburg, threatened to free and arm the slaves, and mounted cannon on the lawn of the Governor's Palace. By October 18, 1775—the day he became one of the twenty grantees in the Wabash purchase—Lord Dunmore was the most hated man in Virginia.

IS THE CROWN THE SOURCE OF TITLE TO LANDS IN AMERICA?

Although only twenty-seven months separated the Illinois purchase and the Wabash purchase, the latter acquisition was conducted under vastly different circumstances. A paradigm shift had taken place between July 1773 and October 1775. A majority of colonists opposed the actions of Parliament, particularly several revenue acts and the Quebec Act, which extended the authority of the Canadian government to the Ohio River. Colonial leaders also questioned the dogma that the Crown was the source of title to all lands in America. Some individuals, such as George Croghan, Samuel Wharton, and Richard Henderson, went further and agreed with Patrick Henry that "a purchase from the natives was as full and ample a title as could be obtained."[19]

The repeal of the Stamp Act led many in the colonies to believe that protests against the Tea Act would yield similar results. Instead Parliament responded to the "Tea Party" by closing Boston's port until the city paid for the jettisoned merchandise. The Boston Port Bill was the first of a series of punitive measures, referred to by the British as the "coercive" acts but characterized by the colonists as the "intolerable acts."[20] In protest, the Virginia House of Burgesses resolved that the first of June would be a day of fasting and prayer.

In May 1774 Lord Dartmouth had presented to the House of Lords a bill to make "more effectual provision for the government of the province of Quebec." The Quebec Act, among other things, extended the boundaries of the province to encompass the entire trans-Appalachian west. Dartmouth claimed the legislation would discourage attempts by British subjects to emulate the Illinois purchasers.[21] On June 17, 1774, the same day that the act passed the House of Lords, the Massachusetts House of Representatives sent forth a call for a colonial congress to meet in Philadelphia. The colonists were upset about "taxation without representation"—perhaps best exemplified by George Washington's comment to Bryan Fairfax that "the Parliament of Great Britain have no more right to put their hands into my pocket, without my consent, than I have to put my hands into yours." When the delegates to the First Continental Congress met in September 1774, they also discussed imperial policies relating to western lands. The Congress called for the repeal of the Quebec Act, which Richard Henry Lee declared to be "the worst grievance" of all. His father, Thomas Lee, surely would have agreed.[22]

Colonial leaders took issue not only with the land policies of the king and Parliament but also with the underlying premise that the Crown was the source of title to lands in America. In February 1773 the governor of Massachusetts, Thomas Hutchinson, had declared that "all our lands and tenements are held mediately, or immediately, of the crown."[23] Not everyone agreed, and it was no coincidence that many of the Americans who challenged Parliament's power to tax the colonies also rejected the notion of Crown ownership of Indian lands. Stuart Banner explains the connection in *How the Indians Lost Their Land: Law and Power on the Frontier*: "One of the arguments offered by defenders of parliamentary authority was that the colonists had obtained their land from the Crown, and that the charters granting the land had incorporated the colonies within a unitary British empire with Parliament at its center. . . . It suddenly made a great deal of difference whether the earliest settlers had obtained their land from the Crown or from the Indians."[24]

In the decade that preceded revolution, the issue of land tenure in America was addressed by three men who would play prominent roles in the formation of the United States: John Adams, Benjamin Franklin, and Thomas Jefferson. Adams, in his 1765 *Dissertation on the Canon and the Feudal Law*, argued that colonial lands were held "allodially," meaning free of any sovereign or superior lord. In response to Governor Hutchinson, Adams published a dozen articles in the *Boston Gazette* under the pseudonym Novanglus between December 1774 and April 1775. The Massachusetts lawyer argued that feudal tenure was based on conquest and pointed out that the Indians had not been conquered by the king. Adams acknowledged that the charters "*suppose* regal authority in the grantor," but he contended that colonial titles did *not* derive from charter grants and were instead traceable to the original proprietors. Overlooking the fact that Rhode Island founder Roger Williams was expelled—not hailed—for his views on Indian rights (chapter 2), Adams argued that early settlers eschewed reliance on charter grants and "honestly purchased their lands of the natives."[25]

Benjamin Franklin, writing in 1767 as "Benevolus," observed that the right to land in America "was supposed to be in the King . . . but in reality was in the tribes of Indians who inhabited it." On March 16, 1773, Franklin published "On Claims to the Soil of America" in the *Public Advertiser* in London. The famed inventor, who was also an avid land speculator, rejected "the king's position as universal landlord" as being "directly contrary to the Nature of Things and to Common-sense."[26]

Thomas Jefferson also disputed the transfer of British feudalism to America. In *A Summary View of the Rights of British America* Jefferson argued that feudal tenure was a Norman exception to "the Saxon laws of possession, under which all lands were held in absolute right." The early settlers—out of either ignorance or indifference—had failed to challenge the notion of Crown ownership of land, but recent events required the colonists to expose this pretension. "It is time," Jefferson wrote, "to lay this matter before his majesty, and to declare that *he has no right to grant lands of himself.*"[27]

Robert Williams, Jr., points out that Jefferson's argument suggests the colonies also lacked the power to control the acquisition of Indian lands.[28] Jefferson himself never contended that private purchase alone sufficed to gain a complete title to Indian lands.[29] Other individuals, however, did endorse the idea that Indians were empowered to sell their lands without government approval. George Croghan and Samuel Wharton immediately come to mind. In the fall of 1770 Croghan began selling portions of his 1749 Indian grant to pay off his debts. In 1773, following his discussion with William Murray regarding the Camden-Yorke opinion, Croghan borrowed six thousand dollars and purchased approximately 1.5 million acres near Fort Pitt from the compliant Iroquois. On July 10, 1775, the irrepressible speculator paid twelve thousand dollars, mostly in Indian goods, to five Iroquois chiefs in exchange for 6 million acres between the Allegheny River and Big Beaver Creek.[30]

At about the same time, Samuel Wharton wrote to Croghan about purchasing lands west of the Ohio. Wharton, who had previously declared that Indians have "an inherent and undoubted power to grant the lands to us," was unaware that his associate had already acted on such principles. The Quaker's belief in the validity of Indian title was strengthened when his cousin, Thomas Wharton of Philadelphia, wrote to Thomas Walpole in September of 1774 and passed along "a very singular anecdote which I yesterday was favored with by Mr. Henry." Patrick Henry "was convinced from every authority that the law knew, that a purchase from the natives was as full and ample a title as could be obtained," and noted that "they had Lord Camden and Mr. York's opinions on that head."[31]

In the spring of 1775 Samuel Wharton and William Trent began to solicit opinions from respected English legal authorities regarding the validity of the "Indiana grant" conveyed by the Iroquois at Fort Stanwix. In March, Henry Dagge of Lincoln's Inn offered his opinion that the Indians "had a right to grant, cede, or transfer" their property and that the recipients of the 1768 grant "hath a good, lawful and sufficient title." A month later, Serjeant-at-Law John Glynn declared that the Six Nations "had a power of alienating and transferring in any manner, or to any persons, unless they had been restrained by their own laws." On April 17, 1775, in a letter to Croghan, Wharton claimed that "Lord Camden entirely agrees in opinion with these Gentlemen . . . and this is also the real opinion of every sound lawyer in Westminister Hall." Camden was apparently reluctant to state his views, a reluctance not shared by Patrick Henry and Benjamin Franklin, who took time from the deliberations of the Second Continental Congress to concur expressly "with Counsellor Dagge and Serjeant Glynn."[32]

Through the efforts of Wharton and Trent, proponents of the right of Indians to sell land to private individuals were equipped, by the summer of 1775, with additional persuasive authority beyond the doctored Camden-Yorke opinion. The inability to obtain Crown approval of the Indiana grant, and the eventual demise of the Vandalia land scheme, had prompted such action. During this same period Richard Henderson of North Carolina pressed forward and, with eight other individuals, purchased most of Kentucky from the Cherokee Indians.

RICHARD HENDERSON AND THE "TREATY" OF SYCAMORE SHOALS

Richard Henderson practiced law in Granville County, North Carolina, and in 1768 became a justice of the highest court in the colony. By then Daniel Boone had reached Kentucky, and according to John Mack Faragher, "there have been suspicions that Henderson and his associates financed Boone's extended hunting expeditions across the mountains in exchange for intelligence." Toward the end of August 1774 Henderson and five other men organized the Louisa Company to "rent or purchase" Indian lands in defiance of colonial statutes and the Proclamation of 1763. On January 6, 1775, the Louisa Company was renamed the Transylvania Company, and three new partners were added—including James Hogg, who began to stockpile trade goods at his store at Cross Creek (Fayetteville).[33]

Reaction to Henderson's proposal was swift. John Stuart, the British superintendent for Indian affairs for the Southern Department, warned Dunmore that "a number of persons from North Carolina were in the

Cherokee Nation negotiating some such purchase." In a letter dated January 28, 1775, the auditor of the colony, Archibald Neilson, exclaimed in a postscript: "Pray, is Dick Henderson out of his head?" Governor Josiah Martin issued a proclamation in February forbidding "Richard Henderson and his Confederates . . . to prosecute so unlawful an Undertaking." Shortly thereafter, Dunmore issued his proclamation, urging officials "to use their utmost endeavours to prevent the unwarrantable and illegal designs of the said *Henderson*, and his abetters."[34]

In the meantime, Henderson had dispatched Daniel Boone and thirty axmen to build a "Wilderness Road" and establish the settlement of Boonesborough on the banks of the Kentucky River. Boone was still blazing his famous trail when, on March 17, 1775, the Cherokees met with "Carolina Dick" at Sycamore Shoals in northeastern Tennessee. Chief Oconistoto agreed to convey lands between the Kentucky and Cumberland rivers (and a corridor east of the Cumberland Gap) in exchange for £10,000 in goods. The tract consisted of about 20 million acres, translating to a price of about two or three cents per acre. Dragging Canoe told the purchasers that Kentucky "was the bloody Ground" and would be difficult to settle. The Cherokee warrior also foretold the Trail of Tears, warning that his people "will be compelled to seek a retreat in some far distant wilderness."[35]

The deed stated that the Indian grantors held an "indefeasible estate of inheritance in fee simple," and were authorized to convey the territory. John Stuart's deputy, Alexander Cameron, reported that Henderson claimed no statute or proclamation could prevent the private purchase of Indian lands.[36] At this time Henderson was presumably unaware of the Camden-Yorke opinion. In the month after the purchase Henderson and his partners wrote to Patrick Henry to express their view "that our purchase is neither against the laws of our country, nor the principles of natural justice and equity." The Camden-Yorke opinion was not mentioned.[37]

After concluding the "treaty" of Sycamore Shoals, Henderson traveled to Boonesborough. On May 23, 1775, he called a convention of the Kentucky settlers, who gathered under a large elm tree. To signify the transfer of title Henderson took possession "of a bit of Kentucky turf in a moment of feudal pageantry." The settlers acknowledged the company as "Lords of the Soil" and agreed to pay quitrents. Opposition would soon emerge—led by a twenty-two-year-old named George Rogers Clark—but "Carolina Dick" seemed to have realized his dream of founding a proprietary colony. When news arrived of the conflict at Lexington and Concord, the company responded by appealing to the Continental Congress for recognition of Transylvania as a separate state. Before Richard Henderson and his associates were to learn the fate of Transylvania, however, another private purchase of Indian lands took place: the Wabash purchase of October 1775.[38]

THE WABASH PURCHASE

The first mention of the Wabash purchase is found in William Murray's letter dated May 16, 1774, in which he notes that "eight in Maryland have signed to the new affair." Beyond this there is virtually no documentation of the events leading up to the purchase of two large tracts of land in October 1775 from the Piankeshaw Indians. In a memorial to Congress, Murray recounted that following the 1773 purchase from the Illinois, he "commenced another negotiation of a similar nature with the several Chiefs of the different Tribes of the Piankashaw nations." This statement is supported by his account of disbursements, which included a charge of twenty-five livres—incurred on September 20, 1775—to Walter Elliot "for writing [a] duplicate of the Indian Deed."[39] The next evidence of the Wabash purchase is the deed itself.

On the other hand, there is a record of activity in 1774 and 1775 with respect to the 1773 Illinois purchase. On May 12, 1774, John Inglis sold his share to William Russell of Maryland, and Robert Callender expressed his desire in June "to convey to any person who will take his share." Murray acquired William Hamilton's share on May 25 and sold it six days later to Samuel Chase of Annapolis. Moses and Jacob Franks transferred their shares during 1774 to David Franks, and by January 1775 an Alexandria merchant named James Kirk and his partner, William Sidebotham of Bladensburg, Maryland, had acquired shares.[40] Kirk and Sidebotham persuaded a recent arrival in America, twenty-four-year-old Nicholas Cresswell of England, to undertake the hazardous journey to the Illinois country in order to survey a portion of the purchase. Cresswell embarked from Fort Pitt, dined with John Campbell, and traveled down the Ohio as far as the mouth of the Kentucky River, but turned back in June when his guide declined to proceed to Illinois.[41]

The Wabash purchase was transacted at "Post Saint Vincent" on the east side of the Wabash River. Thomas Gage had informed Hillsborough in 1769 that "Strollers and Vagabonds . . . have assembled there, to live a lazy kind of Indian Life, or taken shelter there from Justice." When Father Pierre Gibault visited Vincennes in the winter of 1769–70, he wrote that "some cried out: 'Father, save us, we are almost in hell." In 1772 General Gage ordered all residents of the Wabash Valley to relocate "into some one of the colonies of His Majesty." When the Vincennes *habitants* argued that the Piankeshaws had granted lands in 1742, Gage requested verification of their claim.[42] The rebellion of the colonies mooted the issue.

Although Murray states in the 1796 memorial to Congress that he negotiated the purchase with the Piankeshaws, the deed itself declares that it was Louis Viviat who conferred with the Indians. Anna Marks suggests that Murray employed Viviat—an old acquaintance from Kaskaskia—because "the English Crown would not dare oppose such a prominent Frenchman." Viviat was clearly acting as agent for Murray, who paid for "sundries & writing translations and recording."[43] The Native grantors were eleven Piankeshaw chiefs, and the price paid was five shillings and a large assortment of goods, including items of silver jewelry that were not part of the Illinois purchase:

> four hundred blankets, twenty-two pieces of stroud, two hundred and fifty shirts, twelve gross of star gartering, one hundred and twenty pieces of ribbon, twenty-four pounds of vermilion, eighteen pairs velvet laced housings, one piece of malton, fifty-two fusees, thirty-five dozen large buckhorn-handle knives, forty dozen couteau knives, five hundred pounds of brass kettles, ten thousand gun flints, six hundred pounds of gunpowder, two thousand pounds lead, four hundred pounds of tobacco, forty bushels of salt, three thousand pounds of flour, three horses; also, the following quantities of silver ware, viz.: eleven very large armbands, forty wristbands, six whole moons, six half-moons, nine earwheels, forty-six large crosses, twenty-nine hairpipes, sixty pairs of earbobs, twenty dozen small crosses, twenty dozen nose crosses, and one hundred and ten dozen brooches.[44]

Estimates of the value of the merchandise vary: the litigants in *Johnson v. McIntosh* valued the consideration at "31,000 dollars, current money of the United States, and upwards," and the Illinois and Wabash Land Company had previously estimated the goods to be worth $42,477.73.[45]

The amount of land conveyed is also unclear. The two tracts consisted together "of ninety-three leagues in length on the Wabash River, and

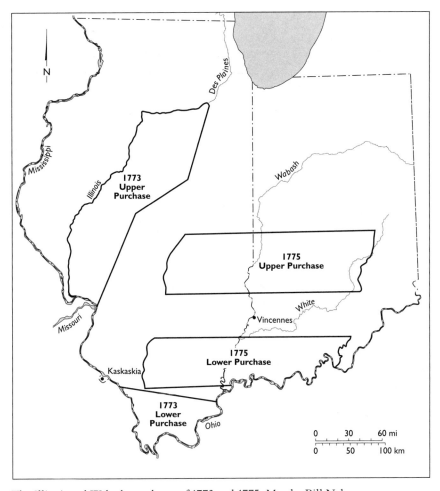

The Illinois and Wabash purchases of 1773 and 1775. Map by Bill Nelson.

on both sides thereof, inclusive, seventy leagues in width or breadth." A large intermediate area was expressly reserved from the conveyance, in conformance with the 1742 "lost" grant made by the Piankeshaws to the French. The tracts have been estimated to amount to 37,497,600 acres, an exaggerated figure, considering that the entire state of Illinois covers just over 37 million acres.[46]

The deed was recorded on December 5, 1775, at Kaskaskia. Although no map or drawing accompanied the deed, the British Museum has a deer-skin map that was likely used during the negotiations. The map is centered "on the long axis of a diagrammatically straightened Wabash River" and is perforated at each corner, suggesting that the skin was nailed to a vertical surface. The tribal names Piankishwa, Kaskaskias, and Wia appear, and the word "Sold" follows Piankishwa in one instance. Cartographer G. Malcolm Lewis hypothesizes that the map "could have been an interim document made and used in discussions between different sub groups of the Piankashaw, between the Piankashaw and French land owners in and around Post Vincennes, or between the latter and Louis Viviat."[47]

Following are the twenty grantees of the Wabash purchase, beginning with the earl of Dunmore, and his son:

John Murray	Virginia
John Murray, Jr.	Virginia
Thomas Johnson, Jr.	Maryland
John Davidson	Maryland
William Russell	Maryland
Matthew Ridley	Maryland
Peter Campbell	Maryland
William Geddes	Maryland
Robert Christie, Sr.	Maryland
Robert Christie, Jr.	Maryland
David Franks	Philadelphia
Moses Franks	Philadelphia
Moses Franks	London
Jacob Franks	London
William Murray	Illinois Country
Nicholas St. Martin	Illinois Country
Francis Perthuis	Illinois Country
Joseph Page	Illinois Country
Daniel Murray	Illinois Country
Louis Viviat	Illinois Country

Five of the grantees were also subscribers to the Illinois purchase: William Murray and the four members of the Franks family. Virginia, which claimed jurisdiction over the land conveyed, was represented by Governor Dunmore and his son. John Murray, Jr., a student at the College of William and Mary, did not outlive his father to become the fifth earl of Dunmore; that title was bestowed on a younger brother in 1809.

The most prominent among the eight Maryland grantees was Thomas Johnson, Jr., of Annapolis. Johnson was "a man of medium stature, with

Thomas Johnson. Courtesy of the Maryland Historical Society (Image ID 1957.20.1).

reddish brown hair," and was described by John Adams as possessing "an extensive knowledge of trade as well as law."[48] A modern biographer has observed that "few men have so conducted their lives to escape historical study better than Thomas Johnson of Maryland." A good deal, however, is known about his public life: he was a delegate to the Continental Congress, where he served on the Committee of Correspondence, and nominated

George Washington to be commander-in-chief, but missed signing the Declaration of Independence due to a temporary absence. He helped draft Maryland's constitution, became the state's first governor in 1777, served three terms, and was thereafter elected to the House of Delegates, where he supported the ratification of the federal constitution. An able lawyer, Johnson became a state court judge in 1790 and, a year later, an associate justice on the United States Supreme Court. On January 16, 1793, Thomas Johnson, Jr., ended the shortest tenure on the bench of any Supreme Court justice by tendering his resignation to President Washington. He thereafter declined an offer to become secretary of state. Johnson was appointed in 1791 as one of three commissioners responsible for overseeing the establishment of the new capital, the District of Columbia.[49]

Edward Delaplaine, in his 1927 biography of Johnson, makes no mention of the Illinois and Wabash Land Company or any of his subject's other speculative ventures. There is no question that Johnson invested heavily in land and became one of the wealthiest men in western Maryland. Nevertheless, Bob Arnebeck claims that Johnson's "one regret was that, despite ample plantation, an ironworks, and thirty-eight slaves, he was not as wealthy as he wished to be."[50] Johnson did not ignore business opportunities during his years of public service. In addition to being a grantee in the Wabash purchase, he acquired a half share in the Illinois purchase in 1775, most likely while serving as a member of the Second Continental Congress. As discussed below, George Mason would accuse "Governor Johnston" in 1779 of opposing Virginia's charter claims in order to profit personally from his investment.

The remaining Maryland investors were primarily men of business. John Davidson, William Russell, Matthew Ridley, and Peter Campbell were merchants, and William Geddes was the royal collector of customs for Kent County.[51] Robert Christie and his namesake son are described in the Piankeshaw deed as merchants, but the younger Christie was appointed sheriff of Baltimore in 1774. As sheriff, Christie was asked on July 29, 1776, to read the Declaration of Independence to a crowd assembled at the courthouse. When he refused, he was suspected of being disloyal and was told in December that "unless you leave this town instantly and the state within six days, your life will be sacrificed by an injured people." Christie soon left for New York.[52]

Little is known about Nicholas St. Martin and Francis Perthuis of the Illinois country, except that both men billed Murray for expenses incurred during the negotiations with the Piankeshaws and neither was associated with the venture by 1779. Joseph Page and Daniel Murray sold their shares to William Murray within a month of the transaction. Daniel Murray, the brother of William, assisted George Rogers Clark during his occupation of Kaskaskia in 1778 and equipped Clark's men for their subsequent conquest of Vincennes. To recover his expenditures, Murray petitioned the Virginia Assembly in 1781 and received partial payment. Within three years he was dead, the result of a bullet wound inflicted during a dispute over a debt.[53] Louis Viviat died two years after negotiating the Wabash purchase. The Frenchman remained loyal to Great Britain, which no doubt contributed to the dissolution of his partnership with the Murray brothers.

The other party to the transaction, the Piankeshaw Indians, had experienced tremendous change within a single generation. The death of Memeskia in 1752 altered the balance of power within the Miami confederacy. The Piankeshaws were able to assist George Croghan during his captivity in 1765, but the tribe exercised far less influence than it did when the settlement at Pickawillany attracted British traders. By the early 1760s the Piankeshaws had returned to their former villages at Vincennes and the mouth of the Vermilion River. At some point during the early 1770s the Delawares moved to southern Indiana with the acquiescence of the Miami confederacy. The territory was no longer needed to sustain the Piankeshaws, who were never a large tribe, numbering between four and six hundred persons prior to the sale of their lands in 1775.[54]

The eleven Piankeshaw chiefs listed as grantors are Tabac (Tobacco); his son, Tabac, junior; Montour; La Grand Couette; Ouaouaijao; La Mouche Noire (Black Fly); Maringoin (Mosquito); Le Petit Castor (Little Beaver); Kiesquibichias; Grelot; and his son, Grelot, junior. Both George Rogers Clark and British general Henry Hamilton conferred with "Old Tobacco" and "Young Tobacco" during their struggle for control of Vincennes. The son—known also as Francis and, more dramatically, as "the Grand Door of the Wabash"—deeded land in southeast Indiana to Clark in 1779. As discussed in chapter 11, the son of Le Petit Castor traveled in 1792–93 with a delegation of Indians to Philadelphia, where he verified his father's signature on the 1775 deed.[55]

The day after the Wabash purchase a conference was concluded at Fort Pitt. The Indians were assured that "we have not the most Distant thought

in Sevalty on unto his said Majesty his Heirs and Successors
to and for the only use benefit and behoof of the said Grantees
their Heirs and Assigns in Sevalty as aforesaid shall and
will Warrent and for ever Defend by these presents
In Witness whereof we the said Chiefs and Sachems
on behalf of Ourselves respectively and on behalf of all
the Other Natives of the several Tribes of the Piankashaw
Nation of Indians as aforesaid have hereunto set our hands
and seals in the presence of the persons Subscribing as
Witness hereunto at a Publick Council held at Post St
Vincent aforesaid this Eighteenth day of October In the
Year of our Lord One Thousand seven hundred & seventy five

Tabac or Tobacco a Chief --- his ⊙ Mark [Seal]

Montour --- a Chief --- his Đ Mark [Seal]

Le Grand Covette a Chief -- his ⟋⫴ Mark [Seal]

Ouacuayao   a Chief --- his ⟜ Mark [Seal]

Tabac Junior a Chief -- his + Mark [Seal]

La Mouche Noir a Chief - his ⟔ Mark [Seal]

Maringoin or Musquitto a Chief his ⟩ Mark [Seal]

Le Petit Castor or little Beaver a Chief his ⟿ Mark [Seal]

Kiesquibichias a Chief --- his ⟁ Mark [Seal]

Grelot Senior a Chief   his (∴) Mark [Seal]

Grelot Junior a Chief   his (⊖) Mark [Seal]

Le fie du Cotonier a Chief   his ⫽ Mark [Seal]

Signatures of the Piankeshaw tribal chiefs in the 1775 deed. *Illinois-Wabash Land Company Manuscript* (Cyrus McCormick, 1915), courtesy of the Abraham Lincoln Presidential Library and Museum.

of Possessing any part of your Lands."[56] The promise did not come from the British government, or from anyone speaking on behalf of the Crown. Rather, the words were spoken by John Walker, the commissioner from Virginia. Also in attendance were commissioners appointed by the Continental Congress "to superintend Indian affairs *in behalf of their colonies.*"[57] In the seven months between the Henderson purchase on March 17, 1775, and the Wabash purchase on October 18, 1775, something happened that had not been anticipated when Lord Dunmore was asked to participate in "the new affair." The colonies were in rebellion, and control over the disposition of western Indian lands, by private purchase or otherwise, hung in the balance.

John Murray: "Our Devil Dunmore"

In the early hours of Friday, April 21, 1775, marines from the *HMS Magdalen* removed fifteen half-barrels of gunpowder from the public magazine in Williamsburg. The following day Governor Dunmore announced that if harm came to any senior British official, he would "reduce the City . . . to ashes." When word of Lexington and Concord reached the Virginia capital, Dunmore barricaded the governor's palace and awaited the advance of Patrick Henry, his former legal adviser and current commander of the Hanover County "volunteers." The confrontation was avoided when the royal governor, his family, and his aides fled during the night to Yorktown, where they boarded the *HMS Fowey.*[58]

This was not the last Virginia would see of her royal governor. In the summer of 1775 Dunmore assembled a small fleet of ships and began raiding coastal towns. Hampered by a lack of resources, he informed Dartmouth in August that, with "a few hundred more" men, he could within a few months reduce the colony "to perfect submission."[59] On the twelfth of October Dunmore destroyed colonial cannon near Norfolk. The attack came just six days *before* the completion of the Wabash purchase in Vincennes.

The other colonies were also in upheaval in the spring and summer of 1775. In Massachusetts, militia forces fought the battle of Bunker Hill, and in New York, Ethan Allen and Benedict Arnold captured Fort Ticonderoga. In May the citizens of Mecklenburg County, North Carolina, declared themselves "a free and independent people." On the other side of the Atlantic, King George III proclaimed on August 23 that the colonies were in "open and avowed rebellion."[60] Shortly thereafter American forces invaded Canada, putting Great Britain on the defensive and exposing its fragile control of the west. However, after capturing Montreal in November, General Richard Montgomery was killed during the assault on Quebec, which failed on New Year's Eve. The king's proclamation had arrived in Philadelphia the first week of November, and coupled with the turn of events in Canada, served to let leaders of the rebellion know that 1776 would be an eventful year.

At about the same time that the king's proclamation reached America, Lord Dunmore issued his own edict, which granted freedom to "all indentured servants [and] negroes . . . that are willing and able to bear arms . . . for the purpose of reducing this colony to a proper sense of their duty to his Majesty's crown and dignity."[61] The proclamation aroused widespread anger. A contributor to the *Virginia Gazette* decried "the *baseness* of lord Dunmore's heart," and George Washington characterized his former theater companion as "that arch-traitor to the rights of humanity." Richard Henry Lee, in a letter to Samuel Adams, referred to him simply as "Our Devil Dunmore."[62] The *Pennsylvania Journal* in December cursed the royal governor in verse, paraphrasing lines from Shakespeare's *MacBeth*:

> Not in the legions
> Of horrid hell, can come a devil more damned,
> In evils, to top Dunmore![63]

In July 1776 the colonial militia bombarded Dunmore's fleet while he regrouped at the mouth of the Piankatank River, forcing him to flee northward to New York. Before departing from Virginia waters, the earl tossed the Great Seal of the colony overboard in a fit of petulance, exclaiming, "There! Let them try to govern without it!"[64]

Before the year 1775 ended John Murray was on a ship to England, and Virginia was finally rid of the "Devil Dunmore." He did return to America in December of 1781, landing at Charleston, South Carolina, but by then Cornwallis had surrendered at Yorktown. Returning to England, Dunmore became a spokesman for loyalists seeking compensation from the Crown. In 1784 he filed his own petition, seeking reimbursement for various items of personal property as well as the loss of lands in Virginia, present-day West Virginia, and present-day Vermont. In addition Dunmore filed a claim for 3.7 million acres along the Wabash River, representing his share of the Wabash purchase. The one item disallowed by the claims commission was for the Piankeshaw lands, but as John Selby notes, "Dunmore apparently expected that, as he had placed no cash value on them." After serving as the governor of the Bahama Islands, Dunmore returned to England in 1796, where he spent the remaining thirteen years of his life. His daughter Virginia corresponded with an American lawyer as late as 1824, regarding "property supposed to have belonged to my late Father."[65] If the inquiry related to the Wabash purchase, the lawyer presumably passed along news of the Supreme Court's 1823 decision in *Johnson v. McIntosh*.

7

VIRGINIA FIGHTS FOR THE
ILLINOIS COUNTRY, 1775–1781

George Croghan, in 1749, 1754, 1773, and again in 1775, purchased large tracts of land in western Pennsylvania from the Iroquois Indians. In November 1768 the "suffering traders" dealt directly with the Iroquois at Fort Stanwix and secured the "Indiana" grant, consisting of land in what is now West Virginia and eastern Kentucky. On July 5, 1773, the remnants of the Illinois confederacy deeded large tracts of land to twenty-two grantees, and on March 17, 1775, the Cherokees conveyed a vast region between the Cumberland and Kentucky Rivers to the proprietors of the Transylvania Company.[1] Seven months later, on October 18, 1775, twenty individuals purchased two tracts of land along the Wabash River from the Piankeshaw Indians.

In each instance the Native grantors transferred title directly to the private purchasers. The grantees, however, faced a common problem: assuring the pertinent authorities, as well as the buying public, that their "Indian title" was valid. For example, when Croghan opened a land office at Pittsburgh in 1770, he was able to convince Barnard Gratz, Joseph Simon, and Alexander Ross to purchase portions of his 1749 grant; but the Irishman did not fare as well with George Washington, who offered to buy fifteen thousand acres only "when a legal title was established."[2] To establish a marketable title that would satisfy Washington, Croghan needed to obtain official acknowledgment of his private purchase.

But from whom? The outbreak of hostilities complicated matters by ushering in a period of uncertainty. Royal confirmation would mean nothing if the colonies achieved independence. Consequently, toward the end of 1775, and throughout the pivotal year of 1776, advocates of Indian title turned away from the Crown. Two choices emerged: Virginia, which claimed jurisdiction by virtue of its expansive charter, and the newly created Congress, whose powers and authority were yet to be determined.[3]

The speculators were at first directed to Virginia, which proved to be as fierce an opponent of private purchase of Indian lands as was the Crown. Between 1775 and 1781 Virginia acted on three fronts to preserve its claim to the Ohio Valley and the Illinois country. In Williamsburg, the government not only rejected memorials seeking confirmation of Indian title; it also enacted legislation proscribing private purchase of Indian lands, and included similar language in its new constitution. In the west, Virginia bolstered its charter claims by authorizing George Rogers Clark to challenge British authority. In Philadelphia, Virginia's delegates challenged the right of Congress to control the disposition of trans-Appalachian lands. By its actions Virginia sought to thwart the speculative ventures that were centered in Pennsylvania and Maryland. George Mason, in a letter to delegate Richard Henry Lee, accused Governor Thomas Johnson of Maryland of delaying the ratification of the Articles of Confederation to save "the great Indian purchase between the Ouabache and the Illinois rivers."[4] Mason's explanation for Maryland's obstinacy is overly simplistic: opposition to confederation was based in part on the popular belief that western lands should be ceded to the national government to finance the war. Nevertheless, there is no question that the private concerns of the newly created Illinois and Wabash Land Company—which combined the holdings of the Illinois and Wabash grantees—impacted the debate regarding the appropriate form of government for the fledgling United States of America.

Virginia Opposes the Speculators

Even prior to the Wabash purchase of October 1775, efforts were under way to obtain confirmation of Indian title from authorities in America. In order to "render our Title a safe and popular one," Samuel Wharton advised his cousin Thomas to take "into partnership" influential members of Congress. William Trent returned to Pennsylvania in June and persuaded Benjamin Franklin and Patrick Henry to endorse the legal opinions of Henry Dagge and John Glynn regarding the validity of the Indiana grant. Shortly thereafter Trent traveled west to convince other "suffering traders" that royal confirmation was unnecessary. At a September meeting in Pittsburgh, Trent argued that the best course of action would be to discontinue efforts to secure the king's approval and instead open a land office and begin selling portions of their grant.[5]

At about the same time, the Transylvania proprietors petitioned the Continental Congress to "be added to the number of the United Colonies." When James Hogg arrived in Philadelphia in October 1775, he met delegates who agreed that Native lands could be purchased by private parties, including a Connecticut merchant named Silas Deane, who argued that Queen Elizabeth—when she granted lands in North America—"had no more right or title than she had to the Empire of China." Hogg sent the Camden-Yorke opinion to Richard Henderson but reported that the Virginia delegation claimed "our purchase was within their charter."[6]

The Virginia delegates responded in a similar fashion when the Indiana Company gave notice in a Philadelphia newspaper, on April 15, 1775, of its intention to sell lands within its 1768 grant. A meeting was arranged the following day at the New Tavern, where Thomas Wharton and George Morgan were informed that the lands had been ceded to Virginia by the 1744 Treaty of Lancaster. The delegates requested that no lands be sold until the issue was resolved by the Virginia Convention.[7] Consequently, the claims of the Transylvania Company and the Indiana Company were first addressed in Williamsburg. As it turned out, the identity of the decision maker—whether it should be Virginia, Congress, or the courts—became as important an issue as the question to be decided: whether a private purchase of Indian lands sufficed to transfer a legal, marketable title.

In the first four months of 1776 several events occurred that pushed the colonies closer to a complete break with Great Britain. Thomas Paine's argument for independence, *Common Sense*, was published in January and distributed throughout the colonies. Congress in February sent Benjamin Franklin, Samuel Chase, John Carroll, and Charles Carroll on a diplomatic mission to Canada and dispatched Silas Deane one month later to Paris to purchase supplies and assess French sentiments. The British evacuated Boston on March 17, 1776, after Washington employed artillery from Fort Ticonderoga. North Carolina thereafter authorized its delegates in Congress to vote for a declaration of independence and—as noted in *Johnson v. McIntosh*—"on the 6th of May, 1776, the colony of Virginia threw off its dependence on the crown and government of Great Britain, and declared itself an independent State."[8]

The delegates to the Continental Congress proclaimed, in July 1776, the inalienable rights of colonial Americans to "life, liberty and the pursuit of happiness"—a phrase that George Mason described as including "the means of acquiring and possessing property." At about the same time, the Virginia Convention denied the basic right of Native Americans to sell their land to whomsoever they pleased. Earlier, in March, disgruntled settlers in Kentucky had prepared a memorial questioning the validity of the purchase from the Cherokees. This memorial was presented in May to the Virginia Convention, as was another petition that complained of the actions of the proprietors. Richard Henderson appeared before the Convention on June 15, 1776, and presented a memorial on behalf of the Transylvania Company. The memorial declared "the right of disposal to be incident to property" and argued that when the Cherokees elected to exercise their unquestioned right to sell their land, the purchasers became "rightful claimants thereof." The proprietors claimed that "disputes to private property do not properly come within the consideration or determination of this Convention," but they expressed willingness to submit "to such government as should be placed by authority over them."[9]

The Convention delegates provided an emphatic response nine days later by resolving "that no purchases of Lands within the chartered limits of *Virginia* shall be made, under any pretence whatever, from any *Indian* tribe or nation, without the approbation of the *Virginia* Legislature." Further asserting authority over the western country, the delegates included a clause in the Constitution of Virginia, adopted on June 29, 1776, that "no purchases of lands shall be made of the Indian natives, but on behalf of the public, by authority of the General Assembly."[10] The Virginia Convention also appointed fifteen commissioners to collect evidence against individuals "pretending to have claims for lands . . . under deeds & purchases from the Indians." As Merrill Jensen notes, Virginia "made plain her intention of maintaining jurisdiction within her charter bounds, and of denying the validity of the Transylvania purchase, the Illinois and Wabash purchases, and the Indiana Company deed."[11]

The commissioners focused their attention on Henderson's transaction with the Cherokees, which likely caused discomfort for Governor Patrick Henry, who had advised that the Transylvania purchase "would stand good." During the summer and fall of 1778, as the Shawnees attacked settlements in Kentucky, the various purchasers of Indian lands renewed their efforts to obtain confirmation of their titles from the Virginia

Assembly.[12] Anticipating a negative result, Henderson backed down and requested only that the proprietors be compensated for their efforts in facilitating settlement. On November 4, 1778, the Virginia House of Delegates passed the following resolutions: "Resolved, That all purchases of lands, made or to be made, of the Indians, within the chartered bounds of this commonwealth, . . . by any private persons not authorized by public authority, are void. Resolved, That the purchase heretofore made by Richard Henderson and Company, of that tract called Transylvania, . . . is void; but . . . it is just and reasonable to allow . . . compensation for their trouble and expense."[13] Virginia and North Carolina eventually awarded the Transylvania proprietors with four hundred thousand acres. The land granted by Virginia encompasses the confluence of the Ohio and Green rivers, the present site of Henderson, Kentucky.

The November 4, 1778, resolution purported to invalidate *prior* purchases "made . . . of the Indians" and thus went beyond the prospective prohibitions set forth in the June 1776 resolution and the state constitution. On the day before its passage, the Illinois and Wabash grantees agreed that William Murray should deliver a memorial to Governor Henry and the Virginia legislature.[14] The memorial was presented on December 26, two weeks after the occupation of Kaskaskia by George Rogers Clark prompted Virginia to pass "An Act for establishing the County of Illinois." The memorial did not request confirmation of title but instead served to inform Virginia of the Wabash purchase and the grantees' intent to settle the lands as soon as feasible: "The said Company think it necessary . . . to notify the Governor, Council & Legislature . . . of their Purchase and that it is the determination of the Proprietors . . . not to dispute the Jurisdiction of the State of Virginia, or any other State, rightly claiming Jurisdiction over any part of the Land purchase in Question."[15]

In response to this memorial—and another petition submitted by the Indiana Company—the General Assembly invited purchasers of Indian land to appear at the May 1779 session. On the appointed date Williamsburg was crowded with speculators, who endured postponement until June. Barnard Gratz presented a memorial on behalf of George Croghan's title, and William Trent and Edmund Randolph argued for the validity of the Indiana grant. George Mason was the most vocal member of the House of Delegates, which sat as a Committee of the Whole.[16] On Wednesday, June 9, 1779, the House specifically declared the Indiana grant "utterly void, and of no effect," and further resolved that "*Virginia* hath the exclusive right of a pre-emption, from the *Indians*, . . . [and] that no person or persons whatsoever have, or ever had, a right to purchase any lands . . . from any *Indian* nation except . . . for the use and benefit of the colony, and lately of the commonwealth."[17] The Senate concurred three days later, and on June 18 a motion to compensate members of the Indiana Company failed, with Speaker Benjamin Harrison casting the tie-breaking vote. The following day an act was passed embodying the resolutions and reiterating that "no person or persons whatsoever have, or ever had, a right to purchase any lands . . . from any Indian Nation, except only persons duly authorized to make such purchases." The General Assembly subsequently established a land office for the purpose of selling western lands. Warrants were issued for large tracts, which provided Virginia with substantial revenue.[18]

Virginia, between 1775 and 1781, consistently opposed the efforts of speculators in Pennsylvania and Maryland to establish marketable title to lands purchased from Indian tribes. During this same period Virginia responded to another threat—Great Britain—by authorizing military action. The daring winter attack on Vincennes in February 1779 by George Rogers Clark is a well-known chapter in American history. By successfully opposing Great Britain in the Illinois country, Virginia was able to buttress its charter claims with conquest.

Virginia Opposes Great Britain

The Quebec Act extended the boundaries of Canada to the Mississippi and Ohio rivers, encompassing much of the territory claimed by Virginia pursuant to its charter. The act also provided for lieutenant-governors to be stationed at Detroit, Kaskaskia, Vincennes, and Michilimackinac. The Vincennes post was assigned to Edward Abbott, who arrived in May 1777. After building Fort Sackville, Abbott grew increasingly fearful of the Indians, who would be expecting—but not receiving—gifts of food and trade goods. He departed in February.[19]

The governorship of Detroit went to Henry Hamilton, who had served under General James Wolfe during the French and Indian War. Hamilton persuaded the Indians to harass frontier settlements by appealing to their fears for their homelands. The Shawnees and other tribes attacked Harrodsburg, Boonesborough, and Morgan's Station, turning 1777 into the "bloody year" in Kentucky. By the end of the year the revolutionary war had spread to the backcountry, and Hamilton was detested as the "hair buyer" who offered rewards for American scalps.[20]

The response to British aggression in the west came from Virginia and was spearheaded by George Rogers Clark. The red-haired Clark was born in 1752 near Jefferson's Monticello and served under Lord Dunmore. In 1776 Clark convinced the Virginia Council to pay for gunpowder in New Orleans, where William Murray had gone after completing the Wabash purchase the previous October. Murray was aware of Clark's intentions and instructed his brother Daniel Murray, in a letter that was carried upriver with the gunpowder shipment, to assist any Americans arriving in Kaskaskia. Two Americans did appear in the spring of 1777, sent by Clark to learn about the town's defenses and the attitude of the French *habitants*. After receiving a favorable report, the twenty-four-year-old Clark traveled to Williamsburg to discuss the conquest of the Illinois country. Governor Henry gave his assent but desired to keep secret the true objectives of Clark's plans.[21]

By approving military action in the Illinois country, Virginia was taking aggressive steps to protect its charter claims. Historians have disagreed as to the principal objective of the Clark campaign. Armstrong Starkey notes that the stated goal—protecting Kentucky settlements from Indian attacks—is at odds with the fact that the threat to Kentucky "was centered several hundred miles to the east" of Kaskaskia and Vincennes. George Chalou suggests the Virginians may have thought that if they controlled "the sources of Indian trade goods, especially arms, gunpowder, and the necessary accoutrements, the Indian forays into Kentucky would be cut down."[22] Another view is that the expedition was undertaken primarily to enhance Virginia's claim to the region. As noted by William Wirt Henry, the grandson of Patrick Henry, the conquest was "by Virginia troops under Clark, who acted not for the United States but *for Virginia alone*." It is telling that Governor Henry discouraged an expedition against Detroit by Continental forces. There is also some evidence that Clark and Henry entered into a partnership regarding the acquisition of western lands.[23] In any event, the occupation of the Illinois country would not only buttress Virginia's charter claims but also help the thirteen states secure their independence from Great Britain.

The campaign was a success. With 175 men, Clark took control of Kaskaskia on July 4, 1778, without firing a shot. In his memoir Clark noted that two local residents, Richard Winston and Daniel Murray, "proved to have been in the american interest." Clark thereafter dispatched Captain Leonard Helm and Father Gibault to Vincennes, to persuade the townspeople to swear their allegiance to Virginia and to convince the neighboring Kickapoos and Piankeshaws "to lay down their Tomahawk." As described by Randolph Downes, "solemn ceremonies were held in which the tribesmen expressed their repentance . . . and pledged peace and friendship with the Big Knife, their new American protectors." At one point the Piankeshaws appeared hostile, but Young Tobacco eventually declared he would "blody the Land no more for the English." According to Clark, this "Valuable negotiation" saved numerous lives.[24] The Virginia legislature, on December 9, 1778, invoked the fact of conquest, as well as its charter claim, and established the County of Illinois.

"THE PURCHASE FROM THE PIANKASHAWS GAVE A GENERAL DISGUST"

When Henry Hamilton learned of Clark's occupation of the Illinois country, he determined to make use of the Wabash purchase of 1775 in order to secure Indian support for an expedition from Detroit. In a letter to General Haldimand outlining his plan, Hamilton declared that "the Savages of the Ouabash . . . cannot relish the invasion of the Virginians, as the purchase from the Piankashaws gave a general disgust." In a second letter Hamilton requested "your Excellency's approbation for a step I mean to take . . . which is to cancel the bargain made for the land of the Peankashaws."[25] Virginia, of course, also considered the Wabash deed to be of no legal effect, but if Hamilton was aware of this, it did not stop him from using the purchase to undermine relations between the Indians and the Americans.

Hamilton left Detroit on the seventh of October. Six weeks later he informed a group of Indians that he would "drive invaders off their lands" and "cancel the Piankashaa contract." In response a Wea chief noted "that the sale of Lands made by *Old Tobacco* . . . had much displeased all the Indians." On December 1 Hamilton held another conference, burned a copy of the deed, and repudiated the transaction as "an irregular proceeding unauthorized by the Crown."[26] The condemnation of the Wabash purchase proved compelling to many Indians in the Wabash Valley. Hamilton was informed that Old Tobacco and his son were "strong with the Virginians" but that La Grande Couette—another signatory to the 1775 deed—now sided with the British. When the expedition arrived at present-day Terre Haute, Indiana, yet another participant in the Wabash purchase—La Mouche Noire (Black Fly)—declared his allegiance to Great Britain.[27] As Hamilton had hoped, Old Tobacco and his son were ostracized and isolated.

Captain Helm surrendered Vincennes to the British on December 17, 1778. When Hamilton reproached Old and Young Tobacco for their conduct "in regard to Lord Dunmore's grant," Young Tobacco declared he was now "glad to join my hand with yours." This change of heart, however, proved to be as short-lived as Henry Hamilton's command of Fort Sackville. Learning that most of the British soldiers had returned to Detroit for the winter, George Rogers Clark informed Patrick Henry on February 3, 1779, of his decision to "risk the whole on a single battle" at Vincennes. "I know the cause is desperate," wrote Clark, "but . . . Great things have been effected by a few men well conducted."[28]

Clark left Kaskaskia two days later. The Little Wabash, Embarrass, and Wabash rivers had overflowed their banks, forcing his men to wade across an expanse of frigid water nearly five miles wide. On February 22, after more than two weeks of marching, Clark's forces reached Vincennes. Hamilton had convened a council the previous day. In his journal the general noted that when Young Tobacco once again professed allegiance to the British, an Ottawa Indian told him "not to speak from the lips outward, but from the heart." The rebuke was well founded, because at some point during the evening of February 22, Young Tobacco offered the services of one hundred warriors to Clark, whose forces had commenced their attack. On February 24, 1779, Henry Hamilton formally surrendered Fort Sackville to George Rogers Clark and became a prisoner of war.[29]

After concluding several treaties with the tribes of the Wabash, Clark returned to Kaskaskia. John Todd, commissioned as county lieutenant by Governor Henry, arrived in the Illinois country in May 1779 and established a court at Vincennes, which proceeded to dispose of a large part of the land purportedly granted in 1742 by the Piankeshaws. As part of his official duties Todd reported on Indian grants in the Illinois country, stating that "they are almost numberless" but noting that only the Illinois and Wabash purchases were "very considerable." "I cannot say," Todd commented, whether it was proper "to make such contracts binding upon the Indians."[30]

Young Tobacco praised George Rogers Clark and on June 16, 1779, granted him land across the Ohio River from present-day Louisville,

Kentucky. Clark did not seek immediate confirmation of this grant, but when Virginia ceded lands north of the Ohio to the United States, it reserved 150,000 acres for Clark and his men.[31] Clark was rewarded because he had taken bold action in defense of Virginia's charter claims. Whether Virginia should be permitted to keep the Illinois country, however, was a question that would be fiercely debated in Congress.

VIRGINIA OPPOSES MARYLAND AND THE "LANDLESS" STATES

Benjamin Franklin, in July 1775, proposed a confederation of "the United Colonies of North America" that would have granted to a national government the authority to resolve differences "about Limits . . . and the Planting of new Colonies." In April 1776 Samuel Chase of Maryland suggested that Congress "appropriate all the Crown Lands" to finance "our Independancy." Two months later a committee headed by John Dickinson of Pennsylvania was appointed to draft articles of confederation. Article XVIII of Dickinson's draft provided that the "United States assembled" would possess the "exclusive Right" of limiting "the Bounds of those Colonies . . . said to extend to the South Sea."[32]

Pennsylvania and Maryland, along with New Hampshire, Rhode Island, New Jersey, and Delaware, were the so-called "landless" states with defined boundaries. In contrast, the seven "landed" states asserted expansive (and conflicting) claims to the west, based on their "sea-to-sea" charters or, in the case of New York, supposed jurisdiction over Iroquois. The most aggressive state, Virginia, not only opposed Great Britain during the American Revolution but also opposed the efforts of speculators, sister states, and Congress either to own or to control the western lands. Timothy Pickering of Massachusetts complained in 1780 that Virginia's conduct was "almost the sole bar to the completion of the Confederation." Thomas Jefferson, James Madison, and George Mason disagreed, blaming Maryland and private purchasers of Indian lands for delaying the formation of a national government. Without question, control of the west "was the issue around which revolved the most bitter controversy during the writing and ratification of the Articles of Confederation."[33]

The movement to curtail the western claims of the "landed" states began in earnest on July 25, 1776, during the debate on Dickinson's proposed Articles. In response to Jefferson's declaration that "the limits of the Southern Colonies are fixed," Samuel Chase retorted that "No Colony has a right to go to the South Sea; they never had; they can't have." In support of this view the combative Chase—who had acquired a share in the Illinois purchase in 1774—argued that upholding Virginia's charter boundaries "would be destructive to her sisters and to herself." James Wilson, the future president of the Illinois and Wabash Land Company, agreed, warning that Pennsylvania "will not confederate unless those claims are cut off." The "knotty problem," as John Adams described it, resurfaced on the second of August, the day set aside for the signing of the Declaration of Independence. When Chase again denounced the idea of a "South Sea" boundary, Benjamin Harrison asked, "How came Maryland by its land, but by its charter?" Samuel Huntington of Connecticut observed that a right "does not cease to be a right because it is large," but Maryland's Thomas Stone countered by arguing that the smaller colonies "would have no safety if the great Colonies were not limited." Jefferson ended the debate by protesting "against the right of Congress to decide upon the right of Virginia."[34]

Maryland refused to drop the issue, and on October 30, 1776, delegates to its state constitutional convention resolved that if dominion over the western lands "should be established by the blood and treasure of the *United States*, such lands ought to be considered as a common stock, to be parcelled out at proper times into convenient, free and independent Governments."[35] Maryland thus staked out its position as early as the fall of 1776, in the midst of setbacks that prompted Thomas Paine to exclaim that "these are the times that try men's souls." The British occupied New York City, Washington's army was in retreat, and Congress fled Philadelphia, not to return until March 1777. A revival of spirits, however, began on Christmas night when Washington and his troops crossed the Delaware River and surprised the Hessians at Trenton. On the third day of the new year the Continental Army prevailed again at Princeton, prompting Congress to order the first printing of the Declaration of Independence that included the affixed signatures.[36]

The fortunes of war in 1777 affected the ratification debate. During the last week of June, as General John Burgoyne prepared to retake Fort Ticonderoga, Charles Carroll of Carrollton complained to his father that Virginia's "absurd claim to the back lands will not be given up."[37] In September, after Washington failed at Brandywine to stop the British advance, Congress fled Philadelphia, moving first to Lancaster and then across the Susquehanna River. Now faced with British occupation of both

New York and Philadelphia, the delegates resumed the confederation debate in York, a town of seventeen hundred.

Edmund Burnett notes that "if the urge to confederate had been strong before the dispersion, it was stronger still amongst the diminished group now huddled at York." On October 15, 1777, only Maryland voted in favor of its motion granting Congress the right "to ascertain and fix the western boundary of such States as claim to the Mississippi or South Sea."[38] Two days later Burgoyne surrendered at Saratoga, and news of the stunning victory soon reached Congress. The delegates amended the Articles to provide "that no State shall be deprived of territory for the benefit of the United States."[39] On November 15, 1777, the Articles of Confederation were adopted without the objectionable provisions granting Congress control over the western lands. Virginia had successfully opposed Maryland's efforts to deny her territorial claims.

Or so it appeared. Congress provided that the Articles would take effect when approved by all states. Samuel Adams predicted that the Articles would be promptly ratified, because confederation "is so necessary for the Support of the great Cause." By August 1778 all but three states had assented. New Jersey voted to ratify in November, and Delaware followed in February 1779. Maryland, however, held out *for two more years.* This renegade stance has been both praised and disparaged: Herbert Adams argues that Maryland prevented the creation of an unbalanced union by opposing "the grasping land claims of Virginia," whereas Merrill Jensen contends that Maryland's actions were dictated "by jealousy and by prominent land speculators."[40]

On December 22, 1777, as the army settled into winter quarters at Valley Forge, the Maryland legislature resolved that the state was entitled—in common with the other states—to the western territory, except for land that was *"vested in, or granted to individuals at the commencement of the present war."* The legislators instructed that private purchases of Indian lands should be upheld, and the remaining lands should constitute "a common estate to be granted out on terms beneficial to all the United States." Pursuant to these instructions, Maryland sought to amend the Articles to empower Congress to ascertain the boundaries of the landed states. The motion failed on June 23, 1778, but four states (Rhode Island, New Jersey, Delaware, and Pennsylvania) voted with Maryland, and the New York delegates were divided.[41] Two days later New Jersey argued that the guarantee in the ninth article—"that no State shall be deprived of territory for the benefit of the United States"—did not encompass "the vacant and unpatented lands, commonly called the crown lands." The French minister, Conrad-Alexandre Gérard, reported that the issue had bred germs of division ("germes de division") between the states and was complicated by the enormous pretensions ("prétentions énormes") of private individuals.[42]

Clark's occupation of the Illinois country enabled Virginia to argue that the western lands were not gained "by the blood and treasure of all" but rather by Virginia alone. Nevertheless, a congressional committee in September 1778 recommended that the landed states cede the western lands to the United States.[43] By this time Virginia was willing to relinquish a portion of its territorial claims, but it remained adamantly opposed to the recognition of prior private purchases of Indian lands. Consequently the stalemate continued into 1779, when on January 9 the delegates for Maryland presented a "Declaration" approved by its legislature the previous December.

The Maryland Declaration argued that the claims of the landed states would "prove ruinous" to the Union and stated that Maryland would join the confederation only if each state was given a right in common "to all the Lands lying to the Westward of the Frontiers aforesaid, *not granted to, surveyed for or purchased by Individuals at the Commencement of the present War.*" No action was taken in Congress with respect to the Declaration, and by the end of February both New Jersey and Delaware had ratified the Articles. "There now only remains Maryland," wrote a New Hampshire delegate, "who you know has seldom done anything with a good Grace. She has always been a froward hussey."[44]

George Mason charged in a letter to Richard Henry Lee that "the secret and true cause of the great opposition" was the Illinois and Wabash purchases, "in which Governor Johnston [*sic*] and several of the leading men in Maryland are concerned." Providing his own underlined emphasis to the Declaration's reference to lands "not granted to, surveyed for, *or purchased by* individuals at the commencement of the present war," Mason directed Lee to "observe the care Governor Johnston . . . has taken to save this Indian Purchase." Mason's allegations were not baseless: the Illinois and Wabash grantees, as discussed in the next chapter, were active in late 1778 and early 1779, planning for settlement and presenting a memorial to Governor Henry and the Virginia legislature. During this time a Maryland delegate reported to Johnson that "these purchases will become objects of great Moment to the parties concerned."[45]

Virginia responded to Maryland's Declaration with a carrot and a stick; first by offering to provide bounty lands for Continental soldiers free of cost out of *its* western territory, and then by proposing that the states confederate *without* Maryland. The Maryland delegates, in turn, warned that Virginia would sell her western lands "on the most moderate terms," enabling her to "lessen her taxes" and depopulate her "less powerful neighbours." In June 1779 Virginia gave credence to such concerns by establishing a land office to sell the "waste and unappropriated lands" in its western territory. Memorials on behalf of the Indiana and Vandalia proprietors were filed in September in protest of Virginia's actions, and on October 30, 1779, Congress "earnestly recommended" that Virginia "forbear settling or issuing warrants for unappropriated lands, or granting the same during the continuance of the present war."[46] Virginia, however, continued to sell western lands.

The submission of memorials to Congress by the Indiana Company and the Vandalia proprietors was troublesome for Virginia. Thomas Jefferson had argued as far back as 1776 that Congress lacked authority to determine the rights of the landed states. The memorialists, however, contended that the western lands were subject to the jurisdiction "of the whole United States in Congress assembled." This "devolution of sovereignty" theory—that the rights and obligations of the Crown passed to the "United States"—would enable speculators to establish, by means of congressional sanction, a legal and marketable title to property acquired from Indians.[47] Virginia's constitution, statutory enactments, and resolutions would no longer control the lands, and the private purchasers, including the Illinois and Wabash grantees, would be free to settle and sell their land.

Consequently, when the Virginia General Assembly learned that Congress had asserted jurisdiction over the memorials of the land companies, it called for the preparation of a remonstrance "firmly asserting the rights of this Commonwealth." The Remonstrance of Virginia was written by George Mason and laid before Congress on April 28, 1780.[48] The document rejects the "devolution of sovereignty" theory and asserts that the United States "hold no territory." If Congress were to "arrogate to themselves a right of adjudication," it would introduce "a most dangerous precedent" and establish a power that in time would "degenerate into an intolerable despotism." To underscore the point, the Remonstrance refers to the Illinois and Wabash purchases and invokes the memory of the "Devil Dunmore": "It is notorious that . . . Men of great influence in some of the neighbouring States, are concerned in partnerships with the Earl of Dunmore, and other Subjects of the British Kind, who under purchases from the Indians, claim extensive tracts of Country between the Ohio and Mississippi Rivers; and that propositions have been made to Congress evidently calculated to secure and guarranty [sic] such purchases."[49]

The Remonstrance of Virginia set forth compelling arguments, but the delegates were influenced by other considerations. The Mohawk leader Joseph Brant was attacking settlements with impunity in upstate New York and western Pennsylvania, and British forces had invaded the southern states. On December 26, 1779, George Washington warned that "there is every appearance that the army will infallibly disband in a fortnight." Members of Congress complained that Virginia was more interested in profiting from the sale of her western lands than in defeating the British. Ezekiel Cornell of Rhode Island reported that "the once patriotic state of Virginia weighs but little at present, in the scale of defence or the furnishing of men or supplies. Her whole attention is engrossed in making sale of her out lands." Even one of her own citizens, Dr. Robert Honeyman of Hanover County, Virginia, complained in 1780 that "the attention of the people of this state is very little taken up with the war at this time, or indeed for a year or two past. . . . The greatest part of the people are entirely taken up in schemes of several kinds. Immense fortunes have been made by trade, or speculation."[50]

Matters became further complicated in March 1780 when New York offered to "restrict the boundaries of this State, in the western parts thereof." Based on its pretended "suzerainty" over the Six Nations, New York maintained a nebulous claim to the lands occupied by the supposed tributaries of the Iroquois. If Congress accepted the proposed cession, the national government could assert ownership to much of the territory claimed by Virginia. The Virginia delegates responded by presenting Mason's Remonstrance, which condemned efforts by Congress to "arrogate to themselves a right of adjudication" over western lands. Congress twice referred the Remonstrance to committees, along with New York's cession offer and Maryland's Declaration. The second committee, appointed on June 26, 1780, produced a report four days later, which was not considered by Congress until September.[51]

The report astutely avoided the merits of the various arguments regarding the western lands, emphasizing instead that a "federal union on a fixed and permanent basis" was necessary to "our very existence as a free, sovereign and independent people." The landed states were requested to cede their western claims and thereby "remove the only obstacle to a final ratification of the articles." For most states the issue was now about survival, and Virginia and the other landed states were asked to surrender their claims, no matter how justified, "for the sake of the common cause." Joseph Jones, one of Virginia's delegates to Congress, agreed that the western lands must be given up, noting in a letter to Governor Thomas Jefferson that "the example of New York is worthy of imitation."[52]

Agreeing to reduce her charter claims, however, did not mean that Virginia would likewise sanction the private purchases of Indian lands. George Mason proposed attaching several conditions to a cession by Virginia, including the "*sine qua non*" requirement that private transactions with Indians for lands within the ceded territory "be deemed and declared absolutely void."[53] Virginia moved that the ceded territory "be laid out in separate and distinct States," and that lands not needed for military bounties "be considered as a common fund." To the consternation of the Illinois and Wabash Land Company, the motion also incorporated Mason's condition that Congress declare as void all private purchases of Indian lands "within any part of such ceded Territory." On September 18, consideration of the controversial provision relating to Indian land purchases was postponed, "with an intention," Madison complained, "of not resuming it."[54]

Edmund Pendleton informed Madison, on September 27, 1780, that Maryland's opposition "proceeds from 5 or 6 Gentlemen there being concerned in an Indian Grant . . . which they hope to preserve." As if to prove his point, on the following day a memorial of the Illinois and Wabash Land Company was read in Congress. Although no action was taken with respect to the memorial, the land companies had considerable support in Congress. On October 10, 1780, Congress agreed with Virginia that ceded lands should be disposed of "for the common benefit of all the United States," but it did *not* approve the provision calling for the annulment of private purchases from Indians.[55] Three years had come and gone since Congress had agreed to the Articles, and delegate Theodorick Bland glumly informed Thomas Jefferson that the Indiana, Vandalia, and Illinois companies had "too great an influence in procrastinating that desireable and necessary event of compleating the Confederation." Nevertheless, on January 2, 1781, the Virginia General Assembly attached several conditions to its proposed cession of territory north and west of the Ohio, including the annulment of private purchases of Indian land within the ceded territory.[56] Virginia's conditional offer of cession was at odds with Maryland's Declaration, and Bland's pessimism regarding the ratification of the Articles appeared well founded.

However, for several reasons, Maryland reversed its position during January 1781 and authorized its delegates to complete the confederation. Once again the fortunes of war influenced the ratification debate. The "turncoat" Benedict Arnold had commenced his invasion of Virginia when the General Assembly passed its act of cession, and three days later British forces set fire to Richmond as Governor Jefferson fled across the James River. Maryland was endangered by the presence of British naval forces in the Chesapeake Bay and appealed to the new French minister, the Chevalier de la Luzerne, to provide military aid. In reply Luzerne coupled his ambivalent assurances of support with a pointed request "that the winter will not come to an end without the accession of your state to the confederation."[57]

Even prior to these events, the Maryland legislature had appointed a joint committee of the two houses to draft new instructions to the delegates in Congress. Thomas Johnson was appointed to the committee, and on January 20, 1781, the House passed a ratification bill that included reservations regarding ownership by the landed states of the western lands. When the Maryland Senate voted against the bill, Johnson was given the task of persuading the senators to reconsider. Edward Delaplaine states that the former governor "emphasized the psychological effect of a favorable action in securing the peace and independence of America." As Merrill Jensen notes, Johnson argued that "Maryland's refusal to confederate would no longer be of service in the Western land question, and she might secure greater justice at the hands of the confederated states than otherwise." Swayed by Johnson's exhortations, the state senate agreed to support ratification, and the bill became law on February 2, 1781. The state of Maryland, Johnson wrote, "sacrificed much . . . to comply with the Desires of the other States."[58]

On March 1, 1781, Congress announced to the public "the final ratification of the Confederation of the United States of America." Cannons were fired on land and from John Paul Jones's frigate on the Delaware River. City bells rang, banquets were held, and the evening "was closed by an elegant exhibition of fireworks." Virginia had successfully opposed Maryland's efforts to limit the landed states' western boundaries and to uphold the private purchases of Indian lands. Theodorick Bland's pessimistic outlook was transformed: on the fifth of March, in a letter regarding Virginia's conditional offer of cession, he expressed "little doubt of the Grants being accepted by Congress," confidently predicting that "the Covert manoeuvres of the land Jobbing Companies are so well known, and so fully discoverd, that few of their abettors will be hardly enough to oppose it in its fullest latitude."[59] The recipient of Bland's letter, Richard Henry Lee, was not as sanguine. A month earlier, he had expressed his doubts to Samuel Adams regarding the acceptance of Virginia's cession offer: "It will bar the hopes, of some powerful confederated Land jobbers, who have long had in contemplation immense possessions in this ceded country, under pretence of Indian purchases, and other plausible, but not solid titles. It is plain therefore, that personal interest, and political views . . . combine members without and within doors, to reject this proffered cession."[60]

With respect to this issue, Lee proved more prescient than Bland. Although ratification was now complete, the issue of ownership of the western territory remained. The instructions that empowered Maryland to ratify the Articles of Confederation expressly declared that *"this State does not relinquish, or intend to relinquish, any right or interest she hath, with the other united or confederated states, to the back country."*[61] By casting votes in favor of ratification, Thomas Johnson, Charles Carroll, and Samuel Chase did not acquiesce to Virginia's demand that the Illinois and Wabash purchases be declared void. Ownership of the west remained unsettled, and the legality of private purchases of Indian lands continued to be a divisive topic of national debate.[62]

8

THE ILLINOIS AND WABASH
PROPRIETORS UNITE

The adoption of the Articles of Confederation on March 1, 1781, did not resolve the territorial claims of the landed states. On the same day that the Articles were ratified, New York presented a cession offer that was *not* conditioned on the annulment of private purchases of Indian land.[1] The New York cession was thus acceptable to the Illinois and Wabash proprietors, since it did not foreclose the possibility that Congress might confirm their 1773 and 1775 acquisitions.

During the next three years Congress considered cession offers from Virginia, New York, and Connecticut, as well as memorials presented on behalf of George Croghan, the Indiana Company, the Vandalia proprietors, and the Illinois and Wabash Land Company. The last-named group was now a mixture of the original grantees and new members, who either purchased or were given shares. Several charter subscribers did not support the American cause, and a few of the new members proved to be controversial figures. On the other hand, the addition of such influential politicians as Robert Morris and James Wilson of Pennsylvania increased the likelihood of favorable treatment. Following the momentous victory at Yorktown in October 1781, Congress devoted much of its time to two issues of critical importance to the Illinois and Wabash Land Company: ownership of the West and the property rights of the Indian inhabitants.

UNION, ORGANIZATION, AND ADVOCACY

The first meeting recorded in the Illinois and Wabash Land Company minutes took place on November 3, 1778, in Philadelphia. Eleven of the original twenty-two Illinois grantees were represented, as well as the interests of five others who purchased shares in the venture.[2] George Ross of Pennsylvania, who signed the Declaration of Independence, was named chairman, and Barnard Gratz was chosen as secretary. Shortly after George Rogers Clark occupied Kaskaskia, a committee made up of Ross, William Murray, and James Hindman drafted a memorial to Virginia. As it turned out, this memorial, which requested recognition of the Illinois purchase, was never submitted. Instead, on December 26, 1778, William Murray presented a memorial regarding the *Wabash* purchase, not requesting confirmation of title, but rather serving to notify Virginia of the grantees' intent to settle "the said Lands."[3]

On the seventh of November the Illinois proprietors agreed to incorporate "for their mutual interest." Ownership was divided into forty shares, enabling current members to admit "persons of influence" into the company. In order to gain favor with Congress it was recommended that the United States be given land sufficient to provide the bounties held by Continental officers and soldiers.[4] With so much at stake, such generosity entailed little sacrifice and could lead to immense profit.

The union of the Illinois and Wabash concerns was discussed at meetings held in January and March 1779. The Virginia General Assembly had raised expectations by inviting purchasers of Indian land to appear at its May session. On March 13 William Murray and James Wilson were requested to draw up articles of incorporation, and two weeks later George Ross sent John Campbell the proposed terms for settlement. Campbell was authorized to offer financial incentives to the first five hundred settlers and was provided detailed instructions for the laying out of towns.[5]

As previously noted, the hope that Virginia would reconsider its prior stance regarding the legality of private purchases of Indian lands was dashed in June 1779, when the General Assembly declared that "no person or persons whatsoever have, or ever had, a right to purchase any lands . . . from any Indian Nation, except only persons duly authorized to make such purchases."[6] Virginia's legislative pronouncement was followed in short order by two additional setbacks. George Ross died unexpectedly, and John Campbell was captured and taken to Detroit, where he was held prisoner until the close of the war. Consequently, the Illinois and Wabash investors were compelled to replace their leader and land agent. On August 20, 1779, James Wilson was elected chair, and William Murray was subsequently named the new agent in the company's revised plan of settlement. Under Wilson's guiding hand the proprietors met more frequently, usually at Philadelphia's City Tavern. Significant progress was made in the fall of 1779 in organizing the company. Ownership of the combined purchases was divided into eighty-four shares: one share each for the original forty-two subscribers, two additional shares to the Wabash proprietors, thirty shares to be sold for the benefit of the existing shareholders, and the remaining ten shares "to be disposed of, as the Companies or a Committee to be appointed for that purpose shall judge most conducive to their general interest."[7]

Murray and two new shareholders—Silas Deane of Connecticut and William Smith of Pennsylvania—outlined the revised settlement plan for the purchased lands. In order to assure the safety of the settlers the proposal called for the temporary presence of army officers and soldiers. This arrangement would end when a government was established "consistent with *the superintending jurisdiction of the United States in Congress assembled.*" In view of developments in Williamsburg, the company intended to renege on the promise set forth in the memorial presented on December 26, 1778, "not to dispute the Jurisdiction of the State of Virginia."[8]

The Illinois and Wabash proprietors voted to incorporate on April 29, 1780, the day after Virginia claimed that Congress lacked "the right of adjudication" over the western lands. William Murray was dispatched to obtain the approval of the Maryland investors, and upon his return the shareholders elected James Wilson as company president. Murray proposed to recruit settlers and then "proceed from Fort Pitt next Spring down the Ohio."[9] Given the fact that Virginia had established a land office and was selling tracts as far west as Kentucky, the shareholders agreed that responsive action was in order.

As it turned out, Murray did not carry out the proposed settlement of the Illinois country in the spring of 1781. During the remaining months of 1780 Congress struggled with the issues of cession and ratification. When Congress debated Virginia's suggestion to vacate all titles held by private purchasers to western Indian lands, the United Illinois and Wabash Companies prepared a memorial in protest, which was presented on September 26, 1780. The Virginia General Assembly continued to press the point, and on January 2, 1781, conditioned its offer to surrender land north of the Ohio River on the annulment of private purchases within the ceded territory. Three days after Maryland authorized its delegates to ratify the Articles of Confederation, the Illinois and Wabash shareholders met at the City Tavern and agreed that James Wilson, Robert Morris, and Colonel John Shee should present a new memorial to Congress. This memorial, set forth in the company minutes for February 5, 1781, asserted that the company's lands were not within the jurisdiction of any state but rather "under the Sovereignty and Jurisdiction of the United States." The memorialists offered to cede a "very considerable proportion of the said Territory" to the United States.[10]

The memorial was referred to the same committee that was considering the offers of cession by New York and Virginia. As described in greater detail in the next chapter, this committee would recommend in June 1781 against accepting any cessions, opining that the western lands already belonged to the United States. Yet another committee of Congress would report the following November on the validity of the acquisitions by George Croghan, the Indiana Company, the Vandalia proprietors, and the Illinois and Wabash grantees. In addition, this five-person committee would report on the cession offers of New York and Virginia, and propose that the national government adopt its own policy regarding the validity of private purchases of Indian lands. Thus, despite the objections of Virginia, the locus of decisional authority regarding ownership of the west was shifting from Williamsburg to Philadelphia. The Illinois and Wabash Land Company was pleased with this result and hoped to persuade Congress—by written word and through the influence of its members—to confirm its title.[11]

LOYALISTS AND EMBARRASSMENTS

Of the forty-six shareholders listed in the Illinois and Wabash Land Company minutes for March 26, 1781, three individuals—Louis Viviat, James Rumsey, and George Ross—were deceased. Many of the remaining investors were merchants who had little or no political influence. But other members served in Congress or were considered to be men of prominence. The united companies had determined in November 1779 to set aside shares in order to "admit a number of persons of influence" and would rely on its new members to help persuade Congress to reject Virginia's demand to annul purchases of Indian lands within its ceded territory.

Unfortunately for the united companies, several of the charter subscribers—and even a few of the new shareholders—were either antagonistic to the American cause or were perceived as controversial figures. Perched at the top of this list was John Murray, the earl of Dunmore, who was despised by patriots and characterized as "a very bad man" by his fellow investor Thomas Johnson. In order to discredit the Illinois and Wabash Land Company, George Mason took care to emphasize that the proprietors were "concerned in partnerships with the Earl of Dunmore, and other Subjects of the British Kind."[12] Dunmore was never involved in the affairs of the united companies, but the fact that he and his son held shares proved to be an embarrassment.

The Illinois and Wabash proprietors selected John Campbell as their land agent, despite the fact that he had been accused of being a Tory. Campbell cleared himself of the charge and appeared to be a loyal American when he was captured by the British. However, Dunmore included Campbell on a list of faithful supporters, and historian Thomas Abernethy asserts that the trader and speculator became a "secret agent of the British authorities in Canada." An inventory of Campbell's papers—when he was taken prisoner in 1779—included a land warrant from Dunmore for two thousand acres.[13]

Other Illinois and Wabash grantees were openly loyal to the Crown. Robert Christie, Jr., left Maryland and relocated in British-occupied New York. Alexander Ross, who had become acquainted with Dunmore during the latter's trip to Pittsburgh in 1774, was arrested by Maryland officials and turned over to Congress. Ross was permitted to leave America for England, but Pennsylvania authorities later confiscated his properties, including land that was once part of George Croghan's 1749 purchase from the Six Nations. Another Scottish loyalist, David Sproat, was "'hiss'd' for his trouble" when he spoke against independence in Philadelphia in 1776. Sproat fled to New York City, where he became the commissary of naval prisoners. Sproat also lost his estate in Pennsylvania when he was proclaimed a traitor by the Provincial Council.[14]

There was never any question that Moses Franks, Jacob Franks, and Moses Franks, Jr., would steadfastly support British efforts to end the rebellion. David Franks was in a more precarious situation. A leading citizen of Philadelphia for over thirty years, Franks was most likely the leading force behind the Illinois and Wabash purchases and was connected—by his daughter's marriage—to the wealthy Hamilton family. Andrew and William Hamilton were also Illinois grantees, but both had sold their shares. Tory by nature, the Hamiltons were no doubt pleased when the British forces occupied Philadelphia in the fall of 1777. David Franks's nineteen-year-old daughter Rebecca was equally delighted. "You can have no idea," she wrote to a friend in Baltimore, "of the life of continued amusement I live in."[15] The patriots remaining in Philadelphia, however, were not amused by the social activities of British sympathizers, particularly when the merriment was contrasted with the grievous conditions at nearby Valley Forge, where the Continental Army endured the rainy winter with insufficient food and shelter.

Resentment of the British occupation was exacerbated when, on May 18, 1778, Major John André staged a twelve-hour farewell extravaganza, called the *Meschianza* or *Mischianza,* for General William Howe, including a tournament of knights in honor of Rebecca Franks and other women chosen for their "youth, beauty and fashion." Elizabeth Drinker, a Philadelphia Quaker who kept a diary throughout the war, criticized the event for its "Scenes of Folly and Vanity."[16] Six weeks later Drinker celebrated the return of Congress from York, noting the "fireing of Cannon on the Occasion." As a result of France's intervention in the war, the British had opted to concentrate their forces in New York. Rebecca Franks remained in Philadelphia with her father, who was arrested in October after letters to family members in London were intercepted. Franks had made disparaging remarks regarding the treatment of William Hamilton, who had been tried for treason but acquitted. Charging that the letters displayed "intentions inimical to the safeties and liberties of the United States," Congress removed Franks from his position as commissary to the British prisoners. Ironically, it was Benedict Arnold who was directed to arrest Franks for his allegedly treasonous behavior.[17]

The jury refused to return an indictment, but several months later Franks was charged with a common law misdemeanor for traitorous correspondence. Franks was likely defended by his friend James Wilson, who had successfully defended William Hamilton. The jury deliberated all night before returning a verdict of acquittal. The outcome prompted an infuriated patriot to publish the letters, with commentary, in a local newspaper. As a consequence, significant portions of Philadelphia were negatively disposed toward the formerly reputable merchant. Nevertheless, during this period of increasing hostility, David Franks regularly attended meetings of the Illinois and Wabash Land Company and was elected, on July 25, 1780, as one of four shareholders to serve on the executive council.[18]

Benedict Arnold's defection in September 1780 gave cause for many patriots to distrust the Franks family further. Major John André, who was hanged as a British spy, had once painted a miniature of Rebecca Franks. Shortly after Arnold's treason both David Franks and William Hamilton were ordered to leave Pennsylvania. Rebecca accompanied her father to New York, where she married Colonel Henry Johnson. David Franks stayed in New York until 1782, when he embarked for England, arriving with no more than £40 or £50 in his pocket. During his absence from Philadelphia he was represented at meetings of the Illinois and Wabash Land Company by either Tench Coxe or Andrew Hamilton.[19]

Three other shareholders were controversial figures who may inadvertently have detracted from the efforts of the Illinois and Wabash Land Company to win congressional favor. Reverend William Smith was the provost of the College of Philadelphia (later to become the University of Pennsylvania) and was considered "a major figure in Philadelphia intellectual circles." He enjoyed a brief friendship with Benjamin Franklin after emigrating from Scotland but soon antagonized the famed inventor. Smith was, paradoxically, "one of the most loathsome and most respected men in eighteenth-century America." Benjamin Rush acknowledged that Smith possessed "genius, taste, and learning" but noted that the minister was "extremely avaricious," someone "who seldom paid a debt without being sued or without a quarrel." When Smith was given the honor of eulogizing General Richard Montgomery, John Adams characterized the address as "an insolent Performance."[20]

When British occupation of Philadelphia ended, Reverend Smith was arrested but paroled. On November 5, 1779, "for 8000 pounds lawful money of Pennsylvania," Smith purchased a share in the Illinois and Wabash venture from William Murray and subsequently became quite active in the affairs of the company. His personality, however, undercut efforts to influence Congress. Pennsylvania Senator William Maclay, in his diary entry for the first of March, 1791, described Smith as "a vile Character," and when Smith died in 1803, Benjamin Rush noted that he "descended to his grave . . . without being lamented by a human creature."[21]

Another controversial figure in the spring of 1781—as well as later in his life—was Samuel Chase of Maryland. Detractors nicknamed the beefy, red-faced man "Bacon Face." He was known for his temper and rough manner; the mayor of Annapolis once described him as "a ring-leader of mobs, a foul-mouthed and inflaming son of discord." Chase emerged as a political leader during the resistance to the Stamp Act and served in the Maryland General Assembly for twenty years until 1784. He also became a prominent lawyer and jurist, eventually serving on the United States Supreme Court. Lacking wealth in land, he was by nature a "plunger" whose failed schemes caused him at one point to declare bankruptcy.[22]

On May 31, 1774, William Murray sold Samuel Chase a share in the Illinois purchase. The Maryland agitator served in the Continental Congress from 1774 to 1778 and traveled to Canada in 1776 with Benjamin Franklin, John Carroll, and Charles Carroll. Described by one historian as "the most uncompromising revolutionary after Sam Adams himself," Chase returned to Philadelphia in time to cast his vote in favor of rebellion.[23] On August 2, 1776, Samuel Chase affixed his signature to the Declaration of Independence. Four other shareholders in the United Illinois and Wabash Land Companies—Charles Carroll, George Ross, Robert Morris, and James Wilson—also signed the historic document.

In two years' time, however, Chase was suspected of disclosing confidential information to his business partners in order to profit from the sale of flour to the Continental Army. He was condemned as "one of the lowest of sharpers in the Revolution's catalog of profiteers." On October 16, 1778, in a letter signed "Publius" in the *New York Journal,* Alexander Hamilton damned Chase "as a traitor of the worst and most dangerous kind."[24] Shortly thereafter Chase lost his seat in Congress. Although he reentered politics at the state level in 1779, he was not able to put the flour scandal behind him. In 1780 Charles Carroll described his former friend as "the most prostituted scoundrel who ever existed." Chase fervently denied that he divulged confidential information, and on January 16, 1782, the Maryland House of Delegates, by a vote of thirty-six to two, declared that Chase was not guilty of "a breach of his duty." However, as biographer Jane Elsmere noted, Chase's political opponents "resurrected the flour scandal whenever they wished to embarrass him and blacken his name."[25]

Perhaps the most controversial member of the Illinois and Wabash Land Company was Silas Deane. The "bizarre turnings" of Deane's career have prompted comparisons with Benedict Arnold and Aaron Burr. Deane represented Connecticut in the Continental Congress; procured supplies essential to the victories at Ticonderoga and Saratoga; commissioned Marquis de Lafayette, Baron de Kalb, and Baron von Steuben; and helped negotiate the treaties of alliance and commerce with France. But Silas Deane also served himself, entering into private schemes with both French and American speculators. By the end of 1781 he was a fallen patriot and a liability to the Illinois and Wabash Company.

The son of a blacksmith, Deane graduated from Yale College, gained property through marriage, and became a merchant. As a member of the Continental Congress, Deane met with James Hogg of the Transylvania Company and offered his favorable assessment of the validity of the Cherokee purchase. John Adams described the incipient speculator in 1775 as "a very ingenious Man and an able Politician." The Connecticut legislature proved to be a better judge of character when it deemed Deane "unteachable and incorrigible" and declined to nominate him for a third term.[26]

When Deane served in the Continental Congress, he associated with men who combined political and commercial interests, such as Robert Morris of Philadelphia. On March 2, 1776, Morris, Thomas Johnson, and the other members of the Committee of Secret Correspondence appointed Deane as a secret envoy to France. "It seems to me," Morris observed in letter to Deane, "the present opportunity of improving our fortunes ought not to be lost, especially as the very means of doing it will contribute to the service of our country." Deane agreed and arranged for French goods to be sent to Philadelphia for resale by the firm of Willing, Morris, and Company.[27]

The high point in Deane's career came in September 1776, when he was appointed as one of three American ambassadors to France. Benjamin Franklin and Arthur Lee of Virginia would soon arrive in Paris and join Deane in carrying out secret negotiations with the French. As a participant in one of the pivotal events in the American Revolution, Silas Deane affixed his signature in February 1778 to two treaties with the French government, one for commerce and the other establishing a military alliance. However, unbeknownst to Deane, Congress had voted the previous November to replace him with John Adams. Richard Henry Lee of Virginia was the leading proponent of the recall. His younger brother, Arthur, disliked his fellow diplomat intensely and accused Deane of profiteering. To defend his honor Deane returned to Philadelphia in July 1779, but he was forced to wait several months for a congressional audience. During this period Deane became a shareholder and an active participant in the Illinois and Wabash Land Company.[28]

The ensuing debate over Deane's conduct sparked a rancorous political struggle. The "commercial interests"—championed by Franklin, Morris, and the French diplomat Conrad-Alexandre Gérard—were opposed by the "old radicals" and "strict republicans" in New England and the South, who believed that Deane and his allies were seeking to establish a mercantile society that would favor private interests. Without voting for either censure or exoneration, Congress granted Deane permission to return to Europe. The Connecticut merchant, however, chose to remain in Philadelphia and promote his land speculations. "I mean to engage in Lands on a large Scale somewhere," he confided in a letter. [29]

As it turned out Silas Deane did return to France in 1780, empowered by the Illinois and Wabash proprietors to bestow up to three shares upon persons "willing to promote the settlement and the interest of the said united companies." His arrival came during a low point in the conflict: the British had taken Charleston and would soon prevail at Camden and advance into Virginia. Prospects for financial gain were meager, and Deane lamented to James Wilson on May 11, 1781, that nothing could be effected "with regard to the Ilinois, or any other lands in America." The despondent Deane began to question the patriot cause and advised friends to reconcile with England. His letters were published in New York— shortly after the victory at Yorktown—and declared to be treasonous. James Madison observed to Edmund Pendleton that the letters "clearly denounce" Deane as "an apostate," and "consign his character to the same infamy with that of his friend Arnold." George Washington expressed his desire "never to hear or see any thing more of so infamous a character."[30]

Deane was now reviled in America, perhaps to a greater extent than his fellow shareholder, the Earl of Dunmore. The American frigate called the *Deane* was rechristened. In April 1783 Deane penned a pathetic letter to James Wilson, confessing "total ignorance" of the affairs of the Illinois and Wabash Company but offering to "dispose of the grants and procure settlers."[31] Six years later Deane unexpectedly died at the outset of a voyage to America to resurrect his reputation. His death, at age fifty-two, may have been due to poisoning by Dr. Edward Bancroft, an acquaintance of Deane who had spied for both sides during the Revolution. Coincidentally, the duplicitous Bancroft was interested in Indian lands, and had once declared to Benjamin Franklin that "Congress should publickly assert & maintain the full and Absolute Right of the Natives to Sell and Convey their Lands."[32]

PATRIOTS AND MEN OF INFLUENCE

Not all of the shareholders proved to be liabilities in the campaign to persuade Congress to affirm the title to the lands purchased from the Illinois and Piankeshaws. The company presumably benefited from the presence of two reputable military officers, John Shee and Daniel Hiester, as well as two prominent French officials, John Holker and Conrad-Alexandre Gérard. John Shee of Pennsylvania fought at Bunker Hill and eventually attained the rank of brigadier general. He was one of four men selected in 1780 to serve on the Illinois and Wabash executive council and was active in the company's affairs as late as 1805. Daniel Hiester became a brigadier general of the Pennsylvania militia and subsequently served in Congress, from 1789 to 1796 and again (as a representative from Maryland) from 1801 until his death on March 7, 1804.[33] John Holker, the consul-general and agent for the French Navy in America, was closely connected to Robert Morris, as was Conrad-Alexandre Gérard, the first French minister to America. Gérard reported to the foreign minister, Comte de Vergennes, that he had been offered a share in the Illinois and Wabash Land Company. In reply, Vergennes informed Gérard that "His Majesty gladly permits you to accept the gift."[34]

The membership of the Illinois and Wabash Land Company in March 1781 also included prominent men of commerce. In contrast to their friend David Franks, the Gratz brothers and William Murray did not equivocate in their support of the American cause. Whereas Franks and his daughter Rebecca were dismayed by the British evacuation of Philadelphia, Michael Gratz celebrated "the good news of our old city being again in our possession." Daniel Murray provided the Clark expedition with food and shelter, and Barnard and Michael Gratz also aided the war effort, supplying blankets and rifles and extending a ten-thousand-dollar line of credit to the financially strapped Virginia delegation. The Maryland merchant Matthew Ridley was another charter subscriber who supported the Revolution. Described by historian Thomas Scharf as one of the "patriotic gentlemen of Baltimore," the English-born Ridley had business dealings during the war with numerous individuals connected with the Illinois and Wabash venture, including Robert Morris, John Davidson, William Russell, Mark Pringle, and Samuel Chase. In the winter of 1780–81 Ridley negotiated a loan from Holland for the benefit of Maryland. He also spent time in Paris and was present on November 30, 1782, when John Adams, John Jay, and Benjamin Franklin signed the preliminary articles of peace between the United States and Great Britain.[35]

Political influence with members of Congress, of course, was the attribute most highly prized by the Illinois and Wabash Land Company. Four

shareholders in particular combined unquestioned patriotism with prominent public service: Thomas Johnson, Charles Carroll of Carrollton, Robert Morris, and James Wilson. The multiple accomplishments of Thomas
Johnson of Maryland are outlined in chapter 6. After participating in the
First Continental Congress and the Second, Johnson was elected by the
state legislature to govern for three consecutive terms during the critical
years 1777–79. Prohibited from serving a fourth term as governor, Johnson
turned down an opportunity to return to Congress and instead retired
to Frederick, where he built "Richfield," his large colonial mansion. In
November 1780 Johnson surprised many by returning to politics and urging his fellow state legislators to ratify the Articles of Confederation. In
contrast to James Wilson, his future colleague on the Supreme Court,
Thomas Johnson did not take an active role in promoting the interests of
the Illinois and Wabash Land Company. However, the lack of controversy
in his personal affairs, his steadfast patriotism, and his enduring friendship
with George Washington made Thomas Johnson a valued shareholder.

Charles Carroll of Carrollton emulated Johnson by maintaining a low
profile in Illinois and Wabash Land Company. Nevertheless, as a signer
of the Declaration of Independence and one of the wealthiest men in
America, Carroll was favorably viewed by members of Congress. John
Adams described Carroll as "a Gentleman of independant Fortune, perhaps the largest in America," who is "a zealous Supporter of the Rights of
America." Even though he was not present in Congress on July 4, 1776,
Carroll elected a month later to sign the Declaration and supposedly added
the words "of Carrollton" to remove any ambiguity regarding his identity.
In 1780 he was again elected to Congress but declined in favor of service
in the Maryland Senate, where he remained until 1800. Carroll did serve
as a United States senator from 1789 to 1792 but resigned after Maryland
prohibited simultaneous service.[36] Carroll died at age ninety-five, outliv-
ing his son-in-law, Robert Goodloe Harper, who had been the driving
force behind *Johnson v. McIntosh*.

The two remaining shareholders—Robert Morris and James Wilson—
merit separate discussion, given their considerable contributions as members of the United Illinois and Wabash Land Companies. Morris and
Wilson both emigrated from Great Britain and settled in Philadelphia. The
two men shared the rarefied status as signatories to both the Declaration
of Independence and the United States Constitution. Robert Morris also

Charles Carroll of Carrollton. Courtesy of the Maryland Historical Society (Image ID 1846.2.1).

signed the Articles of Confederation and became a United States Senator. Equally impressive, James Wilson inspired the text of Jefferson's Declaration, exerted great influence at the Constitutional Convention, and became a justice of the United States Supreme Court. Neither Morris nor Wilson was a charter subscriber, but both were active in promoting the interests of the united companies. Both engaged in massive, unprecedented land speculation. Not coincidentally, both men suffered financial setbacks and ended their lives under tragic circumstances.

Robert Morris: "A new star in our American hemisphere"

Robert Morris, Jr., was born in 1734 in Liverpool, England. At age thirteen he arrived in Maryland, where his father had gone to earn a living by exporting tobacco. Following the death of his father in 1750, Morris became an apprentice to Charles Willing, a wealthy Philadelphia merchant. When Willing died in 1754 the apprentice became a partner with Thomas Willing, who inherited the shipping and banking business. The firm of Willing, Morris, and Company prospered, and Robert Morris became a leading figure in Philadelphia.

In 1765 Morris opposed the Stamp Act but declined to sign the nonimportation agreement in protest of the new tax. A reluctant rebel, Morris was elected in 1775 to the Continental Congress. As a member of the Committee of Secret Correspondence, he helped select Silas Deane as envoy to France. Capitalizing on Deane's presence in Europe, the two men profited from numerous ventures and earned commissions by importing French goods "suitable for the Indians." In the days leading up to the adoption of the Declaration of Independence, Morris sided with the members of the divided Pennsylvania delegation who opposed severing ties with Great Britain. However, when the issue was squarely presented on the second of July, both Morris and John Dickinson were deliberately absent, thus enabling the affirmative votes of John Morton, Benjamin Franklin, and James Wilson to prevail over the two remaining delegates. Morris also abstained two days later from casting a vote in favor of independence, but he stepped forward on August 2, 1776, to add his name to the Declaration. "I think an individual that declines the Service of his Country because its Councils are not conformable to his Ideas," Morris informed Joseph Reed, "makes a bad Subject; a good one will follow if he cannot lead."[37]

Ron Chernow describes Morris as "an impressive-looking man with a wide, fleshy face, an ample paunch, and the sharp, shrewd gaze of a self-made merchant prince." The confident Morris possessed, in the words of John Adams, "vast designs in the mercantile way." Thomas Paine and the Lee brothers of Virginia detested both Silas Deane and Morris and accused the latter of profiteering. In February 1779 a congressional

Robert Morris. National Portrait Gallery, Smithsonian Institution.

committee rejected the charge and concluded that Morris had "acted with fidelity and integrity, and an honorable zeal for the happiness of his country."[38]

On August 20, 1779, the shareholders of the united companies met at the City Tavern in Philadelphia, elected James Wilson as chair, and resolved that Wilson, Deane, and Murray dispose of two shares "in such manner as they shall judge most proper." Two weeks later the members approved an agreement to sell one share each to John Holker and Robert Morris "at the rate of eight thousand pounds currency purchase."[39] Morris quickly became an influential figure in the Illinois and Wabash Land Company. When Maryland authorized its delegates to ratify the Articles of Confederation, the shareholders directed Morris (along with Wilson and John Shee) to present a memorial to Congress offering land in exchange for confirmation of the Illinois and Wabash purchases.

At this point Morris was serving in the state legislature. In 1781 Congress resolved that there be a "Superintendent of Finance" and elected Robert Morris to the position. When he assumed office in May, the treasury was bankrupt, and paper money was nearly worthless. Virginia was now the focal point of the conflict, and Washington and the French general, Comte de Rochambeau, determined to end the war with a decisive victory. In order to underwrite the expedition, Morris embarked on several courses of action. Within days after taking office he proposed that Congress charter a national bank to establish a stable money system and bolster the credit of the United States. The Bank of North America was organized in November 1781 and commenced operations the following January. The initial deposits—primarily gold, silver, and bills of exchange obtained through loans from France and Holland—served to stabilize the paper money, thus avoiding the rapid devaluation that had previously left Congress with a currency "not worth a Continental."[40]

In the meantime, the "Financier of the Revolution" devoted himself to the task of supplying Washington's troops, who on the second of September marched through Philadelphia on their way to Virginia. Morris arranged a loan from General de Rochambeau to pay disgruntled American soldiers, and barrels of silver coins were opened to distribute one month's pay to the grateful troops. The morale of the Continental Army was lifted, and the troops marched with renewed purpose to Virginia.[41]

Even before the victory at Yorktown, Benjamin Rush declared that "Mr. Morris has become a new star in our American hemisphere." While he was serving as superintendent of finance, creditors of the United States accepted "Morris notes"—drafts drawn against the merchant that were secured by his personal credit. Although his detractors complained it was the Revolution that financed Robert Morris—rather than the reverse— the Philadelphia merchant had gained national prominence, the loyalty of George Washington, and the gratitude of most members of Congress.[42]

When Morris tendered his resignation as superintendent of finance in 1783, Congress protested and persuaded the "Great Man" to stay in office until the following year. In 1787 he would nominate General Washington to preside over the Constitutional Convention, and two years later he would decline President Washington's offer to become secretary of the treasury. Robert Morris instead would serve from 1789 to 1795 as a United States senator. As a member of Congress itself, he would be superbly positioned to promote the interests of the Illinois and Wabash Land Company.

James Wilson: Eminent Lawyer, Statesman, Scholar

The eldest son of a Presbyterian farmer, James Wilson was born in Scotland in 1742. Despite the modest wealth of his family, Wilson received an excellent primary education and secured a scholarship at age fifteen to the University of St. Andrews. After four years of undergraduate work and one year in divinity school Wilson was compelled to discontinue his education when his father died. The untimely death caused Wilson to reconsider his future: he decided against a career in the ministry and chose instead to emigrate to America. The Scotsman arrived in 1765 and made his way to Pennsylvania, where he became a Latin tutor at the College of Philadelphia. Wilson thereafter began to study law with John Dickinson and was admitted to the bar in November 1767. He opened his own practice the following year in the town of Reading, sixty miles northwest of Philadelphia.[43]

It was at this time that James Wilson examined the legal relationship between Great Britain and the colonies in a remarkable pamphlet titled *Considerations on the Nature and Extent of the Legislative Authority of British Parliament*. The impetus for the essay was the Stamp Act controversy, but Wilson withheld publication until the "intolerable acts" prompted the convening of the Continental Congress in 1774. Historian Randolph Adams contended that Wilson's pamphlet was superior to essays by Adams and Jefferson in terms of accuracy and presentation. The novice lawyer wrote that the colonies "are not bound by the acts of the British parliament; because they are not represented in it."[44] Wilson remained a loyal subject and took care to note that "a denial of the legislative authority of the British parliament over America is by no means inconsistent with that connexion, which ought to subsist between the mother country and her colonies." The Scottish scholar, however, disagreed with Lord Mansfield

James Wilson. National Portrait Gallery, Smithsonian Institution.

and William Blackstone, who read *Calvin's Case* (1608) as establishing the principle that the authority of Parliament extended over British colonies founded by conquest. Wilson argued that the eminent jurists had not only misconstrued Coke's opinion but had also committed a more fundamental error by misunderstanding "the title by which America is held": "Those . . . in quest of new countries . . . took possession of the country in the *king's* name: they treated, or made war with the Indians by his authority: they held the lands under *his* grants, and paid *him* the rents reserved upon them: they established governments under the sanction of *his* prerogative, or by virtue of *his* charters:—no application for these purposes was made to the parliament."[45]

The statements that the colonists "took possession of the country in the *king's* name" and "held the lands under *his* grants" seem inconsistent with the assertion—later propounded by Wilson—that the indigenous tribes possess the legal capacity to sell land to private individuals. But Wilson was setting forth the history, not the legality, of the British settlements in America, in order to emphasize that it was the colonists who "undertook, at their own expense, expeditions to this distant country, took possession of it, planted it, and cultivated it."[46]

In 1770 Wilson moved farther west to Carlisle, where he married Rachel Bird, a member of a socially prominent family. He became acquainted at this time with George Ross and Robert Morris, who retained Wilson in a property dispute. Thus, in a short span of time, the Scottish emigrant of modest means had vastly improved his prospects through marriage and connections with prominent men in both Philadelphia and western Pennsylvania. Wilson was, in the words of Morton Rosenberg, obsessed "to the point of greed with the desire of acquiring personal wealth." Not surprisingly, given his situation, location, and ambition, James Wilson began almost immediately to speculate in western lands.[47]

Although he was not elected to serve in the First Continental Congress, Wilson nevertheless influenced the proceedings by publishing his pamphlet on August 17, 1774, just a few weeks after Thomas Jefferson set forth similar views in *A Summary View of the Rights of British America.* When members of the Congress deliberated in the fall of 1774, they were well equipped with legal arguments for denying the authority of Parliament over the colonies, and when the Second Continental Congress met in 1775, both Wilson and Jefferson were in attendance. John Adams described Wilson as "a young Gentleman" whose "Fortitude, Rectitude, and Abilities too, greatly outshine his Masters." Benjamin Rush was also impressed with the lawyer from Carlisle, noting that while "his voice was not melodious, it was powerful, and his blue eyes gleamed through heavy spectacles rimmed in metal."[48]

James Wilson at first resisted the move toward independence. "Before we are prepared to build a new house," he cautioned on the tenth of May, "why should we pull down the old one, and expose ourselves to the inclemencies of the season?" Yet when Jefferson began drafting a declaration of independence, the Virginian borrowed from Wilson's pamphlet, which asserted that "all men are, by nature, equal and free."[49] On the first of July Wilson switched his vote in favor of independence. Because Morris and John Dickinson abstained when a formal poll was taken the following day, it was Wilson who cast the deciding vote in the Pennsylvania delegation. A month later—and less than nine years after his arrival in America—James Wilson became one of fifty-six men to sign the Declaration of Independence.

The moderate Wilson opposed the ultra-democratic Pennsylvania constitution, which led to his removal from Congress in September of 1777. Wilson turned to business ventures and land speculation and spent time in Maryland. The first mention of James Wilson in the Illinois and Wabash Land Company minutes occurs in connection with the meeting held on March 13, 1779. Five months later, on August 20, 1779, Wilson was elected chairman of the united companies. Two other events took place in 1779 that were most likely connected: Conrad-Alexandre Gérard was offered a share in the Illinois and Wabash Land Company, and Wilson was appointed as France's advocate-general in America.[50]

By the fall of 1779 James Wilson was a successful lawyer and prominent political leader. Yet, as David Maxey points out, many of his contemporaries "took measure of his ambition and greed." He was "cerebral, bookish, and aloof" and associated with suspected Tories.[51] On October 4, 1779, a handbill was circulated calling for the Philadelphia militia to remove "all disaffected persons and those who supported them." Upset by the high price of food, a depreciated currency, and suspected privateering, a group of men decided to march to Wilson's residence. Elizabeth Drinker noted in her diary that "a Mob . . . stop'd at the Door of Willson the Lawyer who they Intended to take, but mett with opposition." Benjamin Rush informed John Adams that intoxicated individuals attacked "the house of Colonel Wilson, whose only crime was having plead in some cases for the tories."[52] Charles Page Smith, in his article "The Attack on Fort Wilson," notes that Robert Morris was present and that Wilson was "a most unmilitary figure with his thick-lensed glasses."[53] Unable to force entry, the angry mob sent for an artillery piece, but they were turned back when soldiers rescued Wilson and his compatriots. The intended target of what came to be known as the "Fort Wilson riot" was shaken but defiant: he left

Philadelphia reluctantly and went to the country house of Robert Morris, but soon returned. On October 30, 1779, Wilson presided over a meeting of the shareholders of the united companies held at the City Tavern. All participants in the "Fort Wilson riot" were eventually granted "an act of free and general pardon."[54]

In February 1781 the shareholders resolved that "Mr. Wilson be requested to accept one of the unappropriated shares of the Company's land, & that he be assured the Company will entertain a proper sense of any services he may render them." In the fall of the same year Wilson provided legal advice in connection with the formation of the Bank of North America and thereafter served as a director. In 1782 George Washington honored the Scotsman with a request to take on his nephew as a law clerk. Although there is some indication that Washington was displeased by Wilson's fee of one hundred guineas, Bushrod Washington studied law under the tutelage of the man who would one day precede him as a member of the nation's highest court.[55]

After an absence of over five years James Wilson returned in 1783 to serve in the Continental Congress. As a member of Congress, Wilson could combine public service with private interest and act to further the interests of the Illinois and Wabash Land Company. A retiring delegate from Pennsylvania, Thomas Smith, cautioned Wilson in a letter dated December 9, 1782. Smith praised Wilson's achievements but expressed concern that his friend's obsessive pursuit of wealth could lead to ruin: "I never yet knew . . . of any Man who was remarkably eminent in any Science or Profession, who did not prove a Novice to his own loss, when he . . . thinks he has, or can easily be persuaded that he has, found out a shorter road to success."[56]

Wilson received this advice during the struggle between Virginia and Congress over control of the western lands. As president of the Illinois and Wabash Land Company, James Wilson naturally sided with those members in Congress who urged the landed states to cede their territorial claims without qualification. Wilson hoped Congress would not only assert its authority over the lands in question but also confirm prior purchases of Indian lands. Favorable action by Congress would enable the united companies to sell parcels of land to settlers, and the proceeds from such sales would generate tremendous profits for Wilson and his fellow shareholders.

Virginia, however, insisted that any cession of its claims be accompanied by an express nullification of the Illinois and Wabash purchases.

Following the victory at Yorktown, Congress would spend a great deal of its time considering the cession offers of Virginia, New York, and Connecticut as well as the memorials presented by the various land companies. The debate over the western lands was further complicated by the presence in Congress of Arthur Lee, who proved to be a fierce opponent of the land companies as well as a staunch defender of Virginia's territorial pretensions. The "perpetually indignant, paranoid, self-centered" Lee was ultimately unable to convince Congress to nullify expressly the Illinois and Wabash purchases.[57] Consequently when Lee, Jefferson, and the other Virginia delegates executed the deed of cession on March 1, 1784, the possibility still remained that Congress would one day validate the 1773 and 1775 acquisitions, thereby establishing a marketable title to the tracts in question.

9

VIRGINIA GIVES UP THE
ILLINOIS COUNTRY, 1781–1784

In the first five months of 1781, Congress received memorials from the United Illinois and Wabash Companies, the Indiana Company, the Vandalia Company, and from "William Trent and others."[1] At about the same time, two pamphlets with lengthy titles were published that lent support to the speculators. The first to appear was Thomas Paine's *Public Good: Being an Examination into the Claim of Virginia to the Vacant Western Territory, and of the Right of the United States to the Same: To Which is Added Proposals for Laying off a New State, to Be Applied as a Fund for Carrying on the War, or Redeeming the National Debt*. Soon afterward came Samuel Wharton's *Plain Facts: Being an Examination into the Rights of the Indian Nations of America, to Their Respective Countries; and a Vindication of the Grant, from the Six United Nations of Indians, to the Proprietors of Indiana, against the Decision of the Legislature of Virginia; Together With Authentic Documents, Proving That the Territory, Westward of the Allegany Mountain, Never Belonged to Virginia, &c.* The Pennsylvania Quaker Wharton echoed the deist Paine in contesting the justice and legality of Virginia's claims. Wharton went further, however, also discussing the property rights of Indians and asserting that the Natives of America "have an indefeasible right freely to sell, and grant to any person whatsoever."[2]

Both documents were widely disseminated. Paine's *Public Good* was still selling "for a quarter of a dollar" in Philadelphia a year and a half after publication, and William Murray reported in July 1781 that he had purchased two hundred copies of Wharton's pamphlet "on behalf of the Company."[3] The fight in Congress over the western lands was primarily a political struggle, but Virginia's opponents also invoked the legal arguments crafted by Paine and Wharton. Daniel Webster and Robert Goodloe Harper would present similar arguments forty years later in *Johnson v. McIntosh*. Thus in the 1780s, as well as in the 1820s, the property rights of Indians were defended not by Native inhabitants but rather by those who sought to buy America from the Indians.

PUBLIC GOOD AND PLAIN FACTS

The Reverend James Madison, in a letter dated March 9, 1781, informed his son that *Public Good* was "unanswerable as to the main Point." Biographer David Hawke considers Paine's attack on Virginia's charter claims to be "one of his ablest pamphlets." Published in December 1780, *Public Good* divides examination of Virginia's claims into three parts: "first, as to the right, secondly as to the reasonableness, and lastly, as to the consequences." Paine contends that the 1609 charter lapsed when Virginia became a royal province in 1624, and that the colony's boundaries were reduced by the 1763 Proclamation. Following independence, title to the western lands was transferred to the United States "for the benefit of all."[4] This "devolution" of sovereignty, according to Paine, is a commonsense alternative to Virginia's vast territorial claims. When Samuel Huntington of Connecticut observed in 1776 that Virginia's claim "does not cease to be a right because it is large," Maryland's Thomas Stone responded by predicting that the smaller colonies "would have no safety if the great Colonies were not limited." Thomas Paine likewise asserts in *Public Good* that Virginia's claim "has a tendency to create disgust, and sour the minds of the rest of the states."[5]

After denying Virginia's right to the western lands, and dismissing her claim as unreasonable, Paine turns to his final point: the salutary consequences of federal ownership. The lands are "the natural funds of America," he exclaims, and "are capable, under the management of the United States, of repaying the charges of the war." In particular, Paine recommended "laying off a new state" in an area between the Allegheny Mountains and the Ohio River. The preferred site, not coincidentally, encompassed land claimed by the Indiana Company.[6]

Virginia, of course, vigorously disagreed. Edmund Pendleton endeavored to refute Paine's arguments, claiming that the 1763 Proclamation was "designed to restrain present Grants, and not to settle the bounds of any

Colony." When Indiana and Vandalia shareholders petitioned Congress yet again in the fall of 1781, Arthur Lee drafted his own defense of Virginia's charter claims. The document, *A Concise View of the Title of Virginia to the Western Lands in Refutation of the Pamphlet Called Public Good*, argues that Virginia's boundaries were unaffected by the 1624 charter and the Proclamation of 1763, and were confirmed by the 1749 royal grant to the Ohio Company.[7]

Virginians had no qualms about attacking the messenger as well as the message. Pendleton stated that the author of *Public Good* was compensated by individuals "who are contending with Virginia for the greater part of this extensive back Country." Arthur Lee likewise accused Paine of acting on behalf of speculators and dismissed "the profession of *public good*" as "the common practice of knaves." David Hawke disputes these *ad hominem* assertions, concluding that "the interests of the public were uppermost in Paine's mind, and the aid his essay might give friends in the Indiana Company was incidental to the main issue—that Virginia's refusal to abandon its claim to western lands harmed America." The fact remains, however, that George Morgan and other members of the Indiana Company contacted Paine, provided him with many of the historical documents mentioned in *Public Good*, and awarded the essayist with three hundred shares in the company.[8]

The interests of the public clearly were *not* uppermost in the mind of Samuel Wharton when he published *Plain Facts* during the first half of 1781. Although Wharton also challenged Virginia's claim to the western lands, he went far beyond *Public Good* and championed the entitlement of Indians to "all the rights of 'full property' in their several countries."[9] As noted by Robert Williams, Jr., even though Wharton sought to further private interests, his pamphlet represents "the Confederation period's most elaborate legal brief on behalf of the natural-law-based rights of sovereign Indian nations to sell their lands to whomever they pleased."[10] Samuel Wharton's view of Indian land rights was as straightforward—and radical—as the position taken 150 years earlier by Puritan Roger Williams.

Plain Facts denies that Christians possess a right to subjugate heathen Indians and appropriate their lands, noting that the "pervading liberal influence of philosophy, reason, and truth, has since given us better notions of the rights of mankind." Following in the footsteps of Francisco de Vitoria, Wharton also argues that "no European prince could derive a title to the soil of America from *discovery*, because . . . the Continent of America was neither *derelict nor uninhabited*." After rejecting papal grants and European discovery, Wharton presents the central thesis of *Plain Facts*: that the "aborigines of America have an absolute exclusive right to the countries they possess."[11] To support this view Wharton relies in part on the Camden-Yorke opinion. He acknowledges that the "Indians" in the opinion were Asian, rather than American, but maintains that the 1757 opinion should apply with equal force to Native property rights in the New World: "This most respectable opinion in favour of the absolute right of *Heathen Asiatics* to their several territories, applies directly to support the same right, as vested in *Heathen Americans*; for if the title of the latter were defective on account of their infidelity, the same cause must destroy the right of the people of Hindostan, China, and every other Infidel nation, to the countries they inhabit."[12] Wharton also stresses the natural rights of Indians as the first occupants of America. It is a necessary dictate of "the laws of nature," the Quaker asserts, that the "*original* and *just possessors*" enjoy "an absolute, indefeasible title to the . . . *dominion* and *property* of their several countries."[13] In striking contrast to John Marshall, who would declare in *Johnson v. McIntosh* that Indians are "incapable of transferring the absolute title to others," Samuel Wharton in *Plain Facts* maintains that the Indian nations, as free and independent communities, have "*an indefeasible right freely to sell, and grant to any person whatsoever*," and that as a consequence, all conveyances by Indian tribes of their lands "*are in every respect, sufficient to afford the most valid and perfect title to the same*."[14]

It is evident why William Murray purchased two hundred copies of *Plain Facts*. The publication resembles a legal brief, and the arguments Wharton presents served the interests of all purchasers of Indian lands. James Wilson, Robert Morris, and John Shee no doubt relied on *Plain Facts* in preparing the memorial that was read in Congress on March 12, 1781. The memorial asserts that, as "true and lawful owners," the Illinois and Piankeshaws "had a Right to grant" their lands to private purchasers.[15]

Benjamin Franklin endorsed Wharton's pamphlet, stating that "justice is, I think, on the side of those who contracted for the lands." The aged speculator, however, cautioned that "moral and political rights sometimes differ." Franklin was aware that many of the delegates to Congress were predisposed to view the issue differently. One such delegate, James Madison, observed in a letter to Thomas Jefferson that the "pretensions" of Thomas Paine and Samuel Wharton "can be of no avail unless the Jurisdiction of Congress, or N. York at least can be established."[16] With the publication of *Public Good* and *Plain Facts*, the political struggle over the western lands—and the property rights of the Indian inhabitants—intensified in the divided Congress.

VICTORY AT YORKTOWN; SETBACK IN CONGRESS

The opening rounds of the struggle in Congress over control and ownership of the western lands coincided with the last major military action of the Revolutionary War. On October 5, 1781, Admiral de Grasse and Generals Washington and de Rochambeau commenced the siege of Yorktown. Just three days earlier Congress had finally acted with respect to the cession offers of Virginia, New York, and Connecticut as well as the land company memorials. The committee that had been assigned the cessions and memorials had delivered its report on June 27, declaring that it was "inexpedient" for Congress to accept the cessions because of "conditions annexed to them." The committee instead recommended that Congress should fix the limits of the landed states in order to "ascertain what vacant Territory belongs to the United States in common for the general benefit." The matter, however, lay dormant until the second of October, when the delegates resolved that the committee's report be referred to a new committee composed of five designated members.[17]

The five individuals were Elias Boudinot of New Jersey, James Mitchell Varnum of Rhode Island, Samuel Livermore of New Hampshire, Thomas Smith of Pennsylvania, and Daniel (of St. Thomas) Jenifer from Maryland. It was apparent that the committee had been stacked: each member came from a "landless" state, and both Pennsylvania and Maryland were represented. As Levy Andrew Levy noted to fellow shareholder Michael Gratz, the claims of the land companies were "before a Good Committee of Congress."[18]

Chairman Boudinot invited all concerned to testify before the committee. The Virginia delegation refused to appear, insisting that Congress lacked authority under the Articles to adjudicate title claims of either the ceding states or the land companies. On October 16 James Madison moved Congress to declare that the Boudinot committee was without authority to hear evidence from the land companies. Only three states, however, joined Virginia in support of the motion. A week later the Virginia delegation informed Governor Thomas Nelson that the committee members "have been industrious in the . . . investigation of the claims of the several great land-companies." James Wilson and William Trent spoke on behalf of their companies, and Edmund Randolph confided to Theodorick Bland that the committee was "inclined to strike Virginia."[19]

At this point, news of the stunning Yorktown victory reached Philadelphia. On October 17 General Cornwallis sent forth a flag of truce, and two days later George Washington dispatched a message to Congress, informing the delegates "that a Reduction of the British Army . . . is most happily effected." When word of the event reached London, Lord Frederick North exclaimed in distress, "Oh God! It is all over!" Arriving at Charleston with two transports of artillery, Lord Dunmore was informed of the Yorktown defeat and returned to England, where he sought compensation for himself and other loyalists displaced by the war.[20]

The Yorktown victory, combined with the unfolding events in Congress, must have encouraged the shareholders of the United Illinois and Wabash Land Companies. On October 26 the Virginia delegation was unable to secure enough votes in Congress to limit the documents that the land companies could submit on behalf of their claims.[21] After this final challenge to their authority was rejected, the Boudinot committee turned to the task of preparing a report. It seemed likely that the committee would recommend Congress reject Virginia's cession offer, which demanded the annulment of all private purchases of Indian land within the ceded territory. It was less certain, however, whether the committee would affirmatively declare that Indian nations have an absolute right to sell their lands.

The committee delivered its report on Saturday, November 3, 1781. As predicted, Congress was advised to urge Virginia to pass a new act of cession relinquishing all claims "beyond a reasonable western boundary . . . free from any Conditions & Restrictions whatever."[22] The committee preferred the unconditional cession of New York, which was based on its supposed authority over the Six Nations. By accepting the New York offer, "the jurisdiction of the whole western territory belonging to the Six Nations, and their tributaries, will be vested in the United States, greatly to the advantage of the union." To avoid further controversy, the committee urged Virginia, Connecticut, and Massachusetts to cede unconditionally "all claims and pretensions of claim to the said western territory."[23]

The committee then turned to the memorials submitted on behalf of the land companies and George Croghan, who had died in August. With respect to the Vandalia Company, the committee recommended that its American shareholders be reimbursed by a grant of lands "out of the said several tracts." Going even further, the Boudinot committee members urged Congress to confirm the purchases by George Croghan and the Indiana Company. As noted by William Wirt Henry, "had this report been written by the agent of the Indiana Company, it could not have been more entirely in their interest."[24] The committee, however, did *not* endorse Samuel Wharton's view that Indians possess an absolute power to grant their lands, but rather stated that the purchases had been effected with "consent and approbation" of government officials. The Illinois and Wabash purchases, in contrast, had been *disapproved* by both the Crown and the Virginia General Assembly. It was not surprising, therefore, that the Boudinot committee viewed the Illinois and Wabash purchases differently, and recommended that Congress *reject* the claims of the united companies. Five reasons were given:

> 1st. It appeared to the committee by the confession of the agent for the company, that the said purchases had been made without license of the then government or other public authority, and as your committee conceive, contrary to the common and known usage in such case established.
>
> 2nd. That the said purchases were made of certain Indians without any public treaty or other proper act of notoriety.
>
> 3rd. That one of the deeds begins on the north side of the Illinois river, and contains only a number of lines without comprehending any land whatever.
>
> 4th. The Wabash purchase has been made since the present revolution, when Congress had a Commissioner of an agent for Indian affairs residing at Fort Pitt, who had no notice thereof.
>
> 5th. That the Six Nations and their tributaries claim the same lands, in opposition to the Indians conveying the same in the deeds to said companies.[25]

The committee ended its report with general recommendations relating to the acquisition of Indian lands and the creation of new states. With regard to the former issue, the committee urged Congress to declare that the right to purchase Indian lands beyond state boundaries "is necessarily vested in the United States" and that consequently, "no person . . . can or ought to purchase any unappropriated lands belonging to the Indians . . .

under any pretence whatsoever." These proposals—which closely track the Royal Proclamation of 1763 and the prior pronouncements of the Virginia General Assembly—were squarely at odds with the central thesis of *Plain Facts*: that the Native inhabitants possess "absolute" property rights, including "an indefeasible right to sell, and grant to any person whatsoever."

"When the Report was taken up, we had warm debates"

The issue of ownership of the western lands was now before Congress: if it were to adopt the recommendations of the Boudinot committee, Virginia would be stripped of much of its territory, Samuel Wharton and his partners would reap unimaginable riches, and shares in the Illinois and Wabash Land Company would be worthless. It was by no means certain, however, that Congress would endorse the report. Virginia was so confident of the recommendations failing to garner sufficient support that its delegation moved Congress to set aside a day in December to debate the report. But the motion was successfully opposed, and consideration of the Boudinot proposals was delayed until April 1782.[26]

In the intervening months two individuals were elected to Congress who would play leading roles in the debates over the cession offers and the validity of private purchases of Indian lands. On the third of February the Delaware General Assembly elected Samuel Wharton as one of its delegates. The selection of a nonresident was unusual, but not prohibited, and Wharton took his seat in Congress on February 25, 1782. At about the same time, Arthur Lee joined the Virginia delegation. John Adams, like so many others, found the younger brother of Richard Henry Lee to be acrimonious, jealous, and obstinate. A frequent target of such acrimony, Benjamin Franklin, once said that Lee "must either find or make a quarrel wherever he is." Biographer Louis Potts described his subject as "a virtuous revolutionary" but also acknowledged his preoccupation with "office, wealth, position, and power."[27] It incensed Arthur Lee that the "profligate" Wharton was claiming insolvency yet treating his fellow delegates to "magnificent Dinners." Lee deemed the Philadelphia Quaker to be "an Agent for the Enemies to our cause and Country." The remaining members of the Virginia delegation—Joseph Jones, James Madison, and Theodorick Bland—were also determined to protect their state's charter from attacks by "private jobbers."[28]

The deeply divided Congress took up consideration of the Boudinot committee report on April 16, 1782. The Illinois and Wabash shareholders met the same day and prepared a memorial requesting Congress "not determine upon the merits of the Claim of this Company until they have an opportunity of being again heard."[29] The request was not granted, and Congress was about to discuss the report when Arthur Lee surprised the assembled delegates with the following motion: "That previous to any determination in Congress, relative to the cessions of the western lands, . . . each member do declare upon his honour, whether he is, or is not personally interested directly or indirectly in the claims of any company or companies, which have petitioned against the territorial rights of any one of the states, by whom such cessions have been made."[30]

The disclosure motion "caused consternation" and changed the debate on the recommendations. John Morin Scott of New York, in his report to Governor George Clinton, understated the matter by noting that when the report was taken up, "we had warm debates."[31] The primary target of the motion, Samuel Wharton, announced that he would recuse himself when the rights of the Indiana Company were "agitated" in Congress but would participate in any discussion relating to the cession offers and the right of the United States to the western lands. On the first of May, and again on the following day, Theodorick Bland attempted without success to have Congress adopt Lee's disclosure motion. The delegates were at an impasse, and on May 6, 1782, consideration of the Boudinot committee report was postponed indefinitely.[32] As a result, critical issues remained unresolved. Congress had not decided whether to confirm or reject the title claims of the Illinois and Wabash Land Company. The conditional cession offer of Virginia remained on the table. And finally, the chance remained that Congress would declare that the Native inhabitants of America have an absolute right to the lands they possess.

The refusal of Congress to accept the conditions of Virginia's act of cession did not go unnoticed in Richmond, where the state government had relocated to defend itself better against British attack. On June 1, 1782, the General Assembly appointed Arthur Lee, George Mason, Thomas Jefferson, Edmund Randolph, and Thomas Walker to a committee charged with preparing a defense of Virginia's charter claims. The inclusion of George Mason was particularly noteworthy, given his consistent opposition to land companies other than the Ohio Company of Virginia. In 1773 Mason had defended Virginia's title in a tract titled *Extracts from the*

Virginia Charters with Some Remarks on Them. As a state legislator in 1779, Mason had led the opposition in the General Assembly to memorials presented by the land companies, and he was instrumental in the passage of legislation prohibiting private purchases of Indian lands. Most significant, it was Mason who had insisted that Virginia's cession offer include the qualification that Indian deeds for lands within the ceded region be declared "absolutely void and of no effect." In a letter written just prior to his appointment to the committee, Mason reiterated his concern that if the cession was without condition or restriction, the Illinois and Wabash Land Company "wou'd renew their Application, & probably with Success; and thus the most valuable Part of the Lands ceded by Virginia . . . wou'd be converted to private Purposes."[33]

As it turned out, it fell upon the youngest member of the committee—twenty-nine-year-old Edmund Randolph—to prepare the vindication of Virginia's title, which was not completed until the fall of 1783. Meanwhile, on August 5, 1782, Superintendent of Finance Robert Morris submitted a lengthy report to Congress that endorsed the central point of Thomas Paine's *Public Good*: that the western lands were capable, if placed under the management of the United States, of repaying the expenses of the war and redeeming the national debt. One month later, a "grand committee" comprising delegates from each state opined that if the western lands were ceded to the United States, such lands "might contribute towards a fund for paying the debts of these States."[34] In the remaining months of 1782, and throughout the following year, the cession issue would be debated on a regular basis in Congress and would eventually be resolved.

At about the same time that the cession issue resurfaced, members of Congress were discussing the "devolution of sovereignty" doctrine. Arthur Lee considered it "an insult" to Virginia, and James Madison declared the supposition "so extravagant that it could not enter the thoughts of any man." In rejoinder, John Witherspoon of New Jersey pointed out that the notion had entered into his own thoughts as well as "the thoughts of very many sensible men."[35] Witherspoon suggested a compromise: if the states that qualified their cessions would reconsider, Congress would promise not to interfere with any state's determination to annul private purchases of Indian land within the ceded territory. When a committee recommended adoption of the Witherspoon proposal, however, Abraham Clark of New Jersey moved to delete the language that would prevent Congress from altering state determinations of property rights within the ceded territories. In a victory for the purchasers of Indian lands, the motion carried, with Maryland, New Jersey, and Pennsylvania in the majority and Virginia in opposition.[36]

In the minds of many delegates, the time had come to settle the issue of the western territory. On October 29, 1782, Daniel Carroll of Maryland moved that Congress "accept all the right, title, interest, jurisdiction, and claim of the State of New York."[37] Seven states—the minimum necessary for passage—cast votes in favor of the motion. Congress then turned its attention to other pressing matters, such as the provisional articles of peace between the United States and Great Britain. It was not until April 9, 1783, that the delegates were prompted—by a motion from a newly elected member—to appoint a committee to recommend "the measures proper to be taken with respect to the Western Country." The new member was none other than James Wilson, the president of the Illinois and Wabash Land Company, who took his seat in January following his election by the Pennsylvania legislature.[38]

When Theodorick Bland thereafter moved Congress to accept Virginia's conditional cession offer, his motion was referred to a committee, which recommended that Congress resume consideration of the portion of the Boudinot report concerning Virginia. After debate, Congress referred the matter to a reconstituted committee, which added James Madison and Oliver Ellsworth of Connecticut and excluded Daniel Carroll and James Wilson. The committee delivered its report on June 6, 1783, and Madison confided to Edmund Randolph that "a new report has been made which I think a fit basis for a compromise."[39] The committee recommended that Congress respond favorably to most of the conditions attached to Virginia's cession, including that the ceded territory should be "laid out and formed into states"; the inhabitants of Kaskaskia, Vincennes, and "neighbouring villages" should "have their possessions and titles confirmed to them"; and that a quantity of land in the ceded territory should be granted to George Rogers Clark and members of his expedition.[40]

Of particular interest to the Illinois and Wabash Land Company were the committee's recommendations with respect to the sixth and seventh conditions of Virginia's cession offer. The committee endorsed the sixth condition, which provided that the ceded lands be used for the benefit of the United States "and for no other use or purpose whatsoever." With respect to the crucial seventh condition—that private purchases from Indians within the ceded territory be deemed "absolutely void"—the committee suggested that there was no need for Congress to make the requested declaration, because "the 6th condition, engaging how the lands beyond the Ohio shall be disposed of, is sufficient on this point." In other words, in the view of the committee, the language of the sixth condition rendered the controversial seventh condition superfluous. Because the report only "tacitly excludes the pretensions of the companies," Madison cautioned Randolph, "obstacles may arise in Congress from that quarter."[41]

Congress Accepts Virginia's Modified Act of Cession

Contrary to Madison's prediction, Virginia's opponents did not view the new report as "a fit basis for a compromise." When Congress debated the report on June 10, 1783, Alexander Hamilton sought an amendment "in favor of private claims," and Abraham Clark "was strenuous for the right of the U.S." Ten days later New Jersey presented a remonstrance demanding that Virginia "make a more liberal surrender of that territory of which they claim so boundless a proportion."[42] At the end of the day on Friday, June 20, the matter remained unresolved, and further consideration of the report was delayed several weeks due to an unexpected crisis: the presence of rebellious soldiers in Philadelphia and the subsequent evacuation of Congress.

When Congress met on Saturday, June 21, it declared itself "grossly insulted by the disorderly and menacing appearance of a body of armed soldiers." Nine days later Congress reconvened in Princeton, New Jersey, where business was conducted until November, when Congress moved yet again to Annapolis, Maryland. The angry veterans were demanding back pay, and the financially strapped national government was hard-pressed to compensate them. Officers of the Continental Army requested that Congress grant them western lands in lieu of unpaid wages, and when George Washington transmitted their "Newburgh Petition" to Congress, he noted that a settlement of soldiers in the west might induce the Indians "to relinquish *our* Territories; and to remove into the illimitable regions of the West."[43] Thus when Congress finally returned to the report on the Virginia cession, it was under increasing pressure to open the western territory for settlement. Both James Wilson and Samuel Wharton were absent when the debate resumed on September 13, 1783. Eight states voted in favor of the committee's recommendation that "if the legislature of

Virginia make a cession conformable to this report," Congress should accept the cession. It was now incumbent on Virginia to meet the demands of Congress.[44]

Joseph Jones informed Madison in June that it would "be vain to attempt relaxing the clause respecting the companies." However, by the end of October, Jones was optimistic that the Virginia legislature would agree to the new terms.[45] Virginia did so in December 1783, and Congress voted on March 1, 1784, to accept the modified act of cession.[46] By this time James Wilson and Samuel Wharton had completed their terms of service. The deed was signed by Jefferson, Samuel Hardy, James Monroe, and Arthur Lee. Jacob Read of South Carolina, in his report to Governor Benjamin Guerard, stated simply that "this matter has been a business long pending in Congress."[47]

Things had *not* turned out as recommended by the Boudinot committee in November 1781. Virginia retained its extensive claims to land south of the Ohio River—including most of present-day Kentucky and West Virginia—and was able to attach several conditions to its cession of the Northwest Territory. The acceptance by Congress of Virginia's modified act of cession was a defeat for proponents of the "devolution of sovereignty" doctrine, who contended that all trans-Appalachian lands had passed from the Crown to the national government. Even more devastating was the change of fortune for Samuel Wharton, Benjamin Franklin, and others with a financial stake in the Croghan, Indiana, and Vandalia purchases. Whereas the Boudinot committee report had favored such individuals, the areas in question now remained under Virginia's jurisdiction, and the Virginia General Assembly was adamantly opposed to either confirming the purchases or awarding compensation.

In contrast, Virginia relinquished any jurisdiction it may have possessed over the lands located north of the Ohio River, including the lands sold in 1773 and 1775 by the Illinois and Piankeshaw Indians. Consequently the Illinois and Wabash Land Company was no longer subject to Virginia's authority, but its shareholders nevertheless found themselves in a precarious situation. Although the final version of Virginia's act of cession did not include an *express* annulment of all private purchases of Indian lands north of the Ohio River, the committee report recommending that Congress accept the cession of Virginia's claims did so on the understanding that the act, as modified, "*tacitly* excludes the pretensions of the companies." The absence of an express nullification of their purchases, however, left open the possibility that the purchases might still be upheld. This possibility, in fact, had already crossed the mind of George Mason, who worried that the "vague" statements in the act of cession would not "be a sufficient bar to Congress against confirming the claims under Indian purchases."[48]

The shareholders of the united companies faced yet another problem: Congress was preparing to enact laws to facilitate the settlement of the Northwest Territory, which encompassed the Illinois country. Immediately after accepting the deed of cession from Virginia, Congress received the report of a committee, chaired by Thomas Jefferson, that had been appointed to prepare a plan "for the temporary government of the western territory." The United States was now the owner of a vast national domain, and the committee proposed that the ceded territory—"*whensoever the same shall have been purchased of the Indian inhabitants and offered for sale by the U.S.*"—should be formed into distinct states and admitted into the union. As described by John Selby, "this proposal, which became the famous Ordinance of 1784, established the principle that the new lands would enter the confederation as independent states, equal to the original thirteen."[49]

The primary obstacle to American settlement of the Northwest Territory, of course, was the presence of the Native inhabitants, including the Illinois and Piankeshaw Indians. Congress responded in part by formulating a policy with respect to the validity of private purchases of Indian lands. As described in detail in the next chapter, it soon became apparent that the principles set forth in Samuel Wharton's *Plain Facts* would not be adopted as the foundational principles of federal Indian law.

10

CONQUEST, PURCHASE, AND PREEMPTION

The territory Virginia ceded to the United States was a vast area occupied by many tribes, including the Delaware, Eel River, Kaskaskia, Kickapoo, Mascouten, Miami, Ojibwa, Ottawa, Peoria, Piankeshaw, Potawatomi, Shawnee, Wea, and Wyandot peoples. During the French and Indian War many of these tribes allied with France to turn back the "land-hungry" English. When the colonists rebelled two decades later, the western Indians were courted by British general Henry Hamilton, who burned a copy of the 1775 Piankeshaw deed to underscore his promise "to drive invaders off their lands."[1] Although Hamilton surrendered to George Rogers Clark at Vincennes, the Virginians were unable to maintain control over the Illinois country. Nevertheless, in the 1783 Treaty of Paris, diplomats John Adams, Benjamin Franklin, and John Jay succeeded in extending the boundaries of the United States westward to the Mississippi River and north to the Great Lakes.

After securing independence, the Confederation Congress turned its attention to the issue of Indian land rights. In a series of treaties signed in the mid-1780s the government declared that the Indians were defeated nations and announced that the United States owned their lands by right of conquest. However, as Josiah Harmar observed in 1785, the Native inhabitants "still looked upon the lands . . . as their own." In the following decade the United States would reconsider its position and acknowledge that "the property or right of soil" remained "in the Indian nations." As explained by President Washington to the chiefs of the Seneca Nation, "You possess the right to sell, and the right of refusing to sell your lands."[2]

The Illinois and Wabash shareholders were undoubtedly pleased when the United States conceded that Indians had the right to sell their "right of soil." However, the government would *not* agree with the Indians' assertion that they were "free to make any bargain or cession of lands, whenever & to *whomsoever.*" Federal officials instead announced that the United States held a right of "preemption"—that is, an exclusive right "of purchasing of the Indian nations disposed to sell their lands."[3]

In 1790, and again in 1791, the Indians defended their homelands and defeated the United States. In the following year the government elected to avoid further confrontation with hostile tribes and instead negotiated a treaty of peace with the Wabash and Illinois Indians. The 1792 treaty, however, proved to be controversial insofar as it guaranteed that the Native inhabitants had the "right to sell" their lands, without any mention of the government's preemptive rights. The Senate refused to ratify the agreement, and the commissioners appointed to negotiate a subsequent treaty were instructed that they should "carefully guard the general rights of pre-emption of the United States to the Indian country."[4] The tribes, however, objected to this limitation on their land rights, thus setting the stage for further conflict.

Congress Develops a Federal Indian Policy

James Wilson was an active participant in the efforts of the Continental Congress to forge a national policy concerning Indian affairs. On July 13, 1775, the thirty-two-year-old lawyer was named as a commissioner and empowered to treat with the Indians to prevent their involvement in "the present commotions." Wilson invited several tribes, in the fall of 1775, to attend a conference at Fort Pitt, in order to learn about "a Controversy that has Arisen between the White People who live on this Island and some of the English who live on the other side [of] the Great Water." The conference was a success, and Wilson was selected the following April to serve on a standing committee for Indian affairs.[5]

The Indians at Fort Pitt were also addressed by a separate set of commissioners from Virginia, who denied any intention "of making Encroachments on your Lands." Whether the colonies should independently confer with Indian tribes was a question that was debated prior to the adoption of the Articles of Confederation. Benjamin Franklin suggested in 1775 that all purchases of Native lands should be "by the General Congress," and that any *subsequent* "private or Colony Purchases" should be declared invalid. The actual Articles of Confederation, which became effective on March 1, 1781, authorized Congress to regulate "all affairs with the Indians, not members of any of the states, provided, that the legislative right of any state within its own limits be not infringed or violated."[6] The validity of private purchases of Indian lands was not directly addressed.

The extensive claims of the landed states appeared to displace federal authority, yet Congress asserted jurisdiction over the petitions of individuals and land companies holding Indian deeds. The Boudinot committee issued its recommendations on November 3, 1781, and urged Congress to declare that the right to purchase Indian lands beyond state boundaries "is necessarily vested in the United States." Although no action was taken, Hugh Williamson of North Carolina moved, on August 12, 1783, that all persons "be strictly enjoined against making purchases of or settlement on lands claimed by Indians . . . till the further order of Congress shall be known." Six weeks later Congress issued the following proclamation: "The United States in Congress . . . forbid all persons from making settlements on lands inhabited or claimed by Indians, without the limits or jurisdiction of any particular State, and from purchasing or receiving any gift or cession of such lands or claims without the express authority . . . of the United States in Congress assembled."[7] The proclamation provided no criminal sanction for noncompliance, was limited in terms of its application, and was generally ineffective as a deterrent.[8] But it was the first effort by Congress to regulate private purchases of Indian lands.

The siege of Yorktown, while pivotal, did not end the Revolutionary War. In November 1781 George Rogers Clark commanded an expedition that destroyed the Shawnee town of Chillicothe. In March 1782 nearly one hundred peaceful Delaware Indians were killed at Gnadenhutten (Ohio) after spending the night praying and singing hymns in church. A month later George Washington's land agent, William Crawford, was burned at the stake in retaliation for the massacre. Finally, on August 19, 1782, Kentucky militia led by John Todd and Daniel Boone were ambushed and routed at Blue Licks on the Licking River. Indians from various tribes, along with British soldiers and loyalists, killed some seventy men and "cast a gloom over the whole country."[9] Although Clark subsequently destroyed several Shawnee villages on the Great Miami River, the Shawnees did not confront their attackers, and thus the last time the

Indians fought with Americans during the Revolutionary War, the Native warriors prevailed.

At the same time that George Rogers Clark was burning Indian corn in Ohio, the American commissioners in France were in the midst of negotiations that would culminate in the Treaty of Paris. Remarkably, the treaty makes no mention of the Native inhabitants of America. The armistice was proclaimed to the Continental Army on April 19, 1783, and shortly thereafter Congress directed the secretary of war to inform the Indian nations that they must "immediately cease all hostilities."[10] An army officer, Ephraim Douglass, was delegated the task of convincing the Indians to lay down their arms. Douglass attended several councils in the summer of 1783. Rumors of the peace terms preceded him, causing Indians to confront Major Arent De Peyster, the British commandant at Fort Detroit. In his report to General Haldimand, De Peyster observed that the Indians were "impatient to know what is to become of them and their lands" and were "using expressions not proper to be committed to paper." De Peyster, however, did pass along the following speech of a Wea chief: "Father! We are informed that instead of prosecuting the War, we are to give up our lands to the Enemy, which gives us great uneasiness—in endeavouring to assist you it seems we have wrought our own ruin."[11]

The Six Nations in New York complained that General Philip Schuyler had declared the Americans now owned all lands of the hostile Indians. When the British commander at Niagara was so informed, he claimed that the statement was "fabricated by some designing bad people." Shortly thereafter, Sir John Johnson, the son of William Johnson, assured the tribes that the United States would not "deprive you of any part of your country under the pretext of having conquered it." Yet just over a year later members of the Six Nations would listen in sullen silence as American commissioners announced that "by the right of conquest," the United States could "*claim the whole*" of Indian country.[12]

"WE CLAIM THE COUNTRY BY CONQUEST"

The bombastic rhetoric of the "conquest" theory of ownership was tempered by the actual state of affairs at the conclusion of the war. The western tribes had *not* been displaced: they continued to obtain supplies at British forts and were well equipped to defend their homelands against a depleted federal army. In short, the Indian nations of the Northwest

Territory had *not* been conquered. George Washington was aware that the Indians north of the Ohio remained a formidable military opponent. On September 7, 1783, Washington shared his thoughts "relative to Indian affairs" with James Duane, chairman of the Committee of Indian Affairs. The commander in chief advised that the Indians should be told that a "less generous People than Americans" would force the tribes to relocate "beyond the Lakes." Washington also informed Duane, however, that the tribes would not permit their lands to be taken from them "without another struggle." Consequently he advocated "purchasing their Lands in preference to attempting to drive them by force of arms out of their Country." The future president argued that "the gradual extension of our Settlements will as certainly cause the Savage as the Wolf to retire; both being beasts of prey tho' they differ in shape."[13]

The Duane committee adopted many of Washington's proposals in its report to Congress, which acknowledged that the Indians "are not in a temper to relinquish their territorial claims, without further struggles." The report recommended the United States inform the tribes that it would not fully exercise the "right of conquest," but would instead accommodate the Indians by establishing a boundary line "beyond which we will endeavor to restrain our citizens from hunting and settling." The report also urged that commissioners be instructed "not to admit into a treaty . . . any article, stipulation or condition . . . tending to make or confirm to any individual or individuals any grant or grants of land whether real or pretended within the bounds of the United States."[14]

Arthur Lee of Virginia, who was a member of the Duane committee, was named as one of the three commissioners assigned the task of implementing the postwar federal Indian policy in the western territory. On October 20, 1784, at Fort Stanwix in New York, Lee and his fellow commissioners—General Richard Butler and Oliver Wolcott—bluntly rejected the notion that the Iroquois were a free and independent nation: "It is not so. You are a subdued people; you have been overcome in a war which you entered into with us. . . . We shall now therefore declare to you the conditions on which alone you can be received into the peace and protection of the United States."[15] The parties formally agreed, two days later, that the United States would "give peace" to the Iroquois, who in return would "yield to the United States" their claim to the Ohio country. In similar fashion, the Wyandots, Delawares, Chippewas (Ojibwas), and Ottawas were told in January 1785 that they were now subject to the "lenity and generosity" of the United States. The commissioners (with George Rogers Clark in place of Wolcott) emphasized that the United States "claim the country by conquest, and are to *give* not to *receive*." Consequently, the United States did not receive a cession of lands in the Fort McIntosh treaty; rather the United States "allotted" lands to the signatory tribes "to live and to hunt on."[16]

The third and final "conquest" treaty with the northwest Indians was negotiated by Butler, Clark, and Samuel Parsons of Connecticut. Congress hoped that the Shawnee, Potawatomi, Kickapoo, Miami, Wea, and Piankeshaw tribes would acknowledge that the United States owned all lands in Ohio. William Clark, the brother of George Rogers Clark and future expeditional companion of Meriwether Lewis, was dispatched to Vincennes in September 1785 to invite the Wabash Indians to the upcoming treaty conference at Fort Finney, near the mouth of the Great Miami River. Two chiefs of the Piankeshaws—Montour and "the Deaf Man"— proved to be noncommittal, as was Pacanne, a chief of the Miami. "The Indians," Clark observed, "appeared extremely careless and unconcerned about the speeches & messages they received, which together with their behavior, . . . induce me to fear they will not embrace the offers."[17]

Clark's fears were well founded: the Wabash Indians refused to attend, and when the commissioners arrived in late December, they were met by only a handful of Indians. Except for a few Wyandots and Delawares who had been at Fort McIntosh, the only other Indians in attendance were some Shawnees, who informed the commissioners that "they had shut their ears against all that advised them not to come." According to Richard Butler, when the terms of the proposed treaty were explained to the Shawnee chiefs, they complained that "we were putting them to live on ponds, and leaving them no land to live or raise corn on." In response the commissioners agreed to increase the amount of land that the United States would "grant" to the Shawnees.[18]

By this time Indians had begun to challenge the myth of conquest. Corn Tassel declared in 1785 that if a commissioner should claim Cherokee land by right of conquest, "I should retort on him that we had last marched over his territory," and that our warriors "continue to keep his people in fear." The Shawnees, who defeated the Americans at Blue Licks, likewise found it difficult to accept that they had been conquered. Kekewepellethe disputed the commissioners' right to allot portions of the Ohio country to the Indians. "We are Shawnese," he exclaimed, "*and as to the lands, God*

gave us this country, we do not understand measuring out the lands, it is all ours."
In response Richard Butler informed the Shawnees that if they rejected
the terms of peace, the United States would "take the most effectual measures to . . . distress your obstinate nation." With regard to the question
of land rights, Butler flatly denied that the Ohio country belonged to the
Indians: "[T]his country belongs to the United States—their blood hath
defended it, and will forever protect it. Their proposals are liberal and
just, and you should be thankful for the forgiveness and offers of kind-
ness of the United States."[19] The response achieved the desired result: the
Shawnees signed the treaty on January 31, 1786. In a self-congratulatory
note, Butler wrote in his journal that the Indians were "convinced of the
futility of their arguments." He also observed, however, that they appeared
"ready for war."[20] In less than six years after the Fort Finney treaty, Richard Butler would be dead, killed in battle by the Shawnees and the other
"conquered" Indians of the Ohio country.

THE WESTERN TRIBES UNITE TO DEFEND THEIR HOMELANDS

In order to prepare for the impending peace, Great Britain convened a
grand council of Indians at Lower Sandusky (Fremont, Ohio) in September 1783. Representatives from thirty-five Indian nations attended and
were urged by Mohawk leader Joseph Brant to establish a Native confederacy to match the thirteen confederated states of America. The governor
general of British North America, Frederick Haldimand, reported in November that the Indians were determined "to defend their country against
all invaders." Haldimand promoted the idea of a buffer area—extending
to the Ohio River—where neither British nor American subjects would
be allowed to settle. The governor general also recommended that Great
Britain should continue to maintain posts on American soil.[21]

The support of Great Britain helped stiffen the resolve of the Indians
to defend their homelands. It was evident that the United States not only
claimed sovereignty over their territory but also intended to dispossess the
tribes. In its report of April 30, 1784, a committee headed by Thomas Jefferson assumed that settlement north of the Ohio River was inevitable, and
recommended that the territory be "laid off" as new states "*when* the same
shall have been purchased of the Indian inhabitants." The Land Ordinance
of 1785 contained similar language respecting purchase of Indian lands.
George Washington also favored western settlement, but he expressed

concern about settlers who were moving onto lands that belonged to the Indians: "In defiance of the proclamation of Congress, they roam over the Country on the Indian side of the Ohio—mark out Lands—Survey—and even settle them. This gives great discontent to the Indians, and will . . . inevitably produce a war with the western Tribes."[22]

The conquest treaties gave the Indians "great discontent" and failed to remove the Native inhabitants from the Ohio country. "I am well convinced," Josiah Harmar confided to Henry Knox, that "all treaties are farcical as long as the British possess the posts." In July 1786 some 450 warriors descended upon Vincennes to attack American settlers. The Indians ransacked homes and killed livestock but retreated when it became apparent that the French *habitants* would stand with the Americans.[23] Even before Vincennes was besieged, Kentucky settlers had asked George Rogers Clark to mount an attack against the Indians residing along the Wabash River. The expedition failed, however, and the western tribes remained defiant. At the same time, the British and Joseph Brant were preparing for yet another intertribal council, to be held at the mouth of the Detroit River during the final months of 1786. The "Wabash Confederates" were among the tribes in attendance when Brant called upon the Indians to put aside their differences and speak with a common voice: "We were the Lords of the Soil, the great Spirit placed us there! And what is the reason, why we are not still in possession of our forefathers birth Rights? You may Safely Say because they wanted that Unanimity which we now so Strongly and Repeatedly recommend to you."[24]

The "United Indian Nations" set forth the conditions necessary for "effecting a firm and lasting peace." The tribes repudiated the treaties negotiated at Fort Stanwix, Fort McIntosh, and Fort Finney, declaring the treaties to be "of no effect." Congress was informed that future land cessions would be made by "the united voice of the confederacy." The Indians emphasized their desire to prevent "the unnecessary effusion of blood" but warned that "if fresh ruptures ensue, we . . . shall most assuredly, with our united force, be obligated to defend those rights and privileges, which have been transmitted to us by our ancestors."[25]

"THE INDIANS POSSESS THE RIGHT OF SOIL"

Congress did not receive the address of the United Indian Nations until July 18, 1787. Prior to its arrival, two events transpired that underscore the tensions inherent in the government's Indian policy. On the tenth of July Henry Knox provided Congress with an assessment of the escalating conflict between the western tribes and American settlers, noting that "the one side anxiously defend their lands which the other avariciously claim." In one part of his report, the secretary of war candidly noted that "in the present embarrassed state of public affairs and entire deficiency of funds," an Indian war "would most exceedingly distress the United States." Yet in the same report, Knox recommended that—"if peace with the Indians could not be obtained"—the military "should endeavor by force to expel them from their towns or extirpate them."[26]

Three days later Congress enacted "An Ordinance for the Government of the Territory of the United States northwest of the River Ohio." Article III of the 1787 Northwest Ordinance declares that the "utmost good faith shall always be observed towards the Indians," and proclaims that "their lands and property shall never be taken from them without their consent." Congress clearly assumed, however, that "their lands and property" would in fact "be taken from them," as evidenced by the provision for admission into the Union of new states in areas currently occupied by Indians. By enacting the Northwest Ordinance, Congress made it quite clear that the United States would settle the lands north of the Ohio River.[27]

Although the government was committed to the settlement of the Northwest Territory, it was uncertain how to proceed with respect to the Indians. Congress had previously insisted that the tribes were defeated nations who had forfeited their property rights. The western confederacy, however, rejected all treaties based on the premise of conquest. Consequently, federal Indian policy was at a critical juncture, and Congress looked to Henry Knox for counsel. David McCullough, in his book *1776*, notes that "Knox was hard not to notice. Six feet tall, he bulked large, weighing perhaps 250 pounds. He had a booming voice. He was gregarious, jovial, quick of mind, highly energetic." When he was appointed as secretary of war in 1785, the thirty-four-year-old retired major general had little experience in Indian affairs. By July 1787, however, it was evident to Knox that the United States needed to revise its policy. Three days after receiving the address of the United Indian Nations, Knox urged Congress to accede to the request to enter into new negotiations regarding Native claims to the Ohio country, arguing that "it may be wise to extinguish with a small sum of money, a claim which otherwise may cost much blood and infinitely more money."[28]

The Knox report was referred to a committee chaired by Nathan Dane, which reported favorably on the ninth of August. The committee agreed that rather than "attempting to give lands to the Indians," it would be better "to proceed on the principle of fairly purchasing of them and taking the usual deeds." The Dane committee further recommended that a treaty be held with the northwest Indians for the purpose of "settling all affairs concerning lands and boundaries." But the Miami and Wabash tribes refused to yield more lands and declined to attend a treaty conference. At the same time, settlers continued to press forward. Josiah Harmar reported on June 15, 1787, that over twelve thousand persons had passed by the mouth of the Muskingum River in the preceding eight months.[29] The following April General Rufus Putnam and other members of the Ohio Company of Associates established Marietta as the first non-Indian permanent settlement in present-day Ohio. Both lawful and unauthorized settlers were moving into the Northwest Territory in increasing numbers.

The situation at Vincennes, where the American residents had narrowly avoided a massacre in 1786, underscored the increased tensions. In order to "curb the hostile Indians," the federal government established a larger post immediately upriver from the village. Soldiers commanded by Colonel Harmar and Major John Francis Hamtramck arrived in July 1787 and began constructing the garrison that was subsequently named Fort Knox. Shortly after exchanging gifts with eight Piankeshaw Indians "from the *Terre haut*," Harmar learned that Chief Montour and forty Piankeshaws had been "lying in wait" in hopes of attacking supply boats ascending the Wabash River. When a contingent of Piankeshaw and Wea Indians visited Vincennes in September, they were warned that if they engaged in further hostilities, "a body of troops would march to their towns and sweep them off the face of the earth."[30]

Congress awarded Harmer the brevet rank of brigadier general and then ordered him to depart from the Illinois country. Major Hamtramck remained, but his ninety-five men were powerless to prevent Indian raiding to the south and west. In retaliation for an attack led by a Piankeshaw chief named La Grosse Tete, sixty Kentuckians in August 1788 descended on an encampment west of Vincennes on the Embarrass River. The expedition, headed by Patrick Brown, killed nine Piankeshaw and Miami Indians who were friendly to the Americans. General Harmar strongly condemned Brown's "insolent conduct" and expressed to Hamtramck his wish that "you had been strong enough . . . to have severely chastized him and his party."[31] It was evident, however, that the federal troops at Vincennes—and elsewhere—lacked the manpower to prevent either the Indians or the settlers from committing further depredations.

It was under such conditions that Knox set forth his position on Indian affairs. On May 2, 1788, he stated that "the doctrine of conquest is so repugnant to their feelings, that rather than submit thereto, they would prefer continued war." In July 1789 Knox recommended to President Washington that a law be enacted that acknowledged that "the Indians possess the right of soil of all lands within their limits" and "are not to be divested thereof, but in consequence of fair and bona fide purchases." In yet another report, sent to the president on January 4, 1790, Knox asserted that it "cannot be well denied" that "*the Indians possess the natural rights of man*, and that they ought not wantonly to be divested thereof."[32] The sentence is strikingly reminiscent of statements attributed to Roger Williams as well as passages from Samuel Wharton's *Plain Facts*.

The federal government, however, would not accept that the Native inhabitants of America possessed absolute property rights. The idea of ownership by conquest was now a dead letter, replaced by the obligation of purchase. But the government's focus on purchase was intertwined with the ill-defined "right of preemption." Roger Williams had protested against "the *sinne* of the *Pattents*"—that is, the self-proclaimed right of Christian monarchs "to take . . . the Lands and Countries of other men."[33] By rejecting the myth of conquest, the United States could maintain that it was not committing the "*sinne*" of taking Native lands. But by invoking the concept of preemption, the United States could nevertheless deny Indians the valuable right to transact freely with "any person whatsoever."

PREEMPTION AND THE "RIGHT OF REFUSING TO SELL"

On January 9, 1789, Arthur St. Clair—in his dual roles as governor of the Northwest Territory and "commissioner plenipotentiary" of the United States—signed two treaties at Fort Harmar that marked the end of the "conquest" era of federal Indian policy. In the treaty with the Six Nations, the Iroquois agreed to confirm the boundary provisions of the 1784 Fort Stanwix treaty and cede "all the lands west of the said boundary" in exchange for goods valued at three thousand dollars. In a separate treaty, the Wyandot, Delaware, Ottawa, and Chippewa tribes reaffirmed the 1785

Fort McIntosh treaty and agreed to cede part of the Ohio country to the United States in exchange for goods worth six thousand dollars. With regard to lands retained by the Indians, Article III of the treaty states that the tribes shall not "sell or dispose of the same . . . to any sovereign power, except the United States; nor to the subjects or citizens of any other sovereign power, nor to the subjects or citizens of the United States."[34] The treaty thus describes the government's "right of preemption" without expressly employing the term.

Prior to the American Revolution, the word *preemption* was seldom used in connection with Indian land rights.[35] The Royal Proclamation of 1763, for example, does not expressly refer to either a "right of preemption" or a "preemptive right" of the Crown to Indian lands. The Virginia General Assembly, however, expressly declared in 1779 that "this Commonwealth hath the exclusive *right of preemption* from the Indians," and that consequently only "duly authorized" persons could purchase lands from the Native inhabitants. In 1782 delegates to Congress debated whether the United States held the preemptive right to Indian lands west of the Appalachian mountains.[36] Two years later James Madison asserted, in a letter to James Monroe, that the Articles of Confederation reserved to the states the "right of preemption of lands from the Indians," which he described as "the principal right formerly exerted by the Colonies with regard to the Indians."[37]

In his report to the president, dated January 4, 1790, Henry Knox noted that prior to the Fort Harmar treaties, "it seemed a prevailing opinion that the Treaty of Peace with Great Britain, *instead of the pre-emption only*, actually invested the United States with *the absolute right* to the Indian territory."[38] The government's preemptive right to purchase Native lands, and the right of the Indians to refuse to sell, were to become contentious issues in the early 1790s. It soon became apparent that the western tribes would not recognize the Fort Harmar treaties. A few months after the treaties were signed, Major Hamtramck discovered that Indians on the upper Wabash were attacking Kentucky settlers. Arthur St. Clair also expressed concern about the "constant hostilities." In December 1789 Knox communicated to General Harmar that if the Wabash Indians refused to enter into a treaty of peace with the United States, "chastisement must follow."[39]

On September 2, 1790, the secretary of war informed St. Clair that an expedition commanded by General Harmar would punish the Indians for their "hostile depredations" and "for their refusing to treat with the

United States when invited thereto." As it turned out, it was the western tribes who punished the Americans. The Indians were led by a Miami chief, Little Turtle, whose father had attended the 1748 treaty conference at Lancaster, Pennsylvania. Six hundred warriors traveled down the Wabash River to stop a much smaller force led by Major Hamtramck, who had fortuitously returned to Vincennes. The soldiers and militia led by General Harmar were not as fortunate. In two engagements on October 19 and 22 the Indians inflicted heavy losses and forced the Americans to retreat. Although Harmar destroyed several villages, many of his men did not return, and the campaign was soon known as "Harmar's Defeat."[40]

"There is reason to fear," Henry Knox reported in January 1791, that "the defeat of the army on the frontiers will be severely felt." In response, the federal government renewed its strategy of seeking peace with the Indians while simultaneously preparing for war. The Seneca chief, Cornplanter, was instructed to inform the western tribes that the United States "wanted nothing from them but peace," yet at the same time Arthur St. Clair was appointed a major general and instructed to prepare for a fall campaign.[41] In the meantime two expeditions destroyed villages on the Wabash, Tippecanoe, and Eel rivers. In June Brigadier General Charles Scott set fire to Wea and Kickapoo settlements and returned to Kentucky with several dozen prisoners. In August Lieutenant Colonel James Wilkinson achieved similar results in a foray against Miami Indians residing at the mouth of the Eel River near present-day Logansport, Indiana.[42]

The raiding expeditions, while successful, did not inflict losses on the warriors of the western tribes, who continued to harass settlers. John Cleve Symmes complained to fellow land speculator Jonathan Dayton of New Jersey that sales of land along the Miami River were sluggish because the "Indians kill people so frequently that none dare stir into the woods to view the country." In the fall, as St. Clair's army marched north to put an end to such depredations, the Indian confederacy determined that Little Turtle should once again direct their movements. By the evening of November 3, 1791, the American forces had reached a tributary of the Wabash River, and the Miami war chief ordered a dawn attack. Harvey Lewis Carter describes the ensuing battle as "the most overwhelming defeat in American military history," noting that total casualties "were 913 out of 1,400 present, including 68 officers; the dead alone numbered 634." The Indians had successfully defended their homelands at a cost of 21 killed and 40 wounded.[43]

Among the officers killed was General Richard Butler, the commissioner who had dictated the "conquest" treaties. The victorious Indians smashed his skull and reportedly "stuffed dirt into the mouths of the dead Americans that they might have some of the land they so hungered for." As they had promised in December 1786, the tribes united to fight in defense of their rights. Thomas Jefferson, in a letter the previous April to James Monroe, had expressed his hope that "we shall drub the Indians well this summer."[44] Instead, it was the American army that once again received a severe drubbing. The defeat of the American forces under St. Clair constituted the high point of the confederacy of the United Indian Nations.

THE 1792 TREATY WITH THE WABASH AND ILLINOIS INDIANS

Reaction to St. Clair's defeat varied according to location. President Washington, in Philadelphia, acknowledged that "the national loss is considerable" but declared that "it may be repaired without great difficulty." A resident of Vincennes was more circumspect, expressing concern that he and other settlers "will be apt to lose our hair." Henry Knox argued that "an adequate military force should be raised as soon as possible." In April, following the resignation of Arthur St. Clair, Congress created the "Legion of the United States" and placed Major General "Mad" Anthony Wayne in command. Wayne soon established Legionville, the country's first military training facility, in western Pennsylvania.[45]

As Wayne prepared his troops for war, Knox orchestrated peace overtures. John Francis Hamtramck at Vincennes lacked the authority to conclude a formal treaty with the Indians, but he did enter into a peace agreement in March 1792 with the Wea and Eel River tribes, who were promised that no lands would be taken from them "but by a fair purchase and to their satisfaction." Hamtramck secured a similar promise of friendship from the Piankeshaws but informed Knox that "if our Government does not make them presents," the tribes "will go to the British."[46]

At about the same time, Knox met with Iroquois leaders in Philadelphia, who agreed to carry a message of peace to the western tribes. The secretary of war also dispatched Captain Alexander Trueman and Colonel John Hardin to the Ohio country to convince the confederacy to negotiate a cessation of hostilities. An additional emissary, Rufus Putnam of the Ohio Company of Associates, was appointed a brigadier general and was commanded to be present when the Indians convened their grand council. Consistent with language used by Washington in a 1790 speech to the Seneca, Knox emphasized in his instructions to Putnam that the Indians were to be assured that they "*have the right to sell, and the right to refuse to sell*" their lands.[47]

The fifty-four-year-old Putnam arrived at Fort Washington (Cincinnati) on the second of July, accompanied by John Heckewelder, a Moravian missionary. Putnam learned that Trueman and Hardin had been killed, apparently by Wyandot Indians, who cast their bodies into the Maumee River. He suspected that recent hostilities near Fort Washington had been directed at him and informed Knox that there was "little reason" to expect that the northwest Indians would agree to peace terms. As an alternative course of action, Putnam decided to enter into a treaty with the tribes of the lower Wabash in order to detach them from the hostile tribes. The women and children who had been captured the previous summer were transported by boat to Vincennes and, in a gesture of good faith, released.[48]

According to John Heckewelder, when Putnam's party arrived on September 12, the assembled Indians "fired off their guns for joy." During the ensuing treaty negotiations Jean Baptiste DuCoigne served as the chief spokesman and appeared at one point to suggest that only Indians should live north of the Ohio River. A Piankeshaw chief, however, explained that the tribes merely desired that no new white settlements be made north of the Ohio. There was no mention of the 1775 Wabash purchase in the recorded proceedings; however, a Piankeshaw Indian did affirm "that their ancestors had given some lands *to the French*, that it had been put in writing, and that the Piankashaws felt the cessions should be honored." On September 27, 1792, thirty-one "Wabash and Illinois" Indians signed the treaty of "permanent peace and friendship." As instructed by the secretary of war, Putnam included the following language in Article IV of the treaty: "The United States solemnly guaranty to the Wabash, and the Illinois nations, . . . all the lands to which they have a just claim; and no part shall ever be taken from them, but by a fair purchase, and to their satisfaction. That the lands originally belonged the Indians: it is theirs and theirs only. *That they have a right to sell and a right to refuse to sell.* And that the United States will protect them in their said just rights."[49]

At Putnam's request sixteen Indian men, three Indian women, three soldiers, two interpreters, and John Heckewelder set out to confer with President Washington. At least one chief succumbed to smallpox during the trip, but the remaining members of the delegation arrived in Philadelphia on the day after Christmas and "were saluted by the artillery as they came into town."[50] The Indians, however, did not meet with Washington until February. In the meantime a controversy developed with respect to the "right to sell" that was guaranteed by Putnam's treaty. As discussed in detail in the next chapter, the arrival of the delegation was eagerly anticipated by the shareholders of the Illinois and Wabash Land Company, who hoped that the Indians would confirm the 1773 and 1775 purchases. During the second week of January, Washington directed Henry Knox to investigate whether any persons "held any conversations with the Indians since they have been in the City on the subject of Land." On January 28, 1793, Knox approached William Murray's associate Oliver Pollock, who had met with the Indian delegation on behalf of the shareholders. Knox warned Pollock against engaging in future attempts to negotiate with the Indians respecting their lands.[51] Four days later the visiting Indians finally met with Washington, Knox, Arthur St. Clair, Attorney General Edmund Randolph, and Secretary of State Thomas Jefferson. The meeting took place in an elegant mansion owned by Robert Morris, who had offered the residence to President Washington when the federal government returned to Philadelphia.

Thomas Jefferson was on familiar terms with Jean Baptiste DuCoigne, with whom he had conferred, as governor of Virginia, in the spring of 1781. DuCoigne and several other chiefs pledged their friendship but also requested that the United States protect their homelands. A Piankeshaw by the name of Three-Legs presented a white pipe to Washington and declared that if any more of his tribe's land "be taken from us, I will come again to you and complain, for we shall not be able to live."[52] The Indians, who had by then lost several more members of their delegation to smallpox, met with the president on the third and fourth of February and again on the seventh of May.

After the February meetings Knox asked Rufus Putnam "whether it was understood, that any other power, than the United States, had the right of purchasing when the Indians should be disposed to sell their lands?" Putnam replied that "it was never contemplated by me, nor the Indians . . . that the United States conceded to them any right to sell their lands to any other power than the Government of the Union." Two days later, on February 13, 1793, Putnam informed Knox that he had inquired at the treaty conference about the 1775 Wabash purchase and was informed "that the Indians disclaimed the Validity of that pretended Sale." Washington did not ask the visiting Indians to confirm Putnam's assertion but instead transmitted the treaty to the Senate, along with an explanation of the meaning of Article IV and a statement that the Indians disclaimed the 1775 deed. Putnam resigned his commission the following day.[53]

The Senate was requested to advise whether the treaty should be ratified, and if so, "whether it would not be proper . . . to guard, in the ratification, the exclusive pre-emption of the United States to the lands of the said Indians?" On the last day of February the Senate counseled the president to renegotiate the terms of the fourth article and reserve "the pre-emptive right of the United States to the lands of the Indians." However, because more than half of the Indian chiefs had died of smallpox, it was deemed improper to discuss revisions of the treaty with the remaining delegation. On January 9, 1794, the Senate rejected the Putnam treaty, with only four of twenty-five senators voting to ratify, far short of the "two thirds of the Senators present" required by the Constitution.[54]

The federal government was concerned that Article IV could be construed to mean that Indians possessed the right (like everyone else) to sell their lands to purchasers other than the United States. The possibility that the visiting delegation might confirm the 1775 Wabash purchase appeared to have alarmed Washington, and it underscored the need to emphasize the right of preemption. Washington likely discussed the matter with his secretary of state, Thomas Jefferson, who had spent considerable time thinking about the concept of preemption. In 1785 Jefferson published his *Notes on Virginia*, which he had begun shortly after meeting with Du-Coigne in 1781. In his book Jefferson asserts that the state possesses "*a sole and exclusive power* of taking conveyances of the Indian right of soil; since, according to them an Indian conveyance alone could give no right to an individual, which the laws would acknowledge." Although Jefferson did not characterize this "sole and exclusive power" as the "right of preemption," he did write five years later that "the exclusive privilege of acquiring the native right by purchase or other just means . . . is called the right of preemption."[55] In the summer of 1792 George Hammond, the British ambassador to the United States, asked the secretary of state what rights, if any, the United States claimed to lands occupied by Indians. In reply Jefferson stated that the United States did not own the Native lands but rather possessed a preemptive right to purchase such lands:

What did I understand to be our right in the Indian soil? 1st. A right of pre-emption of their lands; that is to say, the sole and exclusive right of purchasing from them whenever they should be willing to sell. 2d. A right of regulating the commerce between them and the whites. Did I suppose that the right of preemption prohibited any individual of another nation from purchasing lands which the Indians should be willing to sell? Certainly.[56]

It was Putnam's failure to assert sufficiently the government's right of pre-emption that caused the Senate to reject the 1792 treaty. However, when the United States did assert its preemption right in treaty negotiations in the summer of 1793, it was the Indians who rejected the notion of preemption as incompatible with *their* property rights.

"WE CONSIDER OURSELVES FREE TO MAKE ANY BARGAIN OR CESSION . . . TO WHOMSOEVER WE PLEASE"

At the same time that President Washington conferred with the Wabash and Illinois Indians, efforts were under way to resolve the conflict with the hostile tribes. On January 23, 1793, Washington asked Charles Carroll to serve as one of three commissioners to attend a tribal council. Carroll declined on grounds of age and health, and the president appointed Benjamin Lincoln, Beverley Randolph, and Timothy Pickering. DuCoigne and the other chiefs in Philadelphia were asked to travel to Ohio and speak on behalf of the United States, but the Indians were fearful, and only two Potawatomis agreed to take part in the venture.

Knox instructed the commissioners that they should "carefully guard the general rights of pre-emption of the United States to the Indian country, against all other nations *and individuals*."[57] British officials escorted the three commissioners to the mouth of the Detroit River but were not permitted to journey further to address the confederated tribes in the Maumee Valley. Negotiations began the last week of July, conducted by the exchange of written messages. It soon became apparent to the commissioners that the western tribes would not agree to the federal government's terms.

The northwest tribes, following the annihilation of St. Clair's army in November 1791, had convened in the fall of 1792 at "the Glaize" near the confluence of the Auglaize and Maumee rivers. In light of the recent achievements of their Indian allies, George Hammond was instructed to suggest that the Muskingum River, in southeastern Ohio, serve as a boundary line between the Indians and the Americans. The Iroquois, under the leadership of Joseph Brant, urged the assembled tribes to accept the Muskingum River as an eastern boundary. However, after contentious debate, it was decided that the Ohio River should be the line of demarcation between the western nations and the settlers. At a subsequent council in November, a representative of the western nations declared that when the Americans "came into our Country, we defeated them, [and] we consider ourselves sole proprietors of this Land."[58]

When negotiations commenced in July 1793, the commissioners were asked to "firmly fix on the Ohio as the Boundary Line between your People and ours," and to "immediately remove all your People from our side of that River." The American response was unequivocal: "We answer explicitly, that . . . it is impossible to make the river Ohio the boundary, between your people and the people of the United States." The commissioners did, however, formally acknowledge that the Indians owned their lands, albeit subject to the right of preemption:

> BROTHERS: . . . We, by express authority of the President of the United States, acknowledge the property, or right of soil, of the great country above described, to be in the Indian nations, so long as they desire to occupy the same. We only claim . . . the right of pre-emption, or the right of purchasing of the Indian nations disposed to sell their lands, to the exclusion of all other white people whatever.[59]

In response the confederacy agreed that the Indians possessed the right of soil but denied that ownership was encumbered by a right of preemption:

> BROTHERS: You have talked, also, a great deal about pre-emption, and your exclusive right to purchase Indian lands, as ceded to you by the King, at the treaty of peace.

> BROTHERS: We never made any agreement with the King, nor with any other nation, that we would give to either the exclusive right of purchasing our lands; and *we declare to you, that we consider ourselves free to make any bargain or cession of lands, whenever and to whomsoever we please.*[60]

A fundamental attribute of property ownership, Samuel Wharton had contended in *Plain Facts*, is the right to sell "to any person whatsoever." The tribes of the Northwest Territory understood this and insisted that "we have never parted with such a power." As noted by Wiley Sword, the document drafted by the western Indians on August 13, 1793, "endures as a classic statement of Indian rights, and is one of the more lucid and poignant documents of this turbulent era."[61]

When Thomas Jefferson learned of the failed negotiations, he predicted in September 1793 that "the war will go on" and that General Wayne would soon be "in motion." In fact, Wayne and the Legion Army were already marching north from Fort Washington and would establish a new camp, Fort Greenville, during the winter of 1793–94. In August 1794, at the Battle of Fallen Timbers, the American army would finally achieve the military success needed in order to compel the northwest tribes to recognize the federal government's right of preemption. As discussed in the next chapter, the 1795 Treaty of Greenville assured the signatory tribes that they have a right to enjoy their lands "so long as they please," but dictated that when the tribes "shall be disposed to sell their lands, or any part of them, *they are to be sold only to the United States.*"[62] Pursuant to this preemptive right to buy America from the Indians, the United States would eventually acquire some of the same land claimed by the United Illinois and Wabash Companies, thus triggering the dispute over Indian land rights that was ultimately resolved by Chief Justice John Marshall in *Johnson v. McIntosh*.

11

A TIME OF TRANSITION

James Wilson, the president of the Illinois and Wabash Land Company, an associate justice of the U.S. Supreme Court, and a signatory to both the Declaration of Independence and the Constitution, was hiding from creditors when he died on August 21, 1798. In the decade prior to his ignominious death several other members of the united companies had passed away, including Silas Deane, Matthew Ridley, Moses and David Franks, Conrad-Alexandre Gérard, and William Murray. In the ten years that followed Wilson's demise, Michael Gratz would become incapacitated, and most of the remaining influential shareholders would draw their last breaths: John Nicholson, Barnard Gratz, William Smith, Daniel Hiester, Joseph Simon, Robert Morris, and John Shee. In addition, the lives of two leading proponents of Indian land rights—Benjamin Franklin and Samuel Wharton—ended during this period.

On several occasions prior to his death, James Wilson and his fellow shareholders presented memorials to Congress, seeking confirmation of the 1773 and 1775 deeds from the Illinois and Piankeshaw Indians. The results were mixed: the purchases were neither confirmed nor rejected, and committee reports were issued that were both favorable and unfavorable. Although the Illinois and Wabash Land Company—under new leadership—continued to press its claims during the first decade of the next century, another problem arose: the cession of the lands at issue, pursuant to treaties the Illinois and Piankeshaws entered into with the United States.

The last part of the eighteenth century was also a time of transition for the Piankeshaw and Illinois Indians. After meeting with President

Washington in 1793, the tribes were caught up in the conflict over the Northwest Territory, which culminated in the American victory at the Battle of Fallen Timbers. Although their involvement was minimal at best, the Kaskaskias and Piankeshaws were parties to the 1795 Treaty of Greenville, which not only ceded a vast territory to the United States but also ratified the government's right of preemption to the lands retained by the signatory tribes. At the same time, the Illinois and Piankeshaws were facing an assortment of social and political problems, including population loss, alcohol abuse, and increased dependence on the United States for sustenance and protection. Under such circumstances, in treaties negotiated by William Henry Harrison between 1803 and 1805, the tribes ceded large portions of the lands that had been previously sold to the Illinois and Wabash grantees.

THE ILLINOIS AND THE PIANKESHAWS PRIOR TO 1795

The diminished Illinois confederacy became predominantly pro-American following the arrival of George Rogers Clark. Kaskaskia Indians assisted Virginia soldiers in 1780 by providing food and joining expeditions against hostile Indians. Jean Baptiste DuCoigne, a signatory to the 1773 deed, served as Clark's emissary to the Chickasaws and also traveled east in 1781 to meet with Thomas Jefferson at Monticello.[1] As British forces were advancing up the James River, Governor Jefferson and members of the General Assembly listened to speeches delivered by the Illinois delegation and commended the Indians for assisting the Virginia troops. In a letter addressed to "Brother John Baptist de Coigne," Jefferson personally thanked the Kaskaskia chief for his "attachment to my country," and encouraged all Illinois Indians to hold fast to "the chain of friendship which binds us together."[2]

In 1787, when Josiah Harmar visited Kaskaskia, DuCoigne delivered a speech "expressive of the greatest friendship for the United States." In his report Harmar identified the five remaining tribes of the confederacy and noted that "they are almost extinct at present." Gilbert Imlay, in his *Topographical Description of the Western Territory of North America* (1792), characterized the "indolent" Kaskaskia Indians as a "debauched tribe" that can barely "produce a sufficiency of skins and furs for clothing."[3] DuCoigne, on the other hand, was considered "a man of good understanding" who would "pass for a Frenchman with strangers." He was a leading spokesman during treaty negotiations in 1792 and traveled thereafter to Philadelphia, where he spoke to Washington and renewed his friendship with Jefferson. The Kaskaskia chief spoke eloquently, requesting the president to "order your people to be just."[4]

Historian Paul Stevens estimates that just eight hundred Piankeshaw Indians were living between Vincennes and the mouth of the Vermilion River in 1777.[5] In July 1783 Ephraim Douglass informed the Piankeshaws, as well as the other tribes assembled at Detroit, that the Americans had prevailed in the conflict with Great Britain. At a council held at Vincennes the following spring, a Piankeshaw chief expressed regret for befriending the British but explained that "poverty forced us to it." The chief accepted the American "peace-belt" and then asked that alcohol be provided to his people, lamenting that "we could never learn to make rum."[6] In 1787 General Harmar reported to Governor St. Clair that the Piankeshaws were "amazingly fond of whisky, and destroyed a considerable quantity of it."[7]

The Piankeshaws at various times allied with the Americans, French, Spanish, the Illinois, and the other tribes of the Miami confederacy. Further complicating the situation was the fact that the "Vermilion" and "Vincennes" Piankeshaws reacted differently to shifts in power. Following the siege of Vincennes in 1786, the local Indians moved farther up the Wabash or into the Illinois country. It was evident that the United States could not protect the "friendly" Piankeshaws, and settlers killed Indians in 1786 and again in 1788. In some instances the raids were carried out in retaliation for attacks by "hostile" Piankeshaws under the direction of two Vermilion chiefs, Montour and La Grosse Tete. Some members of the tribe moved to the Spanish side of the Mississippi River and began to attack nearby American settlements. The "hostile" Piankeshaws went so far as to threaten the life of Jean Baptiste DuCoigne, solely because of his friendship with the United States.[8]

The Kaskaskia chief, however, felt safe enough a few years later to attend the treaty conference with General Rufus Putnam. Over two hundred Piankeshaw men, women, and children were among the nearly seven hundred Indians gathered at Vincennes in September 1792. After the treaty was concluded, two Piankeshaw Indians—M'sekaniah (Three-Legs or Three-Hips) and Le Petit Castor (Little Beaver)—were among the delegation who traveled to Philadelphia. Even though the Putnam treaty was rejected by the Senate, captive Indians had been returned to their families, and no additional tribal lands were surrendered. The first ratified treaty between the United States and the Piankeshaws would be the historic 1795 Treaty of Greenville.

FALLEN TIMBERS AND THE TREATY OF GREENVILLE

The governor of Quebec, Lord Dorchester, informed a delegation of Indians in 1794 that the British have "borne the Language and Conduct of the People of the United States with Patience; but I believe our Patience is almost exhausted." He also said: "I shall not be surprized if we are at war with them in the course of the present year." In response to such provocative words, the assembled tribes gave thanks for what was viewed as a promise to assist the Indians in defending their homelands: "We have long wished and expected you, to send some of your Warriors among us. We your children now assure you that we are still of the same mind and are firmly resolved to defend our Country."[9] In light of the Putnam treaty the Illinois and Piankeshaws were viewed suspiciously by other Indians. Nevertheless, after expressing sorrow "for having listened to the big Knives," it was agreed that the tribes would be readmitted into the confederacy if their warriors would fight the Americans. The decisive Battle of Fallen Timbers, which took place on August 20, 1794, was concluded in two hours: less than forty Indians were killed, but the British refused to participate or provide shelter, which demoralized the western tribes. "We have followed thee to our great loss," exclaimed a vexed Delaware Indian. In November Great Britain promised to evacuate all forts located in the Northwest Territory. By February 1795 most tribes had agreed to meet in the summer with General Wayne at Fort Greenville.[10]

Henry Knox had retired at the end of 1794, and Washington selected Timothy Pickering of Massachusetts as the country's second secretary of war. On April 8, 1795, Pickering wrote to General Wayne regarding the upcoming treaty negotiations. The new war secretary agreed with his predecessor that the "conquest" theory "cannot be too explicitly renounced." Pickering insisted, however, that the federal government claim a right of preemption to the Native lands: "You will carefully explain and maintain the preemption right of the United States. Some delicacy however will be required to state even this claim, without exciting their displeasure. *If the land is theirs (and this we acknowledge) they will say "Why shall we not sell it to whom we please?"*[11] Pickering instructed Wayne to inform the Indians that "each white Nation" has agreed that private individuals "have no right to purchase and possess Indian lands" without approval of their government. "When individuals do such things," Pickering noted, "it is because they wish to cheat not only the Indians but their own nation; which therefore has a right to punish them and to take away the lands so unlawfully obtained."[12]

Although Pickering told Wayne to insist upon the government's preemptive right to purchase lands owned by Indians, the "right of preemption" and "Indian title" were vague and controversial concepts. When Pickering himself—in the guise of a treaty commissioner—ratified a lease of Cayuga lands to a white man in 1791, his action was overturned on the ground that New York's preemptive right "embraces all possible alienations of said lands by the Indians." In the same year, the father of John Marshall argued that a grant by Virginia to George Rogers Clark was void because it was made before the state had purchased the land from the Indians. The Virginia Supreme Court of Appeals, in *Marshall v. Clark*, rejected the argument and held that the existing Indian title "did not impede . . . the power of the legislature to grant the land" to Clark, who held the property subject to the Indian claim but who was entitled to "the benefit of a . . . future extinction thereof." The decision does not mention "preemption" and fails to elaborate on either the nature of the property right granted to Clark, or the "title" held by the tribe prior to its extinguishment by the state. It is apparent, however, that the Virginia court did *not* hold that Clark was granted the state's preemptive right to *acquire* the tribal lands; rather, the court found that Clark was granted the right *to* the tribal lands once the Indian "title" was extinguished by the state.[13]

The Virginia court thus concluded that property rights in Indian lands could be transferred by the state to private individuals *before* the state extinguished the tribe's title by purchase or conquest. In a debate among members of the House of Representatives in January 1795 it was suggested that even a *private* purchase was effective to extinguish Indian title. James Gillespie of North Carolina contended that Richard Henderson's purchase of Kentucky lands from the Cherokees "extinguished the Indian title to those lands."[14] Although the matter was not resolved, the debate surely sparked the interest of the Illinois and Wabash shareholders: if private purchasers could act to extinguish Indian title, then the 1773 and 1775 purchases from the Illinois and Piankeshaws were valuable even if it was determined that the Indians could not convey full ownership rights.

Under such unsettled circumstances, it is not surprising that speculators in Indian lands continued to transact with tribes. One such individual
was John Askin, Sr., a British subject who lived in Detroit. In 1795 and
1796 Askin and his associates entered into several purchase agreements for
considerable portions of present-day Michigan and northern Ohio. In one
instance Askin and his partners obtained "a million acres of land on the
Maumee River, embracing the site of the present city of Toledo." Ottawa
and Chippewa chiefs were prevailed upon to sell another immense parcel,
commencing at the Cuyahoga River and running westward along the south
shore of Lake Erie to Sandusky Lake. In the most astonishing transaction,
the same two tribes (along with the Potawatomis) agreed to convey most of
Michigan's lower peninsula, comprising approximately 20 million acres. To
obtain confirmation of these purchases, it was agreed that Askin's associates
would "transact the business of the concern with the Commissioners of the
American states."[15] Askin was also represented by his son, John Askin, Jr.,
who traveled with a group of Indians to the "Grand Council" hosted by
General Wayne at Fort Greenville.

"I recommend strongly," Askin advised his son, "that the first article of
the Treaty between [the Indians] and the Americans should be that they
are sole Masters of their Lands, *to dispose of them as they think fit without
any restraint Whatsoever.*"[16] It was critically important to Askin as a private
purchaser that the United States agree that tribes were free to sell their
lands "to whomsoever we please." In a letter to a business associate, Askin
expressed hope that the United States would conclude a peace with the
tribes "without laying any Claim to their soil."[17] The United States, however, had rejected Putnam's treaty because it failed to protect expressly the
government's right of preemption, and General Wayne was unlikely to
contravene his explicit instructions on this important subject.

Wayne directed his soldiers to confine the junior Askin at nearby Fort
Jefferson until the conclusion of the treaty negotiations. The treaty was
signed on August 3, 1795, and Askin was released. In his "account of my
Voyage to Fort Greenville" Askin noted that his Indian friends initially
refused to "give up their claims to the disposal of their lands," but did so
"after being intimidated by the threats of the General."[18] According to
Erminie Wheeler-Voegelin, Wayne kept Askin in captivity to prevent
him from taking action "to thwart a pre-emption clause in the Treaty." In
his own report Wayne noted that "influential Characters were employed
to poison the minds" of the Indians by "advising them to insist upon the

Absolute & inherent right of disposing of all their Lands either by sale deed or gift, how When & to whomsoever they please, & to make this right the first Article of the treaty."[19] However, Article V of the Treaty declares that with respect to lands not ceded to the United States, "the Indian tribes who have a right to those lands, are quietly to enjoy them, hunting, planting, and dwelling thereon, so long as they please, . . . *but when those tribes, or any of them, shall be disposed to sell their lands, or any part of them, they are to be sold only to the United States*."[20]

The terms of the treaty proved disastrous for Askin and his associates. Colonel Richard England, the commandant at Detroit, remarked in September that the land speculators "have been severely disappointed by the Treaty, and their purchases of course set aside." When Askin's partner, Alexander Henry of Montreal, heard that the Indians at Greenville had failed to confirm their prior transactions, he observed that "on this sole point depended our fortunes" and exclaimed that "we lost a fortune of at least one Million of Dollars."[21]

A dozen tribes agreed to the 1795 Treaty of Greenville: the Chippewa, Delaware, Eel River, Kaskaskia, Kickapoo, Miami, Piankeshaw, Potawatomi, Ottawa, Shawnee, Wea, and Wyandot Indians. Wayne wrote on June 17 that some Piankeshaw chiefs had arrived at Greenville, yet three Wea Indians signed the treaty in August on behalf of the Piankeshaws.[22] The United States finally achieved what it had hoped to accomplish in the 1789 Treaty of Fort Harmar: ownership and control of the eastern and southern portions of present-day Ohio. In addition to establishing a boundary line between the lands of the United States and the lands retained by the western tribes, the treaty also provided for sixteen separate cessions of land beyond the line, and "excepted" four additional tracts, including the "post of St. Vincennes, on the River Wabash, and the lands adjacent, of which the Indian title has been extinguished."[23] This statement was meant to refer to the 1742 "lost" grant by the Piankeshaws to the French, as opposed to the 1775 grant to Louis Viviat, William Murray, and the other eighteen Wabash grantees.

The 1795 Treaty of Greenville was a pivotal moment for the Indians of the Northwest Territory. As noted by Helen Tanner, the tribes "were confined to reservations within their once extensive lands, and faced resettlement after the Indian Removal Act was passed in 1830." The treaty was also an important event for the United States. In February 1796 cavalry escorted General Wayne into Philadelphia, where fifteen guns saluted his entourage. The publication of the treaty spurred settlement north of the Ohio River, and the towns of Cleveland, Dayton, Youngstown, and Chillicothe were established in places that had recently been inhabited by Shawnee and Wyandot Indians.[24] Within five years of the Treaty of Greenville, the United States Congress would divide the Northwest Territory and create the Indiana Territory, encompassing all of present-day Indiana, Illinois, and Wisconsin as well as portions of Michigan and Minnesota.

The Shareholders Seek Compensation

According to the Illinois and Wabash Land Company minutes, the meeting scheduled for December 11, 1786, was adjourned due to a "sufficient number of shares not being represented." What is significant about this otherwise inconsequential event is that more than four and a half years had passed since the last shareholders' meeting on April 16, 1782. On that day the shareholders had gathered in Philadelphia because Congress was preparing to debate the report of the committee chaired by Elias Boudinot, which recommended that their claims be rejected. Discussion was tabled, however, when Arthur Lee requested a "purifying declaration" by delegates as to their own interests in the pending claims. On March 1, 1784, Congress voted to accept Virginia's offer to cede its claim to territory north of the Ohio River, including lands occupied by the Illinois and Piankeshaws. As previously discussed, while the final version of Virginia's offer did *not* include language expressly annulling all private purchases of Indian lands within the area ceded, it was understood that the act of cession "*tacitly* excludes the pretensions of the companies."[25] Nevertheless, the fact remained that Congress had once again declined to invalidate the 1773 and 1775 purchases, and the Illinois and Wabash shareholders still clung to the hope that their claims would ultimately be upheld.

Consequently James Wilson was requested on January 23, 1787, "to draft a Memorial to Congress stating the Companies' title." No action was taken, however, perhaps because of Wilson's active role in the Constitutional Convention. The esteemed Pennsylvania lawyer spoke more often during the proceedings than any other member except Gouverneur Morris of New York.[26] The Constitution does not directly address the validity of private purchases of Indian lands, but it did expand federal power over Indian affairs, granting to Congress in Article I the power "to regulate

Commerce with foreign Nations, and among the several States, *and with the Indian Tribes.*" On June 21, 1788, New Hampshire became the required ninth state to ratify the document, and on the first of November the final Congress of the Confederation adjourned, leaving the United States without a functioning federal government until the following March.

On the second of May 1788, the Illinois and Wabash Land Company submitted a memorial to the Confederation Congress "stating the claims of the said companies" and "representing their willingness . . . to cede to the [United States] a great proportion thereof."[27] In contrast to the negative recommendation provided by Boudinot's committee in November 1781, the committee that reported on the memorial in June 1788 suggested that it might be appropriate to compensate the united companies for extinguishing Indian title: "However improper it may be in general to countenance private purchases from the Indians, yet, considering all Circumstances attending the purchases . . . and that . . . the United States will be ultimately benefited by an exemption from the expence of purchasing the same Lands, your Committee are of Opinion *a reasonable Compensation in Land should be made to the said Companies.*"[28] The committee suggested that the governor of the Northwest Territory, Arthur St. Clair, and the superintendent of Indian affairs, Richard Butler, should be appointed to investigate "the fairness and validity" of the 1773 and 1775 purchases. Congress postponed consideration of the committee's recommendations on the first of July, however, and no further action was taken.[29]

On March 4, 1789, cannons were fired and bells rang in New York City to celebrate the new federal government. The Illinois and Wabash Land Company was well represented: Daniel Hiester of Pennsylvania was a member of the House of Representatives, Robert Morris and Charles Carroll of Carrollton were two of the twenty-six inaugural senators, and on October 5, 1789, James Wilson was sworn in as an associate justice of the Supreme Court. In January 1790 the shareholders resolved to present another memorial to Congress "in order that a final decision of the Company's claim may be obtained either from Congress, or by a suit in due course of law."[30] Wilson retrieved the 1788 petition from the papers of the Confederation Congress, and on the March 23 he presented a new memorial to the House of Representatives. The matter was referred to the Alexander Hamilton, the secretary of the treasury, who apparently directed the petition to Attorney General Edmund Randolph. No action was taken.[31]

Shortly after the memorial was submitted to the House, the united companies determined that Senator Morris should join with Justice Wilson "to prosecute the business of this Company." On July 22, 1790, Congress passed the "Act to Regulate Trade and Intercourse With the Indian Tribes," which declared that "no sale of lands made by any Indians . . . shall be valid to any person or persons, or to any state, whether having the right of pre-emption to such lands or not, unless the same shall be made and duly executed at some public treaty, held under the authority of the United States." In contrast to the resolutions passed by Virginia in 1778 and 1779, the federal "Nonintercourse" Act did not purport to invalidate *prior* purchases.[32] Moreover, after the defeat of St. Clair's army in November, the possibility that the federal government might acquire the Indian title by conquest appeared to be increasingly remote.[33]

THE ILLINOIS AND PIANKESHAWS IN PHILADELPHIA

On December 12, 1791, Illinois and Wabash Land Company representatives James Wilson, William Smith, and John Shee informed Congress that "the Indians have never denied, and are still ready . . . to acknowledge the honesty of the purchase made from them by your memorialists." The shareholders contended that if the United States were to acknowledge the united companies' claims, "the necessity of a second purchase from the natives would be precluded." In a document entitled "State of Facts," the company asserted that the Illinois and Piankeshaws had "never surrendered their property, nor sold the *right of preemption* thereof to any other people or nation." Reminiscent of Samuel Wharton's "natural rights" argument in *Plain Facts*, the Illinois and Wabash Land Company claimed that the tribes possessed "an absolute right to convey" lands. With regard to the problematic Proclamation of 1763, the shareholders argued that it pertained only to the Iroquois and their subjects, pointing out that the Six Nations had "confined their claims far on this side of the Wabash & Illinois Country."[34]

The December 1791 memorial was referred to committees in both the House of Representatives and the Senate. Shortly thereafter James Wilson presided at a company meeting at Hubley's Tavern in Philadelphia. It was agreed that if the United States would "establish the Company to the right of one fourth or even one eighth if better terms cannot be obtained," the shareholders would cede the remaining lands to the government.[35] Caleb Strong of Massachusetts presented the Senate committee's report on

March 26, 1792. The Senate was advised to reject the Illinois-Wabash proposal because the petitioners "have not a legal title to the said lands." The committee opined that "deeds obtained by private persons from the Indians without any antecedent authority or subsequent confirmation from the Government, could not vest in the grantees mentioned in such deeds a title to the lands therein described." Because it considered unsanctioned private purchases of tribal land to be invalid, the committee found it unnecessary to address the adequacy of the compensation provided to the Illinois and Piankeshaws or whether the tribes were in fact the "owners of the land."[36]

Eight days later the House committee issued an even more succinct report, consisting of just three sentences. The first sentence describes the 1773 and 1775 transactions, and the next sentence restates the offer to convey the land at issue to the United States on condition that "one fourth part of the said lands" be reconveyed to the petitioners. In the concluding sentence, the committee recommended *in favor* of the proposal of the Illinois and Wabash Land Company:

> In the opinion of the committee, the said deeds being given by the Indians, proprietors of the soil, before the declaration of the independence of the United States, for a valuable consideration bona fide paid, are sufficient to extinguish the Indian title to the lands therein described: and, therefore, that, on principles of justice and equity, the United States should agree to the proposal aforesaid.[37]

The favorable recommendation raised the shareholders' hopes and prompted yet another memorial, which Robert Morris presented to the Senate on April 11. This new memorial asserted that the March 26 Senate committee report was based on a principle which "is not founded on the Law of the Land." Consequently, the petitioners requested "that they may be heard . . . in Opposition to the Principle of the said Report."[38] Although no action was taken, the request for a hearing may have forestalled consideration of the negative Senate committee report.

Arthur St. Clair resigned from the army in April and was replaced by Anthony Wayne. Captain Trueman and Colonel Hardin traveled to the Ohio country, never to return, and Henry Knox instructed Rufus Putnam to assure the western tribes that they had "the right to sell, and the right to refuse to sell" their lands. As described in the previous chapter, Putnam went instead to Vincennes and in September 1792 negotiated a treaty of "permanent peace and friendship" with the Illinois and Wabash nations. Shortly thereafter, a contingent of Indians, including Kaskaskia chief Jean Baptiste DuCoigne and two Piankeshaw Indians, traveled east to meet with President Washington. As a result, members of the tribes who had sold land to the Illinois and Wabash grantees would be present in Philadelphia for the first time and would be able to confirm personally that the purchases were publicly and fairly transacted.

On December 20, 1792, just six days prior to the Indians' arrival, a quorum of shareholders met at John Dunwoody's tavern at Eighth and Market streets. Robert Morris was asked to postpone consideration of their memorial in the Senate, while Daniel Hiester was requested to "call up the business" in the House. When Morris announced that the Indians traveling to Philadelphia could acknowledge the validity of the Illinois-Wabash claim, Benjamin Hawkins of North Carolina informed Washington of this, causing the president to instruct his Cabinet to meet the following morning.[39] Seeking to prevent discussion of the land claims, Washington directed Henry Knox to order the interpreters accompanying the delegation "not to communicate to the Indians a single sentence from any person relative to purchasing their Lands."[40] Two weeks later, on January 27, Thomas Jefferson informed the president that a "Mr. O. Pollock" had attempted to negotiate with the Illinois and Wabash Indians "respecting the purchase of land from them." Washington told Knox to meet with Pollock, point out the impropriety of his conduct, and "warn him, in a serious manner, against any such attempts in future."[41] The delegation and their interpreters thereafter met with the president and his Cabinet and discussed matters other than the 1773 and 1775 transactions.

Oliver Pollock had emigrated to America in 1760 and become involved in trade in the West Indies. The Scotch-Irishman moved to New Orleans in 1768 and prospered as a trader and landowner. It is unclear when Pollock became associated with the Illinois and Wabash Land Company. The merchant was acquainted with William Murray, who stayed with him after the Wabash purchase. In 1782 Congress appointed Pollock as its agent in Havana, where he was imprisoned by Spanish officials for debt. By the spring of 1792 the well-traveled merchant was in Pennsylvania and sufficiently wealthy to repay his creditors. According to the minutes for December 17, 1792, Pollock was one of five individuals who agreed to purchase a share for one hundred dollars if the company was unable to sell sufficient shares to other investors.[42]

On February 6, 1793, the shareholders returned to Dunwoody's Tavern to hear from the committee that had been appointed to converse with the visiting Indians. It was reported that the encounter has been postponed for some time "on account of the disease of small pox and the death of many of the Chiefs." Rather than proceed as a group, the committee decided that Pollock alone should speak with the Indians. During his first visit Pollock learned that one of the interpreters knew William Murray and had heard of the purchases. The other interpreter asked to see the pertinent documents, but when Pollock returned the following day, he found both men intoxicated. According to the committee's report, at least one Piankeshaw Indian—the namesake son of Le Petit Castor (Little Beaver)—was willing to acknowledge and confirm the Wabash purchase: "He placed his finger on his father's signature [and] . . . declared he knew it to be his father's signature, that *he had often heard his father speak of it as a fair sale. . . .* A debate then ensued between the two interpreters (Jacques and Myers) the former favoring an enquiry into the Title, the other wishing it to be evaded." The interpreter Myers presumably informed government officials of the visit, because the committee reported to the shareholders that "Mr. Pollock was accosted on the street by the Secretary of War [and] informed that he was directed by the President . . . to refrain him from any further communications whatever with the Indians."[43]

The president also pressed Rufus Putnam on the matter of the Wabash purchase. Although there is no corroborating statement in his notes of the September 1792 negotiations, Putnam declared that the Wabash and Illinois Indians had disclaimed the validity of the 1775 Piankeshaw deed. On February 13, 1793, Putnam elaborated on his assertion: "I made it a point to enquire of Some principle Chiefs with respect to a Sale made to Louis Viviatte and others, and was informed . . . that *the Indians* disclaimed the Validity of that pretended Sale, alleging that it was done by those who had no right to Sell, that none [but] the Piankashaws received the pay or ware concerned in the business and that the lands belonged to all the Wabash Tribes in Common."[44]

It is not clear whether Putnam's reference to "the Indians" was intended to be limited to the Illinois and Piankeshaws only or to encompass all the tribes who signed the treaty. It is possible that the other tribes opposed the views held by the tribes who transacted with William Murray and Louis Viviat. It appears that the matter was not raised with DuCoigne, Le Petit Castor, M'sekaniah, or any other Indian in Philadelphia.[45] Washington presented the treaty to the Senate on February 13, together with "a copy of a paper which has been delivered by a man by the name of John Baptiste Mayée, who has accompanied the Wabash Indians."[46] It is evident that Mayée was the interpreter whom Pollock called Myer, and the "paper" was the 1775 Piankeshaw deed. Washington also informed the Senate that Putnam had certified that "the Wabash Indians disclaimed the validity of the said paper, excepting a certain tract upon the Wabash," which would have been the 1742 "lost" grant to the French.[47] The Senate shared Washington's concern that Putnam had failed to preserve the "exclusive preemption" right of the United States, and they rejected the treaty by a vote of twenty-one to four. On March 8, 1793, six days after the Second Congress had adjourned, the shareholders authorized a committee to ask the president for "a copy of such parts of the late Treaty by General Putnam & the papers thereunto belonging as relates to the rights of this Company." Jefferson, Hamilton, and Randolph advised Washington to decline on the grounds that the treaty had been presented to the Senate, and it fell to Knox to inform the shareholders on March 26, 1793, that "the President does not conceive himself authorized under existing circumstances to permit a copy of the whole or any parts thereof, or the proceedings relative thereto should be given to you."[48]

The president left the next day for Mount Vernon. The shareholders sought to confer with General Putnam, but there is no indication that a meeting took place.[49] It does not appear that members of the Second Congress were ever made aware that Le Petit Castor, while in Philadelphia, acknowledged that his father had not only signed the 1775 Piankeshaw deed but had often spoken of the transaction "as a fair sale." The Senate was instead provided a statement by Putnam—prepared at the request of Knox and Washington—that "*the Indians* disclaimed the Validity of that pretended Sale." It was small solace to the shareholders that the Senate did not adopt the committee report adverse to their interests, because the House of Representatives likewise ended its session without acting on the committee report that favored acceptance of the Illinois-Wabash memorial.

"THESE LAND SPECULATIONS ARE CARRIED ON TO A DEGREE OF MADNESS"

Failure to capitalize on the presence in Philadelphia of the Illinois and Piankeshaw Indians was a setback for the united companies. However, the two most prominent shareholders, Justice James Wilson and Senator

Robert Morris, responded by engaging in even more extensive speculative ventures. Wilson, Morris, and John Nicholson of Pennsylvania—who became an Illinois-Wabash shareholder in 1792—invested heavily in lands located in upstate New York, western Pennsylvania, Virginia, Kentucky, the Carolinas, Georgia, and the newly created District of Columbia. "Vast fortunes, it appears have been made of late years by land speculations," a visiting Englishman noted in 1794, adding that "these land speculations are carried on to a degree of madness."[50] Wilson, Morris, and Nicholson rank among the most aggressive "land jobbers" of their time and were criticized for their grasping behavior even before the real estate "bubble" burst in 1796. Their notoriety and prodigious failures complicated the subsequent efforts of the Illinois and Wabash Land Company to obtain confirmation of the 1773 and 1775 purchases.

The three men were all born in Great Britain. James Wilson left Scotland in 1765 and settled in Pennsylvania, entered into an advantageous marriage, became a successful lawyer, signed the Declaration of Independence, served in the Continental Congress, and played a prominent role at the Constitutional Convention. Although unsuccessful in his efforts to persuade President Washington to appoint him as the first chief justice of the Supreme Court, Wilson was named one of five associate justices. There were no cases on the Court's docket during its first three terms, enabling Wilson not only to attend to the business of the Illinois and Wabash Land Company but also to deliver a series of lectures at the College of Philadelphia. According to the *Pennsylvania Packet*, "a most brilliant and respectable audience" attended his inaugural address in December 1790, including "the President of the United States, with his lady—also the Vice-President, and both houses of Congress, the President and both houses of the Legislature of Pennsylvania, together with a great number of ladies and gentlemen."[51]

As noted by Robert McCloskey, although Wilson "gave much of his heart and mind to the public service, he also wanted with equal passion to be rich." In 1771 he married Rachel Bird, daughter of a prosperous ironworks owner. With the help of family and friends Wilson formed the Canaan Company in 1785 and purchased a hundred thousand acres on the Susquehanna River, including the future site of Binghamton, New York. In addition to his positions as Illinois-Wabash president and Supreme Court justice, the fifty-year-old statesman became the principal agent for the Holland Land Company in 1792, helping Dutch investors acquire property in Pennsylvania and New York. Wilson also joined with Michael and Barnard Gratz, Robert Morris, and others in purchasing land warrants for substantial tracts of land in Virginia and Kentucky. He had become, in the words of Jacob Cooke, "a prince among Pennsylvania's lordly speculators."[52]

Robert Morris was born near Liverpool, England, became a successful merchant in Philadelphia, served as superintendent of finance during the Revolution, and was one of two men to sign the Declaration of Independence, Articles of Confederation, and Constitution. Despite his wealth Morris did not begin to acquire large amounts of land until he became a U.S. senator in 1789. He acquired a million acres in New York for $116,000, which was sold for approximately $330,000. According to one biographer this "handsome return seemed to spur Morris into a mania of land speculation." When his Senate term expired on March 4, 1795, Morris declined to serve again and devoted his time to speculative ventures. At about the same time, he joined with John Nicholson and James Greenleaf of Boston to incorporate the North American Land Company, which has been called "the largest trust ever known in America." Although pressed for cash, Morris and his partners controlled an estimated 6 million acres throughout the United States, and the "Great Man" was thought to be one of the wealthiest men in America. He spent five hundred pounds to acquire a "curious Clock and Organ" from the queen of France and began building a magnificent mansion designed by Pierre Charles L'Enfant.[53]

Throughout the 1790s, Morris entered into numerous partnerships with John Nicholson, who emigrated from Wales and became the state comptroller-general. In the spring of 1792 Nicholson used his position to acquire a substantial part of northwest Pennsylvania, demonstrating "a knack for seeing that state issues of valuable loan warrants and land grants all wound up in his own hands." He formed the Pennsylvania Population Company and sold shares to prominent investors, including Wilson, Morris, and Aaron Burr. Nicholson also joined the Illinois and Wabash Land Company and served on the committee that conferred with the Indians in Philadelphia. In 1794 Nicholson was impeached—but not convicted—for mishandling state funds. He nevertheless resigned in April and joined with Morris in forming the Asylum Company for the purpose of "settling and improving . . . tracts of country within the State." The Welshman soon looked beyond Pennsylvania and amassed large amounts of land, mostly by credit purchases, and no doubt encouraged Robert Morris to do the same.[54]

Wilson, Morris, and Nicholson were also involved—in various combinations—in three other significant speculations: the Indiana Company claim, the creation of the District of Columbia, and the southern "Yazoo" land grants. Wilson and Morris were both shareholders in the Indiana Company as well as major investors in the Yazoo lands that were sold by the state of Georgia. Nicholson likewise speculated in the Yazoo lands and joined with Morris in purchasing lots in the District of Columbia. The failure of these ventures, coupled with the rising cost of credit, proved ruinous for the three overextended Illinois-Wabash shareholders.

On August 11, 1792, a lawsuit against Virginia was filed in the Supreme Court on behalf of William Grayson and other shareholders of the Indiana Company, including David Franks, Joseph Simon, Levy Andrew Levy, James Wilson, and Robert Morris. The plaintiffs in *Grayson v. Virginia* claimed that the 1768 grant by the Iroquois was "good and valid in law, and more especially so in equity, without any subsequent confirmation to render it so." Article III of the Constitution extended federal judicial power to "controversies between . . . a state and citizens of another state," and George Mason had predicted during the ratification debates that the Indiana Company would bring Virginia "to the bar of justice like a delinquent individual."[55]

Mason was correct. The Supreme Court decided the case of *Chisholm v. Georgia* on February 18, 1793, holding that a state could be sued in federal court by a citizen of another state.[56] In light of *Chisholm*, it appeared that the Supreme Court would decide the merits of the Indiana Company claim, which had been renamed *Hollingsworth v. Virginia*. However, efforts were soon afoot to amend the Constitution to provide that federal judicial powers do not extend "to any suit in law or equity, commenced or prosecuted against one of the United States by Citizens of another State, or by Citizens or Subjects of any Foreign State." President Adams notified Congress in 1798 that the Eleventh Amendment had been ratified, and the Supreme Court dismissed the *Hollingsworth* suit.[57]

Although the failure to obtain compensation for the Indiana claim was a disappointment for Wilson and Morris, it was the injudicious acquisition of vast amounts of undeveloped land that ultimately ruined the two men as well as John Nicholson. The speculators were confident that American settlers and European immigrants would purchase western lands and that the ensuing cash flow would more than suffice to satisfy tax obligations and creditors. Morris and Nicholson were also convinced that property values would swiftly rise in the nation's new capital, and they consequently contracted to acquire numerous lots within the projected federal city.

President Washington appointed three commissioners to oversee the creation of a new seat of government—including his good friend Thomas Johnson, who proposed that the site be referred to as the "Territory of Columbia," and the "City of Washington." In 1793 James Greenleaf of Boston assured Morris and Nicholson that he could secure loans in Holland to finance the acquisition of city lots. The commissioners ultimately sold 6,000 of the available 15,000 lots to the three partners, pursuant to a credit arrangement that was contingent upon the building of houses on each lot within a specified time.[58]

James Wilson did not invest but instead traveled to Georgia in the winter of 1794–95 to participate in what has been referred to as "the largest land speculation operation in United States history." On January 7, 1795, Governor George Mathews signed a bill that provided for the sale of 35 million acres to the Upper Mississippi Company, Tennessee Company, Georgia Mississippi Company, and Georgia Company. The state had passed similar legislation in 1789 but refused to grant the lands because the recipients failed to comply with the terms of the agreement.[59] During the intervening years, Eli Whitney had invented the cotton gin, which greatly enhanced the value of southern lands. Even before the legislature had acted, Wilson advanced $25,000 in cash to the Georgia Company in exchange for 750,000 acres of the anticipated grant. The Indians occupying the lands were neither consulted nor compensated.[60]

The name Yazoo was applied to the entire territory, which extended to the Mississippi River and included the Yazoo River. The word *Yazoo* also entered common parlance as a byword for corruption and betrayal of the public trust. Prominent politicians, such as Senator James Gunn of Georgia, Congressman Robert Goodloe Harper of South Carolina, and Judge Nathaniel Pendleton, were among the investors hoping to earn large profits by reselling the granted lands. Although these men were not personally implicated, the land companies to which they belonged secured grants by bribing the state legislators. With just one exception, every member of the Georgia legislature that passed the Yazoo bill received shares in one of the land companies.[61]

Wilson's speculation in the Yazoo land grants was not well received. In the Philadelphia *Aurora* one commentator condemned "Federal Judges . . .

plucking the *state goose*," and another called for Wilson's impeachment, asking whether "a man acting thus [should] deserve the confidence of his country?" In June the position of chief justice became available when John Jay stepped down, but Washington nominated John Rutledge of South Carolina. On the final day of the Court's August session, Wilson acquired an additional 1 million acres of Yazoo lands (which he later resold). In December the Senate declined to confirm Rutledge, which was welcome news to the Illinois-Wabash president, who "ached to be chief justice." However, in what biographer Charles Smith describes as "almost a direct rebuke to Wilson," Washington looked beyond the current justices of the Court and instead nominated a Connecticut Federalist, Oliver Ellsworth, who became the third chief justice in March 1796.[62]

In an effort to raise funds Robert Morris, John Nicholson, and James Greenleaf formed the North American Land Company on February 20, 1795. Turmoil in Europe, brought on by the French Revolution, prevented Greenleaf from obtaining the Dutch loans needed to finance their investments. The three men responded by pooling their land acquisitions and offering shares in the company to creditors and investors. The company's assets were augmented in 1795 when the partners acquired over 2 million acres of Yazoo lands. Prospective purchasers were provided with glowing descriptions of the company lands, including an effusive testimonial from Robert Goodloe Harper. At about the same time, James Wilson prepared a tract titled *On the Improvement and Settlement of Lands in the United States*, which set forth a plan by which "the surplus Labour and Stock and Capital of Europe would be employed on the unimproved Lands of the United States." The overextended Scotsman argued that "the Profits of it would be greater than those, which could be expected from any continued Series of mercantile Speculations—even those to the Indies not excepted."[63]

The wars in Europe, however, discouraged purchasers, limited immigration, and diverted much-needed capital. At the end of January one of Wilson's partners questioned why a bill drawn on the justice had been returned unpaid, noting that "your resources are immense." It would soon become apparent that Wilson could command few resources, and his deteriorating financial situation weighed heavily on his mind. Wilson missed much of the Supreme Court's February session, and James Iredell worried that his colleague "has for some weeks been in very bad health." Wilson's second wife, Hannah Gray of Boston, whom he married in 1793 when she was nineteen, gave birth in May to his seventh child. By then Wilson had no doubt learned that a newly elected Georgia legislature had repealed the Yazoo legislation, declared all purchases null and void, and ordered the "usurped act" to be expunged from the official records of the state.[64] By purchasing a considerable stake in the Yazoo lands, Wilson had exacerbated his financial difficulties.

On August 4, 1796, Edward Burd wrote to Jasper Yeates, his colleague on the Pennsylvania Supreme Court, observing that there were "a great number of Judgments against your friend Wilson lately confessed by him." In December the associate justice suffered the indignity of being jailed for nonpayment of debts. He was released prior to the February 1797 term but was imprisoned again for debt in Burlington, New Jersey, and then again in North Carolina.[65] After his release, he battled malaria and suffered a stroke. On August 21, 1798, the fifty-five-year-old James Wilson, president of the Illinois and Wabash Land Company, died at the Horniblow Tavern in Edenton, North Carolina. His wife stated that "his mind had been in such a state for the last six months, harassed and perplexed, that it was more than he could possibly bear." His attorney had absconded with a large portion of Wilson's remaining funds, and an auction of his belongings produced less than five hundred dollars.[66]

Morris and Nicholson fared no better. The market for their city lots in the District of Columbia was sluggish, hindered by the transitory nature of service in the federal government. Creditors demanded cash instead of shares in the North American Land Company. The commissioners were threatening to attach the properties, interest payments and taxes were overdue, and Pennsylvania was pursuing Nicholson for missing state funds. Construction ceased because workers were not paid, leaving brick houses on South Capitol Street roofless and exposed to the elements. The mansion Morris was building in Philadelphia also had no roof; people called it "Morris's Folly." Morris viewed Wilson's arrest in December 1796 with alarm: "I am seriously uneasy for Wilson's affair will make the vultures more keen after me."[67]

When Wilson was imprisoned in New Jersey in the summer of 1797, Morris retreated to his country estate, where he barred the door and corresponded by lowering a bucket from a second-story window. Creditors lit watch-fires and besieged the former senator. The "Financier of the Revolution" entered the Prune Street debtors' prison in February 1798.[68]

A year and a half later John Nicholson also entered the Prune Street prison, where he died on December 5, 1800, leaving behind a wife, eight children, and debts totaling a staggering $12 million dollars. Morris owed sixty-one creditors $2.9 million but lived long enough to benefit from the Bankruptcy Act of 1800. He died in Philadelphia in 1806, but his financial affairs were not resolved until the end of the nineteenth century.[69]

Passing of the Guard: Grantors and Grantees

By the end of the eighteenth century the Illinois confederacy numbered about five hundred individuals, only one fifth of whom lived east of the Mississippi. Because of their pro-American stance, the Illinois were ostracized and threatened by other tribes. Approximately 420 Peoria and Cahokia Indians resided west of the Mississippi River in Spanish territory, and 80 or so Kaskaskia Natives remained in the Illinois country, among them Jean Baptiste DuCoigne and his son, Louis Jefferson DuCoigne. The elder chief, who had accepted William Murray's offer in 1773 to purchase a large portion of the Illinois homelands, would join his son thirty years later in signing a treaty that ceded the same territory to the United States.[70]

The Piankeshaws were also fighting for survival. A French traveler, Comte de Volney, stayed briefly in Vincennes in 1796 and formed an unfavorable impression of the local Indians: "The men and women roamed all day about the town, merely to get rum, for which they eagerly exchanged their peltry. . . . It was rare for a day to pass without a deadly quarrel, by which about ten men lose their lives yearly."[71] The tribe was clearly entering a period of transition: the first Greenville Treaty annuity, in the amount of five hundred dollars, was delivered on September 12, 1796, and thereafter the Piankeshaws became increasingly dependent upon on the United States. A Virginian traveler named Moses Austin noted in January 1797 that the tribe "had a Town within One Mile of St Vincennes but its now destroyd and there Number reduced to about 120 men."[72] The Piankeshaws and Illinois were nevertheless considered by the United States to be the rightful occupants of much of modern-day Indiana and Illinois. Consequently, after the Indiana Territory was created in 1800, the new territorial governor, William Henry Harrison, devoted a great deal of attention to the tribes in order to obtain treaties of cession that would extinguish Indian title and open up the territory for settlement.

The Illinois-Wabash shareholders, during this time of transition, persisted in their efforts to obtain confirmation of the 1773 and 1775 purchases. The issue was raised during the negotiations that preceded the Treaty of Green-ville. In his report to the secretary of war, Anthony Wayne noted that a 1773 deed that "embraced all the Illinois Country" had been presented for ratification. The report, which is partly illegible, does not provide fur-ther details and unfortunately does not identify the individual who urged Wayne to confirm the transaction. William Henry Harrison later recalled that "a person attended at the treaty of Greenville on behalf of one or both of these companies," but stated that "the subject was not brought before the Indians."[73]

In 1796 the united companies printed *An Account of the Proceedings of the Illinois and Ouabache Land Companies*. The pamphlet contains a description by William Murray of the 1773 and 1775 transactions, the 1780 "Articles of Union" that joined the two companies, copies of the two deeds, the December 1791 "State of Facts," and the 1792 Senate and House reports. The remaining twenty-one pages consist of arguments prepared by James Wilson, William Smith, and John Shee in support of the claims. The shareholders argued that the tribes were never tributaries to the Six Na-tions and had never otherwise relinquished "any preemption right to their territory." They argued further that because the Piankeshaws and Illinois were among the tribes who had not previously "alienated their property or the pre-emption right of the same," they were the "absolute and inde-pendent Proprietors of the Soil" and thus possessed the right to sell their land (or, alternatively, the right of preemption). In support of this position, the pamphlet sets forth the "official opinion of two Lord Chancellors of England, Pratt and York."[74]

On January 13, 1797, another memorial was submitted to Congress, requesting that Congress either act on the shareholders' offer to surrender three-fourths of their claim or "derive some method for a judicial de-cision."[75] The House and Senate committees considering this memorial both adopted the 1792 Senate report, which had concluded that "these companies had no legal title to the said lands." On February 16 the full Senate resolved to deny the Illinois-Wabash petition. The House of Rep-resentatives, however, did not bring the matter to a vote, and the share-holders once again avoided a conclusive rejection of their claims.[76]

The Illinois and Wabash Land Company waited five years before sub-mitting another memorial to Congress, and William Smith and John Shee are described at the end of the 1802 memorial as the "*Survivors* of the Committee" that was appointed to petition Congress.[77] Other shareholders besides James Wilson had died, including David Franks and William Murray. Franks left Philadelphia for a time but returned and attended meetings of the Illinois-Wabash Company between 1786 and 1793. His older brother and fellow shareholder Moses Franks of London passed away in 1789, and on October 13, 1793, Dr. Benjamin Rush informed his wife that "our old neighbor Mr. Franks died last night." According to historian Harry Simonhoff, instead of "an honored grave" in a Jewish cemetery, the "assimilator" David Franks "found his resting place in Potter's Field."[78]

William Murray's active involvement in company affairs had ended in the 1780s, and on December 18, 1786, the shareholders appointed his son, William Murray, Jr., as secretary of the united companies.[79] The elder Murray relocated to Cole's Creek, northeast of Natchez, Mississippi, where he died in 1795. He willed his plantation and eight slaves to his wife Martha and his remaining property "to my beloved son, Wm. Murray," including "drafts and warrants on the State of Virginia" and other "sundry papers" in the possession of Oliver Pollock.[80] His brother Daniel Murray died in 1784 from a bullet wound received in a dispute over collection of a debt. William Murray, Jr., who served as both United States attorney and state attorney general in Kentucky, died in 1805.[81]

On June 11, 1773, when William Murray arrived at Kaskaskia, he had grandly presented the commanding British officer with an edited version of the Camden-Yorke opinion. Charles Yorke died in January 1770, soon after being granted a peerage and appointed lord chancellor. His co-author Charles Pratt (Lord Camden and later Earl Camden) lived until 1794, apparently without public comment on the applicability of the 1757 legal opinion to the Indians of North America.[82] By century's end, most other leading proponents of the absolute right of the Native occupants to own and sell property were also dead: George Croghan (1782), Richard Henderson (1785), William Trent (1787), Silas Deane (1789), Benjamin Franklin (1790), and Patrick Henry (1799).[83] In April 1798 Elizabeth Drinker paid a visit to her "old friends Sammy and Sally Wharton" and noted that "they are both unable to walk." The author of *Plain Facts* died in March 1800.[84]

In the first decade of the nineteenth century, many of the remaining shareholders departed from the scene. Barnard Gratz passed away in 1801 in Baltimore, survived by his younger brother Michael, "a helpless invalid" who would live until 1811.[85] William Smith and John Steinmetz of Philadelphia died in 1803 and Daniel Hiester and Joseph Simon the following year.[86] John Shee made a point of referring to himself in the memorial submitted to Congress in October 1803 as the "*sole survivor* of the committee appointed and authorized to solicit, manage, and negotiate the affairs of the company with Congress." The 1803 memorial did not mention that the most infamous member of the Illinois and Wabash Land Company was still alive: John Murray, the Fourth Earl of Dunmore. However, on February 25, 1809, the former governor of New York, Virginia, and the Bahama Islands died at a seaside resort in Kent, England. He was not survived by John Shee, who passed away the previous year.[87]

Charles Carroll of Carrollton, Thomas Johnson, and Samuel Chase were still living, although the latter came close to death in 1800 when he fell through the ice while crossing the Patapsco River. After 1788 Chase sought "a safe position of honor and dignity."[88] He became the chief justice of the Maryland General Court and in 1796 was appointed by Washington to the U.S. Supreme Court. In December 1797 Justice Chase sought advice regarding his share in the Illinois-Wabash venture from James McHenry, expressing a wish "to be quit of the Business" and offering "to relinquish all Claim for what I have paid with Interest, on 1600£."[89] Chase instead deeded his interest in 1809 to his sons, Samuel and Thomas, to hold as tenants in common. The transaction was witnessed by Justice Brockholst Livingston, who fourteen years later would be present for the case of *Johnson v. McIntosh*.[90]

Thomas Johnson sat with James Wilson on the Supreme Court but departed prior to Chase's appointment. In January 1793 Johnson resigned after just fourteen months—the shortest tenure in the history of the Court. In 1795 and again in 1801 Johnson declined presidential offers of public office. His friend Charles Carroll was never active in the affairs of the land company. Paine Wingate of New Hampshire described Carroll in 1789 as "the richest man in America, worth half a million sterling, but [who] is as plain in his dress & manners & as easy of access any man." Carroll retired from public life in 1801 at age sixty-four. He would live another thirty-one years.[91]

In 1775 Carroll and Johnson had jointly acquired one share in the Illinois purchase. The share mentioned only the latter, a mistake rectified in 1810 when Johnson "for the consideration of one cent" granted Carroll "one undivided moiety as half part of the said share."[92] Robert Goodloe Harper was likely the impetus for this transaction. In May 1801 the ardent Federalist married Catherine Carroll, after finally convincing her father that he was a worthy suitor. Carroll's doubts about Harper concerned his financial situation: due to unwise investments in the Yazoo lands and other speculative ventures, Harper had accumulated large debts. Although Harper readily acknowledged that the primary source of his misfortune was land speculation, he would nevertheless become the foremost champion of the Illinois-Wabash Land Company.

As Sidney Fish has noted, a "second phase of this old contest" began in earnest around 1803. The memorial submitted to Congress by William Smith and John Shee in 1802 was attested by John H. Brinton, the company's new secretary. Brinton was one of several individuals who became involved in the Illinois-Wabash venture by marrying the daughter of a shareholder. Sarah Steinmetz married Brinton in 1795, and their daughter Catherine Ann would wed Edward Ingersoll of Philadelphia in 1816. These two men, along with Robert Goodloe Harper and Solomon Etting, the son-in-law of Barnard Gratz, would vigorously assert the right of the Illinois and Piankeshaw Indians to sell their land. Samuel Chase, Jr., and the sons of Michael Gratz would also actively pursue the claims. The Gratz store would serve as the "general headquarters" in Philadelphia, while Harper, Etting, and Chase would lead the charge in Maryland.[93]

William Henry Harrison would also become an important figure in the affairs of the united companies. Harrison was a friend of Harper and was familiar with the Indian purchases. Correspondence between Treasury Secretary Albert Gallatin and John Badollet, the register of the Vincennes land office, suggests that Harrison may have been more than a disinterested observer. It is uncertain whether the governor of the Indiana Territory ever obtained a financial interest in the Illinois-Wabash concern.[94] What is known, however, is that William Henry Harrison negotiated several treaties with the Illinois and Piankeshaws and convinced the tribes to cede to the United States the same lands that were claimed by the Illinois and Wabash Land Company.

12

CESSION, RESISTANCE, AND REMOVAL

Although reduced in numbers, the Piankeshaws and Illinois still lived within their historic homelands at the beginning of the nineteenth century. However, the tribes soon removed beyond the Mississippi. The Kaskaskias signed three treaties with the United States in 1803 and relinquished almost all their lands, including the tracts sold in 1773 to the Illinois grantees. The Piankeshaws were signatories to four treaties in 1803, 1804, and 1805, ceding the southernmost part of Indiana as well as a large part of southeastern Illinois. These treaties encompassed most, if not all, of the lands that had been deeded in 1775 to the Wabash grantees. William Henry Harrison, the governor of the Indiana Territory, superintendent of Indian affairs, and "commissioner plenipotentiary" of the United States, negotiated a total of twelve treaties between 1803 and 1809, extinguishing Native title to an estimated 50 million acres in the Ohio and Mississippi river valleys.[1]

The Delaware, Eel River, Fox, Kaskaskia, Kickapoo, Miami, Piankeshaw, Potawatomi, Sauk, Shawnee, Wea, and Wyandot tribes all entered into treaties with the United States. Many Indians became dissatisfied with Harrison's aggressive actions and were drawn to the resistance movement initiated by the Shawnee Prophet and carried forward by Tecumseh, his warrior brother. The hostilities with Great Britain ended soon after the death of Tecumseh, and the removal of the northwest Indians began in earnest. The Piankeshaw and Illinois Indians ceded their remaining lands east of the Mississippi River in 1818, and in December of the same year, Illinois was admitted to the Union as the twenty-first state. Shortly thereafter, the secretary of war, John C. Calhoun, reported to the House of Representatives that the western tribes "neither are, in fact, nor ought to be, considered independent nations," and declared that "helplessness has succeeded independence."[2]

Harrison Becomes Governor

William Henry Harrison was born on February 3, 1773, the youngest of seven siblings and the son of former Virginia governor Benjamin Harrison, who died in 1791 while his son was studying medicine in Philadelphia. William Harrison, like James Wilson, changed his career path upon the death of his father and joined the United States army. He arrived in the Northwest Territory just as St. Clair returned from his shattering 1791 defeat on the Wabash by Little Turtle's forces. President Washington appointed Anthony Wayne to replace St. Clair, and Harrison was selected to serve as an aide-de-camp. Lieutenant Harrison witnessed the signing of the Greenville Treaty and was thereafter married to Anna Symmes, the daughter of a prominent landowner. In 1797, at the age of twenty-four, Harrison was given his captain's commission and command of Fort Washington, near the settlement of Cincinnati.[3] He was a young man with a bright future.

When the office of secretary of the Northwest Territory became vacant, Harrison wrote to Robert Goodloe Harper expressing his interest in the position. Harrison received the coveted appointment in 1798 and resigned from the army to begin a second career in politics. In October the following year the General Assembly of the Northwest Territory elected Harrison as their delegate to Congress. He chaired the Committee on Public Lands and was credited with the passage of the "Harrison Land Act." The highly popular Act of May 10, 1800, accelerated western settlement and provided the federal government with substantial revenue.

At about the same time, Congress split the Northwest Territory into two parts, reducing the Northwest Territory and creating the Indiana Territory, which initially included present-day Indiana, Illinois, Wisconsin as well as a large part of Michigan and smaller portions of Ohio and Minnesota. On May 12, 1800, President Adams nominated Harrison to be the governor of the Indiana Territory, and the following day the Senate communicated its consent.[4] The rising politician arrived at the territorial capital in January 1801, a month prior to his twenty-eighth birthday.

William Henry Harrison. National Portrait Gallery, Smithsonian Institution; gift of Mrs. Herbert Lee Pratt, Jr.

Harrison faced numerous obstacles. An immediate political problem stemmed from the fact that he had been appointed by Adams, a Federalist who had lost his bid for another term. The 1800 national election marked the ascendancy of the Republicans, and the new governor adroitly responded to the demise of the Federalist Party by switching his political allegiance. An opponent, who called himself "Decius," condemned such behavior in a letter published in the Vincennes *Gazette*, declaring that "from the firmest Federalist, you wheeled about, like a cock on a steeple, and declared yourself a Republican!!!"[5]

Harrison was criticized often during his tenure as governor. The near absolute power bestowed upon the executive office during the first stage of government placed the governor at the center of factional politics. In particular, a landowner named William McIntosh would become the governor's most vociferous critic. After serving in his native Scotland as a lieutenant in the "Northern Fencibles" from 1778 to 1781, McIntosh had moved to Canada, where his brother Angus was a partner of John Askin.[6] McIntosh moved to Vincennes in 1785, acquired land from the French inhabitants, and served as a witness to Rufus Putnam's 1792 treaty. At first Harrison and McIntosh joined together in business and property transactions, but the Scotsman denounced the governor in 1804, and six years later Harrison sued for slander and recovered four thousand dollars in damages.[7] McIntosh vehemently opposed the governor and his Indian policies, but he is noteworthy for another reason: the combative "tory" in 1820 became the defendant in the case of *Johnson v. McIntosh*.

Harrison was also troubled by demographic and geographic problems. One issue was slavery: the governor and his Virginia associates favored the institution and thus opposed its prohibition in the Northwest Territory. Another concern stemmed from the fact that the non–Indian population of the Indiana Territory numbered less than six thousand and was concentrated in four locations: the French settlements of Cahokia, Kaskaskia, and Vincennes, and Clark's Grant, the area across the Ohio River from Louisville reserved by Virginia for George Rogers Clark and his soldiers. The remaining lands were controlled by hostile Indians, who were in contact with potential European allies. Spain controlled Louisiana but had agreed in the secret Treaty of San Ildefonso (October 1, 1800) to retrocede the territory to France. The British were close at hand in Canada.

The most immediate problem was the limited amount of land available for purchase. Settlement was proceeding at a rapid pace in the Ohio Territory, facilitated by the extensive cessions that were made at Greenville. In contrast, virtually all of the Indiana Territory was subject to Indian claims—particularly if one subscribed to the view that the 1773 and 1775 purchases were ineffective to extinguish the Native title. One exception was Clark's Grant in southeast Indiana, and another area that had been opened to settlement by the Greenville Treaty was the "post of St.

Vincennes . . . *and the lands adjacent,* of which the Indian title has been extinguished." In the 1799 Nonintercourse Act, Congress authorized the marking of boundary lines between the United States and Indian tribes but did not appropriate funds to accomplish the task. In his first official report as governor, Harrison asked of the secretary of war, Henry Dearborn, that the boundary be established "as soon as possible."[8]

THE 1803 TREATIES: THE VINCENNES TRACT
AND THE KASKASKIA CESSION

The delineation of the "Vincennes Tract" was not the only issue Harrison addressed in his initial report to Secretary Dearborn. In language reminiscent of the French traveler Comte de Volney, Governor Harrison described the deplorable state of the local Piankeshaw, Wea, and Eel River Indians, noting that they "are frequently intoxicated" and "kill each other without mercy." Harrison acknowledged that the Indian chiefs held legitimate grievances against certain traders and issued a proclamation that prohibited the sale of "Spirituous Liquors" to Indians within the limits of Vincennes. Harrison also acknowledged that local residents routinely hunted on the lands of the Indians, but he claimed that such actions were "almost impossible to punish" in the absence of clearly marked boundaries.[9]

In the winter of 1801–1802 Little Turtle and other Indian leaders traveled to the new capital city of Washington and requested that the boundary be marked in order to stop further encroachment on Native lands. Dearborn instructed Harrison to determine what "ought to be considered as a fair construction of that part of the Treaty of Greenville," and to enclose "no more land . . . than what the Treaty will fully & fairly justify." Harrison was concerned that the 1775 Piankeshaw deed—which provided the only written evidence of the parameters of the Vincennes Tract—described an area that was "much more extensive than is generally imagined."[10] "I think it would be extremely impolitic to insist on taking the whole of it," the governor cautioned, noting that Putnam had previously assured the Indians "that our claim would not be very extensive." Harrison proposed instead to extend the tract twelve leagues (about thirty miles) in both directions from the Wabash, to form a square of twenty-four leagues. He also recommended convening a general council to comply with the demand of the Indians "that no proposition which relates to their lands can be acceded to without the consent of all the tribes." With respect to claims by individuals to lands outside the Vincennes Tract, the governor informed Dearborn that he was aware only of "those which are made by the Illinois and Wabash companies."[11]

The response of the secretary of war must have surprised Harrison. On June 17, 1802, Dearborn instructed the governor to "sound the Piankishaws" on the validity of the 1775 grant. In particular, Dearborn was interested in learning whether the Indians "would consent to the United States' assuming the right" that was now claimed by the Illinois and Wabash Land Company. If the Indians were reluctant "to agree to such an arrangement," Harrison was told to obtain as much as possible of the Vincennes Tract "as described in the Deed of cession of '75.'" Dearborn also expressed interest in obtaining title to the tract along the Ohio and Mississippi rivers that was conveyed in 1773 to the Illinois grantees, noting that "it would be very desirable that the United States should acquire the exclusive right to this Tract."[12]

There are two possible explanations for the government's interest in the lands purchased by the Illinois and Wabash grantees. As discussed in the following chapter, the shareholders had submitted a memorial to Congress in March 1802, offering to transfer all rights to the United States if the government would agree to reconvey one fourth of the lands. The memorial was quickly rejected by the Senate and House, but the renewal of the Illinois-Wabash claim may have influenced Dearborn to see if Harrison could convince the tribes to cede the same lands to the United States. The recent transfer of the Louisiana territory from Spain to France also sparked the government's interest in securing the title to lands along the Ohio and Mississippi. The terms of the Treaty of San Ildefonso were publicly announced in December 1801, and the retrocession of Louisiana became effective the following March when Great Britain recognized the French Republic. President Jefferson was alarmed about a resurgence of French influence and was aware that American settlement of the Illinois country would provide a sizeable militia to protect the west.[13]

Harrison consequently invited the Eel River, Kaskaskia, Kickapoo, Piankashaw, Potawatomi, and Wea tribes to attend a conference in the fall of 1802 to discuss the Vincennes Tract and to learn whether the Indians, in the words of Secretary Dearborn, would "entertain a disposition to admit the United States in the place of the [Illinois and Wabash] Company." The governor opened the council by announcing that "your father, the

President, desires that you form towns and villages" and "will cause you to be furnished with horses, cattle, hogs, and implements of husbandry." Jefferson had corresponded with Dearborn regarding the northwest Indians and had suggested that "there is perhaps no method more irresistable of obtaining lands from them than by letting them get in debt, which when too heavy to be paid, they are always willing to lop off by a cession of land."[14]

Some five hundred Indians attended the September council. Moses Dawson's "fulsome biography" of William Henry Harrison, published in 1824, provides the only account of the proceedings and appears to confuse the Vincennes Tract with the 1775 purchase.[15] According to Dawson, the governor "urged the claim to the tract granted to the Wabash company as the one which had been set apart for the use of the settlement of Vincennes," which—if true—understandably prompted "marked indignation" by the tribes. The Indians argued that a grant by the Piankeshaws could not bind other tribes as "the Piankishaws owned but a small part of the country." With regard to the 1775 purchase, Dawson states that Harrison concluded that "*the Indians had been imposed upon . . .* [and] that none but the chiefs over whom the French of Vincennes had the greatest ascendency were concerned in the transaction."[16]

Dawson's account may be garbled, but what is certain is that the assembled tribes signed an agreement on September, 17, 1802, that authorized the Miami chiefs Little Turtle and Richardville and the Potawatomi chiefs To-pinee-bik and Winemak to "settle and adjust a treaty" with the United States.[17] According to Moses Dawson, the council "went off much better than was expected from the first appearances." By contrast, Reginald Horsman states that Harrison forced the agreement upon the reluctant Indians and, in doing so, "set the course which was to cause bitter American-Indian relations in the Old Northwest in the next decade."[18]

Jefferson renewed Harrison's commission as governor in February and appointed him as "a commissioner to enter into any treaty . . . which may be necessary with any Indian tribes northwest of the Ohio." Shortly thereafter Harrison received two letters, one official and one private, regarding the northwest Indians. The official missive was from Dearborn, who reported that the Miamis and Delawares were critical of the agreement reached at Vincennes (to which they were not parties). The private correspondence came from Jefferson, who candidly set forth "a more extensive view of our policy respecting the Indians." As he had noted to Dearborn, the president informed Harrison that to facilitate the acquisition of Indian lands, "we shall push our trading houses, and be glad to see the good & influential individuals among them run in debt, because we observe that when these debts get beyond what the individuals can pay, they become willing to lop [them off] by a cession of lands." Jefferson urged Harrison to treat with the Kaskaskias and purchase "their whole country" in light of the impending occupation of Louisiana by the French. "Whatever can now be obtained," he advised, "must be obtained quickly."[19]

Harrison endeavored during the spring of 1803 to persuade the recalcitrant tribes to proceed with the delineation of the Vincennes Tract. The Miamis in particular were opposed, led by Little Turtle and William Wells, a government Indian agent who was married to Little Turtle's daughter. Wells claimed that the Piankeshaws and Kaskaskias never entered into important transactions without the consent of the Miamis. Harrison, in reply, characterized this assertion as "a notorious falsehood" and pointed to the 1792 Putnam treaty. The governor then announced that tribes boycotting the upcoming council at Fort Wayne would not receive the annuities promised by the Treaty of Greenville. The conference began on the first of June and concluded six days later, when nine tribes agreed to a treaty setting forth the boundaries of the Vincennes Tract. In addition to the signatories to the September agreement, the Delawares, Miamis, and Shawnees gave their assent.[20]

The governor then turned his attention to the Kaskaskias. Prior to the conference, France agreed to sell the Louisiana territory to the United States for $15 million. It is not clear whether Harrison was aware of the purchase when he negotiated a treaty of cession with the Kaskaskias on August 13, 1803. Jean Baptiste DuCoigne, his son Louis DuCoigne, and four other Indians signed the treaty, which stated that the Kaskaskias "represent all the tribes of the Illinois Indians, originally called the Kaskaskia, Mitchigamia, Cahokia and Tamaroi." No mention was made of the Peoria, which would cause the United States to enter into a second treaty in 1818 for the same lands. The Kaskaskias, "finding themselves unable to occupy the extensive tract of country which of right belongs to them," ceded to the United States "all the lands in the Illinois country, which the said tribe has heretofore possessed, . . . reserving to themselves however the tract of about three hundred and fifty acres near the town of Kaskaskia . . . and also the right of locating one other tract of twelve hundred and eighty acres within the bounds of that now ceded." In return, the United States gave the tribe $580 and promised to protect the Kaskaskias, who feared extermination by the Potawatomis. In addition, the government agreed to increase the annual annuity payment to one thousand dollars and allow the tribe to live and hunt on the ceded lands owned by the United States.[21] The treaty made no mention of the 1773 transaction with the Illinois grantees.

Thomas Jefferson delivered his third annual message to Congress on October 17, 1803. After discussing the acquisition of Louisiana, the president noted that an "important transaction" had been concluded with the Kaskaskia Indians, and suggested the possibility of immediate settlement of the lands "extending along the Mississippi from the mouth of the Illinois to and up the Ohio." Harrison's 1803 treaties were ratified by the Senate in November. At about the same time, Spain formally transferred the Louisiana Territory to France, which in turn surrendered the vast expanse to the United States. In March 1804 Congress passed "An act making provision for the disposal of the public lands in the Indiana territory, and for other purposes." The act authorized the establishment of land offices at Detroit, Kaskaskia, and Vincennes and provided for the survey and sale of the lands "to which the Indian title has been extinguished." Of particular interest to the Illinois-Wabash shareholders, the 1804 Land Act also empowered the officials to examine prior claims "according to justice and equity" and recommend to Congress whether such claims should be rejected or confirmed.[22]

"THE REMAINING PIANKESHAW CLAIMS CAN BE EASILY PURCHASED"

On June 27, 1804, Secretary of War Henry Dearborn encouraged William Henry Harrison to seek three additional cessions from the Indians: the claims of the Sauk (Sac) Indians to land "on both sides of the Illinois"; the territory of the Piankeshaws between the Vincennes Tract and the Kaskaskia cession; and "the tract between the southern line of the Vincennes territory and the Ohio." Harrison would accomplish all this by the end of 1805. During this same period William McIntosh began to denounce the governor for his advocacy of slavery and partisan administration of territorial affairs. Another critic, of far greater import, emerged among the Indians: the Shawnee Prophet Lalawéthika, who as a youth was nicknamed Wahneshga (the Crazy Fellow) and who would later be known as Tenskwatawa (the Open Door).[23]

When Congress created the Indiana Territory in 1800, it provided that the transition to the "second stage" of government would take place when it was evident to the governor "that such is the wish of a majority of the freeholders."[24] On August 4, 1804, Harrison announced that an election would be held to determine whether to proceed to the next stage of government. In an odd twist of logic, William McIntosh accused Harrison of acting in defiance of popular wishes. The Scotsman also criticized the governor for sponsoring a convention that requested Congress to legalize slavery in the territory for ten years. The accusations, which appeared in a published letter signed by "A Freeholder in Knox County," triggered a rejoinder signed by "Gerald" but authored by Benjamin Parke, the attorney general of the Indiana Territory. Parke declared McIntosh "*an arrant knave, a profligate villain, a dastardly cheat, a perfidious rascal, an impertinent puppy, an absolute liar, and a mean, cowardly poltron.*" In return, McIntosh condemned the "unprincipled slanderer Parke," but declined his offer to duel, and thus avoided the fate that had befallen Alexander Hamilton in the previous month.[25] In December Harrison proclaimed that the voters favored the election of a territorial legislature, which took place the following month. The territory was now entitled to be represented by a delegate in Congress, and the General Assembly elected Benjamin Parke, who served until 1808, when he was appointed as a territorial judge.[26]

Harrison in the meantime heeded his instructions to obtain more land from the Indians. On August 18, 1804, the governor concluded a treaty at Vincennes with the Delawares, who ceded their claim to land located along the Ohio River to the west of Clark's Grant and south of the Vincennes Tract. The treaty acknowledged that the tribe was a recent occupant, and the United States obtained a second cession of the territory nine days later from the Piankeshaws.[27] The area that was ceded overlapped the territory conveyed to the Wabash grantees, yet the 1804 treaty makes no mention of the 1775 transaction. In his fourth annual message to Congress, Jefferson noted that the Delaware and Piankeshaw treaties ceded land along the Ohio and Wabash rivers, and he exulted that "produce of the settled country descending those rivers will no longer pass in review of the Indian frontier but in a small portion."[28] The Piankeshaws retained a "small portion" of riparian land just below the mouth of the Wabash but would relinquish their claim before the end of 1805.

In November 1804 the Sauk and Fox tribes ceded lands located west of the Illinois and Fox rivers and east of the Mississippi. Harrison traveled to St. Louis to acquire this large tract of land, situated north and west of the Kaskaskia cession. The governor took care to secure the federal right of preemption by including a provision whereby the tribes agreed "they will never sell their lands or any part thereof to any sovereign power, but the United States, nor to the citizens or subjects of any other sovereign power, nor to the citizens of the United States." According to the Sauk war chief, Black Hawk, the treaty was "the origin of all our serious difficulties with the whites."[29]

When Harrison returned to Vincennes, he discovered that Little Turtle and the Miami Indians were asserting that the Delawares had no right to sell the lands along the Ohio River, and that the Piankeshaws could not cede the lands without the consent of the other tribes concerned. To make matters worse, some of the Delaware chiefs who had signed the treaty claimed that their understanding of the agreement differed from the actual wording. The treaties, Secretary Dearborn informed Harrison, have "given very great offence to the Miamies and others . . . [who] pretend that the lands ceded by the Piankashaws & Delawares were common property in several nations." An irritated Harrison replied that the Miamis and the other Indians at Fort Wayne "are no more effected [sic] by the Treaties with the Delawares & Piankishaws than the Mandanes of the Missouri."[30]

Another conference was nevertheless arranged, and the Delaware, Eel River, Miami, Potawatomi, and Wea tribes met with the governor at "Grouseland," his two-story brick home. On August 21, 1805, the five tribes signed a treaty that not only confirmed the previous cessions by the Delawares and Piankeshaws but also ceded an additional tract of land located to the north of Clark's Grant in present-day southeastern Indiana.[31] Harrison confessed in his report that the price paid for the new cession was "greater than I could have wished," but he explained that "knowledge of the value of land is fast gaining ground amongst the Indians." The Piankeshaws were not a party to the treaty, but the governor assured Dearborn he could conclude an agreement with the tribe "in ten days" if so instructed. "I have informed the Secretary of War," Harrison wrote to Jefferson, "that *the remaining Piankeshaw claims can be easily purchased.*"[32]

Harrison was authorized in October "to close a bargain . . . with the Piankishaws" and shortly thereafter sent for the tribal leaders, some of whom were as far away as the Mississippi River. On Christmas Eve, Harrison informed Dearborn that he had experienced "more difficulty in assembling the Piankeshaw chiefs and bringing them to reasonable terms than I at first apprehended."[33] The treaty, which was signed on December 30, 1805, was the eighth treaty negotiated by the territorial governor. He would not

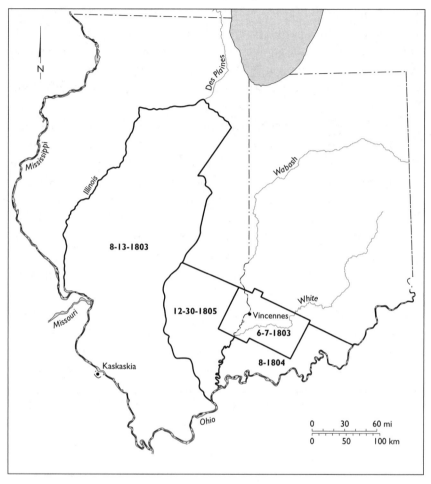

Lands ceded to the United States by the Illinois and Piankeshaw Indians, 1803–1805.
Map by Bill Nelson.

enter into another treaty with either the Piankeshaws or Kaskaskias, and
four years would pass before the Delaware, Eel River, Kickapoo, Miami,
Potawatomi, and Wea tribes would once again agree to cede lands within
the Indiana Territory. The Piankeshaws reserved the right to locate a tract
of two square miles (1,280 acres) but otherwise ceded approximately 2.5
million acres located west of the Wabash River and east of the 1803 Kaskaskia cession. In return the United States paid a sum of one thousand dollars, agreed to provide an additional annuity of three hundred dollars, and
promised to take the tribe "under their immediate care and patronage."

Harrison declared the treaty to be "highly advantageous to the United States" and thought it was not "a bad bargain for the Indians themselves." Jefferson received the news with a great deal of satisfaction and informed Congress that the cession "completes our possession of the whole of both banks of the Ohio from its source to near its mouth."[34]

Harrison and Jefferson were both pleased with the Piankeshaw cession. The views of Montour—one of the three Indians who signed the 1805 treaty—are unknown. We do know that Montour in 1775 had sold tribal lands to private purchasers and three decades later ceded the *same* tribal lands to the United States. We also know that Chief Montour led an eventful life: he received word in April 1784 of the American victory over Great Britain; participated two years later in the sale of the tribal village site just north of Vincennes; moved farther up the Wabash River; coordinated a planned attack in 1787 on supply boats ascending the river; and in 1802 signed the preliminary agreement that led to the demarcation of the Vincennes Tract. The United States by the end of 1805 was steadily engaged in buying America from the Indians, and Chief Montour was one of the many Indians who were compelled to participate.

TIPPECANOE AND MCINTOSH TOO

The relinquishment of title to tribal lands within the Indiana Territory was the primary subject of the treaties negotiated prior to 1806 by William Henry Harrison. The tribes of the Northwest Territory were cut off, at least on paper, from the southern tribes. The cessions engendered a burgeoning resistance movement led by the Shawnee warrior Tecumseh and his younger brother Tenskwatawa, the Shawnee Prophet. Their father had been killed in 1774 at the Battle of Point Pleasant, when the Shawnees fought alone against the Virginia militia. Influenced by the example of Joseph Brant, the two brothers urged the various tribes to unite. Tecumseh championed the idea that Brant had proposed in 1783: that the land was "as the common property of all Indian peoples, and it could be sold to the United States only with the consent of all Indian peoples."[35]

In November 1805 Tenskwatawa had a vision that transformed him from a dissolute alcoholic to a respected religious leader. His message was multifaceted, but in particular the Prophet stressed that white culture was deleterious to the Indians, white people would one day be judged and destroyed, and "virtuous Indians would repossess the land." According to an Ottawa Indian called the Trout, the Prophet proclaimed that the Americans "grew from the scum of the great water, when it was troubled by the Evil Spirit. . . . They have taken away your lands, which were not made for them."[36]

Tenskwatawa established a village in ceded territory at Greenville, Ohio, where his followers killed Indians accused of witchcraft, including Chief Tetapachsit of the Delawares, who had agreed to cede tribal lands. Shortly thereafter, Harrison challenged the "pretended prophet" by demanding that he "cause the sun to stand still" and perform other miraculous acts. Tenskwatawa had been informed that a solar eclipse was to take place on the sixteenth of June, and when he made good on his promise to "darken the sky," his influence spread rapidly among the Indians.[37]

Tenskwatawa moved in 1808 and established Prophet's Town near the confluence of the Tippecanoe and Wabash rivers, just north of the modern city of Lafayette, Indiana. "The Shawnese imposter has acquired . . . an ascendency over the minds of the Indians," Harrison notified Dearborn, adding that "his views are decidedly hostile to the United States." Tenskwatawa, however, protested that he did not intend "to lift up my hand against the Americans," and temporarily won over the governor during a visit to Vincennes in August. "The celebrated Shawnese Prophet . . . is rather possessed of considerable talents," Harrison reported, and "the influence which the Prophet has acquired will prove rather advantageous than otherwise to the United States."[38]

Partisan politics intensified during this period, and Harrison and his "Virginia aristocrats" were challenged both in the press and at the polls. On the side of the governor were men who held appointed positions, such as Benjamin Parke, Henry Hurst, George Wallace, William Prince, and Thomas Randolph. Harrison's leading detractors included John Rice Jones and William McIntosh, both early supporters who no longer held a government office. Upon his death in 1824 Jones was eulogized as "a friend of the indigent, the ignorant and distressed." Harrison, in contrast, described the Welshman as "one of the most abandoned men I ever knew." In a letter sent to the secretary of the treasury, Albert Gallatin, Harrison accused McIntosh of being a faithful servant of King George.[39]

McIntosh and Jones criticized Harrison's participation in the purchase of federal lands, which prompted the issuance of a treasury circular in 1808 that prohibited such activity by territorial officials.[40] The governor also suffered a political setback in 1809 when Jonathan Jennings defeated

Thomas Randolph in a bitter contest to become the territorial delegate to Congress. Harrison complained privately to Gallatin that McIntosh had advised the French residents to vote against Randolph, but the governor's protégé may have been affected more by the formation of the Illinois Territory, a traditional stronghold of support for the administration.

The Indiana Territory had been reduced in 1805 by the creation of the Michigan Territory and again in 1809 when the Illinois Territory was established. In response to Harrison's assertion that settlers "are much Cramped by the Vicinity of the Indian lands," President Madison authorized the purchase of "lands lying east of the Wabash and adjoining south on the lines of the Treaties of Fort Wayne and Grouseland."[41] The treaty conference was held at Fort Wayne in September 1809. The Miamis declared it was time to stop "the encroachments of the whites who were eternally purchasing their lands for less than the real value of them." The Potawatomis, however, stated that they had agreed to the sale of lands for the benefit of the Miamis, and insisted that the Miamis should now sell for their benefit. The Potawatomis had no viable claim to the territory at issue, unlike the Wea, Piankeshaw, and Kickapoo tribes, who were absent. The Shawnees also did not participate, and Tecumseh was away and unaware of the treaty negotiations.[42]

On September 30, 1809, the Delaware, Eel River, Miami, and Potawatomi Indians agreed to cede three tracts of land to the United States. The first was north of the Vincennes Tract; the second was a strip twelve miles wide along the western boundary of the Greenville line; and the third tract was an extension of the first, on the other side of the Wabash River. The first and third cessions were conditioned on the consent of the Weas and Kickapoos, respectively, which Harrison obtained by year's end. The tribes received approximately $10,000 in goods and $3,000 in annuities. The Kickapoos, in addition to providing their consent, separately ceded a tract west of the Wabash. The United States received more than 2.5 million acres for less than two cents per acre, and President Madison extended Harrison's tenure as territorial governor another three years.[43]

John Sugden characterizes the 1809 treaties as "a watershed" event because they "spread dissatisfaction to tribes such as the Miamis, who had previously been counted friends of the Americans, and exhausted what remained of the patience of Tecumseh and Tenskwatawa." The register of the Vincennes land office, John Badollet, called the governor a "moral c[h]ameleon" in a private letter to Albert Gallatin. William McIntosh openly questioned the fairness of the treaties, stating that if Harrison had in fact taken advantage of the Indians, he should be removed from office for inciting further unrest in the territory. This proved too much for Thomas Randolph, who cudgeled McIntosh with a club on the street in Vincennes. The "little Scotchman" carried a dirk, and once again Randolph ended up on the losing side, receiving several stab wounds.[44] McIntosh continued to voice his opposition and attended a meeting held at Badollet's office on the night of June 19, 1810, where he raised the possibility of bypassing official channels and speaking directly with the Indians, in order to ascertain whether they intended to wage war with the settlers. It is not clear when the public learned of this secret gathering, but on July 31, 1810, Harrison sued McIntosh in the General Court of the Indiana Territory, alleging that the defendant had uttered "scandalous words" with regard to his conduct at Fort Wayne. The governor sought nine thousand dollars in damages.[45]

Two weeks prior to filing his slander suit, Governor Harrison sent Tenskwatawa a message denying any wrongdoing by the United States and stating that "if lands have been purchased of those who did not own them they will be restored to the rightful owners." Tecumseh, in response, requested a meeting with Harrison. The Shawnee leader descended the Wabash River with some four hundred warriors, arrived on August 12, 1810, and camped a mile or so above Vincennes. Three days later he led some of his followers into town to a clearing near Grouseland, where Harrison awaited him. Several days passed as Tecumseh set forth his views in speeches that Harrison described as "sufficiently insolent." On August 20 the Shawnee denounced the village chiefs who had signed the 1809 treaties. Tecumseh also spoke about Indian land rights, declaring that "white people have no right to take the land from the Indians, because they had it first; it is theirs." If Indians choose to sell their lands, "all must join" because, according to Tecumseh, all Indians "have equal rights to the unoccupied land."[46]

Harrison, in reply, denied that the United States had treated the tribes unjustly and disagreed that the Indians owned land in common. While the governor was speaking, Tecumseh stood in anger and spoke sharply, creating "a tense moment" that nearly became violent. The next day Tecumseh stated that he had been encouraged by two men who "are endeavouring to fill the minds of the Indians with evil towards the United States." The

first man appeared in Prophet's Town shortly after the Fort Wayne treaties were completed, giving assurances that Harrison would remain in
office for only two years and "would be succeeded by a good man who
was a true friend to the Indians." The second man, Tecumseh informed
the governor, "told me I must go to Vincennes and make my objections
to the purchase of land from the Indians, and not be afraid to speak very
loud to you." Harrison promised to send the words of Tecumseh to the
president but reiterated that the 1809 treaties would remain in place. According to Moses Dawson, the two men met privately that evening, and
Tecumseh ended their conversation by noting that if hostilities occurred,
the president would "sit in his town, and drink his wine, whilst you and
I will have to fight it out."[47]

In his 1939 biography of "Old Tippecanoe," Freeman Cleaves states
that the second man mentioned by Tecumseh was William McIntosh.
Without mentioning McIntosh by name, Harrison reported to Secretary
of War William Eustis that Tecumseh had received information "from
a small factious party here headed by a scotch tory who would not hesi-
tate to adopt any measure that would be likely to do me an injury."
Harrison urged the territorial legislature to impose a penalty on "those
who, by improper interferences and by circulating falsehoods amongst
the Indians, counteract the intentions of the government, and lay the
foundation for distrust and enmities which may produce the most serious
consequences."[48]

McIntosh, who had already shown that he could defend himself, was
not idle. On the third of September he wrote a letter to President Madison, in which he accused Harrison of having "a double interest" in the
1809 cessions. In January 1811 McIntosh submitted depositions that alleged improper conduct by Harrison in business dealings. Harrison in turn
collected testimonials to counter the "barefaced falsehoods." The various
documents were filed in the State Department, "and nothing was heard of
the matter on the floor of Congress."[49]

The stage was set for Harrison's slander suit, which was tried in April
1811. The jury concluded that McIntosh had defamed the governor and
awarded four thousand dollars in damages. McIntosh was forced to sell
land to satisfy the judgment, but two thirds of the property was returned,
and Harrison eventually donated the remaining land to children who became orphans during the War of 1812.[50] Following the conclusion of the
trial, the governor reported with satisfaction to Secretary of War William

Eustis that "the rascally calumniator begg'd for mercy, and his council labour'd only for a mitigation of damages."[51]

Harvey Lewis Carter notes that by prevailing in his slander suit, Harrison "emerged triumphant over his political enemies in the territory." By the end of the year the governor had also dealt a severe blow to the Indian resistance movement. On July 27, 1811, Tecumseh appeared again at Vincennes and informed Harrison that he was about "to set out on a visit to the Southern Tribes to get them to unite with those of the North."[52] When Tecumseh descended the Wabash River, Harrison seized his opportunity. In the last week of September a force of one thousand men marched north from Vincennes. The army camped on November 6 near the confluence of the Wabash and Tippecanoe rivers, just two miles from Prophet's Town. The next day, before dawn, some five hundred Indians—including Chippewa, Kickapoo, Ottawa, Piankeshaw, Potawatomi, Shawnee, Winnebago, and Wyandot tribesmen—attacked at daylight and then withdrew. According to one estimate, sixty-eight soldiers and about fifty warriors were killed. Benjamin Parke and Thomas Randolph both participated in the battle, but only Parke returned to Vincennes.[53]

The Americans entered the deserted Prophet's Town the next day and destroyed it. August Derleth argues that the Battle of Tippecanoe "accomplished nothing for the United States" and caused "a large number of the tribes . . . to throw in their fortunes with the British." John Mahon characterizes the encounter as "the opening battle of the War of 1812."[54] William Henry Harrison and Tecumseh would "fight it out" as predicted, and the disgraced Tenskwatawa would temporarily relocate in Canada. By the end of the war the resistance movement of the northwest Indians was effectively at an end, and Harrison was a hero in the eyes of many Americans. As early as February 1812, his accomplishments were lauded in verse:

> When ruthless savages with impious hands,
> Leagu'd to destroy and lay waste our lands,
> Unterrified amidst the dire alarms,
> Without dismay thou call'd, to arms! to arms![55]

Even though the entirety of the Indiana Territory was not yet *"our lands,"* the poet and his subject shared the belief that it was inevitable that the "ruthless savages" would soon yield. "Is one of the fairest portions of the globe to remain . . . the haunt of a few wretched savages," Harrison asked the territorial legislature prior to Tippecanoe, "when it seems destined by the Creator to . . . be the seat of civilization, of science, and of true religion?" In similar fashion, John Quincy Adams in 1802 had queried whether "the fields and the valleys which a beneficent God has framed to teem with the life of innumerable multitudes [shall] be condemned to everlasting barrenness?"[56] John Winthrop's dehumanizing doctrine of *vacuum domicilium*, as well as John Locke's labor theory of property, were alive and well in nineteenth-century America.

Following the war, Harrison moved to Ohio. After serving in the House of Representatives he was defeated as a candidate for governor in 1820 but was later elected to the Senate. In 1840, at the age of sixty-seven, "Old Tippecanoe" capitalized on his fame to deny Martin Van Buren a second term as president. After delivering the longest inaugural address ever, he developed pneumonia and died on April 4, 1841, just thirty-one days into his term. William Henry Harrison, the first president to die while in office, was eulogized by scores of individuals, including a Pennsylvania politician who praised him for effecting "the surrender of more than sixty millions of acres of land by its savage proprietors."[57]

WAR AND PEACE

The Illinois and Piankeshaws were not immune to the resistance movement. However, following the cession of most of their homelands, their primary concern was survival. In the spring of 1804 the brother-in-law of Chief DuCoigne was killed near Kaskaskia, by either Kickapoo or Potawatomi Indians, and Harrison was informed that "Ducoigne as well as all his people are in a great dread at present." To his credit, the governor made an effort to respond, pointing out that the United States in 1803 had promised the Kaskaskias "protection against every Indian Tribe or Foreign power equal to what is enjoyed by their own Citizens."[58] The government also responded in the fall of 1807 when the last Piankeshaw village on the east side of the Wabash was destroyed by white settlers. The tribal members relocated to the Illinois country, where they successfully repelled a second attack. John Gibson, secretary of the Indiana Territory, instructed Captain William Hargrove to "see what can be done about obtaining a satisfactory adjustment with the Indians," adding that the "Territory is in no shape for a race war with the Indians." Governor Harrison sent tents, blankets, and

kettles, and Hargrove was directed to remind the settlers that "such conduct as this must not occur again."[59]

Some Piankeshaw Indians survived by providing information to the
Americans. A warrior named Yellow Bird informed Gibson in 1807 that
the Indians on the White River were "threatening to drive the Americans back over the Ohio." In the summer of 1810 Harrison reported to
William Eustis that the Piankeshaw chief Gros Bled had warned him
that Tenskwatawa was planning to enter Vincennes under the guise of
friendship and then "surprise this Town."[60] Not all Piankeshaws were
opposed to the Prophet, as indicated by Harrison's statement in 1811 to
Ninian Edwards, governor of the Illinois Territory, that the Prophet's
force included "a few Pankeshaws." Edwards informed Harrison that the
Kaskaskias had been invited "to the Prophet's congress" to discuss "the
subject of recovering their Lands."[61] During 1811 Jean Baptiste DuCoigne
died, and leadership of the Kaskaskias passed to his son, Louis Jefferson
DuCoigne.

Harrison recommended in January 1812 that half of the Piankeshaw
annuity be confiscated "in Consequence of their having permitted their
Warriors to Join the Prophet." In March some of the Piankeshaws who
had allied with Tenskwatawa returned to Vincennes. Other Indians, however, stepped up attacks on isolated settlements. "The hopes which I had
entertained of our being able to avoid a war are entirely dissipated," Harrison told Eustis, noting that a hired hand, four children, and the wife of
Isaac Hutson had been "most Cruelly murdered" just thirty-five miles
northwest of Vincennes (near present-day Hutsonville, Illinois).[62]

The Piankeshaws were physically divided during the ensuing war between the United States and Great Britain. According to Dorothy Libby,
at the outset of the conflict "about half of the Piankashaws (120–150 warriors, or 480–600 persons) had just moved to Peoria . . . and . . . the other
half had joined the hostile Shawnee Prophet." The Kickapoo, Ottawa,
Ojibwa, and Potawatomi tribes also congregated near Peoria. Although
these Indians were removed from most of the hostilities, other Indians
inflicted defeats on the Americans in the fall of 1812: killing soldiers and
others who had evacuated Fort Dearborn (Chicago), decimating the "Pi-
geon Roost" settlement near the Ohio River in southern Indiana, and
besieging both Fort Harrison (Terre Haute, Indiana) and Fort Wayne.
On January 22, 1813, British and Native forces won an important victory at the Raisin River, thirty miles south of Detroit, but provided the

Americans with an emotional rallying cry ("Remember the Raisin!") when captured soldiers were brutalized by inebriated Indians.[63]

In the fall of 1812, as the United States was reeling from defeats at Detroit and elsewhere, Governor Ninian Edwards and Colonel William Russell of Vincennes succeeded in destroying three Kickapoo, Potawatomi, and Piankeshaw villages at Peoria Lake. The following year Iowa, Kickapoo, Mesquakie, Piankeshaw, and Sauk Indians were living near the confluence of the Mississippi and Des Moines rivers. The governor of the Missouri Territory, William Clark, was concerned about this Native presence upriver from St. Louis and urged the Indians to remove farther west. By the summer of 1813 the Piankeshaws and some of the other tribes had relocated on the Missouri River, close to the mouth of the Grand River. These Indians were effectively removed from conflict with the United States but were now within striking distance of another determined foe: the Osage Nation.[64]

"We have met the enemy," Captain Oliver Hazard Perry reported to General William Henry Harrison, "and they are ours—two ships, two brigs, one schooner, and a sloop." By defeating the British Navy on Lake Erie, the U.S. naval commander Perry enabled the Americans to reclaim Detroit on September 30, 1813. Within a week Harrison's troops engaged a combined British and Indian army, led by General Henry Procter and Tecumseh, near the Thames River in southwestern Ontario. On October 5 Tecumseh was killed on the battlefield. The war would continue, but as noted by Armstrong Starkey, the United States "had defeated their most dangerous enemy in the Northwest . . . [and] the era of the removal of the Indian peoples was at hand."[65]

The Delaware, Miami, Ottawa, Seneca, Shawnee, and Wyandot tribes assembled in Greenville in the summer of 1814 and signed a treaty "of peace and friendship." At the same time a delegation of American diplomats was present in Ghent, Belgium, waiting to begin peace negotiations with their British counterparts. When the commissioners from Great Britain finally arrived in August, they informed the Americans that the creation of a "buffer" state for the northwest Indians would be an essential condition of any treaty. The American delegation duly informed the secretary of state, James Monroe, that the British were also insisting "neither the United States nor Great Britain should ever hereafter have the right to purchase or acquire any part of the territory thus recognised as belonging to the Indians." In reply, the American diplomats assured their counterparts that the notion of an Indian buffer state "would be instantaneously rejected." The Americans also argued that the prohibition on purchasing Indian lands "professes to take from Great Britain a privilege which she had not, [and] actually deprives the United States of a right exclusively belonging to them."[66] In support of this claimed exclusive right, the commissioners pointed to the preemption language set forth in the fifth article of the 1795 Treaty of Greenville.

The negotiators in Ghent were not yet aware that the British military had set fire to Washington and were preparing to attack Baltimore. On the fourth of September the British argued that the inclusion of the "preemption" guarantee in the Greenville Treaty actually proved that "but for that stipulation the Indians had a general right to dispose of [their lands]." This "negative inference" argument of the British commissioners touched on the sensitive issue of Indian land rights, and the American delegation responded with a statement that is remarkably similar to the position Chief Justice John Marshall would adopt nine years later in *Johnson v. McIntosh*: "The Indians . . . are so far dependent as not to have the right to dispose of their lands to any private persons, nor to any Power other than the United States. . . . The treaty of Greenville . . . was merely declaratory of the public law, in relation to the parties, founded on principles previously and universally recognised."[67]

The adamant stance of the United States caused the British diplomats to ask for new instructions, and the Crown's advisors eventually dropped their demand for an Indian buffer state. The Americans were asked instead to place the Indian tribes "in every respect in the same situation as that in which they stood before the commencement of hostilities."[68] The commissioners signed the document on Christmas Eve. On January 8, 1815, Andrew Jackson defeated the British at New Orleans, unaware that the two countries had agreed to a cessation of hostilities. The Senate thereafter ratified the treaty on the sixteenth of February, and the United States and Great Britain were at peace. Although the British remained in Canada, they would no longer actively assist the Indians in the United States. The tribes of the Old Northwest were on their own.

REMOVAL

Less than a month after the ratification of the Treaty of Ghent, Secretary of War James Monroe named William Clark, Ninian Edwards, and

René Auguste Chouteau as commissioners to negotiate treaties with the Indians scattered throughout the Illinois and Missouri territories.[69] Given the dislocation and diminishing numbers of the Natives, it was not a simple task to ascertain whether particular tribes were still in existence. "Fifty or sixty years ago," wrote Benjamin Parke, "the Peorias, Cahokias, Micheganians, Kaskaskias, and Peankashaws, especially the two last, were numerous and war-like, [but] three of those tribes are now, I believe, extinct, the others nearly so." Parke was mistaken: the *Missouri Gazette* in St. Louis reported that some Peoria Indians were still residing fifty miles south at Ste. Genevieve, although "reduced to 10 or 15 heads of families." Moreover, when the "tribes of the Illinois nation of Indians" signed a treaty with the United States in 1818, signatories included not only four Kaskaskias but also two Tamaroa, three Michigamea, five Cahokia, and eleven Peoria Indians.[70]

Clark, Edwards, and Chouteau had arrived by the first week of July at Portage des Sioux, located north of St. Louis on the Mississippi River. The commissioners informed Monroe that some of the assembled Indians, including the Sauk, Fox, and Kickapoo tribes, were reluctant to make peace but that "with the Pattawatomies of Illinois river, and the small band of Piankeshaws who are prisoners of war, we shall probably conclude a treaty in a day or two." The Piankeshaws in question had been held as prisoners in St. Louis since the fall of 1814, after being captured in central Missouri during retaliatory raids by the Americans. As predicted, the Potawatomis and Piankeshaws signed separate treaties on July 18, 1818. Five Piankeshaw Indians—none signatories to prior treaties—agreed to "recognize, re-establish, and confirm, all and every treaty, contract, or agreement, heretofore concluded between the United States and the said Piankishaw tribe or nation."[71]

Although the commissioners were told not to seek any cessions, the Piankeshaws in Missouri desired to sell the land that had been reserved in the 1805 treaty, in order to obtain "ploughs, horses, farming utensils, &c., which are necessary to enable them to make a new establishment."[72] The sale of the reserved tract of two square miles, which had never been located, was authorized in October, and the "indenture" was signed on January 3, 1818, by Chekommia (Big River), the "principal chief and head man of the Piankeshaw." The United States paid one thousand dollars to the tribe, which was described as "being reduced in number." The Piankeshaw Indians were now officially a landless people.[73]

In the tradition of Thomas More, John Winthrop, and Emer de Vattel, President James Monroe declared in December 1817 that "no tribe or people have a right to withhold from the wants of others more than is necessary for their own support and comfort." The "others" were American settlers, and what they wanted was to purchase the lands once occupied by the Indians, including the Illinois. William Henry Harrison, however, had failed to extinguish the claims of the Peoria Indians, who had not joined with the other Illinois tribes in signing the treaty of August 13, 1803. To finalize the extinguishment of Native title to the lands of the Illinois confederacy, the Peoria, Kaskaskia, Michigamea, Cahokia, and Tamaroa tribes were invited to a treaty conference in the fall of 1818. On September 25 the United States compensated the tribes with goods worth two thousand dollars and promised "to pay to the said Peoria tribe, for the term of twelve years, an annuity of three hundred dollars, in money, merchandize, or domestic animals." In return, the five tribes ceded "all their land to the United States." In a reversal of roles, the United States agreed in the treaty's final article to cede to the Peoria a tract of land in the Missouri territory consisting of six hundred and forty acres of land.[74] On December 3, 1818, Illinois was admitted into the Union as the twenty-first state.

The tribes that had contracted with the Illinois and Wabash grantees in 1773 and 1775 now resided west of the Mississippi and were under the charge of William Clark, the governor of the Missouri Territory. Clark reported in 1819 that the Piankeshaws who had agreed to peace in 1815 had been sent to southeastern Missouri, where they lived "on scanty subsistence obtained principally from Game out of the Swamps and an annuity of about $800 in merchandise."[75] Piankeshaw and Peoria Indians were also living farther west along the White River in the Ozark Mountains. Indian agent Richard Graham was officially directed in 1821 to move the Indians from Ohio, Indiana, and Illinois as far west as possible, closer to the Osage Nation. Tribal reserves were created for the Delawares, Shawnees, and Kickapoos, but other tribes—such as the Piankeshaws and Peorias—also settled in the same territory. As noted by Stephen Warren, "the forced migration of the Kickapoos, Delawares, Shawnees, Piankashaws, and Peorias into the northwestern Ozarks laid the groundwork for an increasingly desperate struggle with the Osages over diminishing resources."[76]

The case of *Johnson v. McIntosh* was argued before the United States Supreme Court in February 1823. At about the same time, representatives of the Cherokee, Delaware, Kickapoo, Piankeshaw, Peoria, and Shawnee peoples convened a tribal council in northern Arkansas. The tribes hoped that their eastern kinsmen would cross the Mississippi and join them, and that the United States would recognize their proposed confederacy. As Grant Foreman has noted, the assembled tribes also developed a "plan of aggression by which they hoped to wrest from the Osage the fine hunting and agricultural land of the present eastern Oklahoma, with its salt springs and lead mines."[77] Although their efforts were largely unsuccessful, the displaced and diminished tribes were forming alliances and looking to the west for land, sustenance, and survival. The Illinois Indians had crossed the Mississippi, and the Piankeshaws no longer inhabited the Wabash Valley. The tribes were not represented when the issue of Indian land rights was debated in *Johnson v. McIntosh*, and having twice sold their lands, they were not directly affected by the outcome.

13

THE SHAREHOLDERS REGROUP

The Illinois and Wabash Land Company could easily have folded in 1804. Almost all the leading proponents of the company's affairs were gone from the scene. Silas Deane, David Franks, William Murray, James Wilson, John Nicholson, Barnard Gratz, William Smith, and John Steinmetz were dead; Michael Gratz was an invalid; and Robert Morris was bankrupt and disgraced. For more than a quarter of a century, the united companies had tried and failed to obtain confirmation of the land purchases from the Illinois and Piankeshaw Indians. Both Great Britain and Virginia refused to sanction the transactions. The Boudinot committee of the Continental Congress in November 1781 recommended rejection of the claims, and petitions to Congress in 1788, 1790, 1791, and 1797 were unsuccessful. The already dim prospects for success faded even further after the 1800 national election and the ascendancy of the Jeffersonian Republicans. Most of the leading shareholders of the Illinois and Wabash Land Company were Federalists, whose party lost control of the presidency and the House of Representatives in 1800 and of the Senate two years later.[1]

On March 3, 1802, William Smith and John Shee nevertheless submitted yet another memorial on behalf of the "Ilinois and Ouabache Land Companies," which was summarily rejected by a committee of the Senate but never acted upon in the House of Representatives.[2] After Smith died, General Shee once again petitioned Congress on October 17, 1803, prompted by unofficial publications announcing the purchase by a government agent "of a considerable tract of country from the Kaskaskias tribe of Indians."[3] The reports were accurate: Governor Harrison had persuaded

Chief DuCoigne and the Kaskaskias to cede nearly 8 million acres of land to the United States. The Senate indefinitely postponed consideration of the 1803 memorial, but the House took action in February 1804, adopting the following committee recommendation: "The lands claimed by the petitioner have been ceded to the United States by treaty, . . . *and inasmuch as the United States are already rightfully possessed of those lands,* . . . the prayer of the petitioner ought not be granted."[4]

Because both houses of Congress failed to take action in the same session, the Illinois-Wabash Company managed to avoid a conclusive rejection of its claims. Future prospects, however, were bleak. Yet by the fall of 1804 the shareholders were again publicly asserting their claims and would continue to do so until the Supreme Court issued its decision in *Johnson v. McIntosh* in February 1823. Although this persistence appears illogical, there are several reasons why the shareholders continued to press their claims.

First, there was a lot at stake. If the company could somehow persuade Congress to accept its claims—or even to agree to its compromise proposal—the shareholders would become quite wealthy. As long as there was a chance, however slim, it was a chance worth pursuing. Moreover, their petitions had *not* been uniformly rejected: a committee of the Continental Congress had recommended in June 1788 that "a reasonable Compensation in Land should be made," and a committee of the House of Representatives had declared in April 1792 that the deeds were "sufficient to extinguish the Indian title to the lands therein described." Even though Virginia had nullified the Transylvania purchase, Richard Henderson and his colleagues had been rewarded with land, and members of Congress believed the Yazoo lands controversy should be settled by compensating the claimants. Perhaps the Illinois-Wabash claims would be resolved in a similar manner. "We may get nothing," Jacob Gratz told his older brother, Joseph, "but if any will be a fortune."[5]

There was also a new forum in which the shareholders could seek confirmation of the purchases. On March 26, 1804, Congress passed "An act making provision for the disposal of the public lands in the Indiana territory, and for other purposes." Land offices were established at Detroit, Vincennes, and Kaskaskia, and procedures were set forth for the sale of lands recently ceded to the United States.[6] In sections three and four of the 1804 Act, Congress authorized land commissioners to examine prior claims "according to justice and equity" and recommend to Congress whether such claims should be confirmed.[7] Although the jurisdiction of the commissions did not expressly encompass grants from Indian tribes to private individuals, the Illinois-Wabash Land Company filed claims in both the Vincennes and Kaskaskia land offices.

A third reason why the united companies did not fold was that a new generation of individuals emerged to assume leadership roles. As noted at the conclusion of chapter 11, John Brinton of Philadelphia had married John Steinmetz's daughter in 1795 and by 1802 was already serving as the secretary of the Illinois-Wabash Company. Simon Gratz was initially the most involved of Michael Gratz's five sons, although the youngest child, Benjamin, would eventually play an important role as well. In Maryland Samuel Chase, Jr., and Solomon Etting, the son-in-law of Barnard Gratz, became active participants. But without question the driving force of the Illinois and Wabash Land Company in the nineteenth century was Robert Goodloe Harper.[8] Like the late James Wilson, he was a gifted lawyer with many years of experience in speculative ventures involving Indian lands. Most of all, Harper was ambitious, and supremely confident that he possessed the legal skills necessary to establish the validity of the Illinois and Wabash purchases.

ROBERT GOODLOE HARPER

Robert Goodloe Harper for most of his life looked to the west and sought to enrich himself from the purchase and sale of lands that were occupied by Indian tribes. In the summer of 1783 Richard Henderson offered the young man a job on a surveying expedition to Kentucky and Tennessee. Harper purchased five thousand acres and later remarked that the journey "gave me a considerable knowledge of the Western Countries, and a turn for land speculations, which had no inconsiderable influence on my future affairs."[9]

A year later Harper attended the College of New Jersey (Princeton University), where he won a gold medal for his forensic eloquence. Following graduation he moved to South Carolina and was admitted to the bar. But Harper was not accepted by the Charleston aristocracy, and in 1787 he decided to relocate upcountry in South Carolina. When the Georgia legislature contracted in 1789 to sell 20 million acres to three land companies, Harper purchased shares in the South Carolina Yazoo Company. He also traveled to Philadelphia in 1791 to sell stock in the venture. However, because the land companies were unable to fulfill the

Robert Goodloe Harper. Courtesy of the Maryland Historical Society (Image ID 1986.24).

terms of the agreement, the lands were not granted, and Harper found himself deeply in debt due to his speculative investments.[10]

The time spent in Philadelphia gave Harper a "relish for the northern states which contributed not a little . . . towards inducing me to accept a seat in Congress." In the fall of 1794 he won two elections: to fill a vacated seat in the Third Congress, and to serve a full term in the upcoming

Fourth Congress. James Madison suggested to Thomas Jefferson that the new delegate "will be a valuable acquisition," but Harper disappointed the Virginians by becoming a Federalist. During his six years in the House of Representatives, Harper would chair the powerful Committee on Ways and Means, endorse the Alien and Sedition Acts, support the undeclared war with France, and favor Burr over Jefferson. A fellow Federalist, Fisher Ames of Massachusetts, remarked in a letter in 1798 that "Harper is a fine fellow, but praise has half spoiled him."[11]

Biographer Joseph Cox acknowledges that his subject is often represented "as the stereotype of the very worst in Federalism," but argues that undue emphasis of his xenophobia results in an "oversimplified interpretation of Harper's congressional career." Eric Papenfuse notes that Harper "is traditionally remembered as an extreme example of unthinking, reactionary conservatism in an era of intense partisanship and bitter sectional conflict." David Hackett Fischer, who describes Harper as "the McCarthy of his generation," is even less forgiving: "Acquaintances were quick to notice his obsessive egoism and compulsive ambition for wealth, fame, and power. We might take the measure of the man in his characteristic Congressional pose—in his pompous, pretentious, pidgeon-breasted posture, thumbs hooked in figured waistcoat, chin tucked in spotless cravat, mouth turned up at the corners in an infuriating smile of insolent self-satisfaction."[12]

Harper was not yet affiliated with the united companies when the 1797 memorial was submitted to Congress. The House and Senate committees that considered this memorial jointly determined to adopt the 1792 Senate committee report, which concluded that "these companies had no legal title to the said lands." Harper took no public position on the 1797 memorial, which was never put to a vote by the full House of Representatives.

The Upper Mississippi Company, Tennessee Company, Georgia Mississippi Company, and Georgia Company resorted to bribery to obtain Georgia's agreement in 1795 to sell off its claim to the Indian-occupied Yazoo lands. Harper invested in the Georgia Company and also provided testimonials to Robert Morris and John Nicholson to facilitate the sale of Yazoo lands owned by the North American Land Company.[13] A dramatic change of events, however, took place on February 13, 1796, when newly elected state legislators voted to repeal the Yazoo statute, thus precipitating the legal struggle that would eventually reach the Supreme Court.

Harper would be involved in virtually all aspects of this dispute, including the *Fletcher v. Peck* litigation, which not only concerned the validity of the Yazoo purchases but also raised fundamental issues regarding the nature of Indian property rights.

In February 1797 Harper published a lengthy pamphlet, titled *The Case of the Georgia Sales on the Mississippi Considered*, which appended Alexander Hamilton's legal opinion that the repeal of the Yazoo purchases contravened the Constitution's dictate that "no state shall pass a law impairing the obligations of contract." Harper made a similar argument and also rejected the "devolution" theory that the western lands were "Crown lands" that were transferred to the United States. He contended that the 1763 Proclamation did not alter the western limits of the colonies, but he did not go so far as to challenge the king's authority to issue the proclamation.[14] Years later, when arguing on behalf of the Illinois and Wabash shareholders, Harper would assert that "proclamations of the British King, in matters of property, cannot have the force of laws."[15]

Harper's financial dealings were so well-known that the Philadelphia *Aurora* publically commented on "*Mr. Harper's* speculations" in February 1799. Even before the Sixth Congress commenced the following December, the ambitious Federalist had decided to retire from politics at the end of the term. While continuing to represent South Carolina, Harper moved in 1799 to Baltimore, where he opened a law office. He was a friend of Secretary of War James McHenry, who had numerous connections in Maryland, but according to Joseph Cox, there were additional factors that influenced the congressman's decision: "Baltimore was as far north as he could go and still feel comfortable as a southerner, and Maryland was . . . the most solidly Federalist of the southern states. But there were other, purely personal reasons that figured in the choice. In the fall of 1798, as he journeyed to campaign for reelection Harper had been extremely fortunate in being introduced to one of the South's leading families, the Carrolls of Carrollton."[16]

When Harper began courting Catherine Carroll, her father opposed the match due to the fact that Harper owed in excess of thirteen thousand dollars, and perhaps because his daughter's suitor had narrowly avoided a duel.[17] Carroll ordered Harper to stay away from Catherine until his debts were paid, his income was steady, and he owned a house, horse, and carriage. The thirty-six-year-old lawyer responded by preparing an autobiographical sketch, detailing his life and explaining that the cause of his indebtedness was land speculation. Carroll relented, and in 1801 the couple was joined in matrimony by Bishop John Carroll.[18] Their marriage proved unhappy and bittersweet: Catherine was extravagant and demanding, Robert was aloof and often absent, and several of their children died tragically young.[19]

The Harpers entertained guests lavishly at their estate, "Oakland," which featured a bust of Alexander Hamilton in the breakfast room and a dairy designed in the form of a Greek temple. Harper proved a better lawyer than investor, and Charles Carroll soon allowed his son-in-law to manage his extensive legal affairs. Harper also became acquainted with some of Carroll's partners in the Illinois and Wabash Land Company. Supreme Court Justice Samuel Chase offered assistance in securing clients, and Harper developed a friendship with Chase's namesake son. In 1804 Harper was involved in the formation of the Baltimore Water Company and served on the board of directors with the Gratz son-in-law Solomon Etting. It is likely that Harper also met Thomas Johnson and other shareholders residing in Maryland.[20]

Although he had left Congress, Robert Goodloe Harper remained an ardent Federalist. In the fall of 1804 he sought to return to the House of Representatives, but lost to the Republican candidate. By this time the Federalists had relinquished control of the executive and legislative branches but were entrenched in the federal judiciary. President John Adams, in what he later described as "the proudest act of my life," nominated Secretary of State John Marshall to be the fourth chief justice of the Supreme Court. Although Harper and other "High Federalists" were displeased by the choice of the moderate Marshall, the outgoing Sixth Congress confirmed the appointment on January 27, 1801. Shortly thereafter the same legislators passed the Judiciary Act of 1801, enabling Adams to name sixteen loyal Federalists as new federal judges. On the third of March, the last day of Adams's administration, the Senate approved nominations for forty-two justices of the peace, including William Marbury of Maryland.[21]

President Thomas Jefferson famously declared in his inaugural address: "We are all Republicans—we are all Federalists." Despite this conciliatory gesture, the Republican-dominated Congress passed the Judiciary Act of 1802, which repealed the 1801 Judiciary Act and canceled the next scheduled session of the Supreme Court.[22] Political tensions were further exacerbated by William Marbury's lawsuit to force the new secretary of state, James Madison, to deliver his commission as justice of the peace. Although Marbury did not prevail, the Supreme Court held in *Marbury v. Madison* (1803) that the judiciary is empowered to invalidate legislation in conflict with the Constitution.[23]

A few months after the *Marbury* decision Justice Samuel Chase expressed his view, in a charge to a Baltimore grand jury, that "the independence of the National Judiciary [was] shaken to its foundation" by the repeal of the 1801 Judiciary Act. In response, the Republican press resurrected the 1778 flour scandal and otherwise lambasted "this monster in politics." President Jefferson, who had been denounced as an atheist by Chase during the 1800 election, asked a Maryland congressman whether "this seditious and official attack on the principles of our Constitution . . . [should] go unpunished?" On January 5, 1804, Representative John Randolph of Virginia moved for an inquiry into the conduct of Justice Chase, and seven articles of impeachment were reported on March 26. The first session of the Eighth Congress ended the next day, which caused the Senate trial of Samuel Chase to be delayed until the following year.[24]

Chase immediately asked Robert Goodloe Harper to serve as defense counsel. Harper agreed, as did Luther Martin and Philip Barton Key of Maryland, Charles Lee of Virginia, and Joseph Hopkinson of Pennsylvania. When the second session of the Eighth Congress convened in November, the impeachment articles were revised and presented to the Senate. On February 4, 1805, the trial commenced before packed galleries, with Vice President Aaron Burr as the presiding officer. The presence of Burr, who had fatally wounded Alexander Hamilton the previous July, caused someone to remark that formerly it had been the practice *"to arraign the murderer before the judge, but now we behold the judge arraigned before the murderer."* The closing arguments lasted a week, due in part to the delivery by Harper of "a very able speech of some seven hours."[25]

On the first of March Burr announced that the Senate had acquitted Chase. The successful defense enhanced Robert Goodloe Harper's reputation as a skilled lawyer. "I never witnessed, in any place," Senator William Plumer of New Hampshire remarked to his son, "such a display of learning as the counsel for the accused exhibited." Maurice Baxter concurs, characterizing the defense of Chase as "probably Harper's best argument." Although Harper failed again in 1806 in his bid to return to Congress, his legal career was flourishing. In 1807 he successfully defended Erik Bollman, who was accused of treason in connection with Aaron Burr's expedition to the Louisiana Territory.[26] Harper thereafter participated in the celebrated case of *Fletcher v. Peck*, successfully arguing that Georgia could not impair the vested rights of the Yazoo speculators.

At the same time that Harper established himself as one of the nation's preeminent lawyers, the Illinois-Wabash shareholders presented their claims to the Vincennes and Kaskaskia land commissioners. By the Act of March 26, 1804, Congress directed that the register and the receiver at the Detroit, Vincennes, and Kaskaskia land offices assess the validity of preexisting land claims and deliver to the treasury secretary "a full report of all the claims filed."[27] The final decision rested with Congress. Most of the nearly three thousand claims were based on alleged land grants by France, Great Britain, Virginia, and the United States, but in a few instances the claimants relied on Indian deeds.[28] The largest claims presented for consideration were the four tracts sold to the Illinois and Wabash purchasers in 1773 and 1775.

"NOT A SHADOW OF A TITLE TO SUPPORT THEIR CLAIM"

Congress originally required that all claims be filed with the land commissioners by the end of 1804 but later extended the deadline to November 1, 1805. In the fall of 1804 John Shee requested his fellow shareholders to remit thirty dollars per share to treasurer John Brinton in order to defray "the expence attending the prosecution of this business." Shee also notified the public that the Illinois and Wabash companies had purchased lands that "the U. States are about to offer for sale," warning that "the companies are determined as speedily as possible to bring the question of right between the United States and them before the highest judicial tribunal for decision." To protect further the interest of the shareholders, Shee sent a copy of the notice to Secretary of State James Madison, who laid it before President Jefferson.[29]

John Badollet, a Swiss immigrant and childhood friend of Treasury Secretary Albert Gallatin, was the register of the land office at Vincennes, where he worked with Nathaniel Ewing. The register and receiver at Kaskaskia were Michael Jones and Elijah Backus. Badollet and Ewing would eventually oppose the Harrison faction, and Elijah Backus would collaborate in 1808 with William McIntosh in attacking the governor's administration of the Indiana Territory. Consequently, the Illinois and Wabash shareholders may have committed a tactical error in asking Benjamin

Parke to present their claims. Parke had been appointed by Harrison in 1804 as attorney general and was elected the following year to serve as the territory's first representative in Congress. Just a few months prior to serving as the agent of the united companies, Parke had challenged William McIntosh to a duel and had denounced him as being, among other things, a "dastardly cheat," a "perfidious rascal" and "an impertinent puppy."[30]

On the last day of August 1805, John Badollet wrote to Albert Gallatin for advice regarding the Illinois-Wabash claims. Their "immense extent and weighty importance" posed "too much difficulty for the Commissioners," Badollet feared, especially since "high legal authorities will be adduced." In reply Gallatin assured his friend that "the Illinois & Wabash Companies *have not a shadow of a title to support their claim*, which has been repeatedly before Congress." The treasury secretary rejected the suggestion that the 1763 Proclamation applied only to Iroquois lands, arguing instead that the royal edict was an "absolute & general" rule that barred all private purchases of Indian lands located beyond the Appalachian Mountains. "Their whole claim," Gallatin subsequently informed Badollet, "is perfectly ridiculous."[31]

On March 25, 1806, Badollet and Ewing submitted their report, which concluded that the Illinois-Wabash purchase "was a private transaction between the Indians and an individual, in direct violation of the proclamation of the King of Great Britain, dated 7th October, 1763, and, consequently, illegal."[32] On March 3, 1807, Congress confirmed the report of the Vincennes land commissioners and tacitly denied the Illinois and Wabash claims. Shortly thereafter, Gallatin wrote to Michael Jones to inquire whether any persons "claiming under the Wabash or Illinois companies" had attempted to form settlements. The Kaskaskia register was told that "there will be no hesitation in removing persons of that description." No such settlements had yet been attempted, and Jones did his part to ensure that the Illinois-Wabash shareholders would never profit from the 1773 and 1775 purchases. On February 24, 1810, the Kaskaskia commissioners transmitted a "general report" and accompanying documents to the Treasury Department. Among the attachments was a list of rejected claims, which described the Illinois and Wabash purchases as "illegal and unauthorized." The general report concluded that "no grants made during the continuance of the British Government in this country, either by its officers or by the Indian tribes, were either authorized or sanctioned by it."[33]

Although nearly two years would elapse before Congress officially accepted the recommendations of the Kaskaskia land commissioners, it was evident in 1810 that the Illinois and Wabash shareholders had once again failed in their efforts to obtain either confirmation or compensation. By this time, however, Robert Goodloe Harper was actively involved in the affairs of the Illinois and Wabash Land Company and was soliciting prominent individuals to lobby Congress. In the same month that the Kaskaskia commissioners issued their general report, the confident Harper was assuring shareholders that their claims "can be sustained in a court of Law."[34] Soon after this, on March 16, 1810, the future Maryland senator achieved what would prove to be his greatest legal victory. The Supreme Court's decision in *Fletcher v. Peck* is a landmark in the field of constitutional law and is also the first instance in which the Court addressed the nature of Indian land rights in America. The majority opinion, by Chief Justice John Marshall, includes a cursory but important discussion of "the nature of the Indian title." Justice William Johnson wrote separately to argue that the Indians are "the absolute proprietors of their soil." Johnson also suspected that the controversy was feigned, and warned against future collusive litigation, causing Harper to regroup and devise a new strategy to bring the Illinois-Wabash claims before the Court.

FLETCHER V. PECK

The Supreme Court's decision in *Fletcher v. Peck* is noteworthy for several reasons. First, it is evident that Justice Johnson was correct: the parties and their counsel had arranged a "feigned case" in order to obtain a ruling on the constitutionality of the 1796 Georgia rescinding act.[35] Fletcher and Peck were speculators both of whom hoped that the Court would uphold the 1795 Yazoo legislation. The lawyer representing Fletcher—the ostensible champion of Georgia's right to repeal the land grants—made a perfunctory argument and was so intoxicated that the Court was compelled to adjourn temporarily.[36] Despite the nonadversarial nature of the proceedings, the Court decided the case and for the first time invalidated a state law as contrary to the Constitution. In so doing, Chief Justice John Marshall set forth an expansive interpretation of the Contract Clause, which prohibits states from passing laws "impairing the Obligation of Contracts." James Wilson, the acknowledged "author" of the Contract Clause, would undoubtedly have agreed with Marshall's conclusion that "the state of Georgia was restrained . . . from passing a law" that impaired the vested property rights of the Yazoo purchasers and subsequent transferees.[37]

Fletcher v. Peck is notable for another reason: the majority and dissenting opinions set forth divergent views regarding the nature of Indian property rights in America. The chief justice, in the concluding sentences of his opinion, asserts that "a state can be seised in fee of lands, subject to the Indian title." Justice William Johnson disagreed, contending that Georgia had "nothing more than a power to acquire fee-simple by purchase, *when the proprietors should be pleased to sell*," and thus "had *not* a fee-simple in the lands in question." Because Marshall's views ultimately prevailed in *Johnson v. McIntosh*, Robert Williams, Jr., characterizes the *Fletcher* decision as the "preliminary ceremonies in the legal interment of the doctrine that American Indians possessed natural rights to the lands they had occupied since time immemorial."[38]

The Yazoo controversy spanned nearly three decades and touched upon most of the major issues concerning Indian land rights, including the conquest doctrine, the "devolution of sovereignty" theory, and the evolving right of preemption. Georgia was a "landed" state, but much of its claimed territory was controlled by powerful Indian tribes. In 1785 and 1786 the federal government had entered into treaties with the Cherokees, Choctaws, and Chickasaws that "allotted" specified lands to "live and hunt on." However, the United States soon repudiated its fictive theory of ownership by conquest, and in 1790 guaranteed to the Creek Nation "*all their lands* . . . [located] to the westward and southward" of the lands that the Creeks had consented to "relinquish and cede."[39]

When Georgia attempted in 1789 to sell Native-occupied lands to private land companies, President Washington sought the advice of his Cabinet. Jefferson believed that the thirteen states possessed the exclusive right "*to acquire the native title*," but had "relinquished the *means* of doing it to the general government." He concluded that Georgia could convey the right of preemption ("exclusive right to acquire") to the private land companies but "could not convey what she had not herself, that is, the means of acquiring." Washington, on August 25, 1790, issued a proclamation warning the Yazoo purchasers to abide by the treaties that protected the Indians. In his diary the president complained of "Land Jobbers" who sought to "strip the Indns. of all their territory."[40]

In the summer of 1791—while Robert Goodloe Harper was in Phila-delphia selling shares in the South Carolina Yazoo Company—Jefferson expressed his disapproval of a petition submitted by the Yazoo claimants, noting that the southern Indians "have a right to the occupation of their lands . . . until they cede them by treaty or other transaction equivalent to a treaty." As mentioned in chapter 10, Jefferson informed British diplomat George Hammond in June 1792 that "our right in the Indian soil" was "the sole and exclusive right of purchasing from them *whenever they should be willing to sell.*" Eight months thereafter, in the midst of the controversy over Article IV of Putnam's treaty with the Illinois and Wabash tribes, Jefferson declared to Washington that the right of preemption "*gave us no present right whatever*" but merely prevented "other nations from taking possession, and so defeating our *expectancy.*"[41]

Jefferson's views on Indian land rights were by no means universally accepted. The question remained: who owned the Yazoo lands? Was "fee-simple" title held by Georgia (pursuant to its charter), the United States (under the "devolution of sovereignty" doctrine), or the southern tribes (by virtue of occupancy)? If the tribal nations did not "own" their home-lands, then what rights, if any, did they possess? In the wake of resounding victories over Harmar and St. Clair, the northern Indians asserted in 1793 that they were "*free to make any bargain or cession of lands, whenever and to whomsoever we please.*"[42] The United States disagreed and insisted in 1795 that a right of preemption be set forth in the Treaty of Greenville. Going even further than the federal government, Georgia took the position that it could transact with private individuals and transfer title to lands without first extinguishing the rights of the Native occupants.

On March 2, 1795, less than two months after a bribed Georgia legisla-ture sold 35 million acres to four Yazoo land companies, the U.S. Senate directed Attorney General William Bradford to report on the validity of Georgia's title. In an evening session on the same day Fisher Ames declared to the House of Representatives that "it would require a wheelbarrow load of documents and papers to determine whether these lands were the prop-erty of the State of Georgia, or not." In response Robert Goodloe Harper spoke at length to demonstrate that Georgia "actually has a right to the lands in question." According to a summation of his remarks, the Yazoo speculator stated that he "wished that the land did belong to the United States," but he argued that "if the purchasers themselves had completed their rights, he would advise the repurchase from them."[43]

Matters were further complicated on February 13, 1796, when the newly elected Georgia legislators repealed the 1795 Yazoo Act and declared the purchases to be null and void. On the same day, the Georgia Mississippi Company earned nearly 650 percent on its original investment by selling 11 million acres, at ten cents an acre, to the shareholders of the New England Mississippi Land Company.[44] The transferees claimed they were "bona fide" purchasers and relied on legal opinions prepared by Harper and Alexander Hamilton, who argued that Georgia could not lawfully rescind the Yazoo sales and impair vested property rights.

After receiving the attorney general's inconclusive report on Georgia's title to the Yazoo lands, a Senate committee issued its own report on March 2, 1797. The committee relied on the Proclamation of 1763 and the "devolution of sovereignty" doctrine to conclude that the territory in question "belongs to the United States." However, because Georgia "has claimed and exercised jurisdiction over a great portion of this territory," the committee recommended that a "conciliatory plan of accommodating these adverse claims should be adopted" and that federal and state commissioners should "treat, adjust, and determine" the claims of the United States and Georgia. Congress in 1798 authorized the appointment of three commissioners, and also created the Mississippi Territory, with the proviso that its establishment "shall in no respect impair the right of the state of Georgia, or of any person or persons either to the jurisdiction or the soil of the said territory."[45] It is evident that the "person or persons" of concern were claimants to the Yazoo lands *other than* the Indian occupants.

Prospects for a favorable outcome improved when the state and federal commissioners signed a compact titled "Articles of Agreement and Cession" on April 24, 1802. Georgia ceded its claim to the lands in question, and the United States agreed to pay $1.25 million and extinguish the Indian title to lands *within* the State's adjusted borders, "as early as the same can be peaceably obtained on reasonable terms." The question of the validity of the Yazoo land grants was not resolved; but the parties did agree that the United States could dispose of up to 5 million acres of the ceded lands for the purpose of "satisfying quieting, or compensating" land claims.[46]

The federal commissioners who negotiated the Georgia Compact of 1802 compact were also asked to examine the claims of the original and subsequent purchasers of the Yazoo lands. Among the documents considered was a list of Georgia Company shareholders, who included James

Wilson (10 shares, £25,000, 750,000 acres) and Robert Goodloe Harper (1 share, £1,000, 75,000 acres). In their report the commissioners stated that the title of the Yazoo claimants "cannot be supported" but nonetheless urged that "various equitable considerations . . . render it expedient to enter into a compromise on reasonable terms." Congress consequently agreed to set aside 5 million acres in the Mississippi Territory, and it appeared that the Yazoo claimants would obtain what had long eluded the Illinois and Wabash shareholders: compensation in exchange for the extinguishment of their land claims.[47]

Opponents of the Yazoo claims, however, adamantly refused to "give away" either money or property to the land companies. The "Anti-Yazoo" faction contended that the 1795 Georgia legislators "had no right to make the sale" and that the succeeding legislature lawfully exercised "the inalienable right of a people" to "revoke the authority thus abused." A zealous foe of the Yazoo sales, Abraham Bishop of Connecticut, set forth his views on the competing rights of Georgia and the southern tribes to the lands at issue. In *Georgia Speculation Unveiled* (1797), Bishop denied that Georgia owned "the right in fee" to the lands in question. Consequently, the land companies had *not* been granted ownership by the state, but instead received "a mere floating imaginary right to buy land," which "perhaps may never be for sale." Bishop also rejected the "devolution of sovereignty" doctrine and asserted that the southern tribes owned the land "*in fee*, with all the uses belonging to them."[48]

The leading opponent of the proposed settlement was Republican John Randolph of Virginia, who insisted that no part of the 5 million acres set aside in 1802 be used to satisfy the Yazoo claims. Randolph injected politics into the heated debate by associating "the spirit of Federalism" with "the plunder of the public property."[49] One of his supporters, John Baptiste Charles Lucas of Pennsylvania, claimed that if the Yazoo purchasers received a favorable settlement, "all the land companies will find new encouragement to rally round Congress from all quarters, and set forth their claims." Lucas reminded his colleagues of the claims championed by the Illinois and Wabash Land Company and observed that if Congress were to grant the Yazoo claimants 5 million acres of land, "we may as well give as much to the Wabash Company, for they also have a color of title, and a color, too, not darkened by fraud." William Findlay of Pennsylvania, in rejoinder, contended that the Illinois and Wabash purchases "had not the least analogy to the claim in question" because they took place "during the royal Government" and were "contrary to the rules of that Government." The Eighth Congress, after much discussion, was unable to reach a consensus on the Yazoo matter. In the following Congress the Senate did favor indemnification, but the House of Representatives withheld its approval. The vote to reject the Senate bill took place on the twenty-ninth of March, 1806, and immediately thereafter John Randolph moved that the House adjourn, declaring (erroneously) that his supporters had dealt "a death-blow to the Yazoo business."[50]

The shareholders of the New England Mississippi Land Company also sought *judicial* confirmation of their purchases. The claimants, however, were prevented by the Eleventh Amendment from suing a state in federal court, and the Rescinding Act provided that the "usurped law" could not be contested in Georgia's courts. The purchasers could test their title by bringing an "action in ejectment" in the court for the Mississippi Territory, but territorial court decisions were not subject to federal court review.[51] Consequently, a collusive lawsuit between private individuals was filed in federal court in 1803 on the basis of diversity of citizenship. John Peck of Massachusetts sold fifteen thousand acres of Yazoo lands to Robert Fletcher of New Hampshire for three thousand dollars. Soon afterward Fletcher sued Peck in the federal circuit court at Boston for breach of warranty. In the deed utilized to effect the transfer, Peck warranted that he held good title to the lands because Georgia had lawfully conveyed the property in 1795, and also because the subsequent legislature's attempt to nullify the land grants was unconstitutional and ineffective. Fletcher claimed that Peck lacked title by virtue of the 1796 Rescinding Act, and therefore breached the deed's warranties. Fletcher also alleged that Georgia did not have title to lands conveyed.

It is evident that the suit was carefully arranged in a manner that permitted the litigants to raise all issues relating to the validity of the Yazoo land grants. The federal court continued the case until it became clear that a settlement in Congress was not forthcoming. In an unreported decision handed down in October 1807, Supreme Court Justice William Cushing and District Court Judge John Davis found that Georgia held title, transferred title, and lacked authority to nullify the transfer. The United States Supreme Court granted Fletcher's request for a writ of error, and the case was set for the 1809 term.

The oral argument in *Fletcher v. Peck* began on the first of March, 1809, and concluded three days thereafter. Luther Martin of Maryland appeared on behalf of Robert Fletcher, and John Peck was represented by Robert Goodloe Harper and John Quincy Adams. The Supreme Court held that the lower court had "erred in overruling the [plaintiff's] demurrer," but the parties amended the pleadings and returned to Washington in February 1810.[52] In the intervening year two changes had taken place: the Court relocated to the basement floor of the Capitol, and Adams was replaced by thirty-year-old Joseph Story of Massachusetts. The Harvard graduate was a son-in-law of a shareholder in the New England Mississippi Land Company and had been employed as an agent for the Yazoo purchasers. As in the case of Robert Goodloe Harper, Story was elected to fill a vacancy in the House of Representatives; however, he served in Washington for only a short period, from December 1808 to January 1809. In November 1811 the bespectacled legal scholar would become the youngest justice in the history of the Supreme Court. Joseph Story would author several notable decisions during his long career—including *Martin v. Hunter's Lessee* and *United States v. The Amistad*—and would be on the bench in 1823 when Harper and Daniel Webster argued for the Illinois and Wabash purchasers in *Johnson v. McIntosh*.[53]

Luther Martin, whom Thomas Jefferson called "the Federal Bull-Dog," was apparently intoxicated when he appeared before the Court on Fletcher's behalf. One historian of the Supreme Court claims Martin did not present "a single substantive point of law for the Court's edification," but the former (and future) Maryland attorney general did discuss the question of title to the Yazoo lands. Martin contended that the 1763 Proclamation limited the boundaries of the colonies, and consequently the western territory belonged to the Crown and "at the revolution devolved upon the United States."[54] In his view the United States acquired not only the "title of the lands" but also the power to extinguish the Native right of occupancy.

Harper and Story urged the Court to reject the "devolution of sovereignty" doctrine and to hold instead that the lands "belonged to and formed a part of the province of Georgia." With citations to Vattel, Montesquieu, and Adam Smith, the attorneys further contended that Georgia could convey its fee-simple title, notwithstanding the unextinguished occupancy rights of the southern tribes: "The crown of Great Britain granted lands to individuals, even while the Indian claim existed, and there has never been a question respecting the validity of such grants. When that claim was extinguished, the grantee was always admitted to have acquired a complete title. *The Indian title is a mere privilege which does not affect the allodial right.*"[55] Harper and Story also addressed the issue that Martin ignored: the validity of the Rescinding Act. Construing the 1795 grant as both a "contract executed" and "an implied executory contract," the defense drew upon the prior legal opinions of Harper and Alexander Hamilton to argue that the 1796 Georgia legislature "was forbidden by the constitution of the United States to pass any law impairing the obligation of contract."[56]

"THE ABSOLUTE PROPRIETORSHIP OF THEIR SOIL"

Justices Samuel Chase and William Cushing did not participate in *Fletcher v. Peck.* In his opinion for the Court, John Marshall first addressed the constitutionality of the 1796 Rescinding Act and held that Georgia was restrained, by "general principles" and the Contract Clause, "from passing a law whereby the estate of the plaintiff in the premises so purchased could be constitutionally and legally impaired."[57] Working backward, the chief justice concluded that Georgia had title to the lands, rejecting Luther Martin's "devolution" argument. By holding that Georgia instead of the United States held title to the Yazoo lands, Marshall tacitly denied that the *Indians* were the fee-simple owners. In the concluding sentences of his decision Marshall stated that the majority of the court "is of opinion that the nature of the Indian title, which is certainly to be respected by all courts, until it be legitimately extinguished, is not such as to be absolutely repugnant to seisin in fee on the part of the state."[58]

Justice William Johnson of South Carolina set forth his views in a separate opinion. Johnson was thirty-two years old when he was appointed to the court in 1804 by Jefferson, who characterized the state judge as "an excellent lawyer, prompt, eloquent, of irreproachable character, republican connections, and of good nerves in his political principles." Joseph Story praised Johnson as a judge with "considerable soundness of erudition." Described by historians as "a bit of a loose cannon on the early Marshall Court," William Johnson would file over thirty dissenting opinions as an associate justice, yet he shared Marshall's belief in "economic nationalism" and was "highly suspicious of executive power, even when that power was wielded by Republican presidents."[59]

Although he agreed with Marshall that the Georgia legislature could not lawfully rescind the Yazoo land grants, Johnson invoked general principles of natural law instead of the Contract Clause in the Constitution. On the issue of title, however, the South Carolina jurist charted his own path and declared that "Georgia had *not* a fee-simple in the land in question." Johnson claimed that the southern tribes "retain a limited sovereignty, and the absolute proprietorship of their soil," and reasoned that "if the Indian nations be *the absolute proprietors of their soil*, no other nation can be said to have the same interest in it." After determining that the southern tribes owned the lands at issue, Johnson proceeded to describe "the interest of the states in the soil of the Indians within their boundaries" as being "nothing more than . . . a right of conquest or of purchase, exclusively of all competitors within certain defined limits." Georgia held a right of preemption only, and as Johnson noted, if the interest in Georgia "was nothing more than a pre-emptive right, *how could that be called a fee-simple?*" In other words, Justice Johnson viewed Indian land rights in America in a manner quite similar to the position set forth by Thomas Jefferson in the 1790s: the Indians *own* the property they occupy, subject to a "right of pre-emption" that is *not* fee-simple ownership but rather is simply "a power to acquire a fee-simple by purchase, *when the proprietors should be pleased to sell.*"[60]

Milner Ball claims that William Johnson's opinion in *Fletcher v. Peck* "argued for absolute tribal rights." It is true that Johnson referred to the tribes' "*absolute* proprietorship of their soil." However, by acknowledging that "a pre-emptive right" exists with respect to Native lands, Johnson took the position that the Indian tribes can sell "*whenever*" but may not sell "*to whomsoever.*" John Marshall, on the other hand, went far beyond the preemption concept and declared that Georgia was "seised in fee of lands, subject to the Indian title." New York Chancellor James Kent, in the 1832 edition of his influential *Commentaries on American Law*, observed that Marshall's characterization of Indian land rights was "a mere naked declaration, without any discussion or reasoning by the court in support of it." The right to purchase Indian land was transformed into an ownership interest in Indian land that could be transferred even while the Native occupants remained in possession.[61]

The Supreme Court's decision in *Fletcher v. Peck* proved to be a turning point for the Yazoo claimants. In 1814 the Senate passed a bill that would carry into effect the settlement proposed in 1803 by the Jefferson administration.[62] An opponent of compromise, George Troup of Georgia, summarized the sordid affair in one remarkable sentence: "*Not merely were the corrupted corrupted by the corrupters—the corrupters cheated the corrupted—the corrupters cheated one another, and the corrupters, as they say, cheated these claimants.*"[63] On the other side, legislators favoring settlement spoke of "the unfortunate after-purchasers" and "their widows and orphans."[64] The House acceded to the Senate bill, and on March 31, 1814, President Madison signed "An act providing for the indemnification of certain claimants of public lands in the Mississippi Territory."[65]

THE 1810 MEMORIAL

In January 1810, one month prior to the second oral argument in *Fletcher*, a committee of the Illinois and Wabash Land Company authorized Robert Goodloe Harper to make use of four shares in order to engage prominent individuals to lobby Congress. Benjamin Stoddert, who had served as the country's first secretary of the navy under President Adams, accepted a share. Stoddert in turn recruited Walter Jones, Jr., the district attorney in Washington; Nathan Loughborough, a former chief clerk in the Federal Land Office; and Thomas Turner, who was related by marriage to the Lee family of Virginia.[66] To prepare for a possible ejectment action, Harper suggested to John Brinton and Simon Gratz that the company enlist the aid of "some man of talents, activity and influence, in the country where the lands lye."[67] The most logical candidate was William Henry Harrison, who had long enjoyed the support of Congressman Harper. "Governor H of the Western Territory will perhaps be with us," Solomon Etting reported to Simon Gratz. "I am for adding all the weight of mettle & influence possible. *This is between ourselves.*"[68]

Although Etting's letter suggests that Harrison's participation was not to be disclosed, the governor's detractors learned of his involvement. On May 29, 1810, John Badollet informed Albert Gallatin that Harper and the "Wabash company" had solicited Harrison's assistance "to bring an ejectment action against a purchaser" in the territorial courts.[69] The shareholders likely discussed this plan in March when they selected Harper, Stoddert, Simon Gratz, Solomon Etting, and John Brinton to serve as "a Committee to prosecute the claims of the companies before Congress or in the Courts of Law, as may be necessary." However, rather than resort to litigation, the shareholders for several reasons opted in 1810 to return to Congress to seek compensation for their claims. First, as Badollet noted to Gallatin, decisions of the territorial courts could not be appealed to the

Supreme Court.[70] Consequently, even if the united companies prevailed in the territorial courts, there would be no certainty that either Congress or prospective purchasers would respect their title. Furthermore, the tactic employed in *Fletcher v. Peck*—bringing a breach of warranty action in federal court based on diverse citizenship—was foreclosed in view of Justice Johnson's stern warning against collusive litigation.[71] Finally, their local agent, Governor Harrison, had negotiated highly controversial treaties in 1809 and was occupied the following year with defending his actions against the slanderous attacks by William McIntosh and other political opponents.

Harper took the lead and began crafting settlement proposals to be offered to Congress on behalf of the united companies. Solomon Etting brought the new memorial to Philadelphia, and Jacob Gratz shared his favorable reaction with older brother Joseph, who was in Germany: "It is an able well drawn writing done by R. G. Harper who is very earnest in the business. All the objections of the former committees are answered in a very able manner & I think totally refuted. Probably I am blinded. I am too sanguine."[72] The second-generation shareholders were cautiously hopeful that Harper could succeed where James Wilson and others had failed: in convincing Congress to accept the validity of the Illinois and Wabash purchases.

The 1810 memorial sets forth legal arguments that would later be presented to the Supreme Court.[73] In particular, Harper identifies seven past objections to the purchases, which are summarized as follows: (1) the Six Nations were the proprietors of the land sold; (2) the Illinois and Piankeshaw chiefs were not authorized by their respective nations; (3) the private purchases were contrary to the "common and known usage" in such cases as well as the 1763 Proclamation; (4) one of the Illinois deeds contains an inadequate description; (5) the 1775 purchase was made after the Revolution began, and no notice was provided to the agent for Indian affairs at Fort Pitt; (6) the lands at issue have been ceded to the United States, who paid an adequate compensation for them; and (7) the proceeds of all sales of western lands "belonging to the United States" are to be appropriated toward the discharge of the public debt.[74]

The first two objections were readily answered. If the Illinois and Piankeshaws "were not in fact the proprietors of the land sold," then why did George Croghan—the "best informed witness that ever lived"—testify in 1781 that the Iroquois claim extended only as far as "the Big

MEMORIAL

OF THE

UNITED

ILLINOIS AND WABASH

LAND COMPANIES,

TO THE

SENATE AND HOUSE OF REPRESENTATIVES

OF THE

UNITED STATES.

BALTIMORE:

PRINTED BY JOSEPH ROBINSON, 96, MARKET-ST.

1810.

1810 Memorial of the United Illinois and Wabash Land Companies. Indiana Historical Society.

Miami river"? If the Illinois and Piankeshaws were not the rightful owners, then why did the United States treat with these *same tribes* to obtain
large portions of the lands at issue? The "great inadequacy of price" received for the 1803 and 1805 cessions, Harper argued, was itself evidence
that the Indians "remembered the sales made to your memorialists, were
conscious of their fairness and validity, and consequently regarded themselves as selling nothing more to the United States, than a quit claim to
lands before sold."[75]

The final four objections were examined and refuted in an even more
summary fashion. With regard to the imprecise description of the second
tract sold by the Illinois Indians, the memorialists assured Congress that
the natural objects marking the boundaries of the conveyance "can no
doubt be easily found." The 1775 purchase from the Piankeshaws was
concluded *before* the colonies declared independence, and therefore it was
of no consequence that the agent of the Continental Congress at Fort Pitt
was not notified. Likewise, the legal rights of the united companies could
not be affected by the decision of the United States to "purchase land
from the Indians *which those Indians had before sold*." Finally, while it was
true that Congress had determined that the proceeds of sales of western
land "belonging to the United States" should be used to reduce the public
debt, the lands at issue never belonged to the United States, "having been
sold by the legal owners before the United States were in existence, as
an independent or separate Government; *while no law forbidding such sales
existed*."[76]

The shareholders were well aware that Congress and the land commissioners had concluded that laws "forbidding such sales" *did* exist, both
before and after the 1773 and 1775 purchases. In 1805 the House of Representatives declared that the 1779 grant of Piankeshaw lands to George
Rogers Clark was void for failure to comply with the requirements of the
Virginia constitution. Two years later, the House Committee on Public
Lands concluded that a private grant by the Delawares and Shawnees was
contrary to the 1795 Treaty of Greenville and "of course void."[77] Most
important, the Vincennes and Kaskaskia land commissioners squarely held
that the Illinois and Wabash purchases were forbidden by the 1763 Proclamation. Consequently, Harper's response to the third objection—that
the purchases were contrary to "common and known usage" and the royal
proclamation—is longer than the combined responses to the other six
objections.

The 1810 memorial rejects as "utterly untenable" the proposition that the Indians "were divested of their right to sell their lands, by the acts of the British Government, in establishing colonies whose nominal limits included those lands." Proponents of the doctrine of discovery, Harper argues, suggest that "the British Government, by establishing a colony of a few thousand or a few hundred persons, on the Atlantic coast of North America, . . . could divest [the Indians] of their property in the soil . . . or of the right of alienation, which is one of the inherent and essential ingredients of property." Although Harper had embraced the discovery doctrine on behalf of the Yazoo purchasers, he now argued that "so extravagant a proposition" must "surely" be rejected.[78]

According to Harper, the British and colonial governments "always considered and treated these Indians as independent nations, and *absolute owners of the land; from whom individuals or colonies might purchase, and did purchase.*"[79] In support of this assertion, the memorial describes two private purchases of Indian lands: the 1629 sale by the Pisquataqua Indians to John Whelewright of lands along the Merrimack River, and the 1659 purchase by John Mason of land, within the limits of Connecticut, from the Mohegan sachem Uncas and his two sons. Although Great Britain had purchased from the Six Nations the "preemptive right to their lands," this right did not extend to the lands of the Illinois and Piankeshaws: "Of this power of alienation they might divest themselves, as the six nations had done, by a treaty or a sale; but until they did so divest themselves it remained with them, as an inherent and essential part of the right of property, and of the attributes of sovereignty. . . . How indeed . . . could it have ceased to be their own? Not by conquest; for Great Britain never did conquer them or their country."[80]

After arguing that discovery and conquest did not divest the Indians of ownership and the right to sell, the memorial addresses whether the king "had authority to restrain the Indians, by proclamation, from exercising the right of sale, in favour of British subjects." On this same point, Harper had acknowledged in 1797 that "the crown might, and frequently did, . . . prescribe the manner in which [Indian] lands should be purchased or settled."[81] In the 1810 memorial, however, the distinguished lawyer changed course and contended that "the proclamations of the British King, in matters of property, cannot have the force of laws," and that "Parliament is alone competent" to enact legislation restraining British subjects "from the exercise of so dear and natural a right, as that of making purchases."[82]

In support of this position Harper made several dubious assertions. The memorial claims the issuance of the Camden-Yorke opinion in 1772 was proof that the 1763 Proclamation was not considered "as restraining the power of the Indians to sell, or the right of British subjects to buy." The legal opinion, of course, was issued in 1757, six years *prior* to the royal proclamation, and it did *not* concern the right to purchase lands from American Indians.[83]

What is most difficult to comprehend is how Harper hoped to persuade Congress that the 1763 Proclamation did not restrain the right of British subjects to purchase Indian lands. The royal edict reserved the lands west of the Appalachian Mountains to the Indians and prohibited "all our loving subjects from making any purchases or settlements whatever, or taking possession of any of the lands above reserved, without our especial leave and licence for that purpose first obtained." Mustering all of his considerable legal skills, Harper granted that this language prohibited purchases, but he questioned whether the prohibition "extends to purchases from the *Indians*; or is confined to purchases from the King's Governors." After all, in another part of the proclamation, the king barred private persons from making "any purchase *from the said Indians*, of any lands reserved to the said Indians within those parts of our colonies, where we have thought proper to allow settlements." The latter clause, Harper contended, did not encompass the Illinois and Wabash purchases, which were not located within the parts of the colonies where settlements were allowed. Harper thus argued that—because the more general prohibition failed to refer expressly to purchases "from Indians"—it was "at least doubtful whether this proclamation was intended to prohibit such purchases from the Indians as those made by your memorialists."[84]

Although the shareholders expressed "a perfect confidence in the legal and equitable grounds of their claim," they were nonetheless willing to offer "two modes of compromise, . . . one or the other of which they pray Congress to accept." Under the terms of the first proposal, Congress would confirm title to the lands located "east of the Wabash, and south of the tract of land called the Vincennes tract," and in return the shareholders would transfer their remaining claims to the United States. Alternatively, the shareholders would relinquish all claims in exchange for "certificates of debt, transferable and bearing interest, to the amount of what the . . . land east of the Wabash would sell for, at the price of two dollars an acre."[85]

Congress declined both offers. When the memorial was referred to the House Committee on Public Lands, Samuel McKee of Kentucky complained that "it was a subject on which Congress had frequently legislated." Daniel Hiester, whose namesake uncle had become a shareholder prior to 1781, expressed his belief that the shareholders should pursue their claims in court. "I do not think," the Pennsylvania delegate predicted, "that the company can expect much from Congress."[86]

The House Committee on Public Lands issued its report on January 30, 1811, and resolved that the petition "ought not to be granted." After acknowledging Harper's "ingenuity in reasoning," the committee found that the 1763 Proclamation was a lawful exercise of royal authority, which contained "a plain and express prohibition" that applied to the purchasers. Moreover, even prior to 1763, the requirement of government approval of purchases of Indian lands was "part of the law of the land." Amazingly, the shareholders still did not give up. Solomon Etting wrote to Simon Gratz and John Brinton on February 22, 1811, and assured his Philadelphia colleagues that "the more we view this thing the more we are sanguine in our expectation of success." Jacob Gratz informed his brother Jacob of the unfavorable committee report but noted that the shareholders had asked Congress to defer consideration "until the next session when they might be heard with counsel." The young Gratz still hoped that "we will touch the cash" and was cheered by the fact that "Mr. Harper is sanguine as a reasonable person can probably be."[87]

The Eleventh Congress, however, did not hold an additional session and never acted on the 1810 memorial. During the summer of 1811 relations with Great Britain became increasingly strained, and Henry Clay, John Calhoun, and other "War Hawks" advocated aggressive measures. Robert Goodloe Harper favored peace with Great Britain, but when the United States officially declared war on June 18, 1812, he became an active supporter of his country. The hostilities would continue until January 8, 1815, when General Andrew Jackson led the American forces to victory at New Orleans. The Illinois and Wabash Land Company suspended operations during the conflict, but Harper and his fellow shareholders resumed their efforts in 1815 and continued to press their claims for another eight years.

14

LITIGATION

On the first of November 1815, the commissioner of the General Land Office, Josiah Meigs, informed President James Monroe that there was "reason to believe that the Illinois and Wabash companies will resume their efforts to obtain from the United States a confirmation of their claims."[1] Prior to the commencement of hostilities with Great Britain, Robert Harper had written to William Henry Harrison and obtained the assistance of several of his supporters, including George Wallace. In November 1811 John Badollet informed Albert Gallatin that the united companies were planning to bring an ejectment action against a local purchaser of public lands. "George Wallace is the ostensible manager," Badollet wrote, "but the Governor appears to be the real one behind the curtain."[2] However, just as the Revolutionary War had interfered with the plans of the original grantees, the War of 1812 caused the shareholders to postpone efforts to obtain judicial confirmation of their title. By the end of 1815, however, Harper and his colleagues were once again pressing their land claims.

New England Federalists had actively opposed "Mr. Madison's War," and delegates to the Hartford Convention considered secession from the United States. The ill-fated convention, which concluded just prior to Andrew Jackson's victory at New Orleans, hastened the demise of the Federalist Party. Robert Goodloe Harper, in contrast, prospered during the Madison and Monroe administrations. Marriage to Catherine "Kitty" Carroll, while not entirely blissful, had enhanced the lawyer's financial and social standing. In March 1809 Harper attended Madison's first inaugural ball, "perfumed like a milliner, with a large knot of black ribbon on each shoe." Described by an acquaintance as a man of "uncommonly full chest," the self-assured orator addressed the Washington Society of Alexandria shortly after his second argument in *Fletcher v. Peck*, using the occasion to compare the president to Epaminondas of Thebes, Alexander the Great, Scipio Africanus, Pompey, Julius Caesar, Tiberius, Germanicus, Caligula, Trajan, Marcus Aurelius, Julian, Charlemagne, Alfred the Great, Genghis Khan, William Wallace, Tamerlane, King Gustav I of Sweden, and the reigning emperor of France, Napoleon Bonaparte. Never at a loss for words, Harper in 1814 published a four-hundred-page volume, *Select Works*. As biographer Joseph Cox has noted, Robert Goodloe Harper was "never prone to underestimate his own worth."[3]

His ego aside, Harper unquestionably possessed a first-rate command of law and was the most frequent advocate before the U.S. Supreme Court from 1800 to 1815. His name appears in the reports of forty-one decisions during the war years of 1812, 1813, and 1814, including the noteworthy case of *Fairfax's Devisee v. Hunter's Lessee*, which concerned the validity of Lord Fairfax's title to the "Northern Neck" of Virginia. It was not uncommon at this time for the "belles" of Washington society to watch as the nation's leading lawyers demonstrated their rhetorical skills. Attendance decreased when the Court was forced into temporary quarters but picked up in 1819 when the sessions were again held in the basement chambers of the Capitol.[4]

Prior to the summer of 1814 the war had been fought primarily in Canada and the Great Lakes region. Oliver Perry prevailed on Lake Erie in September 1813, and American forces under General Harrison were victorious at the Battle of the Thames. In the following year Great Britain elected to deploy troops to the Chesapeake Bay region. On the evening of August 24, 1814, soldiers entered Washington and set fire to the Capitol, the White House, the War Office, and other public buildings. The invading army left the next day, returned to their transports, and sailed north to Baltimore. On the thirteenth of September British troops landed southeast of the city at North Point, and naval forces commenced bombardment of Fort McHenry. According to the *Niles' Register* magazine, "Robert G. Harper, Esq., who volunteered his services as an aide-de-camp, . . . greatly exerted himself in the hottest part of the fire to encourage and give steadiness to our troops." The forty-nine-year-old Federalist was appointed as major general of the Maryland militia, and the commission was one of his most cherished achievements. As noted by David Fischer, "his only engagements were cornerstone layings, funerals, and receptions, but he was immensely proud of his title, introducing himself as Major General Harper wherever he went."[5]

In addition to the cessation of hostilities, two other events spurred General Harper and the Illinois-Wabash claimants to renew their efforts. Congress's appropriation of $5 million for the Yazoo purchasers in March 1814 was an encouraging sign, but the shareholders were more influenced by the opening of federal land offices in the Illinois territory.[6] Large portions of their acquisitions would soon be sold by the government, greatly complicating matters. One such purchaser was William McIntosh of Vincennes. On April 24, 1815, the seasoned speculator acquired fifty-three tracts in southwestern Illinois. At two dollars an acre, McIntosh paid $23,963.62 for a total of 11,981.81 acres.[7] The Scotsman anticipated an influx of settlers and believed his land would appreciate in value. Indeed, the population of Illinois more than doubled between 1815 and 1818, from 15,000 to over 35,000 persons. By 1820 there were more than 55,000 individuals living in southern Illinois, and the expression "doing a land-office business" emerged as an idiom to describe a successful endeavor. McIntosh himself chose to relocate to the other side of the Wabash River and was listed in the 1820 Illinois census.[8]

Agent Benjamin Stoddert died in 1813 and was replaced by John Law, who was granted a half share in the Company. Law had graduated from Yale College in 1814 and would move to Vincennes in 1817, practice law, serve in a variety of judicial and political positions, and author a history of his adopted city. He suggested that legal opinions be obtained "on the operation of the Proclamation . . . & on the general validity of Indian titles."[9] The more experienced Harper doubted that "mere opinions of counsel would be of much avail," but suggested that favorable opinions from William Rawle and Charles Jared Ingersoll of Pennsylvania, William Wirt and Littleton Tazewell of Virginia, and Thomas Addis Emmet of New York might be helpful.[10]

The shareholders met in December and resolved to submit another memorial to Congress. The Yazoo claimants had been compensated, and it was thought that Congress would likewise settle the Illinois and Wabash claims. On January 25, 1816, Senator Jeremiah Morrow of Ohio presented the memorial of the united companies, which was referred to a committee. The 1816 memorial begins by reproducing the 1810 memorial and then sets forth the legal opinions of Henry Dagge, John Glynn, Benjamin Franklin, and Patrick Henry. On the final page agent Solomon Etting states that the shareholders "would agree, on receiving a just and reasonable compensation, to surrender their claims to the United States." The original purchasers, Etting notes, "had sufficient reason to entertain a just expectation that their rights would have been sanctioned and allowed by the British government; *whose officers encouraged and participated in the purchase.*" The infamous Lord Dunmore is not mentioned by name.[11]

Just two days after the shareholders submitted their memorial, the Maryland legislature elected Robert Goodloe Harper to fill a vacated seat in the U.S. Senate. Encouraged by Harper's election, some of the shareholders expressed hope that "we shall have a favorable Report in the Senate."[12] The Fourteenth Congress, however, adjourned its first session without acting on the memorial. Although their settlement offer was not accepted, the shareholders were pleased that Congress had passed legislation that enabled Indiana, on December 11, 1816, to become the nineteenth state. The Illinois and Wabash Land Company would now be able to litigate the Piankeshaw grant in the federal courts, including the U.S. Supreme Court.[13]

Harper did not vote to admit Indiana, having resigned from the Senate prior to the commencement of the December session. As noted by his biographer, Charles Sommerville, Harper believed "a conscientious discharge of public duties would rob him wholly of time for his private concerns," and consequently decided to retire "to private life and the management of his business." It is not known to what extent the affairs of the Illinois and Wabash Land Company influenced Harper to leave the Senate. His "private concerns" were extensive and wide-ranging. Harper argued ten cases before the Supreme Court in 1816 and participated in the laying of the cornerstone of the Washington Monument. In the national election Harper was one of four Federalist candidates for vice president but received just three electoral votes. The former South Carolina congressman became a charter member in 1817 of the American Colonization Society, which sought to remove freed slaves from the United States. He is credited with establishing the name of the society's African settlement as Liberia, and a town called Harper is located in southern Liberia, just a few miles from the Ivory Coast.[14]

Harper's name appears in nine Supreme Court decisions in 1817 and in seven decisions the following year. After the conclusion of the 1818 winter term Robert and Kitty Harper sailed to Europe for an extended tour. The couple arrived in England and visited Holland, France, Switzerland, and Italy, where Harper commissioned a marble bust of himself. While back in England, General Harper received a sword from the Duke of Wellington.[15] By the fall of 1819 the Harpers were back in Maryland. For several reasons, it was finally time to test the validity of the 1773 and 1775 purchases in a court of law.

The Search for a Defendant

The other Illinois-Wabash shareholders were not idle during Harper's absence. In October 1818 twenty-six-year-old Benjamin Gratz left Pennsylvania for Kentucky, charged with two tasks: supervise the family's western investments, and find a cooperative individual who held title to lands also claimed by the united companies. Benjamin, the youngest of twelve children born to Miriam and Michael Gratz, graduated from the University of Pennsylvania prior to his father's death in 1811. He served as a lieutenant during the war and in 1817 was admitted to the Philadelphia bar. In 1819 he would marry Maria Gist, the niece of Henry Clay and a descendant of the famed explorer Christopher Gist. Benjamin Gratz settled in Lexington, Kentucky, where he lived until 1884, and where his residence still stands, adjacent to the Gratz Park Historic District.[16]

Congress in 1817 confirmed the appointment of Benjamin Parke as the federal district judge for the Indiana District. Consequently, if the shareholders could bring suit in federal court against an Indiana landowner, the presiding judge would be the company's former attorney. Furthermore, because the Indiana court combined the functions of a district and a circuit court, appeals were possible only to the Supreme Court. In all respects the situation held promise: if a compliant defendant could be located, the shareholders would control the factual and legal issues brought before a sympathetic judge and thus better position themselves on appeal to the Supreme Court. In February 1819 Benjamin Gratz reported that Thomas and Cuthbert Bullitt of Louisville might participate in an ejectment action.[17] "I hope to make them defendants in our suit," Gratz wrote, and "as soon as I can arrange the matter with Mr. B. I will leave here for Vincennes."[18] The Bullitt brothers were members of the Terre Haute Land Company, which in 1816 had purchased land fifty miles north of Vincennes on the east bank of the Wabash River. As it turned out, however, the Bullitts would not be named as defendants in an ejectment action brought by the shareholders. Moreover, the lawsuit would not be filed in Indiana, but rather in Illinois, which achieved statehood in December 1818.

Benjamin Gratz did go to Vincennes, which was described by a contemporary as a "dirty village of wooden frame houses, which a fire might much improve." During his stay Gratz received two letters from Philadelphia. One was from his sister Rebecca, who wrote that the Illinois and Wabash claim "seemed like a romance." Rebecca extended her wish "for its success" but cautioned her brother against engaging in "years of toil on an uncertain event."[19] The other letter was from Edward Ingersoll, who had graduated from the University of Pennsylvania a few years before Gratz. Ingersoll was married to Catherine Ann Brinton, the daughter of John Brinton and granddaughter of John Steinmetz. In his letter Ingersoll stated that because the company's finances "are not in very flourishing condition," the Bullitt brothers should receive only "indemnity against expenses." Ingersoll then addressed another problem: the reluctance of Benjamin Parke to try a case involving the land claims of his former client. "As to Judge Parke's scruples," Gratz was counseled, "nothing is left for us but to . . . insist on his trying the cause."[20]

It is not certain why the shareholders altered their plans. However, by the spring of 1819 there was an alternative: Congress had created a federal district court for Illinois, consisting of one judge who was authorized to hold two annual sessions. The position was filled by Nathaniel Pope, who had previously served as a territorial delegate to Congress. During the War of 1812 he was a member of the military expedition that destroyed three Kickapoo, Potawatomi, and Piankeshaw villages at Peoria Lake. His older brother, John Pope, was a former Kentucky senator and the husband to Thomas Johnson's niece.[21]

Benjamin Gratz began a new search to find a defendant with title to lands in Illinois that conflicted with the company's claims. The citizens of Vincennes no doubt suggested William McIntosh, who now resided in a frame house near the "grand rapids" of the Wabash River. On July 20, 1818, the United States granted the lands that McIntosh had contracted to purchase in 1815.[22] Like many speculators at this time, the Scotsman was "land rich but cash poor." In 1817 the Vincennes land district had led the nation in sales, but the "Panic of 1819" ended the economic expansion that followed the war. As noted by Malcolm Rohrbough, the downturn "had a devastating effect on the western portion of the nation and brought a sudden end to the land office business." The sluggish economy may have influenced McIntosh's decision to participate in the Illinois-Wabash lawsuit. In any event, the shareholders had found their man, and William McIntosh—the "scotch tory" who had been verbally abused by Benjamin Parke, attacked in the streets in Vincennes by Thomas Randolph, and successfully sued for slander by William Henry Harrison—would be known to history as the defendant in the "great case" of *Johnson v. McIntosh.*[23]

SIMEON PEACEABLE AND THOMAS TROUBLESOME

It was Robert Harper who decided that Thomas Johnson should serve as plaintiff in the planned lawsuit. Johnson was an original Wabash grantee, and he had also acquired a half share in the Illinois purchase. After the death of his wife in 1794 Johnson lived with his daughter, Ann Jennings Grahame, near Frederick, Maryland. In 1818 the former Supreme Court justice and Maryland governor provided in his will that his residual estate, including the shares in the united companies, should be distributed equally to his son, Joshua Johnson, and his grandson, Thomas Grahame. On October 26, 1819, the elder statesman passed away, ten days prior to his eighty-seventh birthday. Johnson's attorney, Roger Brooke Taney, informed Harper in December that the will had not yet been submitted for probate. Consequently Joshua Johnson and Thomas Grahame did not become Illinois and Wabash shareholders until 1820.[24]

Local counsel would be needed to represent the parties before Judge Pope. The united companies retained Charles Dewey to represent the interests of Johnson and Grahame. Dewey had come to southern Indiana from Massachusetts in 1816 and would later serve as a state legislator, the United States district attorney of Indiana, and on the Indiana Supreme Court.[25] His opposing counsel was Henry Starr, who practiced law in Illinois from 1819 to 1826 and then relocated to Cincinnati. According to one source, Starr "was by far the ablest and most brilliant lawyer then at the bar of the Supreme Court of Illinois."[26]

In contrast to *Fletcher v. Peck*, which used a breach of warranty action to determine the validity of the Yazoo land grants, the *Johnson* litigation was based on the ancient action of ejectment. As Lawrence Friedman explains in *A History of American Law*, the ejectment action is a prime example of the use of legal fictions in Anglo-American lawsuits: "A man named John Doe, it seems, had leased the land from Henry Black. Another man, named William Styles, held a lease from Richard Brown. Styles (it was said) had "ejected" John Doe. *In fact, Doe, Styles, and the two leases were pure figments of legal imagination.* Black and Brown were the only real people in the case. This mummery . . . served the purpose of bringing the issue of title before the court."[27] In similar fashion, the ejectment action brought before Judge Pope involved not only Joshua Johnson, Thomas Grahame, and William McIntosh, but also an imaginary lease and two fictitious litigants: Simeon Peaceable and Thomas Troublesome. Charles Dewey filed the suit on December 4, 1820, in the new capital of Vandalia, situated in the wilderness along the Kaskaskia River in Fayette County.

According to the plea, Joshua Johnson and Thomas "Graham" leased property in Illinois to Simeon Peaceable for a period of twenty years, commencing on the first day of 1820. The land at issue was supposedly sold by the Piankeshaws to Thomas Johnson and nineteen other grantees in 1775, but also conveyed by the United States to William McIntosh in 1818.[28] Harper evidently preferred to argue that the title dispute was between McIntosh and the Wabash grantees, because the Illinois tracts were poorly delineated.

As described in the plea, Simeon Peaceable took possession of the lands but soon encountered trouble. On January 10, 1820, Thomas Troublesome entered "with swords, guns, and knives" and ejected Simeon Peaceable. Consequently the attorney for the peaceful Simeon, Charles Dewey, brought suit against the troublesome Thomas, claiming damages "to the value of two thousand dollars." Soon thereafter, Thomas Troublesome informed William McIntosh that he should "be made defendant in my stead, otherwise I shall suffer judgement to be entered against me, and you will be turned out of possession."[29] William McIntosh, by his attorney Henry Starr, appeared before the court, and was substituted as the defendant. Thomas Troublesome was discharged, and henceforth the suit was brought by Johnson and Grahame's (fictional) lessee against McIntosh.

Two days later, on the sixth of December, the jury was discharged. As noted by Mary Bonsteel Tachau, juries during this period "were often discharged without making a finding," thus enabling the parties to present a statement of the facts for the consideration of the court.[30] The agreed statement of facts was based on the 1810 memorial and was undoubtedly prepared by Robert Harper. By setting forth the circumstances of the purchases in a statement agreed to by the defendant, Harper could eliminate or greatly reduce fact-based objections to the claims.[31] The

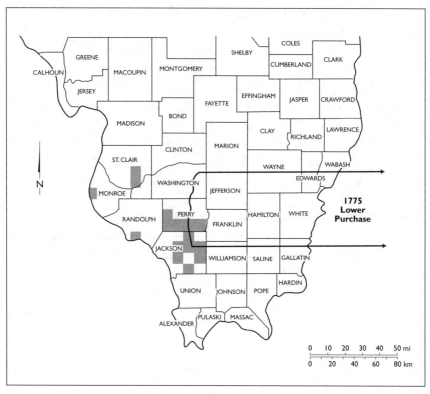

Townships containing land purchased by William McIntosh, and the approximate boundaries of the lower Wabash purchase of 1775. Map by Bill Nelson.

statement of facts presented to Judge Pope is set forth, almost *verbatim*, at the beginning of the Supreme Court's reported decision in *Johnson v. McIntosh*. Several important points are stipulated by the parties. It is agreed that Virginia was occupied by "independent tribes or nations" who were "*the absolute owners and proprietors of the soil thereof.*" It was further agreed that the Piankeshaws and the Illinois were "free and independent" nations, and that each tribe exercised "*absolute ownership, in and over its respective territory.*"[32]

The parties agreed that the tribal chiefs were authorized to sell land for the benefit of their people, and did so for "good and valuable considerations," but only after "open, public, and fair" conferences were held at Kaskaskia and Vincennes. It was further stipulated that the lands were within the limits of the colony of Virginia, that the state of Virginia thereafter transferred its "right, title, and claim" to the United States, and that the United States in 1818 conveyed to William McIntosh certain lands located within one of the tracts sold by the Piankeshaws in 1775. Finally, the parties agreed that Thomas Johnson devised his share in the Wabash purchase to Joshua Johnson and Thomas Grahame of Maryland, and that their lawsuit against William McIntosh of Illinois satisfied the requirements of federal diversity jurisdiction.[33]

"*Upon the facts so stated and agreed it is the opinion of the Court here, that the said William McIntosh is not guilty of . . . trespass and ejectment.*"[34] With these words, Judge Pope found against Johnson and Grahame. The judgment was "*pro forma*"; in other words, a judgment agreed to by the parties and entered for the purpose of hastening an appeal.[35] Although the *pro forma* judgment is "today universally repudiated as a collusive device," it was a permissible means by which Harper could bring the Illinois and Wabash claims before the Supreme Court.

The district court clerk thereafter certified the record, including an order by Judge Pope that granted leave for Johnson and Grahame to appeal. It was now Robert Goodloe Harper's responsibility to ensure that the Supreme Court would hear the case. One issue that was out of his control was the health of William McIntosh. The death of Thomas Johnson had delayed the ejectment action, and the death of McIntosh would require the shareholders to start over again. In the summer of 1820 a "dreadful epidemic" terrified the citizens of Vincennes and nearly depopulated the village. The Wabash River was low and stagnant following an unusual dry spell, and it is likely that the "fatal disease" was yellow fever. The local newspaper reported that half of the houses were vacant due to the contagion and the lingering effects of the Panic of 1819. William McIntosh, however, survived.[36]

Harper's health, as it turned out, was also an issue. Toward the end of his fifty-fifth year he suffered from what was said to be a "bilious" fever, a term often applied to intestinal and malarial afflictions. Moreover, according to David Fischer, the illness "seems to have been complicated by a heart attack." Despite such setbacks, Harper recovered sufficiently to participate in three cases before the Supreme Court during the February 1821 term. This session was the first opportunity for Harper to seek a writ of error from the Court. A "writ of error," as Chief Justice Marshall would explain in *Cohens v. Virginia*, is "a commission by which the judges of one Court are authorized to examine a record upon which a judgment was given in another Court, and, on such examination, to affirm or reverse the same according to law."[37]

On February 5, 1821, the writ of error was issued to the Illinois federal district court, commanding Judge Pope to "send the record and the proceedings aforesaid" to the Supreme Court. But who would represent the Illinois and Wabash Land Company? Harper was the obvious candidate, but his stake in the outcome was a disability. In the spring of 1821 the choice was made: Johnson and Grahame would be represented by William Pinkney, the Maryland attorney whom John Marshall would eulogize as "the greatest man he had ever seen in a Court of Justice."[38]

WILLIAM PINKNEY

According to Henry Wheaton, who served as the reporter of proceedings before the Supreme Court from 1816 to 1827, William Pinkney "*was one of the brightest and meanest of mankind.*" Wheaton was not the only Pinkney contemporary to express conflicting views about the man. William Wirt, the attorney general under James Monroe and John Quincy Adams, noted in 1816 that "Pinkney would make you believe that he knows everything. At the bar he is despotic and cares as little for his colleagues or adversaries as if they were men of wood." Two years later, however, Wirt noted that his frequent adversary "has a fertile and noble mind" and is "a fine creature in his profession." Wirt also praised Pinkney after his death, calling him a "great man" and an "excellent lawyer." Yet even one of his admirers, Theophilus Parsons, Jr., acknowledged that Pinkney was excessively vain, even to the point of being "vain of his vanity."[39]

Pinkney was born in 1764, just a few months before Robert Goodloe Harper. As a young man Pinkney met Samuel Chase, who offered him "the benefit of his library, his instruction, and his table." Pinkney joined Chase in opposing ratification of the Constitution, and their friendship persisted until 1805, when the protégé declined to defend his mentor against charges of impeachment. In 1811 Pinkney became the seventh attorney general of the United States, and a year later he was wounded in battle as British forces approached the nation's capital. After the war Pinkney served in the House of Representatives, then as a foreign minister, and from 1819 until his death as a U.S. senator. He is best remembered as one of the preeminent advocates of the Marshall Court era.[40]

William Pinkney. Courtesy of the Maryland Historical Society (Image ID 1956.75.1).

On February 22, 1819, the Supreme Court heard what would be the first of five days of oral argument in the celebrated case of *McCulloch v. Maryland*, which touched on such core constitutional principles as the supremacy of federal law, the meaning of the "Necessary and Proper" clause, and the notion of implied powers. Daniel Webster spoke first on behalf of McCulloch and the Bank of the United States, followed by Attorney General William Wirt. The State of Maryland was represented by its attorney general, Luther Martin. On the third day of argument William Pinkney stood to deliver argument in rebuttal. The ensuing oration, which lasted three days, was by most accounts the greatest speech of Pinkney's career. The private correspondence of Justice Gabriel Duvall suggests that prior to Pinkney's discourse, the Court had entertained "very strong doubts" about the result. Justice Story later stated that he had "never, in my whole life, heard a greater speech," and Chief Justice Marshall noted in the decision itself that counsel had displayed "a splendor of eloquence, and strength of argument," that had been "seldom, if ever, surpassed."[41]

The fact that William Pinkney was respected by justices of the Supreme Court was of particular importance to the Illinois and Wabash Land Company. Even prior to *McCulloch*, Justice Story observed that "Mr. Pinkney towers above all his competitors." Yet there were issues of concern for the shareholders. First, their chosen attorney did not come cheap: in important cases his fees went as high as $1,500, and Pinkney's annual income as early as 1816 was estimated at $21,000.[42] His haughty manner and personality traits were also an issue. Pinkney donned corsets to minimize his bulk and would stride into the Court's chambers wearing "amber-colored doeskin gloves, a giant cravat, and a blue coat studded with gilt buttons." Speeches were directed not only to the Court but also to the audience. William Wirt once remarked that his rival "could get into his tragical tone in discussing the construction of an act of Congress." An Englishman in 1820 commented on Pinkney's "uncouth and inelegant" habit of "raising one leg on a bench or chair before him, and in thrusting his right arm in a horizontal line from his side to its full length in front."[43] Yet despite such pompous and foppish behavior, the fact remains that many lawyers and judges regarded him as the greatest lawyer of the era. His performance in *McCulloch v. Maryland* (1819) and *Cohens v. Virginia* (1821) had been exemplary, and the shareholders were hopeful that Pinkney could persuade the Court to declare that the Indian tribes owned the lands they occupied and might sell such lands to private purchasers.

The shareholders also sought to secure the services of additional counsel. In January 1822 Francis Walker Gilmer of Richmond confided to an associate that he had been asked to assist Pinkney in arguing the Illinois and Wabash claims. Gilmer noted that the questions would be "as wide as the horizon," and added that Pinkney "was on the same side."[44] As it turned out, Gilmer did not participate in *Johnson v. McIntosh*, but it appears he had previously researched the claim on behalf of a most unlikely person: Virginia Murray, the daughter of Lord Dunmore. Lady Murray corresponded with various persons, both before and after the Supreme Court's decision, in a futile effort to establish rights to her late father's property in America.[45]

The "Devil Dunmore" belonged to another era and had been dead for nearly thirteen years when the Supreme Court convened its winter term on February 4, 1822. To mark the occasion the justices of the Supreme Court were invited to the White House, where the president was holding a reception for a delegation of Kansas, Missouri, Omaha, Oto, and Pawnee Indians. Charles Bird King painted portraits of several of the visitors, which remain on display in the White House. One of the subjects was Chief Sharitarish of the Pawnees, who informed President Monroe that the Indians "have plenty of land, *if you will keep your people off of it.*"[46] It is not known whether Monroe responded, but in his second inaugural address, the president recommended that Indians should dissolve their communal ties, become individual landowners, and sell their excess lands to the United States.[47]

Chief Sharitarish and his companions left Washington a few days after their meeting with President Monroe, and consequently would have missed the chance to watch William Pinkney argue that the Illinois and Piankeshaws were the sovereign owners of their lands and could sell them whenever and to whomsoever they pleased. But as it turned out, Pinkney did not get the chance to make his argument, as the Supreme Court was compelled by a full docket to postpone consideration of *Johnson v. McIntosh* until the following February.[48] Pinkney, however, did appear before the Court in the case of *Ricard v. Williams*. The opposing counsel in *Ricard* was another celebrated orator, Daniel Webster. The Court and Webster watched as the Maryland senator held the floor for two days, speaking for nine hours on the second day and refusing an offer to adjourn on account of his severe hoarseness of voice. The argument was concluded on February 15, and Pinkney fell faint during the following evening. According to

Justice Story, the eminent lawyer was "seized with an apoplexy, or some kindred disease," which led to his death on February 25, 1822.[49] The following day Robert Goodloe Harper declared to the Supreme Court that the bar "has lost one of its brightest ornaments" and moved to adjourn. To show their "profound respect," the justices and counsel wore black armbands for the remainder of the session.[50]

Pinkney's death, in the words of Edward Ingersoll, was "disastrous . . . for the present opportunity of doing business." Even before the funeral, Ingersoll and Harper began to plot a new course of action. As Ingersoll reported on February 26 to John Brinton, it was agreed that Daniel Webster—who "is *now* the most powerful advocate of all that attend the Supreme Court"—would assist Harper. "Mr. Webster . . . would be a very powerful adjunct," Ingersoll noted, given his "thorough knowledge of Indian titles in New England, his great industry and distinguished abilities." As for the opposing counsel, Harper emphasized that "the case must be, *for effect*, thoroughly argued and well argued for the Defendant," and he told Ingersoll that William Winder and Henry Murray should be retained *by the shareholders* to represent McIntosh: "Talk with Mr Murray and Gen. Winder (it seems they know where their fee is to come from), [and] . . . tell them frankly how poor we are and ask them subsequently to name the lowest sum for which they will engage."[51] Ingersoll was instructed to offer Winder and Murray no more than five hundred dollars each. Webster would receive an unknown retainer and a contingent fee of a thousand dollars, and Harper would be compensated in the same manner.[52]

MURRAY, WINDER, WEBSTER

Of the four attorneys who argued *Johnson v. McIntosh*, the least is known about Henry Murray, who was about thirty-three years of age when he appeared in his only case before the Supreme Court. Murray practiced law in Annapolis. His sister, Catherine Eliza Murray, was married to Richard Rush, the son of Benjamin Rush and the eighth attorney general of the United States (serving after William Pinkney and prior to William Wirt). Henry Murray was admitted to the Supreme Court bar on February 22, 1822, the day William Pinkney argued his last case. Although younger than Harper, Winder, and Webster, Henry Murray was the first to die, the victim of a terrible accident.[53]

Murray's co-counsel, William Henry Winder, was born in 1775 in Somerset County, Maryland. Winder graduated from the University of Pennsylvania at age seventeen and studied law with Gabriel Duvall. After a stint in the Department of the Navy under Benjamin Stoddert, Winder established a successful law practice in Baltimore and by 1812 was one of the leading lawyers in Maryland.[54] Both Robert Goodloe Harper and William Winder traded law for military service during the War of 1812. In comparison to Harper, Winder's role in the war was more extensive and of greater importance, but also more controversial.

As described by historian John Mahon, William Winder was a "political general" who owed his appointment to President Madison. On August 24, 1814, Winder's army was soundly defeated at the Battle of Bladensburg (Maryland), the same battle where William Pinkney was wounded. As the American soldiers scattered in a disorganized fashion, the British troops entered Washington and set fire to the White House and other government buildings. Winder insisted on a military court of inquiry, which exonerated him, concluding that he had exhibited a "personal valor highly honorable to himself and worthy of a better fate." Nevertheless, as noted by Arch Blakey, the public associated Winder with the invasion of Washington, and "even his closest friends felt it necessary to refer to Winder as 'that most unfortunate general' of the War of 1812." After being honorably discharged, Winder resumed his law practice; he appeared before the Supreme Court on thirty-seven occasions after the war. Forty-four reported decisions of the Supreme Court include Winder's name, and in exactly half of these cases Robert G. Harper was either co-counsel or on the opposing side. The two men, at different times between 1817 and 1823, also occupied the same seat in the Maryland Senate.[55]

Harper was also quite familiar with his co-counsel, Daniel Webster, although the two men had never previously participated in the same case before the Supreme Court. Born in 1782 in New Hampshire, Webster was seventeen years younger than Harper. After graduating from Dartmouth College in 1801, Webster taught school briefly and then prepared for a career in law. His opposition to war led to two terms in the House of Representatives from 1813 to 1817. During this time Webster began to make a name for himself, serving as chairman of the House Judiciary Committee and arguing a number of cases before the Supreme Court. Rather than seek a third term, Webster decided to focus on his law practice and moved to Boston. In 1822 he returned to the House of Representatives as a Massachusetts delegate.

Daniel Webster. National Portrait Gallery, Smithsonian Institution; gift of Mrs. Gerald B. Lambert.

The Eighteenth Congress, however, would not meet until December of 1823, thus allowing Webster to participate in seven cases—including *Johnson v. McIntosh*—during the Supreme Court's 1823 term.[56]

In 1821 Daniel Webster was counsel in six cases before the Court, including *Prevost v. Gratz*, which involved allegations that Barnard,

Michael, and Simon Gratz committed "sundry breaches of trust" with respect to the property of George Croghan. Webster argued on behalf of the Croghan estate, and William Pinkney defended the Gratz family.[57] Although *Prevost v. Gratz* was important to the Gratz family, it does not rank among Daniel Webster's most notable legal achievements. Prior to 1823, there are three cases that stand out: *Dartmouth College v. Woodward* (1819), *McCulloch v. Maryland* (1819), and *Cohens v. Virginia* (1821). In each instance the Court found in Webster's favor, and each case involved important constitutional issues. In *Cohens*, Chief Justice Marshall once again upheld the authority of the Supreme Court to review state court decisions, and proclaimed that the federal courts possess final authority over constitutional questions. In *McCulloch*, the Court agreed with Webster and Pinkney that the Constitution is the "supreme law of the land," that the "necessary and proper" clause should be broadly construed, and that state taxation of the national bank was unconstitutional because the "power to tax involves the power to destroy." It was *Dartmouth College v. Woodward*, however, that Webster described as the "turning point of my career." Relying on the expansive view of the Contract Clause set forth in *Fletcher v. Peck*, Webster argued that a New Hampshire law altering the college's charter was unconstitutional. The Court and the audience were "wrought up to the highest excitement" by Webster's emotional oration in defense of his alma mater. In the famous summation, Webster paused for effect, looked directly at the Chief Justice, and exclaimed: "Sir, you may destroy this little institution; it is weak, it is in your hands! . . . It is, sir, as I have said, a small college. And yet *there are those who love it!*" Spectators wept uncontrollably, Marshall's eyes "suffused with tears," and the college retained its charter.[58]

With so much at stake, it made perfect sense for the Illinois and Wabash Land Company to replace William Pinkney with Daniel Webster. It was evident that John Marshall held Webster in high esteem, and Joseph Story was both an admirer and a close friend. Webster's oratory, Story marveled, possessed "an almost superhuman influence," such that "it was impossible to listen without increasing astonishment at the profound reaches of the human intellect."[59] Although Robert Goodloe Harper was quite confident of his own abilities, he and the other shareholders were aware of their difficult situation and were no doubt counting on Webster's "almost superhuman influence" to sway John Marshall, Joseph Story, and the remaining Supreme Court justices.

By the end of 1822, if not sooner, Daniel Webster had begun to research the question of Indian land rights in America as well as the related right of private individuals to buy America from the Indians. On December 30, 1822, Webster wrote to David Daggett of Connecticut to request assistance in locating a published account of the "Moheagan Case" that was mentioned in *A Complete History of Connecticut* (1818) by Benjamin Trumbull. "In the course of investigating some ancient Tittles, derived under Indian Deeds," Webster explained, "I have had occasion to look up the history of the purchase of Capt. Mason in Connecticut." As described in chapter 4, the legality of Mason's purchase was reviewed over a span of seven decades by British authorities, who at one point in the proceedings opined that British subjects must make "*fair and honest* purchases of the natives" in order to acquire "the *property of the soil*." Daggett must have told Webster that Harper was in possession of the desired publication, because Webster wrote again a week later to inform Daggett that if "Gen'l Harper has the Moheagan Pamphlet, it is as if I had it, I being in the same cause on the same side."[60]

General Harper, of course, was already well acquainted with most of the legal issues surrounding the Illinois and Wabash purchases, having prepared the statement of facts in the present litigation as well as the 1810 memorial to Congress. In recognition of his essential role, the shareholders in January voted to issue Harper another share for his services. It appears that Harper in turn was advising friends and members of his extended family to invest in the company. Just as the Supreme Court began its 1823 session, Mary Anne Patterson of Baltimore acquired a half share by auction for $460, and John McTavish, David Winchester, and "L. Kimball" of Baltimore paid $820, $640, and $810 each for half shares. Patterson was the daughter of Richard Caton, a son-in-law of Charles Carroll of Carrollton and brother-in-law of Robert Goodloe Harper. Her husband, Robert Patterson, had passed away during the previous year. McTavish, a Scotsman serving as the British consul in Baltimore, was married to Mary Anne's sister. David Winchester was the president of the Baltimore Insurance Company. The last of these unfortunate investors was Leonard Kimball, an attorney who just a few days earlier had married Sarah Yeates Smith, the granddaughter of deceased shareholder William Smith of Philadelphia.[61]

The Supreme Court convened its 1823 term on the third of February. Fortuitously, the proceedings before the Court are described in the diaries of two men: George Brydges Rodney and Charles Jared Ingersoll.[62] Rodney, who was not yet nineteen, was the son of Daniel Rodney, a former governor of Delaware and a current member of the House of Representatives. Charles Jared Ingersoll was also from a prominent family. His father served in the Continental Congress, his brother Edward was an Illinois-Wabash shareholder, and his other brother was attorney Joseph Reed Ingersoll, whose career in Congress would span from 1835 to 1848. Ingersoll himself served in the House of Representatives during the War of 1812 and was currently the U.S. district attorney for Pennsylvania. While in Washington in 1823 he represented a private litigant in a matter before the Supreme Court. His diary and Rodney's focused on the weather, the members of the Supreme Court bar, and the justices in attendance:

Thursday, February 6. George Brydges Rodney: Extremely cold.

Thursday, February 6. Charles Jared Ingersoll: There is an uncommon number of lawyers here this term. . . . Mr. Webster, who, I think, may be considered since Pinkney's death as the most eminent practitioner in this court (I think Genl. Harper has done the most business).

Friday, February 7. George Brydges Rodney: I . . . heard an argument from Mr. Harper upon some insurance case. He is an elderly man, large person, a full red face, grey hair, acquiline nose. . . . There are seven Judges belonging to this Court, but only 6 here. They are Chief Justice Marshall of Va. He is of common stature, head round and small, hair black mixed with grey and cued, skin dark, black eyes and countenance very sedate. Judge Washington . . . is rather small, black hair, sallow complexion, high forehead and black eyes. He looks to be in delicate health. Judge Johnson is a corpulent robust looking man. His head is large, high forehead, hair thin but once light color, healthy appearance and large full face. . . . Livingston of N.Y. . . . is a tall old man with but little hair, long head, large nose and thin face. His appearance is dignified and . . . intelligent. To the extreme right is Duvall. He too is large or tall and slender, quite old looking and with a long cue. To the extreme left is Story of Boston. He is the most pleasant and agreeable looking of all, common size but stout, but little hair, a round fleshy face and a countenance very open and smiling. He is the youngest of any in age and standing. Todd is the last one, but he is [absent].

Saturday, February 8. Charles Jared Ingersoll: This is a bitter cold day.

Tuesday, February 11. George Brydges Rodney: Webster . . . seems to be of a cold dull temperament and his speaking partakes of that character. His chief excellence consists in logical argumentative reasoning.[63]

In addition to George Rodney and Charles Jared Ingersoll, another source of information regarding the events leading up to the arguments in *Johnson v. McIntosh* is Edward Ingersoll, who arrived from Philadelphia on the tenth of February. On the evening of Ingersoll's arrival Webster told him that their case would "probably be reached in the course of three or four days." William Wirt, the attorney general, had been ill for several days, causing cases that did not involve the United States to be moved forward. The younger Ingersoll passed along the news to the shareholders in Philadelphia that Wirt had "received no order from the Government to take any part" in their case—despite the fact that a decision favoring the united companies would remove immense tracts of land from the federal domain. He also reported that "Mr Winder & Mr Murray are both prepared to make hard battle," and that "Mr Harper anticipates a strong argument from Mr Webster on our side."[64]

Edward Ingersoll filed another report on February 13. "I suppose our counsel will make good arguments," he wrote in a letter to Jacob Gratz, "but I do not believe they are so fully prepared as they might be and rather hope the case may not be reached for a week yet." The thirty-two-year-old lawyer assisted Harper and Webster by bringing to their attention the 1774 Quebec Act, "which neither . . . knew anything about."[65] The following evening Harper, Webster, Winder, and Murray were dinner guests of President Monroe, along with several Supreme Court justices and other prominent individuals and officials. Charles Jared Ingersoll, who was seated next to General Harper, noted in his diary that "nearly thirty" judges and lawyers were in attendance. Ingersoll also noted that during the evening Henry Murray made mention of the fact that he had come to Washington to argue against the validity of the Illinois and Wabash purchases: "We had a prodigious shew of Lawyers at dinner at the President's, among them Mrs. Rush's brother who attends the Supreme court to argue a case *in which sevent[y] millions of acres of land are in controversy.*"[66]

The next day was a Saturday, February 15. According to the *Daily National Intelligencer*, the first order of business was the delivery by Justice

Story of the Court's opinion in the *Experiment*—a "prize" case that Daniel Webster argued and lost. Attorney General William Wirt then discussed "some points suggested by the Court . . . in the case of the *Mary Ann*." After Wirt concluded, the case of *Johnson and Graham's Lessee v. McIntosh* was "opened by Mr. Webster for the plaintiff and Mr. Murray for the Defendant."[67] After a day of rest, Murray stood again before the Court on Monday, and was joined by his co-counsel, William Winder. The final two days of argument belonged to Robert Goodloe Harper. On Wednesday, February 19, 1823, after Harper had concluded his rebuttal, George Rodney returned to his lodgings and recorded his thoughts: "Several arguments have been made in the S. Court, and a very long one on the subject of the Indian deed granting a large tract of Illinois to certain individuals. The validity of the deed was maintained by Webster and Harper and opposed by Winder and Murray of Annps. *The court would not give their opinion but it will doubtless [be] against the grant.*[68]

15

THE ARGUMENT AND DECISION
IN *JOHNSON V. McINTOSH*

In the three centuries leading up to the argument in *Johnson v. McIntosh,* most commentators, officials, legislators, and judges took the position that Indians could not sell their lands to private individuals—either because of restrictions placed on the right of disposition or because Indians did not own fee-simple title to the lands they occupied. The array of mostly unfavorable precedents can be sorted into four categories: "positive" law (statutes, regulations, and proclamations); judicial decisions (state and federal); other governmental actions (such as committee reports and decisions of land commissions); and private commentary (set forth in treatises, pamphlets, and other documents). To prevail before the Supreme Court, Daniel Webster and Robert Goodloe Harper would have to convince the justices that prior laws, rulings, and statements that diminished Indian land rights in America were neither binding nor persuasive. The obstacles facing the attorneys for plaintiffs Joshua Johnson and Thomas Grahame were formidable.

THE PRECEDENTS

Even if one agreed that the Native inhabitants of America did possess a "natural" right to own and sell land, such property rights might be restricted by regulations, proclamations, or statutes. The existence of such positive law was problematic for the Illinois and Wabash Land Company. Was the British Crown empowered to prohibit Indian tribes from selling land to private individuals? If the Crown had no such authority, what about Parliament, Virginia, or Congress? Moreover, if the Native grantors could not be controlled, was it nonetheless permissible to regulate the private grantees? The British government, the colonies, the newly independent states, the Continental Congress, and the federal government all exercised such regulatory authority.

Webster and Harper would have to argue that laws prohibiting the sale of Indian lands to private individuals either did not apply to the Illinois and Wabash purchases or were *ultra vires* (beyond legal authority). It was not clear that the sales were prohibited by Virginia law, which at the time declared it unlawful "for an Indian king, *or any other of the said tributary Indians whatever,*" to sell or lease lands to non-Indians.[1] It was also uncertain whether Virginia could retroactively divest property rights, as it had attempted to do in 1779 when the General Assembly asserted that "no person or persons whatsoever have, *or ever had*, a right to purchase any lands . . . from any Indian Nation, except only persons duly authorized to make such purchases."[2] The transactions, of course, occurred *after* the Proclamation of 1763. Harper questioned the applicability and validity of the proclamation in memorials submitted to Congress in 1810 and 1816. Although he did not convince Congress, Harper was confident he could persuade the Supreme Court that the proclamation did not restrain the right of British subjects to purchase the lands of the western tribes.[3]

The second category of precedents consists of judicial decisions that addressed Indian land rights. The Supreme Court itself touched upon this issue in *Fletcher v. Peck*. Although the case did not involve a purchase by private individuals, Chief Justice Marshall stated that "the nature of the Indian title . . . is not such as to be absolutely repugnant to seisin in fee on the part of the state." This assertion in *Fletcher* can be characterized as nonbinding dictum; however, at least two of the other justices viewed Marshall's pronouncement as binding precedent. In oral argument for the case of *Meigs v. McClung's Lessee* (1815), the chief justice asked attorney Charles Lee if the case before the Court raised the issue "whether a grant is good before extinguishment of the Indian title?" Lee said it was not, but Justice Story interjected, "That question has been decided in the case of *Fletcher v. Peck*."[4] Justice Bushrod Washington also asserted that *Fletcher* "resolved" that Indian title was not "absolutely repugnant to seisin; in fee, on the part of the state."[5]

If the Illinois and Piankeshaws did not have seisin to the lands they occupied, then the shareholders could not claim ownership by virtue of the 1773 and 1775 transactions. At best, they acquired "Indian title"—assuming their purchases would be upheld for that limited purpose. John Marshall's views on the "nature of the Indian title" were thus as problematic as the 1763 proclamation. However, Marshall's cursory remarks in *Fletcher* represent just one view of Indian land rights in America. The possessory, ownership, and disposition rights in Native lands can be either aggregated or diffused, leading to differing conceptions of Indian land rights:

1. *Indians own the lands they occupy and are free to sell their lands to whomsoever they please.*
2. *Indians own the lands they occupy but are not free to sell their lands to whomsoever they please.* The holder of the preemption right has the exclusive right to acquire the property rights of the Indians.
3. *Indians possess the land they occupy, but do not own the lands they occupy.* The United States (or one of the original colonies) owns the land subject to the Native right of possession. As owner, the United States (or one of the original colonies) can transfer ownership "notwithstanding the non-extinguishment of the Indian title." Once the "Indian title" is extinguished, the owner of the land also has the right of possession.[6]
4. *Indians have no property rights.* The United States (or one of the original colonies) owns the land *and* the possessory right. The Native occupants are, in effect, trespassers. When payments are made to tribes, it is not done to acquire property rights but rather to expedite the removal of the Indians.

Under the first view, the Illinois and Piankeshaws owed the lands they sold in 1773 and 1775. Under the second view, the 1773 and 1775 transactions were null and void, and the tribes remained the owners until such ownership rights were acquired by the United States by treaty. Under the third view, the reason the tribes could not transfer ownership to the Illinois and Wabash grantees was because the tribes did not own the lands they occupied. The British Crown owned the fee-simple title, which was passed first to Virginia and then to the United States, and the treaties negotiated by William Henry Harrison merely extinguished the Native right of possession. Under the final view, the government paid the Indians only for political (or moral) reasons and for the pragmatic purpose of expediting settlement.

John Marshall's adoption of the third view in *Fletcher v. Peck* was by no means unprecedented. In *Strother v. Cathey* (1807) Judge David Stone of the North Carolina Supreme Court held that "neither the European governments, nor the government of the United States, nor that of North Carolina, have considered the Indian title *other than a mere possessory right*." In his study of Indian land rights Stuart Banner states that "*Strother* . . . appears to be the first reported American court decision holding that unsold Indian land *was owned* by the government, subject only to a lesser right of 'possession' or 'occupancy' held by the Indians."[7] Even before *Strother* and *Fletcher*, however, state courts held that title to Indian lands could be transferred while the Natives occupied the soil. The Supreme Court of Appeals of Virginia held in *Marshall v. Clark* (1791) that "the Indian title did not impede . . . the power of the legislature to grant the land." The Pennsylvania Supreme Court likewise held in *Weiser's Lessee v. Moody* (1796) that if the state knowingly granted Indian lands not yet purchased, the title "would enure for the benefit of the grantee, when the lands came afterwards to be purchased from the Indians." Nine years later, in *Glasgow's Lessee v. Smith and Blackwell* (1805), Tennessee Judge John Overton, Jr., observed that North Carolina was empowered to "contract, sell, and grant lands . . . *before* any treaty was made."[8]

Prominent judges from New York and Pennsylvania also subscribed to this view. The chancellor of New York, John Ten Eyck Lansing, Jr., claimed in *Van Gorden v. Jackson ex dem. Bogardus* (1809) that Indian deeds "were never admitted, as of themselves, to be a source of *legal title*," and that "all titles must be derived, either mediately or immediately, actually or presumptively, from the crown."[9] William Tilghman, the chief justice of the Pennsylvania State Supreme Court, and his fellow justices Jasper Yeates and Hugh Henry Brackenridge, also held negative views of Indian land rights. For example, in *Cox v. Cromwell* (1810) Justice Brackenridge instructed a jury at circuit court that any Indian deed obtained by George Croghan "would have been void, as it would have been in violation of law." Chief Justice Tilghman agreed that if Croghan's title was based on an Indian deed, it "was good for nothing."[10]

The three Pennsylvania justices each authored opinions in *Thompson v. Johnston* (1813), which contains the most detailed discussion of Indian land rights by any American court prior to *Johnson v. McIntosh*. John Thompson had been granted land by Pennsylvania in 1773, two years *before* the state transacted with the Indians. James Johnston, on the other hand, was granted the same land in 1785, after the state purchased it. The state supreme court held that the Thompson grant was invalid—but not on the ground that Pennsylvania in 1773 had nothing to grant. Instead, as Justice Yeates noted, the 1773 grant "was prohibited *by positive law*" because it was "against the uniform practice of the proprietaries to sell lands unpurchased from the Indians." Chief Justice Tilghman emphasized that King Charles "did indeed convey to William Penn an immediate and absolute estate in fee in the province of Pennsylvania," but held that the "good man did not conceive that he had a title in *conscience,* until he had obtained the consent of the natives." Justice Brackenridge dissented, arguing that James Johnston knew of the prior grant and should not be permitted "to avail himself of the mistake." With regard to Indian land rights, however, Brackenridge asserted that the heathen Indians "were not considered as having *any right,*" but were rather viewed by Europeans "as but having a *claim,* which more for the sake of peace than of obligation, it behoved them to extinguish."[11]

Webster and Harper were hard-pressed to find prior decisions upholding Indian land rights. In the dispute between the Mohegan Tribe and Connecticut, the royal commission found for the colony on the merits but did state at one point that the Indians had "*the property of the soil,*" which must be purchased.[12] The most favorable judicial precedent for the Illinois-Wabash shareholders was Justice Johnson's dissenting opinion in *Fletcher v. Peck.* Johnson declared that "Georgia had *not* a fee-simple in the land in question" but also stated that Indian ownership rights are subject to the right of preemption.[13] In other words, Justice Johnson did not adopt the most favorable view of Indian land rights, instead taking the intermediate position that Indians own the lands they occupy but are *not* free to sell their lands to whomsoever they please.

The third category of precedents includes various governmental actions relating to Indian land rights, such as committee reports of the Senate and House of Representatives, decisions of land commissions, and official legal opinions. For the most part, such prior actions were not favorable. The Vincennes and Kaskaskia land commissions recommended that the claims be denied, and Congress consistently declined to grant the petitions of the Illinois and Wabash Land Company. Other persons holding Indian deeds were also unsuccessful in persuading Congress to sustain their claims. In 1819 the Senate refused to confirm the title to land granted to Alexander Macomb by the Potawatomi Nation.[14] A much larger Indian grant was the subject of a negative committee report just prior to the Supreme Court's February 1823 term. On May 1, 1767, Sioux tribal chiefs purportedly granted Jonathan Carver "upwards of ten thousand square miles of land lying in the modern states of Wisconsin and Minnesota." His descendants petitioned Congress in 1806 to confirm the Indian deed but were unsuccessful. The matter was taken up again in 1822, when Representative Reuben Walworth of New York requested information from the executive branch "respecting the pretended titles of the heirs of Jonathan Carver." In response the commissioner of the General Land Office, Josiah Meigs, asserted that the purchase violated the 1763 Proclamation, which embodied a policy that "has been invariably adhered to by the United States."[15]

The matter was referred to the Senate Committee on Public Lands, which issued its report on January 23, 1823, less than a month before the oral arguments in *Johnson v. McIntosh*. The committee relied on the royal proclamation in support of its conclusion that Carver's alleged Indian deed "could not vest the legal title in him." John Marshall and the other justices were likely aware of the immense size of the Carver purchase as well as its similarity to the Illinois and Wabash grants. As it turned out, although the Senate resolved that the prayer of the petitioners should be denied, the House of Representatives did not act on the petition. The Carver claimants persevered for two more years, until the House Committee on Private Land Claims declared in 1825 that the invalidity of private purchases was "settled beyond controversy" in "the case of Johnson against McIntosh."[16]

On the other hand, Webster and Harper could point out that government officials did state in one instance that Indians may sell their lands to private purchasers. Unfortunately, the 1757 Camden-Yorke opinion addressed the property rights of Indians *in India* and was written six years *before* the Proclamation of 1763. In contrast, a more recent opinion by the attorney general of the United States examined Indian land rights *in America*. In 1821 William Wirt was asked whether private individuals could survey lands occupied by the Seneca Nation. The individuals claimed they had been granted the "right of soil" and were "desirous of making partition among themselves." Wirt, however, determined that the proposed survey would be inconsistent not only with the tribe's treaty rights but also with the general nature of the Indian title: "The answer to this question depends on the character of the title which the Indians retain in these lands. . . . *The conquerors have never claimed more than the exclusive right of purchase from the Indians.* . . . They do not hold under the States, nor under the United States; their title is original, sovereign, and exclusive."[17] In light of Wirt's statements, Robert Williams, Jr., has remarked that "even as late as 1821 in this country, legal opinion on the validity of the doctrine of discovery was far from unanimous." By acknowledging the right of preemption, however, William Wirt joined Justice William Johnson in holding that Indians are not free to sell the lands they own to private purchasers.[18]

The final category of precedents was the private commentary set forth in treatises, pamphlets, and other documents. As previously discussed, much ink was spilled in defense of the right of Europeans to claim ownership of the New World. Learned men, such as Hugo Grotius, John Locke, and Emer de Vattel, did not need to cross the Atlantic in order to diminish Indian land rights. Their writings would play a prominent role in the arguments presented by William Winder and Henry Murray in *Johnson v. McIntosh*. The attorneys for McIntosh would also rely on American commentary—such as James Sullivan's *History of Land Titles in Massachusetts* (1801)—that denigrated Indian property rights. Sullivan, who served as a judge, state attorney general, and governor of Massachusetts, contended that the "savages" of North America lack property rights by virtue of their "precarious and transient occupancy." It was "altogether preposterous," Sullivan argued, to believe "that so fair and fertile a part of the terrestrial creation was intended forever to remain in such a savage state."[19]

In response, Webster and Harper could inform the Court that prominent individuals had contended that the Indians of North America owned the land they occupied and might sell the land to whomsoever they pleased. This was the position taken by the Puritan Roger Williams, the Jesuit Thomas Copley, and the Quaker Thomas Chalkley. Jeremiah Dummer of New England and the Newark settlers of New Jersey also championed the right of Indians to own and sell property, as did the English writer Arthur Young. In the 1770s three eminent lawyers—Henry Dagge, John Glynn, and Patrick Henry—asserted that Indians may transfer their property to private individuals. Benjamin Franklin concurred, as did Samuel Wharton, who argued in *Plain Facts* that the Natives of America "have an indefeasible right freely to sell, and grant to any person whomsoever." Even the secretary of war, Henry Knox, conceded in 1790 that "*the Indians possess the natural rights of man, and that they ought not wantonly to be divested thereof.*"[20]

The northern tribes declared in 1793 that "we consider ourselves free to make any bargain or cession of lands, whenever & to whomsoever we please."[21] But would the Supreme Court agree? In 1823, the members of the high court were, in order of seniority, Bushrod Washington,

John Marshall, William Johnson, Brockholst Livingston, Thomas Todd, Gabriel Duvall, and Joseph Story. Todd missed the February 1823 term, and Washington was absent when arguments were presented in *Johnson v. McIntosh*.[22] Consequently the fortunes of the shareholders would be secured if Webster and Harper could persuade just three individuals—a majority of the sitting justices—that American Indians were entitled to the same property rights as non-Native landowners.

THE SUPREME COURT

Although the counsel in *Johnson v. McIntosh* realized that they needed to win the votes of at least three Supreme Court justices, it was generally accepted that the side favored by John Marshall would prevail. Daniel Webster had achieved great success before the Court in part because he recognized Marshall's influence over the other justices, and as a consequence "pitched his legal arguments directly at him." The chief justice was responsible for most of the Court's decisions, including *Marbury v. Madison* (1803), *Dartmouth College v. Woodward* (1819), *McCulloch v. Maryland* (1819), and—most significant–*Fletcher v. Peck* (1810). Marshall was himself a land speculator, having purchased a number of tracts in Kentucky in addition to his investment in the "Fairfax lands" of northern Virginia. Given the importance of Indian land rights in America, it would have been shocking if anyone other than the chief justice spoke for the Court in *Johnson*—the case "at the root of title for most real property in the United States."[23]

A distant cousin of Thomas Jefferson, John Marshall was born in 1755 on the Virginia frontier, the first of fifteen children. In December 1775 he helped defeat the British near Norfolk, hastening Lord Dunmore's departure from Virginia. Marshall was a great admirer of George Washington and fought under the commander-in-chief in several battles, including Brandywine, Germantown, and Monmouth. Both men spent the winter of 1777–78 at Valley Forge, where Marshall earned the nickname "Silverheels" for his running and leaping abilities.[24]

Despite ongoing hostilities with Great Britain, Virginia opened a land office in 1779 to dispose of its western lands. Thomas Marshall, the father of the future chief justice, promptly moved to Kentucky, where he acquired land for himself, his family, and business associates such as Barnard and Michael Gratz. The young John Marshall followed suit and invested in lands in Virginia and Kentucky.[25] After establishing a successful legal practice, Marshall in 1793 joined with his brother, James Markham Marshall, and his brother-in-law, Rawleigh Colston, to purchase approximately 215,000 acres of land in northern Virginia from Denny Martin, the nephew and heir of Lord Fairfax. The debt that was incurred in order to acquire the lands was not extinguished until 1802, and the validity of the title obtained became the subject of several lawsuits, including *Fairfax's Devisee v. Hunter's Lessee* (1812), in which Robert Goodloe Harper was involved.

Marshall and his partners were able to finance the acquisition of the Fairfax lands with the assistance of Robert Morris, who became even more closely connected to the Marshall family when his daughter Hester married James Markham Marshall in 1795. However, as Morris began his descent into bankruptcy, John Marshall acceded to President Adams's request that he participate in a diplomatic mission to France. The subsequent refusal by Marshall, Charles Cotesworth Pinckney, and Elbridge Gerry to submit to French extortion transformed the men into heroes, and when Marshall returned to Philadelphia, he was cheered by hundreds of citizens. At a testimonial dinner on June 18, 1798, fellow Federalist Robert Goodloe Harper exclaimed, "Millions for defense, but not a cent for tribute," and praised Marshall and his colleagues for refusing to dishonor the United States.[26]

In 1799 Marshall's career took a new turn when he was elected as a representative to the Sixth Congress. During this time he prepared a report recommending that Congress accept Connecticut's offer to cede its "Western Reserve" lands. The report contained a detailed discussion of the colonial charters as well as other relevant laws, such as the 1774 Quebec Act. In 1804 Marshall recounted the history of the British settlement of North America in the first volume of his biography of George Washington. Marshall would publish the volume separately in 1824 under the title *A History of the Colonies Planted by the English on the Continent of North America.*[27]

Marshall resigned his seat in June 1800 to become the secretary of state. By the end of the year it was clear that John Adams would not serve another term. In January 1801 Adams nominated Marshall to be the fourth chief justice of the United States Supreme Court. The forty-five-year-old Virginian was sworn into office on the fourth of February. His impact was immediate: between 1801 and 1804 Marshall spoke for the Court in twenty-four of the twenty-six decisions that were accompanied

John Marshall. National Portrait Gallery, Smithsonian Institution; gift of the A. W. Mellon Educational and Charitable Trust.

by opinions. Although William Johnson, Brockholst Livingston, Thomas Todd, Gabriel Duvall, and Joseph Story were appointed by Republican presidents, the chief justice maintained harmonious relations with his colleagues. Following the addition of Justice Story in 1812, there were no changes in personnel for eleven years, and the seven justices began to lodge together. As noted by Dwight Jessup, the bonds among the members of the Court during this time period "were probably stronger than at any other time in Supreme Court history."[28]

Despite such cordiality, the other justices did on occasion part ways with their chief justice. Of the remaining four justices who participated in *Johnson v. McIntosh*, William Johnson and Joseph Story were active members of the Court, whereas Gabriel Duvall and Brockholst Livingston tended to be passive participants. Justice Johnson of South Carolina issued more dissents than any other justice who served with John Marshall and wrote more opinions than any other associate justice besides Joseph Story. In 1822 Johnson published *The Sketches of the Life and Correspondence of Nathaniel Greene*, in which he suggested that former justice James Wilson conspired to remove General Washington from command and promote General Horatio Gates. Bird Wilson, the son of the late justice, enlisted the assistance of Bushrod Washington and obtained a public apology.[29] Although Johnson had besmirched the reputation of James Wilson, there was no reason to believe that he was predisposed to vote against the interests of the Illinois and Wabash shareholders. At one point in his dissent in *Fletcher v. Peck* Johnson referred to the Indians as "*the absolute proprietors of their soil.*"[30] Johnson's views on the nature of Indian property rights gave Webster and Harper hope that the justice could be persuaded to hold that the Illinois and Piankeshaws were empowered to sell their lands to private individuals.

The other justice most likely to take an active role in *Johnson* was Joseph Story of Massachusetts. Story was the youngest justice ever appointed to the high bench, the most productive of the associate justices during Marshall's tenure, and widely considered the "most learned scholar ever to sit on the Supreme Court." As previously noted, the Harvard graduate was a son-in-law of a shareholder in the New England Mississippi Land Company, and he had served both as an agent for the company and as Robert Goodloe Harper's co-counsel in *Fletcher*. As counsel for John Peck, Story and Harper had argued that Indians do not own the land they occupy but rather hold "Indian title," which the two characterized as "a mere privilege which does not affect the allodial right." Story joined the Court in 1812 at thirty-three and became Marshall's closest friend. Story intimated in *Meigs v. McClung's Lessee* (1815) and *Gilman v. Brown* (1817) that he considered the chief justice's statements in *Fletcher* to be the final word on "the nature of the Indian title." Nevertheless, Robert Goodloe

Harper was familiar with Story, having worked with him in the past, and Daniel Webster was a close friend. In fact, two years after *Johnson v. McIntosh*, Daniel and Grace Webster would accompany Joseph and Sarah Story on a six-week summer vacation to Niagara Falls.[31]

The polar opposite of Joseph Story on the Court was Gabriel Duvall, the oldest and least productive justice. Duvall was appointed to the Supreme Court in 1811 following the death of Samuel Chase. Almost sixty years old when he joined the Court, Duvall had served in the House of Representatives, on the Maryland General Court, and as the first comptroller of the United States Treasury. During his twenty-three years on the bench he became progressively more deaf, to the point where he could not hear the oral arguments. In the estimation of Robert Remini, Duvall was "one of the least important justices in the entire history of the Court." G. Edward White, a leading historian of the Marshall Court, agrees, noting that "the few opinions he did write are not memorable: almost none involved major cases, and none was more than a few pages in length."[32]

The fifth and final Supreme Court justice who participated in *Johnson v. McIntosh* was Brockholst Livingston of New York. His father, William Livingston, served as governor of New Jersey during the Revolution and signed the Constitution. His sister Catherine married Matthew Ridley of Maryland, one of the original grantees in the 1775 Wabash purchase. Livingston was nominated by Jefferson in 1806 and occupied the seat once held by Thomas Johnson. Another Illinois-Wabash shareholder, Samuel Chase, asked Livingston in 1809 to witness the granting of his interest in the company to his two sons.

Brockholst Livingston, Gabriel Duvall, and Thomas Todd have been called the "silent justices" of the Marshall Court. In sixteen years on the Court, Livingston produced fewer than fifty opinions, and he usually voted in the same manner as the chief justice, to the disappointment of Jefferson. Livingston's most notable judicial contribution may very well be his dissent in *Pierson v. Post*, written in 1805 as a judge on the New York Supreme Court. The litigants in this dispute—which is required reading for most first year law students in the United States—were a fox hunter and a "saucy intruder" (to quote Livingston) who spoiled the hunt by killing and carrying away the prey. While the majority held that mere pursuit of a wild animal does not confer a property right, Livingston felt that the intruder, "who had not shared in the honours or labours of the chase," should not be permitted to "bear away in triumph the object of pursuit."[33]

Although Brockholst Livingston was on record with respect to the acquisition of property rights in wild animals, his views on the property rights of Indians were not known to the public. Livingston voted with Marshall in *Fletcher v. Peck*, but the New York jurist did not write a separate opinion, and it was not certain that he endorsed the chief justice's position on "the nature of the Indian title." Daniel Webster and Robert Harper would have been greatly pleased to learn that Livingston *had* previously considered the issue of Native land rights and had concluded that Indian tribes were empowered as "Independent Nations" to sell their lands to individuals.

As discussed in chapter 11, John Askin of Detroit joined with other individuals in 1795 and 1796 to purchase considerable portions of present-day Michigan and northern Ohio from local tribes. His son was dispatched to Greenville to ensure that General Anthony Wayne would acknowledge the right of the northwest Indians to sell land to private parties. Wayne, however, detained the younger Askin and negotiated a treaty that ratified the federal government's right of preemption. At about the same time, the senior Askin's partner, Alexander Henry of Montreal, traveled east and discussed the sizable purchases with Alexander Hamilton and Robert Morris. Hamilton was unwilling to declare that the transactions were valid, and Morris was hesitant to invest. Shortly thereafter, Henry asked Brockholst Livingston, in his capacity as a private attorney, to provide legal advice.

Livingston responded in September 1796 in a letter addressed to a "J. Schieffelin," who most certainly was Jonathan Schieffelin, an associate of John Askin. Livingston suggested three options: seek relief as British subjects through diplomatic channels; apply directly to Congress for a confirmation of the title; or settle on the acquired land and then resort to litigation in the courts of the United States. "The third mode," Livingston counseled, "is attended with some risque to the Settlers, but perhaps, is the only one which ought to be pursued." In support of this statement, Livingston strongly endorsed the right of Indians to exercise ownership and disposition rights with respect to their lands: "*I think Congress have no right to say, that the Indians shall grant no lands without their permission.* They have acknowledged them as Independent Nations. They make Treaties, and settle Boundary Lines with them, as such; *It is therefore, interfering with their Sovereignty to declare, that they shall not grant their own lands.*"[34] Justice Livingston, of course, was not obliged to follow legal advice he had provided in a private matter over a quarter century prior to *Johnson v. McIntosh*. As it turned out, the sixty-five-year-old jurist voted with Chief Justice Marshall and did not set forth his own views on Indian land rights. On the February 28, 1823—the same day that the Court announced its decision—Joseph Story confided to a friend that Livingston was "very ill." Two weeks later Brockholst Livingston was dead, the first member of the Court to pass away since the death of Samuel Chase in 1811.[35]

The Argument for Johnson and Grahame

Oral argument in *Johnson and Graham's Lessee v. McIntosh* began on Saturday, February 15, 1823.[36] It is not known whether the litigants were in attendance, but counsel as well as spectators were present when the justices donned robes and seated themselves behind their desks. The Supreme Court was located in the basement of the Capitol, directly below the Senate chamber. The damage inflicted by the British in 1814 had caused the Court to meet for several years in temporary quarters, but the justices returned to their renovated courtroom in 1819, the same year Congress increased the salaries of associate justices to $4,500 and the annual salary of the chief justice to $5,000. In contrast, prominent lawyers such as William Pinkney and Daniel Webster earned as much as $20,000 a year.[37]

It was another cold February day in the nation's capital. The morning session began with Justice Story announcing the Court's decision in a dispute over the cargo of a British sloop seized during the war. The Court relied on an 1816 decision, *The George*, and held that the capture of the *Experiment* by the privateer *Fly* was "fraudulent and collusive" and that the ship's contents were consequently forfeited to the United States. Daniel Webster, on behalf of the American shipowners, had contended that the case was distinguishable from *The George* but failed to convince the Court.[38] Shortly after receiving the bad news, Webster presented the opening argument in *Johnson v. McIntosh*. Once again, Webster would be compelled to argue that his clients' case was distinguishable from a prior decision handed down by the Court—*Fletcher v. Peck*. The presentations by counsel were summarized by the Court reporter, Henry Wheaton, who felt it was unnecessary to reproduce the portions of the arguments that were "fully stated in the opinion." Because there were no written briefs, Wheaton and John Marshall are our primary sources for reconstructing the legal positions taken in the case.[39] Webster and Harper pressed three main points. First and foremost, the two men contended that Indians own

the lands they occupy and may sell their property rights to individuals
in the absence of applicable law to the contrary. The lawyers then asserted
that neither the Proclamation of 1763 nor the laws of Virginia operated to
invalidate the 1773 and 1775 purchases.

Daniel Webster addressed the nature of Indian land rights in his opening remarks on Saturday, and Robert Harper revisited the issue during
his rebuttal on Tuesday and Wednesday. Webster pointed out that "upon
the facts stated in the case, the Piankeshaw Indians were the owners of
the lands in dispute . . . and had the power to sell." The Court, however,
would not to permit the parties to resolve this core issue by stipulation.
Webster and Harper further argued that since the United States itself acquired land from the tribes, it was "unnecessary, and merely speculative,
to discuss the question respecting *the sort of title or ownership*, which may
be thought to belong to savage tribes, in the lands on which they live."
However, it clearly *was* necessary to address the nature of the Indian title,
because if the Illinois and Piankeshaws did not own the lands they occupied, they could not transfer ownership rights to their putative grantees.
Webster and Harper used two different phrases to describe the tribes'
property rights: "title by occupancy" and "right of soil."[40] The former is
not normally equated to ownership, and the latter is ambiguous. Chief
Justice Marshall, of course, had declared in *Fletcher* that the Indians occupying the Yazoo lands held a property right other than the fee-simple
title that is associated with ownership.

After noting that nearly all lands in the United States were held "under
purchases from the Indian nations," Webster and Harper asserted that
"the only question in this case must be, *whether it be competent to individuals
to make such purchases, or whether that be the exclusive prerogative of government.*" In his opinion Marshall states that counsel for the plaintiffs "relied
very much on the opinions expressed by men holding offices of trust,
and on various proceedings in America, to sustain titles to land derived
from the Indians." It is noteworthy, however, that neither Marshall nor
Wheaton mentions the legal opinions of Henry Dagge, John Glynn,
Patrick Henry, and Benjamin Franklin. In support of the right of individuals to purchase Indian lands, Webster and Harper apparently chose
to cite examples of Indian deeds in New England, as well as the "controversy between the colony of Connecticut and the Mohegan Indians,"
and to rely on the "opinion of the Attorney and Solicitor General, Pratt
and Yorke." With somewhat questionable logic, they also contended that

the enactment of laws prohibiting individual purchases of Indian lands proved that "independent of such prohibitions, Indian deeds would be valid."[41]

Their position with respect to the 1763 Proclamation tracked the arguments previously set forth in the memorials to Congress. If the Illinois and Piankeshaw Indians were not British subjects, they could not be bound by the authority of the British government, and if the tribal members were British subjects, they "could not be devested [*sic*] of their rights of property, or any of its incidents, by a mere act of the executive government, such as this proclamation." Furthermore, the king lacked the authority to prohibit his subjects from purchasing Indian lands because "the establishment of a government . . . excludes the power of legislating *by proclamation*."[42] Webster and Harper cited *Campbell v. Hall* (1774) for the proposition that the power to legislate by proclamation "is confined to countries newly conquered, and remaining in the military possession of the monarch." Shortly after France ceded Grenada, King George III imposed a tax on all goods and sugars from the island. An exporter challenged the tax, arguing that it could only be imposed by Parliament. The chief justice of the king's bench, Lord Mansfield, agreed, and held that the king had "precluded himself from the exercise of legislative authority" when he decreed that "legislation over the island should be exercised by an assembly with the consent of the governor and council."[43] Although the case was not directly relevant, Webster and Harper nevertheless argued that if the king lacked the authority to tax British subjects living in Grenada, he likewise was without authority to prohibit his North American subjects from purchasing Indian lands.

The lawyers then turned to Virginia, which on several occasions had passed laws restricting private purchases of Indian lands. According to the plaintiffs, the "old colonial laws on the subject" had been repealed *prior* to the Illinois and Wabash purchases. Furthermore, although the General Assembly declared in 1779 that "no person or persons whatsoever have, *or ever had*, a right to purchase any lands . . . from any Indian Nation, except only persons duly authorized to make such purchases," the Virginia legislation was *ultra vires* to the extent that it purported "to take away private, vested rights."[44] In short, because the purchases were not lawfully prohibited by Virginia law or the 1763 Proclamation, the question before the Court was "*the general inquiry*, whether individuals, in Virginia, at the time of this purchase, could legally obtain Indian titles."[45]

The Argument for McIntosh

Not surprisingly, Henry Murray and William Winder took issue with each of three main points argued by their opposing counsel. The lawyers for McIntosh denied that the Native occupants of America had a natural right to own and sell property, relying in part on the characterization of Indian title put forward by Harper and Story in *Fletcher v. Peck*. In addition, Murray and Winder argued that the purchases were prohibited by the Proclamation of 1763 and also by the laws of Virginia.

Henry Murray spoke first, beginning on Saturday after Webster concluded his remarks and continuing on Monday before yielding to Winder. Both lawyers argued that the Illinois and Piankeshaws did not have "a permanent property in the soil, capable of alienation to private individuals." Because lands occupied by Indians were not used "in such a manner as to prevent their being appropriated by a people of cultivators," the Native occupants of America were merely "perpetual inhabitants with diminutive rights." Citing the commentaries of Grotius, Pufendorf, Locke, Barbeyrac, Vattel, Cadwallader Colden, William Smith, Montesquieu, Blackstone, Jefferson, Adam Smith, Thomas Rutherforth, and George Chalmers, the counsel for McIntosh asserted that "every theory of property" led inexorably to the conclusion that "the Indians had no individual rights to land; nor had they any collectively, or in their national capacity." The defendant's argument focused in particular on the theories propounded by Locke and Vattel. The nomadic North American Indians "acquired no proprietary interest in the vast tracts of territory which they wandered over." The nature of the "Indian title" was "a mere right of usufruct and habitation, without power of alienation."[46] Thirteen years earlier Harper and Story had made a similar argument in *Fletcher v. Peck*, arguing that Indian title "is a mere privilege which does not affect the allodial right."[47] Harper now hoped that Justice Story, as well as the other members of the Court, would take a different view of the matter.

Daniel Webster and Robert Harper urged the Supreme Court to adopt the position that in the absence of lawfully enacted prohibitions, Indian deeds were valid. Henry Murray and William Winder argued that even in the absence of positive law, the Illinois and Wabash grantees could not acquire a fee-simple title from Native grantors because "all existing titles depend on the fundamental title of the crown by discovery." The fact that certain lands in New England were "held under Indian deeds" was dismissed as "an anomaly arising from peculiar local and political causes." The fact that the colonies in the other parts of America also purchased land from the Indians was not proof that Native inhabitants owned the lands they sold, because such transactions were undertaken to promote peaceful relations rather than to obtain title.[48]

Murray and Winder apparently spent only a small portion of their argument discussing the impact of the 1763 Proclamation and the laws of Virginia. They argued that notwithstanding *Campbell v. Hall*, the Crown retained a "direct power of legislation" for the purpose of "prescribing the limits within which grants of land and settlements should be made within the colony." Murray and Winder also contended that an act passed by Virginia in 1662 invalidated the Illinois and Piankeshaw purchases. Rather than argue that the 1779 legislation applied retroactively, defendant's counsel suggested that the statute should "be regarded as a declaratory act, founded upon what had always been regarded as the settled law."[49]

George Rodney, a presumably disinterested observer, was of the opinion that the Supreme Court would not be persuaded that the Illinois and Piankeshaws transferred a fee-simple title to grantees. After the conclusion of the first day of arguments, the eighteen-year-old noted in his diary that Daniel Webster "went into a discussion upon the origin of property and managed it skilfully for a bad cause." Four days later, after Harper concluded his remarks, Rodney observed that the members of the Court "will doubtless [be] against the grant." Edward Ingersoll likewise was not optimistic in his report to Simon Gratz, John Brinton, and Callender Irvine. Ingersoll informed them that Attorney General William Wirt, Treasury Secretary William Crawford, and Secretary of State John Quincy Adams all agreed that the statement of the case was "collusive" and included assertions that "could not be proved by evidence." Ingersoll stated that "Mr. Harper's argument has been everything that could be desired; full, powerful and elegant. I do not believe a better was ever heard in this or in any other Court." On the other hand, Ingersoll was not certain whether Justice Story's absence on the first day that Harper spoke was due to "indisposition or ill will." What likely distressed his Philadelphia colleagues most of all was Ingersoll's statement that if they would issue him another share, he would "sell it immediately without waiting for the rise in value, which in truth I never expect to see." Ingersoll repeated his request the following day. "I wish to sell for present profits," Ingersoll informed Brinton," as "I calculate on an unfavorable decision."[50]

The views of Daniel Webster are unknown. It is doubtful, however, that the New England politician was particularly concerned about the issue of Indian land rights. In a letter written in 1826 Webster declared that "there is as little in the languages of the tribes as in their laws, manners, and customs, worth studying or worth knowing." As Eric Kades has noted, "an index of all of Webster's letters and an even more detailed index of microfilms containing his complete works contain not a single cite to *Johnson v. M'Intosh*."[51] The celebrated lawyer had earned his fee and, unlike Robert Goodloe Harper, did not have a personal stake in the outcome.

It would not be surprising, therefore, if Webster discussed other matters at a dinner party hosted by Commodore Isaac Chauncey on the day after the arguments were concluded. According to Charles Jared Ingersoll, the attendees included Harper, Vice President Daniel Tompkins, Navy Secretary Smith Thompson, and several members of Congress. The *Johnson* case, not surprisingly, was still very much on the mind of Harper, who two days thereafter sent a report to Simon Gratz, John Brinton, and Callender Irvine. He endorsed Edward Ingersoll's request for an additional share, stating that the young lawyer "has been diligent and useful, and *should we obtain a favourable decision*, will be still more so hereafter."[52] Harper was a confident man, but his statement may have been wishful thinking. Elsewhere in the letter, Harper suggested that "the case would be strengthened [by further argument]."[53]

The Decision

Harper was not granted his wish to present further argument in *Johnson v. McIntosh*. John Marshall delivered the Court's opinion on February 28, 1823, affirming the judgment of the District Court of Illinois. In the second paragraph of his opinion he states that the question presented concerns "*the power of Indians to give, and of private individuals to receive, a title which can be sustained in the Courts of this country.*" In the final paragraph of his opinion the chief justice concludes that "*the plaintiffs do not exhibit a title which can be sustained in the Courts of the United States.*"[54] The judgment in favor of McIntosh was affirmed.

The Supreme Court in *Johnson* unequivocally rejects the *most* favorable view of Indian land rights: that the Illinois and Piankeshaws owned the lands they occupied and were free (like everyone else) to sell their lands to private individuals. On the other hand, the Court does not adopt the *least* favorable view of Indian land rights: that the tribes had no property rights and were, in effect, trespassing on the lands they occupied. Two other possibilities have been previously discussed: the "limited owner" and "limited possessor" conceptions of Indian title. Under the former view, the Illinois and Piankeshaws owned the lands they possessed but could transfer ownership only to the holder of the right of preemption. Pursuant to the latter view, Great Britain (and eventually the United States) owned the lands at issue, as well as the exclusive right to extinguish the Indian title, which was limited to the right of possession. Thomas Jefferson, in the 1790s, characterized Indian tribes as landowners with limited disposition rights. John Marshall, in 1810, stated at the conclusion of *Fletcher v. Peck* that Indian tribes do *not* own the lands they occupy. In *Johnson v. McIntosh*, Marshall once again speaks for the Court and adopts the view of Indian land rights set forth in *Fletcher v. Peck*. As the chief justice notes toward the end of his *Johnson* opinion, "this question is not entirely new in this Court."[55]

Most of *Johnson v. McIntosh* is devoted to establishing that the grantees could not have acquired a fee-simple title from their Native grantors even in the absence of a positive prohibition such as the 1763 Proclamation. At the outset of his opinion Marshall selects the source of law that governs the rights of the Native inhabitants. The laws and customs of the various tribal nations were never serious candidates as appropriate sources of law, although Marshall does briefly discuss the possibility that the individuals who transacted with the Illinois and Piankeshaws held "a title dependent on *their* laws." Marshall also eschews "principles of abstract justice," and chooses to focus instead on the principles "which our own government has adopted in the particular case, and given us as the rule for our decision." But what were the principles adopted by "our own government" to define the nature of Indian land rights? John Marshall answers this question by turning directly to the doctrine of discovery, which regulated the "right of acquisition" by European nations in the New World: "This principle was, that *discovery gave title* to the government by whose subjects, or by whose authority, it was made, against all other European governments, which title might be consummated by possession."[56]

In addition to a proprietary title, the discovering nation also obtained "the sole right of acquiring the soil from the natives, and establishing settlements upon it." The transfer of ownership, as well as the accompanying right of preemption, curtailed the rights of the Native inhabitants:

> They were admitted to be the rightful *occupants* of the soil, with a legal as well as just claim to retain *possession* of it, and to use it according to their own discretion; but their rights to complete sovereignty, as independent nations, were necessarily diminished, *and their power to dispose of the soil at their own will, to whomsoever they pleased, was denied by the original fundamental principle, that discovery gave exclusive title to those who made it.*[57]

But *why* did the "discovery" of lands occupied by indigenous peoples give title to the Europeans? And *why* did the discovering nation also obtain the exclusive right of acquiring "the soil" from the Natives? In an attempt to provide convincing answers to these questions, Marshall draws upon his understanding of the history of European settlement of the New World. "The history of America, from its discovery to the present day," the chief justice asserts, "*proves*, we think, the universal recognition of these principles." As discussed in chapter 2, while the practices of colonizing nations lend support to Marshall's assertions, the historical record contradicts his claim of "universal recognition" of the principles underlying *Johnson*. Nevertheless, Marshall maintains that European nations uniformly claimed the right "to grant the soil, while yet in possession of the natives," and thereby "convey a title to the grantees, subject only to the Indian right of occupancy."[58] In an equally sweeping statement, Marshall declares that it "has never been doubted, that either the United States, or the several States, had a *clear title* to all the lands within the boundary lines described in the treaty [of 1783], subject only to the Indian right of occupancy, and that the exclusive power to extinguish that right, was vested in that government which might constitutionally exercise it."[59]

These rights thus predated Virginia's act of 1779, which Marshall suggests should be read as affirming "the broad principle *which had always been maintained*, that the exclusive right to purchase from the Indians resided in the government." The doctrine of discovery and the right of preemption, Marshall concludes, were assented to by all nations (other than the indigenous nations), and consequently serve as "the foundation of all *European* title in America."[60]

After finding that the United States had acceded to the European doctrine of discovery, Marshall addresses whether the doctrine itself was susceptible to judicial review. "We will not enter into the controversy," the chief justice notes, "whether agriculturists, merchants, and manufacturers, have a right, *on abstract principles*, to expel hunters from the territory they possess, or to contract their limits." In *The History of Land Titles in Massachusetts* James Sullivan flatly declared in 1801 that if the Europeans had gained possession of the New World "upon wrong principles, and under the influence of wrong motives, it will by no means follow, that the act was in itself, simply considered, an unjustifiable act." In *Johnson*, John Marshall likewise states that "conquest gives a title which the Courts of the conqueror cannot deny, whatever the private and speculative opinions of individuals may be, respecting the original justice of the claim which has been successfully asserted." The doctrine of discovery was accepted by the European nations and therefore *must* be accepted by the United States Supreme Court. Rather than address the validity of the doctrine of discovery, Marshall views the matter as a *fait accompli*: "It is not for the Courts of this country to question the validity of this title, or to sustain one which is incompatible with it."[61]

Marshall's *ratio decidendi* is both disappointing and disingenuous. Did the Court decide that American Indians do not own the lands they occupy, or did *Johnson v. McIntosh* merely announce that the issue had been previously decided? Marshall states that the doctrine of discovery is "the foundation of all *European* title in America," yet offers only a half-hearted defense of the doctrine. He repeats the argument, made much more forcefully by others, that the transfer of ownership from the tribal nations to the Europeans was justified in part by the "character and habits" of the Indians. The eminent legal theorist Emer de Vattel posited in 1758 that the tribes' "uncertain occupancy of these vast regions can not be held as a real and lawful taking of possession." The chief justice concurs in 1823, observing that the Native inhabitants were "fierce savages . . . whose subsistence was drawn chiefly from the forest," and noting that "to leave them in possession of their country, was to leave the country a wilderness."[62] Yet Marshall also expresses his discomfort with the Eurocentric notion that following "the discovery of an inhabited country," the Native inhabitants of America were reduced to mere occupants and could no longer transfer ownership rights to others: "*However this restriction may be opposed to natural right, and to the usages of civilized nations*, yet, if it be indispensable to that system under which the country has been settled, and be adapted to the actual condition of the two people, *it may, perhaps, be supported by reason, and certainly cannot be rejected by Courts of justice.*"[63]

After establishing that the power of the Indians to dispose of their lands "to whomsoever they pleased" was denied by the "fundamental" doctrine of discovery, Marshall bolsters the holding of the Court with references to prior precedent and positive law. The chief justice notes that his prior characterization of Indian title in *Fletcher* conforms "precisely" to the discovery doctrine as set forth in *Johnson*. In addition, the Proclamation of 1763 was held to constitute "an additional objection to the title of the plaintiffs."[64] Marshall limits the effect of *Campbell v. Hall*—which denied the royal power to impose *taxes* on exports from Grenada—by holding that the separate prerogative powers "of granting, or refusing to grant, vacant lands, and of restraining encroachments on the Indians, have always been asserted and admitted."[65]

Marshall also discounts the precedents relied upon by Webster and Harper. The dispute between Connecticut and the Mohegan Tribe did not, in the view of the Court, establish the principle that individuals "might obtain a complete and valid title from the Indians." The Camden-Yorke opinion was "entirely inapplicable to purchases made in America."[66] The fact that title to certain tracts of land in New England can be traced to Indian deeds was dismissed as aberrational and lacking in judicial sanction. The 1663 Charter of Rhode Island and Providence Plantations merely sanctioned previous unauthorized purchases from Indians, and did not lend support to the proposition that a title acquired from an Indian tribe "would be valid against a title acquired from the crown, or without the confirmation of the crown."[67] The final argument addressed by Marshall was the contention that the enactment of colonial laws prohibiting individual purchases of Indian lands actually proved that Indians could transfer ownership rights to private recipients. The chief justice rejected this negative inference argument and held instead that "the fact that such acts have been generally passed, is strong evidence of the *general opinion*, that such purchases are opposed by the soundest *principles of wisdom and national policy*."[68]

Thomas McKenney, the founder of the semiweekly *Washington Republican* newspaper, described *Johnson v. McIntosh* as "one of the most luminous and satisfactory opinions we recollect ever to have listened to."[69] Nearly fifty years had elapsed since Jean Baptiste DuCoigne and nine other chiefs of the Illinois confederacy agreed in 1773 to sell two large tracts of land to William Murray and twenty-one other British subjects. During the intervening five decades, the thirteen colonies had declared independence, waged war with Great Britain, and created the United States of America. After a long and bitter debate, all thirteen states had agreed to the Articles of Confederation, only to dissolve the Articles and adopt a federal Constitution. The American army fought the northwest tribes and lost, and then regrouped, fought again, and won. The Illinois and Piankeshaws ceded territory to the United States that they had previously sold to the Illinois and Wabash grantees. The United States waged war once again with Great Britain, and once again with the northwest tribes. The few remaining Illinois and Piankeshaws were forced to leave Indiana and Illinois. They had no stake in the controversy over ownership of their historic homelands.

The original grantees, and the subsequent Illinois and Wabash Land Company, failed to persuade Great Britain, Virginia, the Continental Congress, the Vincennes and Kaskaskia land commissions, and the United States Congress to confirm the 1773 and 1775 purchases. The five justices of the United States Supreme Court who decided *Johnson v. McIntosh* agreed with Judge Nathaniel Pope that William McIntosh was not guilty of trespass and ejectment. Justice William Johnson, who dissented in *Fletcher v. Peck*, did not write a separate opinion. Justice Brockholst Livingston, who said privately in 1796 that Indians could "grant their own lands," said nothing publicly in 1823 about their rights.

It was finally over. According to the Supreme Court, Judge Pope had correctly held that the fictitious lessee, Simeon Peaceable, had no basis for complaint, because his supposed lessors, Joshua Johnson and Thomas Grahame, lacked a proper title to the lands in question. The half shares in the Illinois and Wabash Land Company recently purchased by Mary Anne Patterson, John McTavish, David Winchester, and Leonard Kimball were worthless. The other shareholders, including Callender Irvine, Edward Ingersoll, John Brinton, various members of the Gratz family, Solomon Etting, Robert Goodloe Harper, and the venerable Charles Carroll of Carrollton, had nothing to show for the many years devoted to obtaining confirmation of the Illinois and Wabash grants. Lady Virginia Murray, the daughter of Lord Dunmore, would likewise be disappointed in her quest to be compensated for her late father's share in the Wabash purchase. The Illinois and Wabash "mania" had run its course just as Rebecca Gratz feared it would: after engaging in "years of toil on an uncertain event," her brothers and the other shareholders received nothing in return.

16

CLOSURE AND CONTINUITY

The shareholders of the Illinois and Wabash Land Company held at least two meetings after the Supreme Court's decision in *Johnson v. McIntosh*. On May 11, 1824, Edward Ingersoll wrote to Robert Goodloe Harper to inform him that John Brinton, Callender Irvine, and a "Mr. Cohen" had met the previous day in Philadelphia. Nothing was accomplished, however, and another meeting was scheduled for May 24. As Harper subsequently explained in a letter to Simon Gratz, although he was in Philadelphia on the appointed date, he did not join his fellow shareholders because he thought the meeting had been postponed.[1] It is not clear why the shareholders met in the spring of 1824, other than to discuss the possibility of presenting another memorial to Congress. No such memorial was prepared, however, as it became evident to all concerned that it was time to move on to new activities. For some, including Harper, the time that remained would prove to be unexpectedly brief.

The Illinois and Piankeshaw Indians, on the other hand, survived dislocation and eventually banded together with the Wea Indians to create a new tribe called the Confederated Peoria. When *Johnson v. McIntosh* was decided in February 1823, the majority of these Indians were situated in southwestern Missouri, where they often came into conflict with encroaching settlers and the Osage Nation. The transplanted tribes would move twice more, first to Kansas and thereafter to the Indian Territory. In 1936 the Confederated Peoria became the Peoria Tribe of Indians of Oklahoma. Federal recognition of the tribe was "terminated" in 1956 and then "reinstated" in 1978. In the past three decades, the tribe has increased its land base, grown in membership, and initiated several profitable business ventures. The Illinois and Wabash Land Company no longer exists, but the Illinois and Piankeshaw Indians have persevered and—as members of the Peoria Tribe—continue to move forward.

THE LAWYERS

In the July 1824 edition of the *Port Folio*, a monthly magazine published in Philadelphia, the obituary notice for Henry Murray is immediately followed by the obituary notice for William Winder. The lawyers for William McIntosh died within one month of each other and less than fifteen months after John Marshall announced the decision in *Johnson v. McIntosh*.[2] Henry Murray suffered a tragic death at age thirty-five on April 28, 1824. Murray is described in the *Port Folio* as a "distinguished" Maryland lawyer whose "uncommonly fine mind" would have "carried him to the front rank of his profession." The obituary also provides the gruesome details of his death: "Mr Murray was . . . reading in the cabin of the steam boat, *the Eagle*, when the boiler of the steam boat burst, and the cabin was instantly filled with scalding steam. The assault was so sudden and the suffering so dreadful as to deprive him of his recollection; and it was not until, in his confusion, he had crossed the cabin three times, (as was afterwards discovered by the traces of his lacerated flesh,) that he found his way to the deck."[3] Murray suffered for ten days before expiring. The explosion caused one other death and injured several persons.[4]

William Winder also died unexpectedly but of natural causes. He was forty-nine years old when he passed away on May 24. At the time of his death his practice was the largest of the Baltimore bar, and he participated in three cases decided by the Supreme Court during the 1824 term. General Winder was eulogized as "an eminent lawyer and a distinguished citizen," who was "a commanding member of the Legislature." The lawyer-general was buried with "the highest Masonic, civic and military honors," and fifteen thousand persons turned up to pay their last respects.[5]

Robert Harper was in Philadelphia the day Winder died, and he remained for two or three days to attend to business matters. General Harper had suffered an apparent heart attack during the summer of 1823 but recovered and argued five cases before the Supreme Court in 1824, including *Osborn v. Bank of the United States*, in which Chief Justice Marshall broadly construed the power of Congress to grant "federal question" jurisdiction to the federal courts. Prior to his appearance in *Osborn* Harper attended the annual meeting of the American Colonization Society, held at the Capitol, where he proposed that "our African colony" be called Liberia, and that "the principal town in our infant settlement" be named Monrovia in honor of President James Monroe.[6]

Following the conclusion of the Supreme Court's 1824 term, Harper spent the summer months visiting western Pennsylvania and viewing Niagara Falls in New York. By October he was back in Baltimore, where he greeted General Lafayette during the Frenchman's tour of America. In December Harper began to draft a pamphlet to inform the electorate that he intended to offer himself as a candidate for a seat in the House of Representatives. The elder statesman of the Federalist Party, who would turn sixty in January, was determined to return to public service. His life, however, ended on January 14, 1825. On the previous day Harper argued a case for three hours and attended an evening affair. The next morning he awoke, had breakfast, stood before the fireplace with a newspaper in hand, and then collapsed. The likely cause of death was coronary failure. Harper was a leading member of the Baltimore bar and was also remembered as one of the men who repelled the British in September 1814. His funeral, Eric Papenfuse notes, was "a grand affair," and Baltimore lawyers and military officers in the state's First Brigade wore black armbands for a month to honor his memory. General Harper was originally buried at his estate but was later reinterred at Greenmount Cemetery, a few blocks north of Baltimore's Inner Harbor. The monument next to his remains praises Robert Goodloe Harper as a statesman, lawyer, husband, father, and friend. No mention is made of his role in *Fletcher v. Peck* and *Johnson v. McIntosh*, the Supreme Court decisions that first defined the nature and scope of Indian land rights in America.[7]

Daniel Webster lived for thirty years after *Johnson v. McIntosh*, dying in 1852 at the age of seventy. The prominent lawyer had been elected in 1822 to represent Massachusetts in the Eighteenth Congress and would serve in the House of Representatives from 1823 to 1827. During this period Webster also appeared before the Supreme Court in numerous cases, including *Gibbons v. Ogden* (1824), and became known as "Godlike Daniel" following his powerful 1826 eulogy in honor of Adams and Jefferson. The following year Webster began his long and illustrious career in the U.S. Senate (1827–41 and 1845–50), where he was an Anti-Jacksonian, a Whig, and a Unionist. In one of the most famous speeches delivered in the Senate,

Webster in 1830 condemned the Nullification Doctrine by declaring "Liberty *and* Union, now and forever, one and inseparable!"[8] In 1836, 1848, and again in 1852, "Black Dan" campaigned without success to be the Whig nominee for the presidency. He served as secretary of state under Harrison and Tyler and then returned to Senate. On March 7, 1850, the gifted orator urged passage of Henry Clay's compromise proposal and argued once again for the preservation of the Union. Following his resignation from the Senate, Webster served as secretary of state under Millard Fillmore.[9]

In May 1852 "Godlike Daniel" fell from his horse and suffered a severe blow to the head. For several months his health remained poor, exacerbated by abdominal pains and advanced cirrhosis of the liver. On October 24, 1852, Webster died at his home in Marshfield, Massachusetts. More than a century later the U.S. Senate decided to display the portraits of five "outstanding" senators: Robert Taft of Ohio, Robert La Follette of Wisconsin, John Calhoun of South Carolina, Henry Clay of Kentucky, and Daniel Webster of Massachusetts.[10]

THE LITIGANTS

The litigants in *Johnson v. McIntosh* had little at stake in the outcome, either because they were legal fictions (Simeon Peaceable and Thomas Troublesome) or because they were participants in a feigned dispute (Joshua Johnson, Thomas Jennings Grahame, and William McIntosh). Not much is known about the actual plaintiffs. Joshua Johnson, the son of Governor Thomas Johnson, Jr., inherited land from his father in the westernmost part of Maryland. He moved there in 1836, established a residence alongside the National Road, married Harriet Beall late in his life, and died around 1853.[11] Thomas Grahame, the grandson of Thomas Johnson, Jr., married Caroline Worthington Goldsborough Johnson, the daughter of Colonel Baker Johnson. His father-in-law was an officer in the Revolutionary War and later served as a judge on the Maryland General Court. Baker Johnson was a younger brother of Thomas Johnson, Jr., which meant that Thomas Grahame and Catherine Johnson were first cousins once removed. Catherine died in 1831 and Grahame's mother, Ann Jennings (Johnson) Grahame, died in 1837. Thomas Grahame apparently passed away prior to 1884.[12]

William McIntosh's activities prior to 1823 are described in some detail in chapters 12 and 14, including his 1815 purchase of some twelve thousand acres of land in the Illinois Territory. At some point prior to 1820 the Scotsman moved across the Wabash River near the present-day town of Mt. Carmel, Illinois. In 1825 McIntosh was visited by Donald McDonald and William Owen, followers of Robert Owen, the social reformer who was preparing to establish a utopian community in Indiana. Donald McDonald described the visit in his diary: "[Mr. McIntosh] has a black housekeeper by whom he has several children. . . . In consequence of Mr. McIntosh's connection with this black female, his character is lost among the Americans, and he lives quite retired from all society. . . . He gave us an account of the proceedings of the Americans in purchasing & getting possession of the lands of the Indians, and the wars which had taken place. On this subject he had a misunderstanding with General Harrison."[13]

The woman was named Lydia and was the mother of two daughters and a son by McIntosh. According to one account, when McIntosh died, Lydia and her children "were left poor, and others got his land." The son, however, received a good education "in the English and Latin languages and mathematics" and became "a distinguished preacher in the African Methodist Episcopal Church."[14] As for McIntosh, the *Vincennes Gazette* published the following notice on July 14, 1832: "Died—At the Grand Rapids of the Wabash, William McIntosh, Esq. for a long time a resident of Vincennes. He was a native of Scotland, from which country he emigrated at an early age."[15]

THE SHAREHOLDERS

After the death of Robert Goodloe Harper, the two remaining shareholders in Maryland with longstanding connections to the Illinois and Wabash Land Company were Harper's father-in-law, Charles Carroll of Carrollton, and Solomon Etting, the son-in-law of Barnard Gratz. Carroll was never an active participant in the company's affairs, perhaps because of his vast wealth. When Thomas Jefferson and John Adams both died on July 4, 1826, the eighty-eight-year-old Carroll was the sole surviving signer of the Declaration of Independence. This distinction increased his fame and caused Daniel Webster to venerate him publicly as "an aged oak, standing alone on the plain." On November 14, 1832, Carroll died in Baltimore at age ninety-five. In 1901 the State of Maryland chose to honor him with a place in the National Statuary Hall of the United States Capitol.[16]

Whereas Charles Carroll held the distinction of being the only Catholic to sign the Declaration of Independence, Solomon Etting was one of the first Jews elected to public office in Maryland. Etting grew up in Pennsylvania and married Rachel Simon, a daughter of Joseph Simon. After her death in 1790 Etting married Rachel Gratz, the daughter of Barnard Gratz, and moved to Baltimore. When the Maryland General Assembly finally granted Jews the rights of citizenship in 1826, Etting won a seat on the Baltimore City Council and was later elected council president. He was primarily a merchant but also helped found the Baltimore and Ohio Railroad. He died in 1847 at age eighty-three.[17]

The most active shareholders in Pennsylvania in 1823 were John Brinton, Edward Ingersoll, Callender Irvine, and Simon Gratz. Brinton was the first to die, in 1827, and both Ingersoll and Irvine passed away in 1841.[18] Simon Gratz, the oldest son of Michael Gratz, lived from 1773 to 1839 and is buried near his father in the Mikveh Israel Cemetery in Philadelphia. Simon and his brother Hyman inherited the family business, and their store at Seventh and Market streets was the site where Thomas Jefferson wrote the first draft of the Declaration of Independence. Simon was a trustee of the Mikveh Israel Congregation and one of the founders of the Pennsylvania Academy of Fine Arts. Simon Gratz High School in Philadelphia is named after his grandson.[19]

When Joseph Gratz died in 1858 his brother Benjamin became the last person alive who participated in the affairs of the Illinois and Wabash Land Company.[20] After enduring "dull" Vincennes in 1819 and convincing McIntosh to serve as defendant, the youngest Gratz sibling settled in Lexington, Kentucky, where he became a wealthy businessman. Benjamin Gratz died at the age of ninety-one on March 17, 1884, one hundred and forty years after his father, Michael Gratz, was born in Upper Silesia near the German-Polish border.[21]

Although Benjamin Gratz was the last living person actively involved in the affairs of the Illinois and Wabash Land Company, he was not the last laid to rest. That distinction belongs to James Wilson, whose remains were reinterred in 1906. In recognition of his achievements as a jurist and political theorist, the decision was made that Justice Wilson should return to his adopted home, and in November 1906 his remains were brought to Philadelphia. The coffin was placed in the historic east room of Independence Hall, and then moved to Christ Church. The honorary pallbearers were Chief Justice Melville Fuller and Associate Justices William Day,

Oliver Wendell Holmes, Jr., Rufus Peckham, and Edward White. At the committal service the former president of the Illinois and Wabash Land Company was the recipient of lofty praise: "What Jefferson was to the Declaration of Independence, what John Paul Jones was to the navy and George Washington to the army, what Robert Morris was to the finance of the Revolution and Franklin to its diplomacy, that, in fullest measure, James Wilson was to the Constitution of the United States."[22]

It was James Wilson who, at the 1787 Convention, advocated popular election of the president and the Senate. While serving on the Committee of Detail, he came up with the phrase "We the People" and proposed the "necessary and proper" and "contract" clauses. Historian William Ewald describes Wilson as "the principal architect of the executive branch," who successfully argued for "a single President, elected for a relatively short term, eligible for re-election, wielding a veto power, and enjoying authority independently both of the Congress and of the legislatures of the states."[23] James Wilson's body rests in the burial ground immediately adjacent to Christ Church. His fellow shareholder Robert Morris is buried there as well, along with Pierce Butler of South Carolina, who pursued Wilson for unpaid debts and caused him to be jailed for several weeks in 1798.[24]

THE ILLINOIS AND PIANKESHAWS, 1823–1854

At about the same time that the Supreme Court heard arguments in *Johnson v. McIntosh*, a council was held in present-day Arkansas by members of the Cherokee, Delaware, Kickapoo, Peoria, Piankeshaw, Shawnee, and Wea tribes. The tribes were concerned about the hostile Osage Indians, despite the fact that the Osage had signed a peace treaty with most of assembled tribes the preceding September. The council, led by the Cherokee chief Takatoka, explored the possibility of a formal confederacy and also invited tribal members living on the other side of the Mississippi River to remove to the west. In October 1824 the federal government authorized Chief Takatoka to accompany a delegation of "eastern" Indians to Washington to negotiate an exchange of lands to facilitate their removal. As this delegation approached the nation's capital, President Monroe informed Congress that "the removal of the Indian tribes from the lands which they now occupy within the limits of the several States and Territories . . . is of very high importance to our Union."[25]

Consequently, when the delegation arrived in February, the government not only encouraged the Indians to join their western brethren but also urged the tribes in southwestern Missouri and the Arkansas Territory to remove farther west.

In 1824 a chief of the Piankeshaws, No-tack-shin-ga, asked Indian agent Richard Graham to present the tribe's request to be compensated for lands located north and west of Vincennes. The territory had been historically occupied by the Piankeshaws but had been ceded in 1819 by the Kickapoos. The secretary of war, John Calhoun, informed the Piankeshaws that "your Great Father has paid for the land bought of the Kickapoos," but nevertheless agreed to the tribe's request for one thousand dollars and ten square miles of land. "But take my advice," Calhoun counseled, "cultivate the ground, and be industrious and sober, and honest, and you will do well." At this time the Missouri contingent of the Piankeshaws numbered somewhere between 230 and 400 individuals.[26]

In 1826 a party of Osage warriors attacked a Piankeshaw and Delaware village located on the upper White River in Missouri. A few months later a "treaty of peace and amity" was signed by the Delawares, Shawnees, Kickapoos, Piankeshaws, Weas, Peorias, Senecas, and "the several bands of the Big and Little Osage Nation." The tribes agreed that "the unhappy differences which have existed between them within the last fifteen months should cease and terminate." The Delawares paid one thousand dollars to the Osage in compensation "for any depredations or murders they may have committed," and all tribes promised that "no private revenge shall be taken for any property stolen or destroyed, or murders thought to have been committed."[27]

The 1826 treaty was negotiated at St. Louis and signed in the presence of William Clark, the superintendent of Indian Affairs. In a letter written shortly thereafter, Clark recommended to the secretary of war that the Indians leave Missouri and relocate to a "strip of country . . . immediately west of the boundary line of this State." According to Clark, the Indians "seem to be pleased at the idea of being placed upon lands which will be a permanent home to them, and where they will be protected from any further pressure of the white population." Some of the Piankeshaws and Weas moved west the following year and established villages near the present town of Paola, Kansas. A large number of the Illinois Indians eventually settled on the Marais des Cygnes—a tributary of the Osage River—and a number of Shawnees established villages along the Kansas River near the Missouri state line. Among the emigrants was the Shawnee Prophet, Tenskwatawa, who lived apart from his kinsmen near a natural spring in what is today Kansas City, Kansas.[28]

In the fall of 1830 George Catlin made his way to Fort Leavenworth in Kansas, where he painted portraits of Indians from various tribes, including the Kaskaskias, Peorias, Piankeshaws, and Weas. Catlin estimated that there were about 200 Peorias and 200 Weas in Kansas, and approximately 170 Piankeshaws. He described the Iowa, Kansas, Pawnee, Missouri, Omaha, and Otoe Indians as "primitive" in contrast to the Delaware, Kaskaskia, Kickapoo, Peoria, Potawatomie, Shawnee, and Wea Indians, who were the "semi-civilized remnants of tribes that have been removed to this neighborhood by the Government." The latter group of Indians, Catlin observed, lived "principally by ploughing, and raising corn and cattle and horses."[29]

On July 14, 1832, Congress appropriated forty-six thousand dollars to extinguish the title of the Kickapoos, Shawnees, and Delawares to lands in Missouri, and likewise to extinguish the title of the Piankeshaws, Weas, Peorias, and Kaskaskias to their remaining lands in Illinois. By this time the tide had turned in the Black Hawk War, a series of battles in Illinois and Wisconsin fought against the Sauk, Fox, and Kickapoo Indians. During the fall of 1832 representatives of the various tribes assembled near St. Louis at Castor Hill, the home of Superintendent William Clark. On October 24 the Kickapoo Indians agreed to cede their lands east of the Mississippi in return for territory near Fort Leavenworth, Kansas. Over the course of the next five days the United States entered into similar treaties with the Shawnee, Delaware, Illinois, Piankeshaw, and Wea tribes.[30]

The Kaskaskias and Peorias agreed to relinquish all claims to lands in Illinois and Missouri with one exception: 350 acres of land near the town of Kaskaskia reserved "for Ellen Decoigne." The Piankeshaws and Weas also agreed to cede all lands in Illinois and Missouri. In return the government granted the four tribes a total of 400 sections of land, or 256,000 acres. The western 150 sections were set aside for the Illinois Indians. The Piankeshaws and Weas were granted 250 sections, located to the east of the lands assigned to the Kaskaskias and Peorias, and immediately west of the Missouri boundary line. This territory comprised the northern half of present-day Miami County, Kansas.[31]

Approximately 140 Illinois Indians and 300 Piankeshaws and Weas settled along the Marais des Cygnes. The emigrants were led by Christmas

Kee-món-saw, Little Chief (Kaskaskia). Smithsonian American Art Museum; gift of
Mrs. Joseph Harrison, Jr.

Dagnette (or Noel Dashney), a Wea chief who died in 1848, and Baptiste
Peoria, a chief of the Peorias who was fluent in several Indian languages.
Some of the Indians began to farm, while others continued to hunt.
Thomas Farnham passed through in 1839 on his way to Oregon, and
described the living conditions of the Piankeshaws, Weas, and Illinois
in his *Travels in the Great Western Prairies*: "Their fields are enclosed with

Kee-mó-rá-nia, No English (Peoria). Smithsonian American Art Museum; gift of Mrs. Joseph Harrison, Jr.

rails, and they cultivate corn and vegetables sufficient for a comfortable subsistence. The Piankasha band is less improved than the Weas. The former have a field of about fifty acres, made by the government; the latter have made their own improvements."[32] Indian agent Anthony Davis reported in 1842 that the four tribes "depend entirely on agricultural pursuits for a subsistence" and stated that their improvement would be

Men-són-se-ah, Left Hand (Piankeshaw). Smithsonian American Art Museum; gift of Mrs. Joseph Harrison, Jr.

even more rapid "if it was not for the ruinous practice pursued by those lawless individuals who . . . furnish them with whiskey." Non-Indians began to covet their lands, which were located near trails that led settlers to Sante Fe, the Oregon territory, and the California gold fields. Such adversity united the Indians, and Baptiste Peoria encouraged abstinence. The commissioner of Indian Affairs, Luke Lea, noted in his 1851 report that the four tribes "are greatly in advance of the wilder tribes contiguous to them."[33]

The continued presence of so many Indians, however, was an impediment to the organization of the Kansas Territory. Consequently, the new commissioner of Indian Affairs, George Manypenny, was instructed by President Franklin Pierce in 1853 to ask the tribes to sell their lands and remove south to the Indian Territory, or alternatively to cede most of their territory and subsist on the remaining lands. In 1854 and 1855 the "Manypenny treaties" were negotiated with the transplanted and local tribes. On May 30, 1854, the same day Congress enacted the Kansas-Nebraska Act, the treaty with the Kaskaskia, Peoria, Piankeshaw, and Wea Indians was concluded in Washington. In the first article of the 1854 treaty the United States recognized that the four tribes had recently "united themselves into a single tribe," which would become known as the Confederated Peorias. The second article provides for the cession by the four tribes of the lands granted to them in 1832. The tribes, however, reserved a quarter-section of land (160 acres) "for each soul in said united tribe," as well as ten sections (6,400 acres) "to be held as the common property of the said tribe," and one section for the American Indian Mission Association. In addition, the tribes received sixty-six thousand dollars, a portion of which was to be invested in "safe and profitable stocks, the interest to be annually paid to them, or expended for their benefit and improvement."[34]

The treaty lists a total of 259 Indians (142 males and 117 females) as constituting "all the persons and families of the said combined tribe." After the reserved lands were selected by tribal members, the United States was authorized to sell "the residue" for the benefit of the confederated tribe. As it turned out, Indian agents, speculators, railroads, and settlers acquired large tracts of land at minimal prices. In June and July 1857 some 207,758 acres were sold for $346,671, which—after subtracting the land agent's fee of $10,000—comes to approximately $1.62 per acre. According to Grant Foreman, the tribes who signed the Manypenny treaties "parted with title to nearly 18,000,000 acres, leaving them only 1,342,000 acres."[35]

The Confederated Peoria, 1854–1940

The sale of the "residue" lands to non-Indians made life increasingly difficult for the Confederated Peorias, whose situation was further complicated by the violent events that transpired in "Bleeding Kansas" prior to the Civil War. At the center of much of the violence was the abolitionist John Brown, who resided a short distance away from lands retained by the Confederated Peorias. On May 22, 1856, Brown received news that pro-slavery adherents had committed several murders in the town of Lawrence. With four of his sons and two other men, Brown took revenge two days later, using broadswords to kill five men who lived along the Potawatomie Creek in present-day Franklin County. Three months after the "Potawatomie massacre," nearly three hundred Border Ruffians looted and burned Osawatomie, which was defended by Brown and forty men. The small town was located within the former Kaskaskia and Peoria reserve.[36]

In the decade that followed the Manypenny treaties, Kansas exchanged territorial status for statehood and entered the Civil War on the side of the Union. Although the larger tribes in the Indian Territory participated in the war, the Confederated Peorias were not directly involved. When the Cherokee leader Stand Watie—the last Confederate general in the field—signed a ceasefire agreement in June 1865, state officials stepped up their efforts to remove Indians from Kansas. The state had been illegally taxing lands allotted to individual Indians, and trespassing settlers hunted and cut timber with impunity. Rather than resist, members of the Confederated Peorias chose to relocate south of Kansas. In 1866 a delegation from the tribe entered into an agreement with the Quapaws and the Senecas to purchase land located between the Spring and Neosho rivers in present-day Ottawa County, Oklahoma. The Confederated Peorias intended to remove to the Indian Territory, and tribal leaders traveled to Washington to obtain federal approval.[37]

On February 23, 1867, the Confederated Peorias signed a treaty with the United States that authorized the sale of tribal and allotted lands in Kansas as well as the purchase of land in the Indian Territory. Called the "Omnibus Treaty" because of its multiple signatories, the treaty provided that members of the Confederated Peorias who desired to remain in Kansas could elect to do so by declaring their intention to become American citizens.[38] As it turned out fifty-five "Citizen Peorias" remained in Kansas, and a total of 163 men, women, and children moved to the Indian Territory. The Omnibus Treaty of 1867 would be the last treaty between the tribe and the United States, since Congress in 1871 declared that "hereafter no Indian nation or tribe within the territory of the United States shall be acknowledged or recognized as an independent nation, tribe, or power with whom the United States may contract by treaty."[39]

The 1867 Omnibus Treaty also authorized the union of the Miamis and the Confederated Peorias. The two tribes reached an agreement in 1872, and eighty-five Miami Indians joined the Confederated Peorias.[40] The union, however, began to falter after the death in 1873 of Baptiste Peoria, and the Miamis eventually separated and became the Miami Tribe of Oklahoma.[41]

There were fewer than 60 Miami Indians and approximately 150 members of the Confederated Peorias in the Indian Territory in 1885.[42] By this time Chief Joseph of the Nez Perce had surrendered ("I will fight no more forever"); Sitting Bull of the Hunkpapa Lakota Sioux was a performer in Buffalo Bill's Wild West Show, and the Apache leader Geronimo was less than a year away from captivity. The lengthy process of confining Indians to reservations was nearly complete, and the federal government was beginning to implement more aggressive measures to assimilate and "civilize" Indians. In 1887 Henry Dawes of Massachusetts was the driving force behind the enactment of the General Allotment Act, which was designed "to transfer communally owned tribal lands to individual Indians, who presumably would become farmers, Christians, and eventually tax-paying American citizens." Pursuant to the act, individual Indians would receive 80 acres of tribal land, and families would be allotted 160 acres. The remaining communal lands would be available for purchase by non–Indians, and the proceeds of such sales would be held for the use of the tribes, but subject to appropriation by Congress "for the education and civilization of such tribe or tribes of Indians or the members thereof."[43]

Congress exempted the Confederated Peorias and other specified tribes from the 1887 General Allotment Act. However, on March 2, 1889, Congress passed "An act to provide for allotment of land in severalty to United Peorias and Miamis in Indian Territory, and for other purposes." Under its terms, members of the Confederated Peorias and the Western Miamis were authorized to select two hundred acres "out of their common reserve," and all allotted lands would be protected for a period of twenty-five years against "levy, sale, taxation, or forfeiture." The 1889 act also conferred jurisdiction upon the Court of Claims to determine the rights of the "Citizen Peorias" in Kansas with regard to "the invested funds and other common property of the said confederated tribes."[44]

At the same time that the lands of the Confederated Peorias and Western Miamis were being allotted, large portions of the Indian Territory were opened for non-Indian settlement by seven "land runs" that took place between 1889 and 1895. Congress in 1890 organized the western half of the Indian Territory into the Oklahoma Territory and, in 1898, passed the Curtis Act, which set the stage for statehood.[45] During the next nine years Congress moved the two territories closer to statehood by reducing the amount of tribally owned land. Pursuant to the 1889 act, the Confederated Peorias and Miamis were prohibited from selling their communal lands for a period of twenty-five years. However, on May 27, 1902, Congress repealed the prohibition, and most of the land was sold in 1903 and 1904.[46] Following the defeat of a bill to admit the Indian Territory into the Union as the State of Sequoyah, Oklahoma became the forty-sixth state on November 16, 1907.

At the time of statehood there were fewer than two hundred members of the Confederated Peorias. In 1915 the restrictions on their allotted lands expired, which meant that the lands were subject to sale, taxation, and tax liens. In 1932 the last full-blood Piankeshaw, George Washington Finley (Ta-wah-quah-ke-non-guah), died at the age of seventy-four. The loss of land undermined the need for tribal government, and the future of the Confederated Peorias as a sovereign people was uncertain, as was the future of many other Indian tribes. The allotment policy—which Theodore Roosevelt described as "a mighty pulverizing engine to break up the tribal mass"—caused nearly two thirds of all Indian land in America to be transferred to non-Indian ownership. As Robert Miller has noted, the allotment era "was a disaster for tribal governments" that dealt a "near-fatal blow" to American Indians and their culture.[47]

On June 18, 1934, Congress initiated a major shift in federal Indian policy by enacting the Indian Reorganization Act, which applied to tribes outside Alaska and Oklahoma. The act ended future allotments, extended the trust periods for existing allotments, authorized tribes to charter corporations for economic development, and encouraged tribes to adopt constitutions for self-governance. The IRA was a success, and on June 26, 1936, Congress passed the Oklahoma Indian Welfare Act, which provided that "any *recognized* tribe or band of Indians residing in Oklahoma shall have the right to organize for its common welfare and to adopt a constitution."[48] The Confederated Peorias and the Miamis both submitted proposed constitutions to the commissioner of Indian Affairs, who sought legal advice from Nathan Margold, the solicitor for the Department of the Interior. On December 13, 1938, Margold addressed the question of whether the two tribes were "recognized" tribes for purposes of the Oklahoma Indian Welfare Act. "Neither group has any restricted land, either in tribal or allotted status," Margold observed, and very few of the Indians involved have even one-half degree of Indian blood." Margold recommended that consideration of the proposed constitutions be held in abeyance pending the receipt of additional information. Presumably sufficient information was provided, because the tribal members of the Confederated Peorias ratified their proposed constitution on October 10, 1939, and the Department of the Interior issued a proposed charter of incorporation on April 17, 1940. The charter was formally issued on June 1, 1940. The Confederated Peorias were now incorporated under the name of the Peoria Indian Tribe of Oklahoma.[49]

THE PEORIA INDIAN TRIBE: LITIGATION, TERMINATION, AND COMPENSATION

The first chief of the incorporated Peoria Indian Tribe of Oklahoma was George Skye, who served until his death in 1947. Chief Skye was succeeded by Guy Froman, who served for twenty-five years as the Tribe's leader, from 1947 to 1972.[50] The quarter century that Guy Froman led the Tribe can be summed up in three words: litigation, termination, and compensation. On August 13, 1946, Congress created the Indian Claims Commission and granted it jurisdiction to determine claims brought by Indian tribes against the United States for "unconscionable consideration" and lack of "fair and honorable dealings." Decisions of the commission were subject to appeal to the United States Court of Claims and the Supreme Court. Monetary damages, if awarded, were to be appropriated and distributed by Congress. According to one source, "176 tribes and bands lodged 370 claims, which were separated into 617 dockets."[51] The claims filed on behalf of the Illinois, Piankeshaws, Weas, and Confederated Peorias included a request to be fairly compensated for the lands that were first sold in 1773 and 1775 and thereafter ceded to the United States.[52]

Litigation with the United States before the Indian Claims Commission moved slowly. In the meanwhile, federal Indian policy reverted temporarily to assimilation in the 1950s, when Congress passed legislation to "terminate" the federal-tribal relationship with certain tribes, making the members of such tribes "subject to the same laws and entitled to the same privileges and responsibilities as are applicable to other citizens of the United States."[53] Between 1954 and 1966 Congress terminated the federal trust relationship with over one hundred tribes and bands, directly affecting more than eleven thousand Indians and approximately 1.5 million acres of land.

One of the tribes that was "terminated" was the Peoria Indian Tribe of Oklahoma. On August 2, 1956, Congress enacted legislation to end the federal trust relationship with the Peoria Tribe. Under the terms of the act, federal supervision over the Tribe and its members would cease after a grace period of three years, and thereafter tribal members would no longer be entitled "to any of the services performed by the United States for Indians." Because restrictions on the sale of trust or restricted land were removed, tribal landowners were given what was denied to their ancestors: freedom to sell their property to whomsoever they pleased. At this point less than 25 percent of the members of the Peoria Indian Tribe (150 of 640) were living in Ottawa County, Oklahoma. Despite the loss of federal services, the Tribe persevered and continued to litigate its claims before the Indian Claims Commission. Pursuant to section four of the 1956 Termination Act, the Tribe retained its corporate charter until "all claims of the tribe . . . before the Indian Claims Commission or the Court of Claims have been finally adjudicated."[54]

The proceedings were a mixture of history and law, and the formation of new tribes such as the Confederated Peorias complicated matters. For example, on February 16, 1966, the Court of Claims upheld a 1962 decision of the Indian Claims Commission that the Peoria Tribe—suing on behalf of the Weas and the Kickapoos of Kansas and Oklahoma—had recognized title to certain parts of western Indiana and eastern Illinois that were subsequently ceded to the United States in 1809 and 1818.[55] On April 4, 1966, the commission found that the Piankeshaws held recognized title to all of the lands ceded to the United States on December 30, 1805, notwithstanding arguments to the contrary by the Kickapoo Tribe of Kansas. The commission also rejected the contention of the United States that General Anthony Wayne "forged or had others forge parts of [the treaty of] Greenville, especially those mentioning the Piankeshaw Tribe."[56]

The Peoria Tribe successfully pursued most of its claims.[57] For example, after determining that the Piankeshaws received approximately one fourth of a cent per acre for lands ceded pursuant to the Treaty of December 30, 1805, the commission found that the treaty terms were "clearly unconscionable on its face" and awarded the Tribe $3,270,400.[58] However, in *Strong v. United States*, the United States Court of Claims rejected the argument of the Peoria Tribe that the Piankeshaws had aboriginal title to the area around Vincennes until 1803, except for that portion of the land which had been given to the French prior to the Greenville Treaty.[59]

On July 31, 1970, Congress enacted legislation to govern the distribution of awards by the Indian Claims Commission to the members of the Peoria Tribe.[60] The funds were disbursed on four occasions between 1971 and 1984. The fourth award was delayed until an agreement was reached with the descendants of the Citizen Peorias regarding distribution of the funds. The payment roll, when compiled in 1971, listed a total of 2,328 names.[61] The Peoria Indian Tribe, however, was no longer recognized by the United States, and the only remaining land owned by the Tribe was the Peoria cemetery located a few miles east of Miami, Oklahoma.

THE PEORIA INDIAN TRIBE: REINSTATEMENT AND REVITALIZATION

The "termination" policy, which had been abandoned in practice in the early 1960s, was officially discontinued on July 8, 1970, when President Richard Nixon declared that "self-determination among the Indian people can and must be encouraged."[62] On May 15, 1978, Congress passed "An Act to Reinstate the Modoc, Wyandotte, Peoria, and Ottawa Indian Tribes of Oklahoma as Federally Supervised and Recognized Indian Tribes." In support of restoration, Cecil Andrus, the secretary of the interior, noted that Congress did not hold hearings when it "terminated" the four Oklahoma tribes, and further observed that the Peoria and Ottawa tribes were led to believe that if they accepted termination, the federal government would act expeditiously to settle their claims before the Indian Claims Commission.[63] With respect to the Peoria Indian Tribe of Oklahoma, the 1978 statute expressly repealed the Act of August 2, 1956, applied the Oklahoma Indian Welfare Act, and restored the tribe's right to participate in federal programs available to Indian tribes and their members.[64]

In the three decades following the restoration of federal recognition, the Peoria Tribe has increased its land base, strengthened its government, and initiated several profitable business ventures. In 1981 the tribe ratified a new constitution and began acquiring land in Ottawa County to rebuild its land base. By 1994 the tribe owned over eleven hundred acres, including the Peoria Cemetery and the Peoria Schoolhouse, which in 1983 were placed in the National Register of Historic Sites. Some of the newly acquired lands were used as sites for government offices and a health clinic.[65] In 2000 the tribe completed construction of the Peoria Ridge Golf Course, built on nearly three hundred acres near Miami, Oklahoma. The magazine *Golf Digest* has named Peoria Ridge as one of the nation's best public golf courses, and the project—with an accompanying residential development—has greatly benefited the tribe and its members.[66]

In 1988 Congress passed the Indian Gaming Regulatory Act, in part "to provide a statutory basis for the operation of gaming by Indian tribes as a means of promoting tribal economic development, self-sufficiency, and strong tribal governments." On October 27, 2004, the Peoria Tribe spent $10 million to build the Buffalo Run Casino, a 54,000-square-foot gaming and entertainment center. Chief John Froman announced in 2005 that the tribe planned to add an additional 20,000 square feet to the casino at a cost of $2 million. As intended by Congress, the operation of gaming by the Peoria Tribe has promoted tribal economic development and self-sufficiency: according to one source, the tribe in 2006 maintained a payroll "of between $5 million and $6 million" and employed approximately two thousand individuals.[67]

The Peoria Indian Tribe of Oklahoma has significantly increased its membership in the last three decades and at the same time experienced a revitalization of its culture. In 1994 there were about 2,400 individuals in the tribe, with about 400 members living in northeastern Oklahoma. When Oklahoma celebrated its centennial in 2007, there were approximately 2,800 tribal members. During this same period the tribe has taken an active interest in its historic homeland. In 1988 the Peoria Tribe supported efforts to preserve the site of the Grand Village of the Illinois confederacy, which was subsequently designated as a state historic site. In 1998 tribal leaders traveled to Illinois to claim the remains of over one hundred ancestors and also repatriated the remains of two individuals who were offered for sale by a store in New York City. In all, the tribe has recovered more than one thousand funerary objects and has reinterred more than 120 individuals in the Peoria Cemetery. The tribe has determined that certain funerary objects should remain in Illinois and in 2002 collaborated with the Illinois State Museum to establish the Peoria Indian Heritage Collection.[68]

For better or worse, the issue that has brought the Peoria Tribe to the attention of most people in Illinois is the controversy over "Chief Illiniwek," the mascot of the University of Illinois. On April 4, 2000, the tribe passed a resolution requesting "the leadership of the University of Illinois to recognize the demeaning nature of the characterization of Chief Illiniwek, and cease the use of this mascot." The fictitious Chief Illiniwek, who performs a dance in Sioux clothing, was supposedly created by the university's marching band in 1926 to make sporting events more entertaining.[69] In August 2005 the National Collegiate Athletic Association adopted the policy that "mascots, nicknames or images deemed hostile or abusive in terms of race, ethnicity or national origin should not be visible at the championship events that we administer." On November 16, 2005, the NCAA announced that Chief Illiniwek was "hostile" and "abusive" and therefore prohibited from appearing at postseason competitions sponsored by the association. In addition, the University of Illinois was barred from hosting certain events, including football bowl games and postseason tournaments for all NCAA sports. The ban was lifted in 2007 when the university officially retired Chief Illiniwek. The university has retained its "Fighting Illini" nickname, which the NCAA concluded is a reference to the school's competitive spirit and not in violation of its policy.[70]

The Peoria Tribe has survived relocation, allotment, and even termination. A member of Wea descent, Alice Giles Burgess, designed a tribal logo in 1983 that links the Peoria Indians with their Kaskaskia, Peoria, Piankeshaw, and Wea ancestors. In their book *The Peorias: A History of the Peoria Indian Tribe of Oklahoma* (1991), Dorris Valley and Mary Lembcke include a poignant description of the emblem's meaning, which stresses the continuity of the Peoria people:

> Each of the arrows represents one of the four tribes making up the Peoria tribe. The red background symbolizes the tribe's past—the trickery, the tears, the hardships and the heartaches that our ancestors endured.
>
> The large arrowhead of natural color represents our present generation—a promise that we will work, as individuals, and as a tribe to cherish and preserve our heritage and customs. The arrowhead points downward, indicating peace. We will live in peace, but we will not be suppressed.
>
> The turquoise arrow of the Piankeshaws represents our native soil; the red arrow of the Peorias represents the sun; the blue arrow of the Weas represents

the blue waters; and the green arrow of the Kaskaskias represents the green of the grass and the trees.

May the Peorias never forget that these are gifts from the Great Spirit.

The crossing of the arrows represents our promise to future generations that by banding together our spirit cannot be broken and our heritage and customs will never be forgotten.[71]

17

THE LEGACY OF
JOHNSON V. McINTOSH

The impact of *Johnson v. McIntosh* was immediate. When the Supreme Court handed down its decision on February 28, 1823, the Illinois and Piankeshaws no longer occupied their historic homelands, but other tribal nations were actively resisting removal. President Andrew Jackson urged Congress to adopt legislation that would force the southern tribes to leave their homelands. In support of Jackson, politicians from Georgia claimed that *Johnson* established that Indians hold no title to the soil. Their opponents relied on Marshall's statement that the Natives were "the rightful occupants of the soil, with a legal as well as just claim to retain possession of it, and to use it according to their own discretion."[1] On May 28, 1830, Congress narrowly passed the Indian Removal Act, which led to the coerced relocation known as the Trail of Tears.

The impact of *Johnson v. McIntosh* is enduring. In *Worcester v. Georgia* (1832) John Marshall renounced the view that "discovery gave title" and held that discovery conferred only a right of preemption; that is, the right of purchasing lands that the Natives were willing to sell.[2] *Worcester*, however, did not expressly overrule *Johnson*, and soon state and federal courts returned to the "limited possessor" conception of Indian land rights. Although the Supreme Court has said that the Native right of possession is "as sacred as the fee simple of the whites," the fact remains that Indian title—as defined in *Johnson*—is not a proprietary title. In *Tee-Hit-Ton Indians v. United States* (1955) Justice Stanley Reed relied on *Johnson v. McIntosh* to hold that Indian title may be terminated by the United States "without any legally enforceable obligation to compensate the Indians."

The *Johnson* version of the discovery doctrine still reigns supreme, as evidenced by the decision in *City of Sherrill v. Oneida Indian Nation* (2005), which reaffirmed that "fee title to the lands occupied by Indians when the colonists arrived became vested in the sovereign—first the discovering European nation and later the original States and the United States."[3]

The impact of *Johnson v. McIntosh* has also been far-reaching. In addition to the discovery doctrine, *Johnson* is closely connected to such basic principles as diminished tribal sovereignty, the federal trust duty (and authority), and the plenary power doctrine. According to Chief Justice Marshall, the adverse consequences of European discovery for the Native inhabitants were twofold: "their power to dispose of the soil at their own will, to whomsoever they pleased, was denied," and "their rights to complete sovereignty, as independent nations, were necessarily diminished."[4] Marshall could not have anticipated the allotment of tribal lands, suppression of Native cultures, and the forced assimilation of Indian peoples.[5] As the author of *Worcester v. Georgia*, he would be amazed by decisions such as *Oliphant v. Suquamish Indian Tribe* (1978) and *Montana v. United States* (1981), which have eviscerated the authority of Indian tribes over activities by nonmembers.[6]

The Marshall Court recognized—and yet undermined—Native land rights and tribal sovereignty. Pursuant to the trust and plenary power doctrines, Congress has curtailed tribal government and regulated Indian affairs. Even when Congress has not acted, the Supreme Court has held that Indian tribes have been implicitly divested of the right to exercise certain governmental powers. Federal Indian law today is marred by "doctrinal incoherence and a tendency toward judicial subjectivism which threatens to undermine foundational principles of tribal political status and tribal governmental authority."[7] American Indians in the twenty-first century continue to struggle with the legacy of *Johnson v. McIntosh*.

JOHNSON V. McINTOSH AND THE REMOVAL DEBATE

Johnson v. McIntosh figured prominently in the debate over the Indian Removal Act.[8] The United States in 1802 had promised Georgia that it would extinguish the Indian title within the state's borders "as early as the same can be peaceably obtained on reasonable terms." Most southern Indians, however, did not wish to give up their homelands and sought some form of permanent coexistence. The majority of the Cherokee people were *not* interested in ceding their remaining homelands, as evidenced by the fact that the original Cherokee Constitution declared that the "boundaries of this nation . . . shall forever hereafter remain unalterably the same." As Tim Garrison notes in *The Legal Ideology of Removal*, the Cherokees were "proclaiming to the world that they considered themselves an independent, sovereign nation of people beyond the reach and jurisdiction of the federal and state governments of the United States."[9]

The Cherokee Constitution was ratified in October 1827. In December the same year a joint committee of the Georgia Legislature issued a report stating that the Indians lacked permanent property rights, possessed their lands by permission, and "were *mere tenants at will*."[10] The assertion that Indians have no property rights provoked Jeremiah Evarts of New England to publish a series of essays in the *Washington National Intelligencer*. Under the name of "William Penn," Evarts offered up a contrary description of Indian land rights that is reminiscent of the position set forth two hundred years earlier by Roger Williams: "The Cherokees are human beings, endowed by their Creator with the same natural rights as other men. . . . If the Cherokees are interrogated as to their title, they can truly say, 'God gave this country to our ancestors. . . . *We own the land which we now occupy*, by the right of the original possessors.'"[11] In support of his expansive view of Indian property rights, Evarts relied on the statement in *Johnson v. McIntosh* that the Natives "were admitted to be the rightful occupants of the soil, with a legal as well as just claim to retain possession of it, and to use it according to their own discretion." While acknowledging that private individuals were prohibited by "municipal law" from purchasing Indian land, Evarts argued that it was "both absurd and cruel to construe this necessary limitation of the natural rights of the Indians . . . as a denial that the Indians have any rights at all."[12]

In his first annual message Andrew Jackson requested legislation that would set apart "an ample district west of the Mississippi . . . to be guaranteed to the Indian tribes as long as they shall occupy it."[13] During the ensuing debate over the Indian Removal Act, the nature of Indian land rights, the doctrine of discovery, and the meaning of *Johnson v. McIntosh* would be topics of discussion. In the midst of the debate, on the ninth of April, 1830, Senator Theodore Frelinghuysen of New Jersey addressed whether Indian land rights were affected by European discovery. He argued that "ever since the first colonies of white men found an abode on these Western shores, we have distinctly recognized their title; *treated with them as owners*, and in all our acquisitions of territory, applied ourselves to these ancient proprietors, by purchase and cession alone, to obtain the right of soil." In response Senator John Forsyth of Georgia declared that it was "well known" that "the lands, the streams, the woods, . . . were all the property of, or subject to, the Government of the fortunate navigator, who, by accident or design, first saw the before unknown country."[14] Senator John McKinley of Alabama went even further, stating that "the case of Johnson and McIntosh" held that "the natives had no title to the soil."[15]

Both proponents of removal were well versed in the law: Forsyth was a former attorney general of Georgia (and future secretary of state under Jackson and Van Buren), and McKinley would be appointed in 1837 as an associate justice of the U.S. Supreme Court. Their arguments were answered in turn by another lawyer, Senator Peleg Sprague of Maine, who would later become a federal district judge in Massachusetts. Sprague acknowledged that Indians had been prohibited from freely alienating their lands, but contended that it was wrong to conclude from this fact that discovery had deprived the Natives of title: "The rights which the United States have claimed with respect to the territory of the aborigines have been two-fold—pre-emptive and reversionary; a right to purchase, to the exclusion of all others; and to succeed the natives, should they voluntarily leave the country or become extinct. . . . *They cannot indeed transfer their country to others, but this does not impair their title, although it may diminish its value in the market.*"[16]

The removal bill passed the Senate by a vote of 28 to 19 and was taken up in the House of Representatives. Henry Storrs of New York belittled the "pretension" that the Indians had lost their lands by conquest and discovery, and relied on an exhaustive array of historical sources—including the 1791 and 1793 opinions of Thomas Jefferson—to establish that the British Crown had held a mere "naked right of pre-emption."[17] William Ellsworth of Connecticut, who later served his state as governor and as a supreme court justice, claimed discovery was "a mere political arrangement" among European nations that had nothing to do with the prior possessors of the land. "I can hardly conceive," Ellsworth noted, "how sailing along our coast for a few miles should, in the first instance, have given a right to North America."[18] In less than two years' time, John Marshall would express the same doubts in *Worcester v. Georgia*.

The chief proponents of removal in the House, as one might expect, were the representatives from Georgia. The future governor, Wilson

Lumpkin, contended that "the fundamental principle, that Indians had no right either to the soil or sovereignty of the countries they occupied, has never been abandoned." Thomas Foster quoted at length from *Johnson* to refute the assertion that discovery merely conferred an exclusive right to acquire territory from the Indians. Henry Lamar invoked *Johnson* and *Fletcher v. Peck* and argued that "the speculations of the theorist have been . . . reduced to order and regularity." James Wayne, whom Andrew Jackson would appoint to the U.S. Supreme Court, reminded his New England opponents that Roger Williams, the celebrated Puritan, "would never have been banished, if, in the zeal for Indian rights, he had not said that the charter of Massachusetts was good for nothing, as the soil and sovereignty were not purchased from the Indians."[19]

When the debate finally ended, the House of Representatives voted 102 to 97 in favor of the Removal Act. Proponents of Native land rights stressed that Indians are "the rightful occupants of the soil," whereas their opponents emphasized that "discovery gave exclusive title to those who made it." The Cherokees, under mounting pressure to relocate, would turn to the Supreme Court for protection. In *Cherokee Nation v. Georgia* (1831) and *Worcester v. Georgia* (1832), the Court would revisit the issues of Native sovereignty and land rights.

THE MOVEMENT AWAY FROM *JOHNSON V. MCINTOSH*

On September 18, 1828, Joseph Story celebrated his birthday by delivering a speech in commemoration of the first settlement of Salem, Massachusetts. Although Story had silently assented to Marshall's opinion in *Johnson*, the forty-nine-year-old scholar chose the occasion to repudiate the notion that European discovery of the New World could lawfully deprive the Native inhabitants of their property rights. Even if discovery could confer title, "the natives already possessed it by such prior discovery. . . . *In short, it is clear, that, upon the principles generally recognized by European nations, as between themselves, the natives could not be rightfully displaced.*"[20] Story assured his audience, however, that the Pilgrims of New England "respected the Indians in their settlements and claims of soil," and only occupied lands that were either vacant or purchased. "Our forefathers," he exclaimed, "did not attempt to justify their own emigration and settlement upon the European doctrine of discovery" and consequently "did not precipitate *the evil days.*"[21]

It is evident that Justice Story not only disagreed with Marshall's view of the discovery doctrine but also opposed the "evil" policy of relocating the southern tribes beyond the Mississippi. Story sent his Salem speech to his colleague and sought his reaction. The chief justice, in reply, made no mention of the doctrine of discovery but did observe that "the conduct of our forefathers in expelling the original occupants of the soil grew out of so many mixed motives that any censure which philanthropy may bestow upon it ought to be qualified." On the other hand, Marshall noted that "every oppression now exercised on a helpless people depending on our magnanimity and justice for the preservation of their existence impresses a deep stain on the American character."[22]

Marshall and the Supreme Court would soon become involved in the polarizing controversy. Shortly after the enactment of the Indian Removal Act, the Cherokee Nation enlisted the services of William Wirt, who had served as attorney general for both James Monroe and John Quincy Adams. Chief John Ross instructed Wirt to challenge the legality of Georgia "extension" statutes, which purported to annex tribal lands, abolish the Cherokee government, and generally extend state criminal and civil jurisdiction into Indian country. On December 27, 1830, William Wirt and his associates filed *Cherokee Nation v. The State of Georgia* in the U.S. Supreme Court.[23]

The lawsuit was primarily concerned with safeguarding tribal sovereignty against state incursion, but Indian land rights were also addressed. In particular, the tribe's complaint makes five points regarding the "pretended" doctrine of discovery. First, the complaint questions the applicability of the doctrine to inhabited lands, noting that the Cherokees had long been "the *occupants and owners* of the territory on which they now reside." Second, it challenges the Eurocentric assumption that "this earth was designed only for the purpose of agriculture, and that no title could be acquired to any portion of it in any other manner." Third, the complaint points out that—even if title is "derivable only from cultivation"—the Cherokee people "have become *civilized, Christians, and agriculturists.*"[24]

The remaining arguments relate to the core principles of the discovery doctrine. In 1793 the Indians of the Northwest Territory defiantly informed the United States that "we consider ourselves free to make any bargain or cession of lands, whenever & to whomsoever we please." The Cherokee Nation, in their complaint filed with the Supreme Court in 1830, also denied that Indian nations are no longer free to sell their lands

to whomsoever they please: "[The principle that] the first European discoverer has the prior and exclusive right to purchase these lands from the
Indian proprietors . . . [is] *a principle to which the Indian proprietors have never
given their assent, and which they deny to be a principle of the natural law of nations, or as in any manner obligatory on them.*"[25] The Cherokee Nation took
direct aim at the central holding of *Johnson v. McIntosh*, arguing that "this
pretended title by prior discovery . . . can have no effect in divesting the
prior title of the Indian occupants and settlers of this country."[26]

The Supreme Court issued its decision in *Cherokee Nation v. Georgia* on
March 18, 1831. Pursuant to Article 3, Section 2 of the Constitution, the
original jurisdiction of the Court extends to disputes "between a State . . .
and foreign States." The six justices who participated in the decision could
not agree as to whether the Cherokee Nation was a "foreign state" within
the meaning of the Constitution. Smith Thompson of New York, who was
joined by Joseph Story, concluded that "the Cherokees compose a foreign
state . . . and constitute a competent party to maintain a suit against the
state of Georgia." Henry Baldwin and William Johnson both declared
that Indian tribes were neither sovereign nations nor foreign states. John
Marshall, who was joined by John McLean, characterized Indian tribes
residing within the boundaries of the United States as "domestic dependent nations," but held that the suit must be dismissed because "an Indian
tribe or nation within the United States is not a foreign state in the sense
of the constitution."[27]

In his oral argument William Wirt insisted that the Native right of
occupancy described in *Johnson* was neither a permissive nor temporary
occupancy but was rather a legally enforceable right to retain the property
permanently.[28] Thompson, in his dissent, stated that it was unnecessary to
determine whether the tribe held "a mere right of occupancy, or an absolute right to the soil." Baldwin, on the other hand, declared that *Johnson*
"is too explicit to be misunderstood," and clearly established that "from
the time of discovery" the Indians held occupancy rights only, and that
consequently "the ultimate absolute fee, jurisdiction and sovereignty was
in the government."[29]

The remaining opinions in *Cherokee Nation* were authored by William Johnson and John Marshall, who had both previously set forth their
views on Indian land rights. In *Fletcher v. Peck*, Johnson claimed that the
southern tribes retained "the absolute proprietorship of their soil," and
further reasoned that "if the interest in Georgia was nothing more than

a pre-emptive right, how could that be called a fee-simple?"[30] In *Chero-kee Nation v. Georgia*, Johnson took a much different view: "It cannot be questioned that the right of sovereignty, as well as soil, was notoriously asserted and exercised by the European discoverers. . . . [Indians are not] able to alienate without permission of the remainder-man or lord . . . [and are] without land that they can call theirs in the sense of property."[31] Marshall, who delivered the opinion of the Court, made no mention of *Johnson* but did acknowledge that Indians possess "an unquestionable . . . right to the lands they occupy, until that right shall be extinguished by a voluntary cession to our government." The chief justice also recognized the existence of a trust relationship between the United States and the native inhabitants: "[The Indians] occupy a territory to which we assert a title independent of their will, which must take effect in point of posses-sion when their right of possession ceases. Meanwhile they are in a state of pupilage. Their relation to the United States resembles that of a ward to his guardian."[32]

Although the result in *Cherokee Nation* was favorable to Georgia, the Supreme Court had not accepted the state's characterization of Indians as "mere tenants at will." The Cherokees were soon presented with another chance to challenge the Georgia extension statutes. Samuel Worcester and Elizur Butler were convicted in 1831 for "residing within the limits of the Cherokee nation without a license" and for failure to take an oath "to support and defend the constitution and laws of the state of Georgia." The imprisoned missionaries filed a writ of error in the Supreme Court, arguing that the state statute was unconstitutional. At about the same time, John Marshall survived a surgical procedure that removed over one thousand small stones from his bladder.[33] The seventy-six-year-old jurist made a remarkable recovery and was present in February when the Court heard three days of argument from William Wirt and his associate, John Sergeant. The State of Georgia declined, once again, to appear or other-wise participate.

Chief Justice John Marshall's opinion in *Worcester v. Georgia*, handed down on March 3, 1832, has been described as "the most important deci-sion in federal Indian law."[34] The Court, by a six to one margin, not only held the Georgia statute in question to be "repugnant to the constitution, treaties, and laws of the United States," but also declared that Indian tribes are sovereign entities with retained property rights and inherent powers of self-government:

> *The Indian nations had always been considered as distinct, independent political com-*
> *munities, retaining their original natural rights, as the undisputed possessors of the*
> *soil,* from time immemorial, with the single exception of that imposed by
> irresistible power, which excluded them from intercourse with any other
> European potentate than the first discoverer of the coast of the particular
> region claimed. . . .
>
> *The Cherokee nation, then, is a distinct community occupying its own territory,*
> *with boundaries accurately described, in which the laws of Georgia can have no force,*
> and which the citizens of Georgia have no right to enter, but with the assent
> of the Cherokees themselves, or in conformity with treaties, and with the
> acts of congress.[35]

As John Hurley has observed, *Worcester v. Georgia* "examines in detail
the doctrine of discovery, the system of Crown property grants, British
and American policy regarding Native land rights, and, of particular importance, the political status of American Indian nations."[36] In *Worcester*
Marshall downplays the effect of the discovery doctrine, discounts the
pretentious claims of the colonial charters, and describes Indian land rights
in a manner that differs in significant respects from his earlier statements in
Johnson. In fact, one can credibly argue that *Worcester v. Georgia* implicitly
overruled *Johnson v. McIntosh.*

In both decisions Marshall candidly acknowledges the "pretension" of
applying the doctrine of discovery to inhabited lands, but he concludes
that the principle had been "acknowledged by all Europeans" and "cannot be rejected."[37] In *Worcester* Marshall goes so far as to quote his prior
holding in *Johnson* that "'discovery gave title to the government by whose
subjects or by whose authority it was made, against all other European
governments, which title might be consummated by possession.'"[38] But
what was the nature of the "title" bestowed upon the Europeans by virtue
of discovery? In *Johnson,* Marshall noted that the "*absolute ultimate title* has
been considered as acquired by discovery, subject only to the Indian title
of occupancy." In *Worcester* the chief justice dropped the "limited possessor" view of Indian title in favor of the "limited owner" conception:

> This principle . . . gave to the nation making the discovery . . . the sole right
> of acquiring the soil and of making settlements on it. . . . It regulated the right
> given by discovery among the European discoverers; but could not affect the
> rights of those already in possession. . . . *It gave the exclusive right to purchase, but*
> *did not found that right on a denial of the right of the possessor to sell.*"[39]

In other words, Indians continue to "own" the lands they occupy, but are no longer free to sell their lands to whomsoever they please, because discovery created a "pre-emptive privilege" in the discoverer; to wit, the exclusive right to acquire the property rights of the Indians *should they choose to sell*. This marks an important departure from the "limited possessor" view of Indian title, whereby the Indians possess, but do not own, the lands they occupy.[40] Under the "limited possessor" view, the United States (or one of the original colonies) owns the land and can either extinguish the Indian possessory rights or transfer ownership *subject to* the Native right of possession. In *Worcester* the chief justice returns the ownership of Native lands to the Indians, subject to the right of preemption. In so doing Marshall accepts the arguments presented by Peleg Sprague and Henry Storrs during the removal debates and adopts the position set forth by William Johnson in *Fletcher v. Peck*.[41]

The shift in Marshall's articulation of Indian land rights is also evidenced by his discussion of the colonial charters, such as Virginia's "sea-to-sea" charter. In *Johnson* Marshall stated that the colonial charters contained "an actual grant of the soil, as well as of the powers of government."[42] In *Worcester* he repudiates this notion, stating that the charters "were well understood to convey the title which, according to the common law of European sovereigns respecting America, they might rightfully convey, and no more. *This was the exclusive right of purchasing such lands as the natives were willing to sell*."[43] The "truth" of the matter, Marshall stated, was that the grants in the colonial charters "*were considered as blank paper so far as the rights of the natives were concerned*." As Howard Berman has noted, the interpretation of the discovery doctrine set forth in *Johnson v. McIntosh*—"that the European discovery of the continent instantly brought into being a fee simple property right in the common law sense to all the lands in the western hemisphere"—was "justly ridiculed" nine years later by Marshall in *Worcester v. Georgia*.[44] The Cherokee Nation *owns* the lands its members occupy, subject only to the federal government's preemptive right to purchase their territory *should they choose to sell*. The Court's decision in *Worcester* endorses tribal sovereignty and Native ownership rights. The Cherokees had won.

And yet the Cherokees lost. Initially, there was considerable doubt as to whether the Supreme Court's decision would be respected by President Jackson and the Congress. It is at this point that historians tell us Andrew Jackson did not in fact say, "John Marshall has made his decision. Now let him enforce it!"[45] The fact remains, however, that the *Worcester* decision did not please the president, who had previously claimed *Johnson* established that the "Indian tribes, east of the Mississippi, are a conquered and dependant people."[46] It appeared that Georgia would refuse to abide by the Supreme Court's decision, but a constitutional crisis was narrowly avoided when, after a series of events, Samuel Worcester and Elizur Butler were released in 1833.[47] The Cherokees had prevailed, but tribal members were divided regarding the wisdom of further resistance. On December 29, 1835, a dissident faction signed the Treaty of New Echota and consented to removal. The agreement was not approved by the Cherokee National Council but was ratified in the U.S. Senate by the margin of a single vote. In 1838 federal troops began forcibly removing Indians from their homes. On the first of August imprisoned members of National Council defiantly resolved that "the title of the Cherokee people to their lands is the most ancient, pure, and absolute known to man," and that its validity was confirmed "by possession and enjoyment antecedent to all pretense of claims by any other portion of the human race."[48]

One quarter to one half of the Cherokee, Creek, and Seminole populations died as a direct consequence of removal. The Choctaws and Chickasaws, who traveled shorter distances to the Indian Territory, also suffered terrible losses.[49] The forced expulsion of the Cherokee Nation has ensured that in a literal sense, the holding in *Worcester* remains good law: the Cherokee people today occupy lands—in Oklahoma and North Carolina—"in which the laws *of Georgia* can have no force." But Marshall's restatement of Indian land rights in *Worcester* has not prevailed. State and federal courts soon returned to the "limited possessor" view of Native property rights articulated in *Johnson v. McIntosh*. In more ways than one, *Worcester v. Georgia* proved a Pyrrhic victory.

THE RETURN TO *JOHNSON V. MCINTOSH*

John Walker was a Cherokee who believed his people could survive as a nation only by relocating west of the Mississippi. In the fall of 1834 Walker was killed by James Foreman and Anderson Springston, tribal members who opposed removal. The murder took place near present-day Cleveland, Tennessee, and the state indicted the two men for murder. The circuit judge, however, held that Tennessee could not lawfully assert jurisdiction over crimes committed in Cherokee territory. The matter was appealed to the state Supreme Court of Errors and Appeals, which heard argument in July 1835. Counsel for the defendants relied on *Worcester v. Georgia* and contended that the laws of Tennessee could have no force within the boundaries of the Cherokee Nation. The state relied on *Johnson v. McIntosh* and argued that Chief Justice Marshall's more recent statements regarding Indian land rights "are wholly incompatible with previous determinations of the same tribunal." The two decisions, the state argued, "are as diametrically opposed to each other as light is to darkness."[50]

By a vote of two to one in *State v. Foreman* (1835), the highest court of Tennessee repudiated *Worcester* and upheld the state's extension of jurisdiction over the Cherokee Nation.[51] Jacob Peck noted in dissent that the controlling legal issue had already "been before the federal judiciary, *to whom, in my opinion, it belongs to decide it.*" Judges Nathan Green and John Catron, however, were convinced that John Marshall got it right in *Johnson* and then went astray in *Worcester.* The colonial charters, Judge Green wrote, "were *not* mere blank paper in reference to the Indians." Rather, as set forth in *Johnson,* "the principle is well settled 'that discovery gave an exclusive right to extinguish the aboriginal right of occupation, either by conquest or purchase, and to assume such jurisdiction over the savages as circumstances might require.'"[52]

John Catron's views are particularly noteworthy, given his subsequent appointment by Andrew Jackson to the Supreme Court, where he would author several decisions concerning Indian land rights. Catron had fought alongside Jackson against the Upper Creeks and remained loyal to his commander, mentor, and president. In prior cases involving disputes over Native lands, Catron had cited *Johnson* with approval.[53] In *State v. Foreman* he likewise praised the 1823 decision as "an authority . . . of unequalled merit." Catron correctly predicted that the central holding of *Worcester*—that Indian tribes are distinct and sovereign political communities, independent of the states—would eventually be abandoned. With respect to Indian land rights, Catron rejected *Worcester* and endorsed the doctrine of discovery as articulated in *Johnson.* The refusal of the Tennessee Supreme Court to follow *Worcester,* Tim Garrison has noted, "represented the final and fatal strike against the idea of Native American sovereignty for the Cherokees and the other southeastern tribes." In a letter to Vice President Martin Van Buren, Catron openly acknowledged that his *Foreman* opinion "attempted to disencumber" the authority of *Worcester v. Georgia.*[54]

In state court cases involving Indian land rights, the U.S. Supreme Court decision that is cited most often is *Johnson v. McIntosh*. Although *Worcester v. Georgia* is still considered the starting point for any discussion of tribal sovereignty, Marshall's reformulation of Native property rights is rarely acknowledged by state courts.[55] *Worcester* was stillborn in the federal courts as well. Marshall's statements about the limited effect of the colonial charters have *never* been quoted in subsequent Supreme Court decisions. His assertion that discovery "could not affect the rights of those already in possession" has been quoted only once—in *Holden v. Joy* (1872), a case that otherwise endorsed the *Johnson* discovery rule. Finally, the statement in *Worcester* that discovery "gave the exclusive right to purchase, but did not found that right on a denial of the right of the possessor to sell," has been quoted just twice by the Court: in *Holden v. Joy* and *United States v. Alcea Band of Tillamooks* (1946), a case that was strongly criticized, if not overruled, in a subsequent decision.[56]

Why did the *Johnson* version of Indian land rights prevail? It was due in part to Marshall's departure from the Court.[57] As it turned out, the next Supreme Court case to discuss the discovery doctrine—*Mitchel v. United States* (1835)—was the last decision in which John Marshall participated. In *Mitchel* the high court considered the rights of private individuals who purchased Indian lands in Florida with the permission of Spanish officials, who subsequently confirmed the grants. In his opinion for the Court, Justice Henry Baldwin ignored *Worcester*, proclaiming that "the view taken by this court of Indian rights in the case of *Johnson v. M'Intosh* . . . has received universal assent." Baldwin did state that "their right of occupancy is considered *as sacred as the fee simple of the whites*," and further noted that Indian title could be alienated with permission. The *Mitchel* decision does not, however, accede to Marshall's position in *Worcester* that Indian land rights are rights of ownership, limited only by the government's preemptive privilege.[58]

In 1835, when *Mitchel* was decided, there were three Jackson appointees on the high court: John McLean, who had opined in *Worcester* that tribal self-government was "undoubtedly" a temporary measure; Henry Baldwin, who had consistently endorsed the *Johnson* discovery rule; and James Wayne of Georgia, a recent addition to the Court who had voted for the Indian Removal Act as a member of the House of Representatives. After John Marshall died on July 6, 1835, Andrew Jackson nominated Roger Taney as the fifth chief justice of the Supreme Court. In 1837 the Court was enlarged to nine members, and it was populated in 1838 by seven justices who had been nominated by either Jackson or his chosen successor, Martin Van Buren:

1835 Term	*1838 Term*
John Marshall (Adams appt.)	Roger Taney (Jackson appt.)
James Wayne (Jackson)	James Wayne (Jackson)
[vacant]	Philip Barbour (Jackson)
Joseph Story (Madison)	Joseph Story (Madison)
Smith Thompson (Monroe)	Smith Thompson (Monroe)
John McLean (Jackson)	John McLean (Jackson)
Henry Baldwin (Jackson)	Henry Baldwin (Jackson)
	John Catron (Jackson)
	John McKinley (Van Buren)

Philip Barbour of Virginia and John McKinley of Georgia both voted for the Indian Removal Act as members of the House of Representatives, and McKinley had claimed *Johnson* established that "the natives had no title to the soil." John Catron, as earlier noted, regarded *Johnson* with approval; he believed that *Worcester* was "greatly in conflict" with the "well-considered case" of *Johnson v. McIntosh.*[59]

The Jackson appointees dominated the reconfigured Court and proceeded to ignore Marshall's statements in *Worcester v. Georgia* regarding Indian land rights.[60] Henry Baldwin relied on *Johnson* in *United States v. Fernandez* (1836), as did James Wayne in *Mitchel v. United States* (1841). Chief Justice Roger Taney cited *Johnson* in *Martin v. Waddell's Lessee* (1842) and *Scott v. Sandford* (1856), and he declared in *United States v. Rogers* (1846) that the Indian tribes of America "have never been acknowledged or treated as independent nations by the European governments, nor regarded as the owners of the territories they respectively occupied." John Catron applied the *Johnson* discovery rule in *Clark v. Smith* (1839), *Marsh v. Brooks* (1850), and again in *Doe v. Wilson* (1859).[61]

In *United States v. Cook* (1873) the Supreme Court declared that the authority of *Johnson v. McIntosh* "has never been doubted."[62] Indeed, Charles Royce remarked, in his treatise *Indian Land Cessions in the United States* (1900), on "the *absurdity* of admitting the Indians' claim to the absolute right of the soil of the whole country." Nevertheless, the "limited owner" conception of Indian property rights has not entirely disappeared. In *Shoshone Tribe v. United States* (1937), the United States Court of Claims held that "the right of occupancy is the real ownership. It is the full title, or as much title, as . . . any other than the sovereign usually holds."[63] Nine years later, in *United States v. Alcea Band of Tillamooks* (1946), the Supreme Court was presented with the question of whether a cause of action exists "for compensation arising out of an involuntary taking of lands held by original Indian title." The Court cited Marshall's statement in *Worcester*—that discovery "gave the exclusive right to purchase, but did not found that right on a denial of the right of the possessor to sell"—and held that Indians must be compensated in such circumstances: "As against any but the sovereign, original Indian title was accorded the protection of complete ownership. . . . Admitting the undoubted power of Congress to extinguish original Indian title compels no conclusion that compensation need not be paid. . . . The Indians have more than a merely moral claim for compensation."[64] The notion that Indian title is a compensable right was short-lived. In *Tee-Hit-Ton Indians v. United States* (1955) the Court relied on *Johnson* to hold that Indian title is "not a property right" but is instead a "right of occupancy" that may be terminated "without any legally enforceable obligation to compensate the Indians."[65] As Lindsay Robertson has argued, the *Tee-Hit-Ton* decision is based on a "fundamentally flawed" understanding of British colonial policy, American history, and "the legal consequences of discovery."[66]

Under the "limited ownership" conception of Indian land rights, as set forth by John Marshall in *Worcester*, the tribe's ownership rights are constrained by the government's right of preemption. The preemptive right is *not* itself title to land but rather a right to acquire the Indians' property. Yet in some cases the federal courts have characterized the right of preemption *as* fee-simple title. For example, in *Oneida Indian Nation of New York v. County of Oneida, New York* (1974), the Supreme Court at one point equates "fee title to Indian lands" with "the pre-emptive right to purchase from the Indians."[67] The United States Court of Appeals for the Second Circuit has also held that the term "fee title," as used in the context of Indian lands, is "used interchangeably with 'right of preemption,' or the preemptive right over all others to purchase the Indian title or right of occupancy from the inhabitants."[68] Equating the ownership right ("fee simple") with the right to purchase ("preemption") serves only to confuse the issue of Indian land rights further. As William Johnson noted in 1810, if the government's interest is "nothing more than a pre-emptive right, how could that be called a fee-simple?" Yet the Supreme Court, in

City of Sherrill, New York v. Oneida Indian Nation of New York (2005), again equated "fee title to Indian lands" with "the pre-emptive right to purchase from the Indians." In the same decision the Court notes that "under the doctrine of discovery, . . . fee title to the lands occupied by Indians when the colonists arrived became vested in the sovereign—first the discovering European nation and later the original States and the United States."[69] This statement conflicts with the "limited owner" conception of Indian lands rights in *Worcester* but is consistent with the "limited possessor" view of Indian lands rights in *Johnson*.

The lack of ownership rights has, in some instances, proved to be a benefit to Indians. In 1990 the Black Hills Institute of Geological Research paid five thousand dollars to Maurice Williams, a member of the Cheyenne River Sioux Tribe, for the right to excavate fossil remains from his property. The bones that were removed, which have been described as "the most valuable *Tyrannosaurus rex* skeleton known to man," were eventually sold to Chicago's Field Museum of Natural History for $8.36 million dollars. Unfortunately for the Black Hills Institute, the bones were not "owned" by Maurice Williams. Instead, as held by the United States Court of Appeals for the Eighth Circuit, the fossil remains were found "on land to which the United States holds legal title in trust for Williams." By virtue of the doctrine of discovery, Maurice Williams did not have the right to convey his property rights to whomsoever he pleased. Because the secretary of the interior had not approved the transaction, the transaction with the Black Hills Institute was held to be void. When the dinosaur was subsequently sold at auction, the trustee United States transferred its legal title to the Field Museum. Maurice Williams, as beneficiary, received approximately $7.6 million.[70]

In 2007 a federal district court held that the United States is liable, under the Comprehensive Environmental Response, Compensation and Liability Act, as an "owner" of the Midnite Mine Superfund Site, a former open-pit uranium mine located on the Spokane Indian Reservation. Citing *Johnson v. McIntosh*, the court held that it "has long been recognized . . . that title to the lands of this nation, originally occupied by the Indians, became vested in the colonial European nations and then the United States of America through 'discovery' and 'conquest.'" The court rejected the contention that the United States lacked sufficient "indicia of ownership" to warrant liability under the Superfund law. Because the

United States is the owner of the mining site, the federal government must share responsibility with other liable parties for remediating the ground and water contamination. In 2008 the costs of cleanup were estimated to be $152 million.[71]

THE IMPACT OF *JOHNSON V. MCINTOSH* ON FEDERAL INDIAN LAW

The impact of *Johnson v. McIntosh* extends far beyond Indian land rights. As noted by Robert Laurence, "at the heart of Indian law—at least the domestic, federal Indian law of the United States—lies the so-called Discovery Doctrine." In contrast to Canada, New Zealand, and Australia, the United States has always acknowledged that Indian title "includes governmental authority as well as land rights."[72] The Marshall Court, in *Johnson* (1823), *Cherokee Nation* (1831), and especially *Worcester* (1832), established that Indian tribes not only retained property rights after European discovery but also retained territorial sovereign authority. On the other hand, the "limited possessor" conception of Indian land rights has led the Court to craft principles of federal Indian law that have severely curtailed tribal sovereignty. In particular, there are three judicial doctrines that are closely connected to the *Johnson* discovery rule: the diminished tribal sovereignty doctrine, the trust doctrine, and the plenary power doctrine. Each warrants discussion.

The diminished tribal sovereignty doctrine (or "implicit divestiture" doctrine) can be traced to Chief Justice Marshall's statement in *Johnson* that as a consequence of European discovery, the rights of the original inhabitants "to complete sovereignty, as independent nations, *were necessarily diminished.*" *Johnson* not only denied Indians the right to sell their land "whenever and to whomsoever" they pleased but also established the principle that "discovery divested tribes of their authority *as sovereigns* to have government-to-government relations with anyone but their discoverer (or its successor in interest)."[73] The *Johnson* discovery rule "is the well-spring of the idea of Diminished Sovereignty," Robert Miller has explained, "because tribal sovereign and real property rights were assumed to have been limited automatically and immediately by Discovery when Europeans or Americans first encountered native territories."[74] The diminished tribal sovereignty doctrine runs counter to one of the most basic tenets of federal Indian law: the "reserved rights" principle that Indian tribes retain the "inherent powers of a limited sovereignty which has never been extinguished."[75]

The Supreme Court did not expand the scope of the diminished sovereignty doctrine for the next 155 years. However, in *Oliphant v. Suquamish Indian Tribe* (1978), the Court relied on the diminished tribal sovereignty doctrine to conclude that Indian tribes in the United States have been *implicitly* divested of criminal jurisdiction over non-Indians. Justice William Rehnquist cited *Johnson v. McIntosh* and held that tribes—by virtue of their "dependent status"—had lost the right to exercise certain governmental powers, such as freely alienating to non-Indians the land they occupy; entering into direct commercial or governmental relations with foreign nations; and exercising criminal jurisdiction over non-Indians in tribal courts.[76] Three years later, in *Montana v. United States* (1981), the Court announced "the general proposition that the inherent sovereign powers of an Indian tribe do not extend to the activities of nonmembers of the tribe."[77] In subsequent decisions, the Court has further circumscribed the adjudicatory and regulatory authority of Indian tribes over activities by non-members.[78]

Although there is lack of consensus regarding the origins and purpose of the trust doctrine, some scholars and jurists associate the trust concept with the *Johnson* discovery rule.[79] Marshall held in *Johnson* that the discoverer's title was encumbered by the Native right of occupancy, and by the end of the nineteenth century the Supreme Court had adopted the position that the United States owned Indian lands "in trust" for the Native inhabitants. Courts have invoked the trust concept to protect tribes from state intrusion and to impose affirmative obligations upon the federal government. In addition, in limited circumstances, Indians and Indian tribes have been permitted to sue the United States for damages resulting from a breach of trust.[80] Viewed most favorably, the trust doctrine represents the "central protective principle of Indian tribal rights under our law" and serves as a basis for judging the government's conduct "by the most exacting fiduciary standards."[81]

The trust doctrine, on the other hand, has also been employed to justify federal regulation of the internal affairs of Indian tribes.[82] In *United States v. Kagama* (1886) the Supreme Court held that Congress could extend federal criminal jurisdiction to crimes committed by Indians in Indian country: "These Indian tribes are the wards of the nation. . . . From their very weakness and helplessness, so largely due to the course of dealing of the federal government with them, and the treaties in which it has been promised, there arises the duty of protection, *and with it the* power."[83] In *Lone Wolf v. Hitchcock* (1903) the Supreme Court went even further and held that Congress may abrogate treaties with Indian tribes whenever "circumstances . . . demand, in the interest of the country and the Indians themselves, that it should do so."[84] As bluntly stated by the Court in *United States v. Rowell* (1917), when Congress exercises its control over Indians, the "wish of the ward [has] to yield to the will of the guardian."[85]

The *Kagama* and *Lone Wolf* decisions also gave rise to the plenary power doctrine. The Court in *Lone Wolf* stated that authority over tribal relations "has been exercised by Congress from the beginning, and the power has always been deemed a political one, not subject to be controlled by the judicial department of the government." The plenary power doctrine is a logical outgrowth of the diminished tribal sovereignty, trust, and discovery doctrines.[86] In light of his statements in *Worcester v. Georgia*, it is evident that Chief Justice John Marshall did not believe the United States could exercise unqualified dominion over Indian affairs. Yet in *Santa Clara Pueblo v. Martinez* (1978) Justice Thurgood Marshall acknowledged that "Congress has plenary authority to limit, modify or eliminate the powers of local self-government which the tribes otherwise possess."[87]

Courts have justified the diminished tribal sovereignty, trust, and plenary power doctrines on the supposed inferiority and dependency of "conquered" Indians. As noted by Alex Tallchief Skibine, judges have "juxtaposed the civilized whites against the savage Indians and invoked the notion of trust because Indians were said to be incompetent and in need of a guardian."[88] *Johnson v. McIntosh* lends support to the Eurocentric and Christian-based idea that the rights of "uncivilized" and "heathen" Indians can be disregarded. In the 1823 decision the U.S. Supreme Court characterized the indigenous inhabitants as "fierce savages" whose "character and religion . . . afforded an apology for considering them as a people over whom the superior genius of Europe might claim an ascendency."[89] In *United States v. Lucero* (1869) the Supreme Court of the New Mexico Territory was less circumspect: "The idea that a handful of wild, half-naked, thieving, plundering, murdering savages should be dignified with the sovereign attributes of nations, enter into solemn treaties, and claim a country five hundred miles wide by one thousand miles long as theirs in fee simple, because they hunted buffalo and antelope over it, might do for beautiful reading in Cooper's novels or Longfellow's Hiawatha, but is unsuited to the intelligence and justice of this age, or the natural rights of mankind."[90] Such overtly racist statements belong to a different age of American jurisprudence.[91] Yet the doctrine of discovery, the diminished tribal sovereignty doctrine, the trust doctrine, and the plenary power doctrine are all still with us. In 2004 a Justice of the U.S. Supreme Court remarked that "what transformed the tribes from independent sovereigns to dependent sovereigns was not a decision of this Court and the act of Congress. . . . It's the result of historical events."[92] This statement, of course, ignores the obvious: the Supreme Court's decision in *Johnson v. McIntosh*, and the Court's subsequent refusal to accept John Marshall's restatement of the discovery doctrine in *Worcester v. Georgia*, are themselves among the "historical events" that have curtailed tribal sovereignty and diminished Indian land rights.

The Impact of *Johnson v. McIntosh* Outside the United States

Johnson v. McIntosh has also influenced indigenous rights in Australia, New Zealand, and Canada.[93] The eminent British lawyer William Burge cited *Johnson* in 1836 in support of his opinion that a private purchase from the Australian Aborigines was invalid. In 1847 the New Zealand Supreme Court decided *The Queen v. Symonds*, the first judicial decision outside the United States to invoke Marshall's Indian jurisprudence. Likewise, when the existence and scope of Aboriginal title was finally litigated in Canada in the 1880s, the *Johnson* decision played a major role. In the twentieth and twenty-first centuries, Australian, New Zealand, and Canadian courts continue to cite John Marshall's views on Native land rights and the doctrine of discovery.

On June 6, 1835, the Dutigalla Aborigines sold approximately 600,000 acres of land near present-day Melbourne, Australia. The grantees were fifteen men from Van Diemen's Land (Tasmania), who later formed the Port Phillip Association. Their leader, John Batman, was in many respects the George Croghan of the Antipodes, and his attempt to acquire a "good" title from the indigenous inhabitants met a fate similar to that of Croghan's effort.[94] Like Croghan, the syndicate initially sought royal confirmation of the transaction but was informed that it would be contrary to British practice to recognize the private purchase. The governor of New South Wales, Richard Bourke, also issued a proclamation, declaring that "every such treaty, bargain, and contract with the Aboriginal Natives . . . is void and of no effect against the rights of the Crown."[95]

In order to overcome such opposition, the Port Phillip Association resorted to the time-honored tradition of seeking opinions from eminent lawyers with expertise in colonial law. One such individual was William Burge, a former attorney general of Jamaica. Burge's opinion, dated January 16, 1836, relied on "the case of Johnson v. M'Intosh," which established that "Indian title was subordinate to the absolute ultimate title of the Government, and that the purchase made otherwise than with the authority of the Government was not valid."[96] The Port Phillip Association purchase was never confirmed, and the British government instead adopted the view that the Crown had acquired *all* rights of ownership and possession upon settlement of the continent. The doctrine of *terra nullius*—the most extreme application of the doctrine of discovery—would remain a cornerstone of Australian law until 1992.

Five years after John Batman transacted with the Aborigines, Sydney lawyer William Charles Wentworth and four other individuals met with visiting Mâori chiefs from New Zealand and purchased approximately 20 million acres, consisting of the South Island and most of the adjacent islands. When Governor George Gipps introduced a bill in the New South Wales legislature to invalidate unauthorized purchases of Mâori land, Wentworth argued that "until such a law is made and passed by this Council, the right of British subjects to buy land from the natives is as indisputable as the right of the natives to sell it to them."[97] Gipps disagreed, asserting that the Mâori "have not the right of granting the soil to individuals because they themselves have not individual possession."[98] When Gipps stressed that the subject at hand "was discussed at great length in the celebrated case of *Johnson v. M'Intosh*," Wentworth argued, without success, that the Legislative Council should reject the "principle of usurpation" that had diminished Native land rights in the New World.[99]

In 1847 the New Zealand Supreme Court decided *The Queen v. Symonds*, which was a feigned dispute designed to produce a judicial determination regarding indigenous land rights. As Mark Hickford has noted, the *Symonds* decision "introduced the Marshall Court jurisprudence of the United States to imperial New Zealand."[100] Justice Henry Chapman held that private purchases of Mâori lands are "good as against the Native seller, but not against the Crown."[101] The Natives of New Zealand retained their customary rights to use and occupy their lands, but their title was necessarily "modified" when Great Britain claimed sovereignty over the islands and acquired the preemptive right to extinguish the Native title.[102] Aboriginal title was thus afforded limited recognition in New Zealand only twenty-four years after *Johnson v. McIntosh*.

Aboriginal land rights were denied in the nineteenth century in western Canada, where, "as in Australia, the government simply allocated the land to settlers without obtaining the consent of its previous occupants."[103] The *Johnson* decision, however, did have an impact on Native land rights in eastern Canada. In *St. Catherine's Milling and Lumber Company v. The Queen* (1885–88), lawyers and jurists on both sides argued that their view of indigenous land rights had been endorsed by the United States Supreme Court.[104] The Ontario Court of Appeal (1886) and the Supreme Court of Canada (1887) agreed that the province held legal title to the lands in question. In one of four opinions handed down by the Court of Appeal, Justice George Burton noted the "very interesting and instructive" discussion in *Johnson* of the relationship of "the Indian right of occupancy" to "the absolute title of the Crown." Without mentioning *Worcester v. Georgia* by name, Burton acknowledged that other American decisions "would seem to place the so called Indian title on a higher footing" but argued that *Johnson* was better reasoned.[105] Justices Samuel Strong and Jean-Thomas Taschereau of the Supreme Court also cited *Johnson* with approval, and Chief Justice William J. Ritchie quoted from Joseph Story's discussion of the discovery doctrine in his *Commentaries on the Constitution of the United States*.[106] "I think the Crown owns the soil of all unpatented lands," Ritchie held, "the Indians possessing only the right of occupancy, and the Crown possessing the legal title subject to that occupancy, with the absolute exclusive right to extinguish the Indian title either by conquest or by purchase."[107]

Indigenous land rights in Australia, New Zealand, and Canada have not remained static. In the 1973 decision of *Calder v. British Columbia* the Supreme Court of Canada acknowledged that the indigenous inhabitants held an "aboriginal title" at the time the Crown acquired sovereignty.[108] The impact of *Johnson* on *Calder* is evident. Justice Emmett Hall described the 1823 decision as "the outstanding judicial pronouncement on the subject of Indian rights" and "the *locus classicus* of the principles governing aboriginal title."[109] In subsequent decisions Canadian courts have continued to look to *Johnson* for guidance in defining the nature and scope of aboriginal title. In *Guerin v. The Queen* (1984), Justice Robert Dickson noted that *Calder* was consistent with "the leading American cases."[110] The Canadian Supreme Court in *Guerin* then endorsed *Johnson's* "limited possessor" conception of indigenous land rights, holding that "Indians have a legal right to occupy and possess certain lands, the ultimate title to which is in the Crown."[111] Twelve years later, in *Van der Peet v. The Queen* (1996), the Court again cited *Johnson*, noting that "the view of aboriginal rights as based in the prior occupation of North America by distinctive aboriginal societies, finds support in the early American decisions of Marshall C.J." Speaking for the Court, Chief Justice Antonio Lamer acknowledged that Canadian aboriginal law "has developed in unique directions," but nevertheless approved of legal scholar Brian Slattery's statements that the Marshall decisions provide "structure and coherence to an untidy and diffuse body of customary law based on official practice" and are "as relevant to Canada as they are to the United States."[112]

Although the 1847 *Symonds* decision held that the Māori retained "modified" rights to use and occupy their lands, subsequent legislation and judicial pronouncements were less respectful of indigenous land rights. In *Wi Parata v. Bishop of Wellington* (1877), Chief Justice James Prendergast declared that the Māori had "no regular system of territorial rights nor any definite ideas of property in land," and characterized the cession of sovereignty in the Treaty of Waitangi as "a simple nullity."[113] New Zealand has only recently rejected *Wi Parata* and returned to the views expressed in *Symonds*. In *Attorney-General v. Ngati Apa* (2003), the New Zealand Court of Appeal addressed whether customary Māori title extends to lands that are either temporarily or permanently under salt water. Judges Noel Anderson and Sir Kenneth Keith noted that *Johnson v. McIntosh* recognized existing Native rights, which were characterized as a "right of occupancy" and which remained a burden on title until extinguished. Judge Dame Sian Elias cited *Johnson* for the proposition that Native rights are "rights at common law, not simply moral claims against the Crown."[114] The court reaffirmed Māori land rights and held that the "radical title of the Crown is a technical and notional concept" and is "not inconsistent with common law recognition of native property."[115]

The most significant change has occurred in Australia. On June 3, 1992, the High Court of Australia held, in *Mabo v. Queensland (No 2)*, that "the common law of this country recognizes a form of native title."[116] Although the High Court was careful to note the "special constitutional and historical considerations" that influence American cases, it also expressly acknowledged that "the notion of native or Indian title owes much to the celebrated judgment of Marshall C.J. in the case of *Johnson v McIntosh*."[117] Richard Bartlett has stated that "the rhetoric in *Mabo No. 2* was of justice and equality before the law, but the conclusions reflect the pragmatism employed by Marshall CJ in 1823."[118] Peter Russell reaches a similar conclusion in his book on the *Mabo* case: "The moral structure of . . . the High Court's decision . . . is reminiscent of the jurisprudence of Chief Justice John Marshall, . . . who tried to square recognition of Indigenous peoples' rights with acceptance of their colonization. . . . The same utilitarian subordination of the fundamental human rights of Indigenous peoples to the interests of the settler majority is evident in the majority's position in *Mabo*."[119] Although the High Court held that "a mere change in sovereignty does not extinguish native title to land," it also held that the common law did not recognize a right of compensation for extinguishment of Native title.[120] Australia is *terra nullius* no more, but the Crown is still acknowledged to be the owner of the underlying title to indigenous lands.

Johnson v. McIntosh has continued to play a role in shaping Australia's Aboriginal land rights jurisprudence. In *Wik Peoples v. Queensland* (1996) the High Court cited *Johnson* for the proposition that a sovereign may extinguish Native title, but held (by a 4–3 vote) that the issuance of pastoral leases did not necessarily extinguish all incidents of Native title.[121] Marshall's views on the extinguishment of Native title were also noted by the High Court in *Fejo v. Northern Territory* (1998) and by the Federal Court of Australia in *Western Australia v. Ward* (2000).[122]

The High Court's decision in *Mabo v. Queensland (No 2)* can be read as an apology to the Aborigines of Australia. Justices William Deane and Mary Gaudron acknowledge in the 1992 decision that "the dispossession and oppression of the Aborigines" was premised on two legal fictions: that the continent in 1788 was *terra nullius* and that ownership of all the lands vested in the Crown, unaffected by any claims of the Aboriginal inhabitants. By means of a simple declaration—that *"the lands of this continent were not terra nullius or "practically unoccupied" in 1788"*—the justices rejected the longstanding legal theories that had constituted "the darkest aspect of the history of this nation."[123]

18

THE CRITICAL RESPONSE TO
THE DOCTRINE OF DISCOVERY

The *Johnson* discovery rule and the "limited possessor" conception of in-digenous land rights have never enjoyed universal acclaim. In *Fletcher v. Peck* Justice William Johnson disagreed with the notion that discovery con-ferred ownership, arguing that Georgia had "nothing more than a power to acquire fee-simple by purchase, when the proprietors should be pleased to sell," and thus "had *not* a fee-simple in the lands in question."[1] Justice Joseph Story, in his *Commentaries on the Constitution*, questioned the applica-tion of the discovery doctrine to occupied lands. Most significant, Chief Justice John Marshall renounced the "limited possessor" view in *Worcester v. Georgia* and held instead that Indians own their lands, subject to the govern-ment's right of preemption. It is *Johnson v. McIntosh*, however, that remains the leading decision on Native property rights in the United States.

The 1823 decision is still cited with approval by the Supreme Court. The response of legal scholars, however, has not remained constant. In 1974 Native historian Vine Deloria, Jr., inaugurated the modern era of scholarship on Indian land rights by including a critique of the discov-ery doctrine in *Behind the Trail of Broken Treaties: An Indian Declaration of Independence*. Since that time law professors and historians have produced numerous publications examining the legal, political, economic, moral, religious, and racial underpinnings of the doctrine of discovery. As Simon Young of Australia notes, debate over *Johnson* "has become an important 'cottage industry' in US legal scholarship."[2]

There is a virtual consensus among critics that Marshall's restatement of the discovery doctrine in *Worcester* is preferable to the position set forth in

Johnson. However, scholars disagree on *Johnson*'s underlying rationale, the deleterious effects of the decision, and the precise nature of the property interests created by Marshall's opinion. There is also lack of unanimity with respect to the appropriate response to *Johnson*. Two proposed courses of action have garnered significant support in recent years: (1) reliance on international human rights law as a source of legal protection for indigenous rights; and (2) repudiation of *Johnson v. McIntosh* and the doctrine of discovery. Advocates for Native land rights have pursued claims before international tribunals, and both the Organization of American States and the United Nations have addressed the rights of indigenous peoples. In 2007 the UN General Assembly adopted its Declaration on the Rights of Indigenous Peoples, which asserts that indigenous peoples "have the right to the lands, territories and resources which they have traditionally owned, occupied or otherwise used or acquired."[3]

The future for indigenous land rights is uncertain. The Supreme Court has shown no inclination to overturn *Johnson v. McIntosh*, the Vatican has ignored requests to rescind the papal bulls that sanctioned European discovery and control of the New World, and in 2007 the United States, Canada, Australia, and New Zealand voted against the Declaration on the Rights of Indigenous Peoples. Yet in a remarkable turn of events, Australia changed course in 2009 and endorsed the UN Declaration, and in 2010 New Zealand, Canada, and the United States followed suit. Although the Catholic Church has taken no action, other religious organizations have now repudiated the discovery doctrine, including the Episcopal Church of the United States, which has declared the "Christian Doctrine of Discovery" to be "fundamentally opposed to the Gospel of Jesus Christ and our understanding of the inherent rights that individuals and peoples have received from God."[4]

THE RESPONSE OF LEGAL SCHOLARS

The "celebrated case of *Johnson v. M'Intosh*" is discussed by Justice Joseph Story in his *Commentaries on the Constitution of the United States* (1833) and also by New York chancellor James Kent in his *Commentaries on American Law* (1st ed., 1826–30). Both men offer mild critiques of Marshall's jurisprudence. Story questions his reliance on the discovery doctrine, stating that "in respect to countries then inhabited by the natives, it is not easy to perceive how . . . it can be successfully vindicated."[5] In similar fashion

Kent notes the "pretension" in *Johnson* of converting the discovery of a country into a conquest, but he agrees with Marshall that "it is now too late to draw into discussion the validity of that pretension, or the restrictions which it imposes." In his second edition (1832) Kent includes a footnote criticizing Marshall's discussion of Indian title in *Fletcher* as "a mere naked declaration, without any discussion or reasoning by the court in support of it."[6]

Subsequent discussions of *Johnson v. McIntosh* in the nineteenth century and early twentieth century were predominantly positive. Emory Washburn, in his 1868 *Treatise on the American Law of Real Property*, endorsed the *Johnson* discovery rule without comment.[7] John Westlake distinguished between "civilized and uncivilized humanity" in his *Chapters on the Principles of International Law* (1894) and noted that the American Indians held a limited right of occupancy because they "knew no greater right among themselves."[8] Joseph Cotton praised *Johnson* in 1905 "for its freedom from petty palliation for the hardships of conquest." Other scholars described *Johnson v. McIntosh* as a "masterly" statement of law and a "great and fearless opinion."[9]

The notable exception was George Bryan, a lawyer from Richmond who practiced commercial law and served as president of the Virginia Bar Association. In his 1924 book *The Imperialism of John Marshall: A Study in Expediency*, Bryan argued that the Supreme Court "bowed to expediency rather than to right" and defined Indian land rights in a manner that was "morally wrong."[10] According to Bryan, *Johnson v. McIntosh* was concerned with "a flat question of right and wrong," and by refusing to acknowledge the absolute right of Indians to own and sell property, the Supreme Court failed to do the "right" thing: "Justice to the American Indian demanded that his title to his property be recognized and, if . . . the property of the Indian was deemed necessary to the public use, it should have . . . been duly condemned and the fair value paid to the owner."[11] But Bryan was unable to convince his audience. "If Marshall was an imperialist," one reviewer wrote, "then it is safe to say that nine-tenths of his contemporaries, including Mr. Jefferson, were also imperialists." Attitudes that were prevalent in the prior century still lingered, as is evident in another review of Bryan's book: "It [is] denied that a savage race, by being prior in time in a large and fertile territory has a moral right to preempt it to its wasteful uses, and shut out from it civilized peoples needing it for its and for their fullest development. *To hold that the Indians owned the lands would mean that they could keep them if they so desired, as well as convey them to whom they pleased.*"[12]

George Bryan's critique of *Johnson v. McIntosh* was ahead of its time. In the half century that followed the publication of his book, federal Indian law underwent dramatic changes. In 1934 Congress enacted the Indian Reorganization Act, and in 1946 the Indian Claims Commission was established to adjudicate tribal land claims. During the 1950s Congress "terminated" the federal trust relationship with numerous tribes, but in 1970 President Richard Nixon called for a new era of self-determination. During his administration the country witnessed the rise of the American Indian Movement, the occupation of Alcatraz Island, the "Broken Treaties" march on Washington, and the standoff between Indians and law enforcement at Wounded Knee, South Dakota. In 1975 Congress enacted the Indian Self-Determination and Assistance Act and established the American Indian Policy Review Commission. The commission's 1977 report emphasized that indigenous peoples depend on land for their economic security and the survival of their cultures.[13]

During this same period legal scholars began to examine the doctrine of discovery. In 1974 Vine Deloria, Jr., published an insightful analysis of *Johnson v. McIntosh* and noted that "for the first time in history, American Indians are exploring the old legal doctrines."[14] One such Native scholar was James Youngblood Henderson, a tribal citizen of the Oklahoma Chickasaw Nation and graduate of Harvard Law School. In his 1977 law review article "Unraveling the Riddle of Aboriginal Title," Henderson contended that Indian title "slowly but perceptibly changed from its original concept as established in the Marshall Court," and was transformed by the Supreme Court from a property right "as sacred as the fee simple of the whites" into noncompensable "naked possession." The "modern paradigm of Indian title," Henderson argued, "demands reappraisal."[15]

The academic community responded with a number of articles and books exploring the historical and legal treatment of indigenous land rights in the United States.[16] In 1978 Howard Berman published an article titled "The Concept of Aboriginal Rights in the Early Legal History of the United States," and in 1987 Milner Ball presented a new way of looking at *Johnson* in his article "Constitution, Court, Indian Tribes." Other American scholars provided new insights regarding Indian title, and authors from outside the United States made important contributions.[17] Two books stand out in terms of depth and originality: *Common Law*

Aboriginal Title (1989), by Canadian Kent McNeil, and *The American Indian in Western Legal Thought: The Discourses of Conquest* (1990), by Robert Williams, Jr., of the Lumbee Indian Tribe.

In some respects *Common Law Aboriginal Title* can be read like a legal brief: it was written to solve the "riddle of aboriginal title" and demonstrate that "even by the colonizers' own rules indigenous people did—and in some cases no doubt still do—have title to the lands occupied by them." McNeil contends that acquisition of British sovereignty over discovered lands did *not* mean that the Crown acquired *title* to the lands occupied by indigenous peoples. Rather, in situations where Native inhabitants can prove they held title by virtue of their own customary laws, the Crown is compelled to acknowledge such "customary" aboriginal title.[18] Where Natives had no customary property laws, but occupied distinct areas, McNeil argues that the Crown is obliged to recognize a "common law" aboriginal title that gives the inhabitants "fee simple estates" under English law.[19]

McNeil points out that "the American situation is in many ways anomalous" because Indians in the United States are viewed as members of "domestic dependent nations," whereas Natives in Canada have always been considered to be British subjects. In his estimation John Marshall erred when he created "Indian title"—a property right that is "unknown to the common law"—on the basis of "doubtful premises" drawn from a misunderstanding of international law.[20] McNeil's principal criticism of *Johnson v. McIntosh* is that Marshall failed to explain *how* discovery could give title to lands that the Indians occupied. Based on his study of English property law, McNeil argues that when lands in the New World were claimed for the Crown, a "right to fee simple estates" vested in the indigenous inhabitants pursuant to the doctrine of continuity and the common law.[21]

Robert Williams's 1990 book *The American Indian in Western Legal Thought* can be read like a criminal indictment: it presents evidence of the western world's "discourses of conquest" and charges the United States with preserving "the legacy of 1,000 years of European racism and colonialism directed against non-Western peoples."[22] Williams, a 1980 graduate of Harvard Law School, has written extensively in the fields of federal Indian law, indigenous people's rights, international law, and critical race and postcolonial theory. In a 1987 article Williams echoed George Bryan by arguing that "expediency, not the rule of law, ultimately informed and determined Revolutionary era legal discourse on the natural law rights and status of the Indian."[23] Williams's central contention is that the doctrine of discovery is a *racist* discourse, and that the result in *Johnson* was foreordained in view of the history of European subjugation of indigenous peoples. Because history had "determined the inescapable framework for Marshall's legal discourse," the task that remained was "merely to fill in the details and rationalize the fictions by which Europeans legitimated the denial of the Indians' rights in their acquisition of the Indians' America."[24]

Kent McNeil and Robert Williams published their books at a time when preparations were under way to acknowledge the five-hundred-year anniversary of the first trans-Atlantic voyage of Christopher Columbus. In many parts of the world, reaction to the anniversary was problematic. Advocates for indigenous rights seized the opportunity to condemn the negative effects of "discovery," and the National Council of Churches of Christ in the United States declared that "for the descendants of the survivors of the subsequent invasion, genocide, slavery, 'ecocide' and exploitation of the wealth of the land, a celebration is not an appropriate observation."[25] In late 1993 the United Nations General Assembly proclaimed the International Decade of the World's Indigenous People. In the academic community, legal scholars in the United States and elsewhere continued to produce articles on Native land rights.[26] In addition, several books have been published since 1990 that explore the historical and legal bases for the limitation of the rights of indigenous peoples.[27]

Modern scholars disagree on *Johnson*'s underlying rationale, the deleterious effects of the decision, and the precise nature of the property interests created by Marshall's opinion. Why did John Marshall rely on the doctrine of discovery to deny the claims of the Illinois and Wabash Land Company? His critics and defenders have variously argued that Marshall adopted the "limited possessor" conception of indigenous land rights in *Johnson v. McIntosh* because he was (1) a Eurocentric racist; (2) a "chosen" Christian; (3) a loyal Virginian; (4) an efficient imperialist; and (5) a pragmatic realist.

Robert Williams is the most prolific proponent of the view that *Johnson* is a racist decision. In articles and books, Williams has condemned the doctrine of discovery as "an instrument of racial discrimination against indigenous tribal peoples' rights of self-determination" and has depicted John Marshall as "one of the most Indianophobic, racist justices of all time."[28] In *Like a Loaded Weapon: The Rehnquist Court, Indian Rights, and the Legal History of Racism in America* (2005), Williams offers similar criticism: "*Johnson v. McIntosh* has to be considered one of the most thoroughly racist, nonegalitarian, undemocratic, and stereotype-infused decisions ever issued by the Supreme Court. It elevates a European colonial-era fantasy of white racial supremacy and dictatorship over entire continents of nonconsenting non-European peoples into a skeletal principle of the U.S. legal system."[29] Other scholars likewise have accused John Marshall and the Supreme Court of exhibiting an "ethnocentric and racist tone," manifesting "religious, cultural, and racial biases," harboring "racist disdain for Indians," and failing "to recognize the inherent equality of all human beings."[30]

A related criticism of *Johnson v. McIntosh* is that it lends credence to the view that the United States may dispossess and control Indians "simply because Christians 'discovered' non-Christian lands and simply because Christians supposedly succeeded in conquering the 'heathen' nations of North America." In *Pagans in the Promised Land: Decoding the Doctrine of Christian Discovery* (2008), Steven Newcomb argues that "the so-called right of discovery in the *Johnson* ruling is grounded in the background cultural and religious belief that the chosen people will one day fulfill God's will by taking over all the non-Christian parts of the earth as a promised and everlasting possession." Newcomb is a Shawnee/Lenape Indian and co-founder of the Indigenous Law Institute. His view is that in order to understand Marshall's opinion, one must "decode the hidden biblical, or, more specifically, Old Testament, background of the *Johnson* ruling."[31]

Other scholars have focused less on the racial and religious aspects of *Johnson v. McIntosh*, emphasizing instead how the doctrine of discovery furthered the imperial designs of the United States by facilitating the removal of Indians from desirable lands. This was the basic theme of George Bryan's 1924 book. A modern proponent of this view is Eric Kades, who argues that the rule against private purchases of Indian lands "makes perfect sense as a tool of efficient expropriation," and that the *Johnson* decision "is best explained as one element of a calculated, rational, unemotional effort to obtain Indian lands at the least cost."[32] Jedediah Purdy has described *Johnson* as "an exercise in imperial jurisprudence," and Robert Porter has similarly characterized the opinion as a leading example of "America's Indian control jurisprudence."[33]

A fourth explanation for the adoption in *Johnson* of the "limited possessor" conception of indigenous land rights focuses on Marshall's concern for the claims of Virginians who held militia land warrants in lands burdened by Indian occupancy. In *Conquest by Law: How the Discovery of*

America Dispossessed Indigenous Peoples of Their Lands (2005), Lindsay Robertson theorizes that *Johnson v. McIntosh* "achieved landmark status as a result of political circumstances unrelated to its origins."[34] Robertson points out that Virginia militiamen in 1823 were pursuing claims to Chickasaw lands in Kentucky, and that the validity of such claims depended in part on whether the Natives held a proprietary title or merely a right of occupancy.[35] By basing the *Johnson* decision on the doctrine of discovery, and by endorsing the "limited possessor" conception of indigenous land rights, Marshall was able to strengthen the claims of the holders of militia warrants for tribal lands.[36] Stuart Banner, in *How the Indians Lost Their Land: Law and Power on the Frontier* (2005), also argues that Marshall—in order to "firm up" western land titles—deliberately transformed *Johnson* into a case about the validity of grants of land that had not yet been purchased from the Indians.[37] Indian land rights, Banner argues, transitioned between 1790 and 1820 "from ownership to occupancy" because the prevalent state practice of selling "preemption rights" caused lawyers and prospective settlers "to think of the Indians as tenants on the land rather than owners of it."[38]

The fifth explanation for why Marshall adopted the "limited possessor" conception of indigenous land rights in *Johnson v. McIntosh* is that recognition of a right of occupancy was the optimal result achievable for the Indians given prior practices and political realities. There is an obvious problem with this view: in *Worcester v. Georgia*, Marshall discarded the "limited possessor" version of the discovery doctrine and held that Indians own the lands they occupy, subject to the government's right of preemption. On the other hand, the Court never endorsed the most extreme version of doctrine of discovery—*terra nullius*—and thus rejected the idea that Indians held no property rights and were "tenants at will" or trespassers.[39] Moreover, it is not self-evident that the "unaffected" view of indigenous land rights—the notion that European "discovery" did not impair the absolute right of Native landowners to sell or transfer their property rights—would have been the preferable choice. Alex Tallchief Skibine suggests that "by allowing non-Indians to bargain directly with the tribes, much more pressure would have been brought on the tribes to sell their lands."[40]

Marshall's defenders stress the fact that the statement in *Johnson*—that the Indians are the "rightful occupants of the soil, with a legal as well as just claim to retain possession"—is not only "an unequivocal recognition of an Indigenous title" but is also "one of the most quoted (and adopted) passages in Indigenous rights jurisprudence."[41] David Wilkins, who is a critic of the doctrine of discovery, has nevertheless acknowledged the pragmatic nature of Marshall's "compromise" solution: "Marshall had cleverly reached a political/legal compromise that avoided two contrasting visions of Indian title: (1) that the doctrine of discovery completely vanquished Indian title *in toto* or (2) that tribes held a title equal to the fee-simple title that was wholly unaffected by the claims of the European and U.S. 'discoverers.' The former would have left the tribes with no enforceable interests whatsoever; the latter would have nullified state and federal grants derived from Indians."[42]

Milner Ball argues that Marshall's version of the discovery doctrine did *not* significantly impact Native land rights. He notes that Indian title—although described as "occupancy"—is a property right that "has all the indicia of fee simple except this: unless a non-Indian purchaser is licensed by the discovering sovereign or that sovereign's successor, the non-Indian purchaser takes only the Indian's interest."[43] According to Ball, the reason the shareholders lost was because the Illinois and Piankeshaws repudiated the prior purchases when the same lands were ceded to the United States. This line of reasoning was adopted by the "American Indian Nations Supreme Court" when *Johnson v. McIntosh* was "reargued" in 2000 by legal scholars.[44]

Michael Blumm also contends that the discovery doctrine "left Indian tribes with nearly all of their proprietary rights."[45] The problem, according to Blumm, is that the Supreme Court subsequently "misinterpreted the Marshall Court's language and undermined the principles it laid down." Overlooking the fact that *Johnson* holds that "discovery gave title"—or perhaps urging adoption of the "limited owner" view of indigenous land rights in *Worcester*—Blumm argues that Marshall's "Indian title" is a proprietary "fee simple absolute" estate that is subject to a partial restraint on alienation.[46]

Even prior to *Johnson v. McIntosh*, confusion abounded with respect to the precise nature of the property rights held by the indigenous inhabitants and the European discoverers. Over time, the property right of the discovering European nation has been characterized as a "mere possibility" of ownership, an expectancy, a potential interest, an exclusive option, a right of first refusal, a right of preemption, a reversionary right, a remainder, an executory interest, a contingent fee-simple, naked fee title, fee simple absolute, seisin in fee, and the absolute, ultimate title.

The Native land right, in turn, has either been denied or variously described as a tenancy at sufferance, a tenancy at will, a usufructuary right, a leasehold interest, the right of occupancy, full beneficial ownership, a fee simple subject to an executory limitation, or absolute proprietorship. Michael Blumm chooses to describe the Native right as a "fee simple subject to the government's right of preemption," or alternatively as a "fee simple with a partial restraint on alienation."[47] Either description is consistent with the "limited owner" conception of indigenous land rights set forth in *Worcester v. Georgia*.

It stands to reason that, given such divergent viewpoints, there is also disagreement regarding the appropriate response to *Johnson* and the doctrine of discovery. One course of action is to undermine the discovery doctrine by developing principles of international human rights law that promote indigenous land rights. Another course of action is to seek official repudiation of the doctrine of discovery.

THE RESPONSE OF INTERNATIONAL LAW

Even if one accepts that *Johnson*'s version of the doctrine of discovery was a faithful application of prevailing principles of international law, the current application of the doctrine is difficult to justify in view of contemporary norms of international indigenous rights. Robert Williams, James Anaya, Alex Skibine, Frank Pommersheim, and others advocate reliance on international law as a means to undermine foundational federal Indian law principles such as the doctrines of plenary power and discovery.[48] The "emerging international legal discourse of indigenous human rights holds significant transformative potential," Williams argued in a 1990 article.[49] Although international tribunals occasionally addressed the discovery doctrine in the first half of the twentieth century, the primary sources for international protection of indigenous land rights have been developed after World War II by the United Nations and the Organization of American States.[50]

The 1945 Charter of the United Nations sets forth two principles relevant to indigenous peoples: the right of self-determination and the duty of all states to promote human rights. In 1957 the International Labor Organization adopted Convention 107, the first multilateral treaty "devoted specifically to recognizing and protecting indigenous peoples' human rights."[51] In 1989 the ILO replaced Convention 107 with Convention

109, which urges all governments to respect the cultural and spiritual importance of land to indigenous peoples. This convention has been ratified by several nations with significant Native populations but has not been endorsed by either Canada or the United States.[52] Prior to the adoption of the 2007 UN Declaration on the Rights of Indigenous Peoples, ILO No. 109 was "international law's most concrete manifestation of the growing recognition of indigenous peoples' rights to property in lands."[53]

The Organization of American States formed in 1948 and immediately adopted the American Declaration of the Rights and Duties of Man, which in Article XXIII generally affirms the right of all persons "to own such private property as meets the essential needs of decent living and helps to maintain the dignity of the individual and the home."[54] In 1959 member states of the OAS created the Inter-American Commission on Human Rights, which today is empowered (along with the OAS Inter-American Court of Human Rights) to address individual human rights complaints under either the American Declaration or the 1969 American Convention on Human Rights. Indigenous land rights are protected by Article 21 of the American Convention, which provides that "everyone has the right to the use and enjoyment of his property." Neither the United States nor Canada is a party to the American Convention; however, the Inter-American Commission on Human Rights may adjudicate petitions against states that are not parties to the American Convention on Human Rights by reference to the 1948 American Declaration on the Rights and Duties of Man.[55]

Advocates of indigenous land rights have had mixed success before international tribunals. The International Court of Justice, in *Judgment on North Sea Continental Shelf Cases* (1969), held that disputes regarding the continental shelf are to be settled by agreement, and not by the doctrine of discovery. Six years later the ICJ issued its *Advisory Opinion on Western Sahara*, which declared that the Western Sahara was not *terra nullius* at the time of Spanish colonization in 1884. The decision expressly repudiated the notion that lands of indigenous peoples could be legally regarded as "belonging to no one" under contemporary international law.[56] More recently the OAS Inter-American Commission on Human Rights (IACHR) and the UN Committee for the Elimination of Racial Discrimination (UN CERD) have both criticized the United States with regard to its treatment of the indigenous land rights of the Western Shoshone peoples.

On December 27, 2002, the IACHR concluded that the United States failed to ensure the rights of Mary and Carrie Dann, citizens of the Western Shoshone Nation, as required by the 1948 American Declaration of the Rights and Duties of Man. The Danns filed their complaint with the commission in 1993, contending that the United States interfered with the use and occupation of their ancestral lands.[57] In support of their argument that the United States acted contrary to international law, the Dann sisters cited the 1969 (OAS) American Convention on Human Rights, ILO Convention No. 169, Article XVIII of the proposed (OAS) American Declaration on the Rights of Indigenous Peoples, and Article 26 of the proposed UN Declaration on the Rights of Indigenous Peoples. It is noteworthy that even though the United States had not agreed to any of these instruments, the IACHR stated that it was appropriate to evaluate the complaint "in the context of the evolving rules and principles of human rights law in the Americas and in the international community more broadly, as reflected in treaties, custom and other sources of international law."[58]

The Dann sisters argued that the United States law discriminates against indigenous peoples insofar as it fails to accord Indian title the same constitutional protections granted to non-indigenous forms of property. The commission agreed and recommended that the United States review its laws, procedures, and practices "to ensure that the property rights of indigenous persons are determined in accordance with the rights established in the American Declaration."[59] The United States, however, has refused to accede to the decision and "respectfully declines to take any further actions to comply with the Commission's recommendations."[60]

Indigenous peoples remain hopeful that emerging principles of international law will produce tangible benefits in terms of safeguarding rights to land and natural resources. The most significant development in recent years was the adoption of the UN Declaration on the Rights of Indigenous Peoples.[61] Despite the opposition of the United States, Canada, Australia, and New Zealand, the UN General Assembly voted overwhelmingly on September 13, 2007, to adopt the declaration.[62] The OAS will likely follow suit and adopt its proposed American Declaration on the Rights of Indigenous Peoples, which complements the UN Declaration but also addresses the particular needs and issues of indigenous peoples in the western hemisphere.[63]

The UN Declaration contains several provisions that acknowledge the rights of indigenous peoples to their lands. Article 26 states that indigenous peoples "have the right to the lands, territories and resources which they have traditionally owned, occupied or otherwise used or acquired," and that nation states "shall give legal recognition and protection to these lands, territories and resources . . . with due respect to the customs, traditions and land tenure systems of the indigenous peoples concerned." Article 28 provides that indigenous peoples "have the right to redress, by means that can include restitution or, when this is not possible, just, fair and equitable compensation, for the lands, territories and resources which they have traditionally owned or otherwise occupied or used, and which have been confiscated, taken, occupied, used or damaged without their free, prior and informed consent."[64] The language of Article 28, Walter Echo-Hawk has argued, "seemingly repudiates the discovery doctrine of *Johnson v. M'Intosh*."[65]

The UN Declaration on the Rights of Indigenous Peoples is an aspirational set of principles that lack binding effect. In its 2007 statement in opposition to the declaration, the United States emphasized that the document does not provide a basis for legal actions, complaints, or other claims in any international or domestic forum. Nevertheless, international law scholars contend that the UN Declaration "signifies a broad customary international law norm that indigenous peoples do have land rights."[66] For example, the Supreme Court of Belize acknowledged the persuasive force of Article 26 of the declaration in support of its recognition of customary Mayan land rights.[67]

In April 2009 the Australian government changed course and endorsed the UN Declaration, acknowledging that the document "sets important international principles for nations to aspire to." One year later New Zealand reversed its position and announced qualified support for the UN Declaration. Several months later, on November 12, 2010, the Canadian government gave its formal endorsement, stating that "Canada can interpret the principles expressed in the Declaration in a manner that is consistent with our Constitution and legal framework." Finally, on December 16, 2010, President Barack Obama announced that the United States "is lending its support" to the Declaration. According to the president, "the aspirations it affirms—including the respect for the institutions and rich cultures of Native peoples—are one[s] we must always seek to fulfill."[68]

John Marshall transformed the doctrine of discovery into American law in *Johnson v. McIntosh.* It stands to reason that if international norms of the nineteenth century are no longer accepted, the legal doctrines based on such norms should be reconsidered. The High Court of Australia, in *Mabo (No. 2),* stated that the evolution of international law lent support to the Court's rejection of the *terra nullius* doctrine.[69] In similar fashion, the U.S. Supreme Court should acknowledge the UN Declaration on the Rights of Indigenous Peoples and revisit the "limited possessor" conception of indigenous land rights set forth in 1823.

THE FUTURE OF THE DOCTRINE OF DISCOVERY

The 1985 draft of the UN Declaration declared that discovery and *terra nullius* "are never legitimate bases for States to claim or retain the territories of indigenous nations or peoples."[70] The 1988 and 1989 drafts also denounced discovery and *terra nullius,* but such references were removed from the 1993 draft, and the words do not appear in subsequent versions.[71] Consequently, although the 2007 Declaration supports indigenous land rights, it does not expressly renounce the doctrine of discovery.

"This remnant of the white man's Old World vision," Robert Williams argued in 1986, "must be rejected."[72] Williams has been joined by other scholars, such as David Wilkins and K. Tsianina Lomawaima, who contend that the discovery doctrine must be "explicitly stricken from the federal government's political and legal vocabulary."[73] The movement has not been restricted to the academic community. During the Columbus Quincentenary commemoration, the Traditional Circle of Indian Elders and Youth called on Pope John Paul II to repudiate the papal bulls of 1453 and 1493.[74] The Canadian Royal Commission on Aboriginal Peoples in 1996 urged federal, provincial, and territorial governments to acknowledge that *terra nullius* and the doctrine of discovery "are factually, legally, and morally wrong."[75] In 2006 delegations of indigenous nations and nongovernmental organizations met in South Dakota and requested the Catholic Church and the Church of England to disavow all doctrines "that have been relied thereon for the dispossession of lands and the subjugation of non-Christian peoples."[76]

The royal charters and papal bulls that sanctioned discovery of the New World remain in effect. On the other hand and as earlier noted, the Episcopal Church of the United States officially renounced the discovery doctrine in 2009 as "fundamentally opposed to the Gospel of Jesus Christ and our understanding of the inherent rights that individuals and peoples have received from God."[77] The Anglican Church of Canada approved an identical resolution in June 2010.[78] At about the same time, the UN Permanent Forum on Indigenous Issues released its preliminary study of the discovery doctrine, which concludes that the doctrine "lies at the root of the violations of indigenous peoples' human rights."[79]

John Chaffee, a history professor in New York, and John Dieffenbacher-Krall, the executive director of the Maine Indian Tribal State Commission, were both advocates of the Episcopal Church resolution. According to Chaffee, the resolution can "provide important legal ammunition in terms of pending and future legal cases that might be brought by Native Americans." His colleague Dieffenbacher-Krall is even more hopeful: "I want to see an all out effort to overturn *Johnson v. M'Intosh*, just as the NAACP legal defense fund and many civil rights activists worked strategically to overturn *Plessy v. Ferguson*."[80]

Yet despite calls for repudiation, the discovery doctrine and the royal charters that legitimized the colonization of the New World remain in effect. For too long the United States, Australia, New Zealand, and Canada have invoked the doctrine of discovery to diminish Native land rights. By endorsing the UN Declaration on the Rights of Indigenous Peoples, however, these countries have taken a significant step in the right direction. The United States declared in December 2010 that it "aspires to improve relations with indigenous peoples by looking to the principles embodied in the Declaration in its dealings with federally recognized tribes, while also working, as appropriate, with all indigenous individuals and communities in the United States."[81] In his accompanying remarks President Barack Obama acknowledged that "what matters far more than words . . . are actions to match those words."[82] It is time for the United States to take action and formally reject the discovery doctrine.

Conclusion

As Jedediah Purdy has noted, the 1823 U.S. Supreme Court decision in *Johnson v. McIntosh* "continues to fascinate in no small part because of its strangeness: Marshall's embrace of a legal conclusion he apparently concedes to be deeply unjust, the half-disowned apologetics of his *dicta*, and the unclear relationship between the legal conclusion and the historical narrative of the long aside."[83] There was an established practice of buying America from the Indians, but for what purpose—to secure rights of property or to pacify the indigenous inhabitants? Moreover, what rights were purchased, and what rights (if any) were reserved? Confusion still reigns, as evidenced by the different terms used to describe the rights and title of the "discoverer" and the "discovered": no ownership rights; limited ownership rights; full ownership rights; rights of preemption; sovereign rights; rights of soil; usufructuary rights; possessory rights; leasehold rights; rights of occupancy; beneficial title; Native title, indigenous title, Indian title; customary aboriginal title; common law aboriginal title; allodial title; radical title; absolute title; and fee-simple title.

If the Indians and other Native inhabitants held property rights prior to European discovery, how were such rights divested? In some instances, the discovered lands were deemed to be *terra nullius*, and in other instances acquisitions of preexisting Native property rights were justified by discovery, conquest, treaty, purchase, proclamation, statute, and judicial fiat. Europeans claimed Native lands on the basis of feudal law, canon law, common law, natural law, positive law, and international law. Native laws and customs were rarely, if ever, consulted.

I suggest in this book that the possessory, ownership, and disposition rights in Native lands can be either aggregated or diffused, leading to four different conceptions of indigenous land rights:

1. The indigenous inhabitants held preexisting rights of ownership and possession that were *unaffected* by European discovery.
2. The indigenous inhabitants continued to own their lands after discovery but held *limited ownership* rights, because they were no longer free to sell their lands to whomsoever they pleased.
3. The indigenous inhabitants continued to possess their lands after discovery but held *limited possessor* rights, because they now occupied their lands subject to the discoverer's rights of ownership and preemption.
4. The indigenous inhabitants had *no property rights* after discovery, either because they had no property rights prior to discovery or because discovery divested them of all rights of possession and ownership.

The U.S. Supreme Court, in *Johnson v. McIntosh*, finally put an end to one of the largest land speculations in American history by holding that the Illinois and Piankeshaw Indians lacked the power to grant to private individuals "a title . . . which can be sustained in the courts of this coun-try."[84] David Franks, William Murray, James Wilson, and Robert Morris actively promoted the cause without success, and Robert Goodloe Harper devised the litigation strategy that brought the matter to its final resolution. The Illinois and Wabash Land Company disbanded in defeat. The Illinois and Piankeshaws did *not* disband, but instead joined with the Kaskaskias and Weas to become the Peoria Tribe of Indians of Oklahoma. In March 2009 Chief John Froman and Second Chief Jason Dollarhide traveled to the University of Illinois to discuss the Peoria Tribe's history, culture, gov-ernmental structure, and the programs it offers its citizens. "A lot of the student body doesn't know that the Peoria Tribe of Indians of Oklahoma even exists," Dollarhide said. "We want to get our name out there and let these folks know that we do exist and we are striving as a tribe."[85]

In his study of Indian title in British Columbia, Hamar Foster states that "as a moral idea, Indian title can be grasped by the average third grade schooler in three seconds flat."[86] Understanding the historic treatment and limitation of indigenous land rights, however, is not an elementary task. For a fuller sense of the adverse consequences of the discovery doctrine, as set forth in *Johnson v. McIntosh*, I have examined the history of Native land speculations that preceded the Illinois and Wabash purchases, the efforts to obtain confirmation of the 1773 and 1775 grants, and the effect the sales had on the Indians, the purchasers, and their successors. My hope is that an understanding of the roots and history of the Illinois-Wabash purchases will facilitate a critical assessment of the impact of *Johnson v. McIntosh* on indigenous land rights in the United States and elsewhere.

It is also not easy to predict the future of the doctrine of discovery. Advocates for the rights of indigenous peoples continue to press for the repudiation of this doctrine.[87] In 1924 George Bryan presented his read-ers with the following challenge: "What has another century in store for us and for those who are to follow us? Perhaps, among other things, the repudiation in terms of the doctrine of *Johnson and Graham's Lessee v. McIntosh*; perhaps the judicial, legislative and executive recognition of the property rights of an Indian, or of one claiming under a conveyance from an Indian, upon precisely the same basis accorded the rights of a member of the so-called dominant race."[88]

Bryan's century has not yet elapsed.

NOTES

ABBREVIATIONS

1810 Memorial	Illinois and Wabash Land Company, *Memorial of the United Illinois and Wabash Land Companies, to the Senate and House of Representatives of the United States*, 1810
ASP	*American State Papers*
HSP	Historical Society of Pennsylvania
IWC Minutes	Illinois and Wabash Land Company, United Illinois and Wabash Land Companies Minutes, 1778–1812
JCC	Continental Congress, *Journals of the Continental Congress*
NYCD	O'Callaghan, ed., *Documents Relative to the Colonial History of the State of New York*

PREFACE

1. *Johnson*, 21 U.S. at 574.

2. Bobroff, "Indian Law in Property," 521; Berman, "Concept of Aboriginal Rights," 648 ("fiat"); and Porter, "Two Kinds of Indians," 637 ("subjugation").

3. *Tee-Hit-Ton Indians v. United States*, 348 U.S. (1955) at 279.

4. Wilson, *History of DuBois County,* 88 ("place of roots"); McCafferty, *Native American Place-Names*, 142 ("root-land place"); and Kades, "Dark Side," 1068 (quoting *Tee-Hit-Ton Indians v. United States*, 348 U.S. at 279).

CHAPTER 1. FEBRUARY 28, 1823

1. Biskupic and Witt, *Supreme Court*, 116; Remini, *Webster*, 115–24; White, "Working Life of the Marshall Court," 1–4; Warren, *History of the American Bar*, 376; and Maroon, *Supreme Court*, 20.

2. Quoted in Robertson, *Conquest by Law*, 3, citing Meigs, *Ingersoll*, 123 (Henry Murray).

3. Robertson, *Conquest by Law*, 72 and 74, citing Rodney, *Diary*, 28–29, and United Illinois and Wabash Land Companies Collection, http://digital.libraries .ou.edu/IWLC/docs/r1823-02-20.pdf (Ingersoll to John Brinton, Feb. 20, 1823). Lindsay Robertson is responsible for making publicly available hundreds of documents relating to the United Illinois and Wabash Land Companies. See Robertson, *Conquest by Law*, x–xi (explaining his discovery of papers held by Jasper Brinton, whose ancestor John Hill Brinton served as the companies' secretary from 1805 to 1823). The documents (hereafter cited as Illinois and Wabash Collection) are now part of the University of Oklahoma Law Digital Collections and are available at http://digital.libraries.ou.edu/IWLC/.

4. Robertson, *Conquest by Law*, 73, citing Illinois and Wabash Collection (Ingersoll to Simon Gratz, Brinton, and Callender Irvine, Feb. 19, 1823).

5. *Johnson*, 21 U.S. at 571–74 (emphasis added).

6. Webster, *Papers of Daniel Webster, Correspondence*, 1:322.

7. *Johnson*, 21 U.S. at 574; *Fletcher v. Peck*, 10 U.S. 87 (1810); Wirt, *Memoirs*, 2:119 (Wirt to wife, Apr. 7, 1821); Rodney, *Diary*, 25; Cox, *Champion*, 215–16; Story, *Life and Letters of Joseph Story*, 1:161.

8. Cox, *Champion*, 205, 216–17; Sommerville, *Harper*, 10, 30; and Scharf, *Chronicles*, 351, 418.

9. Robertson, *Conquest by Law*, 200 n.77, citing Illinois and Wabash Collection, (Ingersoll to Simon Gratz, Feb. 19, 1823).

10. On Harper's involvement with the Illinois and Wabash Companies and his marriage to Catherine Carrol, see Robertson, *Conquest by Law*, 32.

11. Cox, *Champion*, 20–23, 211–13; and Sommerville, *Harper*, 7.

12. Robertson, "*Johnson v. M'Intosh*," 79 n.27, citing Illinois and Wabash Collection (letter from Benjamin Stoddert to Solomon Etting, Feb. 28, 1810); Robertson, *Conquest by Law*, 40, citing Gratz Family of Philadelphia Papers, American Jewish Historical Society, Waltham, Mass. (letter from Jacob Gratz to Joseph Gratz, Mar. 10, 1811); and Gratz Collection, case 1, box 37 (letter from Harper to Simon Gratz, Feb. 22, 1823), Historical Society of Pennsylvania, Philadelphia (hereafter cited as HSP).

13. *Johnson*, 21 U.S. at 574, 588, 591.

14. Ibid., 586, 594–97.

15. Ibid., 573, 604.

16. Ibid., 591–92 (emphasis added).

17. Berman, "Concept of Aboriginal Rights," 655 ("misunderstood"); Newton, "Whim of the Sovereign," 1223 ("compromise"); Ball, "Constitution, Court, Indian Tribes," 24 ("little or no restriction"); Williams, Jr., "Algebra of Federal Indian Law," 297; Newcomb, "Christian Nationalism in Federal Indian Law," 304; and Robertson, *Conquest by Law*, xii.

18. Baxter, *Webster*, 143 (emphasis added).

19. Ibid.; and *Johnson*, 21 U.S. at 592.

20. Williams, "Jefferson, the Norman Yoke," 165.

CHAPTER 2. "THE *SINNE* OF THE *PATTENTS*"

1. Marshall, *Life of George Washington*, 1:xi. The parallels between volume 1 of Marshall's biography of Washington and portions of Marshall's decision in *Johnson v. McIntosh* were first noted by Lindsay Robertson in his article "John Marshall as Colonial Historian." See also Robertson, *Conquest by Law*, 101–103, and 206–207 n.12. This chapter is otherwise based on Watson, "John Marshall and Indian Land Rights: A Historical Rejoinder."

2. Gaustad, *Liberty*, 28; and MacLeod, *American Indian Frontier*, 199.

3. Juricek, "English Territorial Claims," 18; and Thorpe, *Constitutions*, 3:1834.

4. Gaustad, *Liberty*, 19–20 ("little respect"); and Thorpe, *Constitutions*, 3:1849–50.

5. Cronon, *Changes*, 56 (Cushman); and Vaughan, *New England Frontier*, 110 (Winthrop, emphasis added).

6. Deane, *Massachusetts Charter*, 5 (Winthrop); and Cronon, *Changes*, 56 (Cotton).

7. Anderson and McChesney, "Raid or Trade?" 54 (Pemaquids); Robertson, "*Johnson v. M'Intosh*, Brief for Appellants," 865 (Whelewright); Dickason, "Concepts," 236 (Winthrop); and Deane, *Massachusetts Charter*, 10 (instructions).

8. Parrington, "Roger Williams, Seeker," 35; Brockunier, *Irrepressible Democrat*, 47; and Gaustad, *Liberty*, 28.

9. Williams, *Key into the Language of America*, 53, 95.

10. Grinde, and Johansen, *Exemplar*, 74; and Andrews, *Colonial Period*, 1:472 n.4. Williams presented his book to Governor John Winthrop of the Massachusetts Bay Colony, who shared it with his council and others. Deane, *Massachusetts Charter*, 3–4.

11. Deane, *Massachusetts Charter*, 8; Washburn, "Moral and Legal Justifications," 25 ("from whom alone"); and Vaughan, *New England Frontier*, 119.

12. Deane, *Massachusetts Charter*, 7 (letter from Winthrop to John Endicott, Jan. 3, 1633).

13. Winthrop, "Journal," 1 (Dec. 27, 1633); and Ernst, *Roger Williams: Firebrand*, 104 ("gave satisfaction").

14. Salisbury, *Manitou*, 195; Winthrop, "Journal," 2; Ernst, *Roger Williams: Firebrand*, 100; and Gaustad, *Liberty*, 37.

15. Grinde and Johansen, *Exemplar*, 76; Andrews, *Colonial Period*, 2:4–5; and Gaustad, *Liberty*, 46 ("would occupy").

16. Ernst, *Roger Williams: Firebrand*, 185, 399; Deane, *Massachusetts Charter*, 17; Andrews, *Colonial Period*, 2:25; and Thorpe, *Constitutions*, 6:3211.

17. Williams, *Key Into the Language of America*, 167.

18. Eisinger, "Puritan's Justification," 141.

19. Worthen, "Book Review, Sword or Shield," 1375 ("Catholic conceptualization"); Williams, Jr., *American Indian in Western Legal Thought*, 44–45, 71; and Dickason, "Concepts," 151.

20. Williams, Jr., *American Indian in Western Legal Thought*, 41; and Dickason, "Concepts," 242.

21. Collis, *Columbus*, 81 ("free gift").

22. Washburn, *Red Man's Land*, 5 (Spain); Green, "Claims to Territory," 4 (Portugal).

23. Dickason, "Concepts," 232; and Hamilton, *Political Thought*, 179 ("Pope did not grant").

24. Falkowski, *Indian Law/Race Law*, 22 ("true owners"); Vitoria, *De Indis*, 128–39; and Williams, Jr., "Medieval and Renaissance Origins," 73.

25. Cohen, "Original Indian Title," 45 (*Sublimis Deus*); Savelle, *Origins of American Diplomacy*, 199–200 ("simply by"); Hanke, *Spanish Struggle*, 122 (Sepúlveda); and Christian, "Introduction," ix–xi (Las Casas).

26. *Johnson*, 21 U.S. at 574; and Williams, Jr., "Medieval and Renaissance Origins," 70 n.300.

27. Knecht, *Francis I*, 340.

28. *Johnson*, 21 U.S. at 574–75 (emphasis added).

29. Parkman, *La Salle*, 307.

30. White, *Middle Ground*, at x, 342; Eccles, *French Imperial Policy*, 25; and Gage, *Correspondence*, 1:348 (Gage to Dartmouth, Apr. 7, 1773).

31. O'Callaghan, ed., *Documents Relative to the Colonial History of the State of New York*, 6:610 (hereafter cited as *NYCD*).

32. *NYCD*, 6:610.

33. MacLeod, *American Indian Frontier*, 195 (emphasis added); and Cohen, "Original Indian Title," 39 (patroons).

34. Revera, "Making of a Civilized Nation," 31.

35. Williamson, *Cabot Voyages*, 52 ("pious"), 204–205 (1496 patent); Mackie, *Earlier Tudors*, 226; and *Johnson*, 21 U.S. at 576.

36. Williamson, *Cabot Voyages*, 133 (1502 patent, emphasis added); von der Heydte, "Discovery," 458 (Elizabeth); and Juricek, "English Territorial Claims," 21–22.

37. Hoffer, *Colonial America*, 10; Robertson, "Marshall as Colonial Historian," 761; and Commager, *Documents*, 11.

38. Bond, *Quit-Rent System*, 439; Adams and Sewall, *Novanglus*, 94–116; and Jefferson, *Summary View*, 27–28.

39. Dane, *General Abridgement*, 4:69; George et al., *Charter to William Penn*, 81–83 (emphasis added); Penn, *Account of the Lenni Lenape*, 58–60 (emphasis added); and Merritt, *Crossroads*, 25.

40. Goebel, *Falkland Islands*, 105.

41. Juricek, "English Territorial Claims," 18 n.45 (Coke); and Taylor, *American Colonies*, 192 (resolves).

42. More, *Complete Works*, 4:137; Vaughan, *New England Frontier*, 112; Locke, *Two Treatises*, book II, chapter V, §49; Arneil, *Locke*, 18–19; and Tully, *Approach to Political Philosophy: Locke*, 139.

43. Bulkley, Preface, 53–54.

44. *Johnson*, 21 U.S. at 590; and Golson, *Playboy Interview*, 269.

45. Berman, "Concept of Aboriginal Rights," 653; Boorstin, *The Americans*, 260; Baker, "Scratch with a Bear's Paw," 236; De Forest, *Indians of Connecticut*,

177 (Ludlow); MacLeod, *American Indian Frontier*, 200 (Harvard, Winslow); Bronner, "Indian Deed," 111 (Kinsey); and Merritt, *Crossroads*, 36 (Cartlidge).

46. Dummer, *Defence of the New-England Charters*, 13–14; and Hofstra, *New Virginia*, 122 (Chalkley).

47. Robinson, "Conflicting Views," 89.

48. De Forest, *Indians of Connecticut*, 176; and Kades, "Dark Side," 1079–80.

49. Vaughn and Rosen, *Early American Indian Documents*, 15:43–44 (1652 law); Virginia, *Colony Laws of Virginia*, 2:396 (1654 and 1656 laws), 468 (similar law passed by the General Assembly, 1658).

50. Priestley, "Communal Title," 158 (1662 law, emphasis added); Robertson, "*Johnson v. M'Intosh*, Brief for Appellants," 866 (emphasis added).

51. Robertson, "*Johnson v. M'Intosh*, Brief for Appellants," 866; Virginia, *Proceedings of the Convention,* 154 (emphasis added); Butler, *History of Kentucky*, lxvi (Virginia Constitution).

52. Pomfret, *Colonial New Jersey*, 12; Fleming, *New Jersey*, 6–8; McConville, *Daring Disturbers*, 12–13.

53. Cunningham, *Newark*, 24 (1667 purchase); Fleming, *New Jersey*, 14; Pomfret, *New Jersey Proprietors*, 18 (quitrents); *NYCD*, 13:486–87 (1675 opinion); Edsall, *Journal*, 127 (1683 Act); and MacLeod, *American Indian Frontier*, 202 (1703 Act).

54. Klein, *American Whig*, 134 (lawsuit); and Cunningham, *Newark*, 64 ("flooded").

55. Whitehead et al., *Archives of the State of New Jersey*, 6:284 (Jenkins), 6:319–22 (proprietors).

56. Kemmerer, *Path to Freedom*, 200 n.58 (newspaper); Whitehead et al. *Archives of the State of New Jersey,* 7:31–32, 34–36 (settlers).

57. Young, *Political Essays*, 472.

58. See Robertson, "John Marshall as Colonial Historian," 766.

Chapter 3. The Illinois and Piankeshaws

1. *Johnson*, 21 U.S. at 553, 557.

2. Temple, *Indian Villages*, 11; Hoxie, *Encyclopedia*, 266; Balesi, *Time of the French*, 234; and Blasingham, "Depopulation," 193.

3. *Johnson*, 21 U.S. at 590; and Dussias, "Squaw Drudges," 669–70.

4. Hinderaker, *Elusive Empires*, 12; Scott, *Illinois Nation*, 21.

5. Kellogg, *Early Narratives*, 214 (Lusson); Hinderaker, *Elusive Empires*, 13; Hoffman, *Guide to the History of Illinois*, 33; and Franza, *Old Ste. Genevieve*, 11–13.

6. Tanner, *Atlas*, 5; and Spindel, *Dancing*, 60.

7. Chesnel, *History of Cavelier de La Salle*, 132–33; and Parkman, *La Salle*, 219–30, 235 ("speedily assailed").

8. Scott, *Illinois Nation*, 21.

9. Parkman, *La Salle*, 307; Hinderaker, *Elusive Empires*, 14; and Franza, *Old Ste. Genevieve*, 16.

10. Tanner, *Atlas*, 31; White, *Middle Ground*, 49, 136; Blasingham, "Depopulation," 199; and McConnell, *Country Between*, 56.

11. Hinderaker, *Elusive Empires*, 16; Temple, *Indian Villages*, 29–39; Hoffman, *Guide to the History of Illinois*, 34; and Valley and Lembcke, *Peorias*, 7.

12. Brown, *Cultural Transformations*, 230; Jablow, *Illinois, Kickapoo, and Potawatomi*, 140–44, 151; and Temple, *Indian Villages*, 42, 47.

13. Valley and Lembcke, *Peorias*, 8; Brown, *Cultural Transformations*, 230; Scott, *Illinois Nation*, 4; Temple, *Indian Villages*, 48; Hoxie, *Encyclopedia*, 207; and Spindel, *Dancing*, 43.

14. Tanner, *Atlas*, 42.

15. Alvord and Carter, "Critical Period," at 450 (emphasis added); and Jablow, *Illinois, Kickapoo, and Potawatomi*, 240 (emphasis added).

16. Gipson, *British Empire*, 11:420; and Dunn, *Documents*, 9, 13 (Report of May 4, 1766).

17. Libby, *Piankashaw and Kaskaskia*, 102; and Croghan, "Letters and Journals," 148.

18. Jablow, *Illinois, Kickapoo, and Potawatomi*, 250 (letter from Stirling to Gage, Dec. 15, 1765).

19. Temple, *Indian Villages*, 50–51; Tanner, *Atlas*, 63; and White, *Middle Ground*, 313. Following Pontiac's death, the Illinois supposedly gathered on the high rock where Fort St. Louis once stood, where they were trapped and killed. This fanciful tale caused the site to be renamed "Starved Rock."

20. Marks, "Murray," 201.

21. Temple, *Indian Villages*, 52.

22. Scott, *Illinois Nation*, 8. But see McCafferty, *Native American Place-Names*, 126 ("Piankashaw is an English language spelling of Miami-Illinois *peeyankihšia*, "torn-ears person").

23. Parkman, *La Salle*, 316; Moses, *Illinois*, 1:45; and Hinderaker, *Elusive Empires*, 35.

24. Jablow, *Illinois, Kickapoo, and Potawatomi*, 144 (Vaudreuil); Balesi, *Time of the French*, 113; Barnhart and Riker, *Indiana to 1816*, 73; Carter, *Little Turtle*, 24; Peckham, *Indiana*, 19; and Libby, *Piankashaw and Kaskaskia*, 89.

25. Alvord, *Illinois Country*, 165–66; Franklin, "Pennsylvania-Virginia Rivalry," 464; and Anson, *Miami Indians*, 36.

26. Peckham, *Indiana*, 5; and Shannon, *Indians and Colonists*, 67 (rats in cheese).

27. Anson, *Miami Indians*, 36; Carter, *Little Turtle*, 26; Cayton, *Frontier Indiana*, 20; and Barnhart and Riker, *Indiana to 1816*, 89.

28. Barnhart and Riker, *Indiana to 1816*, 327; Wilson, "Early Indiana Trails,"410; and Cayton, *Frontier Indiana*, 6 ("arable strips").

29. Cayton, *Frontier Indiana*, 20. See also McCafferty, *Native American Place-Names*, 129–30, 214–15 (*meemeehšikia*, the "Piankashaw King," may have been Miami).

30. Cayton, *Frontier Indiana*, 21; Bond, "Foundations," 110; and Balesi, *Time of the French*, 255.

31. Tanner, *Atlas*, 44.

32. Edmunds, *American Indian Leaders*, 5; Edmunds, "Pickawillany," 171; and Gipson, *British Empire*, 4:205.

33. Slick, *Trent*, 12; Hurt, *Ohio Frontier*, 37–38; and Carter, *Little Turtle*, 33 ("moved").

34. Peckham, *Colonial Wars*, 123–24 ("metal sign"); Galbreath, *Expedition of Céleron*, 50–53 (La Galissonière, emphasis added), and 57 ("devoted").

35. Goodman, "Historical Sketch," 43; Libby, *Piankashaw and Kaskaskia*, 90; Thwaites, *French Regime in Wisconsin*, 67 (letter from La Jonquière to Comte de Jouy, Minister of the Marine, Sept. 30, 1750); Wheeler-Voegelin, "Ethnohistory," 320; and Hurt, *Ohio Frontier*, 38.

36. Darlington, *Gist's Journal*, 47–48; Croghan, "Letters and Journals," 90; and *Minutes of the Provincial Council of Pennsylvania*, 5:523.

37. *Minutes of the Provincial Council of Pennsylvania*, 5:522 (May 7, 1751, "publick matters"); Mulkearn, *Mercer Papers*, 616; Hurt, *Ohio Frontier*, 38–39; McDonnell, "Langlade," 81; Edmunds, *American Indian Leaders*, 15–16; and Rawlyk, "'Rising French Empire,'" 54.

38. Edmunds, *American Indian Leaders*, 16.

39. Goodman, "Journal of *Trent*," 88; and Slick, *Trent*, 19–20.

40. Stagg, *Royal Proclamation*, at 96; and McDonnell, "Langlade," at 81 ("first battle").

41. Hinderaker, *Elusive Empires*, xi, 134; and Scott, *Illinois Nation*, 28.

42. Galbreath, *Expedition of Céleron*, 21 (July 31, 1749, "invade the territories" and La Galissonière, emphasis added), 47 (Aug. 23, 1749, "drive you away"), and 22 (July 31, 1749, "our lands").

43. Jennings, "Conquest and Legal Fictions," 142 ("your comming"); Volwiler, *Croghan*, 68 ("nott Like"); McConnell, *Country Between*, 91 ("Indians' land"); Ellis, *Washington*, 15 ("maintain your rights"); and *NYCD*, 6:868 (Hendrick).

CHAPTER 4. "AN UNACCOUNTABLE THIRST
FOR LARGE TRACTS OF LAND"

1. Gleeson, *Millionaire*, 138, 156–157, 187.

2. Jensen, "Cession," 28; Wilkinson, *Land Policy*, iv; and *NYCD*, 7:17 (Wraxall).

3. Wharton, "Selections from Letter Books," 445 (letter from Thomas Wharton to Thomas Walpole, Sept. 23, 1774, setting forth Patrick Henry's opinion on Indian title).

4. Nagel, *Lees of Virginia*, 31–46; and Hendrick, *Lees of Virginia*, 58–63.

5. Nagel, *Lees of Virginia*, 39 ("proud"). The Five Nations became the Six Nations in 1720 when the Tuscaroras united with the Iroquois.

6. Nagel, *Lees of Virginia*, 45; Hendrick, *Lees of Virginia*, 65 ("key"); Hofstra, *New Virginia*, 174 (cession); and Bond, "Foundations," 104 (deed).

7. Gipson, *British Empire*, 4:227; and Nester, *Frontier War*, 32.

8. Wallace, *Jefferson and the Indians*, 29; Hinderaker and Mancall, *Edge of Empire*, 128; Alvord, *Mississippi Valley*, 1:87; and Billington, *Westward Expansion*, 140.

9. Nagel, *Lees of Virginia*, 45 ("California"); Billings et al., *Colonial Virginia*, 249 ("strongest frontier); and Darlington, *Gist's Journal*, 31–32.

10. Nester, *Frontier War*, 36 ("come to settle"); and McConnell, *Country Between*, 91 ("where the Indians' land lay").

11. Mulkearn, *Mercer Papers*, 63–65; James, *Ohio Company*, 64; Slick, *Trent*, 14–18; Wainwright, *Croghan*, 50–51; Anson, *Miami Indians*, 52; Alvord, *Mississippi Valley*, 1:89 (proclamation); Friedenberg, *Pursuit of Land*, 173; and Ellis, *Washington*, 262.

12. James, *Ohio Company*, 101; and Wallace, *Jefferson and the Indians*, 33.

13. Sosin, *Whitehall*, 32; and Hinderaker and Mancall, *Edge of Empire*, 117.

14. Sosin, *Whitehall*, 42; and James, *Ohio Company*, 126–28.

15. Carter, "Documents," 312 (letter from William Lee, Secretary, to Thomas Cumming, London agent, Sept. 26, 1763); Livermore, *Early American Land Companies*, 102; Jensen, *American Colonial Documents*, 642 (1763 Proclamation, emphasis added).

16. Merrell, *Into the American Woods*, 82 ("King of the Traders"); Volwiler, *Croghan*, 13; and Hinderaker, *Elusive Empires*, 40.

17. Wainwright, *Croghan*, 42–49.

18. Volwiler, *Croghan*, 254 (1749 sales); Wainwright, *Croghan*, 84 (Aughwick Creek); Slick, *Trent*, 24; Penn Letter Book, 4:38, HSP (letter from Thomas Penn to Richard Peters, Feb. 21, 1755).

19. Volwiler, *Croghan*, 85, 98; and Fish, *Barnard and Michael Gratz*, 42 ("surprized").

20. Volwiler, *Croghan*, 138 ("knocked"); and Wainwright, *Croghan*, 160, 179, 201.

21. Wainwright, *Croghan*, 111; Bailey, *Ohio Company*, 225; and Fish, *Barnard and Michael Gratz*, 82–83.

22. Volwiler, *Croghan*, 169; and Lewis, *Indiana Company*, 42.

23. Stagg, *Royal Proclamation*, 18; Clinton, "Proclamation of 1763," 331; Cushing, *Laws and Liberties of Massachusetts*, 1:110; Shurtleff, *Records*, 4:194, 4:213 ("country is theirs"); and Hawke, *Colonial Experience*, 199.

24. Smith, *Appeals to Privy Council*, 426 (1705 Commission), 434, 442; Walters, "*Mohegan Indians*," 803–805; Henderson, "Unraveling the Riddle," 98; and Tully, *Approach to Political Philosophy: Locke*, 167–68. See also Yirush, "Claiming the New World."

25. Hawke, *Colonial Experience*, 335–39; Steele, "Metropolitan Administration," 8; Alvord, *Mississippi Valley*, 1:153–54; and Olson, "Board of Trade," 38.

26. Stagg, *Royal Proclamation*, 23 (1697 instructions); Labaree, *Royal Instructions*, 2:519 (1702 instructions); *NYCD*, 6:855 (1753 instructions), and 888 (Albany Congress).

27. *NYCD*, 7:17 (1756 report); Barck and Lefler, *Colonial America*, 471; Bailey, *Ohio Company*, 222–23 (Bouquet proclamation); and Stagg, *Royal Proclamation*, 260 (December 1761 instructions).

28. Tucker and Hendrickson, *Fall of the First British Empire*, 90 ("formalized"); Alvord, *Illinois Country*, 253; Billington, *Westward Expansion*, 145; and Humphreys, "Shelburne," 254.

29. Stagg, *Royal Proclamation*, 348–49; MacDonald, *Select Charters*, 270–71.

30. Bailyn, *Voyagers*, 29–30 (Hillsborough); Gage, *Correspondence*, 1:11 (Gage to Halifax, Jan. 7, 1764); Sosin, *Revolutionary Frontier*, 15 (Halifax to Amherst, Oct. 11, 1763); and Dowd, *War under Heaven*, 178 ("horrified").

31. Sosin, "Britain and the Ohio Valley," 63.

32. Butterfield, *Washington–Crawford Letters*, 3 (letter, Sept. 21, 1767); and Sosin, "Britain and the Ohio Valley," 63.

33. *Johnson*, 21 U.S. at 594 (emphasis added); Bennett, "Aboriginal Title," 624.

34. Robertson, *Conquest by Law*, 56.

35. Cooper, *Last of the Mohicans*, 177–220.

36. Wilbur, *East India Company*, 267; Hufton, *Europe: Privilege and Protest*, 88; and Lambert, *House of Commons Sessional Papers*, 26:5 (petition, transmitted on Dec. 2, 1757, by William Pitt to Charles Pratt and Charles Yorke).

37. Lambert, *House of Commons Sessional Papers*, 26:5 (petition); Campbell, *Lord Chancellors*, 6:361–400, 7:78–99.

38. Lambert, *House of Commons Sessional Papers*, 26:7–8.

39. *Johnson*, 21 U.S. at 599.

40. Clinton, "Dormant Indian Commerce Clause," 1093; Wainwright, *Croghan*, 208–209; and Friedenberg, *Pursuit of Land*, 150 ("pay taxes").

41. Volwiler, *Croghan*, 257–58; Fish, *Barnard and Michael Gratz*, 83; Wainwright, *Croghan*, 210–13; and Hinderaker, *Elusive Empires*, 167.

42. Libby, *Piankashaw and Kaskaskia*, 96; Carter, *Great Britain and the Illinois Country*, 39–41; Dunn, *Opening New Markets*, 119–22; and Doerflinger, *A Vigorous Spirit*, 149.

43. Peckham, *Indiana*, 23–24 (Croghan to William Murray, July 12, 1765).

44. Volwiler, *Croghan*, 183 (separate journals); Croghan, "Letters and Journals," 142 ("would not be concerned"), 148 ("settled all matters"), 159 (Aug. 30, 1765, "never conquered").

45. Franklin, "Pennsylvania-Virginia Rivalry," 476–77.

46. Thomas, "Successful and Unsuccessful Merchants," 433 ("universally hated"); Fish, *Barnard and Michael Gratz*, 50; Dunn, Jr., *Opening New Markets*, 134; Marshall, "Lord Hillsborough, Samuel Wharton and the Ohio Grant," 717; and Byars, *B. and M. Gratz*, 347.

47. Molovinsky, "Maryland and the American West," 358 (journal entry, Feb. 25, 1766); Nester, *Frontier War*, 35; Anderson, *Thomas Wharton*, 160; and Philbrick, *Rise of the West*, 16 (letter from Croghan to Johnson, Mar. 30, 1766).

48. Sosin, *Whitehall*, 144 (Benjamin Franklin to William Franklin, June 13, 1767); Brands, *First American*, 384; Savelle, *Morgan*, 58; and Marshall, "William Johnson and the Treaty of Fort Stanwix," 167.

49. Savelle, *Morgan*, 59; and *NYCD*, 7:725 (May 2, 1765, "Considerable Present").

50. Lewis, *Indiana Company*, 58.

51. Billington, "Fort Stanwix Treaty," 194; and Fish, *Barnard and Michael Gratz*, 95.

52. McConnell, "Peoples 'In Between,'" 111.

53. Wainwright, *Croghan*, 256.

54. Cadwallader Collection, George Croghan Papers, series IV, box 31, HSP (Wharton to Croghan, Sept. 4, 1770, *"undoubted power,"* emphasis added); and *Diaries of George Washington*, 3:152.

55. Byars, *B. and M. Gratz*, 344; Marshall, "Lord Hillsborough, Samuel Wharton and the Ohio Grant," 719–20; Friedenberg, *Pursuit of Land*, 121; Lewis, *Indiana Company*, 86; and Franklin, *Papers*, 16:167 (petition).

56. Billington, *Westward Expansion*, 154; and Brands, *First American*, 431.

57. Franklin, *Papers*, 18:75–76; Sosin, *Whitehall*, 201; Wainwright, *Croghan*, 266–72; Anderson, *Thomas Wharton*, 168 ("feared arrest"); and Marshall, "Lord Hillsborough, Samuel Wharton and the Ohio Grant," 724.

58. Another candidate is George Croghan. William Murray, in a letter to Michael Gratz dated May 15, 1773, stated that Croghan "assured me that Lords Camden and York personally confirmed to [the Administration] the opinion respecting Indian titles when Croghan was last in England." Byars, *B. and M. Gratz*, 130. Croghan went to England in 1764, seven years after the Camden-Yorke opinion. The Irishman, however, did not mention the opinion in any known correspondence between 1764 and 1773.

59. Dowd, *War under Heaven*, 230 (Pontiac); and Quaife, "Carver," 11.

60. Johnson, *Papers*, 11:925–26 (Johnson to John Tabor Kempe, Sept. 7, 1765).

61. Adams and Sewall, *Novanglus*, 97 (letter addressed "To the Inhabitants of the Colony of Massachusetts Bay," Mar. 13, 1775).

62. Young, *Political Essays*, 472.

63. Bowen, *Revenue and Reform*, 49–55; Lawson, *East India Company*, 120; Franklin, *Papers*, 14:111 ("territory and dominion"), 115 ("in the tribes"); and Franklin, *Papers*, 16:291–92 ("False!"). See also Franklin, *Papers*, 17:380.

64. Franklin, *Papers*, 20:302. Franklin noted that the 1757 opinion "has been lately printed here at large in Bolts's Book on Indian Affairs." The merchant William Bolts was involved in several lawsuits with the East India Company. The second edition of his book includes the Camden-Yorke opinion in an appendix. Bolts, *Considerations on India Affairs*, 181.

65. Franklin, *Papers*, 20:302–303.

66. Franklin, *Papers*, 20:304 ("no Right"); and Cadwallader Collection, Croghan Papers, series IV, box 31, HSP (Wharton to Croghan, Sept. 4, 1770).

67. Cadwallader Collection, Croghan Papers, series IV, box 33, HSP; and box 31.

68. Slick, *Trent*, 146; Bailey, *Ohio Company*, 225; and Randall, *Franklin and His Son*, 246–47.

69. Byars, *B. and M. Gratz*, 349 (Mason); Wharton, "Selections from the Letter Books," 445 (Wharton); and Marshall, "Lord Hillsborough, Samuel Wharton and the Ohio Grant," 736.

70. Alvord, *Mississippi Valley*, 2:164–65.

71. Philbrick, *Rise of the West*, 42; Wainwright, *Croghan*, 293; Buck and Buck, *Planting of Civilization*, 140–41; Bouquet, *Papers*, 5:439 n.17; and Crumrine, *Court Records*, 252–73.

72. Wainwright, *Croghan*, 301–10.

Chapter 5. The Illinois Purchase of 1773

1. Gratz-Joseph Papers, American Jewish Archives, Cincinnati, Ohio, reel 107 ("soon as convenient"); Bailey, *Ohio Company*, 461–62 (letter from Murray to Michael Gratz, May 15, 1773); Marks, "Murray," 200; *Johnson*, 21 U.S. at 550.

2. Alvord and Carter, "Trade and Politics," 222; Byars, *B. and M. Gratz*, 71; Marks, "Murray," 191 (suggesting Captain Murray became merchant Murray). Myles Murray and Robert Zoba assert that the speculator William Murray was the nephew of John Murray, the 1st Duke of Atholl. Murray and Zoba, *William Murray, Esq.*, 9. One reviewer has dismissed this assertion as a "conspiracy theory . . . without a shred of evidence." Furlong, "Book Review," 338–39.

3. Keltie, *History of the Scottish Highlands*, 6:340–41 (commission); and Bouquet, *Papers*, 6:577, 720 n.2 (Fort Pitt).

4. Keltie, *History of the Scottish Highlands*, 6:350.

5. Bouquet, *Papers*, 5:76 n.1; and Byars, *B. and M. Gratz*, 102 (letter from Michael Gratz to William Murray, Sept. 1, 1769).

6. Bouquet, *Papers*, 6:418–21 (letter from Bouquet to Plumsted and Franks, Sept. 30, 1763); and Linn and Egle, "Pennsylvania Marriages," 468.

7. Illinois and Wabash Land Company, United Illinois and Wabash Land Companies Minutes, 1778–1812, 177–78 (May 31, 1774); hereafter cited as IWC Minutes.

8. Alvord and Carter, "Trade and Politics," 447; Byars, *B. and M. Gratz*, 84–119, 342–47; McBee, *Natchez Court Records*, 120–21; and Bailey, *Ohio Company*, 459–60.

9. James, *Pollock*, 49; and Byars, *B. and M. Gratz*, 100 (letter from Michael Gratz to Barnard Gratz, Aug. 21, 1769).

10. Hinderaker, *Elusive Empires*, 170; Sosin, *Whitehall*, 222; and Marks, "Murray," 198.

11. Gratz-Joseph Papers, reel 107.

12. Illinois and Wabash Land Company, *Illinois-Wabash Land Company Manuscript*, 2.

13. Another possible source is James Robertson, a Scot who served as royal governor of New York during the Revolution. Robertson had shown Thomas Gage a copy of the opinion "some time" before Gage left America in June of 1773. Shy, *Toward Lexington*, 71, 337.

14. Davidson and Stuvé, *Complete History of Illinois*, 168; and Gratz-Joseph Papers, reels 106 and 107. At some point prior to November 1778, Castles sold half of his share to Thomas Johnson and the other half to Charles Carroll of Carrollton.

15. Alvord, *Kaskaskia Records*, 2:90 n.1; and Alvord, *Illinois Country*, 284. It appears that Rumsey sold one-fourth of his share to William Murray and another one-fourth share to Alexander Ross. Murray provided in his will that a portion of his estate should go to "Anna Maria Rumsey," presumably the wife (or daughter) of James Rumsey. McBee, *Natchez Court Records*, 120–21.

16. Byars, *B. and M. Gratz*, 100, 342; Marcus, *Colonial American Jew*, 2:596 (Milligan); and Alvord and Carter, "Trade and Politics," 525 (Ross).

17. General Thompson was captured in 1776 and exchanged in 1780. John Campbell was captured by the British in 1779 and held prisoner until 1782. Campbell, who was suspected of being a loyalist, died in 1799. "Notes and Queries" (1922), 251.

18. IWC Minutes, 203 (Inglis); Stern, *David Franks*, 74 (Inglis). Byars, *B. and M. Gratz*, 76, 95, 102, 126, 140; Alvord and Carter, "Trade and Politics," 438 (Sproat); and Palmer, *Biographical Sketches*, 817 (Sproat).

19. Byars, *B. and M. Gratz*, 6, 14, 33–35, 133; Lebeson, *Pilgrim People*, 95, 110; and Marcus, *Colonial American Jew*, 2:554, 740, 744.

20. Byars, *B. and M. Gratz*, 8, 32; and Faber, *Jewish People of America*, 24–25.

21. Byars, *B. and M. Gratz*, 5, 10–11, 33; "Addenda to Watson's Annals," 131, 142; and Marcus, *Colonial American Jew*, 2:556.

22. Fish, *Barnard and Michael Gratz*, 37, 78–79; Byars, *B. and M. Gratz*, 76, 108; and Marcus, *Colonial American Jew*, 2:557, 596.

23. Alvord and Carter, "Critical Period," xxii; and Marcus, *Colonial American Jew*, 2:761.

24. Faber, *Jewish People of America*, 39; and Marcus, *Colonial American Jew*, 2:555, 568, 593, 717.

25. Bouquet, *Papers*, 6:12, 562 n.1, 583 n.1; "Addenda to Watson's Annals," 131, 149; Bailey, *Ohio Company*, 11; and Wolf and Whiteman, *Jews of Philadelphia*, 91.

26. Marcus, *Colonial American Jew*, 2:545; and Palmer, *Biographical Sketches*, 290. Jacob (John) Franks, the son of David Franks, provided his father a home when he arrived in England in 1782. Marcus, *American Jewry*, 289–90; and Hershkowitz and Meyer, *Letters of the Franks Family*, 79 (genealogy chart).

27. Marks, "Murray," 192; Marcus, *Early American Jewry*, 2:37; and Fish, *Barnard and Michael Gratz*, 118 (letter, dated May 15, 1773).

28. Marks, "Murray," 199; Alvord, *Kaskaskia Records*, 2:4 n.4; and Alvord and Carter, "Trade and Politics," 474.

29. Gratz-Joseph Papers, reel 107 (letter from Murray, Illinois Country, July 14, 1773).

30. Kades, "Dark Side," 1081; Jablow, *Illinois, Kickapoo, and Potawatomi*, 240 ("these lands").

31. A handwritten version of the 1773 deed is reproduced in the *Illinois-Wabash Land Company Manuscript* published by Cyrus McCormick, 8–9.

32. *ASP: Public Lands*, 2:117 (1834). Stroud is coarse wool. Vermilion is a red pigment. A gun-worm was a corkscrew device used to remove unspent charges from a musket barrel.

33. Gratz-Joseph Papers, reels 106 and 107.

34. *ASP: Public Lands*, 2:117–18; *Johnson*, 21 U.S. at 552–53 (deed descriptions). I am indebted to Michael McCafferty, Duane Esarey, and Mark Walcynzski for their insights regarding the two tracts described in the 1773 deed. For different depictions of the tracts, see Kades, "Dark Side," 1067, and Robertson, *Conquest*

by Law, xiii–xvi (1805 copies of maps submitted to Vincennes land commissioners). The 1805 map of the upper Illinois purchase extends eastward from the confluence of the Illinois River and Chicagou Creek (Des Plaines River). This is a mistake, as the site of the 1730 battle between the Pewaria and Renard Indians was Arrowsmith, Illinois, south of the Des Plaines. The deed refers to "a northerly course," which is also a mistake.

35. *Johnson*, 21 U.S. at 553; Kades, "Great Case," 82; and Gratz-Joseph Papers, reel 106 (letter from Murray, Illinois Country, July 14, 1773).

36. *ASP: Public Lands*, 2:117 (emphasis added); *Johnson*, 21 U.S. at 553; and Gratz-Joseph Papers, reel 106 (letter from Murray, July 14, 1773).

37. Davies, *Documents*, 6:181 (emphasis added).

38. Dunn, *Documents*, 31–32 (letter from Haldimand to Gage, Jan. 5, 1774, describing the letter written by Lord to Haldimand, Sept. 3, 1773).

39. Johnson, *Papers*, 8:885 (letter from Haldimand to Johnson, Sept. 15, 1773), 898–99 (letter from Johnson to Haldimand, Sept. 30, 1773).

40. Davies, *Documents*, 6:228–29 (letter from Haldimand, New York, to Dartmouth, Oct. 6, 1773, "dangerous tendency"). Charles Yorke became Baron Morden just prior to his death in January 1770.

41. Johnson, *Papers*, 8:931–32 (partial); and *NYCD*, 8:404 (letter from Dartmouth to Johnson, Dec. 1, 1773).

42. Henderson, "Pre-Revolutionary Revolt," 199; Sioussat, "Breakdown," 69; Bailyn, *Voyagers*, 56; and Friedenwald, "Declaration of Independence," 227.

43. Davies, *Documents*, 8:58–60 (Haldimand, New York, to Dartmouth, Mar. 2, 1774, "clandestine"); Marks, "Murray," 203; Johnson, *Papers*, 8:1074–76 (proclamation); and Robertson, *Conquest by Law*, 10.

44. Kades, "Great Case," 83; and Gratz-Joseph Papers, reel 106 ("wait upon the Earl").

Chapter 6. Dunmore, the Wabash Purchase of 1775, and Revolution

1. *Johnson*, 21 U.S. at 557; Kades, "Great Case," 84–85; and Alvord, *Mississippi Valley*, 2:204.

2. Shy, "Dunmore," 14 ("only money talked"); and Smith, *Historical Memoirs*, 1:91 (diary entry, Dec. 1, 1770).

3. Jensen, *American Colonial Documents*, 215 (instructions); and Smith, *Historical Memoirs*, 1:106 (diary entry, July 9, 1771).

4. Alvord, *Mississippi Valley*, 2:181–82.

5. *NYCD*, 8:357 (instructions, dated Apr. 7, 1773, to colonial governors); and Caley, "Dunmore," 187–88 (gift).

6. Hamilton, *Letters to Washington*, 4:76 (letter from William Crawford, Jan. 10, 1774, regarding Croghan's grant).

7. Marcus, *Early American Jewry*, 2:39 (petition); and Fish, *Barnard and Michael Gratz*, 132 ("new affair").

8. Davies, *Documents*, 8:113–15 (letter from Dunmore to Dartmouth, May 16, 1774).

9. Johnson, *Papers*, 12:1082 (McKee); and Force, *American Archives*, 1:277 (Mar. 24, 1774, "Virginius").

10. Volwiler, *Croghan*, 302; and Oaks, "Impact of British Western Policy," 184.

11. Dreer Autograph Collection, 21:2, page 54, HSP (Ross); Skidmore and Kaminsky, *Dunmore's Little War*, 1; and Donoughue, *British Politics*, 116 n.3.

12. Achenbach, *Grand Idea*, 109 (marker); and Thwaites and Kellogg, *Lord Dunmore's War*, 438 (poem).

13. Force, *American Archives*, 1:1019 ("grateful hearts"); and Steuart, "Letters from Virginia," 157 (letter from James Parker, Norfolk, to Charles Steuart, Jan. 27, 1775).

14. Davies, *Documents*, 8:144 (letter from Dartmouth to Dunmore, July 6).

15. Davies, *Documents*, 8:195; and Aspinall, *Aspinall Papers*, 724–28.

16. Davies, *Documents*, 8:252–55; Curtis and Gill, "Cresswell's American Odyssey," 178–80; and Aspinall, *Aspinall Papers*, 737 (letter from Dartmouth to Dunmore, Mar. 3, 1775).

17. Force, *American Archives*, 2:174; Laub, "Revolutionary Virginia," 304–305; and Friedenwald, *Declaration of Independence*, 227.

18. Gipson, *British Empire*, 11:454 (resolution); and Laub, "Revolutionary Virginia," 304.

19. Wharton, "Selections from the Letter Books," 445 (letter from Thomas Wharton to Thomas Walpole, Sept. 23, 1774, setting forth Henry's opinion).

20. Vaughan, *Chronicles*, 5–6; and Selby, *Chronology*, 12.

21. Newman, *Britain in the Hanoverian Age*, 581; Shortt and Doughty, *Canadian Archives*, 554 (letter from Dartmouth to Hillsborough, May 1, 1774).

22. Henderson, "Pre-Revolutionary Revolt," 191 (letter from Washington to Fairfax, July 20, 1774); Vaughan, *Chronicles*, 18; Metzger, *Quebec Act*, 146–47; and Holton, *Forced Founders*, 36 (Lee).

23. Vaughan, *Chronicles*, 43 (speech to the colonial House of Representatives, Feb. 16, 1773).

24. Banner, *How the Indians Lost Their Land*, 115.

25. Adams, *Political Writings*, 5, 11; and Adams and Sewall, *Novanglus*, 97–98 (Mar. 13, 1775).

26. Franklin, *Papers*, 14:115 ("in the King"), 20:115 ("directly contrary").

27. Jefferson, *Summary View*, 20–21 (emphasis added).

28. Williams, Jr., *American Indian in Western Legal Thought*, 182–83 ("If American land was unencumbered by Norman-derived feudal incidents, then why could not Americans purchase directly from the Indians?").

29. Katz, "Jefferson and the Right to Property," 467; and Miller, *Native America*, 59–76.

30. Volwiler, *Croghan*, 290–97; and Wainwright, *Croghan*, 293–96.

31. Cadwallader Collection, Croghan Papers, series IV, box 31, HSP (Wharton to Croghan, Sept. 4, 1770); Sosin, *Whitehall*, 248; Wharton, "Selections from the Letter Books," 444–46 (letter from Wharton to Walpole, Sept. 23, 1774).

32. Wharton, *View of the Title to Indiana*, 22–24 (Dagge), 24 (Glynn); Gipson, *British Empire*, 11:483 n.105 (Henry and Franklin), 11:483 n.106 (letter from Wharton to Croghan, April 17, 1775).

33. Faragher, *Boone*, 74; Henderson, "Richard Henderson," 348 ("settling"); Alden, *John Stuart*, 290–91; Gipson, *British Empire*, 11:492; Saunders, *Colonial Records*, 9:1129; and Bailyn, *Voyagers*, 535–37.

34. Saunders, *Colonial Records*, 9:1106 (Stuart), 1116 (Neilson), 1122 (proclamation of Feb. 10, 1775); and Force, *American Archives*, 2:174 (Dunmore's proclamation).

35. Bailyn, *Voyagers*, 537–38; Livermore, *Early American Land Companies*, 92; Hammon and Taylor, *Virginia's Western War*, 2 ("bloody Ground"); and Faragher, *Boone*, 111 (Dragging Canoe).

36. Ranck, *Boonesborough*, 151–54 (deed); and Henderson, "Pre-Revolutionary Revolt," 207 (letter from Alexander Cameron to John Stuart, Mar. 21, 1775).

37. Ranck, *Boonesborough*, 195 (letter from Henderson to Patrick Henry, Apr. 26, 1775).

38. Faragher, *Boone*, 124–25; Stoebuck and Whitman, *Law of Property*, 807 (describing the oral ceremony known as "feoffment with livery of seisin"); and Saunders, *Colonial Records*, 9:1275 (Journal of the Proceedings of the House of Delegates or Representatives of the Colony of Transylvania, May 27, 1775).

39. Byars, *B. and M. Gratz*, 140–41 (letter from Murray to Barnard Gratz, May 16, 1774); Illinois and Wabash Land Company, *An Account of the Proceedings of the Illinois and Ouabache Land Companies* [1796], 3; and Gratz-Joseph Papers, reel 107 (disbursement).

40. IWC Minutes, 203 (Inglis and Callender), 177–78 (Hamilton's share); Marcus, *Colonial American Jew*, 3:1516 n.20 (Moses and Jacob Franks); and Curtis and Gill, "Cresswell's American Odyssey," 175 (Kirk and Sidebotham).

41. Kiker, "Loyalism in Eighteenth Century Alexandria," 7; Cresswell, *Journal*, 52, 69; and Curtis and Gill, "Cresswell's American Odyssey," 185.

42. Gage, *Correspondence*, 1:212 (letter, Jan. 6, 1769); Shea, *Life and Times of John Carroll*, 128 ("hell"); Cayton, *Frontier Indiana*, 63–64 (Gage's order), 65 (verification).

43. Deloria and DeMallie, *Documents*, 2:1203 (deed, Oct. 18, 1775); Marks, "Murray," 204; and Gratz-Joseph Papers, reel 107 (disbursements).

44. Deloria and DeMallie, *Documents*, 2:1203.

45. *Johnson*, 21 U.S. at 557; Kades, "Great Case," 84–85; and Alvord, *Mississippi Valley*, 2:204.

46. Deloria and DeMallie, *Documents*, 2:1204; Dillon, *History of the Early Settlement*, 123; Cayton, *Frontier Indiana*, 38; Nester, *Frontier War*, 81; and U.S. Census Bureau, *Statistical Abstract of the United States*, 215. The "Riviere du Chat" that is mentioned in the 1775 deed is the Big Raccoon Creek, which flows into the Wabash below Montezuma, Indiana. McCafferty, *Native American Place-Names*, 140–41.

47. Lewis, "Early Map on Skin," 79. See also Warhus, *Another America: Native American Maps*, 15–17; and King, *Stonyhurst Mullanphy Collection*. The artifact was

taken to England in 1825 and given to Stonyhurst College by Bryan Mullanphy, an American who later served as the mayor of St. Louis.

48. Cushman, *Supreme Court Justices*, 32; and Delaplaine, *Thomas Johnson, Maryland and the Constitution*, 112, 98 (description by Adams, Oct. 10, 1774).

49. Johnson, "Thomas Johnson," 96 ("escape historical study"); Atkinson, *Leaving the Bench*, 15; Cushman, *Supreme Court Justices*, 35; and Chernow, *Morris*, 133.

50. Arnebeck, *Fiery Trial*, 34.

51. Hoffman, *Princes of Ireland*, 387. Geddes sold his share to William Murray, who in turn sold it to Barnard Gratz. IWC Minutes, 185–93.

52. Hoffman, *Spirit of Dissension*, 190; and Scharf, *Chronicles*, 147, 163.

53. *ASP: Public Lands*, 2:123–27 (Report of the Board of Commissioners, Feb. 24, 1810); and Madison, *Papers*, 3:342–45 (Daniel Murray).

54. Libby, *Piankashaw and Kaskaskia*, 92, 118–20; and Cayton, *Frontier Indiana*, 52.

55. Deloria and DeMallie, *Documents*, 2:1203–1207; and Fish, *Barnard and Michael Gratz*, 171.

56. Calloway, *Documents*, 18:103 (Oct. 10, 1775); and Thwaites and Kellogg, *Revolution on the Upper Ohio*, 94, 98–99.

57. Continental Congress, *Journals of the Continental Congress*, 2 *JCC* 175 (July 12, 1775, emphasis added; hereafter cited as *JCC*, preceded by volume number).

58. Holton, *Forced Founders*, 143–44; Reardon, *Randolph*, 18; and Selby, *Dunmore*, 1.

59. Caley, "Dunmore," 557 (letter from Dunmore to Dartmouth, Aug. 2, 1775).

60. Saunders, *Colonial Records*, 9:1263 (Mecklenburg Declaration, May 20, 1775); Commager, *Documents*, 96 (Proclamation).

61. Moore, *Diary of the American Revolution*, 1:159. The proclamation was issued on November 15, 1775.

62. Rhodehamel, *American Revolution: Writings*, 81 (*Virginia Gazette*, Nov. 24, 1775); Washington, *Writings*, 4:167 (letter to Joseph Reed, Dec. 15, 1775); and Lee, *Letters of Richard Henry Lee*, 1:208 (letter to Samuel Adams, July 6, 1776).

63. Caley, "Dunmore," 630.

64. Hagemann, *Lord Dunmore*, 75; and Whitney, *Founders*, 2:301.

65. Selby, *Dunmore*, 68 ("expected that"); Caley, "Dunmore," 904–906 (final years); and "Lady Virginia Murray," 93 ("late Father"). Dunmore died on February 25, 1809, in Kent, England.

CHAPTER 7. VIRGINIA FIGHTS FOR THE ILLINOIS COUNTRY, 1775–1781

1. For examination of the Transylvania Purchase and its influence on subsequent Illinois and Wabash claims, see Robertson, *Conquest by Law*, 14–16.

2. Volwiler, *Croghan*, 292.

3. Robertson, *Conquest by Law*, 14–16.

4. Byars, *B. and M. Gratz*, 363 (letter from Mason to Richard Henry Lee, Apr. 12, 1779).

5. Slick, *Trent*, 153–56; "Notes and Queries," 394 (letter from Samuel Wharton to Thomas Wharton, Aug. 7, 1775); and Fish, *Barnard and Michael Gratz*, 130.

6. Ranck, *Boonesborough*, 212 (Resolution of the Transylvania Proprietors, Sept. 25, 1775); Saunders, *Colonial Records*, 10:300 (letter from Silas Deane to James Hogg, Nov. 2, 1775); and Ranck, *Boonesborough*, 226–27 (letter from Hogg to Henderson, Jan. 1776).

7. Savelle, *Morgan*, 87.

8. Barthelmas, *Signers*, 44; McCullough, *Adams*, 98; and *Johnson*, 21 U.S. at 558.

9. Rowland, *Mason*, 1:434; and Virginia, *Proceedings of the Convention of Delegates*, 39–40, 66–67, 124–27.

10. Force, *American Archives*, 6:1588 (Virginia Convention resolution, June 24, 1776); and Thorpe, *Constitutions*, 7:3819.

11. Palmer et al., *Calendar of Virginia State Papers*, 1:272; and Jensen, *Articles of Confederation*, 122.

12. Hammon and Taylor, *Virginia's Western War*, 13 (Henry); and Lewis, *Indiana Company*, 210.

13. Ranck, *Boonesborough*, 253 (emphasis added).

14. Alvord, *Illinois Country*, 340; IWC Minutes, 3–5.

15. Palmer et al., *Calendar of Virginia State Papers*, 1:314.

16. Lewis, *Indiana Company*, 214; Palmer et al., *Calendar of Virginia State Papers*, 6:11; Marcus et al., *Documentary History of the Supreme Court*, 5:277; and Selby, *Revolution in Virginia*, 158.

17. Virginia, *Journal of the House of Delegates*, 45–46.

18. Hening, *Statutes at Large; Being a Collection of All the Laws of Virginia*, 10:97; and Virginia, *Journal of the House of Delegates*, 73 (land office).

19. Alvord, *Illinois Country*, 312–13; and Barnhart, *Hamilton and Clark*, 14–15.

20. Mohr, *Federal Indian Relations*, 50; and Barnhart, *Hamilton and Clark*, 14–15.

21. Bakeless, *Background to Glory*, 49; and James, *Clark*, 112–14.

22. Starkey, *European and Native American Warfare*, 125; and Chalou, "Clark and Indian America," 35.

23. Henry, *Patrick Henry*, 2:105 (emphasis added); Thom, "Clark and the American Indian," 43; and Harrell, "Some Neglected Phases of the Revolution," 163.

24. Clark, "Papers," 229; Jablow, *Illinois, Kickapoo, and Potawatomi*, 289 ("lay down"); Downes, *Council Fires*, 235; Calloway, *Documents*, 18:157 ("blody"); and Barnhart, *Hamilton and Clark*, 112 ("Valuable negotiation").

25. Haldimand, *Papers*, 9:475 (letter from Hamilton, Sept. 16, 1778, emphasis added); and Beckwith, "Clark's Conquest," 339 (letter from Hamilton to Haldimand, Sept. 26, 1778).

26. Barnhart, *Hamilton and Clark*, 124–34.

27. Ibid., 142–43.

28. Ibid., 152 (Dec. 20, 1778, "their conduct"), 153 (Young Tobacco), 71–73; and Smith, *Historical Sketches*, 38 ("risk the whole").

29. Harrison, *Clark and the War in the West*, 49 (journey across Illinois); and Barnhart, *Hamilton and Clark*, 176 (council).

30. Davidson and Stuvé, *Complete History of Illinois*, 208; and Jefferson, *Papers*, 3:71 (letter from John Todd, Jr., Kaskaskia, to Jefferson, Aug. 18, 1779).

31. Clark, "Papers," 153 (letter to George Mason, Nov. 19, 1779); and Deloria and DeMallie, *Documents*, 2:1206–1207 (grant).

32. Franklin, *Papers*, 22:120; Smith, *Letters of Delegates*, 3:597 (letter from Chase to John Adams, Apr. 28, 1776); and 5 *JCC* 550–51 (July 12, 1776).

33. Onuf, *Origins of the Federal Republic*, 88 (letter from Timothy Pickering to John Pickering, June 13, 1780); and Haw et al., *Stormy Patriot*, 80.

34. 6 *JCC* 1076–77 (notes of John Adams for July 25, 1776), 1082–83 (notes for Aug. 2, 1776).

35. Jensen, *Articles of Confederation*, 156–57 n.61.

36. Vaughan, *Chronicles*, 260 (Paine); and Whitney, *Founders*, 2:332–34.

37. Hoffman, *Dear Papa, Dear Charley*, 2:1024 (letter from Carroll to his father, June 23, 1777).

38. Burnett, *Continental Congress*, 248; and Adams, "Maryland's Influence," 22.

39. 9 *JCC* 843 (Oct. 27, 1777).

40. Adams, *Writings of Samuel Adams*, 4:6; Adams, "Maryland's Influence," 8; and Jensen, *Articles of Confederation*, 124.

41. Jensen, *Documentary History of the Ratification of the Constitution*, 1:97–98 ("vested in," emphasis added); and 11 *JCC* 636–37 (June 23, 1778).

42. 11 *JCC* 649–50 (June 25, 1778); and Meng, *Despatches*, 208–209 (letter from Gérard to Vergennes, Aug. 12, 1778).

43. 12 *JCC* 931 (Sept. 19, 1778).

44. Robertson, "*Johnson v. M'Intosh*," 28; Jefferson, *Papers*, 3:627 (Maryland Declaration, Dec. 15, 1778, emphasis added); and Burnett, *Letters*, 4:60 (letter from William Whipple to Josiah Bartlett, Feb. 7, 1779).

45. Robertson, *Conquest by Law*, 17, citing Rowland, *Mason*, 1:321 (letter from Mason to Lee, Apr. 12, 1779); and Smith, *Letters of Delegates*, 12:358 (letter from Henry to Johnson, Apr. 20, 1779).

46. 13 *JCC* 115–17 (Jan. 26, 1779); 14 *JCC* 617–19 (May 20, 1779), 620–21 (May 21, 1779); Adams, "Maryland's Influence," 25; and 15 *JCC* 1229–30 (Oct. 30, 1779).

47. See 15 *JCC* 1063 (Sept. 14, 1779); Jensen, "Cession," 40; and Savelle, *Morgan*, 96.

48. Rowland, *Mason*, 1:340–41 (Nov. 13, 1779, "firmly asserting"); and 16 *JCC* 398 (Apr. 28, 1780).

49. Jefferson, *Papers*, 3:631.

50. Vaughan, *Chronicles*, 260 (letter from Washington, Dec. 26, 1779, to Caesar Rodney); Staples, *Rhode Island in the Continental Congress*, 294 (letter from Ezekiel Cornell, June 18, 1780 to William Greene); and Isaac, *Transformation of Virginia*, 276 (journal entry of Dr. Robert Honeyman, Mar. 16, 1780).

51. 16 *JCC* 236 (Mar. 7, 1780); Jefferson, *Papers*, 3:631; Henry, *Patrick Henry*, 2:80; 17 *JCC* 558–63 (June 26, 1780), 580 (June 30, 1780); and , 802–808 (Sept. 2, 1780, debated and adopted).

52. Madison, *Papers*, 2:72; Burnett, *Continental Congress*, 496; Jefferson, *Papers*, 3:633–34; and Jones, *Letters of Joseph Jones*, 15 (letter to Jefferson, June 30, 1780).

53. Rowland, *Mason*, 1:363–67 (letter to Joseph Jones, July 27, 1780).

54. 17 *JCC* 806–808 (Sept. 2, 1780), 808 (Sept. 6, 1780); Jensen, *Articles of Confederation*, 231; and Madison, *Writings*, 1:68 (letter to Joseph Jones, Sept. 19, 1780).

55. Pendleton, *Letters and Papers*, 1:308 (letter to Madison, Sept. 25, 1780); 18 *JCC* 862 (Sept. 26, 1780, Illinois-Wabash memorial); and 18 *JCC* 915 (Oct. 10, 1780).

56. Smith, *Letters of Delegates*, 16:375 (letter from Theodorick Bland to Jefferson, Nov. 22, 1780); Hening, *Statutes at Large; Being a Collection of All the Laws of Virginia*, 10:564–65; and Sosin, *Revolutionary Frontier*, 158.

57. Sioussat, "Chevalier De La Luzerne," 394 (letter, Jan. 10, 1781).

58. Delaplaine, *Thomas Johnson, Maryland and the Constitution*, 7; Jensen, *Articles of Confederation*, 237; and *Publications of the Southern History Association*, 9:399 (letter from Johnson to James Duane, Feb. 2, 1781).

59. Konkle, *Thomas Smith*, 136; Burnett, *Continental Congress*, 500; 19 *JCC* 223 (Mar. 2, 1781); and Smith, *Letters of Delegates*, 17:14 (letter from Bland to Richard Henry Lee, Mar. 5, 1781).

60. Lee, *Letters of Richard Henry Lee*, 2:214 (letter to Samuel Adams, Feb. 5, 1781).

61. Delaplaine, *Thomas Johnson, Maryland and the Constitution*, 8 (emphasis added); and 19 *JCC* 139 (Feb. 12, 1781).

62. Robertson, *Conquest by Law*, 18.

Chapter 8. The Illinois and Wabash Proprietors Unite

1. 19 *JCC* 208–13 (Mar. 1, 1781).

2. IWC Minutes, 1.

3. IWC Minutes, 2–5 (Illinois draft memorial); and Palmer et al., *Calendar of Virginia State Papers*, 1:314 (Wabash memorial).

4. IWC Minutes, 9–15 (Nov. 7, 1778).

5. IWC Minutes, 18–25.

6. Hening, *Statutes at Large; Being a Collection of All the Laws of Virginia*, 10:97.

7. Barthelmas, *Signers*, 226; Haldimand, *Papers,* 19:376 (Campbell); IWC Minutes, 26–27 (Aug. 20, 1779), 59 (Nov. 10, 1779).

8. IWC Minutes, 50–57 (Nov. 10, 1779); and Palmer et al., *Calendar of Virginia State Papers*, 1:314.

9. IWC Minutes, 61–67 (Apr. 29, 1780), 74 (June 12, 1780) and , 76–77 (July 25, 1780).

10. 18 *JCC* 862 (Sept. 26, 1780); IWC Minutes, 79–81 (Sept. 25, 1780), and 84 (Feb. 5, 1781).

11. Robertson, "*Johnson v. M'Intosh*," 31–33.

12. 3 *JCC* 482 (Oct. 6, 1775) (Johnson); and Jefferson, *Papers*, 3:631 (Mason).

13. Kellogg, *Frontier Advance*, 51 n.3; Caley, "Dunmore," 880; Abernethy, *Western Lands*, 240; and Haldimand, *Papers*, 19:376–77 (inventory).

14. Hoffman, *Spirit of Dissension*, 190 (Christie); 4 *JCC* 286 (Apr. 16, 1776), 316–17 (Apr. 29, 1776), 347 (May 10, 1776); 5 *JCC* 652 (Aug. 13, 1776), 740 (Sept. 7, 1776, Ross); Bailey, *Ohio Company*, 405 (Ross); Morton, "Diary," 16 (Sproat); and Ranlet, "Tory David Sproat," 187–201.

15. Jackson, *With the British Army in Philadelphia*, 213 (letter from Rebecca Franks to Anne Paca, Feb. 26, 1778).

16. Jackson, *With the British Army in Philadelphia*, 235–49; and Drinker, *Diary*, 1:306 (May 18, 1778).

17. Drinker, *Diary*, 1:314, 332; Marcus, *American Jewry*, 246; and 12 *JCC* 1032–33 (Oct. 21, 1778).

18. Marcus, *American Jewry*, 242; Larson, "Revolutionary American Jury," 1493, 1501; and IWC Minutes, 76 (July 25, 1780).

19. Marcus, *Colonial American Jew*, 3:1247; Marcus, *American Jewry*, 243; Simonhoff, *Jewish Notables*, 39; IWC Minutes, 82 (Feb. 5, 1781), 85 (Feb. 20, 1781), 97 (Mar. 26, 1781), and 81 (Jan. 7, 1781).

20. Bowling and Veit, *First Federal Congress*, 9:177 ("major figure"); Armentrout, "William Smith," 306 ("loathsome"); Starr, "William Smith," 356–57 ("seldom paid"); and Butterfield, *Abigail and John: Selected Letters of the Adams Family*, 125 (letter, Apr. 28, 1776, eulogy).

21. Wood, *Creation of the American Republic*, 333 (arrest and parole); and Starr, "William Smith," 356 (Rush).

22. Barthelmas, *Signers*, 44; Haw et al., *Stormy Patriot*, 14; and Elsmere, *Justice Samuel Chase*, 5.

23. IWC Minutes, 177–78 (May 31, 1774); and Quinn, *Signers*, 72 ("uncompromising").

24. Haw et al., *Stormy Patriot*, 106; and Hamilton, *Papers of Alexander Hamilton*, 1:562 (Oct. 16, 1778).

25. Hoffman, *Princes of Ireland*, 330 (May 11, 1780, Carroll); Haw et al., *Stormy Patriot*, 115 (House of Delegates); and Elsmere, *Justice Samuel Chase*, 22.

26. Butterfield, *Abigail and John: Selected Letters of the Adams Family*, 110 (letter to Abigail Adams, Oct. 19, 1775); and Potts, "Deane," 296.

27. McCullough, *Adams*, 98; Deane, *Papers*, 4:172 (letter from Morris to Deane, Aug. 11, 1776); and Potts, *Arthur Lee*, 161–62.

28. Abernethy, "Commercial Activities of Silas Deane," 484; and Boyd, "Deane," 533.

29. Wood, *Creation of the American Republic*, 420; "Letters to Thomas Adams," 32 (letter from Deane, June 25, 1779).

30. IWC Minutes, 49 (Nov. 8, 1779); Deane, *Papers*, 4:317; Burnett, *Letters*, 6:262–63 (letter from Madison to Pendleton, Nov. 13, 1781); and Washington, *Writings*, 24:259 (letter to Benjamin Tallmadge, May 15, 1782).

31. Burnett, *Letters*, 6:364; and Deane, *Papers*, 5:149 (letter to Wilson, Apr. 1, 1783).

32. Boyd, "Deane"; and Franklin, *Papers*, 22:152 (letter from Bancroft, Aug. 7, 1775).

33. IWC Minutes, 76 (July 25, 1780); Fish, *Barnard and Michael Gratz*, 175; and 4 *JCC* 24 (Jan. 3, 1776, Shee).

34. Meng, *Despatches*, 914 (letter to Vergennes, May 5, 1780), 917 (letter from Vergennes, May 19, 1780).

35. Byars, *B. and M. Gratz*, 171 (letter from Michael Gratz to his wife Miriam, July 15, 1778, "good news"); Fish, *Barnard and Michael Gratz*, 133–41 (line of credit); Scharf, *Chronicles*, 185; Papenfuse, *In Pursuit of Profit*, 104–105; and Mc-Cullough, *Adams*, 283.

36. Butterfield, *Abigail and John: Selected Letters of the Adams Family*, 116 (letter from Adams to Abigail Adams, Feb. 18, 1776).

37. Chernow, *Morris*, 14; and Smith, *Letters of Delegates*, 4:512 (letter from Morris to Joseph Reed, July 21, 1776).

38. Chernow, *Hamilton*, 155; and 13 *JCC* 164, 167 (Feb. 11, 1779).

39. IWC Minutes, 126–27 (Aug. 20, 1779), 46 (Oct. 2, 1779).

40. 19 *JCC* 126 (Feb. 7, 1781), 180 (Feb. 20, 1781); and Whitney, *Founders*, 2:168.

41. Hallahan, *Day the Revolution Ended*, 152; and Ver Steeg, "Morris," 908.

42. Rush, *Letters of Benjamin Rush*, 1:264 (letter to Horatio Gates, Sept. 5, 1781); Abernethy, *Western Lands*, 173; Chernow, *Morris*, 25–27; and Rappleye, *Morris*, 520–21.

43. Alexander, "Wilson," 586; Hall, "Wilson," 126–27; Wilson, *Works*, 1:7–12; and Wilson, *Collected Works*, 1: xv–xvi.

44. Wilson, *Works*, 2:721–23, 738, 745; Zweiben, *How Blackstone Lost the Colonies*, 122; Adams, *Political Ideas of the American Revolution*, 53; and Wilson, *Collected Works*, 1:4, 22, 30.

45. Wilson, *Works*, 2:740–42.

46. Ibid., 2:740.

47. Rosenberg, "In Search of James Wilson," 110; and Friedenberg, *Pursuit of Land*, 350.

48. Butterfield, *Adams Family Correspondence*, 1:253 (letter to Abigail Adams, July 23, 1775); and Barthelmas, *Signers*, 288 (Rush).

49. 4 *JCC* 1076 (May 10, 1776); Wilson, *Works*, 2:711.

50. Cooke, *Tench Coxe*, 85 (removal from Congress); IWC Minutes, 20 (Mar. 13, 1779), 26 (Aug. 20, 1779).

51. Maxey, "Translation of James Wilson," 29; Ewald, "James Wilson," 925; and "Addenda to Watson's Annals," 144.

52. Barthelmas, *Signers*, 287 (handbill); Drinker, *Diary*, 1:361; and Rush, *Letters of Benjamin Rush*, 1:240 (letter to Adams, Oct. 12, 1779).

53. Smith, "Attack on Fort Wilson," 182–85.

54. Rush, *Letters of Benjamin Rush*, 1:240 (letter to Adams, Oct. 12, 1779); IWC Minutes, 47 (Oct. 30, 1779); and Smith, "Attack on Fort Wilson," 186–88.

55. IWC Minutes, 85; Ver Steeg, "Morris," 85; Hall, "Wilson," 127; and Maxey, "Translation of James Wilson," 30.

56. Konkle, *Thomas Smith*, 154–55.

57. Nagel, *Lees of Virginia*, 133.

CHAPTER 9. VIRGINIA GIVES UP THE ILLINOIS COUNTRY, 1781–1784

1. 19 *JCC* 253 (Mar. 12, 1781), 264 (Mar. 16, 1781); and 20 *JCC* 534 (May 25, 1781).

2. Wharton, *Plain Facts*, 28.

3. IWC Minutes, 98 (July 2, 1781).

4. Madison, *Papers*, 3:11; Hawke, *Paine*, 107; and Wheeler, *Paine*, 8:152.

5. 6 *JCC* 1082–83 (Aug. 2, 1776); and Hawke, *Paine*, 109.

6. Wheeler, *Paine*, 8:164–73.

7. Pendleton, *Letters and Papers of Edmund Pendleton*, 1:328 (letter to Joseph Jones, Feb. 10, 1781); and Hoffman and Molyneaux, *Lee Family Papers*, reel 7.

8. Pendleton, *Letters and Papers of Edmund Pendleton*, 1:328 (letter to Joseph Jones, Feb. 10, 1781); Hoffman and Molyneaux, *Lee Family Papers*, reel 7; Hawke, *Paine*, 108–109; and Williams, Jr., "Jefferson, the Norman Yoke," 189.

9. Wharton, *Plain Facts*, 28.

10. Williams, Jr., *American Indian in Western Legal Thought*, 298.

11. Wharton, *Plain Facts*, 3–16.

12. Ibid., 9.

13. Ibid., 26–27.

14. Ibid., 28 (emphasis added).

15. IWC Minutes, 84 (Feb. 5, 1781).

16. Byars, *B. and M. Gratz*, 371 (letter from Franklin to Richard Bache, Sept. 13, 1781); and Madison, *Papers*, 4:154 (letter to Jefferson, Apr. 16, 1782).

17. 20 *JCC* 704 (June 27, 1781); and 21 *JCC* 1032 (Oct. 2, 1781).

18. Fish, *Barnard and Michael Gratz*, 164 (letter from Levy to Gratz, Oct. 17, 1781).

19. 21 *JCC* 1058 (Oct. 16, 1781); Henry, *Patrick Henry*, 2:88; Burnett, *Letters*, 6:246 (letter to Governor Nelson, Oct. 23, 1781), 247 (letter from Randolph to Bland, Oct. 23, 1781).

20. 21 *JCC* 1071 (Oct. 24, 1781); Wraxall, *Historical Memoirs*, 2:103; Vaughan, *Chronicles*, 303.

21. 21 *JCC* 1076–78 (Oct. 26, 1781).

22. Mason, *Papers*, 2:718; 22 *JCC* 228 (May 1, 1782). The report of the Boudinot committee was not set forth in the *Journals* until May, 1, 1782, when Congress took the report under consideration.

23. Mason, *Papers*, 2:717; and 22 *JCC* 226 (May 1, 1782).

24. 22 *JCC* 228–29 (May 1, 1782); and Henry, *Patrick Henry*, 2:92.

25. Mason, *Papers*, 2:719–20; and 22 *JCC* 230 (May 1, 1782).

26. 21 *JCC* 1113–14 (Nov. 14, 1781); and 22 *JCC* 190–95 (Apr. 18, 1782).

27. Hendrick, *Lees of Virginia*, 265 (Adams' description of Lee); Potts, *Arthur Lee*, 1 (letter from Franklin to Wharton, June 17, 1780), 56–57.

28. Burnett, *Letters*, 6:331 (letter from Lee to Samuel Adams, Apr. 21, 1782); and Onuf, *Origins of the Federal Republic*, 90 (letter from a Virginia delegate to an unnamed correspondent, Dec. 10, 1781, "private jobbers").

29. IWC Minutes, 100 (Apr. 16, 1782).

30. 22 *JCC* 191 (Apr. 18, 1782).

31. Bodley, *Our First Great West*, 193 ("consternation"); and Burnett, *Letters*, 6:333 ("warm debates").

32. Munroe, "Nonresident Representation," 179 (letter from Wharton to Simon Kollock of Delaware, June 10, 1782); 22 *JCC* 223–25 (May 1, 1782), 234–35 (May 2, 1782), and 240–41 (May 6, 1782).

33. Rowland, *Mason*, 1:363 (letter to Joseph Jones, July 27, 1780, "void"); and Mason, *Papers*, 2:715 (letter to Samuel Purviance, May 20, 1782, "renew their Application").

34. 22 *JCC* 445 (Aug. 5, 1782); and 23 *JCC* 545 (Sept. 4, 1782).

35. Corwin, *French Policy*, 231 (Lee); and Thomson, *Papers of Charles Thomson*, 108, 145 (Madison and Witherspoon).

36. 23 *JCC* 552 (Sept. 6, 1782, compromise), 605 (Sept. 25, 1782) (motion).

37. 23 *JCC* 694 (Oct. 29, 1782).

38. 25 *JCC* 955 (Apr. 9, 1783).

39. 24 *JCC* 272–73 (Apr. 23, 1783, Bland motion), 381 (June 4, 1783, report); and Madison, *Writings*, 1:476 (letter to Randolph, June 10, 1783).

40. 25 *JCC* 559–62 (Sept. 13, 1783). Although the report was delivered on the sixth of June, it was not printed in the *Journals* until September 13, when it was approved.

41. 25 *JCC* 561–63 (Sept. 13, 1783); and Madison, *Writings*, 1:476 (letter to Randolph, June 10, 1783).

42. 25 *JCC* 968–69 (June 10, 1783, notes of Madison); and 24 *JCC* 408–409 (June 20, 1783).

43. 24 *JCC* 410 (June 21, 1783, "insulted"); and Washington, *Writings*, 27:17–18 (letter to the President of Congress, June 17, 1783, emphasis added).

44. 25 *JCC* 563–64 (Sept. 13, 1783); Selby, *Chronology*, 48; and Lewis, *Indiana Company*, 261.

45. Jones, *Letters of Joseph Jones*, 125 (letter to Madison, June 28, 1783), 132 (letter to Madison, Oct. 30, 1783).

46. 26 *JCC* 117 (Mar. 1, 1784).

47. Ibid., 397 (letter from Read to Guerard, Mar. 1, 1784).

48. Rowland, *Mason*, 2:51 (letter to Alexander Henderson and Charles Broadwater, May 30, 1783).

49. Selby, *Chronology*, 48.

CHAPTER 10. CONQUEST, PURCHASE, AND PREEMPTION

1. Barnhart, *Hamilton and Clark*, 125 (journal entry, Nov. 19, 1778).

2. Calloway, *Documents*, 18:329 (letter from Harmar to John Dickinson, Jan. 15, 1785); "Canadian Archives," 585 (Reply of the Commissioners to the Indians, July 31, 1793) ("right of soil"); and Washington, *Washington: A Collection*, 551 (address to the Seneca, Dec. 29, 1790).

3. Simcoe, *Correspondence*, 2:19, Message from the Western Indians to the Commissioners of the United States, Aug. 13, 1793, "free to make any bargain,"

emphasis added); *ASP: Indian Affairs*, 1:354 (speech of the Commissioners, July 31, 1793, right of preemption).

4. *ASP: Indian Affairs*, 1:341 (instructions from Secretary of War, Henry Knox, Apr. 26, 1793).

5. 2 *JCC* 175 (July 12, 1775), 183 (July 13, 1775); Thwaites and Kellogg, *Revolution on the Upper Ohio*, 78; and 4 *JCC* 319 (Apr. 30, 1776).

6. Thwaites and Kellogg, *Revolution on the Upper Ohio*, 98; 2 *JCC* 198 (July 21, 1775, Franklin); and 5 *JCC* 919 (Nov. 15, 1777, Articles).

7. 22 *JCC* 228–31 (May 1, 1782, Nov. 1781 report of the Boudinot committee); 24 *JCC* 503 (Aug. 12, 1783); and 25 *JCC* 602 (Sept. 22, 1783, proclamation).

8. Sword, *Washington's Indian War*, 56.

9. Sugden, *Blue Jacket*, 64 (quoting a letter from William Christian to Benjamin Harrison, Sept. 28, 1782).

10. 24 *JCC* 319–20 (May 1, 1783); and Mohr, *Federal Indian Relations*, 94.

11. Haldimand, *Papers*, 11:372 (letter from De Peyster to Haldimand, June 28, 1783), 370 (speech by tribal chief, June 28, 1873).

12. Calloway, *Documents*, 18:285 (report by Ephraim Douglass of a council with the Six Nations, July 2, 1783, "fabricated"); Haldimand, *Papers*, 20:177 (John Johnson speech read to Indians at Sandusky, Sept. 6, 1783); and Craig, *Olden Time*, 2:426 (Oct. 20, 1784, "*claim the whole*," emphasis added).

13. Washington, *Writings*, 27:134 (letter to James Duane, Sept. 7, 1783), 140.

14. 25 *JCC* 681 (Oct. 15, 1783, "temper"), 683–86 (recommendation), and 692 ("not to admit").

15. Craig, *Olden Time*, 2:424–25.

16. Fort Stanwix Treaty with the Six Nations, 7 Stat. 15, Oct. 22, 1784; Denny, *Journal*, 212 (letter from Harmar to John Dickinson, Jan. 15, 1785, "lenity"); Pickering, *Timothy Pickering Papers*, 122–23 ("give not to receive"); Fort McIntosh Treaty with the Wyandot, etc., 7 Stat. 16, Jan. 21, 1785; and Horsman, "American Indian Policy," 38–39.

17. Papers of the Continental Congress, reel 69, item 56, 299 (report of Clark, Oct. 5, 1785); and Edmunds, *Potawatomis*, 116.

18. Denny, *Journal*, 63 (Dec. 20, 1785, "disappointed"); Calloway, *Documents*, 18:341 (Butler's journal, Jan. 14, 1786, "shut their ears"), 344–45 (Jan. 30, 1786, Shawnee complaints and response).

19. Nabokov, *Native American Testimony*, 122–23 (Corn Tassel); Calloway, *Documents*, 18:344 (Butler's journal, Jan. 30, 1786, "We are Shawnese"), 347 ("belongs to the United States").

20. Fort Finney Treaty with the Shawnee, 7 Stat. 26, Jan. 31, 1786; and Calloway, *Documents*, 18:347 (Butler's journal, Jan. 30, 1786).

21. Burt, *British North America*, 93.

22. 26 *JCC* 324 (Apr. 30, 1784, emphasis added); 25 *JCC* 375 (May 30, 1785, Land Ordinance); and Washington, *Papers*, 2:119–20 (letter to Jacob Read, Nov. 3, 1784).

23. Denny, *Journal*, 215 (letter from Harmar to Knox, May 7, 1786); and Kinnaird, "Spain in the Mississippi Valley," 175–79.

24. Kelsay, *Brant*, 403.

25. *ASP: Indian Affairs*, 1:8–9 (speech of the United Indian Nations, given in council at the mouth of the Detroit River, Dec. 18, 1786).

26. Carter, *Territorial Papers*, 2:31 ("anxiously defend"), 34 ("distress").

27. Commager, *Documents*, 128, 131; Ellis, *Ordinance of 1787*, 124, 127; and Horsman, *Expansion*, 37.

28. McCullough, *1776*, at 58; and 33 *JCC* 388–89 (July 21, 1787).

29. 33 *JCC* 480 (Aug. 9, 1787); and Sugden, *Blue Jacket*, 73.

30. Thornbrough, *Outpost*, 37 (letter from Harmar to Henry Knox, Aug. 7, 1787), 51 (letter from Harmar to Knox, Nov. 24, 1787, describing a speech delivered on Sept. 5, 1787).

31. Thornbrough, *Outpost*, 114, 117 (letter from Hamtramck to Harmar, Aug. 31, 1788), 150 (letter from Harmar to Hamtramck, Feb. 15, 1789).

32. 34 *JCC* 125 (May 2, 1788); *ASP: Indian Affairs*, 1:53 (communication from Knox to Washington, July 7, 1789), 1:61 (letter from Knox to Washington, Jan. 4, 1790, emphasis added). After the Constitution became effective on March 4, 1789, Knox served in the newly formed Executive Branch.

33. Eisinger, "Puritan's Justification," 141.

34. Fort Harmar Treaty with the Six Nations, 7 Stat. 33, Jan. 9, 1789; and Fort Harmar Treaty with the Wyandot, etc., 7 Stat. 28, Jan. 9, 1789.

35. Jeremiah Dummer argued in 1721 that the Crown could only give "a bare Right of Preemption." Dummer, *Defence of the New-England Charters*, 14. The New Jersey claimants argued in 1752 that the "Letters Patent" from King Charles did not "grant an absolute Property in the Lands . . . but rather the Right of Pre-emption." Bond et al., *An Answer to a Bill in the Chancery of New Jersey*, 5.

36. Hening, *Statutes at Large; Being a Collection of All the Laws of Virginia*, 10:97 (Act of June 19, 1779); Wait, *Secret Journals*, 3:154 (Jan. 2, 1782); and Thomson, *Papers of Charles Thomson*, 148 (Aug. 27, 1782). When asked in 1782 why United States had a right to lands possessed by Indians, John Jay answered that the United States "claimed the right of pre-emption with respect to them." Jay, *Life of John Jay*, 2:471–74 (exchange with Spanish ambassador in Paris).

37. Madison, *Papers*, 8:156 (letter to Monroe, Nov. 27, 1784).

38. *ASP: Indian Affairs*, 1:61 (letter from Knox to Washington, Jan. 4, 1790, emphasis added).

39. Jablow, *Illinois, Kickapoo, and Potawatomi*, 303 (Hamtramck); *ASP: Indian Affairs*, 1:58 (letter from St. Clair to Washington, Sept. 14, 1789, "constant hostilities"); and Thornbrough, *Outpost*, 211 (letter from Knox to Harmar, Dec. 19, 1789, "chastisement").

40. *ASP: Indian Affairs*, 1:100 (letter from Knox to St. Clair, Sept. 12, 1790); and Carter, *Little Turtle*, 95.

41. *ASP: Indian Affairs*, 1:107 (report from Knox to Washington, Jan. 5, 1791).

42. Ibid., 129–35 (expeditions); and Jablow, *Illinois, Kickapoo, and Potawatomi*, 312–13.

43. Symmes, *Correspondence*, 143 (letter from Symmes to Dayton, June 19, 1791); and Carter, *Little Turtle*, 108 (St. Clair's defeat).

44. Taylor, "Land and Liberty," 96; and Horsman, "American Indian Policy," 44 (letter from Jefferson to Monroe, Apr. 17, 1791).

45. *Annals of Congress*, 3:1052, 2nd Cong., 1st Sess. (message, dated Dec. 12, 1791, from Washington to Congress); Wright, *Britain and the American Frontier*, 69 (quoting a letter, June 15, 1792, from Vincennes, published Sept. 28, 1792, in the *Bahama Gazette*); *ASP: Indian Affairs*, 1:198 ("Statement Relative to the Frontiers Northwest of the Ohio," Dec. 26, 1791); and Carter, *Little Turtle*, 124.

46. Carter, *Territorial Papers*, 2:374 (Articles of Agreement with the Wabash Indians, Mar. 14, 1792), 380 (letter from Hamtramck to Knox, Mar. 31, 1792).

47. *ASP: Indian Affairs*, 1:229–30 (instructions from Knox to Trueman, Apr. 3, 1792), 234 (instructions from Knox to Putnam, May 22, 1792).

48. Buell, *Memoirs of Rufus Putnam*, 275 (letter from Putnam to Knox, July 5, 1792), 293 (letter from Putnam to Knox, July 11, 1792); and Wallace, *Thirty Thousand Miles*, 268, 278.

49. Libby, *Piankashaw and Kaskaskia*, 194 ("their ancestors," emphasis added); and *ASP: Indian Affairs*, 1:338 (treaty, emphasis added).

50. *ASP: Indian Affairs*, 1:319; and *National Gazette* (Dec. 26, 1792, "saluted").

51. Twohig, *Journal of the Proceedings of the President*, 11 (Jan. 12, 1793), 37 (Jan. 28, 1793, warning).

52. Jefferson, *Writings*, 16:382 (notes of the speeches by Indian chiefs, Feb. 1, 1793).

53. Buell, *Memoirs of Rufus Putnam*, 377 (letter from Knox to Putnam, Feb. 11, 1793), 378 (letter from Putnam to Knox, Feb. 11, 1793), 379 (letter from Putnam to Knox, Feb. 13, 1793), and 120–22 (resignation).

54. *ASP: Indian Affairs*, 1:338 (message from Washington to the Senate, Feb. 13, 1793, "not be proper"); *Journal of the Senate*, 5:115 (Feb. 28, 1793), 6:216 (Jan. 7, 1794). See also *ASP: Indian Affairs*, 1:440 (letter from Knox to Washington, Jan. 2, 1794).

55. Jefferson, *Writings*, 1:188–89 (emphasis added), 3:19 (opinion, dated May 3, 1790).

56. Jefferson, *Writings*, 17:328–29 (notes, dated June 3, 1792, of Jefferson's conversation with Hammond). Jefferson analogized the right of preemption to an Anglo-American property right called a "remainder." See Jefferson, *Writings*, 1:340 ("I consider our right of preemption of the Indians lands . . . in the nature of a remainder after the extinguishment of a present right"). A "remainder" is a property interest that is owned by someone other than the person who is presently entitled to possess the property. More recently, Stuart Banner has compared the right of preemption to a different property right, called an "executory interest," which he describes as "the right to take possession of the land at some point in the future, should a particular event transpire." Banner, *How the Indians Lost Their Land*, 163. Banner's analogy is more apt, because remainders follow possessory interests that are measured in finite terms, whereas executory interests depend on events that may never occur. It is telling that Jefferson equated the preemption right to a remainder, because even though he stated that the Indians

might choose to keep the land, it is apparent that he believed the Indians would inevitably give up their rights.

57. *ASP: Indian Affairs*, 1:341 (Apr. 26, 1793, emphasis added).

58. Ritcheson, *Aftermath of Revolution*, 245–50 (Hammond's proposal); and "Canadian Archives," 512 (proceedings of an Indian council, Nov. 13, 1792, at "Buffaloe Creek").

59. "Canadian Archives," 571 (message given in council); *ASP: Indian Affairs*, 1:353 (response of the Commissioners, July 31, 1793), 353–54.

60. *ASP: Indian Affairs*, 1:356 (reply of the confederated tribes, Aug. 13, 1793, emphasis added).

61. Ibid.; and Sword, *Washington's Indian War*, 245. See also Sugden, *Blue Jacket*, 153 ("defiant and frank sentiments of proud, undefeated peoples").

62. Jefferson, *Writings*, 9:236–37 (letter to Gouverneur Morris, Sept. 11, 1793); and Treaty of Greenville, Article V, 7 Stat. 52 (Aug. 3, 1795, emphasis added).

CHAPTER 11. A TIME OF TRANSITION

1. Blasingham, "Depopulation," 213, 380; and Clark, *Papers*, 456–57 (letter from John Montgomery to Clark, Sept. 22, 1780).

2. Jefferson, *Writings*, 16:371–77; and Onuf, "'We shall all be Americans,'" 103.

3. Thornbrough, *Outpost*, 46 (letter from Harmar to Knox, Nov. 24, 1787); and Imlay, *Topographical Description*, 501.

4. Austin, "Journal," 539 (Jan. 1797, DuCoigne); and Jefferson, *Papers*, 25:113 (Indian conference held on Feb. 1, 1793).

5. Stevens, "'One of the Most Beautiful Regions of the World,'" 375 n.15.

6. Filson, *Discovery, Settlement and Present State of Kentucke*, 82; and Imlay, *Topographical Description*, 359–62 (council held by Thomas Dalton at Vincennes, Apr. 15, 1784).

7. Thornbrough, *Outpost*, 52.

8. Libby, *Piankashaw and Kaskaskia*, 160–76; Thornbrough, *Outpost*, 14, 46–58, 114–20, 136–42; and Cayton, *Frontier Indiana*, 95, 140–41.

9. Simcoe, *Correspondence*, 2:149–50 (speech by Dorchester to the Seven Nations of Canada, Feb. 10, 1794); and "Canadian Archives," 656 (speech "of the Shawanese, Delawares, Miamis, Mingoes &ca together with Deputies from the Wabash Nations," Apr. 14, 1794).

10. "Canadian Archives," 697 (report from McKee to Simcoe, July 26, 1794, regarding the tribal council held July 14, 1794); and Zeisberger, *Diary*, 2:378 (entry for Oct. 15, 1794, "great loss").

11. Knopf, *Wayne*, 398 (letter from Pickering to Wayne, Apr. 8, 1795, emphasis added).

12. Ibid., 398–99; and 25–26.

13. *ASP: Indian Affairs*, 1:169 (letter from Knox to George Clinton, Aug. 17, 1791, "all possible alienations"); and *Marshall v. Clark*, 8 Va. 268 (1791).

14. [Benton], *Abridgement of the Debates of Congress*, 1:576 (Jan. 29, 1795). The representatives debated whether North Carolina—prior to ceding Indian lands to the United States—held a right of preemption or "fee-simple" ownership. Compare *Abridgement*, 577 (William Smith of South Carolina declaring that North Carolina had "absolute title to the lands") with 578 (Elias Boudinot of New Jersey arguing that North Carolina only had "the privilege of pre-emption"). A similar debate took place in the House of Representative in April 1796. *Annals of Congress*, 5:895, 4th Cong., 1st Sess. (Apr. 9, 1796, statement by James Holland of North Carolina that Indians "were tenants at will"); 897 (statement by William Cooper of New York that "the idea that our citizens can acquire the fee of their lands without their consent, was not only new, but contrary to natural justice"); 899 (statement of James Hillhouse of Connecticut that the right of preemption "is not a title, but a right only of becoming, in preference to all others, owners of the land, by some future grant or cession to be made by the Indians," and statement of James Madison that the Natives hold "a qualified property only in the land"); and 900 (statement by William Lyman of Massachusetts that the land occupied by Indians "was the property of the United States, which they were suffered to enjoy, but to which they had no real title").

15. Bald, *Detroit's First American Decade*, 12 (lower peninsula); and Askin, *John Askin Papers*, 1:546 ("transact"). See also Simcoe, *Correspondence*, 4:50 (letter from Joseph Brant to John Butler, July 23, 1795, "Land Jobbers are now gone . . . to Wayne with their Deeds to get them confirmed").

16. Simcoe, *Correspondence*, 4:35 (letter from John Askin, Sr., to his son, July 5, 1795, emphasis added).

17. Askin, *John Askin Papers*, 1:553–54 (letter from Askin to W. D. Powell, July 11, 1795).

18. Simcoe, *Correspondence*, 4:70 (report from John Askin, Jr., to Col. Richard England, commandant at Detroit, Aug. 19, 1795).

19. Wheeler-Voegelin, "Ethnohistory," 414; and Knopf, *Wayne*, 461.

20. Treaty of Greenville, 7 Stat. 49, Aug. 3, 1795 (emphasis added).

21. Simcoe, *Correspondence*, 4:92 (letter from England to Simcoe, Sept. 8, 1795), 99–100 (letter from Alexander Henry to Askin, Oct. 7, 1795).

22. Treaty of Greenville, 7 Stat. 49, Aug. 3, 1795. It is possible that no Piankeshaw chiefs were present. Libby, *Piankashaw and Kaskaskia*, 203 (Harrison in 1803 stated the Piankeshaws and Kaskaskias thought it unnecessary to go "as one of them had never been at war with the United States and the other had made peace three years before").

23. Treaty of Greenville, 7 Stat. 51, Aug. 3, 1795.

24. Tanner, "Greenville Treaty of 1795," 56; Cayton, "'Noble Actors',"268; and Elkins and McKitrick, *Age of Federalism*, 439. Wayne died on December 15, 1795.

25. IWC Minutes, 101 (Dec. 11, 1786); and Madison, *Writings*, 1:476 (letter to Randolph, June 10, 1783).

26. IWC Minutes, 102 (Jan. 23, 1787); and Hall, "James Wilson," 128–29.

27. See 34 *JCC* 133 (May 5, 1788).

28. 34 *JCC* 270–71 (June 27, 1788, emphasis added).

29. 34 *JCC* 276 n.4 (July 1, 1788).

30. IWC Minutes, 105 (Jan. 21, 1790).

31. De Pauw, *First Federal Congress*, 3:337–42; Bowling et al., *First Federal Congress*, 8:204–206; and Jefferson, *Papers*, 22:5 (letter from Tench Coxe, Aug. 6, 1791, stating that the attorney general had the claims "under official Consideration").

32. IWC Minutes, 107 (Apr. 12, 1790); and 1 Stat. 137 (July 22, 1790).

33. Robertson, *Conquest by Law*, 19–20.

34. *ASP: Public Lands*, 1:21; and Illinois and Wabash Land Company, *An Account of the Proceedings of the Illinois and Ouabache Land Companies* (1796), 27–29. The "State of Facts" prepared in December of 1791 is printed in the 1796 memorial.

35. IWC Minutes, 110 (Dec. 17, 1791). See also Robertson, *Conquest by Law*, 20.

36. *ASP: Public Lands*, 1:27.

37. Ibid., 1:27 (Apr. 3, 1792).

38. Carter, *Territorial Papers*, 2:387; and Washington, *Papers*, 11:620 n.1.

39. IWC Minutes, 112–13 (Dec. 20, 1792); Carter, *Territorial Papers*, 2:428 (letter from Benjamin Hawkins to Washington, Jan. 11, 1793); Washington, *Papers*, 11:620 n.1 (letter from Tobias Lear, Washington's secretary, to Henry Knox, Jan. 11, 1793); and Twohig, *Journal of the Proceedings of the President*, 9–11. The letter from Senator Hawkins included the Illinois-Wabash petition and the adverse Senate committee report of March 1792.

40. Twohig, *Journal of the Proceedings of the President*, 12 (Jan. 12, 1793); and Washington, *Papers*, 11:621 n.2.

41. Twohig, *Journal of the Proceedings of the President*, 37 (Jan. 27, 1793, Jan. 28, 1793).

42. IWC Minutes, 111–12 (Dec. 17, 1792).

43. IWC Minutes, 116–17 (Feb. 6, 1793, "on account," 118–19 (Little Castor), and 119 ("accosted"). The committee report was authored by Pollock and John Nicholson.

44. Buell, *Memoirs of Rufus Putnam*, 378–79 (letter from Putnam to Knox, Feb. 13, 1793, emphasis added).

45. The Illinois and Piankeshaws had acknowledged the sales as recently as 1789. In the company minutes is a report by George Morgan to Henry Knox dated September 10, 1789. The report describes a gift of a pipe from the Piankeshaws and Kaskaskias to Morgan on March 28, 1789. It goes on to state that "although the Piankeshaw and Kaskaskia Indians *confess that they formerly sold their lands to one Murray*," they hoped that Congress "will not remember that foolish transaction." When Morgan asked them if the sale was fairly transacted, "*they confessed that it was*." IWC Minutes, 120–21 (Feb. 6, 1793, emphasis added).

46. *ASP: Indian Affairs*, 1:338 (statement by Washington to the Senate, Feb.13, 1793).

47. *Journal of the Senate*, 5:108 (Feb. 13, 1793).

48. Buell, *Memoirs of Rufus Putnam*, 120–22 (resignation); IWC Minutes, 157 (Mar. 8, 1793, request for a copy of "the late Treaty"), 159 ("does not conceive").

49. IWC Minutes, 160 (Apr. 12, 1793).

50. Strickland, *Journal*, 59, 165 (entries for Sept. 24, 1794, and Oct. 22, 1794).

51. Whitney, *Founders*, 2:229; Marcus, "Federal Judicial Selection," 802; Hall, "James Wilson," 42 (quoting *Pennsylvania Packet and Daily Advertiser*, Dec. 25, 1790, "brilliant"); and Zweiben, *How Blackstone Lost the Colonies*, 3.

52. Wilson, *Works*, 1:7; Friedenberg, *Pursuit of Land*, 352; Wilkinson, *Land Policy*, 71; and Cooke, *Tench Coxe*, 314.

53. Ver Steeg, "Morris," 911 ("handsome return"); and Drinker, *Diary*, 1:689 ("Clock and Organ").

54. Arbuckle, "John Nicholson," 406; Arnebeck, *Fiery Trial*, 147 ("knack"); and Arbuckle, *Pennsylvania Speculator*, 79.

55. Palmer et al., *Calendar of Virginia State Papers*, 6:5 (bill of equity in *Grayson v. Virginia*); and Kaminski and Saladino, *Documentary History of the Ratification of the Constitution*, 10:1406 (June 18, 1788).

56. *Chisholm v. Georgia*, 2 U.S. 419, 449 (1793, opinion of Justice Iredell). James Wilson, who held three hundred shares in the Indiana Company, authored a lengthy opinion supporting the notion that states may be sued in federal court. Although Wilson's participation in *Chisholm* would be inappropriate today, his failure to recuse himself was not criticized in private correspondence or the press. Casto, *Supreme Court in the Early Republic*, 195.

57. *Annals of Congress*, 7:809, 5th Cong., 2nd Sess. (message from Adams, Jan. 8, 1798); and Henry, *Patrick Henry*, 2:96.

58. Delaplaine, *Thomas Johnson, Maryland and the Constitution*, 473 (letter to Pierre L'Enfant from Thomas Johnson, David Stuart, and Daniel Carroll, Sept. 9, 1791); and Arnebeck, *Fiery Trial*, 90, 186.

59. Bishop, *Georgia Speculation Unveiled*, foreword ("largest land speculation"); *ASP: Indian Affairs*, 1:114 (Georgia Act, Dec. 21, 1789); Haskins, *Yazoo Land Companies*, 73; and Magrath, *Yazoo*, 5.

60. Friedenberg, *Pursuit of Land*, 265.

61. Arbuckle, *Pennsylvania Speculator*, 172; and Haskins, *Yazoo Land Companies*, 84.

62. Marcus et al., *Documentary History of the Supreme Court*, 5:505–506 (quoting the *Aurora*, Feb. 11 and 16, 1795); and Smith, *Wilson*, 379.

63. Abernethy, *South in the New Nation*, 138; and Wilson, *Collected Works*, 1:372.

64. Smith, *Wilson*, 378 (letter from a Mr. Saylor of Richmond to Wilson, Jan. 30, 1796, "your resources"), 380 (letter from Iredell to his wife, Mar. 18, 1796, "bad health"); and Wilson, *Works*, 1:44 (second marriage). The Georgia lawmakers in February 1793 summoned fire from the heavens (with a magnifying glass) to destroy the "records of corruption." Magrath, *Yazoo*, 13.

65. Burd, *Papers*, 191–92 (letter from Edward Burd to Jasper Yeates, Aug. 4, 1796); and Smith, *Wilson*, 382–84; Friedenberg, *Pursuit of Land*, 354.

66. Atkinson, *Leaving the Bench*, 17; Wilkinson, *Land Policy*, 251 (Hannah Wilson to Bird Wilson, Sept. 1, 1798); and McRee, *Life and Correspondence of James Iredell*, 2:533.

67. Rappleye, *Morris*, 496–507; Young, *Forgotten Patriot*, 217 ("Morris's Folly"); and Arnebeck, *Fiery Trial*, 411 ("vultures").

68. Chernow, *Morris*, 103, 199, 211; and Rappleye, *Morris*, 506.

69. Arbuckle, *Pennsylvania Speculator*, 199–202; Chernow, *Morris*, 222; Arnebeck, *Fiery Trial*, 467; and Rappleye, *Morris*, 507–515.

70. Temple, *Indian Villages*, 52; Blasingham, "Depopulation," 370–81; and Treaty with the Kaskaskia, 7 Stat. 78 (Aug. 13, 1803).

71. Volney, *View of the Soil and Climate of the United States*, 354.

72. Austin, "The Journal," 530 (Jan. 1, 1797).

73. Harrison, *Messages and Letters*, 1:46 (letter to Secretary of War Henry Dearborn, Feb. 26, 1802); .

74. Illinois and Wabash Land Company, *An Account of the Proceedings of the Illinois and Ouabache Land Companies* (1796), 31–36. The shareholders included an affidavit from George Croghan, dated Oct. 20, 1781, that states that the Six Nations never claimed lands occupied by the Piankeshaws and Illinois. Ibid., 43–44.

75. Illinois and Wabash Land Company, *Memorial of the Illinois and Wabash Land Company* (1797), 8.

76. *Annals of Congress*, 6:2064, 4th Cong., 2nd Sess. (House committee report, Feb. 3, 1797), 6:1551–52 (Senate adoption of committee report, Feb. 16, 1797); *ASP: Public Lands*, 1:73 (Feb. 16, 1797); and Robertson, *Conquest by Law*, 22.

77. Illinois and Wabash Land Company, *Memorial of the Illinois and Ouabache Land Companies to the Honourable Congress of the United States* (1802), 20 ("*Survivors* of the Committee," emphasis added).

78. Marcus, *Colonial American Jew*, 3:1299; Rush, *Letters of Benjamin Rush*, 2:714 (letter to Mrs. Rush, Oct. 13, 1793); and Simonhoff, *Jewish Notables*, 40. On March 21, 1793, Franks sold his stake in the company to Michael Gratz for 500 Spanish milled dollars. Stern, *David Franks*, 172.

79. IWC Minutes, 101 (Dec. 18, 1786).

80. McBee, *Natchez Court Records*, 63, 115, 116, 147, 153, 192, 272, 279 (references to Murray as plantation owner and *alcalde*, or Spanish justice of the peace). Murray's estate was valued at $2,862. His will also provided for Anna Maria Rumsey, presumably the wife or daughter of James Rumsey. McBee, *Natchez Court Records*, 120–21; and Stern, *David Franks*, 89.

81. Madison, *Papers*, 3:344 (Daniel Murray); and Tachau, *Federal Courts in the Early Republic*, 44, 69–70 (William Murray, Jr.).

82. Campbell, *Lord Chancellors*, 7:49, 78–99.

83. Conrad-Alexandre Gérard, the first French minister to America, died on April 16, 1790. His brother subsequently corresponded with Thomas Jefferson regarding the Illinois and Wabash Land Company. Jefferson informed him that the claim lacked merit. Meng, *Despatches*, 122, 917; and Jefferson, *Writings*, 8:19–21 (letter, Mar. 20, 1801).

84. Drinker, *Diary*, 2:1020 (Apr. 10, 1798); and Wharton, "Wharton Family," 457.

85. Fish, *Barnard and Michael Gratz*, 174. Rachel Gratz was Solomon Etting's second wife; his first wife, a daughter of Joseph Simon, had died in 1790. Another daughter of Simon, Miriam, married Michael Gratz in 1769 and was therefore Rachel (Gratz) Etting's aunt. Ashton, *Gratz*, diagram of the Gratz family tree, after page 12.

86. Joseph Simon, the father-in-law of Michael Gratz and Levy Andrew Levy, began business in Lancaster in 1742 and was likely present in 1744 when Thomas Lee met with the Iroquois and negotiated a land cession. John Steinmetz, a Philadelphia merchant and shipowner, was the great-grandfather of Union General George McClellan, the Democratic nominee for president in 1864.

87. *ASP: Public Lands*, 1:161 (Oct. 17, 1803, Illinois-Wabash memorial, emphasis added); Miller, *Irish Immigrants in the Land of Canaan*, 299; and Selby, *Dunmore*, 74.

88. Haw et al., *Stormy Patriot*, 156–57.

89. Steiner, *James McHenry*, 273–74 (letter from Chase, Dec. 10, 1797).

90. IWC Minutes, 176–84 (Feb. 4, 1809).

91. Delaplaine, *Thomas Johnson, Maryland and the Constitution*, 464, 470, 497; Adams, *Maryland's Influence*, 181; Hoffman, "Charles Carroll," 467–69; and Bickford et al., *First Federal Congress*, 15:536 (letter from Senator Paine Wingate to Jeremy Belknap, May 12, 1789).

92. Maryland State Archives, M4708-3577 (deed, dated Apr. 28, 1810, from Johnson to Carroll).

93. Fish, *Barnard and Michael Gratz*, 175–76.

94. Robertson, *Conquest by Law*, 32.

CHAPTER 12. CESSION, RESISTANCE, AND REMOVAL

1. Baer, "William Henry Harrison and the Indian Treaty Land Cessions," 168.

2. Calhoun, *Papers of John C. Calhoun*, 3:342 (Dec. 5, 1818).

3. Cayton, *Frontier Indiana*, 167–75; and Goebel, *Harrison*, 14–37.

4. See 2 Stat. 58–59 (May 7, 1800).

5. Harrison, *Papers of William Henry Harrison*, reel 1:381 (*Gazette*, Oct. 15, 1805).

6. Bulloch, *Territorial Soldiering*, 114–18; Alvord, *Cahokia Records*, 2:510; and Askin, *John Askin Papers*, 1:279, 293, 308, 328.

7. Askin, *John Askin Papers*, 1:344, 477 (correspondence between McIntosh and Askin); Buell, *Memoirs of Rufus Putnam*, 362, 366 n.1 (Putnam's treaty); Harrison, *Messages and Letters*, 1:23–24 (letter "with great Regard" to McIntosh, Apr. 3, 1801), 509–10 (letter to Secretary of War William Eustis, Apr. 23, 1811, describing the slander suit); and Robertson, *Conquest by Law*, 51–52.

8. 1 Stat. 743, 749 (Mar. 3, 1799); and Harrison, *Messages and Letters*, 1:26 (letter to Henry Dearborn, July 15, 1801).

9. Harrison, *Messages and Letters*, 1:28 (letter to Dearborn, July 15, 1801, "intoxicated," 25–31 (hunting).

10. Carter, *Territorial Papers*, 7:46–47 (letter from Dearborn to Harrison, Jan. 23, 1802, "considered"); and Harrison, *Messages and Letters*, 1:41 (letter to Dearborn, Feb. 26, 1802, "extensive").

11. Harrison, *Messages and Letters*, 1:41–46 (letter to Dearborn, Feb. 26, 1802).

12. Carter, *Territorial Papers*, 7:53–54 (letter from Dearborn to Harrison, June 17, 1802). See also Bayard, *Development of the Public Land Policy*, 197 ("Dearborn recommended that Harrison might try to obtain Piankashaw and Kickapoo recognition of their cession to the Illinois-Wabash Land Company. This recommendation was made at the same time that the central government was refusing to recognize this claim").

13. Erney, *Dearborn*, 258; and Wright, *Britain and the American Frontier*, 131.

14. Carter, *Territorial Papers*, 7:53 (letter, from Dearborn to Harrison June 17, 1802, "disposition"); Harrison, *Messages and Letters*, 1:547 (address to Indian council); and Carter, *Territorial Papers*, 7:69–70 (letter from Jefferson to Dearborn, Aug. 12, 1802).

15. Smith, "Indian Land Cessions," 126 n.42 ("Dawson gives the only account of this phase of the council"); and Libby, *Piankashaw and Kaskaskia*, 216 (Dawson was "an apologist for Harrison").

16. Dawson, *Historical Narrative*, 25–26 (emphasis added).

17. Harrison, *Messages and Letters*, 56 (agreement with the Eel River, Kaskaskia, Kickapoo, Piankeshaw, Potawotami, and Wea, Sept. 17, 1802).

18. Dawson, *Historical Narrative*, 27; and Horsman, *Expansion*, 144.

19. *Journal of the Executive Proceedings of the Senate*, 7th Cong., 2nd Sess., 441 (Feb. 4, 1803, Harrison's commission); Horsman, *Expansion*, 144–45 (describing a letter, dated Feb. 21, 1802, from Dearborn to Harrison); and Carter, *Territorial Papers*, 7:91–92 (letter from Jefferson to Harrison, Feb. 27, 1803).

20. Harrison, *Messages and Letters*, 1:78 (letter to Dearborn, Mar. 3, 1803, "falsehood"); Treaty with the Delawares, etc., 7 Stat. 74, June 7, 1803; and Treaty with the Eel River, etc., 7 Stat. 77, Aug. 7, 1803.

21. Treaty with the Kaskaskia, 7 Stat. 78, Aug. 13, 1803.

22. Jefferson, *Writings*, 3:352–54 (message to Congress, Oct. 17, 1803); 2 Stat. 277–83 (Mar. 26, 1804); and Robertson, *Conquest by Law*, 25.

23. Harrison, *Messages and Letters*, 1:101 (letter from Dearborn, June 27, 1804); and Sugden, *Tecumseh*, 23, 53, 168.

24. 2 Stat. 59 (May 7, 1800).

25. Robertson, *Conquest by Law*, 25.

26. Purcell, "Survey of Early Newspapers," 360 (*Indiana Gazette*, Aug. 27, 1804); Cayton, *Frontier Indiana*, 236–37 (McIntosh-Parke debate); and Dunn, Jr., *Indiana: Redemption from Slavery*, 305 (slavery issue). See also Chernow, *Hamilton*, 18 ("impertinent puppy" were "fighting words that prompted duels").

27. Treaty with the Delawares, 7 Stat. 81, Aug. 18, 1804; and Treaty with the Piankeshaws, 7 Stat. 83, Aug. 27, 1804. In addition to relinquishing their claim, the Piankeshaws acknowledged "the right of the Kaskaskia tribe to sell the country which they have lately ceded to the United States." In return, the

Piankeshaws received an annuity of two hundred dollars for ten years and goods valued at seven hundred dollars.

28. Rodriguez, *Louisiana Purchase*, 437 (Jefferson's message to Congress, Nov. 8, 1804).

29. Patterson, *Black Hawk's Autobiography*, 27; and Davis, *Frontier Illinois*, 119.

30. Harrison, *Papers of William Henry Harrison, 1800–1815*, reel 2:79 (letter from Dearborn, Jan. 17, 1805), 2:200 (letter to Dearborn, May 27, 1805).

31. Treaty with the Delawares, etc., 7 Stat. 91, Aug. 21, 1805.

32. Carter, *Territorial Papers*, 7:302 (letter from Harrison to Jefferson, Aug. 29, 1805, emphasis added).

33. Harrison, *Messages and Letters*, 1:181 (letter to Dearborn, Dec. 24, 1805).

34. Wallace, *Jefferson and the Indians*, 232 (message to Congress, Dec. 3, 1805); Harrison, *Messages and Letters*, 1:184 (letter to Dearborn, Jan. 1, 1806); Treaty with the Piankeshaws, 7 Stat. 100, Dec. 30, 1805; Edmunds, *Potawatomis*, 156; and Libby, *Piankashaw and Kaskaskia*, 241–43.

35. Sugden, *Tecumseh*, 44.

36. Ibid., 119, 144–45; and Dowd, *Spirited Resistance*, 124–32, 141.

37. Wallace, *Jefferson and the Indians*, 232–34; Harrison, *Messages and Letters*, 1:183 (message, written "early in 1806," to the Delawares); Harrison, *Papers of William Henry Harrison, 1800–1815*, reel 2:518–22 (noting that Harrison's message to the Delaware was referred to in the April 12, 1806, edition of the Vincennes *Gazette*). See also Edmunds, "Tecumseh, the Shawnee Prophet, and American History," 269 (discussing how the Prophet may have learned of the eclipse).

38. Harrison, *Messages and Letters*, 1:290 (letter to Dearborn, May 19, 1808, "imposter"); and Harrison, *Papers of William Henry Harrison, 1800–1815*, reel 3:228 (letter to Dearborn, Sept. 1, 1808, "celebrated").

39. Houck, *History of Missouri*, 3:257 (eulogy); Harrison, *Messages and Letters*, 1:297 (letter to Jefferson, July 16, 1808), 112 (letter to Gallatin, Aug. 29, 1809).

40. Carter, *Territorial Papers*, 8:94–101; and Rohrbough, *Land Office Business*, 33 (Circular to Land Offices, Apr. 30, 1808).

41. Harrison, *Papers of William Henry Harrison, 1800–1815*, reel 3:79–85 (letter to Secretary of War William Eustis, May 16, 1809, assertion); and Harrison, *Messages and Letters*, 356–57 (letter from Eustis, July 15, 1809, Madison).

42. Harrison, *Papers of William Henry Harrison, 1800–1815*, reel 3:504; and Sugden, *Tecumseh*, 182–83.

43. Treaty with the Delawares, at Fort Wayne, 7 Stat. 113, Sept. 30, 1809; Supplemental Treaty with the Miami and Eel River Indians, at Fort Wayne, 7 Stat. 115, Sept. 30, 1809; Treaty with the Weas, at Vincennes, 7 Stat. 116, Oct. 26, 1809; and Treaty with the Kickapoos, at Vincennes, 7 Stat. 117, Dec. 9, 1809.

44. Sugden, *Tecumseh*, 185; Thornbrough, *Badollet and Gallatin*, 116–17 (letter from Badollet to Gallatin, Nov. 13, 1809); and Harrison, *Papers of William Henry Harrison, 1800–1815*, reel 3:135.

45. Carter, *Territorial Papers*, 8:29 (meeting); and Harrison, *Papers of William Henry Harrison, 1800–1815*, reel 4:122, 193–95 (lawsuit).

46. Harrison, *Messages and Letters*, 1:448 (message to Tenskwatawa, July 19, 1810); and Harrison, *Messages and Letters*, 1:460 (letter to Eustis, Aug. 22, 1810, describing the encounter).

47. Harrison, *Messages and Letters*, 1:461 (letter to Eustis, Aug. 22, 1810, "tense moment"), 468 ("fill the minds"); Carter, *Little Turtle*, 192–93; and Dawson, *Historical Narrative*, 158–59.

48. Harrison, *Messages and Letters*, 1:462 (letter to Eustis, Aug. 22, 1810), 491 (message to the territorial legislature, Nov. 12, 1810).

49. United States, Record Group 107, Secretary of War/Letters Received/ Registered Series, microfilm M 221, National Archives, reel 38:5285 (letter from McIntosh to Madison, Sept. 3, 1810); Carter, *Territorial Papers*, 8:76–85 (letter from John Eppes to Robert Smith, Jan., 1811, with depositions supporting Harrison), 87–102 (letter to Eppes, Jan. 22, 1811, with enclosures); and Cleaves, *Old Tippecanoe*, 77.

50. Robertson, *Conquest by Law*, 53 and 196 n.21.

51. Harrison, *Messages and Letters*, 1:509–10 (letter to Eustis, Apr. 23, 1811). See also Harrison, *Papers of William Henry Harrison, 1800–1815*, reel 4:193–95, 449, 457, 464–65, 476; and Cleaves, *Old Tippecanoe*, 77.

52. Carter, *Little Turtle*, 212; and Harrison, *Messages and Letters*, 544 (letter to Eustis, Aug. 6, 1811).

53. Sugden, *Tecumseh*, 228–36; and Woolen, *Biographical and Historical Sketches*, 385, 398 (Randolph and Parke).

54. Derleth, *Vincennes*, 181; and Mahon, *War of 1812*, 27.

55. Harrison, *Papers of William Henry Harrison, 1800–1815*, reel 5:386 (poem by James Shannon of St. Clairsville, Ohio, published in the Vincennes *Western Sun*, Feb. 22, 1812, emphasis added).

56. Harrison, *Messages and Letters*, 1:492–93 (Harrison's annual message, Nov. 12, 1810); and Eisinger, "Puritan's Justification," 373 (oration by John Quincy Adams, Dec. 22, 1802).

57. Konkle, *Thomas Williams*, 1:154 (eulogy delivered before the Pennsylvania legislature, Apr. 17, 1841).

58. Burton, *Manuscripts*, 129 (letter from Michael Jones to Harrison, May 4, 1804); and Ibid., 130 (letter from Harrison to Col. Pierre Menard, May 18, 1804).

59. Harrison, *Messages and Letters*, 1:277 (letter from John Gibson to William Hargrove, Nov. 18, 1807).

60. Harrison, *Papers of William Henry Harrison, 1800–1815*, reel 3:345 (letter from John Gibson to William Hargrove, Nov. 12, 1807); and Harrison, *Messages and Letters*, 1:424–25 (letter to Eustis, June 14, 1810).

61. Harrison, *Papers of William Henry Harrison, 1800–1815*, reel 4:414 (letter to William Eustis, July 25, 1810, relaying information from Ninian Edwards), 4:614 (letter to Ninian Edwards, dated July 4, 1811).

62. Ibid., reel 5:309 (letter to Eustis, Jan. 29, 1812), 5:487–88 (letter to Eustis, Apr. 14, 1812).

63. Libby, *Piankashaw and Kaskaskia*, 286; Sugden, *Tecumseh*, 322–23; and Mahon, *War of 1812*, 67.

64. Libby, *Piankashaw and Kaskaskia*, 251.

65. Mahon, *War of 1812*, 175; and Starkey, *European and Native American Warfare*, 163. Perry prevailed on September 10, 1813.

66. Treaty with the Wyandots, etc., 7 Stat. 18, July 22, 1814; *ASP: Foreign Relations*, 3:709 (report of the commissioners to Monroe, Aug. 19, 1814), 712 (reply of the American commissioners to the British, Aug. 24, 1814).

67. *ASP: Foreign Relations*, 3:716 (reply of the American commissioners, Sept. 9, 1814).

68. Ibid., 724 (reply of the American commissioners, Oct. 13, 1814).

69. Foreman, "Illinois and Her Indians," 83. In August of 1814 Monroe became secretary of war as well as secretary of state.

70. Harrison, *Messages and Letters*, 2:671 (letter from Parke to Thomas Posey, Nov. 18, 1814); Ekberg, *Colonial Ste. Genevieve*, 113; and Treaty with the Peoria, etc., 7 Stat. 181, Sept. 25, 1818. Thomas Posey was appointed in 1813 to serve as governor of the Indiana Territory.

71. *ASP: Indian Affairs*, 2:8 (letter to Monroe from Clark, Edwards, and Chouteau, July 16, 1815, "day or two"); and Treaty with the Piankeshaws, 7 Stat. 124, July 18, 1815.

72. *ASP: Indian Affairs*, 2:10 (letter to Monroe from Clark, Edwards, and Chouteau, Oct. 18, 1815).

73. Kappler, *Indian Affairs: Laws and Treaties*, 2:1031–32 (Agreement with the Piankeshaws, Jan. 3, 1818). The agreement was never ratified.

74. Monroe, *Writings*, 6:40 (First Annual Message to Congress, Dec. 2, 1817); and Treaty with the Peorias, etc., 7 Stat. 181, Sept. 25, 1818.

75. Foreman, *Last Trek*, 35 (letter from Clark to Calhoun, Mar. 27, 1819).

76. Warren, *Shawnees and Their Neighbors*, 87.

77. Foreman, *Indians and Pioneers*, 188.

Chapter 13. The Shareholders Regroup

1. Robertson, *Conquest by Law*, 23, 26.

2. Illinois and Wabash Land Company, *Memorial of the Ilinois and Ouabache Land Companies to the Honourable Congress of the United States* (1802); *Annals of Congress* 11:199, 7th Cong., 1st Sess. (Senate), and 11:1163, 7th Cong., 1st Sess. (House of Representatives); and Robertson, *Conquest by Law*, 24–25.

3. *ASP: Public Lands*, 1:160 (Oct. 17, 1803, communication of John Shee to the House of Representatives).

4. *ASP: Public Lands*, 1:189 (Feb. 14, 1804, (committee report, emphasis added). See also *Journal of the House of Representatives*, 8th Cong., 1st Sess. 577 (Feb. 14, 1804, petition "ought not be granted").

5. 34 *JCC* 270–71 (June 27, 1788); *ASP: Public Lands*, 1:27 (Apr. 3, 1792); and Gratz Family of Philadelphia Papers (letter from Jacob Gratz to Joseph Gratz, Hamburg, Germany, July 4, 1810).

6. Robertson, *Conquest by Law*, 25.

7. 2 Stat. 278–279 (Mar. 26, 1804).

8. Robertson, *Conquest by Law*, 26–27.

9. Cox, *Champion*, 7.

10. Fischer, "Harper," 6–10; Sommerville, *Harper*, 5–7; and Cox, *Champion*, 20–23.

11. Cox, *Champion*, 23; Madison, *Papers*, 15:380 (letter to Jefferson, Nov. 16, 1794); and Sommerville, *Harper*, 11 (letter from Ames to Christopher Gore, July 28, 1798).

12. Cox, *Champion*, ix; Papenfuse, *Evils of Necessity*, back cover; and Fischer, *Revolution of American Conservatism*, 36–37.

13. Arbuckle, *Pennsylvania Speculator*, 172; and Wilkinson, *Land Policy*, 180–93.

14. Harper, *Case of the Georgia Sales on the Mississippi Considered*, 1–2, 26. See also 107–109 (Hamilton's opinion).

15. Illinois and Wabash Land Company, *Memorial of the United Illinois and Wabash Land Companies, to the Senate and House of Representatives of the United States*, 1810, 23–24 (hereafter cited as *1810 Memorial*).

16. Fischer, "Harper," 95 (noting that the Philadelphia *Aurora*, on February 4, 1799, erroneously reported that Harper owed $17,000, when in fact he owed $13,450, a smaller but still "staggering figure"); and Cox, *Champion*, 172.

17. Harper exchanged words in 1800 with John Francis Mercer, who accused him of being a "houseless adventurer" who was wooing Catherine Carroll for her father's fortune. Harper challenged Mercer to a duel, but the men later exchanged mutual apologies. Fischer, "Harper," 103.

18. Cox, *Champion*, 197 n.1, 208–11; and Sommerville, *Harper*, 24–25.

19. Hoffman, *Princes of Ireland*, 389; Marks, *Guide to Harper Family Papers*, 8; and Mason, "Charles Carroll," 31–32.

20. Cox, *Champion*, 213 (furniture); Hamilton, "Harper," 286; Marks, *Guide to Harper Family Papers*, 5; and Scharf, *Chronicles*, 295–96.

21. Cassell, "Structure of Baltimore's Politics," 286 (1804 election); Smith, *Marshall*, 14–15; Newmyer, *Marshall and the Heroic Age*, 128–29; and Forte, "Marbury's Travail," 353.

22. Hall, *Magic Mirror*, 80; and Simon, *What Kind of Nation*, 148.

23. *Marbury v. Madison*, 5 U.S. 137, 178 (Feb. 24, 1803); and Jefferson, *Writings*, 8:311 (letter to Abigail Adams, Sept. 11, 1804).

24. Haw et al., *Stormy Patriot*, 215–16 (Philadelphia *Aurora*, May 27, 1803, "monster"), 208 (Chase denouncing Jefferson as an atheist); Jefferson, *Writings*, 10:390 (letter to Joseph Nicholson, May 13, 1803); Horsnell, "Chase," 744; and Elsmere, *Justice Samuel Chase*, vii.

25. Appleby, *Jefferson*, 97 (witticism); and Haw et al., *Stormy Patriot*, 238 (speech).

26. Smith, *Marshall*, 346 (quoting from a letter, dated Mar. 3, 1805, from William Plumer to Daniel Plumer); Baxter, *Webster*, 29; and *Ex Parte Bollman*, 8 U.S. 75 (1807).

27. 2 Stat. 278–79 (Mar. 26, 1804).

28. Davis, *Frontier Illinois*, 120; and Esarey, *History of Indiana*, 150–52.

29. Carter, *Territorial Papers*, 7:220; and Fish, *Barnard and Michael Gratz*, 175 (describing a similar notice published in April 1805 in the *General Advertiser Aurora*).

30. Purcell, "Survey of Early Newspapers," 360 (*Indiana Gazette*, Aug. 27, 1804).

31. Thornbrough, *Badollet and Gallatin*, 47–48 (letter from Badollet to Gallatin, Aug. 31, 1805), 51 (letter from Gallatin to Badollet, Oct. 25, 1805); and Carter, *Territorial Papers*, 7:312 (letter from Gallatin to Badollet, Oct. 23, 1805, emphasis added).

32. *ASP: Public Lands*, 1:279 (Mar. 25, 1806); and Robertson, *Conquest by Law*, 26.

33. 2 Stat. 446–48 (Mar. 3, 1807); Carter, *Territorial Papers*, 7:445 (letter from Gallatin to Jones, Mar. 28, 1807); *ASP: Public Lands*, 2:102 (commissioners' general report, Feb. 24, 1810), 113–14, 165–66 (list of rejected claims, Dec. 31, 1809).

34. 2 Stat. 677–78 (Feb. 20, 1812, action on Kaskaskia report); and Robertson, "*Johnson v. M'Intosh*," 79, citing Illinois and Wabash Collection (letter from Benjamin Stoddert to Solomon Etting, Feb. 28, 1810, setting forth the views of Harper).

35. For insight into this case and its "feigned" structure, see Robertson, "'A Mere Feigned Case,'" and Robertson, *Conquest by Law*, 31–36.

36. Ibid., 35, citing Magrath, *Yazoo*, 69.

37. *Fletcher v. Peck*, 10 U.S. at 139. See also Article I, section 10, clause 1 (Contract Clause); and *Sturges v. Crowninshield*, 17 U.S. 122, 151 (1819, statement by Marshall that Wilson was "the author" of the Contract Clause).

38. *Fletcher*, 10 U.S. at 142, 146–47 (emphasis added); and Williams, Jr., *American Indian in Western Legal Thought*, 309.

39. Compare Treaty with the Cherokees, 7 Stat. 18, Nov. 28, 1785; Treaty with the Choctaws, 7 Stat. 21, Jan. 3, 1786; and Treaty with the Chickasaws, 7 Stat. 24, Jan. 10, 1786; with Treaty with the Creeks, 7 Stat. 35, Aug. 7, 1790.

40. Jefferson, *Writings*, 3:20 (opinion, dated May 3, 1790); *ASP: Indian Affairs*, 1:112 (Proclamation, Aug. 25, 1790); and Washington, *Diaries*, 4:196 (June 4, 1791).

41. Robertson, *Conquest by Law*, 108–109, citing Jefferson, *Papers*, 22:27 (letter to Knox, Aug. 10, 1791); and Jefferson, *Writings*, 1:340 (Feb. 26, 1793, emphasis added).

42. *ASP: Indian Affairs*, 1:356 (reply of the confederated tribes to the Commissioners of the United States, dated Aug. 13, 1793, and received Aug 16, 1793).

43. *Annals of Congress*, 4:844, 3rd Cong., 2nd Sess. (Senate resolution), 1278 (Ames), 1279 (Harper).

44. Haskins and Johnson, *Foundations of Power*, 341; and Haskins, *Yazoo Land Companies*, 88. The Georgia Mississippi Company purchased the lands for approximately one and one-half cents per acre. Magrath, *Yazoo*, 15.

45. Carter, *Territorial Papers*, 5:79–80 (committee report, March 2, 1797); 1 Stat. 549–50 (Act of Apr. 7, 1798); and Carter, *Territorial Papers*, 5:18–22.

46. Carter, *Territorial Papers*, 5:142–44.

47. *ASP: Public Lands*, 1:122 (report of the commissioners, Feb. 16, 1803), 128 (list of Georgia Company shareholders); and 2 Stat. 229, 232 (Act of Mar. 3, 1803). The federal commissioners were Secretary of State James Madison, Secretary of the Treasury Albert Gallatin, and Attorney General Levi Lincoln.

48. *Annals of Congress*, 14:1029, 8th Cong., 2nd Sess. (Jan. 29, 1805, Representative John Randolph of Virginia, "had no right"), 13:1039, 8th Cong., 1st Sess. (February 20, 1804, Randolph, "inalienable right"); and Magrath, *Yazoo*, 168 (Bishop, emphasis added).

49. *Annals of Congress*, 14:1032, 8th Cong., 2nd Sess. (Jan. 29, 1805); *Annals of Congress*, 13:1039–40, 8th Cong., 1st Sess. (Feb. 20, 1804, Randolph's resolutions); and Malone, *Jefferson and His Time*, 4:246–48.

50. *Annals of Congress*, 14:1046–47, 8th Cong., 2nd Sess. (Jan. 30, 1805, Lucas),and (Jan. 31, 1805, Findlay); and *Annals of Congress*, 15:921, 9th Cong., 1st Sess. (Mar. 29, 1806, Randolph).

51. Robertson, "'Feigned Case,'" 259; and Magrath, *Yazoo*, 51–53. In 1807 Congress enacted legislation that prevented the claimants from entering upon the Yazoo lands to try their title. 2 Stat. 445–46 (Mar. 3, 1807).

52. *Fletcher v. Peck*, 10 U.S. at 127.

53. Magrath, *Yazoo*, 68; McClellan, *Justice Story*, 36–37; *Martin v. Hunter's Lessee*, 14 U.S. 304 (1816); and *United States v. The Amistad*, 40 U.S. 518 (1841).

54. Magrath, *Yazoo*, 69; Newmyer, *Marshall and the Heroic Age*, 227 ("single substantive point"); and *Fletcher v. Peck*, 10 U.S. at 115 ("devolved").

55. *Fletcher v. Peck*, 10 U.S. at 116–20 (argument of Harper and Story), 121–23 ("*mere privilege*," emphasis added).

56. Ibid., 123.

57. Ibid., 139.

58. Ibid., 142–43.

59. Story, *Life and Letters of Joseph Story*, 168 (letter to Samuel Fay, Feb. 25, 1808); Hunt, "Office-Seeking," 282 (Jefferson memorandum, Feb. 17, 1804); Newmyer, *Marshall and the Heroic Age*, 404; Morgan, "William Johnson," 359; and Magrath, *Yazoo*, 63.

60. *Fletcher*, 10 U.S. at 143–49 (emphasis added).

61. Ball, "Constitution, Court, Indian Tribes," 39 n.171; and Kent, *Commentaries*, 3:378 note (c).

62. *Annals of Congress*, 27:643, 13th Cong., 2nd Sess. (Feb. 28, 1814).

63. Ibid., 27:1839, 13th Cong., 2nd Sess. (Mar. 8, 1814).

64. Ibid., 25:1069–71, 12th Cong., 2nd Sess. (Feb. 15, 1813, John Adams Harper of New Hampshire).

65. 3 Stat. 116–20 (Mar. 31, 1814).

66. See Robertson, *Conquest by Law*, 32–34.

67. Robertson, *Conquest by Law*, 34, citing Illinois and Wabash Collection (letter from Harper to Brinton and Gratz, Jan. 26, 1810).

68. Robertson, "*Johnson v. M'Intosh*," 74, citing Illinois and Wabash Collection (letter from Etting to Gratz, Jan. 26, 1810; emphasis added).

69. Thornbrough, *Badollet and Gallatin*, 149 (letter from Badollet to Gallatin, May 29, 1810). Although no lawsuit was filed in 1810 or 1811, Badollet continued to inform Gallatin of his suspicions that Harrison and his supporters were preparing for litigation. In September 1810 Badollet suggested to Gallatin that the 1809 treaties negotiated by Harrison were somehow connected to the Illinois-Wabash claims. Ibid., 168–69 (letter from Badollet to Gallatin, Sept. 25, 1810). Badollet also stated that "hundreds of the Pamphlets containing the Indian deeds, petitions to, & reports of Committees, Congress and other documents, relative to that gigantic claim," were being distributed by a Harrison supporter, presumably "to create in the public a prejudice in favour of the claimants & to prepare thus before hand a propitious Jury," 169.

70. IWC Minutes, Mar. 5, 1810, in Fish, *Barnard and Michael Gratz*, 176–77 n.80 ("prosecute the claims"). The 1801 Judiciary Act had created a new federal circuit that included the Indiana Territory and provided for appeals to the Supreme Court. 2 Stat. 89, 98–99 (Feb. 13, 1801). However, the circuit was abolished when the 1801 Act was repealed by the Seventh Congress. 2 Stat. 156 (Apr. 29, 1802). In 1803 Congress considered allowing writs of error and appeals from territorial courts to the Supreme Court but took no action after a House committee recommended against the proposal. *Annals of Congress*, 14:1577–79, 8th Cong., 1st Sess. (Dec. 29, 1803). In the spring of 1810 there was once again a bill before Congress to provide for appeals from the territorial courts to the Supreme Court, but the bill did not pass. Robertson, *Conquest by Law*, 36.

71. Robertson, *Conquest by Law*, 35.

72. Gratz Family of Philadelphia Papers (letter from Jacob Gratz to Joseph Gratz, Hamburg, Germany, July 4, 1810).

73. For examination of this memorial as precedent for Harper's Supreme Court strategy, see Robertson, *Conquest by Law*, 36–39.

74. *1810 Memorial*, 6–7.

75. Ibid., 9–10 (Iroquois claim), 14 (1803 and 1805 cessions).

76. Ibid., 29 (emphasis added).

77. *Annals of Congress*, 15:301, 9th Cong., 1st Sess. (Dec. 23, 1805); *ASP: Public Lands*, 1:229 (report on Clark's petition, dated Dec. 23, 1805, by the Committee on Public Lands); and *ASP: Public Lands*, 1:533 (report of the House Committee on Public Lands, dated Feb. 17, 1807, on the application by George Ash to confirm an Indian grant). Although the conveyance was declared void, Congress granted Ash the right to purchase 640 acres, encompassing the land he settled.

78. *1810 Memorial*, 15–16.

79. Ibid., 16 (emphasis added).

80. Ibid., 20.

81. Ibid., 20 ("authority to restrain"); and Harper, *Case of the Georgia Sales on the Mississippi Considered*, 23.

82. *1810 Memorial*, 23.

83. The 1810 memorial notes that "eminent lawyers," "informed merchants," and the Earl of Dunmore were among the purchasers and that such men "cannot

be supposed to have been ignorant of what was the law and practice of the British Government, on a subject of so much importance, where they were about to expend such large sums of money." *1810 Memorial*, 24. These men were not ignorant of the prohibition against private purchases; rather, they proceeded despite such constraints.

84. Jensen, *American Colonial Documents*, 642 (1763 Proclamation, emphasis added); and *1810 Memorial*, 26–27.

85. *1810 Memorial*, 30 (settlement proposal). The interest from the debt certificates, and the principal, would be extinguished "out of the funds to arise from such parts of the lands included in both deeds, as the United States shall first sell."

86. Robertson, *"Johnson v. M'Intosh,"* 91–92, citing Illinois and Wabash Collection (letter from Daniel Hiester to John Brinton, dated Dec. 21, 1810).

87. *ASP: Public Lands*, 2:219–20 (report of the House Committee on Public Lands, Jan. 30, 1811); Illinois and Wabash Collection (letter from Solomon Etting to Simon Gratz and John Brinton, Feb. 22, 1811); and Robertson, *Conquest by Law*, 42, citing Gratz Family of Philadelphia Papers (letter from Jacob Gratz to Joseph Gratz, Mar. 10, 1811).

CHAPTER 14. LITIGATION

1. Carter, *Territorial Papers*, 17:235.

2. Thornbrough, *Badollet and Gallatin*, 205 (letter from Badollet to Gallatin, Nov. 6, 1811).

3. Wharton, *Social Life in the Early Republic*, 135 ("perfumed"); Sommerville, *Harper*, 27 (Harper's speech, Feb. 22, 1810, to the Washington Society of Alexandria); Harper, *Select Works*; and Cox, *Champion*, 164.

4. Warren, *History of the American Bar*, 260; White, *History of the Supreme Court*, 3:289; and *Fairfax's Devisee v. Hunter's Lessee*, 11 U.S. 603 (1812).

5. Mahon, *War of 1812*, 300–301; Scharf, *Chronicles*, 351; and Fischer, "Harper," 154.

6. For an analysis of the companies' wartime hiatus and particular reasons for resumption, see Robertson, *Conquest by Law*, 41.

7. See http://www.ilsos.gov/GenealogyMWeb/landsrch.html (Illinois Public Domain Land Tract Sales Database). The fifty-three tracts are in Jackson, Randolph, Perry, Monroe, and St. Clair counties.

8. Meyer, *Heartland Quilt*, 116; Buck, *Illinois in 1818*, 97; Cunliffe, *Nation Takes Shape*, 86 ("land-office business"); and Norton, *Illinois Census Returns*, 59.

9. Robertson, *Conquest by Law*, 41; and Robertson, *"Johnson v. M'Intosh,"* 100–101, citing Illinois and Wabash Collection (letter from Law to Henry Hurst, Oct. 25, 1815).

10. Robertson, *Conquest by Law*, 41, citing Illinois and Wabash Collection (letter from Harper to Solomon Etting, Dec. 28, 1815).

11. Illinois and Wabash Land Company, *Memorial of the United Illinois and Wabash Land Companies to the Senate and House of Representatives of the United States* (1816), 48 (emphasis added).

12. Fischer, "Harper," 157–61; and Robertson, *Conquest by Law*, 42, citing Illinois and Wabash Collection (letter from John Brinton, Simon Gratz, and Callender Irvine to Harper and Solomon Etting, Feb. 28, 1816).

13. Robertson, *Conquest by Law*, 42–43.

14. Sommerville, *Harper*, 30; Papenfuse, *Evils of Necessity*, 55; Cox, *Champion*, 144; and Robertson, *Conquest by Law*, 43.

15. Fischer, "Harper," 168–69.

16. Ashton, *Gratz*, 17, 41–42; Friedenberg, *Pursuit of Land*, 376 n.11; and Osterweis, *Gratz*, 135–36.

17. Robertson, *Conquest by Law*, 49–50.

18. Benjamin Gratz Papers, American Jewish Historical Society, Waltham, Mass. (letter from Benjamin Gratz, Louisville, to unknown recipient, Feb. 8, 1819).

19. Faux, *Memorable Days*, 214 (entry for Oct. 1819, "dirty village"); and Philipson, *Letters of Rebecca Gratz*, 18 (letter to Benjamin Gratz, Mar. 24, 1819).

20. Rush, *Letters of Benjamin Rush*, 2:1018 (describing Ingersoll); Benjamin Gratz Papers (Ingersoll to Gratz, Mar. 20, 1819).

21. 3 Stat. 503 (Mar. 3, 1819). Nathaniel Pope's son, John, would command Union forces during the Civil War and suppress the Sioux Indians during the Dakota War of 1862.

22. Faux, *Memorable Days*, 225 (entry for Nov. 1819, "Squire M'Intosh"); and National Archives, Appellate Case Files of the Supreme Court of the United States, call no. Record Group (RG) 267, Cases 1100–1113 (Feb. 16–Mar. 8, 1821), microcopy no. 214, roll no. 56, No. 1105, frames 0409–14 (grant).

23. Rohrbough, *Land Office Business*, 131, 137; and *Tee-Hit-Ton Indians v. United States*, 348 U.S. 272, 279 (1955, "great case").

24. Robertson, *Conquest by Law*, 47–49. The statement of the case in *Johnson* mistakenly gives October 1, 1819, as the date of Johnson's death. 21 U.S. at 561 (1823).

25. Geib and Kite, *Federal Justice in Indiana*, 24; and Woolen, *Biographical and Historical Sketches*, 37, 360–63; and Robertson, *Conquest by Law*, 49 and 201 n.83.

26. Scott, *Supreme Court of Illinois*, 286–87.

27. Friedman, *History of American Law*, 18–19. See also Robertson, *Conquest by Law*, 53–54.

28. See Kades, "Dark Side," 1092 (arguing there is no overlap of the 1775 purchase and the lands purchased by McIntosh). By its terms, the lower Wabash purchase extended 75 leagues westward from the Wabash River where it meets the White River and the Ohio River. Because a French league is measured at 2.422 miles, or approximately 2.5 miles, it appears that the 1775 purchase did in fact encompass the lands subsequently purchased by McIntosh that are situated in modern-day Perry and Jackson counties. See Wilson, "First Public Land Surveys in Indiana," 7–8 (French league). See also Robertson, *Conquest by Law*, 196 n.15 (describing the use of a French league to measure the purchases).

29. National Archives, Appellate Case Files of the Supreme Court of the United States, call no. Record Group (RG) 267, Cases 1100–1113 (Feb. 16–Mar. 8, 1821), microcopy no. 214, roll no. 56, No. 1105, frame 0344.

30. Tachau, *Federal Courts in the Early Republic*, 88.

31. Robertson, *Conquest by Law*, 58.

32. National Archives, Appellate Case Files of the Supreme Court of the United States, call no. Record Group (RG) 267, Cases 1100–1113 (Feb. 16–Mar. 8, 1821), microcopy no. 214, roll no. 56, No. 1105, frames 0350–51, and frames 0355–56 (emphasis added).

33. Ibid., frames 0361, 0378, 0402–17. Pursuant to diversity jurisdiction, federal courts were empowered to hear disputes between citizens of different states.

34. Ibid., frame 0420.

35. Robertson, *Conquest by Law*, 56 and 58.

36. Somes, *Old Vincennes*, 183; and Cauthorn, *History of Vincennes*, 67.

37. Fischer, *Revolution of American Conservatism*, 170–72; *Cohens v. Virginia*, 19 U.S. 264, 409–11 (1821).

38. National Archives, Appellate Case Files of the Supreme Court of the United States, call no. Record Group (RG) 267, Cases 1100–1113 (Feb. 16–Mar. 8, 1821), microcopy no. 214, roll no. 56, No. 1105, frame 0332; and Tyler, *Memoir of Roger Brooke Taney*, 141 (eulogy).

39. Ireland, "Pinkney," 235 (statements by Wheaton and Parsons); Wirt, *Memoirs*, 1:403 (letter to Francis Gilmer, Apr. 1, 1816), 2:807 (letter to Mrs. Wirt, Aug. 12, 1818); and Warren, *History of the American Bar*, 367 (Wirt's eulogy, May 9, 1882).

40. Haw et al., *Stormy Patriot*, 120 (Pinkney and Chase); Sterling, "Pinkney," 548; and Ireland, *Legal Career of William Pinkney*, 1, 20, 33, 201.

41. Ireland, "Pinkney," 239–44; Ireland, *Legal Career of William Pinkney*, 186–87 (Duvall); Warren, *History of the American Bar*, 380 (letter from Joseph Story, Mar. 3, 1819); and *McCulloch v. Maryland*, 17 U.S. 316, 426 (1819).

42. Warren, *History of the American Bar*, 281 (letter from Joseph Story to W. Sampson, Feb. 22, 1815, "towers"); and Sterling, "Pinkney," 548 (fee and salary figures).

43. Shapiro, "Pinkney," 43 (gloves); Davies, *Gilmer*, 108 (corset); Wirt, *Memoirs*,1:358 (letter from Wirt to Francis Gilmer, Apr. 1, 1816, "tragical"); and Faux, *Memorable Days*, 362 ("uncouth").

44. Robertson, *Conquest by Law*, 4, citing Davies, *Gilmer*, 150 (quoting a letter from Francis W. Gilmer to Judge Dabney Carr, Jan. 12, 1822).

45. According to one source, a "Francis Geo. Gilmer" of Richmond wrote to "J. Stevens, Washington" on April 17, 1820, to report that he had searched certain journals (without success) in connection with Lady Virginia Murray's efforts to recover her father's American property. Although the names do not precisely match, Francis Walker Gilmer practiced law in Richmond in 1820. See "Lady Virginia Murray," 85, 97.

46. Gunn, *New World Metaphysics*, 281 (emphasis added).

47. Ammon, *Monroe*, 474 (second inaugural address, Mar. 5, 1821).

48. Robertson, *Conquest by Law*, 60.

49. *Ricard v. Williams*, 20 U.S. 59 (1822); and Story, *Life and Letters of Joseph Story*, 1:412–13 (letter to Sarah Story, Feb. 21, 1822).

50. 5 L.Ed. 579–580 (Feb. 26, 1822, Harper's remarks, found only in Michie's Lawyers' Edition); and Shapiro, "Pinkney," 45 (armbands).

51. Robertson, "*Johnson v. M'Intosh*," 141–42, and Robertson, *Conquest by Law*, 60, 62–64, citing Illinois and Wabash Collection (letter from Edward Ingersoll to John Brinton, Feb. 26, 1822).

52. Robertson, *Conquest by Law*, 62, citing Illinois and Wabash Collection (letter from Edward Ingersoll to Simon Gratz, John Brinton, and Callender Irvine, Feb. 19, 1823).

53. Kades, "Great Case," 102 n.69; and Robertson, *Conquest by Law*, 62, 198 n.38 and 200 n.83.

54. Blakey, *Winder*, 11–13; Palmer, *Stoddert's War*, 126; and Robertson, *Conquest by Law*, 35.

55. Mahon, *War of 1812*, 103, 149, 300; Standiford, *Washington Burning*, 266–83; Scharf, *Chronicles*, 417 ("personal valor"); and Blakey, *Winder*, 27.

56. Baxter, "Daniel Webster," 865; Remini, *Webster*, 16; and Baxter, *Webster*, 1, 4.

57. *Prevost v. Gratz*, 19 U.S. 481, 482 (1821). The Court held that Simon Gratz did not engage in improper behavior when he foreclosed on and purchased certain lands of George Croghan located in central and western Pennsylvania.

58. *McCulloch v. Maryland*, 17 U.S. 316, 431 (1819); Remini, *Webster*, 163 ("turning point"), 156 (argument in *Dartmouth College,* emphasis added).

59. Remini, *Webster*, 157–58 n.84 (undated document written by Joseph Story).

60. Henderson, "Unraveling the Riddle," 98; Smith, *Appeals to Privy Council*, 434; Webster, *Papers of Daniel Webster on Microfilm*, reel 4, frame 3384 (letter from Webster to David Daggett, Dec. 30, 1822), frame 3394 (letter, dated Jan. 7, 1823, from Webster to Daggett).

61. IWC Minutes, Jan. 23, 1823; Hoffman, *Princes of Ireland*, 390; Smith, *Charles Carroll*, 302–304; Rowland, *Life of Charles Carroll*, 321; Scharf, *Chronicles*, 298, 439; "Descendants of the Rev. William Smith," 380–81; and Smith, *Life and Correspondence of the Rev. William Smith*, 2:548. See also Robertson, *Conquest by Law*, 65 and 198 n.47.

62. Lindsay Robertson discovered and drew on these diaries to construct his account of the proceedings. See esp. Robertson, *Conquest by Law*, 68–75.

63. Rodney, *Diary*, 25–27; and Meigs, *Ingersoll*, 109, 113.

64. Robertson, "*Johnson v. M'Intosh*," 148, citing Illinois and Wabash Collection (letter from Edward Ingersoll to Simon Gratz, John Brinton, and Callender Irvine, Feb. 11, 1823).

65. Ibid., 149, citing Gratz Collection, case 1, box 37, HSP (letter from Edward Ingersoll to Jacob Gratz, Feb. 13, 1823).

66. Quoted in Robertson, *Conquest by Law*, 3 and 68, citing Meigs, *Ingersoll*, 123–24 (emphasis added).

67. *Daily National Intelligencer,* Feb. 17, 1823, 3.

68. Robertson, *Conquest by Law*, citing Rodney, *Diary*, 29 (emphasis added).

CHAPTER 15. THE ARGUMENT AND DECISION IN *JOHNSON V. MCINTOSH*

1. Robertson, "*Johnson v. M'Intosh*, Brief for Appellants," 866 (emphasis added).

2. Hening, *Statutes at Large; Being a Collection of All the Laws of Virginia*, 10:97 (Act of June 19, 1779, emphasis added).

3. Robertson, *Conquest by Law*, 64.

4. *Fletcher v. Peck*, 10 U.S. at 142–43; *Meigs v. McClung's Lessee*, 13 U.S. 11, 16 (1815). Two years later Justice Story made the same point in *Gilman v. Brown*, a case argued by Daniel Webster that involved the Yazoo land claims. "That the state of Georgia was seised in fee simple, and had a capacity to convey, notwithstanding the non-extinguishment of the Indian title," Story declared in his capacity as a circuit judge, "is completely established by the case of *Fletcher v. Peck*." *Gilman v. Brown*, 10 F.Cas. 392, 399 (Circuit Court, D. Massachusetts, May Term, 1817).

5. *Bleecker v. Bond*, 3 F.Cas. 687, 692 (Circuit Court, E.D. Pennsylvania, Oct. Term 1819).

6. Anglo-American property law utilizes "future interest" terminology to describe various ways by which one can own land but lack the right of present possession. Thomas Jefferson employed one such future interest term—"remainder"—to describe the government's self-proclaimed right of preemption in Indian lands. Jefferson, *Writings*, 1:340 ("I consider our right of preemption of the Indians lands . . . in the nature of a remainder"). Stuart Banner prefers another future interest term: the "executory interest," defined as "the right to take possession of the land at some point in the future, should a particular event transpire." Banner, *How the Indians Lost Their Land*, 163. The preemption right can also be analogized to a right of first refusal or an option to purchase property. A right of first refusal is "a right to elect to take specified property at the same price and on the same terms and conditions as those contained in a good faith offer by a third person if the owner manifests a willingness to accept the offer." *Pearson v. Fulton*, 497 So.2d 898, 900 (Fla. 2nd Dist. Ct., 1986). An "option" has been described as "a privilege given by the owner of property to another to buy the property at his election." *Western Union Telegraph Co. v. Brown*, 253 U.S. 101, 110 (1920). The right of first refusal analogy suffers from the fact that—given the prohibition on private purchases—there will be no "good faith offer by a third person." An option grants the power to compel an unwilling owner to sell, which is inconsistent with the notion that the Indian inhabitants could not be compelled to sell their lands. In reality, however, the tribes were forced to sell their lands.

7. *Strother v. Cathey*, 5 N.C. (1 Mur.) 162, 168 (N.C. Sup. Ct., July Term 1807, emphasis added); and Banner, *How the Indians Lost Their Land*, 169 (emphasis added).

8. *Marshall v. Clark*, 8 Va. (4 Call.) 268 (Va. Sup. Ct. of Appeals, November 1791); *Weiser's Lessee v. Moody*, 2 Yeates 127, 127 (Pa. Sup. Ct., 1796); *Glasgow's Lessee v. Smith and Blackwell*, 1 Tenn. (1 Overt.) 144, 167 (Superior Court of Law and Equity of Tennessee, 1805, emphasis added). The Pennsylvania court tacitly

invokes the "estoppel by deed" doctrine, which "prevents a grantor of a warranty deed, who does not have title at the time of the conveyance but who later
acquires title, from denying that he or she had title at the time of the transfer."
Black's Law Dictionary, 590 (8th ed. 2004). See *Weiser's Lessee v. Moody, supra*, at
127 (the situation "might be compared to a person's selling lands without title,
and afterwards obtaining a right thereto, where the vendor would hold in trust
for the vendee").

9. *Van Gorden v. Jackson ex dem. Bogardus*, 5 Johns. 440, 460–61 (N.Y. Ct. for
the Correction of Errors, Feb. 1809, emphasis added). In an earlier decision of
the New York Supreme Court (a trial court of general jurisdiction), Chief Justice
James Kent stated that "the abstract right of granting lands in the possession of
the native *Indians*, without their previous consent, as original lords of the soil, is
a political question with which we have at present nothing to do." *Jackson ex dem.
Klock v. Hudson*, 3 Johns. 375, 384–85 (N.Y. Sup. Ct., Aug. Term, 1808). The
courts of New York during this period also invoked the positive law set forth in
the state constitution and legislative enactments to hold that Indians within the
state could not alienate property rights. See, e.g., *Jackson ex dem. Gilbert v. Wood*,
7 Johns. 290, 296 (N.Y. Sup. Ct., Nov. Term, 1810, Chief Justice Kent); *St. Regis
Indians v. Drum*, 19 Johns. 127, 128 (N.Y. Sup. Ct., May Term 1821, Justice Jonas
Platt); and *Goodell v. Jackson ex dem. Smith*, 20 Johns. 693, 719 (N.Y. Ct. for the
Correction of Errors, Feb. Term 1823, Chancellor James Kent, "by the constitution and statute law of this state, no white person can purchase any right or title
to land from any one or more *Indians*, either individually or collectively, without
the authority and consent of the legislature").

10. *Cox v. Cromwell*, 3 Binn. 114, 115, 119 (Pa. Sup. Ct., Oct. 2, 1810).

11. *Thompson v. Johnston*, 6 Binn. 68, 70, 76–78 (Pa. Sup. Ct., Sept. 11, 1813,
Chief Justice Tilghman), 72–73 (Justice Yeates, emphasis added).

12. Henderson, "Unraveling the Riddle," 98 (Commissioner Daniel Hors-
manden); Smith, *Appeals to Privy Council*, 442; and Walters, "*Mohegan Indians v.
Connecticut*," 805.

13. *Fletcher v. Peck*, 10 U.S. at 146–47 (emphasis added).

14. Macomb claimed six small islands based on a grant or gift made at Detroit
in 1781 by the Potawatomis with the approbation of the British. *ASP: Public
Lands*, 3:360 (report of the Senate Committee on the Public Lands, Jan. 15, 1819).
Although Congress did not recognize his deed, it did confirm title to one of the
six islands based on the doctrine of adverse possession. Ibid., 3:360; and 6 Stat.
228 (Mar. 2, 1819).

15. Quaife, "Carver," 11; *Annals of Congress*, 38:826, 17th Cong., 1st Sess. (Jan.
29, 1822, Walworth); and *ASP: Public Lands*, 3:484 (letter from Josiah Meigs to
Treasury Secretary William Crawford, Feb. 8, 1822).

16. *ASP: Public Lands*, 3:534 (report, Jan. 23, 1823, "could not vest"), and
4:84 (report, Jan. 28, 1825). See Quaife, "Carver," 24; *Annals of Congress*, 40:159,
17th Cong., 2nd Sess. (Jan. 29, 1823, Senate vote to deny the Carver claim); and
Robertson, *Conquest by Law*, 65.

17. *Official Opinions of the Attorneys General*, 1:466–67 (Apr. 26, 1821, emphasis added).

18. Williams, Jr., "Medieval and Renaissance Origins," 70 n.300. At one point in his opinion, Wirt states that the individuals who were assigned the right of preemption "hold only a remainder, depending on a contingency which may be very remote." *Official Opinions of the Attorneys General*, 1:467. Wirt had previously expressed a much less generous view of Indian land rights, declaring in a letter in 1819 that Indians "have no more right to sell the standing timber . . . than they have to sell the soil itself." McCluggage, "The Senate and Indian Land Titles," 471.

19. Sullivan, *Land Titles in Massachusetts*, 23, 26, 29.

20. Wharton, *Plain Facts*, 28–29; and *ASP: Indian Affairs*, 1:61 (letter from Henry Knox to President Washington, Jan. 4, 1790, emphasis added).

21. Simcoe, *Correspondence*, 2:19.

22. Minutes of the Supreme Court of the United States (Feb. 1, 1790–Aug. 4, 1828), National Archives, Washington, D.C., reprinted in National Archives Microfilm Publications, microcopy no. 215, roll no. 1 (entries for Feb. 15, 17, 18, and 19, 1823).

23. Remini, *Webster*, 118; and Bobroff, "Indian Law in Property," 521.

24. Tomlins, *United States Supreme Court*, 498; Simon, *What Kind of Nation*, 24; and Elkins and McKitrick, *Age of Federalism*, 558.

25. Baker, *Marshall*, 79–80.

26. Sommerville, *Harper*, 10; and Smith, *Marshall*, 236–37.

27. Oster, *Political and Economic Doctrines of John Marshall*, 206–207; *Annals of Congress*, 10:638, 6th Cong., 1st Sess. (Mar. 21, 1800); Marshall, *Life of George Washington*, 372; and Marshall, *History of the Colonies*.

28. Tomlins, *United States Supreme Court*, 47–48; Simon, *What Kind of Nation*, 138; Morgan, "Origin of Supreme Court Dissent," 355; Hobson, *Great Chief Justice*, 10; and Jessup, *Reaction and Accommodation*, 106.

29. White, *History of the Supreme Court*, 3:336; and Schroeder, "Life and Judicial Work of Justice William Johnson, Jr.," 170–71.

30. *Fletcher*, 10 U.S. at 147 (emphasis added).

31. Schwartz, *History of the Supreme Court*, 59 ("most learned"); *Fletcher*, 10 U.S. at 121–23; Tomlins, *United States Supreme Court*, 516–17; White, *History of the Supreme Court*, 3:355; Jessup, *Reaction and Accommodation*, 90; and Baxter, *Webster*, 21.

32. Remini, *Webster*, 117; and White, *History of the Supreme Court*, 3:326.

33. Tomlins, *United States Supreme Court*, 494; Ketchum, *Saratoga*, 183; and *Pierson v. Post*, 3 Cai. R. 175 (N.Y. Sup. Ct., 1805).

34. Askin, *John Askin Papers*, 2:61–62. See also Burton, *History of Cleveland*, 17.

35. Story, *Life and Letters of Joseph Story*, 1:424 (letter to Nathaniel Williams, Feb. 28, 1823). Livingston died on March 14, 1823.

36. *Daily National Intelligencer*, Feb. 17, 1823, 3. See also Robertson, *Conquest by Law*, 68 and 199 n.53.

37. See 3 Stat. 484 (Feb. 20, 1819); and White, "Working Life of the Marshall Court," 9.

38. *The Experiment*, 21 U.S. 261 (1823); and *The George*, 14 U.S. 408 (1816).

39. *Johnson*, 21 U.S. at 562; White, *History of the Supreme Court*, 3:247; and Robertson, *Conquest by Law*, 68.

40. *Johnson*, 21 U.S. at 562 ("facts stated"), 562–63 ("*sort of title or ownership*," emphasis added), 543 ("title by occupancy"), and 563 ("right of soil").

41. Ibid., 563 ("only question," emphasis added), and 598–604 ("independent").

42. Ibid., 563–64 ("could not be"), and 564 ("legislating *by proclamation*," emphasis added).

43. *Johnson*, 21 U.S. at 565 ("confined"); and *Campbell v. Hall*, 1 Cowp. Rep. 204 (1774).

44. Hening, *Statutes at Large; Being a Collection of All the Laws of Virginia*, 10:97 (Act of June 19, 1779, emphasis added); *Johnson*, 21 U.S. at 566–67.

45. *Johnson*, 21 U.S. at 566 (emphasis added).

46. Ibid., 567, 569–70 (emphasis added). Jean Barbeyrac was a French jurist who translated Samuel von Pufendorf and Hugo Grotius. Cadwallader Colden was a lieutenant governor for New York Province and author of *The History of the Five Indian Nations*. The jurist William Smith—not to be confused with speculator William Smith—wrote *The History of the Province of New York from its Discovery in 1532* (1757). Thomas Rutherforth taught philosophy at Cambridge University, and George Chalmers was a Scotsman who set forth a political history of the American colonies in his *Political Annals of the Present United Colonies from Their Settlement to the Peace of 1763* (1780).

47. *Fletcher v. Peck*, 10 U.S. at 121–23. See also *Johnson*, 21 U.S. at 569 (argument by Murray and Winder); and Robertson, *Conquest by Law*, 72.

48. *Johnson*, 21 U.S. at 569–70 ("existing titles"), 567 ("held under"), and 570–71 ("anomaly").

49. Ibid., 571 ("power of legislation"), and 569 ("regarded").

50. Rodney, *Diary*, 28–29 (Feb. 15 and 19, 1823); Robertson, *Conquest by Law*, 73, citing Illinois and Wabash Collection (letter, dated Feb. 19, 1823, from Edward Ingersoll to Simon Gratz, John Brinton, and Callender Irvine); ibid., 74, citing Illinois and Wabash Collection (letter, dated Feb. 20, 1823, from Ingersoll to Brinton).

51. Remini, *Webster*, 259 (quoting a letter, dated Mar. 1, 1826, from Webster to George Ticknor); and Kades, "Great Case," 102 n.67.

52. Meigs, *Ingersoll*, 132–33 ("pleasant entertainment"); Gratz Collection, case 1, box 37, HSP (Harper to Simon Gratz, John Brinton, and Callender Irvine, Feb. 22, 1823, emphasis added).

53. Gratz Collection, case 1, box 37, HSP (Harper to Simon Gratz, John Brinton, and Callender Irvine, Feb. 22, 1823). Harper's doubts may have increased when, on the twenty-seventh of February, the Court announced its decision in *Green v. Biddle*, 21 U.S. 1 (1823). According to Lindsay Robertson, the *Green* litigation "is essential to understanding *Johnson*." Robertson, *Conquest by Law*, 81. One aspect of the controversy involved the validity of military

land warrants that were granted to Virginia soldiers at a time when the lands in question were occupied by the Chickasaw Nation. *Green* did not involve the right of Indian tribes to sell land to private individuals and was decided just one day before *Johnson*—which does not cite *Green* or otherwise refer to it. Nevertheless, Robertson theorizes that Marshall's concern about the rights of the holders of Virginia militia land warrants caused him "to convert *Johnson* from a case about the effect of the Proclamation of 1763 on pre–Revolutionary War Indian purchases into a case covering as well the validity of Revolutionary War–era state lands grants," 92. It should be noted, however, that *Johnson* was never solely about the effect of the proclamation on pre–Revolutionary War Indian purchases. Counsel for both sides addressed the broader question of the nature of Indian land rights in America, and it stands to reason that—even if the *Green* litigation had never occurred—Marshall would still have focused his attention on "the power of Indians to give, and of private individuals to receive, a title which can be sustained in the Courts of this country." *Johnson*, 21 U.S. at 572.

54. *Johnson*, 21 U.S. at 572, 604–605 (emphasis added). The date of the decision in the official reports is erroneously stated as March 10, 1823. See Robertson, *Conquest by Law*, 200 n.81. According to contemporary and official sources, the date of the decision was February 28. See *Daily National Intelligencer*, March 1, 1823, 3; and National Archives and Records Administration, Records of the Supreme Court of the United States, Record Group 276, Microfilm Publications, M215, roll 1 (Minutes of the U.S. Supreme Court, Feb. 28, 1823).

55. Ibid., 592.

56. Ibid., 593 ("title dependent on *their* laws," emphasis added), 572 ("own government has adopted"), and ("*discovery gave title*," emphasis added).

57. Ibid., 574 (emphasis added).

58. Ibid. ("universal recognition," emphasis added, and "grant the soil").

59. Ibid., 585.

60. Ibid. ("unequivocal," emphasis added), and 588 ("foundation").

61. Ibid. ("not enter," emphasis added), 588 ("gives a title"), 589 ("not for the Courts"); and Sullivan, *Land Titles in Massachusetts*, 30.

62. *Johnson*, 21 U.S. at 590.

63. Ibid., 591–92 (emphasis added).

64. Ibid., 592 ("precisely"), 594 ("additional objection"). Similar reasoning was employed in *Halloway and King v. Doe on the Demise of Buck*, 4 Litt. 293, 14 Ky. 293 (Ky. Ct. App., Nov. 28, 1823), which concerned the validity of the Indian deed given to Richard Henderson and Company. The Kentucky court noted that such purchases were prohibited by the 1763 Proclamation and Virginia's Act of 1779 but observed that "all such sales and deeds were in their origin void, and the Act of 1779 was only declaratory of what the law was." The reported version of *Halloway* includes an editorial note stating that *Johnson v. McIntosh* "decides the same principle, as to purchases from the Indians."

65. *Johnson*, 21 U.S. at 597. In support of this conclusory statement, Marshall offered up an equally conclusory observation: "The authority of this

proclamation, so far as it respected this continent, has never been denied, and the titles it gave to lands have always been sustained in our Courts."

66. 21 U.S. at 598 ("might obtain"), 598–99 (British and French in 1755), and 599 ("entirely inapplicable"). Marshall stresses that Samuel Wharton acknowledged in *Plain Facts* that the Camden-Yorke opinion related to purchases in the East Indies, but he ignores Wharton's contention that the 1757 legal opinion applies with equal force to Native property rights in the New World. See Wharton, *Plain Facts*, 9.

67. 21 U.S. at 600–601 (Indian deeds in New England), 604 ("would be valid"). See also Thorpe, *Constitutions*, 6:3211 (1663 Rhode Island royal charter).

68. *Johnson*, 21 U.S. at 604 (emphasis added). Marshall emphasizes that either the states, or the United States, held the exclusive and preemptive right to acquire Indian title. See 585 ("exclusive right to purchase from the Indians resided in the government"). However, Marshall also notes that "if an individual might extinguish the Indian title for his own benefit, or, in other words, might purchase it, still he could acquire only that title," 593. "The grant derives its efficacy from their will," Marshall observes, "and, if they choose to resume it, and make a different disposition of the land, the Courts of the United States cannot interpose for the protection of the title," 593. The chief justice then notes that Illinois and Piankeshaws ceded "the lands in controversy . . . to the United States, without any reservation of their title," 594. Thus, even if one assumes that the Illinois-Wabash grantees could acquire the Indian title, the tribes had the right to annul their grants, and did so when they subsequently ceded the same lands to the United States.

69. *Niles' Register* (Mar. 8, 1823, quoting from the *Washington Republican*).

CHAPTER 16. CLOSURE AND CONTINUITY

1. Gratz Collection, case 1, box 37, HSP (Harper to Simon Gratz, Nov. 24, 1824).

2. See Robertson, *Conquest by Law*, 200–201 n.83.

3. Hall, "Obituary," 85–86 (*Port Folio*, July–December, 1824).

4. See Holly, *Tidewater by Steamboat*, 22.

5. Hall, "Obituary," 86 (*Port Folio*, July–December, 1824, "commanding member"); and Scharf, *Chronicles*, 415–17.

6. *Osborn v. Bank of the United States*, 22 U.S. 738 (1824); and American Colonization Society, *The African Repository*, 37:247 (description of the society's meeting held on Feb. 20, 1824).

7. Fischer, "Harper," 177–78; Sommerville, *Harper*, 40; Cox, *Champion*, 1, 214; Scharf, *Chronicles*, 418; and Papenfuse, *Evils of Necessity*, 71.

8. *Gibbons v. Ogden*, 22 U.S. 1 (1824); Remini, *Webster*, 263–68 ("Godlike Daniel"); and Webster, *Papers of Daniel Webster, Speeches*, 1:348 (Jan. 26, 1830).

9. Remini, *Webster*, 335 ("sat mum"); Satz, *American Indian Policy in the Jacksonian Era*, 40 (Panic of 1837); Lodge, *Webster*, 347 ("beyond his means"); and Remini, *supra*, at 743 ("I wish to speak").

10. Remini, *Webster*, 335 (death); and Peterson, *Great Triumvirate*, 6.

11. Hoye, *Pioneer Families*, 330–31; Williams and McKinsey, *History of Frederick County*, 1:102; Kirkwood, *They Came to Kentucky*, 424–26; and Hanson, *Old Kent*, 53.

12. Kirkwood, *They Came to Kentucky*, 409–10.

13. Robertson, *Conquest by Law*, 202 n.83, citing McDonald, "Diaries," 284–86 (Feb. 10, 1825).

14. See Robertson, *Conquest by Law*, 14 and 202–203 n.83.

15. Woolen, *Biographical and Historical Sketches*, 381 ("left poor"); Askin, *John Askin Papers*, 1:281; and *Vincennes Gazette* (July 14, 1832).

16. Webster, *Works*, 1:146 (eulogy of Adams and Jefferson, Aug. 2, 1826); Baxter, "Daniel Webster," 469; and Hanley, *Revolutionary Statesman*, 404.

17. Baroway, "Etting," 14–15; and Scharf, *Chronicles*, 420.

18. University of Pennsylvania, Society of the Alumni, *Catalogue*, 38. Although he sold his share in 1778, Levy Andrew Levy of Lancaster was still alive when the Supreme Court decided *Johnson v. McIntosh* in 1823. Levy died in 1829 at age ninety-five.

19. Donaldson, *The House in Which Thomas Jefferson Wrote the Declaration of Independence*, 69; Marcus, *American Jewry*, 65; and Byars, *B. and M. Gratz*, 265.

20. Joseph Gratz died in 1858, two years after his older brother Jacob. Both men were involved with the Philadelphia Institution for the Deaf and Dumb. Jacob was president of the Union Canal Company and served in the state legislature. Byars, *B. and M. Gratz*, 259.

21. Rose, "Interfaith Families," 239; and Byars, *B. and M. Gratz*, 263–64. In her letter to her brother Benjamin, dated Mar. 24, 1819, Rebecca Gratz remarked that "Vincennes must be a dull place." Philipson, *Letters of Rebecca Gratz*, 18.

22. Konkle, "Wilson Memorial," 11.

23. Ewald, "James Wilson," 922, 988, 991, 1001–1005. See also Pedersen, "The Lost Founder," 268–72.

24. Author Walter Semkiw suggests that Robert Morris has been reincarnated as actress Shirley MacLaine and James Wilson has "returned" as media mogul Oprah Winfrey. Semkiw, *Return of the Revolutionaries*, 332–45 (MacLaine), 382 (observing that Wilson and Winfrey share "a tendency to be loose with their money").

25. Prucha, *Documents*, 39 (Jan. 27, 1825).

26. Calhoun, *Papers of John C. Calhoun*, 9:258 (letter to the Piankeshaw, Aug. 1, 1824), 8:498–500 (letter from Richard Graham, Jan. 23, 1824); Hodge, *Handbook*, 2:240; and Libby, *Piankashaw and Kaskaskia*, 274.

27. *ASP: Indian Affairs*, 2:673–74 (treaty, concluded at St. Louis, Missouri, on Oct. 7, 1826, between the Osage and the Delaware, Shawnee, Kickapoo, Wea, Piankeshaw, and Peoria tribes); and Ingenthron, *Indians of the Ozark Plateau*, 123.

28. *ASP: Indian Affairs*, 2:673 (letter from William Clark to James Barbour, Secretary of War, Oct. 12, 1826, "seem to be pleased"), 2:674 (estimate by Clark of costs of removal); Cutler, *History of Kansas*, 876; and Foreman, *Last Trek*, 62. Tenskwatawa died in 1836.

29. Catlin, *Catlin's Indians*, 434–35.

30. 4 Stat. 594 (July 14, 1832, appropriation); Treaty with the Kickapoos, 7 Stat. 391, Oct. 24, 1832; Treaty with the Shawnees and Delawares, 7 Stat. 397, Oct. 26, 1832; Treaty with the Kaskaskias and Peorias, 7 Stat. 403, Oct. 27, 1832; and Treaty with the Piankeshaws and Weas, 7 Stat. 410, Oct. 29, 1832.

31. Treaty with the Kaskaskias and Peorias, 7 Stat. 403, Oct. 27, 1832; Treaty with the Piankeshaws and Weas, 7 Stat. 410, Oct. 29, 1832; and Cutler, *History of Kansas*, 875–76.

32. Farnham, "Travels," 134.

33. Libby, *Piankashaw and Kaskaskia*, 283 (quoting report of Anthony Davis, Sept. 30, 1842); Ingenthron, *Indians of the Ozark Plateau*, 146 ("advancement"); and Washburn, *American Indian and the United States*, 1:50 (report of Luke Lea, Commissioner of Indian Affairs, Nov. 27, 1851).

34. Treaty with the Kaskaskias, Peorias, Piankeshaws, and Weas, 10 Stat. 1082, May 30, 1854; Foreman, *Last Trek*, 206; and Cutler, *History of Kansas*, 876.

35. Foreman, *Last Trek*, 232.

36. Warren, *Shawnees and Their Neighbors*, 155.

37. Spindel, *Dancing*, 45; Valley and Lembcke, *Peorias*, 79–80; Cutler, *History of Kansas*, 876; and *The Kansas Indians*, 72 U.S. 737, 757–59 (1866, Wea lands in Kansas could not be taxed by the state).

38. Treaty with the Senecas, Mixed Senecas and Shawnees, Quapaws, Confederated Peorias, Miamis, etc., 15 Stat. 513, Feb. 23, 1867.

39. 16 Stat. 566 (Mar. 3, 1871).

40. Deloria and DeMallie, *Documents*, 1:721–22 (agreement between the Western Miamis and the Confederated Weas, Peorias, Kaskaskias, and Piankeshaws, Jan. 15, 1872); and 17 Stat. 631, 633 (Act of Mar. 3, 1873).

41. Valley and Lembcke, *Peorias*, 117.

42. Blair, *Indian Tribes of the Upper Mississippi Valley*, 1:317; and Brown, *Cultural Transformations*, 232.

43. Watson, "Thrust and Parry," 488 ("transfer communally"); and 24 Stat. 388–91 (Act of Feb. 8, 1887). The federal government would hold title to the allotments for the first twenty-five years on behalf of the allottees, who would thereafter own their land in fee simple absolute as citizens of the United States, subject to state regulation and taxation.

44. 25 Stat. 1013–15 (Mar. 2, 1889); and Valley and Lembcke, *Peorias*, 104, 111–13.

45. 25 Stat. 495–519 (June 28, 1898).

46. 32 Stat. 246 (May 27, 1902); Valley and Lembcke, *Peorias*, 113–14; Scott, *Illinois Nation*, 56; and Blasingham, "Depopulation," 216.

47. Alvord, *Illinois Country*, 435 n.16; Valley and Lembcke, *Peorias*, 116, 197; Roosevelt, *Presidential Addresses*, 2:594 (State of the Union Address, Dec. 3, 1901); and Miller, *Native America*, 175. Indian land holdings were reduced from 138 million acres in 1887 to 48 million acres in 1934. Getches et al., *Cases and Materials on Federal Indian Law*, 171.

48. 49 Stat. 1967 (June 26, 1936, emphasis added).

49. *Opinions of the Solicitor of the Department of the Interior*, 1:864 (Dec. 13, 1938); and Valley and Lembcke, *Peorias*, 118–19.

50. Ibid., 206–208; and Scott, *Illinois Nation*, 66, 70. When Chief Froman stepped down in 1972, he was made an honorary chief. He died at age ninety-two on March 5, 1994.

51. 60 Stat. 1049 (Aug. 13, 1946), codified at 25 U.S. Code § 70a (Indian Claims Commission); and Wishart, *Encyclopedia of the Great Plains*, 453. When the Indian Claims Commission expired in 1978, all pending cases were transferred to United States Court of Claims.

52. See generally Valley and Lembcke, *Peorias*, 128–38.

53. H.R. Con. Res. 108, 83d Cong., 1st Sess., 67 Stat. B132 (1953). See also Act of Aug. 15, 1953, ch. 505, 67 Stat. 588 (commonly referred to as Public Law 280).

54. 70 Stat. 937 (Aug. 2, 1956), codified at 25 U.S.C. §§ 821–26.

55. *United States v. Kickapoo Tribe of Kansas and the Peoria Tribe of Indians of Oklahoma on Behalf of the Wea Nation*, 174 Ct.Cl. 550 (Feb. 18, 1966).

56. *Peoria Tribe of Indians of Oklahoma v. United States*, 16 Ind. Cl. Comm. 574, 589–92, 600 (1966).

57. For the most part, the claims presented by the Peoria Tribe were resolved by either the commission or the Court of Claims. However, in one instance, the Peoria Tribe successfully presented its claim to the Supreme Court. The issue concerned the promise, made in the 1854 Manypenny treaty, to invest the proceeds from the sale of Native lands "in safe and profitable stocks, the interest to be annually paid to them, or expended for their benefit and improvement." See *Peoria Tribe of Indians of Oklahoma v. United States*, 390 U.S. 468, 471 (1968).

58. *Peoria Tribe of Indians v. United States*, 22 Ind. Cl. Comm. 186 (1969); and *Peoria Tribe of Indians v. United States*, 22 Ind. Cl. Comm. 442 (1970, final award).

59. *Strong v. United States*, 518 F.2d 556 (U.S. Court of Claims, 1975). The court also upheld the commission's conclusion that the Piankeshaws did not have either an aboriginal or a recognized title interest in the land known as Clark's Grant.

60. 84 Stat. 688 (July 31, 1970), codified at 25 U.S.C. §§1221–27. Congress authorized the determination of a membership roll, included provisions for minors and next of kin, and specified that the judgment funds are exempt from federal and state income taxes.

61. Valley and Lembcke, *Peorias*, 130–33; and Scott, *Illinois Nation*, 62.

62. Prucha, *Documents*, 257–58 (President Nixon, Special Message on Indian Affairs, July 8, 1970).

63. U.S. Code (1978), Congressional and Administrative News, 95th Cong., 2nd Sess., Legislative History (Public Law 95–281, Vol. 3), at 762–63 (letter to Morris Udall, Chairman, Committee on Interior and Insular Affairs, July 13, 1977).

64. 92 Stat. 246–47 (May 15, 1978), codified at 25 U.S.C. §§ 861–861c.

65. Hoxie, *Encyclopedia*, 475. See also "Peoria Tribe Chief to Begin Second Term," *Tulsa World*, Feb. 4, 1994 ("The tribe has 1,164 acres of agriculture land

in the Miami area, including a recently acquired 706-acre farm"); "Peoria Tribe Stakes Economic Future on Land," *Tulsa World,* June 18, 1990; and Valley and Lembcke, *Peorias,* 120, 157–60.

66. Tiller, *Guide to Indian Country,* 864; and "Peoria Tribe Plans Casino Near Miami," *Tulsa World,* Sept. 25, 2003.

67. Pub. L. No. 100-497, 102 Stat. 2467 (Oct. 17, 1988), codified at 25 U.S.C. §§ 2701–21 (Indian Gaming Regulatory Act); and "Miami Begins Rolling Back after Tire Plant Shutdown," *Daily Oklahoman,* Feb. 5, 2006.

68. Hoxie, *Encyclopedia,* 267 (Grand Village); "Oklahoma Tribe Reclaims Skeletons from Museum," *State Journal-Register* (Springfield, Ill.), Oct. 8, 1998; and "Peoria Tribe Set to Accept Remains," *Peoria Journal Star,* Aug. 1, 1999 ("Sacred burial objects and bones more than 1,000 years old are to be returned to the Peoria Tribe of Oklahoma after being used in recent years by researchers at the University of Arkansas").

69. Carol Spindel, "Frequently Asked Questions, Answers about Chief Illiniwek," *Champaign News-Gazette,* May 28, 2000. Another source states that the dance performed by Chief Illiniwek was created in 1926 by the Boy Scouts. "The Resurrection of Chief Illiniwek; Though Banned as a Mascot, He Was Cheered at U. of I.'s Homecoming Parade," *Chicago Sun-Times,* Nov. 4, 2007.

70. "U. Illinois Illiniwek Appeal Denied by NCAA," *University Wire* (Champaign), Nov. 16, 2005 (quoting Chief John Froman, who informed the NCAA that Chief Illiniwek "was not representative of our tribe and culture, mainly because the costume is Sioux"); and "University of Illinois Drops Indian Mascot," *Washington Times,* Feb. 21, 2007.

71. Valley and Lembcke, *Peorias,* 124.

CHAPTER 17. THE LEGACY OF *JOHNSON V. MCINTOSH*

1. *Johnson,* 21 U.S. at 574.

2. See Robertson, *Conquest by Law,* 133–34 and 212 n.45.

3. *Tee-Hit-Ton Indians v. United States,* 348 U.S. 272, 279 (1955); and *City of Sherrill, New York v. Oneida Indian Nation of New York,* 544 U.S. 197, 203 n.1 (2005, quoting *County of Oneida, New York v. Oneida Indian Nation of New York,* 470 U.S. 226, 234 [1985]).

4. *Johnson,* 21 U.S. at 574.

5. Robertson, *Conquest by Law,* 143.

6. *Oliphant v. Suquamish Indian Tribe,* 435 U.S. 191 (1978); and *Montana v. United States,* 450 U.S. 544 (1981).

7. Watson, "Thrust and Parry," 442.

8. For analysis of the influence of *Johnson v. McIntosh* on the Removal Act debates in Congress, see Robertson, *Conquest by Law,* 126–29.

9. Perdue, "Conflict Within," 63–64 (Cherokee Constitution); and Garrison, *Legal Ideology of Removal,* 34.

10. Evarts, *Cherokee Removal,* 170 ("*tenants at will,*" emphasis added).

11. Ibid., 53–54 (emphasis added).

12. Ibid., 166 (quoting *Johnson*, 21 U.S. at 574, "rightful occupants"), 167 ("absurd and cruel"). See also 171–72 ("The exclusive right of extinguishing the Indian title, or what has usually been called the right of preemption, is a totally different thing from this all-absorbing and overwhelming right of discovery").

13. Remini, *Jackson*, 133.

14. Congressional Debates, 21st Cong., 1st Sess. 312 (Apr. 9, 1830, emphasis added, Frelinghuysen), 333 (Apr. 15, 1830, Forsyth). Without referring explicitly to *Johnson*, Forsyth observed that the Supreme Court had "pronounced upon the condition of the Indians and the Indian lands" and had held that the Indian lands are "owned in fee simple by the Governments of the United States, or by State Governments," 337.

15. Ibid., 353 (Apr. 17, 1830, speech by Senator Peleg Sprague of Maine, describing prior remarks by Senator John McKinley of Alabama).

16. Ibid., 345, 352 (Apr. 17, 1830, emphasis added); and Robertson, *Conquest by Law*, 321. The *Johnson* decision, Sprague argued, does *not* hold that Natives lack title to the soil, as contended by the proponents of removal, but rather "sustains my position" that the Indians are entitled "to the *perpetual and exclusive occupancy of all their lands*," 352–53 (emphasis added).

17. Ibid., 1009–10 (May 15, 1830).

18. Ibid., 1028 (May 17, 1830).

19. Ibid., 1024 (May 17, 1830, Lumpkin), 1031–33 (May 17, 1830, Foster), 1116 (May 19, 1830, Lamar), and 1127 (May 24, 1830, Wayne).

20. Story, *Miscellaneous Writings*, 460 (emphasis added).

21. Ibid., 461–65 (emphasis added).

22. Oster, *Political and Economic Doctrines of John Marshall*, 125 (letter from Marshall to Story, Oct. 29, 1828).

23. Before Wirt could file the Cherokee Nation suit, the Georgia laws were put to the test when the state asserted jurisdiction over George Tassels (or Tassel), a Cherokee who had been arrested for killing a tribal member within the borders of the Cherokee Nation. In *Georgia v. Tassels*, the state court cited *Fletcher* and *Johnson* for the proposition that Georgia "is seized in fee of all lands within its chartered limits, notwithstanding the land may be in the occupancy of the Indians." The state appellate court upheld the assertion of jurisdiction, and soon thereafter the death sentence was carried out, thus mooting any review by the Supreme Court. *Georgia v. Tassels*, 1 Dud. 229, 234 (Ga. 1830); and Norgren, *Cherokee Cases*, 155–64 (2004, court's opinion).

24. Peters, *Case of the Cherokee Nation against the State of Georgia*, 3 ("the *occupants and owners*," emphasis added), 11 ("earth was designed"), and 12 ("become *civilized*"). Peters, the official reporter of the Supreme Court, published the pleadings in *Cherokee Nation v. Georgia* and related materials.

25. Ibid., 4 (emphasis added). Wirt acknowledged that the Cherokee Nation could sell its lands only to the United States but insisted that this limitation was a condition of their treaties with the federal government and was not imposed on the Cherokee by the doctrine of discovery.

26. Ibid., 4.

27. *Cherokee Nation v. Georgia*, 30 U.S. 1, 54 (1831, Thompson), 14 (Marshall).

28. Peters, *Case of the Cherokee Nation Against the State of Georgia*, 124–25, and 128 (Georgia "chooses to consider a future contingent title, as a present, absolute one, a mere possibility, as a certainty").

29. *Cherokee Nation*, 30 U.S. 1, 47 (1831, Thompson), 32–33 (Baldwin).

30. *Fletcher v. Peck*, 10 U.S., 143, 146–47.

31. *Cherokee Nation*, 30 U.S. 1, 16, 19 (1831).

32. Ibid., 30 U.S. 1, 13 (1831).

33. *Worcester v. Georgia*, 31 U.S. 515, 528–29 (1832, Worcester and Butler); Baker, *Marshall*, 746–49; and Smith, *Marshall*, 512–14 (surgery).

34. Frickey, "A Common Law for Our Age of Imperialism," 10.

35. *Worcester*, 31 U.S. at 559, 561. Duvall, Thompson and Story joined Marshall. McLean concurred but warned that "the exercise of the power of self-government by the Indians, within a state, is undoubtedly contemplated to be temporary" and would end when the Indians became "incapable of self-government, either by moral degradation or a reduction of their numbers," 593–94. Baldwin dissented for the reasons given in his *Cherokee Nation* opinion, 596.

36. Hurley, "Aboriginal Rights," 430.

37. *Johnson*, 21 U.S. at 591–92; and *Worcester*, 31 U.S. at 542–43.

38. *Worcester*, 31 U.S. at 543–44 (quoting *Johnson*, 21 U.S. at 573).

39. *Johnson*, 21 U.S. at 592; and *Worcester*, 31 U.S. at 544 (emphasis added).

40. Robertson, *Conquest by Law*, 99.

41. See Garrison, *Legal Ideology of Removal*, 178 ("Marshall adopted precisely the position that Justice William Johnson had pronounced in his dissent in *Fletcher v. Peck* twenty years before"); Robertson, *Conquest by Law*, 133; and Hurley, "Aboriginal Rights," 433. William Johnson did not participate in the *Worcester* decision.

42. *Johnson*, 21 U.S. at 592, 603.

43. *Worcester*, 31 U.S. at 544–45 (emphasis added).

44. *Worcester*, 31 U.S. at 546 ("*blank paper,*" emphasis added); Berman, "Concept of Aboriginal Rights," 655. See also Robertson, *Conquest by Law*, 134–35.

45. Boller and George, *They Never Said It*, 53. Jackson did observe, a month after *Worcester*, that "the decision of the Supreme court has fell still born, and they find that it cannot coerce Georgia to yield to its mandate." Howe, *What Hath God Wrought*, 412 (letter to John Coffee, Apr. 7, 1832).

46. Jackson, *Correspondence*, 4:219–20 (letter, undated but likely written in 1831, to either John Eaton or Lewis Cass).

47. Bass, *Cherokee Messenger*, 156–59. In 1992 the Georgia Board of Pardons and Paroles "unconditionally" pardoned Samuel Worcester and Elizur Butler in order "to remove a stain on the history of criminal justice in Georgia." Norgren, *Cherokee Cases*, 2 (quoting the state's pardon).

48. Woodward, *Cherokees*, 214.

49. Thornton, "Cherokee Losses," 289; and Twibell, "Rethinking *Johnson v. M'intosh*," 168.

50. *State v. Foreman*, 16 Tenn. (8 Yer.) 256, 558–59 (Tenn. Sup. Ct. of Errors and Appeals, 1835).

51. Alabama had also upheld the extension of state jurisdiction into Indian country. In *Caldwell v. State*, 1 Stew. & P. 327 (Ala. Sup. Ct., 1832), the defendant was a white man who killed a Creek Indian within the borders of the Creek Nation. All three supreme court justices cited *Johnson v. McIntosh* with approval; see *Caldwell v. State*, 338, 346, 354, 389, 409–416, 419, 425–426. The court rejected "the pretension of empire in the Indian tribes, within the chartered limits of the states," 355. The *Caldwell* decision was issued after *Cherokee Nation* (1831) but before *Worcester* (1832). Any possibility that the Supreme Court might review *Caldwell* was mooted when Alabama pardoned the defendant in February of 1832. Garrison, *Legal Ideology of Removal*, 151–68.

52. *State v. Foreman*, 16 Tenn. (8 Yer.) 256, 366 (Tenn. Sup. Ct. of Errors and Appeals, 1835, "*it belongs,*" emphasis added), 256, 338, 342 (Green and Catron).

53. See *Cornet v. Winton's Lessee*, 10 Tenn. (2 Yer.) 143, 145, 149–50 (Tenn. Sup. Ct. of Errors and Appeals, 1826); and *Blair v. Pathkiller's Lessee*, 10 Tenn. (2 Yer.) 407, 408 (Tenn. Sup. Ct. of Errors and Appeals, 1830). In *Cornet*, Catron's fellow judge, John Haywood, stated that the "infidel Indians" were "*tenants at sufferance*" and that the "pretended title of the Indians was mere moonshine." 10 Tenn. (2 Yer.) at 154, 156. Catron, on the other hand, described the Indians at issue, the Cherokee, as "a conquered people . . . with acknowledged rights . . . which the courts of justice are bound to regard," 150. In *Blair*, Catron held that after discovery, Indians retained a "right of possession," and further noted that *Johnson v. McIntosh* "is the best examination within the knowledge of this court upon the subject, and to which, perhaps, nothing material could be added." 10 Tenn. (2 Yer.) at 408; and Huebner, *Southern Judicial Tradition*, 41–42, 55, 58.

54. *State v. Foreman*, 16 Tenn. (8 Yer.) 256, 287, 334–35 (Catron); Garrison, *Legal Ideology of Removal*, 217, 229–33; and Huebner, *Southern Judicial Tradition*, 59 (quoting a letter, dated Dec. 12, 1835, from Catron to Van Buren). The defendants in *Foreman* were released, mooting any possibility of Supreme Court review.

55. A Mississippi court in 1840 implicitly acknowledged Marshall's views in *Worcester* when it observed that the Indian "right of occupancy" is really an ownership right encumbered by a right of preemption. *Newman v. Doe ex dem. Harris & Plummer*, 4 Howard 522, 5 Miss. 522 (High Court of Errors and Appeals of Mississippi, 1840). The Supreme Court of the Utah Territory in 1889 quoted the statement in *Worcester* that discovery "gave the exclusive right to purchase, but it did not found that right on a denial of the right of the possesser to sell," but then proceeded to cite *Johnson* for the proposition that discovery vested fee-simple title in the government, subject to the Native right of occupancy. *Utah Mining & Manufacturing Co. v. Dickert & Myers Sulphur Co.*, 21 P. 1002, 1007 (Sup. Ct. of the Territory of Utah, 1889). Likewise, a 1914 New York decision includes several quotes from *Worcester* concerning Indian land rights but then cites *Johnson* and concludes that the discoverer held "the fee of the lands occupied by [the Indians]

and the sole right of pre-emption to the same." *George v. Pierce*, 148 N.Y.S. 230, 231–32 (N.Y. Sup. Ct., 1914, emphasis added). See also *Brown v. Smathers*, 188 N.C. 166, 126 S.E. 22, 25 (N.C. Sup. Ct., 1924, citing *Worcester*'s statement that discovery transferred only the "exclusive right of purchasing such lands as the natives were willing to sell," and thereafter stating that Indian title was "a mere possessory right, or right of occupancy"). More recently, the Appellate Court of Connecticut quoted the statements in *Worcester* that declared the colonial charters to be "blank paper so far as the rights of the natives were concerned" and described the discoverer's "title" as the "exclusive right of purchasing such lands as the natives were willing to sell." *Schaghticoke Indians of Kent, Connecticut, Inc. v. Potter*, 577 A.2d 719, 726 (Conn. App., 1990), rev'd, 587 A.2d 139 (Conn. Sup. Ct. 1991). The dispute, however, did not concern Indian land rights but rather involved an effort by the state to assert civil regulatory jurisdiction on activities taking place within the reservation.

56. See *Holden v. Joy*, 84 U.S. 211, 244 (1872); and *United States v. Alcea Band of Tillamooks*, 329 U.S. 40, 47 (1946). The Supreme Court cited *Worcester* in two other passages that concern Indian land rights (as opposed to sovereign powers), but in both instances the Court was actually endorsing *Johnson*'s "limited possessor" conception of Native property. See *Francis v. Francis*, 203 U.S. 233, 238 (1906); and *United States v. Shoshone Tribe*, 304 U.S. 111, 117 (1938). Marshall's statements in *Worcester* have been cited in only a few instances in the lower federal courts. In *Coleman v. United States*, 715 F.2d 1156 (7th Cir. 1983), the court of appeals noted in dicta that *Worcester* held that discovery gave only "the exclusive right of purchasing such lands as the natives were willing to sell," 1158 (quoting *Worcester*, 31 U.S. at 545). In *Bear v. United States*, 611 F.Supp. 589 (D. Neb. 1985), the district court noted that the Supreme Court "qualified its analysis" in *Worcester* and held that discovery "did not itself pass title to the land" but instead gave the discoverer "the exclusive right of purchasing such lands as the natives were willing to sell," 596 n.11. Yet the court cites *Johnson* for the proposition that "tribes do not hold, and thus cannot convey, fee interests in the lands they occupy," 595–96. In *Shoshone Tribe of Indians v. United States*, 35 Ct. Cl. 331 (1937), the United States Court of Claims cites *Holden* and *Worcester* for the proposition that discovery granted only a right of preemption to the discoverer, 363, 367.

57. For analysis of the influence of Jackson appointees on Supreme Court decisions involving Indian land rights, see Robertson, *Conquest by Law*, 138–41.

58. *Mitchel v. United States*, 34 U.S. 711, 746 (1835, *Mitchel I*, "universal assent"), 745 ("ultimate fee"), 746 ("sacred as the fee simple," emphasis added), and 758–59 (Indians can alienate their lands, "subject only to ratification and confirmation by the license, charter, or deed from the governor representing the king"); Fletcher, "The Iron Cold of the Marshall Trilogy," 647; and Robertson, *Conquest by Law*, 122, 139. David Wilkins contends that *Mitchel* "goes far towards undermining, although not explicitly disavowing, the disastrous doctrines unleashed in *M'Intosh*." Wilkins, "*Johnson v. M'Intosh* Revisited," 171. See also Wilkins and Lomawaima, *Uneven Ground*, 60–61.

59. Congressional Debates, 21st Cong., 1st Sess., 324 (Apr. 13, 1830, Mc-Kinley's remarks); and *State v. Foreman*, 16 Tenn. (8 Yer.) 256, 287 (Tenn. Sup. Ct. of Appeals, 1835, Catron).

60. Robertson, (*Conquest by Law*, 141) notes that "in five decisions between 1836 and 1842 . . . the Jackson members of the Supreme Court thus hammered the discovery doctrine into law."

61. *United States v. Fernandez*, 35 U.S. 303, 304 (1836); *Mitchel v. United States*, 40 U.S. 52, 89 (1841, *Mitchel II*); *Martin v. Waddell's Lessee*, 41 U.S. 367, 409–10 (1842); *Scott v. Sandford*, 60 U.S. 393, 501 (1856); *United States v. Rogers*, 45 U.S. 567, 572 (1846); *Clark v. Smith*, 38 U.S. 195, 201 (1839); *Marsh v. Brooks*, 49 U.S. 223, 232 (1850); and *Doe ex dem. Mann and Hannah v. Wilson*, 64 U.S. 457, 463–64 (1859). See also Robertson, *Conquest by Law*, 138–42.

62. *United States v. Cook*, 86 U.S. 591, 593 (1873). Just one year earlier, in *Holden v. Joy*, 84 U.S. 211 (1872), the Court had repeated Marshall's statements in *Worcester* that discovery "could not affect the rights of those already in possession," and that the discoverer acquired "the exclusive pre-emption right to purchase," 244. However, at the same time, the Court cited *Johnson* and noted that European nations had agreed that "discovery should give title to the government by whose subjects, or by whose authority, it was made, against all other governments, and that the title so acquired might be consummated by possession," 243. For the remainder of the nineteenth century, the Supreme Court relied on the *Johnson* discovery rule. See, e.g., *Beecher v. Wetherby*, 95 U.S. 517, 525 (1877); *Buttz v. Northern Pacific Railroad Co.*, 119 U.S. 55, 66–67 (1886); *Shively v. Bowlby*, 152 U.S. 1, 14 (1894); and *Jones v. Meehan*, 175 U.S. 1, 8 (1899).

63. Royce, *Indian Land Cessions*, 537 ("*absurdity*," emphasis added); and *Shoshone Tribe v. United States*, 85 Ct. Cl. 331 (1937).

64. *United States v. Alcea Bank of Tillamooks*, 329 U.S. 40, 46–47 (1946).

65. *Tee-Hit-Ton Indians v. United States*, 348 U.S. 272, 279 (1955, emphasis added). The Court limited its holding in *Alcea Band of Tillamooks* by noting that recovery in that case "was based upon statutory direction to pay for the aboriginal title in the special jurisdictional act to equalize the Tillamooks with the neighboring tribes, rather than upon a holding that there had been a compensable taking under the Fifth Amendment," 284.

66. Robertson, "*Johnson v. M'Intosh*, Brief for Appellants," 871.

67. *Oneida Indian Nation of New York v. County of Oneida, New York*, 414 U.S. 661, 670 (1974).

68. *Oneida Indian Nation of New York v. State of New York*, 691 F.2d 1070, 1075 (2nd Cir. 1982). See also *Seneca Nation of Indians v. New York*, 206 F.Supp.2d 448, 504 (W.D. N.Y. 2002, equating the "underlying fee title to Indian land" and "the right of preemption"); and *Seneca Nation of Indians v. New York*, 382 F.3d 245, 248 n.4 (2d Cir. 2004), *cert. denied*, 547 U.S. 1178 (2006, same).

69. *Fletcher v. Peck*, 10 U.S. at 143, 146–47 (*Johnson*); *City of Sherrill, New York v. Oneida Indian Nation of New York*, 544 U.S. 197, 203 n.1 (2005, quoting both *Oneida Indian Nation of New York v. County of Oneida, New York*, 414 U.S. 661,

670 [1974], and *County of Oneida, New York v. Oneida Indian Nation of New York*, 470 U.S. 226, 234 [1985]).

70. *Black Hills Institute of Geological Research v. South Dakota School of Mines and Technology*, 12 F.3d 737, 739–43 (8th Cir. 1993), *cert. denied*, 513 U.S. 810 (1994); and Fiffer, *Tyrannosaurus Sue*, 210, 233.

71. *United States v. Newmont USA Ltd.*, 504 F.Supp.2d 1050, 1061, 1067–74 (E.D. Wash. 2007).

72. Laurence, "Learning to Live with the Plenary Power," 416; and McNeil, "Judicial Treatment of Indigenous Land Rights," 263.

73. *Johnson*, 21 U.S. at 574 ("*necessarily diminished*," emphasis added); and Sappington, "Is *Lara* the Answer to Implicit Divestiture?" 154 (emphasis added).

74. Miller, "Doctrine of Discovery in American Indian Law," 109.

75. Cohen, *Handbook of Federal Indian Law*, 122.

76. *Oliphant v. Suquamish Indian Tribe*, 435 U.S. 191, 208–209 (1978); see also *United States v. Wheeler*, 435 U.S. 313, 326 (1978).

77. *Montana v. United States*, 450 U.S. 544, 565 (1981). The Court carved out two "exceptions" to its general rule and held that tribes may exercise civil authority over nonmembers (1) when non-Indians are engaged in "consensual relationships with the tribe or its members, through commercial dealing, contracts, leases, or other arrangements," 565; and (2) when "the conduct of non-Indians on fee lands within [the] reservation . . . threatens or has some direct effect on the political integrity, the economic security, or the health or welfare of the tribe," 566.

78. See, e.g., *Brendale v. Confederated Tribes and Bands of the Yakima Indian Nation*, 492 U.S. 408 (1989); *Duro v. Reina*, 495 U.S. 676 (1990); *South Dakota v. Bourland*, 508 U.S. 679 (1993); *Strate v. A-1 Contractors*, 520 U.S. 438 (1997); *Atkinson Trading Company, Inc. v. Shirley*, 532 U.S. 645 (2001); *Nevada v. Hicks*, 533 U.S. 353 (2001); and *Plains Commerce Bank v. Long Family Land and Cattle Co.*, 554 U.S. 316 (2008).

79. Skibine, "Indian Gaming," 259–60; and *Friends of East Willits Valley v. County of Mendocino*, 123 Cal. Rptr.2d 708, 713 (Cal. App. 1 Dist., 2002, "the trust power finds its roots in *Johnson*").

80. See, e.g., *United States v. Mitchell*, 445 U.S. 535 (1980); *United States v. Mitchell*, 463 U.S. 206 (1983); *United States v. White Mountain Apache Tribe*, 537 U.S. 435 (2003); *United States v. Navajo Nation*, 537 U.S. 488 (2003); and *United States v. Navajo Nation*, 556 U.S. 287 (2009).

81. Williams, Jr., "'People of the States Where They Are Found,'" 997; and *Seminole Nation v. United States*, 316 U.S. 286, 297 (1942).

82. Skibine, "Indian Gaming," 257 (describing two versions of the trust doctrine, one "aimed at giving control to the federal government over Indian tribes," and the other "aimed at protecting tribal self-government while at the same time giving power to the federal government over the states in the area of Indian affairs").

83. *United States v. Kagama*, 118 U.S. 375, 383–84 (1886, emphasis added). See also Deloria, "Conquest," 103–104 (The suggestion in *Kagama* that the power to

deal with Indians might derive from ownership of the land is "perhaps the most radical interpretation of the Doctrine of Discovery ever articulated").

84. *Lone Wolf v. Hitchcock*, 187 U.S. 553, 565–66 (1903).

85. *United States v. Rowell*, 243 U.S. 464, 468 (1917).

86. *Lone Wolf v. Hitchcock*, 187 U.S. 553, 565 (1903); Miller, "Doctrine of Discovery in American Indian Law," 106; Skibine, "Book Review, *Braid of Feathers*," 564; and Williams, Jr., "Jefferson, the Norman Yoke," 168.

87. *Santa Clara Pueblo v. Martinez*, 436 U.S. 49, 56 (1978).

88. Skibine, "Reconciling Federal and State Power inside Indian Reservations," 1128–29.

89. *Johnson*, 21 U.S. at 573, 590. See also 589 ("Although we do not mean to engage in the defence of those principles which Europeans have applied to Indian title, they may, we think, find some excuse, if not justification, in the character and habits of the people whose rights have been wrested from them").

90. *United States v. Lucero*, 1 N.M. 422, 425–26 (Sup. Ct. of the Territory of N.M., 1869).

91. See *Beecher v. Wetherby*, 95 U.S. 517, 525 (1877, "ignorant and dependent race"); *Montoya v. United States*, 180 U.S. 261, 265 (1901, "Owing to the natural infirmities of the Indian character, their fiery tempers, impatience of restraint, their mutual jealousies and animosities, their nomadic habits, and lack of mental training, they have as a rule shown a total want of that cohesive force necessary to the making up of a nation in the ordinary sense of the word"); and *United States v. Sandoval*, 231 U.S. 28, 39 (1913, Indians are "a simple, uninformed, and inferior people"). As recently as 1955, the Court referred to "savage" tribes. *Tee-Hit-Ton Indians v. United States*, 348 U.S. 272, 322–23 (1955).

92. Transcript of the oral argument in *United States v. Lara*, 2004 Westlaw 193036, at *36 (Jan. 21, 2004). The transcript does not identify the source of the comment.

93. Robertson points to the global influence of *Johnson v. McIntosh* in his afterword to *Conquest by Law* (144). The following discussion is an abridged version of Watson, "The Impact of the American Doctrine of Discovery on Native Land Rights in Australia, Canada, and New Zealand."

94. Billot, *Batman*, 97. See generally Attwood and Doyle, *Possession: Batman's Treaty*.

95. Billot, *Batman*, 153–54 (Bourke proclamation, Aug. 26, 1835).

96. Bonwick, *Port Phillip Settlement*, 378 (Burge's opinion, Jan. 16, 1836).

97. Sweetman, *Unsigned New Zealand Treaty*, 86 (remarks, on June 30, 1840, before the New South Wales Legislative Council). Wentworth also argued that the Crown could not claim New Zealand by virtue of discovery because the islands were "a country previously peopled." Ibid., 97 (July 1, 1840).

98. Ibid., 107–108 (July 9, 1840).

99. Ibid., 121–22, 141–46. Wentworth also pointed out that Marshall expressed doubts, in *Worcester v. Georgia*, about applying the doctrine of discovery to inhabited lands.

100. Hickford, "'Settling Some Principles': Three 'Forgotten' Cases of the 1840s," 2. See also Miller et al., *Discovering Indigenous Lands*, 214–16.

101. *The Queen v. Symonds* (1847) [1840–1932] NZPCC 387, 390.

102. Belgrave, *Historical Frictions*, 69. Justice Chapman described the Crown's ownership as "technical seisin" and stated that the Mâori hold a "modified title" that "is not theoretically inconsistent with the Queen's seisin in fee as against her European subjects." *Symonds*, 391.

103. Banner, *Possessing the Pacific*, 195. In 1887 the premier of British Columbia, William Smithe, characterized Indians prior to European contact as "little better than wild beasts of the field" and declared that as a consequence of discovery, the land "all belongs to the Queen." Tennant, *Aboriginal Peoples and Politics*, 58.

104. Oliver Mowat, the premier and attorney general of Ontario, argued that *Johnson* held that Indian title is only a moral claim and not a title that is recognized in law. 10 *Ontario Reports* 196, 199–201 (1885). This interpretation of *Johnson*—which was similar to the position taken by Georgian politicians during the debate over the 1830 Indian Removal Act—was disputed by the attorney for St. Catherine's Milling and Lumber Company. 10 *Ontario Reports* 196, 202 (1885). See also Miller et al., *Discovering Indigenous Lands*, 119–25.

105. 13 App. Rep. 148, 160–61 (1886).

106. 13 Can. S.C.R. 577 (1887), at 610 (Strong), 643 (Taschereau), and 600 (Ritchie).

107. Ibid., 599–600. The Privy Council in London affirmed the prior decisions and accepted Ontario's contention that "before and after the treaty of 1873 the title to the lands in suit was in the Crown and not in the Indians." 14 App. Cas. 46, 49 (1888). Lord Watson rejected the notion that the Ojibway had been "the owners in fee simple of the territory which they surrendered" and instead held that the Crown "has all along had a present proprietary estate in the land, upon which the Indian title was a mere burden." Ibid., 58.

108. *Calder v. British Columbia* (1973), S.C.R. 313, 422.

109. Ibid., 313, 346, 380. Following *Calder*, the Canadian Constitution was amended in 1982 to provide in Section 35(1) that "the existing Aboriginal and treaty rights of Canada's Aboriginal peoples are . . . recognized and affirmed."

110. *Guerin v. The Queen* (1984), 2 S.C.R. 335, 377.

111. Ibid., 382.

112. *Van der Peet v. The Queen* (1996), 2 S.C.R. 507, at ¶ 35. See also Slattery, "Understanding Aboriginal Rights," 739; and Miller et al., *Discovering Indigenous Lands*, 126–70.

113. *Wi Parata v. Bishop of Wellington* (1877), 3 NZ Jur (NS) 72 (SC), at 77–78. See also Miller et al., *Discovering Indigenous Lands*, 219.

114. *Attorney-General v. Ngati Apa* (2003), NZCA 117, 3 N.Z.L.R. 643, at ¶ 136 (Anderson and Keith), ¶ 19 (Elias).

115. Ibid., ¶ 13. See generally Miller and Ruru, "An Indigenous Lens into Comparative Law."

116. *Mabo v. Queensland (No 2)* [1992], HCA 23; 175 CLR 1, 15.

117. Ibid., 135 (Dawson).

118. Bartlett, "Native Title in Australia," 414.

119. Russell, *Recognizing Aboriginal Title*, 249.

120. *Mabo v. Queensland (No 2)* [1992], HCA 23; 175 CLR 1, 57 (Brennan).

121. *Wik Peoples v. Queensland* (1996), 187 CLR 1, 123 n.456 (Toohey).

122. *Fejo v. Northern Territory* (1998), HCA 58, 195 CLR 96, 153; and *Western Australia v. Ward* (2000), 170 ALR 159; 99 FCR 316, 519.

123. *Mabo v. Queensland (No 2)* [1992], HCA 23; 175 CLR 1, 40 (Brennan), 108 (Deane and Gaudron).

Chapter 18. The Critical Response
to the Doctrine of Discovery

1. *Fletcher v. Peck*, 10 U.S. at 142, 146–47 (emphasis added).

2. Young, *Trouble with Tradition*, 22.

3. Article 26, United Nations Declaration on the Rights of Indigenous Peoples, G.A. Res. 61/295, U.N. GAOR, 61st Sess., 107th plen. mtg., U.N. Doc. A/RES/61/295 (Sept. 13, 2007), available at http://www.unhcr.org/refworld/docid/471355a82.html.

4. The July 2009 resolution of the 76th General Convention of the Episcopal Church is set forth at http://gc2009.org/ViewLegislation/view_leg_detail.aspx?id=983&type=Final. See also "Episcopal Church Repudiates Doctrine of Discovery—Urges US Adoption of UN Declaration," *Indian Country Today*, July 26, 2009, updated July 27, 2009, available at http://www.indiancountrytoday.com/home/content/51572857.html.

5. Story, *Commentaries*, § 2 (1833).

6. Kent, *Commentaries*, 3:310 (1828, "now too late"); and Kent, *Commentaries* 3:378 note c (1832, "mere naked declaration"). In the 1848 edition Kent noted that the Northwest Indians had declared in 1793 that they were "free to make any bargain or cession of lands whenever and to whomsoever they pleased." Kent, *Commentaries* 3:380 note a (1848).

7. Washburn, *Treatise*, 3:164–68 (164–66).

8. Westlake, *Chapters on the Principles of International Law*, 147–48.

9. Cotton, *Constitutional Decisions of John Marshall*, 2: at I; Scott, *United States of America: A Study in International Organization*, 91 ("masterly"); and Wise, *Red Man in the New World Drama*, 347 ("great and fearless opinion"). Even as late as 1968, *Johnson* was lauded as "stern but humane judicial statesmanship." Faulkner, *Jurisprudence of John Marshall*, 52.

10. Bryan, *Imperialism of John Marshall*, 91.

11. Ibid., 94.

12. "Review," 463 ("cannot discover"); Ribble, "Review," 414 ("*hold that*," emphasis added).

13. American Indian Policy Review Commission, *Final Report*, 1:308.

14. Deloria, *Behind the Trail of Broken Treaties*, 249.

15. Henderson, "Unraveling the Riddle," 75–78.

16. The importance of grasping the historical and political context of Supreme Court decisions had been demonstrated by Joseph Burke's study of the *Cherokee Nation* and *Worcester* decisions. See Burke, "Cherokee Cases."

17. See, e.g., Berman, "Concept of Aboriginal Rights" (1978); Clinton and Hotopp, "Judicial Enforcement of the Federal Restraints on Alienation of Indian Land" (1979); Barsh and Henderson, *The Road* (1980); Newton, "Whim of the Sovereign" (1980); Bloxham, "Aboriginal Title" (1980); Williams, Jr., "Medieval and Renaissance Origins" (1983); Newton, "Federal Power over Indians" (1984); Springer, "American Indians and the Law of Real Property in Colonial New England" (1986); Williams, Jr., "Algebra of Federal Indian Law" (1986); Williams, Jr., "Jefferson, the Norman Yoke" (1987); Ball, "Constitution, Court, Indian Tribes" (1987); Norgren, "Protection of What Rights They Have" (1988); and Williams, Jr., "Documents of Barbarism" (1989). Foreign authors from this period include Mickenberg, "Aboriginal Rights" (1971); Cummings and Mickenberg, *Native Rights in Canada* (1972); Hookey, "Gove Land Rights Case" (1972); Hookey, "Marshall and the English Oak" (1974); Priestley, "Communal Title and the Common Law" (1974); Bennett, "Aboriginal Title" (1978); Hurley, "Aboriginal Rights" (1982–83); Green and Dickason, *Law of Nations and the New World* (1989); and McNeil, *Common Law Aboriginal Title* (1989).

18. McNeil, *Common Law Aboriginal Title*, 304, 306.

19. Ibid., 4–6, 160, 206–208, 221, 298. McNeil acknowledges that the Crown possessed sovereignty (lordship) and possibly a right of preemption (the right to acquire Native land rights if and when Native inhabitants choose to sell), but argues that the Indians "had fee simple estates by virtue of their occupation of lands," 192, 240–41.

20. Ibid., 236, 245, 264, 301.

21. Ibid., 228–29, 304. The *Johnson* dispute should have been resolved by reference to the 1763 Proclamation and other applicable prohibitions of private purchases, without mention of the doctrine of discovery; see 227.

22. Williams, Jr., *American Indian in Western Legal Thought*, 317. As noted by Kevin Worthen, Williams traces "the lineage of the Discovery Doctrine from medieval crusades, through imperial Spain and England, and ultimately to the United States," and "attempts to lay bare the moral (or perhaps immoral) underpinnings of contemporary federal Indian law." Worthen, "Book Review, Sword or Shield," 1372.

23. Williams, Jr., "Jefferson, the Norman Yoke," 184.

24. Williams, Jr., *American Indian in Western Legal Thought*, 312.

25. Daniels, "Immigration," 215–16. See also Summerhill and Williams, *Sinking Columbus*.

26. See, e.g., Singer, "Sovereignty and Property" (1991); Williams, Jr., "Columbus's Legacy" (1991); Newton, "Courts of the Conqueror" (1992); Newcomb, "Christian Nationalism in Federal Indian Law" (1993); Singer, "Increasing Weight of History in American Indian Land Claims" (1994); Burch, "How Much Diversity" (1994); Wilkins, "*Johnson v. M'Intosh* Revisited" (1994); Skibine,

"Reconciling Federal and State Power inside Indian Reservations" (1995); Wilkins, "Quit-Claiming the Doctrine of Discovery" (1998); Worthen, "Grand Experiment" (1998); McNeil, "Aboriginal Rights in Canada" (1998); Russell, "High Courts and the Rights of Aboriginal Peoples" (1998); Slattery, "Thoughts on Aboriginal Title" (1999); Frickey, "A Common Law for Our Age of Colonialism" (1999); Ball, "Marshall and Indian Nations" (2000); Kades, "Dark Side" (2000); Kades, "Great Case" (2001); Carbone, "Back to the Future" (2002); Porter, "Two Kinds of Indians" (2002); Blumm, "Retracing the Discovery Doctrine" (2004); McHugh, "Aboriginal Title in New Zealand" (2004); Miller, "Doctrine of Discovery in American Indian Law" (2005); Watson, "John Marshall and Indian Land Rights: A Historical Rejoinder" (2006); Fletcher, "The Iron Cold of the Marshall Trilogy" (2006); McNeil, "Aboriginal Title and the Supreme Court" (2006); Purdy, "Property and Empire" (2007); Twibell, "Rethinking *Johnson v. M'intosh*" (2008); and Miller and Ruru, "An Indigenous Lens into Comparative Law" (2009).

27. See, e.g., Falkowski, *Indian Law/Race Law* (1992); Pommersheim, *Braid of Feathers* (1995); Norgren, *Cherokee Cases* (1996); Anaya, *Indigenous Peoples in International Law* (1996); Wilkins, *American Indian Sovereignty and the U.S. Supreme Court* (1997); Wilkins and Lomawaima, *Uneven Ground* (2001); Banner, *How the Indians Lost Their Land* (2005); Robertson, *Conquest by Law* (2005); Williams, Jr., *Loaded Weapon* (2005); Barker, *Sovereignty Matters* (2005); Slattery, *Paper Empires* (2005); Russell, *Recognizing Aboriginal Title* (2005); Miller, *Native America* (2006); Henderson, *Indigenous Diplomacy and the Rights of Peoples* (2008); Newcomb, *Pagans in the Promised Land* (2008); Young, *Trouble with Tradition* (2008); and Richardson et al., *Indigenous Peoples and the Law* (2009).

28. Williams, Jr., "Columbus's Legacy," 67 ("instrument"); and Williams, Jr., *Loaded Weapon*, 57 ("Indianophobic").

29. Williams, Jr., *Loaded Weapon*, 56.

30. Wilkins, "Quit-Claiming the Doctrine of Discovery," 311; Miller, "Doctrine of Discovery in American Indian Law," 117; Twibell, "Rethinking *Johnson v. M'intosh*," 153; and Falkowski, *Indian Law/Race Law*, 99.

31. Newcomb, *Pagans in the Promised Land*, 117 ("simply because"), 45–46 ("so-called right"), and xv ("decode").

32. Kades, "Dark Side," 1080, 1109. See also Kades, "Great Case," 111; Skibine, "Marshall and the Doctrine of Discovery," 132; Blumm, "Retracing the Discovery Doctrine," 776 n.414; Wilkins, *American Indian Sovereignty and the U.S. Supreme Court*, 4; and Pommersheim, *Braid of Feathers*, 43.

33. Purdy, "Property and Empire," 341; and Porter, "Two Kinds of Indians," 646.

34. Robertson, *Conquest by Law*, xiii.

35. Ibid., 95.

36. Ibid., 116; see also 141, and Fletcher, "The Iron Cold of the Marshall Trilogy," 634–35.

37. Banner, *How the Indians Lost Their Land*, 181.

38. Ibid., 150, 190.

39. As noted by Eric Kades, the fact that the Supreme Court did not deny Indians all property rights "presents difficulties for those who portray American Indian policy as intentionally genocidal." Kades, "Dark Side," 1109.

40. Skibine, "Marshall and the Doctrine of Discovery," 133. See also Blumm, "Retracing the Discovery Doctrine," 776 n.414.

41. Young, *Trouble with Tradition*, 22, 76 n.8. See also Getches, "Conquering the Cultural Frontier," 1580 n.24 ("It is difficult to imagine the young nation's Court being less restrictive of Indian rights in such hotly charged cases").

42. Wilkins, *American Indian Sovereignty and the U.S. Supreme Court*, 34–35. See also Kades, "Dark Side," 1108–1109 ("At one extreme, Marshall could have given the Indians a full loaf: European title, with an absolute right to alienate to anyone. At the other extreme, Marshall could have given the Indians no loaf by declaring them truly tenants at sufferance subject to ejection at the will of the United States").

43. Ball, "Constitution, Court, Indian Tribes," 25.

44. See Clinton, "There Is No Federal Supremacy Clause for Indian Tribes," 237 n.434. Lindsay Robertson represented the appellants and argued that *Johnson* was without historical support and was rejected in *Worcester*. Robertson acknowledged that private purchases were regulated by colonial legislation but argued that Virginia had not acted to prohibit the purchases. Robertson, "*Johnson v. M'Intosh*, Brief for Appellants," 861–66. Lew Millenbach, for McIntosh, argued that the doctrine of discovery and the nature of Indian land rights were nonjusticiable political doctrines. Millenbach, "*Johnson v. M'Intosh*, Brief for Respondents," 886. The fictitious American Indian Nations Supreme Court declared that a "true" doctrine of discovery was inapplicable to inhabited lands but held for McIntosh because the Indians failed to reserve the lands when they ceded their territory to the United States. Rice, "*Johnson v. M'Intosh*, Decision," 899, 903.

45. Blumm, "Retracing the Discovery Doctrine," 718.

46. Ibid., 773 ("Indian title—with all rights of use, possession, and development—should have been identified as a fee simple. But it is true that this fee simple was burdened with the government's right of preemption, imposing a severe, but partial restraint on alienation. Yet this sort of property interest is well within the confines of traditional Anglo-American law").

47. Blumm, "Retracing the Discovery Doctrine," 740 and n.183.

48. See, e.g., Williams, Jr., *American Indian in Western Legal Thought*, 328; Skibine, "Reconciling Federal and State Power inside Indian Reservations," 1109; Pommersheim, *Braid of Feathers*, 123–26; Anaya and Williams, "Protection of Indigenous Peoples' Rights," 33; Smelcei, Comment, "Using International Law More Effectively," 303; and Gilbert, "Historical Indigenous Peoples' Land Claims," 584.

49. Williams, Jr., "Encounters," 670.

50. International tribunals in the 1920s and 1930s declined to recognize indigenous territorial rights. See *Cayuga Indians (Great Britain v. United States)*, 6 R.

Int'l Arb. Awards 173 (1926); *Island of Palmas Case (United States v. Netherlands)*, 2 R. Int'l Arb. Awards 829 (1928); and *Legal Status of E. Greenland (Denmark v. Norway)*, 1933 P.C.I.J. (ser. A/B) No. 53 (Apr. 5), discussed in Anaya, "Rights of Indigenous Peoples and International Law," 208–11; and Williams, Jr., "Encounters," 675 n.49. In the *Island of Palmas Case*, the Permanent Court of Arbitration held that Spain had title over the islands derived from discovery, even though the islands were inhabited at the time of the supposed discovery. Charters, "Indigenous Peoples and International Law and Policy" 162.

51. Anaya and Williams, "Protection of Indigenous Peoples' Rights," 33–34, 56. The International Labor Organization is a specialized UN agency focused on the promotion of social justice and labor rights.

52. See Smelcer, Comment, "Using International Law More Effectively," 309 ("ILO Convention No. 169 abandons the ILO's former assimilationist posture toward indigenous peoples, and instead affirms indigenous peoples' aspirations to land and natural resource rights, rights to be free from discrimination in national social policies, and, most importantly, the right to cultural integrity").

53. Anaya and Williams, "Protection of Indigenous Peoples' Rights," 56. Advocates for indigenous peoples' rights have also relied on the UN International Covenant on Civil and Political Rights and the UN International Convention on the Elimination of All Forms of Racial Discrimination.

54. Ibid., 42.

55. Ibid., 35–42; and Tittemore, "Dann Litigation," 594–95.

56. *Judgment on North Sea Continental Shelf Cases*, I.C.J. 3 (1969); and *Advisory Opinion on Western Sahara*, I.C.J. 3 (1975).

57. In particular, the Danns alleged that the United States violated Article II (right to equality before the law), Article XVIII (right to a fair trial), and Article XXIII (right to property) of the 1948 Declaration "by purporting to have appropriated the lands as federal property through an unfair procedure before the Indian Claims Commission ("ICC"), by physically removing and threatening to remove the Danns' livestock from the lands, and by permitting or acquiescing in gold prospecting activities within Western Shoshone traditional territory." *Mary and Carrie Dann v. United States*, Case 11.140, Report No. 75/02, Inter-Am. C.H.R., Doc. 5 rev. 1 at 860, ¶ 2 (Dec. 27, 2002).

58. Ibid., ¶ 124 ("evolving rules").

59. Ibid., ¶ 55 ("reflected in judicial decisions"), ¶ 175 ("ensure").

60. Ibid., ¶ 176. In 2006 the UN Committee for the Elimination of Racial Discrimination expressed concern that the "Western Shoshone peoples' legal rights to ancestral lands have been extinguished through gradual encroachment." Decision 1(68) (United States of America), U.N. ESCOR, CERD, 68th Sess., U.N. Doc. CERD/C/USA/DEC/1 (Apr. 11, 2006).

61. The origins of the declaration can be traced back to 1982, when the UN Economic and Social Council established the Working Group on Indigenous Populations to draft a declaration of the rights of indigenous peoples for consideration by the UN General Assembly. The draft was referred to the Commission

on Human Rights in 1994, which established another Working Group to examine its terms. On June 29, 2006, the Human Rights Council (the successor body to the Commission on Human Rights) approved the revised declaration and referred it to the General Assembly.

62. United Nations Declaration on the Rights of Indigenous Peoples, G.A. Res. 61/295, Annex, United Nations Document A/RES/61/295 (Sept. 13, 2007), available at http://www2.ohchr.org/english/issues/indigenous/declaration .htm. See Newcomb, *Pagans in the Promised Land*, xxviii ("new era for indigenous human rights"); and Anaya and Williams, "Protection of Indigenous Peoples' Rights," 34. The declaration passed with 114 nations in favor, four opposed (United States, Canada, Australia, and New Zealand), and eleven abstentions.

63. In 1989 the OAS General Assembly resolved to "request the Inter-American Commission on Human Rights to prepare a juridical instrument relative to the rights of indigenous peoples." Anaya, *Indigenous Peoples in International Law*, 66. In 2009 the working group was close to finalizing the American Declaration on the Rights of Indigenous Peoples. "Draft American Declaration on the Rights of Indigenous Peoples Moves Forward," *Indian Country Today*, Jan. 9, 2009.

64. United Nations Declaration on the Rights of Indigenous Peoples, G.A. Res. 61/295, U.N. Doc. A/RES/61/295 (Sept. 13, 2007). See also Prasad, "The UN Declaration on the Rights of Indigenous Peoples," 316.

65. Echo-Hawk, *Courts of the Conqueror*, 84.

66. Stevenson, Comment, "Indigenous Land Rights and the Declaration on the Rights of Indigenous Peoples," 324, 327.

67. *Cal v. Attorney General* (Belize Sup. Ct., Oct. 18, 2007). The Court noted that states are not expected to disregard principles of general international law contained in UN declarations.

68. Speech by Jenny Macklin, Minister for Families, Housing, Community Services and Indigenous Affairs, delivered in the Parliament House, Canberra, Australia (Apr. 3, 2009), available at http://www.jennymacklin.fahcsia .gov.au/internet/jennymacklin.nsf/print/un_declaration_03apr09.htm; "New Zealand Supports the UN Declaration," *Indian Country Today*, Apr. 19, 2010, available at http://www.indiancountrytoday.com/internal?st=pri nt&id=91543409&path=/home/content; Canada's Statement of Support on the United Nations Declaration on the Rights of Indigenous Peoples, November 12, 2010, available at http://www.ainc-inac.gc.ca/ap/ia/dcl/stmt-eng .asp; and "Remarks by the President at the White House Tribal Nations Conference, Department of the Interior, Washington, D.C.," press release, Dec. 16, 2010, available at http://www.whitehouse.gov/the-press-office/2010/12/16/ remarks-presidentwhite-house-tribal-nations-conference.

69. See Gilbert, "Historical Indigenous Peoples' Land Claims," 594; and Anaya and Williams, "Protection of Indigenous Peoples' Rights," 69.

70. E/CN.4/Sub.2/AC.4/1985/WP.4/Add.4, at 6 (1985 draft declaration), available at http://www.akha.org/content/humanrightsdocs/rightsofindigenous populations.html.

71. See Williams, Jr., "Encounters," 689–90; http://worldebookfair.org/ Members/CWIS/FWDP/International/draft88.pdf, at 15 (1988 draft); and http://worldebookfair.org/Members/CWIS/FWDP/International/draft89.pdf (1989 draft). See also http://worldebookfair.org/Members/CWIS/FWDP/Inter national/draft93.pdf (1993 draft declaration); http://www1.umn.edu/humanrts/ instree/declra.htm (1994 draft declaration); and http://www.un.org/esa/socdev/ unpfii/en/drip.html (2007 final version of the *Declaration*).

72. Williams, Jr., "The Algebra of Federal Indian Law," 290. Robert Laurence has argued that Williams's proposals are neither achievable nor advisable. Laurence, "Learning to Live with Plenary Power," 422–23 ("I am not sure that such a system is achievable in today's legal and political world. . . . Even if it is, I am not sure it is the wisest system. . . . For the United States to cut the Turtle Mountain Chippewa Tribe loose to sink or swim as an independent sovereign would be . . . neglectful"). See also Worthen, "Book Review, Sword or Shield," 1376 n.6 ("the complete restructuring of the American legal system advocated by Professor Williams seems both undesirable and unachievable"). In response, Williams contends that "Indian people will never secure the most fundamental of human rights, the right to true self-determination, until the lie of words sustained by Federal Indian legal law and its blind obeisance to the Discovery Doctrine and its closely related Congressional plenary power doctrine can no longer be lived with as 'the actual state of things.'" Williams, Jr., "Learning Not to Live with Eurocentric Myopia," 457.

73. Wilkins and Lomawaima, *Uneven Ground*, 63. See also Skibine, "Reconciling Federal and State Power inside Indian Reservations," 1109; and Miller, *Native America*, xiv.

74. Newcomb, "Christian Nationalism in Federal Indian Law," 338.

75. *Looking Forward, Looking Back*, 1:696.

76. Resolution of the Summit of Indigenous Nations Calling for a Rescission of the Conceptual Doctrine of Discovery and Related Documents, Specifically the Inter Caetera Bull (Papal Bulls) of 1493 and the 1496 Royal Charter of the Church of England, Summit of Indigenous Nations, Resolution # 2006-01, at Bear Butte, South Dakota (Aug. 1–4, 2006), available at http://www.gopetition .com/petitions/rescind-the-papal-bulls.html. See also "Indigenous in Americas Just Say 'No' to Papal Bull," *Indian Country Today*, Aug. 14, 2006, (signatories included "a cross-section of indigenous and non-indigenous organizations and nations").

77. See http://gc2009.org/ViewLegislation/view_leg_detail.aspx?id=983 &type=Final (July 2009). Indigenous peoples attending the 2009 Parliament of the World's Religions in Australia called upon the Vatican to repudiate the decrees that legitimized activities that "evolved into the dehumanizing Doctrine of Christian Discovery." "Indigenous Delegates Ask Pope to Repudiate Doctrine of Discovery," *Indian Country Today*, Dec. 21, 2009, at http://www.indiancountry today.com/home/content/79636552.html.

78. See http://www.anglicanjournal.com/nc/news-items/article/reality -check-9220.html (June 9, 2010).

79. See http://www.un.org/esa/socdev/unpfii/documents/E.C.19.2010 .13%20EN.pdf (April 2010).

80. "Episcopal Church Repudiates Doctrine of Discovery–Urges US Adoption of UN Declaration," *Indian Country Today*, July 26, 2009, updated July 27, 2009; and "Episcopal Church Repudiates Doctrine of Discovery, Calls on US to Do Same," available at http://weiwentg.blogspot.com/2009/07/episcopal -church-repudiates-doctrine-of.html (July 29, 2009).

81. U.S. Department of State, *Announcement of U.S. Support for the United Nations Declaration on the Rights of Indigenous Peoples* (Dec. 16, 2010), available at http://usun.state.gov/documents/organization/153239.pdf.

82. "Remarks by the President at the White House Tribal Nations Conference, Department of the Interior, Washington, D.C.," press release, Dec. 16, 2010, available at http://www.whitehouse.gov/the-press-office/2010/12/16/ remarks-presidentwhite-house-tribal-nations-conference.

83. Purdy, "Property and Empire," 340 n.49.

84. *Johnson*, 21 U.S. at 572.

85. Peoria Tribe Representatives Travel to U. Illinois Campus (Mar. 11, 2009), at http://www.dailyillini.com.

86. Foster, "Letting Go the Bone," 36.

87. Scholars suggest various ways to repudiate or modify the doctrine of discovery. See, e.g., Williams, Jr., *Loaded Weapon*, 166 (confront judges "with the racist stereotypes and patterns of thought they perpetuate"); Miller, *Native America*, 176–78 (extend "the commendable goals of the self-determination era"); Newcomb, *Pagans in the Promised Land*, 136 (effect a "positive cognitive paradigm shift away from the mentality and behaviors of empire and domination"); and Twibell, "Rethinking *Johnson v. M'intosh*," 195–98 (United States should overturn *Johnson* and issue an apology for the forced relocation of indigenous populations). Robert "Tim" Coulter, a Potawatomi and founder of the Indian Law Resource Center, has drafted "principles of law relating to Indian land and resources," which include the following statements: (1) Native nations have complete ownership of their aboriginal lands—not some limited or partial right; (2) discovery did not give the discovering country any ownership of Native lands or resources; and (3) Congress cannot take Native lands and resources without fair compensation and without following a genuine legal process. "Expert Offers Principles to Fix Inequities in Federal Indian Law," *Indian Country Today*, Apr. 9, 2010, at http://www.indiancountrytoday.com/archive/90353444 .html.

88. Bryan, *Imperialism of John Marshall*, 112.

BIBLIOGRAPHY

Manuscripts and Archival Collections

British Library, London.
Croghan, George. Papers. Historical Society of Pennsylvania, Philadelphia.
Dreer Autograph Collection. Historical Society of Pennsylvania, Philadelphia.
Gratz, Benjamin. Papers. American Jewish Historical Society. Waltham, Mass.
Gratz Collection. Historical Society of Pennsylvania, Philadelphia.
Gratz Family of Philadelphia. Papers. American Jewish Historical Society. Waltham, Mass.
Gratz-Joseph Papers. American Jewish Archives, Cincinnati, Ohio.
Illinois and Wabash Land Company. United Illinois and Wabash Land Companies Minutes, 1778–1812. Historical Society of Pennsylvania, Philadelphia.
Maryland State Archives, Annapolis.
Papers of the Continental Congress.
Penn Letter Book. Vol. 4. Historical Society of Pennsylvania, Philadelphia.
Public Archives of Canada, Ottawa.
United Illinois and Wabash Land Companies Collection. University of Oklahoma, Norman, Oklahoma.

Government Documents and Publications

American Indian Policy Review Commission. *Final Report*. Vol. 1. Washington, D.C.: U.S. Government Printing Office, 1977.
American State Papers: 1–2, Indian Affairs; 1–2, Public Lands; 3 Foreign Relations.
Annals of the Congress of the United States, 1789–1824. 42 Vols. Washington, D.C., 1834–56.

[Benton, Thomas Hart, ed.]. *Abridgement of the Debates of Congress, from 1789 to 1856*. Vol. 1. New York: Appleton, 1857.

Carter, Clarence Edwin, ed. *The Territorial Papers of the United States*. Vols. 2, 5, 7–8, 17. Washington, D.C.: U.S. Government Printing Office, 1934–50.

Continental Congress. *Journals of the Continental Congress, 1774–1789*. Edited by Worthington C. Ford et al. 34 vols. Washington, D.C., 1904–37.

Hening, William Waller, comp. *The Statutes at Large; Being a Collection of All the Laws of Virginia, from the First Session of the Legislature in 1609*. 1819–1823; reprint, Charlottesville: University Press of Virginia, 1969.

Journal of the Senate, Including the Journal of the Executive Proceedings of the Senate, George Washington Administration 1789–1797. Vols. 5–6. Ed. Martin P. Claussen. Wilmington, Del.: M. Glazier, 1977.

Kappler, Charles J. *Indian Affairs: Laws and Treaties*. Vol. 2. Washington, D.C.: U.S. Government Printing Office, 1904.

Minutes of the Provincial Council of Pennsylvania. Vol. 5. Harrisburg: Theo. Fenn and Company, 1851.

Minutes of the Supreme Court of the United States (Feb. 1, 1790–Aug. 4, 1828). National Archives, Washington, D.C.

Official Opinions of the Attorneys General of the United States. Vol. 1. Washington, D.C.: U.S. Government Printing Office, 1852.

Opinions of the Solicitor of the Department of the Interior. Vol. 1. Washington, D.C.: U.S. Department of the Interior, 1979.

Palmer, William P., et al., eds. *Calendar of Virginia State Papers and Other Manuscripts Preserved in the Capitol at Richmond*. Vols. 1, 6. Richmond, 1875, 1886.

Register of Debates in Congress. 14 vols. Washington, D.C., 1824–38.

Twohig, Dorothy, ed. *The Journal of the Proceedings of the President, 1793–1797*. Charlottesville: University Press of Virginia, 1981.

United States. Record Group 107. Secretary of War/Letters Received/Registered series, microfilm M 221, cited by reel and frame. National Archives, Washington, D.C.

———. Record Group 267. Appellate Case Files of the Supreme Court of the United States, cases 1100–1113, microcopy no. 214, cited by roll and frame. National Archives, Washington, D.C.

———. Record Group 267. Minutes of the Supreme Court of the United States [Feb. 1, 1790–Aug. 4, 1828], microcopy no. 215, cited by roll and frame. National Archives, Washington, D.C.

U.S. Census Bureau. *Statistical Abstract of the United States*, 129th ed. Washington, D.C.: U.S. Government Printing Office, 2010.

U.S. Congress. *Congressional Debates*, 21st Cong., 1st Sess.

U.S. *House Journal*.

U.S. *Senate Journal*.

Virginia. *Colony Laws of Virginia, 1642–1660*. Vol. 2. Wilmington, Del.: Michael Glazier, 1978.

———. Convention. *The Proceedings of the Convention of Delegates*. Williamsburg, Va.: Alexander Purdie, 1776.

———. *Journal of the House of Delegates*. Williamsburg, Va.: Clarkson and Davis, 1779.

———. *Journal of the House of Delegates*. Richmond, Va.: Davis, 1792.

NEWSPAPERS

[Champaign, Ill.] *News-Gazette*.
[Champaign, Ill.] *University Wire*.
[Chicago] *Sun-Times*.
Daily National Intelligencer.
Indian Country Today.
Niles' Weekly Register.
[Peoria, Ill.] *Journal Star*.
[Philadelphia] *National Gazette*.
[Springfield, Ill.] *State Journal-Register*.
Tulsa World.
[Vincennes] *Indiana Gazette*.
Washington Times.

BOOKS AND ARTICLES

Abernethy, Thomas P. "Commercial Activities of Silas Deane of France." *American Historical Review* 39 (1934): 477.

———. *The South in the New Nation, 1789–1819*. Baton Rouge: Louisiana State University Press, 1961.

———. *Western Lands and the American Revolution*. New York: Appleton-Century, 1937.

Achenbach, Joel. *The Grand Idea: George Washington's Potomac and the Race to the West*. New York: Simon and Schuster, 2004.

Adams, Herbert B. "Maryland's Influence on Land Cessions to United States." *Historical and Political Sciences* 3 (1885): 22.

Adams, John. *The Political Writings of John Adams*. Edited by George W. Carey. Washington, D.C.: Regnery, 2000.

Adams, John, and Jonathan Sewall. *Novanglus and Massachusettensis*. New York: Russell and Russell, 1968.

Adams, Randolph G. *Political Ideas of the American Revolution: Britannic-American Contributions to the Problem of Imperial Organization, 1765–1775*. Durham, N.C.: Trinity College Press, 1922.

Adams, Samuel. *The Writings of Samuel Adams*. Edited by Harry Alonzo Cushing. Vol. 4. New York: Octagon Books, 1968.

"Addenda to Watson's Annals of Philadelphia: Notes by Jacob Mordecai, 1836." *Pennsylvania Magazine of History and Biography* 98 (1974): 131.

Alden, John Richard. *John Stuart and the Southern Colonial Frontier: A Study of Indian Relations, War, Trade, and Land Problems in the Southern Wilderness, 1754–1775*. New York: Gordian Press, 1966.

Alexander, John K. "James Wilson." In *American National Biography*, vol. 23, edited by John A. Garraty and Mark C. Carnes. New York: Oxford University Press, 1999.

Alvord, Clarence W. *The Illinois Country, 1673–1818*. Urbana: University of Illinois Press, 1920.

———. *The Mississippi Valley in British Politics: A Study of the Trade, Speculation, and Experiments in Imperialism Culminating in the American Revolution*. Vols. 1–2. Cleveland, Ohio: Arthur H. Clark Company, 1917.

Alvord, Clarence W., ed. *Cahokia Records*. Vol. 2. Springfield: Trustees of the Illinois State Historical Library, 1907.

———. *Kaskaskia Records*. Vol. 2. Springfield: Trustees of the Illinois State Historical Library, 1909.

Alvord, Clarence W., and Clarence Edwin Carter, eds. *The Critical Period, 1763–1765*. Collections of the Illinois State History Library, vol. 10. Springfield: Trustees of the Illinois State Historical Library, 1915.

———. *Trade and Politics, 1767–1769*. Collections of the Illinois State History Library, vol. 16. Springfield: Trustees of the Illinois State Historical Library, 1921.

American Colonization Society. *The African Repository* [August 1861]. Vol. 37. Washington, D.C.: William H. Moore, 1861.

Ammon, Harry. *James Monroe: The Quest for National Identity*. New York: McGraw-Hill, 1971.

Anaya, S. James. *Indigenous Peoples in International Law*, 1st ed. New York: Oxford University Press, 1996.

———. *Indigenous Peoples in International Law*, 2nd ed. New York: Oxford University Press, 2004.

Anaya, S. James, and Robert A. Williams, Jr. "The Protection of Indigenous Peoples' Rights over Lands and Natural Resources under the Inter-American Human Rights System." *Harvard Human Rights Journal* 14 (2001): 33.

Anderson, James D. "Thomas Wharton, 1730/31–1784: Merchant in Philadelphia." Ph.D. thesis, Department of History, University of Akron, 1977.

Anderson, Terry L., and Fred S. McChesney, "Raid or Trade? An Economic Model of Indian-White Relations." *Journal of Law and Economics* 37 (1994): 39.

Andrews, Charles M. *The Colonial Period of American History: The Settlements*. Vols. 1–2. New Haven: Yale University Press, 1934–36.

Anson, Bert. *The Miami Indians*. Norman: University of Oklahoma Press, 1970.

Appleby, Joyce Oldham. *Thomas Jefferson*. New York: Times Books, 2003.

Arbuckle, Robert D. "John Nicholson." In *American National Biography*, vol. 16, edited by John A. Garraty and Mark C. Carnes. New York: Oxford University Press, 1999.

———. *Pennsylvania Speculator and Patriot: The Entrepreneurial John Nicholson, 1757–1800*. University Park: Pennsylvania State University Press, 1975.

Armentrout, Donald S. "William Smith." In *American National Biography*, vol. 20, edited by John A. Garraty and Mark C. Carnes. New York: Oxford University Press, 1999.

Arnebeck, Bob. *Through a Fiery Trial: Building Washington, 1790–1800.* Lanham, Md.: Madison Books, 1991.

Arneil, Barbara. *John Locke and America: The Defence of English Colonialism.* New York: Oxford University Press, 1996.

Ashton, Dianne. *Rebecca Gratz: Women and Judaism in Antebellum America.* Detroit: Wayne State University Press, 1997.

Askin, John. *The John Askin Papers.* Vols. 1–2. Edited by Milo M. Quaife. Detroit: Detroit Library Commission, 1928–31.

Aspinall, Thomas, ed. *Aspinall Papers.* Collections of the Massachusetts Historical Society, vol. 40. Boston: Massachusetts Historical Society, 1871.

Atkinson, David N. *Leaving the Bench: Supreme Court Justices at the End.* Lawrence: University Press of Kansas, 1999.

Attwood, Bain, and Helen Doyle. *Possession: Batman's Treaty and the Matter of History.* Carlton, Australia: Miegunyah Press, 2009.

Austin, Moses, "The Journal." *American History Review* 5 (1900): 523.

Baer, M. Teresa. "William Henry Harrison and the Indian Treaty Land Cessions." In *The Indiana Territory, 1800–2000: A Bicentennial Perspective*, edited by Darrel E. Bigham. Indianapolis: Indiana Historical Society, 2001.

Bailey, Kenneth P. *The Ohio Company of Virginia and the Westward Movement, 1748–1792: A Chapter in the History of the Colonial Frontier.* Glendale, Calif.: Arthur H. Clark, 1939.

Bailyn, Bernard. *Voyagers to the West.* New York: Knopf, 1986.

Bakeless, John. *Background to Glory: The Life of George Rogers Clark.* Philadelphia: Lippincott, 1957.

Baker, Emerson W. "A Scratch with a Bear's Paw: Anglo-Indian Deeds in Early Maine." *Ethnohistory* 36 (1989): 235.

Baker, Leonard. *John Marshall: A Life in Law.* New York: Macmillan, 1974.

Bald, F. Clever. *Detroit's First American Decade, 1796–1805.* Ann Arbor: University of Michigan Press, 1948.

Balesi, Charles J. *The Time of the French in the Heart of North America: 1763–1818.* Chicago: Alliance Française Chicago, 1992.

Ball, Milner S. "Constitution, Court, Indian Tribes." *American Bar Foundation Research Journal* 1987 (1987): 1.

———. "John Marshall and Indian Nations in the Beginning and Now." *John Marshall Law Review* 33 (2000): 1183.

Banner, Stuart. *How the Indians Lost Their Land: Law and Power on the Frontier.* Cambridge, Mass.: Belknap Press of the Harvard University Press, 2005.

———. *Possessing the Pacific: Land, Settlers, and Indigenous People from Australia to Alaska.* Cambridge, Mass.: Harvard University Press, 2007.

Barck, Oscar Theodore, Jr., and Hugh Talmage Lefler. *Colonial America*, 2nd ed. New York: Macmillan, 1968.

Barker, Joanne, ed. *Sovereignty Matters: Locations of Contestation and Possibility in Indigenous Struggles for Self-Determination.* Lincoln: University of Nebraska Press, 2005.

Barnhart, John D., ed. *Henry Hamilton and George Rogers Clark in the American Revolution with the Unpublished Journal of Lieut. Henry Hamilton.* Crawfordsville, Ind.: R. E. Banta, 1951.

Barnhart, John D., and Dorothy Riker, *Indiana to 1816: The Colonial Period.* Indianapolis: Indiana Historical Bureau, 1971.

Baroway, Aaron. "Solomon Etting, 1764–1847." *Maryland Historical Magazine* 15 (1920): 1.

Barsh, Russel L., and James Youngblood Henderson. *The Road: Indian Tribes and Political Liberty.* Berkeley: University of California Press, 1980.

Barthelmas, Della Gray. *The Signers of the Declaration of Independence: A Biographical and Genealogical Reference.* Jefferson, N.C.: McFarland, 1997.

Bartlett, Richard H. "Native Title in Australia: Denial, Recognition, and Dispossession." In *Indigenous Peoples' Rights in Australia, Canada, and New Zealand,* edited by Paul Haveman. New York: Oxford University Press, 1999.

Bass, Althea. *Cherokee Messenger.* Norman: University of Oklahoma Press, 1936.

Baxter, Maurice G. "Daniel Webster." In *American National Biography,* vol. 22, edited by John A. Garraty and Mark C. Carnes. New York: Oxford University Press, 1999.

———. *Daniel Webster and the Supreme Court.* Amherst: University of Massachusetts Press, 1966.

Bayard, Charles Judah. *The Development of the Public Land Policy, 1783–1820, with Special Reference to Indiana.* New York: Arno Press, 1979.

Beckwith, Hiram Williams, ed. *General George Rogers Clark's Conquest of the Illinois.* Collections of the Illinois State Historical Library, vol. 1. Springfield, Ill.: H. W. Rokker, 1903.

Belgrave, Michael. *Historical Frictions: Maori Claims and Reinvented Histories.* Auckland, New Zealand: Auckland University Press, 2005.

Bennett, Gordon I. "Aboriginal Title in the Common Law: A Stony Path through Feudal Doctrine." *Buffalo Law Review* 27 (1978): 617.

Berman, Howard R. "The Concept of Aboriginal Rights in the Early Legal History of the United States." *Buffalo Law Review* 27 (1978): 637.

Bickford, Charlene Bangs, Kenneth R. Bowling, Helen E. Veit, and William Charles diGiacomantonio, eds. *Documentary History of the First Federal Congress of the United States of America.* Vol. 15. Baltimore: Johns Hopkins University Press, 2004.

Billings, Warren M., John E. Selby, and Thad W. Tate, *Colonial Virginia: A History.* White Plains, N.Y.: KTO Press, 1986.

Billington, Ray A. "The Fort Stanwix Treaty of 1768." *New York History* 25 (1944): 182.

———. *Westward Expansion: A History of the American Frontier,* 4th ed. New York: Macmillan, 1974.

Billot, C.P. *John Batman: The Story of John Batman and the Founding of Melbourne.* Melbourne, Australia: Hyland House, 1979.

Bishop, Abraham. *Georgia Speculation Unveiled.* Ann Arbor, Mich.: University Microfilms, 1966.

Biskupic, Joan, and Elder Witt. *The Supreme Court at Work*, 2d ed. Washington, D.C.: Congressional Quarterly, 1997.

Blair, Helen, ed. *The Indian Tribes of the Upper Mississippi Valley and Region of the Great Lakes*. Vol. 1. Lincoln: University of Nebraska Press, 1996.

Blakey, Arch Fredric. *General John H. Winder*. Gainesville: University of Florida Press, 1990.

Blasingham, Emily J. "The Depopulation of the Illinois Indians." *Ethnohistory* 3 (1956): 193.

Bloxham, Steven John. "Aboriginal Title, Alaskan Native Property Rights, and the Case of the Tee-Hit-Ton Indians." *American Indian Law Review* 8 (1980): 299.

Blumm, Michael C. "Retracing the Discovery Doctrine: Aboriginal Title, Tribal Sovereignty, and Their Significance to Treaty-Making and Modern Natural Resources Policy in Indian Country." *Vermont Law Review* 28 (2004): 713.

Bobroff, Kenneth H. "Indian Law in Property: *Johnson v. M'Intosh* and Beyond." *Tulsa Law Review* 37 (2001): 521.

Bodley, Temple. *Our First Great West: In Revolutionary War, Diplomacy and Politics*. Louisville, Ky.: J. P. Morton, 1938.

Boller, Paul F., Jr., and John H. George. *They Never Said It: A Book of Fake Quotes, Misquotes, and Misleading Attributions*. New York: Oxford University Press, 1989.

Bolts, William. *Considerations on India Affairs; Particularly Respecting the Present State of Bengal and Its Dependencies*, 2nd ed. London: J. Almon, P. Elmsly, and Brotherton and Sewell, 1772.

Bond, Benjamin, William Smith, and William Livingston. *An Answer to a Bill in the Chancery of New Jersey, at the Suit of John Earl of Stair, and others, commonly called Proprietors, of the Eastern Division of New Jersey, against Benjamin Bond, and Others Claiming under the Original Proprietors and Associates of Elizabeth-Town*. New York: James Parker, 1752.

Bond, Beverley W., Jr. "The Foundations of Ohio." In *History of the State of Ohio*, vol. 1, edited by Carl Wittke. Columbus: Ohio State Archaeological and Historical Society, 1941.

———. *The Quit-Rent System in the American Colonies*. New Haven: Yale University Press, 1919.

Bonwick, James. *Port Phillip Settlement*. London: Sampson Low, Marston, Searle, and Rivingston, 1883.

Boorstin, Daniel J. *The Americans: The National Experience*. New York: Random House, 1965.

Bouquet, Henry. *The Papers of Henry Bouquet*. Vol. 5. Edited by Louis M. Waddell. Harrisburg: Pennsylvania Historical and Museum Commission, 1984.

———. *The Papers of Henry Bouquet*. Vol. 6. Edited by S. K. Stevens, Donald H. Kent and Autumn L. Leonard. Harrisburg: Pennsylvania Historical and Museum Commission, 1994.

Bowen, Huw V. *Revenue and Reform: The Indian Problem in British Politics, 1757–1773*. New York: Cambridge University Press, 1991.

Bowling, Kenneth R., and Helen E. Veit, eds. *Documentary History of the First Federal Congress of the United States of America*. Vol. 9. Baltimore: Johns Hopkins University Press, 1988.

Bowling, Kenneth R., William Charles DiGiacomantonio, and Charlene Bangs Bickford, eds. *Documentary History of the First Federal Congress of the United States of America*. Vol. 8. Baltimore: Johns Hopkins University Press, 1998.

Boyd, Julian P. "Silas Deane: Death by a Kindly Teacher of Treason?" *William and Mary Quarterly* 16 (1959): 165.

Brands, H. W. *The First American: The Life and Times of Benjamin Franklin*. New York: Doubleday, 2000.

Brockunier, Samuel Hugh. *The Irrepressible Democrat, Roger Williams*. New York: Ronald Press, 1940.

Bronner, Edwin B. "Indian Deed for Petty's Island." *Pennsylvania Magazine of History and Biography* 89 (1965): 111.

Brown, Margaret Kimball. *Cultural Transformations among the Illinois: An Application of a Systems Model*. East Lansing: Michigan State University, 1979.

Bryan, George. *The Imperialism of John Marshall: A Study in Expediency*. Boston: Stratford, 1924.

Buck, Solon J. *Illinois in 1818*. Urbana: University of Illinois Press, 1967.

Buck, Solon J., and Elizabeth Hawthorn Buck. *The Planting of Civilization in Western Pennsylvania*. Pittsburgh: University of Pittsburgh Press, 1939.

Buell, Rowena, ed. *The Memoirs of Rufus Putnam and Certain Official Papers and Correspondence*. Boston: Houghton, Mifflin and Company, 1903.

Bulkley, Rev. John. Preface. In *Poetical Meditations*, by Roger Wolcott. New London, Conn.: T. Green, 1725.

Bulloch, John Malcolm. *Territorial Soldiering in the North-East of Scotland during 1759–1814*. Aberdeen, Scotland: New Spalding Club, 1914.

Burch, Jordan. "How Much Diversity Is the United States Really Willing to Accept?" *Ohio Northern University Law Review* 20 (1994): 957.

Burd, Edward. *The Burd Papers*. Edited by Lewis Burd Walker. Pottsville, Pa.: Standard Publishing Company, 1899.

Burke, Joseph C. "The Cherokee Cases: A Study in Law, Politics, and Morality." *Stanford Law Review* 21 (February 1969): 500.

Burnett, Edmund C. *The Continental Congress*. New York: Macmillan, 1941.

Burnett, Edmund C., ed. *Letters of Members of the Continental Congress*. Vols. 4, 6. Washington, D.C.: Carnegie Institution of Washington, 1928, 1933.

Burt, A. L. *The United States, Great Britain, and British North America from the Revolution to the Establishment of Peace after the War of 1812*. New York: Russell and Russell, 1961.

Burton, Clarence Monroe. *A Chapter in the History of Cleveland*. Detroit: Wilton-Smith Company, 1895.

Burton, M. Agnes, ed. *Manuscripts from the Burton Historical Collection*. Detroit, Mich.: C. M. Burton, 1916.

Butler, Mann. *A History of the Commonwealth of Kentucky*, 2nd ed. Cincinnati: J. A. James and Company, 1836.

Butterfield, C. W., ed. *The Washington–Crawford Letters, Being the Correspondence Between George Washington and William Crawford, from 1767 to 1781, Concerning Western Lands.* Cincinnati: Robert Clarke and Company, 1877.

Butterfield, L. H., ed. *Adams Family Correspondence.* Vols. 1–2. Cambridge, Mass.: Belknap Press of Harvard University Press, 1963.

———. *The Book of Abigail and John: Selected Letters of the Adams Family, 1762–1784.* Cambridge, Mass.: Harvard University Press, 1975.

Byars, William V. *B. and M. Gratz: Merchants in Philadelphia, 1754–1798.* Jefferson City, Mo.: Hugh Stephens Printing, 1916.

Caley, Percy B. "Dunmore: Colonial Governor of New York and Virginia, 1770–1782." Ph.D. diss., University of Pittsburgh, 1939.

Calhoun, John C. *The Papers of John C. Calhoun.* Vols. 3–4, 8–9. Edited by W. Edwin Hemphill. Columbia: University of South Carolina Press, 1967–76.

Calloway, Colin G., ed. *Early American Indian Documents: Treaties and Laws, 1607–178,.* vol. 18: *Revolution and Confederation.* Washington, D.C.: University Publications of America, 1994.

Campbell, John C. *Lives of the Lord Chancellors and Keepers of the Great Seal of England, from the Earliest Times Till the Reign of King George IV.* Vols. 6–7. London: J. Murray, 1868.

"Canadian Archives." *Michigan Pioneer and Historical Society Historical Collections.* Vol. 24. Lansing: Robert Smith and Company, 1895.

Carbone, June. "Back to the Future: Intellectual Property and the Rediscovery of Property Rights—and Wrongs." *St. Louis University Law Journal* 46 (2002): 629.

Carter, Clarence Edwin. "Documents Relating to the Mississippi Land Company, 1763–1769." *American History Review* 16 (1911): 311.

———. *Great Britain and the Illinois Country, 1763–1774.* Washington, D.C.: American Historical Association, 1910.

Carter, Harvey Lewis. *The Life and Times of Little Turtle: First Sagamore of the Wabash.* Urbana: University of Illinois Press, 1987.

Cassell, Frank A. "The Structure of Baltimore's Politics in the Age of Jefferson, 1795–1812." In *Law, Society, and Politics in Early Maryland,* edited by Aubrey C. Land, Lois Green Carr, and Edward C. Papenfuse. Baltimore: Johns Hopkins University Press, 1977.

Casto, William R. *The Supreme Court in the Early Republic: The Chief Justiceships of John Jay and Oliver Ellsworth.* Columbia: University of South Carolina Press, 1995.

Catlin, George. *Catlin's Indians.* Philadelphia: Hubbard Brothers, 1891.

Cauthorn, Henry S. *A History of the City of Vincennes, Indiana, from 1702 to 1901.* Vincennes, Ind.: M. C. Cauthorn, 1902.

Cayton, Andrew R. L. *Frontier Indiana.* Bloomington: Indiana University Press, 1996.

———. *The Frontier Republic: Ideology and Politics in the Ohio Country, 1780–1825.* Kent, Ohio: Kent State University Press, 1986.

———. "'Noble Actors' upon 'the Theatre of Honour': Power and Civility in the Treaty of Greenville." In *Contact Points: American Frontiers from the Mohawk Valley to the Mississippi, 1750–1830,* edited by Andrew R. L. Cayton and Fredrika J. Teute. Chapel Hill: University of North Carolina Press, 1998.

Chalmers, George. *Political Annals of the Present United Colonies from Their Settlement to the Peace of 1763.* London: J. Bowen, 1780.

Chalou, George C. "George Rogers Clark and Indian America, 1778–1780." In *The French, the Indians, and George Rogers Clark in the Illinois Country.* Indianapolis: Indiana Historical Society, 1977.

Charters, Claire. "Indigenous Peoples and International Law and Policy." In *Indigenous Peoples and the Law,* edited by Benjamin J. Richardson, Shin Imai, and Kent McNeil. Portland, Ore.: Hart, 2009.

Chernow, Barbara Ann. *Robert Morris: Land Speculator, 1790–1801.* New York: Arno Press, 1978.

Chernow, Ron. *Alexander Hamilton.* New York: Penguin Press, 2004.

Chesnel, Paul. *History of Cavelier de La Salle, 1643–1687.* Translated by Andrée Chesnel Meany. New York: G. P. Putnam's Sons, 1932.

Christian, Timothy J. "Introduction." In *The Law of Nations and the New World,* by L. C. Green and Olive P. Dickason. Edmonton, Canada: University of Alberta Press, 1989.

Clark, George R. *George Rogers Clark Papers, 1771–1781.* Collections of the Illinois State Historical Library, vol. 8. Edited by James Alton James. Springfield: Illinois State Historical Library, 1912.

Cleaves, Freeman. *Old Tippecanoe: William Henry Harrison and His Time.* New York: Charles Scribner's Sons, 1939.

Clinton, Robert N. "The Dormant Indian Commerce Clause." *Connecticut Law Review* 27 (1995): 1055.

———. "The Proclamation of 1763: Colonial Prelude to Two Centuries of Federal-State Conflict over the Management of Indian Affairs." *Boston University Law Review* 69 (1989): 329.

———. "There Is No Federal Supremacy Clause for Indian Tribes." *Arizona State Law Journal* 34 (2002): 237.

Clinton, Robert N., and Margaret Tobey Hotopp, "Judicial Enforcement of the Federal Restraints on Alienation of Indian Land: The Origins of the Eastern Land Claims." *Maine Law Review* 17, no. 31 (1979): 17.

Cohen, Felix. *Handbook of Federal Indian Law.* Washington, D.C.: U.S. Government Printing Office, 1945.

———. "Original Indian Title." *Minnesota Law Review* 32 (1947): 28.

Collis, John Stewart. *Christopher Columbus.* New York: Stein and Day, 1977.

Commager, Henry Steele, ed. *Documents of American History,* 4th ed. New York: Appleton-Century-Crofts, 1948.

Cooke, Jacob E. *Tench Coxe and the Early Republic.* Chapel Hill: University of North Carolina Press, 1978.

Cooper, James Fenimore. *The Last of the Mohicans: A Narrative of 1757*. Edited by W. K. Wickes. New York: Macmillan, 1921.

Corwin, Edward S. *French Policy and the American Alliance of 1778*. New York: B. Franklin, 1970.

Cotton, Joseph P. *The Constitutional Decisions of John Marshall*. Vol. 2. New York: G. P. Putnam's Sons, 1905.

Cox, Joseph W. *Champion of Southern Federalism: Robert Goodloe Harper of South Carolina*. Port Washington, N.Y.: Kennikat Press, 1972.

Craig, Neville B. *The Olden Time*. Vol. 2. Pittsburgh: Wright and Charlton, 1848.

Cresswell, Nicholas. *The Journal of Nicholas Cresswell, 1774–1777*. Port Washington, N.Y.: Kennikat Press, 1968.

Croghan, George. *George Croghan's Journal of His Trip to Detroit in 1767*. Edited by Howard H. Peckham. Ann Arbor: University of Michigan Press, 1939.

———. "A Selection of George Croghan's Letters and Journals Relating to Tours into the Western Country (November 16, 1750–November, 1765)." In *Early Western Travels, 1748–1846*, vol. 1, edited by Reuben Gold Thwaites. Cleveland, Ohio: Arthur H. Clark Co., 1904.

Cronon, William. *Changes in the Land: Indians, Colonists, and the Ecology of New England*. New York: Hill and Wang, 1983.

Crumrine, Boyd, ed. *Virginia Court Records in Southwestern Pennsylvania: Records of the District of West Augusta and Ohio and Yohogania Counties, Virginia, 1775–1780*. Baltimore: Genealogical Publishing Company, 1981.

Cumming, Peter A., and Neil H. Mickenberg, eds. *Native Rights in Canada*, 2nd ed. Toronto: Indian-Eskimo Association of Canada, 1972.

Cunliffe, Marcus. *The Nation Takes Shape, 1789–1837*. Chicago: University of Chicago Press, 1959.

Cunningham, John T. *Newark*. Newark: New Jersey Historical Society, 1966.

Curtis, George M., III, and Harold B. Gill, Jr. "A Man Apart: Nicholas Cresswell's American Odyssey, 1774–1777." *Indiana Magazine of History* 96 (2000): 169.

Cushing, John D., ed. *The Laws and Liberties of Massachusetts 1641–1691*. Vol. 1. Wilmington, Del.: Scholarly Resources, 1976.

Cushman, Clare, ed. *The Supreme Court Justices: Illustrated Biographies, 1789–1995*, 2d ed. Washington, D.C.: Congressional Quarterly, 1995.

Cutler, William G. *History of the State of Kansas*. Chicago: A. T. Andreas, 1883.

Dane, Nathan. *A General Abridgement and Digest of American Law*. Vol. 4. Boston: Cummings, Hilliard and Company, 1824.

Daniels, Roger. "Immigration." In *A Companion to 20th-Century America*, edited by Stephen J. Whitfield. Malden, Mass.: Blackwell Publishers, 2004.

Darlington, William M. *Christopher Gist's Journals, with Historical, Geographical and Ethnological Notes and Biographies of His Contemporaries*. Pittsburgh: J. R. Weldin and Company, 1893.

Davidson, Alexander, and Bernard Stuvé. *A Complete History of Illinois from 1673 to 1873*. Springfield, Ill.: D. L. Phillips, 1877.

Davies, K. G., ed. *Documents of the American Revolution (Colonial Office Series).* Vols. 4, 6, 8. Shannon: Irish University Press, 1972–74.

Davies, Richard Beale. *Francis Walker Gilmer: Life and Learning in Jefferson's Virginia.* Richmond, Va.: Dietz Press, 1939.

Davis, James E. *Frontier Illinois.* Bloomington: Indiana University Press, 1998.

Dawson, Moses. *Historical Narrative of the Civil and Military Services of Major-General William H. Harrison.* Cincinnati: By the author, 1824.

Deane, Charles. *Roger Williams and the Massachusetts Charter.* Cambridge, Mass.: John Wilson and Son, 1873.

Deane, Silas. *The Deane Papers.* Edited by Charles Isham. Collections of the New York Historical Society, vols. 19–20. New York: New York Historical Society, 1889–90.

De Forest, John W. *History of the Indians of Connecticut.* Hartford, Conn.: W. J. Hamersley, 1852.

Delaplaine, Edward S. *The Life of Thomas Johnson.* New York: F. H. Hitchcock, 1927.

———. *Thomas Johnson, Maryland and the Constitution.* Baltimore: Maryland State Bar Association, 1925.

Deloria, Vine, Jr. *Behind the Trail of Broken Treaties: An Indian Declaration of Independence.* New York: Delacorte Press, 1974.

———. "Conquest Masquerading as Law." In *Unlearning the Language of Conquest,* edited by Wahinkpe Topa (Four Arrows) aka Don Trent Jacobs. Austin: University of Texas Press, 2006.

Deloria, Vine, Jr., and Raymond J. DeMallie, *Documents of American Indian Diplomacy.* Vols. 1–2. Norman: University of Oklahoma Press, 1999.

Denny, Ebenezer. *Military Journal of Major Ebenezer Denny, an Officer in the Revolutionary and Indian Wars.* Philadelphia: Historical Society of Pennsylvania, 1859.

De Pauw, Linda Grant, ed. *Documentary History of the First Federal Congress of the United States of America.* Vol. 3. Baltimore: Johns Hopkins University Press, 1977.

Derleth, August. *Vincennes: Portal to the West.* Englewood Cliffs, N.J.: Prentice-Hall, 1968.

"Descendants of the Rev. William Smith, D.D., First Provost of the College of Philadelphia." *Pennsylvania Magazine of History and Biography* 4 (1880): 373.

Dickason, Olive P. "Concepts of Sovereignty at the Time of First Contacts." In *The Law of Nations and the New World,* edited by L. C. Green and Olive P. Dickason. Edmonton, Canada: University of Alberta Press, 1989.

Dillon, John B. *History of the Early Settlement of the North-Western Territory.* Indianapolis: Sheets and Braden, 1854.

Doerflinger, Thomas M. *A Vigorous Spirit of Enterprise: Merchants and Economic Development in Revolutionary Philadelphia.* Chapel Hill: University of North Carolina Press, 1986.

Donaldson, Thomas. *The House in Which Thomas Jefferson Wrote the Declaration of Independence.* Philadelphia: Avil Printing, 1898.

Donoughue, Bernard. *British Politics and the American Revolution: The Path to War, 1773–75*. London: Macmillan, 1964.

Dowd, Gregory Evans. *War under Heaven: Pontiac, the Indian Nations and the British Empire*. Baltimore: Johns Hopkins University Press, 2002.

Downes, Randolph C. *Council Fires on the Upper Ohio: A Narrative of Indian Affairs in the Upper Ohio Valley until 1795*. Pittsburgh: University of Pittsburgh Press, 1940.

Drinker, Elizabeth. *The Diary of Elizabeth Drinker*. Edited by Elaine Forman Crane. Vols. 1–2. Boston: Northeastern University Press, 1991.

Dummer, Jeremiah. *A Defence of the New-England Charters*. London: W. Wilkins, 1721.

Dunn, Jacob Piatt. *Documents Relating to the French Settlements on the Wabash*. Indianapolis: Bowen-Merrill, 1894.

Dunn, J. P., Jr., *Indiana: A Redemption From Slavery*. Boston: Houghton, Mifflin, 1905.

Dunn, Walter S., Jr. *Opening New Markets: The British Army and the Old Northwest*. Westport, Conn.: Praeger, 2002.

Dussias, Allison M. "Squaw Drudges, Farm Wives, and the Dann Sisters' Last Stand: American Indian Women's Resistance to Domestication and the Denial of Their Property Rights." *North Carolina Law Review* 77 (1999): 637.

Eccles, W. J. "French Imperial Policy for the Great Lakes Basin." In *The Sixty Years' War for the Great Lakes, 1754–1814*, edited by David Curtis Skaggs and Larry L. Nelson. East Lansing: Michigan State University, 2001.

Echo-Hawk, Walter R. *In the Courts of the Conqueror: The 10 Worst Indian Law Cases Ever Decided*. Golden, Colo.: Fulcrum, 2010.

Edmunds, R. David. "Pickawillany: French Military Power versus British Economics." *Western Pennsylvania Historical Magazine* 58 (1975): 169.

———. *The Potawatomis: Keepers of the Fire*. Norman: University of Oklahoma Press, 1978.

———. "Tecumseh, the Shawnee Prophet, and American History: A Reassessment." *Western History Quarterly* 14 (1983): 261.

Edmunds, R. David, ed. *American Indian Leaders: Studies in Diversity*. Lincoln: University of Nebraska Press, 1980.

Edsall, Preston W., ed. *Journal of the Courts of Common Right and Chancery of East New Jersey, 1683–1702*. Philadelphia: American Legal History Society, 1937.

Eisinger, C. E. "The Puritan's Justification for Taking the Land." *Essex Institute Historical Collections* 84 (1948): 131.

Ekberg, Carl J. *Colonial Ste. Genevieve*. Gerald, Mo.: Patrice Press, 1985.

Elkins, Stanley, and Eric McKitrick, *The Age of Federalism: The Early American Republic, 1788–1800*. New York: Oxford University Press, 1993.

Ellis, Joseph J. *His Excellency: George Washington*. New York: Alfred A. Knopf, 2004.

Ellis, William Donohue. *The Ordinance of 1787: The Nation Begins*. Dayton, Ohio: Landfall Press, 1987.

Elsmere, Jane Shaffer. *Justice Samuel Chase.* Muncie, Ind.: Janevar Publishing Company, 1980.

Erney, Richard Alton. *The Public Life of Henry Dearborn.* New York: Arno Press, 1979.

Ernst, James. *Roger Williams: New England Firebrand.* New York: AMS Press, 1969.

Esarey, Logan. *A History of Indiana from Its Exploration to 1922.* Vol. 1. Dayton, Ohio: Dayton Historical Publishing Company, 1922.

Evarts, Jeremiah. *Cherokee Removal: The "William Penn" Essays and Other Writings.* Edited by Francis Paul Prucha. Knoxville: University of Tennessee Press, 1981.

Ewald, William. "James Wilson and the Drafting of the Constitution." *University of Pennsylvania Journal of Constitutional Law* 10 (2008): 901.

Faber, Eli. *The Jewish People of America—A Time for Planting: The First Migration, 1654–1820.* Baltimore: Johns Hopkins University Press, 1992.

Falkowski, James E. *Indian Law/Race Law: A Five-Hundred-Year History.* New York: Praeger, 1992.

Faragher, John Mack. *Daniel Boone: The Life and Legend of an American Pioneer.* New York: Holt, 1992.

Farnham, Thomas J. "Travels in the Great Western Prairies." In *Early Western Travels, 1748–1846,* vol. 28, edited by Reuben Gold Thwaites. Cleveland, Ohio: Arthur H. Clark Company, 1906.

Faulkner, Robert Kenneth. *The Jurisprudence of John Marshall.* Princeton, N.J.: Princeton University Press, 1968.

Faux, William. *Memorable Days in America: Being a Journal of a Tour to the United States.* New York: AMS Press, 1969.

Fiffer, Steve. *Tyrannosaurus Sue: The Extraordinary Saga of the Largest, Most Fought Over T. Rex Ever Found.* New York: W. H. Freeman, 2000.

Filson, John. *The Discovery, Settlement and Present State of Kentucke.* Wilmington, Del.: James Wilson, 1784.

Fischer, David Hackett. *The Revolution of American Conservatism: The Federalist Party in the Era of Jeffersonian Democracy.* New York: Harper and Row, 1965.

————. "Robert Goodloe Harper." Senior history thesis, Princeton University, 1958.

Fish, Sidney M. *Barnard and Michael Gratz: Their Lives and Times.* Lanham, Md.: University Press of America, 1994.

Fleming, Thomas. *New Jersey: A Bicentennial History.* New York: Norton, 1977.

Fletcher, Matthew L. M. "The Iron Cold of the Marshall Trilogy." *North Dakota Law Review* 82 (2006): 627.

Force, Peter, ed. *American Archives, Fourth Series.* Vols. 1–2, 6. Washington, D.C.: Published under authority of Congress, 1837–46.

Foreman, Grant. "Illinois and Her Indians." *Papers in Illinois History and Transactions for the Year 1939.* Springfield: Illinois State Historical Society, 1940.

————. *Indians and Pioneers: The Story of the American Southwest Before 1830.* New Haven: Yale University Press, 1936.

————. *The Last Trek of the Indians*. Chicago: University of Chicago Press, 1946.

Forte, David F. "Marbury's Travail: Federalist Politics and William Marbury's Appointment as Justice of the Peace." *Catholic University Law Review* 45 (1996): 349.

Foster, Hamar. "Letting Go the Bone: The Idea of Indian Title in British Columbia, 1849–1927." In *Essays in the History of Canadian Law: British Columbia and the Yukon*, edited by Hamar Foster and John McLaren. Vol. 6. Toronto: University of Toronto Press, 1995.

Franklin, Benjamin. *The Papers of Benjamin Franklin*. Vol. 14. Edited by Leonard W. Labaree. New Haven: Yale University Press, 1970.

————. *The Papers of Benjamin Franklin*. Vols. 16–18, 20, 22. Edited by William B. Willcox. New Haven: Yale University Press, 1972–82.

Franklin, W. Neil. "Pennsylvania-Virginia Rivalry for the Indian Trade of the Ohio Valley." *Mississippi Valley Historical Review* 20 (1934): 463.

Franza, Gregory M. *The Story of Old Ste. Genevieve*. St. Louis, Mo.: Patrice Press, 1967.

Frickey, Phillip P. "A Common Law for Our Age of Imperialism: The Judicial Divestiture of Indian Tribal Authority over Nonmembers." *Yale Law Journal* 109 (1999): 1.

Friedenberg, Daniel M. *Life, Liberty, and the Pursuit of Land*. Buffalo, N.Y.: Prometheus Books, 1992.

Friedenwald, Herbert. *The Declaration of Independence: An Interpretation and an Analysis*. New York: De Capo Press, 1974.

Friedman, Lawrence M. *A History of American Law*. New York: Simon and Schuster, 1973.

Friedman, Leon, and Fred L. Israel, eds. *The Justices of the United States Supreme Court, 1789–1969: Their Lives and Major Opinions*. Vol. 1. New York: R. R. Bowker Company, 1969.

Furlong, Patrick J. "Book Review." *Indiana Magazine of History* 86 (1990): 338.

Gage, Thomas. *The Correspondence of General Thomas Gage with the Secretaries of State, 1763–1775*. Edited by Clarence Edwin Carter. Vol. 1. Hamden, Conn.: Archon Books, 1969.

Galbreath, C. B., ed. *Expedition of Céleron to the Ohio Country in 1749*. Columbus, Ohio: F. J. Heer, 1921.

Garrett, John. *Roger Williams: Witness beyond Christendom*. New York: Macmillan, 1970.

Garrison, Tim Alan. *The Legal Ideology of Removal: The Southern Judiciary and the Sovereignty of Native American Nations*. Athens: University of Georgia Press, 2002.

Gaustad, Edwin S. *Liberty of Conscience: Roger Williams in America*. Grand Rapids, Mich.: W. B. Eerdmans Publishing Company, 1991.

Geib, George W., and Donald B. Kite, Sr. *Federal Justice in Indiana: The History of the United States District Court for the Southern District of Indiana*. Indianapolis: Indiana Historical Society, 2007.

George, Staughton, et al., eds. *Charter to William Penn and Laws of the Province of Pennsylvania.* Harrisburg, Pa.: L. S. Hart, State Printer, 1879.

Getches, David H. "Conquering the Cultural Frontier: The New Subjectivism of the Supreme Court in Indian Law." *California Law Review* 84 (1996): 1573.

Getches, David H., Charles F. Wilkinson, and Robert A. Williams, Jr. *Cases and Materials on Federal Indian Law,* 4th ed. St. Paul, Minn.: West Publishing Company, 1998.

Gilbert, Jérémie. "Historical Indigenous Peoples' Land Claims: A Comparative and International Approach to the Common Law Doctrine on Indigenous Title." *International and Comparative Law Quarterly* 56 (2007): 583.

Gillingham, Harrold E. "The Cost of Old Silver." *Pennsylvania Magazine of History and Biography* 54 (1930): 32.

Gipson, Lawrence Henry. *The British Empire before the American Revolution.* Vols. 4, 11. New York: Alfred A. Knopf, 1961, 1965.

Gleeson, Janet. *Millionaire: The Philanderer, Gambler, and Duelist Who Invented Modern Finance.* New York: Simon and Schuster, 1999.

Goebel, Dorothy Burne. *William Henry Harrison: A Political Biography.* Indianapolis: Historical Bureau of the Indiana Library and Historical Department, 1926.

Goebel, Julius, Jr. *History of the Supreme Court of the United States: Antecedents and Beginnings to 1801.* Vol. 1. New York: Macmillan, 1971.

———. *The Struggle for the Falkland Islands: A Study in Legal and Diplomatic History.* New Haven: Yale University Press, 1927.

Golson, G. Barry, ed. *The Playboy Interview.* New York: Wideview Books, 1981.

Goodman, A. T. "Historical Sketch of the English Post at Pickawillany." In *The First American Frontier.* New York: Arno Press, 1971.

Green, L. C. "Claims to Territory in Colonial America." In *The Law of Nations and the New World,* edited by L. C. Green and Olive P. Dickason. Edmonton, Canada: University of Alberta Press, 1989.

Green, L. C., and Olive P. Dickason, eds. *The Law of Nations and the New World.* Edmonton, Canada: University of Alberta Press, 1989.

Grinde, Donald A., Jr., and Bruce E. Johansen. *Exemplar of Liberty: Native America and the Evolution of Democracy.* Los Angeles: American Indian Studies Center, University of California–Los Angeles, 1991.

Grotius, Hugo. *The Freedom of the Seas.* Translated by Ralph Van Deman Magoffin. Edited by James Brown Scott. New York: Oxford University Press, 1916.

———. *The Law of War and Peace.* Vol. 2. Translated by Francis W. Kelsey. New York: Oceana, 1964.

Gunn, Giles B. *New World Metaphysics: Readings on the Religious Meaning of the American Experience.* New York: Oxford University Press, 1981.

Hagemann, James A. *Lord Dunmore: Last Royal Governor of Virginia, 1771–1776.* Hampton, Va.: Wayfarer Enterprises, 1974.

Haldimand, Frederick. *The Haldimand Papers.* Michigan Pioneer and Historical Society Historical Collections, vols. 9, 11, 19–20. Vol. 9, Lansing: Thorp and Godfrey, 1886; vol. 11, Lansing: Thorp and Godfrey, 1888; vols. 19–20, Lansing: Robert Smith and Company, 1892.

Hall, John E., ed. "Obituary." *Port Folio* (Philadelphia: Harrison Hall), vol. 18, July–December, 1824.

Hall, Kermit L. *The Magic Mirror: Law in American History*. New York: Oxford University Press, 1989.

Hall, Mark D. "James Wilson: Democratic Theorist and Supreme Court Justice." In *Seriatim: The Supreme Court before John Marshall*, edited by Scott Douglas Gerber. New York: New York University Press, 1998.

Hallahan, William H. *The Day the Revolution Ended: 19 October 1781*. Hoboken, N.J.: Wiley, 2004.

Hamilton, Alexander. *The Papers of Alexander Hamilton*. Vol. 1. Edited by Harold C. Syrett. New York: Columbia University Press, 1961.

Hamilton, Bernice. *Political Thought in Sixteenth-Century Spain: A Study of the Political Ideas of Vitoria, De Soto, Suárez, and Molina*. Oxford: Clarendon Press, 1963.

Hamilton, J. G. de R. "Robert Goodloe Harper." In *Dictionary of American Biography*, vol. 8, edited by Dumas Malone. New York: Charles Scribner's Sons, 1932.

Hamilton, Stanislaus Murray, ed. *Letters to Washington and Accompanying Papers*. Vol. 4. New York: Houghton, Mifflin and Company, 1901.

Hammon, Neal, and Richard Taylor. *Virginia's Western War, 1775–1786*. Mechanicsburg, Pa.: Stackpole Books, 2002.

Hanke, Lewis. *The Spanish Struggle for Justice in the Conquest of America*. Philadelphia: University of Pennsylvania Press, 1949.

Hanley, Thomas O'Brien. *Revolutionary Statesman: Charles Carroll and the War*. Chicago: Loyola University Press, 1983.

Hanson, George A. *Old Kent: The Eastern Shore of Maryland*. Baltimore: J. P. Des Forges, 1876.

Harper, Robert G. *The Case of the Georgia Sales on the Mississippi Considered*. Philadelphia: Richard Folwell, 1797.

———. *Select Works of Robert Goodloe Harper*. Baltimore: O. H. Neilson, 1814.

Harrell, Isaac S. "Some Neglected Phases of the Revolution in Virginia." *William and Mary Quarterly*, 2nd ser., 5 (1925): 159.

Harrison, Lowell H. *George Rogers Clark and the War in the West*. Lexington: University Press of Kentucky, 1976.

Harrison, William H. *Messages and Letters of William Henry Harrison*. Vols. 1–2. Edited by Logan Esarey. Indianapolis: Indiana Historical Commission, 1922.

———. *The Papers of William Henry Harrison, 1800–1815* (microfilm). Edited by Douglas E. Clanin. Indianapolis: Indiana Historical Society, 1999.

Haskins, Charles Homer. *The Yazoo Land Companies*. New York: Knickerbocker, 1891.

Haskins, George L., and Herbert A. Johnson. *Foundations of Power: John Marshall, 1801–1815*. New York: Macmillan, 1981.

Haw, James, Francis F. Beirne, Rosamond R. Beirne, and R. Samuel Jett. *Stormy Patriot: The Life of Samuel Chase.* Baltimore: Maryland Historical Society, 1980.

Hawke, David Freeman. *The Colonial Experience.* Indianapolis: Bobbs–Merrill, 1966.

———. *Paine.* New York: Harper and Row. 1974.

Henderson, Archibald. "A Pre-Revolutionary Revolt in the Old Southwest." *Mississippi Valley Historical Review* 17 (1930): 191.

———. "Richard Henderson and the Occupation of Kentucky, 1775." *Mississippi Valley Historical Review* 1 (1914): 341.

Henderson, J. Youngblood. *Indigenous Diplomacy and the Rights of Peoples: Achieving UN Recognition.* Saskatoon, Canada: Purich Publishing, 2008.

———. "Unraveling the Riddle of Aboriginal Title." *American Indian Law Review* 5 (1977): 75.

Hendrick, Burton J. *The Lees of Virginia: Biography of a Family.* Boston: Little, Brown, 1935.

Henry, William Wirt. *Patrick Henry: Life, Correspondence and Speeches.* Vol. 2. New York: Charles Scribner's Sons, 1891.

Hershkowitz, Leo, and Isidore S. Meyer, eds. *Letters of the Franks Family, 1733–1748.* Waltham, Mass.: American Jewish Historical Society, 1968.

Hickford, Mark. "'Settling Some Very Important Principles of Colonial Law': Three 'Forgotten' Cases of the 1840s." *Victoria University of Wellington Law Review* 35 (2003): 1.

Hinderaker, Eric. *Elusive Empires: Constructing Colonialism in the Ohio Valley, 1673–1800.* New York: Cambridge University Press, 1997.

Hinderaker, Eric, and Peter C. Mancall. *At the Edge of Empire: The Backcountry in British North America.* Baltimore: Johns Hopkins University Press, 2003.

Hobson, Charles F. *The Great Chief Justice: John Marshall and the Rule of Law.* Lawrence: University Press of Kansas, 1996.

Hodge, Frederick Webb, ed. *Handbook of American Indians North of Mexico.* Vol. 2. New York: Pageant Books, 1959.

Hoffer, Peter Charles. *Law and People in Colonial America.* Baltimore: Johns Hopkins University Press, 1992.

Hoffmann, John, ed. *A Guide to the History of Illinois.* New York: Greenwood Press, 1991.

Hoffman, Paul P., and John L. Molyneaux, eds. *The Lee Family Papers, 1742–1795* (microfilm). Charlottesville: University of Virginia Library, 1966.

Hoffman, Ronald. "Charles Carroll of Carrollton." In *American National Biography*, vol. 4, edited by John A. Garraty and Mark C. Carnes. New York: Oxford University Press, 1999.

———. *Princes of Ireland, Planters of Maryland: A Carroll Saga, 1500–1782.* Chapel Hill: University of North Carolina Press, 2000.

———. *A Spirit of Dissension: Economics, Politics, and the Revolution in Maryland.* Baltimore: Johns Hopkins University Press, 1973.

Hoffman, Ronald, ed. *Dear Papa, Dear Charley.* Vols. 2–3. Chapel Hill: University of North Carolina Press, 2001.

Hofstra, Warren R. *The Planting of New Virginia: Settlement and Landscape in the Shenandoah Valley.* Baltimore: Johns Hopkins University Press, 2004.

Holly, David C. *Tidewater by Steamboat: A Saga of the Chesapeake.* Baltimore: Johns Hopkins University Press, 1991.

Holton, Woody. *Forced Founders: Indians, Debtors, Slaves, and the Making of the American Revolution in Virginia.* Chapel Hill: University of North Carolina Press, 1999.

Hookey, John. "Chief Justice Marshall and the English Oak: A Comment." *Federal Law Review* 6 (1974): 174.

———. "The Gove Land Rights Case: A Judicial Dispensation for the Taking of Aboriginal Rights in Australia?" *Federal Law Review* 5 (1972): 85.

Horsman, Reginald. "American Indian Policy in the Old Northwest, 1783–1812." *William and Mary Quarterly*, 3rd ser., 18 (1961): 35.

———. *Expansion and American Indian Policy, 1783–1812.* East Lansing: Michigan State University Press, 1967.

Horsnell, Margaret. "Samuel Chase." In *American National Biography*, vol. 4, edited by John A. Garraty and Mark C. Carnes. New York: Oxford University Press, 1999.

Houck, Louis. *A History of Missouri from the Earliest Explorations and Settlements until the Admission of the State into the Union.* Vol. 3. Chicago: R. R. Donnelley and Sons, 1908.

Howe, Daniel Walker. *What Hath God Wrought: The Transformation of America, 1815–1848.* New York: Oxford University Press, 2007.

Howe, William. "General Orders by Major General The Honorable William Howe." *New York Historical Society Publication Fund, Collections of the New York Historical Society for the Year 1883.* Vol. 16. New York: New-York Historical Society, 1884.

Hoxie, Frederick E., ed. *Encyclopedia of North American Indians.* Boston: Houghton Mifflin Company, 1996.

Hoye, Charles E. *Hoye's Pioneer Families of Garrett County.* Parsons, W.V.: McClain Printing Company, 1988.

Huebner, Timothy S. *The Southern Judicial Tradition: State Judges and Sectional Distinctiveness, 1790–1890.* Athens: University of Georgia Press, 1999.

Hufton, Olwen. *Europe: Privilege and Protest, 1730–1789*, 2nd ed. Malden, Mass: Blackwell Publishers, 2000.

Humphreys, R. A. "Lord Shelburne and the Proclamation of 1763." *English History Review* 49 (1934): 241.

Hunt, Gaillard. "Office-Seeking during Jefferson's Administration." *American History Review* 3 (1898): 270.

Hurley, John. "Aboriginal Rights, the Constitution and the Marshall Court." *Revue Juridique Thémis* 17 (1982–83): 403.

Hurt, R. Douglas. *The Ohio Frontier: Crucible of the Old Northwest, 1720–1830.* Bloomington: Indiana University Press, 1996.

Illinois and Wabash Land Company. *An Account of the Proceedings of the Illinois and Ouabache Land Companies, In Pursuance of Their Purchases Made of the*

Independent Natives, July 5th, 1773, and 18th October, 1775. Philadelphia: William Young, 1796.

———. *An Account of the Proceedings of the Illinois and Oubache Land Companies, In Persuance of Their Purchases made of the Independent Natives, July 5th, 1773, and 18th October, 1775.* Philadelphia: William Duane, 1803.

———. *The Illinois-Wabash Land Company Manuscript.* [Chicago?]: Privately printed by Cyrus H. McCormick, 1915.

———. *Memorial of the Ilinois and Ouabache Land Companies to the Honourable Congress of the United States.* Philadelphia, 1802.

———. *Memorial of the Illinois and Wabash Land Company.* Printed by order of the House of Representatives, 1797.

———. *Memorial of the United Illinois and Wabash Land Companies, to the Senate and House of Representatives of the United States.* Baltimore: Joseph Robinson, 1810.

———. *Memorial of the United Illinois and Wabash Land Companies, to the Senate and House of Representatives of the United States.* Baltimore: Joseph Robinson, 1816.

Imlay, Gilbert. *A Topographical Description of the Western Territory of North America,* 3rd ed. London: Printed for J. Debrett, 1792.

Ingenthron, Elmo. *Indians of the Ozark Plateau.* Point Lookout, Mo.: School of the Ozarks Press, 1970.

Ireland, Robert M. *The Legal Career of William Pinkney.* New York: Garland, 1986.

———. "William Pinkney: A Revision and Re-emphasis." *American Journal of Legal History* 14 (1970): 235.

Isaac, Rhys. *The Transformation of Virginia, 1740–1790.* Chapel Hill: University of North Carolina Press, 1982.

Jablow, Joseph. *Illinois, Kickapoo, and Potawatomi Indians.* New York: Garland, 1974.

Jackson, Andrew. *Correspondence of Andrew Jackson.* Vol. 4. Edited by John Spencer Bassett. Washington, D.C.: Carnegie Institution of Washington, 1929.

Jackson, John W. *With the British Army in Philadelphia, 1777–1778.* San Rafael, Calif.: Presidio Press, 1979.

James, Alfred P. *The Ohio Company: Its Inner History.* Pittsburgh: University of Pittsburgh Press, 1959.

James, James Alton. *The Life of George Rogers Clark.* Chicago: University of Chicago Press, 1928.

———. *Oliver Pollock: The Life and Times of an Unknown Patriot.* New York: Appleton-Century, 1937.

Jay, William. *The Life of John Jay with Selections from His Correspondence and Miscellaneous Papers.* Vol. 2. New York: J. and J. Harper, 1833.

Jefferson, Thomas. *The Papers of Thomas Jefferson.* Vol. 3. Edited by Julian P. Boyd. Princeton, N.J.: Princeton University Press, 1950–51.

———. *The Papers of Thomas Jefferson.* Vol. 22. Edited by Charles T. Cullen. Princeton, N.J.: Princeton University Press, 1986.

———. *The Papers of Thomas Jefferson*. Vol. 25. Edited by John Catanzariti. Princeton, N.J.: Princeton University Press, 1992.

———. *A Summary View of the Rights of British America*. 1774; reprint, New York: Burt Franklin, 1971.

———. *The Writings of Thomas Jefferson*. Vols. 1, 3, 9–10, 16–17. Edited by Albert Ellery Bergh. Washington, D.C.: Thomas Jefferson Memorial Association of the United States, 1903–1904.

———. *The Writings of Thomas Jefferson*. Vol. 8. Edited by Paul Leicester Ford. New York: G. P. Putnam's Sons, 1897.

Jennings, Francis. "Conquest and Legal Fictions." *Oklahoma City University Law Review* 23 (1998): 141.

Jensen, Merrill. *The Articles of Confederation*. Madison: University of Wisconsin Press, 1962.

———. "The Cession of the Old Northwest." *Mississippi Valley Historical Review* 23 (1936): 27.

———. "The Creation of the National Domain, 1781–1784." *Mississippi Valley Historical Review* 26 (1939–40): 323.

Jensen, Merrill, ed. *American Colonial Documents to 1776*. New York: Oxford University Press, 1962.

———. *The Documentary History of the Ratification of the Constitution: Constitutional Documents and Records, 1776–1787*. Vol. 1. Madison: State Historical Society of Wisconsin, 1976.

Jessup, Dwight Wiley. *Reaction and Accommodation: The United States Supreme Court and Political Conflict, 1809–1835*. New York: Garland, 1987.

Jones, Joseph. *Letters of Joseph Jones of Virginia, 1777–1787*. Edited by Worthington Chauncey Ford. New York: New York Times, 1971.

Johnson, Herbert Alan. "Thomas Johnson." In *The Justices of the United States Supreme Court 1789–1978: Their Lives and Major Opinions*, vol. 1, edited by Leon Friedman and Fred L. Israel. New York: R. R. Bowker Company, 1969.

Johnson, William. *The Papers of Sir William Johnson*. Vol. 8. Edited by Alexander C. Flick. Albany: University of the State of New York, 1933.

———. *The Papers of Sir William Johnson*. Vols. 11–12. Edited by Milton W. Hamilton. Albany: University of the State of New York, 1953, 1957.

Juricek, John T. "English Territorial Claims in North America under Elizabeth and Early Stuarts." *Terrae Incognitae* 7 (1975): 7.

Kades, Eric. "The Dark Side of Efficiency: *Johnson v. M'Intosh* and the Expropriation of American Indian Lands." *University of Pennsylvania Law Review* 148 (2000): 1065.

———. "History and Interpretation of the Great Case of *Johnson v. M'Intosh*." *Law and History Review* 19 (2001): 67.

Kaminski, John P., and Gaspare J. Saladino, eds. *The Documentary History of the Ratification of the Constitution*. Vols. 8, 10. Madison: State Historical Society of Wisconsin, 1988, 1993.

Katz, Stanley N. "Thomas Jefferson and the Right to Property in Revolutionary America." *Journal of Law and Economics* 19 (1976): 467.

Kellogg, Louise Phelps, ed. *Early Narratives of the Northwest, 1634–1699.* New York: C. Scribner's, 1917.

———. *Frontier Advance on the Upper Ohio, 1778–1779.* Madison: Wisconsin Historical Society, 1916.

Kelsay, Isabel Thompson. *Joseph Brant, 1743–1807: Man of Two Worlds.* Syracuse, N.Y.: Syracuse University Press, 1984.

Keltie, John S. *A History of the Scottish Highlands, Highland Clans and Highland Regiments.* Vol. 6. London: A. Fullarton and Company, 1875.

Kemmerer, Donald L. *Path to Freedom: The Struggle for Self-Government in Colonial New Jersey, 1703–1776.* Cos Cob, Conn.: J. E. Edwards, 1968.

Kent, James. *Commentaries on American Law,* 1st ed. Vols. 1, 3. New York: O. Halsted, 1826–28.

———. *Commentaries on American Law,* 2nd ed. Vol. 3. New York: O. Halsted, 1832.

———. *Commentaries on American Law,* 3rd ed. Vol. 1. New York: E. B. Clayton, James van Norden, 1836.

———. *Commentaries on American Law,* 6th ed. Vol. 3. New York: W. Kent, 1848.

Ketchum, Richard M. *Saratoga: Turning Point of America's Revolutionary War.* New York: H. Holt, 1997.

Kiker, Marshall Stopher. "Loyalism in Eighteenth Century Alexandria, Virginia." *Historic Alexandria Quarterly* (Winter 2001): 1.

King, J. C. H. *Native American Art, Irish American Trade: The Stonyhurst Mullanphy Collection.* London: British Museum, 2004.

Kinnaird, Lawrence, ed. "Spain in the Mississippi Valley, 1765–1794." In *Annual Report of the American Historical Association.* Washington, D.C.: U.S. Government Printing Office, 1945.

Kirkwood, Alberta Carson. *They Came to Kentucky.* Baltimore: Gateway Press, 1976.

Klein, Milton M. *The American Whig: William Livingston of New York.* New York: Garland, 1993.

Knecht, R. J. *Francis I.* New York: Cambridge University Press, 1982.

Knopf, Richard C., ed. *Anthony Wayne: A Name in Arms, Soldier, Diplomat, Defender of Expansion Westward of a Nation: The Wayne-Knox-Pickering-McHenry Correspondence.* Pittsburgh: University of Pittsburgh Press, 1960.

Konkle, Burton Alva. "The James Wilson Memorial." *American Law Register* 55 (1907): 1.

———. *The Life and Speeches of Thomas Williams.* Vol. 1. Philadelphia: Campion and Company, 1905.

———. *The Life and Times of Thomas Smith, 1745–1809.* Philadelphia: Campion and Company, 1904.

Labaree, Leonard Woods, ed. *Royal Instructions to British Colonial Governors, 1670–1776.* Vol. 2. New York: Octagon Books, 1967.

"Lady Virginia Murray and Her Alleged Claim against the State of Virginia." *William and Mary Quarterly Historical Magazine* 24 (1915): 85

Lambert, Sheila, ed. *House of Commons Sessional Papers of the Eighteenth Century.* Vol. 26. Wilmington, Del.: Scholarly Resources, 1975.

Larson, Carlton F. W. "The Revolutionary American Jury: A Case Study of the 1778–1779 Philadelphia Treason Trials." *Southern Methodist University Law Review* 61 (2008): 1441.

Laub, C. H. "Revolutionary Virginia and the Crown Lands." *William and Mary Quarterly*, 2nd ser., 11 (1931): 304.

Laurence, Robert. "Learning to Live with the Plenary Power of Congress over the Indian Nations." *Arizona Law Review* 30 (1988): 413.

Law, John. *The Colonial History of Vincennes.* Vincennes, Ind.: Harvey, Mason and Company, 1858.

Lawson, Philip. *The East India Company: A History.* New York: Longman, 1987.

Lebeson, Anita Libman. *Pilgrim People.* New York: Minerva Press, 1975.

Lee, Richard Henry. *The Letters of Richard Henry Lee.* Vols. 1–2. Edited by James Curtis Ballagh. New York: Macmillan, 1911–14.

———. *Life of Arthur Lee.* Vol. 1. Boston: Wells and Lilly, 1829.

"Letters to Thomas Adams." *Virginia Magazine of History & Biography* 6 (1968): 30.

Lewis, George E. *The Indiana Company, 1763–1798.* Glendale, Calif.: Arthur H. Clark, 1941.

Lewis, G. Malcolm. "An Early Map on Skin of the Area Later to Become Indiana and Illinois." In *Images and Icons of the New World: Essays on American Cartography*, edited by Karen Severud Cook. London: British Library, 1996.

Libby, Dorothy. *Piankashaw and Kaskaskia Indians.* New York: Garland, 1974.

Linn, John B., and Wm. H. Egle, eds. "Record of Pennsylvania Marriages Prior to 1810." In *Pennsylvania Archives*, 2nd series, vol. 9. Harrisburg, Pa.: Benjamin Singerly, 1896.

Livermore, Shaw. *Early American Land Companies: Their Influence on Corporate Development.* New York: Octagon Books, 1968.

Locke, John. *Two Treatises of Government, book II: The Second Treatise on Civil Government.* Amherst, N.Y.: Prometheus Books, 1986.

Lodge, Henry Cabot. *Daniel Webster.* Boston: Houghton, Mifflin, 1899.

Looking Forward, Looking Back. Report of the Royal Commission on Aboriginal People, vol. 1. Ottawa, Canada: Royal Commission on Aboriginal People, 1996.

MacDonald, William, ed. *Select Charters and Other Documents Illustrative of American History, 1606–1775.* New York: Macmillan, 1914.

Mackie, J. D. *The Earlier Tudors, 1485–1558.* Oxford: Clarendon Press, 1966.

MacLeod, William Christie. *The American Indian Frontier.* New York: Alfred A. Knopf, 1928.

Madison, James. *The Papers of James Madison.* Vols. 2–4. Edited by William T. Hutchinson and William M. E. Rachel. Chicago: University of Chicago Press, 1962–65.

——. *The Papers of James Madison*. Vol. 8. Edited by Robert A. Rutland and William M. E. Rachal. Chicago: University of Chicago Press, 1973.

——. *The Papers of James Madison*. Vol. 15. Edited by Thomas A. Mason, Robert A. Rutland, and Jeanne K. Sisson. Charlottesville: University Press of Virginia, 1985.

——. *The Writings of James Madison*. Vol. 1. Edited by Gaillard Hunt. New York: G. P. Putnam's Sons, 1900.

Magrath, C. Peter. *Yazoo: Life and Politics in the New Republic*. Providence, R.I.: Brown University Press, 1966.

Mahon, John K. *The War of 1812*. Gainesville: University of Florida Press, 1972.

Malone, Dumas. *Jefferson and His Time: Jefferson the President—First Term, 1801–1805*. Vol. 4. Boston: Little, Brown, 1970.

Marcus, Jacob R. *American Jewry: Eighteenth Century Documents*. Cincinnati: Hebrew Union College Press, 1959.

——. *The Colonial American Jew, 1492–1776*. Vols. 2–3. Detroit: Wayne State University Press, 1970.

——. *Early American Jewry*. Vol. 2. Philadelphia: Jewish Publication Society of America, 1955.

Marcus, Maeva. "Federal Judicial Selection: The First Decade." *University of Richmond Law Review* 39 (2005): 797.

Marcus, Maeva et al., eds. *The Documentary History of the Supreme Court of the United States, 1789–1800*. Vol. 5. New York: Columbia University Press, 1994.

Marks, Anna Edith. "William Murray, Trader and Land Speculator in the Illinois Country." *Transactions of the Illinois State Historical Society* 26 (1919): 188.

Marks, Bayly Ellen. *Guide to the Microfilm Edition of the Robert Goodloe Harper Family Papers*. Baltimore: Maryland Historical Society, 1970.

Maroon, Suzy. *The Supreme Court of the United States*. New York: Thomasson-Grant, 1996.

Marshall, John. *A History of the Colonies Planted by the English on the Continent of North America*. Philadelphia: A. Small, 1824.

——. *The Life of George Washington*. Philadelphia: C. P. Wayne, 1804.

Marshall, Peter. "Lord Hillsborough, Samuel Wharton and the Ohio Grant, 1769–1775." *English History Review* 80 (1966): 717.

——. "Sir William Johnson and the Treaty of Fort Stanwix, 1768." *Journal of American Studies* 1 (1967): 149.

Mason, George. *The Papers of George Mason*. Vol. 2. Edited by Robert A. Rutland. Chapel Hill: University of North Carolina Press, 1970.

Mason, Sally D. "Charles Carroll of Carrollton and His Family, 1688–1832." In *"Anywhere So Long as There Be Freedom": Charles Carroll of Carrollton and His Maryland*, edited by Ann C. Van Devanter. Baltimore: Baltimore Museum of Art, 1975.

Maxey, David W. "The Translation of James Wilson." *Journal of Supreme Court History* 14 (1995): 29.

McBee, May Wilson, ed. *Natchez Court Records, 1767–1805: Abstracts of Early Records*. Greenwood, Miss.: M. W. McBee, 1953.

McCafferty, Michael. *Native American Place-Names of Indiana*. Urbana: University of Illinois Press, 2008.

McClellan, James. *Justice Story and the American Constitution*. Norman: University of Oklahoma Press, 1971.

McCluggage, Robert W. "The Senate and Indian Land Titles, 1800–1825." *Western Historical Quarterly* 1 (1970): 415.

McConnell, Michael N. "Peoples 'In Between': The Iroquois and the Ohio Indians, 1720–1768." In *Beyond the Covenant Chain: The Iroquois and Their Neighbors in Indian North America, 1600–1800*, edited by Daniel K. Richter and James H. Merrell. Syracuse, N.Y.: Syracuse University Press, 1987.

———. *A Country Between: The Upper Ohio Valley and Its Peoples, 1724–1774*. Lincoln: University of Nebraska Press, 1992.

McConville, Brendan. *These Daring Disturbers of the Public Peace: The Struggle for Property and Power in Early New Jersey*. Ithaca: Cornell University Press, 1999.

McCord, Shirley S. *Travel Accounts of Indiana, 1679–1961*. Indianapolis: Indiana Historical Bureau, 1970.

McCullough, David. *John Adams*. New York: Simon and Schuster, 2002.

———. *1776*. New York: Simon and Schuster, 2005.

Mcdonald, Donald. *The Diaries of Donald Mcdonald, 1824–1826*. Indiana Historical Society Publications, vol. 14. Indianapolis: Indiana Historical Society, 1942.

McDonnell, Michael A. "Charles-Michel Mouet de Langlade: Warrior, Soldier, and Intercultural "Window" on the Sixty Years' War for the Great Lakes." In *The Sixty Years' War for the Great Lakes, 1754–1814*, edited by David Curtis Skaggs and Larry L. Nelson. East Lansing: Michigan State University, 2001.

McHugh, P. G. "Aboriginal Title in New Zealand: A Retrospect and Prospect." *New Zealand Journal of Public and International Law* 2 (2004): 139.

McNeil, Kent. "Aboriginal Rights in Canada: From Title to Land to Territorial Sovereignty." *Tulsa Journal of Comparative & International Law* 5 (1998): 253.

———. "Aboriginal Title and the Supreme Court: What's Happening?" *Saskatchewan Law Review* 69 (2006): 281.

———. *Common Law Aboriginal Title*. New York: Oxford University Press, 1989.

———. "Judicial Treatment of Indigenous Land Rights in the Common Law World." In *Indigenous Peoples and the Law*, edited by Benjamin J. Richardson, Shin Imai, and Kent McNeil. Portland, Ore.: Hart, 2009.

McRee, John Griffith. *Life and Correspondence of James Iredell*. Vol. 2. New York: P. Smith, 1949.

Meigs, William M. *The Life of Charles Jared Ingersoll*. Philadelphia: J. B. Lippincott, 1897.

Meng, John J. *Despatches and Instructions of Conrad Alexandre Gérard, 1778–1780*. Baltimore: Johns Hopkins University Press, 1939.

Merrell, James H. *Into the American Woods: Negotiators on the Pennsylvania Frontier.* New York: W. W. Norton, 1999.

Merritt, Jane T. *At the Crossroads: Indians and Empires on a Mid-Atlantic Frontier, 1700–1763.* Chapel Hill: University of North Carolina Press, 2003.

Metzger, Charles H. *The Quebec Act: A Primary Cause of the American Revolution.* New York: United States Catholic Historical Society, 1936.

Meyer, Douglas K. *Making the Heartland Quilt: A Geographical History of Settlement and Migration in Early-Nineteenth-Century Illinois.* Carbondale: Southern Illinois University Press, 2000.

Mickenberg, Neil H. "Aboriginal Rights in Canada and the United States." *Osgoode Hall Law Journal* 9 (1971): 119.

Millenbach, Lew A. "*Johnson v. M'Intosh*, Brief for Respondents." *Kansas Journal of Law and Public Policy* 9 (2000): 873.

Miller, Kerby A. *Irish Immigrants in the Land of Canaan: Letters and Memoirs from Colonial and Revolutionary America.* New York: Oxford University Press, 2003.

Miller, Robert J. "The Doctrine of Discovery in American Indian Law." *Idaho Law Review* 42 (2005): 1.

———. *Native America, Discovered and Conquered: Thomas Jefferson, Lewis and Clark, and Manifest Destiny.* Westport, Conn.: Praeger Publishers, 2006.

Miller, Robert J., and Jacinta Ruru. "An Indigenous Lens into Comparative Law: The Doctrine of Discovery in the United States and New Zealand." *West Virginia Law Review* 111 (2009): 849.

Miller, Robert J., Jacinta Ruru, Larissa Behrendt, and Tracey Lindberg. *Discovering Indigenous Lands: The Doctrine of Discovery in the English Colonies.* New York: Oxford University Press, 2010.

Mohr, Walter H. *Federal Indian Relations, 1774–1788.* Philadelphia: University of Pennsylvania Press, 1933.

Molovinsky, Lemuel. "Maryland and the American West at Independence." *Maryland Historical Magazine* 72 (1977): 353.

Monroe, James. *The Writings of James Monroe.* Vol. 6. Edited by Stanislaus Murray Hamilton. New York: G. P. Putnam's Sons, 1902.

Moore, Frank. *Diary of the American Revolution from Newspapers and Original Documents.* Vol. 1. New York: C. T. Evans, 1863.

More, Thomas. *The Complete Works of St. Thomas More.* Vol. 4. New Haven, Conn.: Yale University Press, 1963.

Morgan, Donald G. "The Origin of Supreme Court Dissent." *William and Mary Quarterly*, 3rd ser., 10 (1953): 353.

Morton, Robert. "The Diary of Robert Morton, Kept in Philadelphia While That City Was Occupied by the British Army in 1777." *Pennsylvania Magazine of History and Biography* 1 (1877): 1.

Moses, John. *Illinois, Historical and Statistical: Comprising the Essential Facts of Its Planting and Growth as a Province, County, Territory, and State.* Vol. 1. Chicago: Fergus Printing Company, 1889.

Mulkearn, Lois, ed. *George Mercer Papers, Relating to the Ohio Company of Virginia*. Pittsburgh: University of Pittsburgh Press, 1954.

Munroe, John A. "Nonresident Representation in the Continental Congress: The Delaware Delegation of 1782." *William and Mary Quarterly*, 3rd ser., 9 (1952): 166.

Murray, Myles N., and Robert V. Zoba. *William Murray, Esq.: Land Agent in the Illinois Territory before the Revolutionary War*. New York: Theo. Gaus, 1987.

Nabokov, Peter, ed. *Native American Testimony: A Chronicle of Indian-White Relations from Prophecy to the Present, 1492–1992*. New York: Penguin, 1992.

Nagel, Paul C. *The Lees of Virginia: Seven Generations of an American Family*. New York: Oxford University Press, 1990.

Nester, William R. *The Frontier War for American Independence*. Mechanicsburg, Pa.: Stackpole Books, 2004.

———. *The Great Frontier War: Britain, France, and the Imperial Struggle for North America, 1607–1755*. Westport, Conn.: Praeger, 2000.

Newcomb, Steven T. "The Evidence of Christian Nationalism in Federal Indian Law: The Doctrine of Discovery, *Johnson v. McIntosh*, and Plenary Power." *New York University Review of Law and Social Change* 20 (1993): 303.

———. *Pagans in the Promised Land: Decoding the Doctrine of Christian Discovery*. Golden, Colo.: Fulcrum, 2008.

Newman, Gerald, ed. *Britain in the Hanoverian Age, 1714–1837: An Encyclopedia*. New York: Garland, 1997.

Newmyer, R. Kent. *John Marshall and the Heroic Age of the Supreme Court*. Baton Rouge: Louisiana State University Press, 2001.

Newton, Nell J. "'At the Whim of the Sovereign': Aboriginal Title Reconsidered." *Hastings Law Journal* 31 (1980): 1215.

———. "Federal Power over Indians: Its Sources, Scope, and Limitations." *University of Pennsylvania Law Review* 132 (1984): 195.

———. "Indian Claims in the Courts of the Conqueror." *American University Law Review* 41 (1992): 753.

Nichols, Roger L. *The American Indian: Past and Present*. Norman: University of Oklahoma Press, 2008.

Norgren, Jill. *The Cherokee Cases: The Confrontation of Law and Politics*. New York: McGraw-Hill, 1996.

———. *The Cherokee Cases: Two Landmark Federal Decisions in the Fight for Sovereignty*. Norman: University of Oklahoma Press, 2004.

———. "Protection of What Rights They Have: Original Principles of Federal Indian Law." *North Dakota Law Review* 64 (1988): 73.

Norton, Margaret Cross, ed. *Illinois Census Returns, 1820*. Collections of the Illinois State Historical Library Statistical Series, vol. 26. Springfield: Trustees of the Illinois State Historical Library, 1934.

"Notes and Queries." *Pennsylvania Magazine of History and Biography* 24 (1900): 393.

"Notes and Queries." *Western Pennsylvania Historical Magazine* 5 (1922): 251.

Oaks, Robert F. "The Impact of British Western Policy on the Coming of the American Revolution in Pennsylvania." *Pennsylvania Magazine of History and Biography* 101 (1977): 171.

O'Callaghan, E. B., ed. *Documents Relative to the Colonial History of the State of New York*. Vols. 1, 6–9, 13. Albany, N.Y.: Weed, Parsons, 1855–81.

Olson, Alison G. "The Board of Trade and London-American Interest Groups in the Eighteenth Century." In *The British Atlantic Empire before the American Revolution*, edited by Peter Marshall and Glyn Williams. Totowa, N.J.: Cass, 1980.

Onuf, Peter S. *The Origins of the Federal Republic*. Philadelphia: University of Pennsylvania Press, 1983.

———. "'We shall all be Americans': Thomas Jefferson and the Indians." *Indiana Magazine of History* 95 (1999): 103.

Oster, John Edward. *The Political and Economic Doctrines of John Marshall*. New York: Neale Publishing Company, 1914.

Osterweis, Rollin G. *Rebecca Gratz: A Study in Charm*. New York: G. P. Putnam's Sons, 1935.

Palmer, Gregory. *Biographical Sketches of Loyalists of the American Revolution*. Westport, Conn.: Meckler, 1984.

Palmer, Michael A. *Stoddert's War: Naval Operations during the Quasi-War with France, 1798–1801*. Columbia: University of South Carolina Press, 1987.

Papenfuse, Edward C. *In Pursuit of Profit: The Annapolis Merchants in the Era of the American Revolution, 1763–1805*. Baltimore: Johns Hopkins University Press, 1975.

Papenfuse, Eric Robert. *The Evils of Necessity: Robert Goodloe Harper and the Moral Dilemma of Slavery*. Philadelphia: American Philosophical Society, 1997.

Parkman, Francis. *La Salle and the Discovery of the Great West*. Boston: Little, Brown, 1915.

Parrington, Vernon L. "Roger Williams, Seeker." In *Main Currents in American Thought*, vol. 1. New York: Harcourt, Brace, 1927.

Patterson, J. B. *Black Hawk's Autobiography: Through the Interpretation of Antoine LeClaire*. Rock Island, Ill.: American Publishing Company, 1912.

Peckham, Howard H. *The Colonial Wars: 1689–1762*. Chicago: University of Chicago Press, 1964.

———. *Indiana: A Bicentennial History*. New York: Norton, 1978.

———. *Pontiac and the Indian Uprising*. Princeton, N.J.: Princeton University Press, 1947.

Pedersen, Nicholas. "The Lost Founder: James Wilson in American Memory." *Yale Journal of Law and the Humanities* 22 (2010): 257.

Pendleton, Edmund. *The Letters and Papers of Edmund Pendleton*. Vol. 1. Edited by David John Mays. Charlottesville: University Press of Virginia, 1967.

Penn, William. *William Penn's Own Account of the Lenni Lenape or Delaware Indians*. Edited by Albert Cook Myers. Somerset, N.J.: Middle Atlantic Press, 1970.

Perdue, Theda. "The Conflict Within: Cherokees and Removal." In *Cherokee Removal: Before and After*, edited by William L. Anderson. Athens: University of Georgia Press, 1992.

Peters, Richard. *The Case of the Cherokee Nation against the State of Georgia*. Philadelphia: J. Grigg, 1831.

Peterson, Merrill D. *The Great Triumvirate: Webster, Clay, and Calhoun*. New York: Oxford University Press, 1987.

Philbrick, Francis S., ed. *The Laws of Illinois Territory, 1809–1818*. Collections of the Illinois State Historical Library, vol. 25. Springfield: Illinois State Historical Library, 1950.

———. *The Rise of the West, 1754–1830*. New York: Harper and Row, 1965.

Philipson, David, ed. *Letters of Rebecca Gratz*. Philadelphia: Jewish Publication Society of America, 1929.

Pickering, Timothy. *The Timothy Pickering Papers*. Edited by Frederick S. Allis, Jr. Boston: Massachusetts Historical Society, 1966.

Pomfret, John E. *Colonial New Jersey: A History*. New York: Scribner, 1973.

———. *The New Jersey Proprietors and Their Lands*. Princeton, N.J.: Van Nostrand, 1964.

Pommersheim, Frank. *Braid of Feathers: American Indian Law and Contemporary Tribal Life*. Berkeley: University of California Press, 1995.

Porter, Robert B. "Two Kinds of Indians, Two Kinds of Indian Nation Sovereignty: A Surreply to Professor Lavelle." *Kansas Journal of Law and Public Policy* 11 (2002): 629.

Potts, Louis W. *Arthur Lee: A Virtuous Revolutionary*. Baton Rouge: Louisiana State University Press, 1981.

———. "Silas Deane." In *American National Biography*, vol. 6, edited by John A. Garraty and Mark C. Carnes. New York: Oxford University Press, 1999.

Prasad, Viniyanka. "The UN Declaration on the Rights of Indigenous Peoples: A Flexible Approach to Addressing the Unique Needs of Varying Populations." *Chicago Journal of International Law* 9 (2008): 297.

Price, Monroe E. *Law and the American Indian: Readings, Notes and Cases*. Indianapolis: Bobbs-Merrill, 1973.

Priestley, L. J. "Communal Title and the Common Law: Further Thoughts on the Gove Land Rights Case." *Federal Law Review* 6 (1974): 150.

Prucha, Francis Paul. *Documents of United States Indian Policy*. Lincoln: University of Nebraska Press, 1975.

Publications of the Southern History Association. Vol. 9. Washington, D.C.: Southern History Association, 1905.

Purcell, George W. "A Survey of Early Newspapers in the Middle Western States." *Indiana Magazine of History* 20 (1924): 347.

Purdy, Jedediah. "Property and Empire: The Law of Imperialism in *Johnson v. M'intosh*." *George Washington Law Review* 75 (2007): 329.

Quaife, Milo M. "Jonathan Carver and the Carver Grant." *Mississippi Valley Historical Review* 7 (1920): 3.

Quinn, Brother C. Edward. *The Signers of the Declaration of Independence*. Bronx, N.Y.: Bronx County Historical Society, 1988.

Ranck, George W. *Boonesborough*. New York: Arno Press, 1971.

Randall, Willard Sterne. *A Little Revenge: Benjamin Franklin and His Son*. Boston: Little, Brown, 1984.

Ranlet, Philip. "Tory David Sproat of Pennsylvania and the Death of American Prisoners of War." *Pennsylvania History* 61 (1994): 185.

Rappleye, Charles. *Robert Morris: Financier of the American Revolution*. New York: Simon and Schuster, 2010.

Rawlyk, George A. "The 'Rising French Empire' in the Ohio Valley and Old Northwest." In *Contest for Empire, 1550–1775*, edited by John B. Elliott. Indianapolis: Indiana Historical Society, 1975.

Reardon, John J. *Edmund Randolph: A Biography*. New York: Macmillan, 1974.

Reed, Joseph. *Life and Correspondence of Joseph Reed*. Vol. 2. Edited by William B. Reed. Philadelphia: Lindsay and Blakiston, 1847.

Remini, Robert V. *Andrew Jackson*. New York: Harper and Row, 1969.

———. *Daniel Webster: The Man and His Time*. New York: W. W. Norton, 1997.

Revera, Margareta. "The Making of a Civilized Nation: Nation-Building, Aristocratic Culture, and Social Change." In *New Sweden in America*, edited by Carol E. Hoffecker et al. Newark: University of Delaware Press, 1995.

"Review." *Virginia Law Register* 10 (October 1924): 463.

Rhodehamel, John, ed. *The American Revolution: Writings from the War of Independence*. New York: Library of America, 2001.

Ribble, F. D. G. "Review." *Virginia Law Review* 11 (1925): 413.

Rice, G. William. "*Johnson v. M'Intosh*, Decision from American Indian Nations Supreme Court." *Kansas Journal of Law and Public Policy* 9 (2000): 889.

Richardson, Benjamin J., Shin Imai, and Kent McNeil, eds. *Indigenous Peoples and the Law*. Portland, Ore.: Hart, 2009.

Ridge, Martin. "Book Review, William Murray, Esq.: Land Agent in the Illinois Territory before the Revolutionary War." *Illinois Historical Journal* 82 (1989): 275.

Ritcheson, Charles R. *Aftermath of Revolution: British Policy toward the United States, 1783–1795*. Dallas: Southern Methodist University Press, 1969.

Robertson, Lindsay G. *Conquest by Law: How the Discovery of America Dispossessed Indigenous Peoples of Their Lands*. New York: Oxford University Press, 2005.

———. "John Marshall as Colonial Historian: Reconsidering the Origins of the Discovery Doctrine." *Journal of Law and Politics* 13 (1997): 759.

———. "*Johnson v. M'Intosh*: Land, Law, and the Politics of Federalism, 1773–1842." Ph.D. diss., University of Virginia, 1997.

———. "*Johnson v. M'Intosh*, Brief for Appellants." *Kansas Journal of Law and Public Policy* 9 (2000): 852.

———. "'A Mere Feigned Case': Rethinking the *Fletcher v. Peck* Conspiracy and Early Republican Legal Culture." *Utah Law Review* 2000 (2000): 249.

Robinson, W. Stitt. "Conflicting Views on Landholding: Lord Baltimore and the Experiences of Colonial Maryland with Native Americans." *Maryland Historical Magazine* 83 (1988): 85.

Rodney, George Brydges. *Diary of George Brydges Rodney.* National Society of the Colonial Dames of America in the State of Delaware. N.p., n.d.

Rodriguez, Junius P. *The Louisiana Purchase: A Historical and Geographical Encyclopedia.* Santa Barbara, Calif.: ABC-CLIO, 2002.

Rohrbough, Malcolm J. *The Land Office Business.* New York: Oxford University Press, 1968.

Roosevelt, Theodore. *Presidential Addresses and State Papers,* vol. 2: *December 3, 1901 to January 4, 1904.* New York: Review of Books Company, 1910.

Rose, Anne C. "Interfaith Families in Victorian America." In *Moral Problems in American Life: New Perspectives on Cultural History,* edited by Karen Halttunen and Lewis Perry. Ithaca, N.Y.: Cornell University Press, 1998.

Rosenberg, Morton M. "In Search of James Wilson." *Pennsylvania History* 55 (1988): 107.

Rowland, Kate M. *The Life of Charles Carroll of Carrollton.* New York: G. P. Putnam's Sons, 1898.

———. *The Life of George Mason.* Vols. 1–2. New York: Putnam's, 1892.

Royce, Charles C. *Indian Land Cessions in the United States.* Washington, D.C.: Government Printing Office, 1900.

Rush, Benjamin. *The Autobiography of Benjamin Rush.* Edited by George W. Corner. Princeton, N.J.: Princeton University Press, 1948.

———. *Letters of Benjamin Rush.* Vols. 1–2. Edited by L. H. Butterfield. Princeton, N.J.: Princeton University Press, 1951.

Russell, Peter H. "High Courts and the Rights of Aboriginal Peoples: The Limits of Judicial Independence." *Saskatchewan Law Review* 61 (1998): 247.

———. *Recognizing Aboriginal Title: The Mabo Case and Indigenous Resistance to English-Settler Colonialism.* Buffalo, N.Y.: University of Toronto Press, 2005.

Salisbury, Neal. *Manitou and Providence.* New York: Oxford University Press, 1982.

Sappington, Anna. "Is *Lara* the Answer to Implicit Divestiture? A Critical Analysis of the Congressional Delegation Exception." *Wyoming Law Review* 7 (2007): 149.

Satz, Ronald H. *American Indian Policy in the Jacksonian Era.* Lincoln: University of Nebraska Press, 1975.

Saunders, William L., ed. *The Colonial Records of North Carolina.* Vols. 9–10. Raleigh, N.C.: P. M. Hale, 1890.

Savelle, Max. *George Morgan, Colony Builder.* New York: Columbia University Press, 1932.

———. *The Origins of American Diplomacy: The International History of Angloamerica, 1492–1763.* New York: Macmillan, 1967.

Scharf, J. Thomas. *The Chronicles of Baltimore.* Baltimore: Turnbull Brothers, 1874.

Schroeder, Oliver, Jr. "The Life and Judicial Work of Justice William Johnson, Jr." *University of Pennsylvania Law Review* 95 (1946): 164.

Schwartz, Bernard. *A History of the Supreme Court.* New York: Oxford University Press, 1993.

Scott, James. *The Illinois Nation: A History of the Illinois Nation of Indians from Their Discovery to the Present Day.* Streator, Ill.: Streator Historical Society, 1973.

Scott, James Brown. *The United States of America: A Study in International Organization.* New York: Oxford University Press, 1920.

Scott, John M. *Supreme Court of Illinois, 1818: Its First Judges and Lawyers.* Bloomington, Ill., 1896.

Selby, John E. *A Chronology of Virginia and the War of Independence, 1763–1783.* Charlottesville: University Press of Virginia, 1973.

———. *Dunmore.* N.p.: Virginia Independence Bicentennial Commission, 1977.

———. *The Revolution in Virginia, 1775–1783.* Williamsburg, Va.: Colonial Williamsburg Foundation, 1988.

Semkiw, Walter. *Return of the Revolutionaries: The Case for Reincarnation and Soul Groups Reunited.* Charlottesville, Va.: Hampton Roads Publishing, 2003.

Shannon, Timothy J. *Indians and Colonists at the Crossroads of Empire: The Albany Congress of 1754.* Ithaca, N.Y.: Cornell University Press, 2000.

Shapiro, Stephen M. "William Pinkney: The Supreme Court's Greatest Advocate." *Journal of Supreme Court History* 12 (1988): 43.

Shea, John Gilmary. *Life and Times of the Most Rev. John Carroll.* New York: J. G. Shea, 1888.

Shortt, Adam, and Arthur G. Doughty, eds. *Canadian Archives: Documents Relating to the Constitutional History of Canada, 1759–1791.* Ottawa, Canada: Printed by S. E. Dawson, 1918.

Shurtleff, Nathaniel B., ed. *Records of the Governor and Company of the Massachusetts Bay in New England.* Vol. 4. Boston: W. White, 1853.

Shy, John W. "Dunmore, the Upper Ohio Valley, and the American Revolution." In *Ohio in the American Revolution*, edited by Thomas H. Smith. Columbus: Ohio Historical Society, 1976.

———. *Toward Lexington: The Role of the British Army in the Coming of the American Revolution.* Princeton, N.J.: Princeton University Press, 1965.

Simcoe, John Graves. *Correspondence of Lieutenant-Governor John Graves Simcoe.* Edited by E. A. Cruikshank. Vols. 2, 4. Toronto: Ontario Historical Society, 1924, 1926.

Simon, James F. *What Kind of Nation: Thomas Jefferson, John Marshall, and the Epic Struggle to Create a United States.* New York: Simon and Schuster, 2002.

Simonhoff, Harry. *Jewish Notables in America, 1776–1865: Links of an Endless Chain.* New York: Greenberg, 1956.

Singer, Joseph William. "Sovereignty and Property." *Northwestern University Law Review* 86 (1991): 1.

———. "Well Settled? The Increasing Weight of History in American Indian Land Claims." *Georgia Law Review* 28 (1994): 481.

Sioussat, St. George. "The Breakdown of the Royal Management of Lands in the Southern Provinces, 1773–1775." *Agricultural History* 3 (1929): 67.

———. "The Chevalier De La Luzerne and the Ratification of the Articles of Confederation by Maryland, 1780–1781, with Accompanying Documents." *Pennsylvania Magazine of History and Biography* 60 (1936): 391.

———. "Review, The Conquest of the Old Southwest." *Mississippi Valley Historical Review* 7 (1921): 378.

Skibine, Alex Tallchief. "Book Review, *Braid of Feathers*: Pluralism, Legitimacy, Sovereignty, and the Importance of Tribal Court Jurisprudence (*Braid of Feathers*, by Frank Pommersheim)." *North Dakota Law Review* 96 (1996): 557.

———. "Chief Justice John Marshall and the Doctrine of Discovery: Friend or Foe to the Indians?" *Tulsa Law Review* 42 (2006): 125.

———. "Indian Gaming and Cooperative Federalism." *Arizona State Law Journal* 42 (2010): 253.

———. "Reconciling Federal and State Power inside Indian Reservations with the Right of Tribal Self-Government and the Process of Self-Determination." *Utah Law Review* 1995 (1995): 1105.

———. "Teaching Indian Law in an Anti-Tribal Era." *North Dakota Law Review* 82 (2006): 777.

Skidmore, Warren, and Donna Kaminsky. *Lord Dunmore's Little War of 1774: His Captains and Their Men Who Opened up Kentucky and the West to American Settlement*. Bowie, Md.: Heritage Books, 2002.

Slattery, Brian. "Some Thoughts on Aboriginal Title." *University of New Brunswick Law Journal* 48 (1999): 19.

———. *Paper Empires: The Legal Dimensions of French and English Ventures in North America*. Vancouver, Canada: University of British Columbia Press, 2005.

———. "Understanding Aboriginal Rights." *Canadian Bar Review* 66 (1987): 727.

Slick, Sewell Elias. *William Trent and the West*. Harrisburg, Pa.: Archives Publishing Company, 1947.

Smelcer, John D. Comment, "Using International Law More Effectively to Secure and Advance Indigenous Peoples' Rights: Towards Enforcement in U.S. and Australian Domestic Courts." *Pacific Rim Law and Policy Journal* 5 (2006): 301.

Smith, Charles Page. "The Attack on Fort Wilson." *Pennsylvania Magazine of History and Biography* 78 (1974): 177.

———. *James Wilson: Founding Father, 1742–1798*. Westport, Conn.: Greenwood, 1956.

Smith, Dwight L. "Indian Land Cessions in the Old Northwest, 1795–1809." Ph.D. diss., Indiana University, 1949.

Smith, Ellen Hart. *Charles Carroll of Carrollton*. Cambridge, Mass.: Harvard University Press, 1945.

Smith, Horace Wemyss. *Life and Correspondence of the Rev. William Smith, D.D.* Vol. 2. Philadelphia: S. A. George, 1880.

Smith, Hubbard Madison. *Historical Sketches of Old Vincennes*, 2nd ed. Vincennes, Ind.: N.p., 1903.

Smith, Jean Edward. *John Marshall: Definer of a Nation*. New York: H. Holt and Company, 1996.

Smith, Joseph. *Appeals to the Privy Council from the American Plantations*. New York: Octagon Books, 1965.

Smith, Paul, ed., *Letters of Delegates to Congress*. Vols. 3, 11–12, 16–17, 21. Washington, D.C.: U.S. Government Printing Office, 1978–98.

Smith, William. *Historical Memoirs from 16 March 1763 to 25 July 1778 of William Smith*. Vol. 1. Edited by William H. W. Sabine. New York: New York Times and Arno Press, 1969.

———. *The History of the Province of New York from its Discovery in 1532*. London: Printed for Thomas Wilcox, 1757.

Somes, Joseph Henry Vanderburgh. *Old Vincennes: The History of a Famous Old Town and Its Glorious Past*. New York: Graphic Books, 1962.

Sommerville, Charles W. *Robert Goodloe Harper*. Washington, D.C.: Neale, 1899.

Sosin, Jack M. "Britain and the Ohio Valley, 1760–1775: The Search for Alternatives in a Revolutionary Era." In *Contest for Empire, 1550–1775*, edited by John B. Elliott. Indianapolis: Indiana Historical Society, 1975.

———. *The Revolutionary Frontier, 1763–1783*. New York: Holt, Rinehart and Winston, 1967.

———. *Whitehall and the Wilderness: The Middle West in British Colonial Policy, 1760–1775*. Lincoln: University of Nebraska Press, 1961.

———. "The Yorke-Camden Opinion and American Land Speculators." *Pennsylvania Magazine of History and Biography* 85 (1961): 38.

Spindel, Carol. *Dancing at Halftime: Sports and the Controversy over American Indian Mascots*. New York: New York University Press, 2000.

Springer, James Warren. "American Indians and the Law of Real Property in Colonial New England." *American Journal of Legal History* 39 (1986): 25.

Stagg, Jack. *Anglo-Indian Relations in North America to 1763, and an Analysis of the Royal Proclamation of 7 October 1763*. Ottawa: Indian and Northern Affairs Ministry of Canada, 1981.

Standiford, Les. *Washington Burning*. New York: Crown Publishers, 2008.

Staples, William R. *Rhode Island in the Continental Congress*. Providence: Providence Press Company, 1870.

Starkey, Armstrong. *European and Native American Warfare, 1675–1815*. Norman: University of Oklahoma Press, 1998.

Starr, Harris Elwood. "William Smith." In *Dictionary of American Biography*, vol. 17, edited by Dumas Malone. New York: Charles Scribner's Sons, 1935.

Steele, Ian K. "Metropolitan Administration of the Colonies, 1696–1775." In *A Companion to the American Revolution*, edited by Jack P. Greene and J. R. Pole. Malden, Mass.: Blackwell Publishers, 2000.

Steiner, Bernard C. *The Life and Correspondence of James McHenry*. New York: Arno Press, 1979.

Sterling, David L. "William Pinkney." In *American National Biography*, vol. 17, edited by John A. Garraty and Mark C. Carnes. New York: Oxford University Press, 1999.

Stern, Mark Abbott. *David Franks: Colonial Merchant.* University Park: Pennsylvania State University Press, 2010.

Steuart, A. Francis. "Letters from Virginia." *The Magazine of History* 3 (1906): 151.

Stevens, Paul L. "'One of the Most Beautiful Regions of the World': Paul Des Ruisseaux's Memoire of the Wabash-Illinois Country in 1777." *Indiana Magazine of History* 83 (1987): 360.

Stevenson, Sarah M. Comment, "Indigenous Land Rights and the Declaration on the Rights of Indigenous Peoples: Implications for Maori Land Claims in New Zealand." *Fordham International Law Journal* 32 (2008): 298.

Stoebuck, William B., and Dale A. Whitman, *The Law of Property*, 3rd ed. St. Paul, Minn.: West Publishing Group, 2000.

Story, Joseph. *Commentaries on the Constitution of the United States.* Vol. 1. Boston: Hilliard, Gray, and Company, 1833.

———. *Miscellaneous Writings of Joseph Story.* Edited by William W. Story. Boston: Little, Brown, 1852.

Story, William W., ed. *Life and Letters of Joseph Story.* Vols. 1–2. Boston: Little, Brown, 1851.

Strickland, William. *Journal of a Tour in the United States, 1794–1795.* Edited by Rev. J. E. Strickland. New York: New York Historical Society, 1971.

Sugden, John. *Blue Jacket: Warrior of the Shawnees.* Lincoln: University of Nebraska Press, 2000.

———. *Tecumseh: A Life.* New York: Henry Holt and Company, 1997.

Sullivan, James. *The History of Land Titles in Massachusetts.* New York: Arno Press, 1972.

Summerhill, Stephen J., and John Alexander Williams. *Sinking Columbus: Contested History, Cultural Politics, and Mythmaking during the Quincentenary.* Gainesville: University Press of Florida, 2000.

Sweetman, Edward. *The Unsigned New Zealand Treaty.* Melbourne: Arrow Printery, 1939.

Sword, Wiley. *President Washington's Indian War: The Struggle for the Old Northwest, 1790–1795.* Norman: University of Oklahoma Press, 1985.

Symmes, John. *The Correspondence of John Cleves Symmes.* Edited by Beverley W. Bond, Jr. New York: Macmillan, 1926.

Tachau, Mary K. Bonsteel. *Federal Courts in the Early Republic: Kentucky, 1789–1816.* Princeton, N.J.: Princeton University Press, 1978.

Tanner, Helen Hornbeck. "The Greenville Treaty of 1795." *Indians of Ohio and Indiana Prior to 1795.* Vol. 1. New York: Garland, 1974.

Tanner, Helen Hornbeck, ed. *Atlas of Great Lakes Indian History.* Norman: University of Oklahoma Press, 1987.

Taylor, Alan. *American Colonies.* New York: Viking, 2001.

————. "Land and Liberty on the Post-Revolutionary Frontier." In *Devising Liberty: Preserving and Creating Freedom in the New American Republic*, edited by David Thomas Konig. Stanford, Calif.: Stanford University Press, 1995.

Temple, Wayne C. *Indian Villages of the Illinois Country*. Springfield: Illinois State Museum, 1987.

Tennant, Paul. *Aboriginal Peoples and Politics: The Indian Land Question in British Columbia, 1849–1989*. Vancouver: University of British Columbia Press, 1991.

Thom, James Alexander. "George Rogers Clark and the American Indian." In *The Life of George Rogers Clark, 1752–1818*, edited by Kenneth C. Carstens and Nancy Son Carstens. Westport, Conn.: Praeger, 2004.

Thomas, Charles M. "Successful and Unsuccessful Merchants in the Illinois Country." *Journal of the Illinois State Historical Society* 30 (1938): 429.

Thomson, Charles. *The Papers of Charles Thomson, Secretary of the Continental Congress*. Collections of the New York Historical Society for the Year 1878. New York: New York Historical Society, 1879.

Thornbrough, Gayle, ed. *The Correspondence of John Badollet and Albert Gallatin, 1804–1836*. Indianapolis: Indiana Historical Society, 1963.

————. *Outpost on the Wabash, 1878–1791*. Indianapolis: Indiana Historical Society, 1957.

Thornton, Russell. "Cherokee Losses during the Trail of Tears: A New Perspective and a New Estimate." *Ethnohistory* 31 (1984): 289.

Thorpe, Francis N., ed. *Federal and State Constitutions, Colonial Charters, and Other Organic Laws of the States, Territories, and Colonies Now or Heretofore Forming the United States of America*. Vols. 3, 6, 7. Washington, D.C.: Government Printing Office, 1909.

Thwaites, Reuben Gold. *French Regime in Wisconsin, 1743–1760*. Collections of the State Historical Society of Wisconsin, vol. 18. Madison: Wisconsin Historical Society, 1908.

Thwaites, Reuben Gold, and Louise Phelps Kellogg, eds. *Documentary History of Lord Dunmore's War, 1774*. Madison: Wisconsin Historical Society, 1905.

————. *The Revolution on the Upper Ohio, 1775–1777*. Madison: Wisconsin Historical Society, 1908.

Tiller, Veronica E. Velarde, ed. *Tiller's Guide to Indian Country: Economic Profiles of American Indian Reservations*. Albuquerque, N.M.: Bow Arrow Publishing Company, 2005.

Tittemore, Brian D. "The Dann Litigation and International Human Rights Law: The Proceedings and Decision of the Inter-American Commission on Human Rights." *American Indian Law Review* 31 (2006–2007): 593.

Tomlins, Christopher, ed. *The United States Supreme Court: The Pursuit of Justice*. Boston: Houghton, Mifflin, 2005.

Tucker, Robert W., and David C. Hendrickson. *The Fall of the First British Empire: Origins of the War of American Independence*. Baltimore: Johns Hopkins University Press, 1982.

Tully, James. *An Approach to Political Philosophy: Locke in Contexts.* New York: Cambridge University Press, 1993.

Twibell, T. S. "Rethinking *Johnson v. M'Intosh* (1823): The Root of the Continued Forced Displacement of American Indians Despite *Cobell v. Norton* (2001)." *Georgetown Immigration Law Journal* 23 (2008): 129.

Tyler, Samuel. *Memoir of Roger Brooke Taney.* Baltimore: J. Murphy, 1872.

University of Pennsylvania, Society of the Alumni. *Catalogue of the Trustees, Officers, and Graduates of the Departments of Arts and Science and of the Honorary Graduates of the University of Pennsylvania, 1749–1880.* Philadelphia: J. B. Lippincott and Company, 1880.

Valley, Dorris, and Mary M. Lembcke. *The Peorias: A History of the Peoria Indian Tribe of Oklahoma.* Miami, Okla.: Peoria Tribe of Oklahoma, 1991.

Vaughan, Alden T. *New England Frontier: Puritans and Indians, 1620–1675.* Boston: Little, Brown, 1965.

Vaughan, Alden T., ed. *Chronicles of the American Revolution.* New York: Grosset and Dunlap, 1965.

Vaughan, Alden T., and Deborah A. Rosen, eds. *Early American Indian Documents: Treaties and Laws, 1607–1789,* vol. 15: *Virginia and Maryland Laws.* Washington, D.C.: University Publications of America, 1998.

Ver Steeg, Clarence L. "Robert Morris." In *American National Biography,* vol. 15, edited by John A. Garraty and Mark C. Carnes. New York: Oxford University Press, 1999.

———. *Robert Morris: Revolutionary Financier.* New York: Octagon, 1972.

Vitoria, Francisco de. *De Indis et de Ivre Belli Relectiones.* Edited by Ernest Nys. New York: Oceana, 1964.

Volney, Constantin François. *A View of the Soil and Climate of the United States of America.* New York: Hafner Publishing Company, 1968.

Volwiler, Albert T. *George Croghan and the Westward Movement, 1741–1782.* Cleveland, Ohio: Arthur H. Clark Co., 1926.

Von der Heydte, Friedrich August Freiher. "Discovery, Symbolic Annexation and Virtual Effectiveness in International Law." *American Journal of International Law* 29 (1935): 448.

Wainwright, Nicholas B. *George Croghan: Wilderness Diplomat.* Chapel Hill: University of North Carolina Press, 1959.

Wait, Thomas B. *Secret Journals of the Acts and Proceedings of Congress.* Vol. 3. Boston: Thomas B. Wait, 1821.

Wallace, Anthony F.C. *Jefferson and the Indians: The Tragic Fate of the First Americans.* Cambridge, Mass.: Belknap Press of Harvard University Press, 1999.

Wallace, Paul A., ed. *Thirty Thousand Miles with John Heckewelder.* Pittsburgh: University of Pittsburgh Press, 1958.

Walters, Mark D. "*Mohegan Indians v. Connecticut* (1705–1773) and the Legal Status of Aboriginal Customary Laws and Government in British North America." *Osgoode Hall Law Journal* 33 (1995): 785.

Warhus, Mark. *Another America: Native American Maps and the History of Our Land.* New York: St. Martin's Press, 1997.

Warren, Charles. *A History of the American Bar.* Boston: Little, Brown, 1911.

Warren, Stephen. *The Shawnees and Their Neighbors, 1795–1870.* Urbana: University of Illinois Press, 2005.

Washburn, Emory. *Treatise on the American Law of Real Property,* 3rd ed. Vol. 3. Boston: Little, Brown, 1868.

Washburn, Wilcomb E. *The American Indian and the United States.* Vol. 1. New York: Random House, 1973.

———. "The Moral and Legal Justifications for Dispossessing the Indians." In *Seventeenth-Century America: Essays in Colonial History,* edited by James Morton Smith. Chapel Hill: University of North Carolina Press, 1959.

———. *Red Man's Land/White Man's Law: A Study of the Past and Present Status of the American Indian.* New York: Scribner, 1971.

Washington, George. *The Diaries of George Washington.* Vol. 3. Edited by Donald Jackson and Dorothy Twohig. Charlottesville: University Press of Virginia, 1978.

———. *The Diaries of George Washington.* Vol. 4. Edited by John Fitzpatrick. Boston: H. Mifflin Company, 1925.

———. *George Washington: A Collection.* Edited by William B. Allen. Indianapolis: Liberty Classics, 1988.

———. *The Papers of George Washington: Confederation Series.* Vol. 2. Edited by W. W. Abbot and Dorothy Twohig. Charlottesville: University Press of Virginia, 1992.

———. *The Papers of George Washington: Presidential Series.* Vol. 11. Edited by Christine Sternberg Patrick. Charlottesville: University Press of Virginia, 2002.

———. *The Writings of George Washington.* Vols. 4, 24, 27. Edited by John C. Fitzpatrick. Washington, D.C.: U.S. Government Printing Office, 1931, 1938.

Watson, Blake A. "The Impact of the American Doctrine of Discovery on Native Land Rights in Australia, Canada, and New Zealand." *Seattle University Law Review* 34 (2011): 507.

———. "John Marshall and Indian Land Rights: A Historical Rejoinder to the Claim of 'Universal Recognition' of the Doctrine of Discovery." *Seton Hall Law Review* 36 (2006): 481.

———. "The Thrust and Parry of Federal Indian Law." *University of Dayton Law Review* 23 (1998): 437.

Webster, Daniel, *The Papers of Daniel Webster on Microfilm.* Reel 4. Edited by Charles M. Wiltse. Ann Arbor, Mich.: University Microfilms, 1971.

———. *The Papers of Daniel Webster (Speeches and Formal Writings).* Vol. 1. Edited by Charles M. Wiltse. Hanover, N.H.: University Press of New England, 1986.

———. *The Works of Daniel Webster,* 20th ed. Vol. 1. Boston: Little, Brown, 1890.

Westlake, John. *Chapters on the Principles of International Law.* Cambridge, U.K.: Cambridge University Press, 1894.

Wharton, Anne H. *Social Life in the Early Republic*. Philadelphia: J. P. Lippincott, 1902.

———. "The Wharton Family." *Pennsylvania Magazine of History and Biography* 1 (1877): 455.

Wharton, Samuel. *Plain Facts: Being an Examination into the Rights of the Indian Nations of America, to Their Respective Countries; and a Vindication of the Grant, from the Six United Nations of Indians, to the Proprietors of Indiana, against the Decision of the Legislature of Virginia; Together with Authentic Documents, Proving that the Territory, Westward of the Allegany Mountain, Never Belonged to Virginia, &c.* Philadelphia: R. Aitken, 1781.

———. *View of the Title to Indiana, a Tract of Country on the River Ohio.* [Philadelphia?], 1775.

Wharton, Thomas. "Selections from the Letter Books of Thomas Wharton, of Philadelphia, 1773–1783." *Pennsylvania Magazine of History and Biography* 33 (1909): 319.

Wheeler, Daniel Edwin., ed. *Life and Writings of Thomas Paine.* Vol. 8. New York: V. Parke and Company, 1908.

Wheeler-Voegelin, Erminie. "Ethnohistory of Indian Use and Occupancy in Ohio and Indiana Prior to 1795." *Indians of Ohio and Indiana Prior to 1795.* Vol. 1. New York: Garland, 1974.

White, G. Edward. *History of the Supreme Court of the United States: The Marshall Court and Cultural Change, 1815–35.* Vols. 3–4. New York: Macmillan, 1988.

———. "The Working Life of the Marshall Court, 1815–1835." *Virginia Law Review* 70 (1984): 1.

White, Richard. *The Middle Ground: Indians, Empires, and Republics in the Great Lakes Region, 1650–1815.* New York: Cambridge University Press, 1991.

Whitehead, William A., et al., eds. *Archives of the State of New Jersey, First Series.* Vols. 6–7. Newark, N.J.: Daily Advertiser Printing House, 1882–83.

Whitney, David C. *Founders of Freedom in America: Lives of the Men Who Signed the Declaration of Independence and So Helped Establish the United States of America.* Vol. 2. Chicago: Encyclopaedia Britannica Educational Corporation, 1971.

Wilbur, Marguerite Eyer. *The East India Company and the British Empire in the Far East.* Stanford, Calif.: Stanford University Press, 1945.

Wilkins, David E. *American Indian Sovereignty and the U.S. Supreme Court: The Masking of Justice.* Austin: University of Texas Press, 1997.

———. "*Johnson v. M'Intosh* Revisited: Through the Eyes of *Mitchel v. United States.*" *American Indian Law Review* 19 (1994): 159.

———. "Quit-Claiming the Doctrine of Discovery: A Treaty-Based Reappraisal." *Oklahoma City University Law Review* 23 (1998): 277.

Wilkins, David E., and K. Tsianina Lomawaima. *Uneven Ground: American Indian Sovereignty and Federal Law.* Norman: University of Oklahoma Press, 2001.

Wilkinson, Norman B. *Land Policy and Speculation in Pennsylvania, 1779–1800: A Test of the New Democracy.* New York: Arno Press, 1979.

Williams, Robert A., Jr. "The Algebra of Federal Indian Law: The Hard Trial of Decolonizing and Americanizing the White Man's Indian Jurisprudence." *Wisconsin Law Review* 1986 (1986): 219.

———. *The American Indian in Western Legal Thought: The Discourses of Conquest.* New York: Oxford University Press, 1990.

———. "Columbus's Legacy: Law as an Instrument of Racial Discrimination against Indigenous Peoples' Rights of Self-Determination." *Arizona Journal of International and Comparative Law* 8 (1991): 51.

———. "Documents of Barbarism: The Contemporary Legacy of European Racism and Colonialism in the Narrative Traditions of Federal Indian Law." *Arizona Law Review* 31 (1989): 237.

———. "Encounters on the Frontiers of International Human Rights Law: Redefining the Terms of Indigenous Peoples' Survival in the World." *Duke Law Journal* 1990 (1990): 660.

———. "Jefferson, the Norman Yoke, and American Indian Lands." *Arizona Law Review* 29 (1987): 165.

———. "Learning Not to Live with Eurocentric Myopia." *Arizona Law Review* 30 (1988): 439.

———. *Like a Loaded Weapon: The Rehnquist Court, Indian Rights, and the Legal History of Racism in America.* Minneapolis: University of Minnesota Press, 2005.

———. *Linking Arms Together: American Indian Treaty Visions of Law and Peace, 1600–1800.* New York: Oxford University Press, 1997.

———. "The Medieval and Renaissance Origins of the Status of the American Indian in Western Legal Thought." *Southern California Law Review* 57 (1983): 1.

———. "'The People of the States Where They Are Found Are Often Their Deadliest Enemies': The Indian Side of the Story of Indian Rights and Federalism." *Arizona Law Review* 38 (1996): 981.

Williams, Roger. *A Key into the Language of America,* 5th ed. Bedford, Mass.: Applewood Books, 1997.

Williams, T. J. C., and Folger McKinsey, *History of Frederick County, Maryland.* Vol. 1. Frederick, Md.: L. R. Titsworth and Company, 1910.

Williamson, James A. *The Cabot Voyages and Bristol Discovery under Henry VII.* Cambridge, U.K.: Cambridge University Press, 1962.

Wilson, George R. "Early Indiana Trails and Surveys." *Indiana Historical Society Publications* 6 (1919): 348.

———. "The First Public Land Surveys in Indiana: Freeman's Lines." *Indiana Magazine of History* 12 (1916): 1.

———. *History of DuBois County from Its Primitive Days to 1910.* Jasper, Ind.: By the author, 1910.

Wilson, James. *Collected Works of James Wilson.* Vol. 1. Edited by Kermit L. Hall and Mark David Hall. Indianapolis: Liberty Fund, 2007.

———. *The Works of James Wilson.* Vols. 1–2. Edited by Robert Green McCloskey. Cambridge, Mass.: Belknap Press of Harvard University Press, 1967.

Winthrop, John. "John Winthrop's Journal." In *Roger Williams and the Massachusetts Magistrates*, edited by Theodore P. Greene. Boston: Heath, 1964.

Wirt, William. *Memoirs of the Life of William Wirt*. Vols. 1–2. Edited by John P. Kennedy. Philadelphia: Lea and Blanchard, 1849.

Wise, Jennings C. *The Red Man in the New World Drama*. Washington, D.C.: W. F. Roberts Company, 1931.

Wishart, David J. *Encyclopedia of the Great Plains*. Lincoln: University of Nebraska Press, 2007.

Wolf, Edwin, and Maxwell Whiteman. *The History of the Jews of Philadelphia from Colonial Times to the Age of Jackson*. Philadelphia: Jewish Publication Society of America, 1956.

Wood, Gordon S. *The Creation of the American Republic, 1776–1787*. Chapel Hill: University of North Carolina Press, 1969.

Woodward, Grace Steele. *The Cherokees*. Norman: University of Oklahoma Press, 1963.

Woolen, William Wesley. *Biographical and Historical Sketches of Early Indiana*. Indianapolis: Hammond, 1883.

Worthen, Kevin J. "Book Review, Sword or Shield: The Past and Future Impact of Western Legal Thought on American Indian Sovereignty (*The American Indian in Western Legal Thought*. By Robert A. Williams, Jr.)." *Harvard Law Review* 104 (1991): 1372.

———. "The Grand Experiment: Evaluating Indian Law in the 'New World.'" *Tulsa Journal of Comparative and International Law* 5 (1998): 299.

Wraxall, Nathaniel William. *Historical Memoirs of My Own Time*. Vol. 2. London: K. Paul, Trench, Trubner, 1904.

Wright, J. Leitch, Jr. *Britain and the American Frontier, 1783–1815*. Athens: University of Georgia Press, 1975.

Yirush, Craig Bryan. "Claiming the New World: Empire, Law, and Indigenous Rights in the Mohegan Case, 1704–1743." *Law and History Review* 29 (2011): 333.

Young, Arthur. *Political Essays Concerning the Present State of the British Empire*. London: Printed for W. Strahan and T. Cadell, 1772.

Young, Eleanor. *Forgotten Patriot: Robert Morris*. New York: Macmillan, 1950.

Young, Simon. *The Trouble with Tradition: Native Title and Cultural Change*. Annandale, N.S.W., Australia: Federation Press, 2008.

Zeisberger, David. *Diary of David Zeisberger*. Vol. 2. Edited by Eugene F. Bliss. Cincinnati: R. Clarke and Company, 1885.

Zweiben, Beverly. *How Blackstone Lost the Colonies: English Law, Colonial Lawyers, and the American Revolution*. New York: Garland, 1990.

INDEX

Chauncey, Isaac, 290
Chekommia (Big River; Piankeshaw chief), 221
Cherokee Nation v. Georgia, 322–25, 334; and the doctrine of discovery, 323–24
Cherokees, 57, 159, 223, 302, 309; resist removal, 319–20, 322, 323–29, 413n23, 413n25; sell land to private purchasers, 77, 87–88, 100, 103, 126, 178; sign treaties, 235, 328
Cheyenne River Sioux Tribe, 333
Chickasaws, 34–35, 175, 328, 345, 349, 407n53; sign treaty, 235
Chief Illiniwek, 316, 412nn69–70
Chippewas, 28, 158, 216; sell land to private purchasers, 179; sign treaties, 164–65, 180
Chisholm v. Georgia, 190, 388n56
Choctaws, 235, 238
Chouteau, René Auguste, 221
Christie, Robert, Jr., 92, 94, 122
Christie, Robert, Sr., 92, 94
Church of England, 355
City of Sherrill v. Oneida Indian Nation, 319, 322–23
City Tavern (Philadelphia), 120, 132, 138
Clark, Abraham, 149, 151
Clark, George Rogers, 95, 101, 104–107, 112, 119, 128, 154, 159, 175, 178; captures Vincennes, 108; Clark's Grant, 109, 150, 202, 208, 209, 411n59; deeded land by the Piankeshaws, 95, 246; fights Indians, 156–57, 161; opposes the Transylvania Company, 88, 108–109
Clark, William, 159, 219, 220, 221, 222, 303, 304
Clark v. Smith, 331
Clay, Henry, 249, 254, 299

Cleaves, Freeman, 215
Clement VII (pope), 17
Clinton, George, 148
Clive, Robert, 52
Coercive Acts (1774), 75, 84
Cohens v. Virginia, 259–60, 262, 267
Coke, Edward, 21, 135
Colbrooke, Nesbitt, and Franks, 65
Colden, Cadwallader, 30, 288, 406n46
College of Philadelphia, 124, 134, 188. *See also* University of Pennsylvania
College of William and Mary, 82, 92
Colston, Rawleigh, 280
Columbus, Christopher, 16, 347; quincentenary commemoration, 355
Committee of the Privy Council on Trade and Plantations, 49. *See also* Privy Council
Company of the Indies (Compagnie des Indes), 41
Comprehensive Environmental Response, Compensation and Liability Act (1980), 333–34
Confederated Peorias, 296, 308, 312–13; sign treaties, 309–10
Congress, U.S. *See* U.S. Congress
Connecticut: dispute with Mohegans, 48–49, 268, 276, 286, 294
Constitution, U.S. *See* U.S. Constitution
Continental Congress, 62, 83, 84, 87, 89, 97, 102, 103, 136; considers memorials of the Illinois and Wabash Land Companies, 108, 120–21, 133, 140, 143–48, 174, 181, 182, 225, 295; debates ownership of western lands, 101, 109–17, 118, 120, 140–53; develops an Indian land policy; 102, 146–47, 155–58, 162–63, 273